"This new edition of Adrien Nocent's *The Liturgical Year* dappers up an old friend! The passing of time and the introduction of the new translation of the Roman Missal had made the original edition of Nocent's work more difficult to use. Now Paul Turner has done us a favor with this thorough revision: he has replaced prayer texts with the new translation, explained the context of some issues that have faded in the almost forty years since Nocent wrote the book, and emended Matthew J. O'Connell's fine translation to make it more accessible to readers today. The virtues of Nocent's original work (namely, his opening up of the reformed liturgical year through the lens of the lectionary and prayer texts of the Missal in the light of the history of the liturgy) can again serve preachers, liturgists, and lovers of the liturgy because of Turner's fine work. It promises to be a key resource for another forty years."

> Rev. Michael Witczak, Associate Professor of Liturgical Studies, Catholic University of America

"Adrien Nocent's *The Liturgical Year* offers the reader a wealth of biblical, liturgical, pastoral, and theological inspiration. The general introductions to the season, whether Lent, Holy Week, or Easter, as well as the profound reflections more specifically on the Sunday lectionary readings always serve to draw out the great Judeo-Christian themes of revelation: salvation history, creation in the image and likeness of God, sin, redemption, divinization, transformation into Christ, etc. Nocent manages marvelously to place the word in the dynamic context of the church's liturgy, giving powerful expression to the word as Living Word, ancient and ever new. The writing style, so accessible in this fine translation, allows the author's insights to stir the imagination, drawing us into a new wonder at the God who not simply entered into the human drama but ever walks the paths of our human story and stories. This fresh presentation of Nocent's work seems particularly timely with the increasing calls of the church's magisterium to a New Evangelization and Pope Francis' own emphasis on the need to focus more intentionally on what is essential to the Gospel message. This resource will serve preachers well in giving vivid and substantial expression to the central and essential realities of our Catholic faith Sunday by Sunday."

> Rev. Anthony Oelrich, Pastor, St. Mary's Cathedral, St. Cloud, Minnesota

The Liturgical Year

Volume Two

LENT, THE SACRED PASCHAL TRIDUUM,
EASTER TIME

by

Adrien Nocent, OSB

Translated by

Matthew J. O'Connell

Introduced, Emended, and Annotated by

Paul Turner

LITURGICAL PRESS
Collegeville, Minnesota

www.litpress.org

Nihil Obstat: Reverend Robert Harren, *Censor deputatus.*
Imprimatur: ✠ Most Reverend Donald J. Kettler, J.C.D., Bishop of Saint Cloud, Minnesota, December 11, 2013.

Cover design by Ann Blattner. Illustration by Frank Kacmarcik, OblSB. Saint John's Abbey, Collegeville, Minnesota. Used with permission.

Available in three volumes, *The Liturgical Year* is the authorized English version of *Célébrer Jésus-Christ, L'année Liturgique,* published by Jean-Pierre Delarge, 10, rue Mayet, 75006 Paris, France. The English translation of *The Liturgical Year* was first published by Liturgical Press in four volumes in 1977.

Volume 2: ISBN 978-0-8146-3570-4   ISBN 978-0-8146-3595-7 (e-book)
Volume 3: ISBN 978-0-8146-3571-1   ISBN 978-0-8146-3596-4 (e-book)

1	2	3	4	5	6	7	8	9

Library of Congress Cataloging-in-Publication Data

Nocent, Adrien.
    [Célébrer Jésus-Christ. English]
    The liturgical year : Advent, Christmas, Epiphany / by Adrien Nocent, OSB ; Translated by Matthew J. O'Connell ; Introduced, Emended, and Annotated by Paul Turner.
        volumes cm
    Includes bibliographical references.
    ISBN 978-0-8146-3569-8 (v. 1 : pbk. : alk. paper) —
    ISBN 978-0-8146-3594-0 (v. 1 : e-book)
    1. Church year.   I. Title.

BV30.N6213   2013
263'.9—dc23   2013011152

Contents

Lent

The Sacred Paschal Triduum

Easter Time

Solemnities and Feasts of the Lord

Abbreviations

AAS   *Acta Apostolicae Sedis*

CCL   *Corpus Christianorum, Series Latina.* Turnhout, 1953–

CL   *Constitution on the Sacred Liturgy*

CSEL   *Corpus Scriptorum Ecclesiasticorum Latinorum.* Vienna, 1866

LII   *Liturgy of the Hours*

PG   *Patrologia Graeca*, ed. J. P. Migne. Paris, 1857–66

PL   *Patrologia Latina*, ed. J. P. Migne. Paris, 1844–64

SC   *Sources Chretiennes.* Paris, 1942–

TPS   *The Pope Speaks.* Washington, 1954–

TDNT   *Theological Dictionary of the New Testament.* Grand Rapids, 1964–74

Series Introduction

When the postconciliar lectionary first fell into the hands of priests, musicians, and parish liturgists in 1970, few could fully grasp the significance of the event. The vast selection of readings, the nimble choice of responsorial psalms, and the blossoming of the liturgical year would become clearer only in time.

One of the first companions to the revised lectionary was composed by Adrien Nocent, a Belgian monk who became a consultor for the Sacred Congregation for Divine Worship in 1969. In 1964 he had served as a consultor for the Consilium for the Implementation of the Constitution on the Sacred Liturgy of the Second Vatican Council. He was the secretary for the Consilium's Study Group 17, which worked on the revision of Holy Week, and, among other responsibilities, was part of Study Group 11, which revised the Lectionary for Mass. He drew up the preliminary schemas for Advent, the Sundays after Epiphany, and the Sundays following Pentecost.

For Nocent, a commentary on the lectionary could not be a mere commentary on a book but an exploration of the dialogue between the Word of God and humanity in every culture and time. The Church had been through only one complete three-year cycle of the lectionary when Nocent was writing this book. He shared his vision of this project for eager readers, students, and worshipers.

On the occasion of the fiftieth anniversary of the Constitution on the Sacred Liturgy, Liturgical Press is proud to reissue Nocent's work. I was deeply honored at the invitation to contribute annotations— honored because when I was in the seminary, *The Liturgical Year* was the main resource I consulted to prayerfully approach my participation in the Sunday Mass; honored because as a young priest, I used *The Liturgical Year* to help prepare my homilies; honored because as a liturgical catechist, my brain had been hardwired to Nocent's approach to the lectionary: Start with the gospel, then look at the first reading, then the psalm, and be ready to discard the second reading from your treatment of the Sunday lectionary.

Readers today may criticize Nocent's approach as too "thematic" in content. He presumes that each Sunday carries a theme and that he knows what it is. In reality, there is no single theme, and the second reading deserves its place in the sun. Still, in practice, Nocent's ability to explain the layout of the lectionary is still vital. Although a specialist in liturgy, he reveals himself as a most capable biblical exegete; although a man of philosophical depth, he constantly returns to the question of relevance: What does this passage have to say to us today? I have added a few annotations where I thought the reader needed a bridge between Nocent's day and our own, but I have kept these at a minimum to let the author's voice speak.

I have also refrained from changing too much of Matthew J. O'Connell's fine original translation. He wrote before issues of gender-inclusive language became important, however, and I felt that the book could not be reissued without attention to this detail. The greatest number of changes I introduced to the translation have to do with this concern. I have also emended O'Connell's work where I thought it needed greater clarity due to the length of sentences, obscure vocabulary, or theological imprecisions. Otherwise, again, I wanted his voice to win.

Nocent's seven-volume work in French, which had been rearranged into four volumes in English, is now redistributed again into three. All the material is here, along with Nocent's desire to share his profound faith and scholarship. I am confident that you, the reader, will meet a friend, a spiritual father, and a compelling mentor in Adrien Nocent.

Paul Turner

Lent

Introduction

This volume on the liturgical year will follow the pattern adopted in the other two volumes. First, we shall attempt to give the reader greater access to the theology of Lent by asking as honestly as we can whether that theology has anything to say to us and our contemporary concerns. Then, we shall examine the texts used in the celebrations and the manner in which they complement one another. Finally, we shall point out the various ways in which Lent was celebrated by the Roman Church and other Churches in centuries past.

It hardly needs to be said that we cannot aim at completeness. Lent, after all, has six Sundays, each with a three-year cycle of readings; it also has a special celebration for each weekday. On the other hand, we think that what should be important for us is not so much the details but a mentality we ought to make our own. The purpose of acquiring this mentality is not to abandon our contemporary outlook and adopt an older one but to enrich what we now have and to achieve a personal synthesis that can guide our lives.

It seems worth recalling here a point we made in volume 1 with regard to the reading of Scripture in the liturgy. The liturgy must, of course, take into account the data of scientific exegesis and find support in it. At the same time, however, if we wish to grasp the message being conveyed in the liturgical proclamation of a passage from the gospels, we must keep in mind that the liturgical vision of such a passage is not the same as the exegetical vision of the same text. One and the same text receives different emphases when it is proclaimed in different celebrations, since the other two readings provide a new context and point to the primary meaning the gospel has in a particular liturgy. In other words, the liturgical season and the first two readings of the Mass—or at least one of these two readings—will lead us to read the gospel from a special point of view. This does not mean that we elaborate a new exegesis each time the same passage recurs; it means simply that the Church approaches the text from a new angle of vision. This, at any rate, is the way we shall be looking at the texts in each of the celebrations we are studying.

3

Biblico-Liturgical Reflections on Lent

1. THE ANTHROPOLOGY OF LENT

What God Creates Is Divine

We are so used to seeing the defects and faults of the beings and the things around us that we find it difficult to pass an accurate judgment on the value, meaning, and purpose of creation. It may also be that a certain kind of religious education and a poorly understood liturgy have contributed to our having a rather pessimistic view of the created world.

On the First Sunday of Lent, for example, the first reading (Year A) tells us of the Fall and thus of the inability of the first human couple to resist temptation (Gen 2.7-9, 3.1-7). When we hear it often enough, we end up thinking that it is describing humanity's natural condition. Once we acquire this mentality, life becomes difficult. Either we succumb to a kind of fatalism with regard to sin and accustom ourselves to accepting the disastrous situation of sin and its effects, or else we live with a constant sense of overwhelming anxiety and of the shadowy character of human existence.

Are such attitudes a proper response to the true meaning of creation? Certainly not. But, on the other hand, can we be surprised to find people abandoning in despair a religion that is presented to them as a kind of poultice applied to an incurable wound, a religion that looks upon a human as a fallen being, a weak thing who is offered Christian morality as a crutch or a form of opium for the people?

We must admit that some presentations of Lent utterly fail to give people a proper sense of what they really are in the midst of God's creation. The formula, "Remember that you are dust, and to dust you shall return," which for centuries accompanied the imposition of ashes, was not calculated to give the recipient a positive vision of Lent, any more than was the account of the Fall, read on the First Sunday of Lent. If people have only this one-sided vision of things, they will see humanity and its history as a failure and will not be encouraged to try to patch up a situation so radically compromised.

If, then, we are to understand the real situation of humanity and of the world, we must tackle the problem afresh. We must bear in mind, however, that the Church presents her interpretation of the world's history only to believers. It is not that she refuses to speak of it to others but rather that in her liturgy she handles these problems, not as merely intellectual challenges, but as problems whose answers are to influence the way we live. Consequently, when she describes the Fall, her concern is to make us understand our human condition, not merely or primarily as wretched, but also and above all as marked by the great certainty that has power to deliver us from our wretchedness; for she shows us that God is capable of creating only what is divine.

The liturgy, like the Bible, is therefore offering us not an explanation but a sign; it tells us that creation is a language in which God expresses himself. We might even say that creation is a process wherein God reveals himself. And often he reveals himself as a Father.

We can see immediately that the facile contrast between the distant, terrible God of the Old Testament and the God of the New Testament who is so close to us has no solid foundation. Ever since the final age, the time of salvation, began, the Church has been urging us to read the account in Genesis, even while she shows us the Father of our Lord Jesus Christ. The fact that she can do both without any sense of a tension between them shows us what she is about. She is not presenting us with a religious philosophy or a humanism or a method for developing humanity's powers. No, she is urging upon us a bold project legitimated by a command of Christ himself: "[B]e perfect, just as your heavenly Father is perfect" (Matt 5:48).

The account in Genesis tells us that we are made in God's image. Here, in the New Testament, we are told more specifically just what this image is. A paradox, is it not? On the one hand, a God who is the inaccessible, transcendent Creator; on the other, ever since the time of Abraham, a gracious, condescending God who draws closer and closer to us and to whom we in turn can draw ever closer, to the point where we receive the command to imitate him. But the apparent contradiction is resolved by the fact that it is Christ who gives this order. For he is our salvation, and in him we discover the humanity of God. St. John records these most meaningful words of Christ: "Whoever has seen me has seen the Father" (John 14:9).

Consequently, when the Church reads the account of creation to us each year during the Easter Vigil, she thinks of it not as an isolated episode but rather as the culmination of the revelation begun in that account. She thinks of the Trinity, into whose life we enter by way of the humanity of the Risen Christ. Though the account in Genesis speaks only of God as Creator and Father of the universe, the Church has before her eyes the whole history of salvation. In the account of creation, she contemplates the germinal presence of all the great and wonderful deeds that God will perform for the salvation of the world, especially the sending of his Son and the activity of his Spirit. This Creator-God, Father of the universe, is the God whom Jesus will show us and who is already revealing himself in the initial act of creation.

How can we belong to the people of God and become part of the "wonderful deeds" that mark this people's history if we do not believe in the fatherhood of God as revealed by his Son? The Church indicates to us how the new creation is already implied in the account of the first creation. For, in the story of Jesus' baptism, we see the Spirit descending on the waters, just as he did at the beginning of the world, except that in his descent at the Jordan he officially appoints Christ, the new Adam, to his messianic role.

> Christians have to relearn that they belong to the family of God. A more habitual reading of Paul and John will give them a sense of their divine adoption and of their divinization by the filial Spirit of God's Son. At the same time, they will be able to understand the strength of the bonds that link them to Christ, and the transcendent unity whereby all Christians are gathered into one body so that they may share in the very life of God.
>
> Yet, even this renewed awareness may remain abstract or be inspired simply by humanity's age-old yearning for immortality unless, with the help of the Old Testament, it recovers a sense of its authentic human roots. The family of God is, first of all, Israel. When the Son of God became a human, he was "born of a woman, born under the law" (Gal 4:4), and was "descended from David according to the flesh" (Rom 1:3). The entire people of God was of one race with its Christ, and every word in the Bible is a stammering of his Word. If, then, we are to belong to the race or family of God, we must belong by adoption to the race or family of the spiritual Israel.[1]

The Inaccessible God in Our Midst

Such a reading of Genesis evidently looks beyond the level of mere story. It shows us what our God is like and how we are to relate to him. We glimpse the face of God, but that face, close to us though it is, is never fully unveiled.

Thus, to be aware of God's nearness and humanness does not mean that we abandon our attitude of respect, reverential fear, and adoration. We retain always a clear vision of our total dependence on him whose "thoughts are not our thoughts" and who always remains incomprehensible and inaccessible. The Church does not hesitate to remind the faithful of this again and again. "Perhaps the most difficult thing required of the Christian is to accept the inaccessibility of God. But when one does so, one will also understand the nearness and the humanness of God."[2]

Father of the Universe

There is a further point that we cannot pass over in silence, for unless we grasp it, we may radically misunderstand the plan of redemption and the life of the Church. The point is this: The Church preaches to us a God who is the Creator not only of the isolated individual but also of all other human beings and of the entire universe. Adam was placed in paradise as a person intimately involved with the beings that surrounded him. In fact, in the view of the fathers, God created the whole of humankind as a single totality, and it is this unity, which extends to the uttermost depths of every being, that explains how one man's sin could implicate the whole human race. But the same unity also explains how redemption could be accomplished by the sacrifice of the new Adam: "By the sacrifice of Christ the first human was saved, that human who is in us all."[3]

Christians cannot, therefore, have the right attitude toward their Creator unless they stand before him with a soul that is open not only to other human beings but to all created things, animate and inanimate, and indeed to the universe in its entirety. For the latter, like humanity itself, has been redeemed. To put it another way, it is the whole person, and not just one's soul, that God has created and that Christ has redeemed, and the resurrection of the flesh implies in turn the restoration of the universe as a whole. In his letter to the Romans, St. Paul gives us his thinking on these matters, and there is no reason to believe that he is simply indulging in metaphor:

> I consider that the sufferings of this present time are as nothing compared with the glory to be revealed for us. For creation awaits with

eager expectation the revelation of the children of God; for creation was made subject to futility, not of its own accord but because of the one who subjected it, in hope that creation itself would be set free from slavery to corruption and share in the glorious freedom of the children of God. We know that all creation is groaning in labor pains even until now; and not only that, but we ourselves, who have the firstfruits of the Spirit, we also groan within ourselves as we wait for adoption, the redemption of our bodies. (Rom 8:18-23)

It is important for Christians to bear in mind that salvation embraces our whole being, body no less than soul, and also the whole of creation, including all that is subhuman in it. In setting our sights on the definitive kingdom to come, we must therefore not separate into watertight compartments the spiritual and the fleshly, the soul and the body, the things of the spirit and material things. The world to come presupposes that all the various orders of being are given their proper value and brought into perfect harmony and balance.

Humanity is indeed the center of creation, and everything else was created for its sake. This means, however, that subhuman creation has a place in an overall unity willed by God. It means too that Adam was put into the world as a cosmic personage, one linked to the rest of creation by an ontological bond. From the very beginning of Lent, therefore, the Church already has in mind the night of the Easter Vigil, when she will read the opening pages of Genesis to those who are about to be buried with Christ in death in order that they may rise with him to new life. Then the newly baptized will understand those pages with minds reborn.

The Fall

We must acknowledge, however, that the Fall is indeed a central focus of the Lenten liturgy. It is not the only theme, as we have seen, but certainly the fact of the Fall and its consequences are everywhere present in the celebrations of this season.

It is, then, the Church's wish that her faithful, present and future, should be confronted with the fact of sin. Here again, however, the book of Genesis cannot be properly understood except in the context provided by the other books of Scripture. In point of fact, it was only through concrete experience and the enlightenment bestowed by the Spirit that Israel came to understand original sin.[4] A series of disillusionments, cataclysms, and personal and collective failures made people aware of the existence of a single, first sin in which all shared. St. Paul would later say that "Jews and Greeks alike . . . are all under the domination of sin" (Rom 3:9) and that "through one transgression condemnation came upon all" (Rom 5:18).

We are all prisoners of sin. The Old Testament had various descriptive words for sin, but gradually it tended toward a single, unequivocal understanding of it. Sin is an action that fails of its end. More concretely, it is an action in which we fail with regard to another person. It is "a violation of the bond which unites persons to each other, an act which, because it does not respect this organic bond, only affects the person concerned by injuring him."[5]

Yet, there is nothing pessimistic about the liturgy's very realistic vision of a world destroyed by sin. The aim is rather that Christians should become aware of their sinful state and have a concrete grasp of the deficiencies, failures, and humiliating limitations of their wounded nature. The liturgy does not indulge in extremist presentations that provide preachers with ready-made sermons in which the period before the Fall is described in language from the *Arabian Nights* while the ages after the Fall are uniformly black and catastrophic. The Church knows only too well, from long experience, that such contrasts arouse only a passing emotion and cannot lead to radical changes in the soul's outlook. Something more is needed for a genuine conversion.

Preoccupation with Paradise

If the Church likes to tell us of the paradisal state (it is a frequent theme of the fathers), she does so not for the pleasure of reminding us of what we have lost but to remind us that we must return to that paradise. If we are to properly comprehend the whole paschal liturgy and its rich typology, and if we are to understand properly the spirit in which the Church will reread the account of paradise in Genesis to those about to be baptized during the Easter Vigil, we must begin now to enter into her mentality as she proclaims the story at the moment when she wishes us to begin to live, with her, the history of salvation. Paradise, in her way of thinking, is not so much a paradise that has been lost as it is a paradise we are to regain and, in fact, have already regained. In describing to us paradise when it was first created, the Church already has in mind the words Christ will speak to the Good Thief while hanging on the cross: "Amen, I say to you, today you will be with me in Paradise" (Luke 23:43).

This is a point we must insist on: The Church cannot read the narrative of creation and paradise to us without taking into account all that happened later on, any more than she can fail to remember at every moment what she is and where she comes from. She is herself both an image of paradise and the beginning of paradisal fulfillment. In an ancient text entitled *The Odes of Solomon*, which may have been used in liturgical celebrations, the splendor of that regained paradise, of which the Church is an image, is described in poetic terms. The text tells us that our paradise is now to be found in Christ:

> Eloquent water from the fountain of the Lord was given me to drink; I drank and was intoxicated by the living water that does not die. I abandoned the madness widespread on the earth, stripped it from me and cast it away. The Lord gave me his own new garment and clad me in his light. I drew glad breath in the pleasant breeze of the Lord. I adored the Lord because he is glorious, and I said: Happy they who have their roots in the earth and for whom there is a place in his paradise.[6]

The reader will recognize in the sentence "The Lord gave me his own new garment and clad me in his light" an allusion to the grace of baptism, which consists, according to St. Paul, in "clothing oneself in Christ." And, in fact, it is baptism into the death and resurrection of Christ that fulfills the prophecy: "Today you will be with me in Paradise." The fathers vie with one another for developing the theme of the return to paradise through baptism. Similarly, a favorite motif in the mosaics that decorate the early baptisteries is the portrayal of paradise, whose running ("living") waters symbolize baptism. The sheep drinking at the stream are the faithful who have been made one within the bosom of the Church, and among them walks Christ, the new Adam.

Everything said of Adam in the Genesis narratives must be carefully noted, since the fathers like to compare him with the new Adam as with his infinitely superior counterpart. The parallel between the two Adams, so dear, for example, to St. Irenaeus, leads in turn to a parallel between Eve and the new Eve, Mary, and between Eve and the Church. Thus, the birth of Eve from Adam's side becomes the image of the Church's birth, as Spouse of Christ, from the side of the new Adam.

Sin in the Light of Redemption

Evidently the Church, in her reflection on sin, does not concentrate primarily on the Adam who fell but sees sin rather in the light of the redemption wrought by Christ. The Church here shows a healthy realism, for though she wants us to be fully aware of all that sin implies, she refuses to make sin the center of religion. The focus of Christianity is not on sin but on Christ who conquered sin and death. Consequently, in the theology of Lent, the promise of redemption is more important than sin. Christianity is not a dualist religion that sees the good and evil spirits locked in conflict; it is the religion of the God who overcomes all evil.

Original Sin?

For quite some time now, we have been uneasy with the concept of "original sin." Our uneasiness has two causes: the concept of original sin seems to undermine our human dignity, and it seems to involve a basic injustice. The first thing the modern world does, therefore, when it turns its attention to Christianity, is to reject the idea of original sin. By so doing it involves itself in all sorts of misunderstandings about Christianity, but at least its attitude is an intelligible one. For there can be no doubt that the presentation of original sin has too often been morbid and that it is morbid at times even today. Few concepts have, in fact, been so distorted and ruined by countless misunderstandings as has the concept of original sin.

On the other hand, in order to repress the anxiety that the concept of original sin can arouse, people at times transform the Genesis narrative into a bedtime story for clever or naughty children. Once it is turned into a myth, it is much easier to reject the reality that has thus been cleverly hidden.

We do not intend to enter here into the thicket of theological discussion on original sin. After all, Christians who lack specialized training nonetheless have the right to an intelligent grasp of the essentials of a problem that affects them very deeply. Let us therefore leave aside the question of what elements each of the various sources of Genesis 2–3 has contributed to the story. We may also leave aside the question of whether the "human" who sinned was an individual; even in the story itself, after all, two human beings sin!

Before proceeding, however, we should advert to the fact that the word "Adam" is not a proper name applied to a single person but signifies "human being," in the sense of humankind or all humans. The Hebrew for "Adam" occurs 539 times, and in every case the translators are justified in translating it simply as "the human." Ezekiel, for example, uses "Adam" several times, and the translation "human" is quite legitimate. Thus, Ezekiel 19:3, "a young lion he became; / He learned to tear apart prey, / he devoured people"; a more literal translation would be: "he devoured Adam." The reader may also consult Ezekiel 20:11, 13, 21; 25:13; etc. (and see Gen 7:21; 9:5).

To repeat, we may leave this problem aside; for even if we maintain that a couple sinned, or even a multiplicity of couples, this creates no real difficulty. The important, and the more difficult, thing is to put our finger on the essential theology of Genesis 2–3. Adequate treatment would, of course, require a whole book. We can at least give a short synthesis, a series of points that can provide food for reflection and stir our interest in pursuing the question further, while supplying in the interim a sufficient foundation for our vital experience of the liturgical season we are here endeavoring to understand.

We noted earlier that what God creates is divine. This means that when he created a human, his only thought was to create a being that would eventually share in the divine nature. The only qualification to this is that God wanted this creature to share in the divine nature in a free and fully personal way. In other words, humans must freely accept such a participation and attain it along the lines set down by the Creator. There was to be nothing automatic in this creation of a divinized human being: humans must freely consent to divinization; they must assent to this divinized state and cooperate fully with it.

There can be no doubt, of course, that every gift is from God and that the whole work of divinization, like that of creation itself, depends entirely on him. The point we are emphasizing here is that when God created a human, he was not creating a mere thing; humans must cooperate in shaping their own being and in making themselves what they are meant to be in the divine plan: *the image and likeness of God*. When God created humans, he set participation in the divine nature before them as a goal, but he did not simply impose it on them without their consent. This means that the possibility of failure is inherent in the plan of creation.

At the same time, we must remember that in God's plan human beings were endowed with supernatural powers. Humans then lost these powers by refusing to act as God wished. But the Lord continues to invite us to live a life like his. That life is a possibility for us; it is not forced upon us, since a being compelled to be divine would really not be divine after all! The invitation and the possibility, however, are freely given by God, just as the grace to follow the invitation and to become "divine" is likewise God's gift.

There was, then, a catastrophe at the beginning of human history. Humanity lost the gift of divinization that it had refused to accept, despite the clarity of mind and the strength of will with which people were then endowed. After that catastrophe, each human born, without being radically corrupt (as Luther maintained), would be born into a world that is sick in every respect: physically, physiologically, intellectually, and spiritually. Humans no longer possess sufficient strength to confront and master the world into which they are born. They must indeed grow and gradually achieve divinization or else reject it; yet, if left to their own resources, they are incapable of entering upon the true way that leads to divinization.

Every human depends on the human race, past and present, of which he or she is a part. The individual is not an isolated entity; every enrichment and every perversion of humanity is social in character. We do not inherit the personal guilt of our family ancestors, but we do inherit their defects. The inclination to evil is perennial; it precedes the present state of humanity. We cannot but admit that of all the beings that make up the world, humans alone have the power to destroy themselves, and "evil" consists in this self-destruction. Evil is the contrary of creation; it is opposed to creation, not as one being to another, but as negation. At the same time, however, this evil flows from the human will, and humans are responsible for it.

Evil Today

Here we have the permanent stumbling block: How is the existence of God, who is necessarily good and just, compatible with the evil in the world? Of what value have the long centuries of Christianity been?

In earlier times people were tempted to solve the basic problem by dualism: an ultimate source of evil alongside an ultimate source of good. Our contemporaries adopt a more radical solution: atheism. The existence of evil has, of course, always been regarded as the clinching argument against Christianity, but this is only because evil has been misunderstood.

Take, for example, death. According to a pagan vision of reality, death is evil supreme and unqualified. Consequently, the opposition between paganism and Christianity emerges most clearly at this point. For the Christian, death is not an annihilation of the person but only a stage or phase in the ongoing completion of the creation of humanity. Therefore, there is no contradiction between death and the goodness of God. On the contrary, we may even say that death is a manifestation of God's goodness, inasmuch as he thereby continues his work of creation despite the resistance people offer.

The same can be said for all the failures and setbacks that mark one's life. There is genuine "failure" only when we adopt the worldly perspective that makes "success" all-important. In the Christian vision, "success" can be measured only in relation to a final, future destiny. Evil, then, can also be defined only in terms of the definitive goal to which we are called.

Sin and Reparation

God is concerned about people, but if he is to divinize people, he must allow them the responsibility for their actions. Divinization is always the end that God has in view, but he gives us the means of freely attaining that end. This is the point of the Adam-Christ antithesis that is so favored a theme in the New Testament (Mark 1:13; Rom 5:12-21; 1 Cor 15:22, 45-49).

We shall have occasion later on, in connection with the First Sunday of Lent, to attend to Mark 1:13, the temptation of Christ by Satan. The text clearly intends to contrast Christ, as head of a new human race, with the first Adam and to show Christ as overcoming where the first Adam succumbed. The parallelism also involves both Adam and Jesus being tempted by Satan. It is reasonable that the Adam-Christ parallel accounts for Luke's tracing the genealogy of Jesus all the way back to Adam (Luke 3:38) and for his placing the genealogy immediately before his account of the temptation (4:1-13).[7]

We are hereby invited to read Genesis with reparation and the new creation in mind. There is an air of triumph about the way St. Paul develops the contrast between Christ and Adam. We can sense it in Romans 5:12-21, which comprises the second reading for the First Sunday of Lent (Year A). Where sin abounded, grace has abounded still more. Adam was a figure of him who was to come (Rom 5:14), that is, of the Christ who has bestowed life-giving grace on all humankind (Rom 5:15). Grace is universal in its compass, so that wherever death laid its hand, there shall be resurrection (1 Cor 15:22), and those who rise to eternal life will have a body that is glorious and incorruptible (1 Cor 15:44-49). At that point we will lay aside our likeness to the mortal, corruptible Adam and acquire the likeness to Christ and his spiritual body.

St. Paul here cites Genesis 2:7 in the Septuagint version: "The first man, Adam, became a living being," and then he draws his parallel: "the last Adam a life-giving spirit" (1 Cor 15:45). In our material, earthly bodies we resemble the first Adam; in our glorious, heavenly bodies we shall resemble the last Adam (see 1 Cor 15:48).

The Optimism of Lent

Lent, then, offers us an optimistic vision of the world; for though it sees the world as sinful because of humanity's beginnings, it always links sin to redemption, and the destruction of the world to its renewal.

To those not yet converted, Lent offers entry into the new creation through baptism. To those already baptized, it proposes a reformation of life and thus an advance toward the divinization that is already theirs in principle but that they must make truly their own in an ever more conscious and radical way.

Sincerity and Honesty

Lent thus summons us to something more than an artificial asceticism or a set of supplementary observances. It asks of all people that they have the courage sincerely and honestly to reform their lives and to judge where they are, what they are seeking, and how much they have really understood of Christian life. These forty days lived with Israel in the desert, with Moses, with Elijah, and above all with Christ are a time of deep spiritual significance.

We all know that we must face temptation. We all know too that we are capable of overcoming with Christ. The question is, do we sincerely and honestly want to overcome? The fact that we are capable of overcoming does not do away with our inherent weakness or with the various physiological and psychological influences at work in us. It does mean, however, that we are not tempted beyond our strength.

There is, then, a sense of risk but also an optimism because we are assured of victory, provided we use the means Christ offers us. For the person preparing for baptism, Lent is a time for the deliberate acquisition of these means. For those who are already Christians, it is a time for learning anew how to use the means wisely and to develop or renew them. In short, Lent is a time when we are to collaborate with God in creating something divine.

2. THE EXPERIENCE OF LENT IN THE FATHERS

It is evident that the fathers of the Church attached great importance to Lent. In fact, we find it quite normal that they should have been preoccupied with this season of penance. After all, was it not part and parcel of the religious mentality of their times, somewhat as the garment of camel's hair and the meals of grasshoppers and wild honey were part of the religious personality of John the Baptist? The fathers lived in an age that called for a strict and rather dour asceticism; harsh temperaments required a harsh asceticism.

Many are inclined, therefore, to let the dust of history rest undisturbed on patristic ideas and attitudes, for it is assumed that these must be irrelevant to people today. And yet, if we familiarize ourselves with some of the fathers, we will soon find that the human and spiritual physiognomy of the Christians of that time is surprisingly similar to our own.

It is remarkable that our contemporaries almost always associate Catholicism of the early centuries with men and women of iron temperament, armor-clad souls, unremitting energy, and unimaginative minds. Fasting and mortification seem to have been so much a part of that world that we would be almost scandalized to discover any laxity in the practice of these virtues. Their absence would introduce a false shading into the picture.

But the picture is, in fact, one that we have simply created for ourselves with little if any foundation; it represents only our own preconceived ideas. It is an almost totally false picture, drawn in unconscious justification of our contemporary rejection of asceticism. The Christians of the patristic age were in reality very much like us and the Christians around us today. The homilies of the fathers offer clear proof of this. Indeed, the topicality and relevance of these compositions are perhaps the most striking thing about them. We are the contemporaries of the fathers; they speak to us, and no sincere Catholic is dispensed from heeding them.

A Balanced Asceticism

Our contemporaries will find the ascetic demands of the fathers acceptable because the fathers are very much concerned that this asceticism be both down-to-earth and utterly permeated by the authentic Christian spirit. For the fathers, practices as such are secondary and a means to an end. Practices are valid only on certain conditions. The first condition is union with the community through love; this is to find concrete expression in the practice of almsgiving. The second condition is authentic union with God through prayer that is selfless and derives its power from the dispositions created by fasting. If these two conditions are not met, the asceticism of fasting degenerates into selfishness and self-delusion; it becomes a means of turning in, unconsciously, on oneself and creates an atmosphere of spiritual inauthenticity.

Prayer and Fasting

Prayer is the chief activity of Lent, and Lent is a time for renewal in the practice of prayer. The spiritual life, after all, is a coherent whole. A period of fasting requires that we give ourselves to prayer. In turn, the ascetical effort to liberate the self from the downward pull of the flesh and the effort to go out of ourselves to our neighbor in generous selfless charity will affect the quality and power of our prayer. St. Augustine observes:

> No one can doubt, then, that fasting is profitable; for when you impose on yourself the burden of fasting, you show that you really want what you are asking for. That is why it is said that "prayer is good when accompanied by fasting" (Tob 12:8). Therefore, prayer seeks fasting for a companion so that it may be heard1[1]

In a Lenten sermon, St. Augustine told his hearers:

> By almsgiving and fasting we add wings of fervor to our prayers so that they may more easily fly up and reach God. . . . Through humility and charity, fasting and almsgiving, abstaining and forgiving, avoiding evil and doing good, our prayer seeks peace and achieves it. For such prayer takes its flight on the wings lent it by these virtues and easily reaches heaven, where Christ our Peace has gone on ahead.[2]

The same image occurs in another Lenten sermon: "During these days our prayer rises aloft because it is borne up by pious almsgiving and austere fasting."[3]

It is clear that St. Augustine closely associates fasting with prayer and almsgiving. In his view, Lent is to be chiefly a time for prayer but also a period in which prayer is greatly enriched and refined because it receives the "food" it needs if it is to rise up to God: "Prayer has a food of its own which it is bidden to take without interruption. Therefore, let it always fast from hatred and feed on love."[4]

Charity

While St. Augustine, in his Lenten asceticism, insists very much on the quality of prayer during this season, St. Leo the Great concentrates more on the charity that is given concrete expression in almsgiving. Almost all of St. Leo's twelve sermons on Lent that have come down to us speak of love, the forgiveness of offenses, and almsgiving.

> Therefore, beloved, mindful of our weakness that makes us readily fall into all kinds of sins, let us not neglect this powerful remedy and most efficacious means of healing our wounds. Let us forgive so that we may be forgiven; let us grant others the pardon we seek for ourselves. We pray for forgiveness; let us not seek revenge.[5]

The saint reminds his hearers of the custom by which emperors released prisoners in honor of the passion and resurrection of the Lord:

> Therefore let the Christian peoples imitate their princes and be spurred by the royal example to a domestic clemency. The laws that govern private life should not be more severe than those that govern public life. Forgive sins, break fetters, wipe out offenses, and eliminate vengefulness so that the sacred feast may be marked by pardon human and divine, and thus find everyone joyous and beyond reproach.[6]

> Beloved, remove the causes of discord and the thorns of enmity. Let hatred cease and rivalries disappear, and let all the members of Christ meet in loving unity.[7]

The concluding theme in most of St. Leo's Lenten sermons is that we should forgive the offenses done to us by others so that we may ourselves win pardon from God. This great pope constantly urges his hearers to pray the Our Father and emphasizes the fact that what we say in that prayer imposes an obligation on us, for it sets a condition for the forgiveness we ask of God: "If we say, 'Forgive us our sins as we forgive those who sin against us,' but do not act according to our words, we fasten heavy chains upon ourselves."[8]

Our forgiveness must be given not only to our peers but also to our subordinates: "Beyond any doubt, you may promise yourselves God's sure mercy if, in dealing with those subject to you, you make every offense an occasion for pardon."[9]

St. Leo begs mercy for offenders and, for all his reserve, does not hesitate to make an emotional appeal: "If you are keeping people prisoner for some offense or other, remember that you yourself are a sinner! If you wish to receive forgiveness for yourself, rejoice that you have someone whom you yourself may forgive."[10] "What you decide with regard to others, you also decide, by that very fact, for yourself."[11]

Such forgiveness is in no sense demeaning. On the contrary, it is an action by which we share in the exercise of a divine power: "Forgiveness is a perfectly just and good action whereby a human being shares in God's own power, so as to determine by one's own free act the sentence God will pass in return, and to bind the Lord to the same judgment that one passes on one's fellow servant."[12]

St. Augustine turns to similar themes in his seventh sermon on Lent, which is wholly devoted to the subject of charity and the forgiveness of offenses. The sermon begins with a vigorous assertion of the fact that the soul's salvation, as it struggles against the many temptations besetting it, depends on forgiving the offenses done to it by others:

> These holy days, which we spend in the observance of Lent, make it our duty to speak to you of the harmony that must reign in the community. Those who have any quarrel with another must put an end to it lest an end be put to them. . . . We have made an agreement with God and have submitted to a condition that must be fulfilled if our debt to him is to be written off.[13]

The forgiveness of offenses, according to Augustine, is necessary if we are to attain illumination and freedom of spirit. Appealing to 1 John 3:15, "Everyone who hates his brother is a murderer," the saint tells his hearers: "Those who hate others walk, go out and in, and travel where they wish; they seem burdened by no chains, locked in no prison, but they are nonetheless enchained by their crime. Do not believe that they are not in prison; their prison is their own heart!"[14]

Almsgiving

One of the most concrete forms of charity is almsgiving, a practice inseparable from authentic fasting. But almsgiving is by no means limited to the material action whereby one gives away one's money. St. Augustine warns against such a narrow interpretation: "It is your duty to intensify your almsgiving during these days. . . . There is a further work of mercy in which one takes nothing from one's store or purse but expels from the heart that which it is more harmful to keep than to give away. I am referring to the anger one stores up in one's heart against another."[15]

Almsgiving, joined to fasting, also makes possible our union with God in prayer. Commenting on what Isaiah says of fasting (58:3), the saint concludes: "These are the two wings on which prayer mounts up to God: forgiveness of offenses and alms to the needy."[16]

When St. Augustine speaks of almsgiving, he makes it a condition for union with God in prayer. St. Leo the Great looks upon it rather as a work of mercy that wins us God's forgiveness. "Let us not pass the poor by, deaf to their groans, but with ready goodwill show mercy to the needy so that we ourselves may find mercy at the Judgment."[17]

The duty of almsgiving is not limited to helping those who share our faith: "Though the poverty of the faithful should be alleviated first, yet those who have not yet accepted the gospel are to be pitied in their distress, for we must love the one nature that all people share."[18]

To give alms is to participate in the generosity of God himself: "Nothing is worthier of humans than to imitate their Creator and to be, as far as they can, agents of the divine work."[19]

The tenth and eleventh sermons on Lent both end with an exhortation to almsgiving. When people act mercifully, Pope St. Leo tells us, God sees his own image realized in them: "No zeal on the part of the faithful gives greater joy to God than that which is devoted to his poor. Where he finds a concern for mercy, he sees his own love imaged forth in humanity."[20]

In a paradoxical turn of phrase, the saint makes it clear that in his eyes fasting involves far more than mere abstinence from food: "Let fasting Christians grow fat through the distribution of alms and the care of the poor. Let them give to the weak and the poor what they refuse to spend on their own pleasures."[21]

St. Leo's exhortations during Lent are all marked by his major concerns: charity, forgiveness, and almsgiving. He evidently thinks that Christians may easily slip into misunderstandings. Perhaps there was danger that a formalistic practice of exterior fasting would become an excuse for a tepid spiritual life. St. Leo does not want this to happen, and he points out the danger in straightforward fashion: "Let us engage in this solemn fast with alert faith and celebrate it, not as a sterile abstinence from food (as bodily weakness or the disease of avarice may suggest), but as a form of great-hearted generosity."[22]

The saint never tires of emphasizing the real nature and purpose of fasting: "Our fasting does not consist merely in abstinence from food; in fact, there is no profit in depriving the body of nourishment unless the spirit turns from injustice and the tongue abstains from quarreling."[23] To fail in this further abstinence would be hypocrisy, and Pope Leo does not hesitate to agree with non-Christians who criticize Christians in this regard: "Unbelievers will rightly criticize us, and the tongues of the wicked will have a weapon against religion if we fast but our manner of life lacks the purity that perfect abstinence requires."[24]

In these pages we have been drawing only upon sermons dealing with Lent. There are, of course, many other sources we could cite, but these will be enough to show how realistically two important Latin fathers deal with fasting and how much at one they are with our contemporaries in their demand for sincerity and the elimination of all formalism. In a moment, as we endeavor to put our finger on the essential point in fasting, we shall see how John Chrysostom, for example, likewise rejects formalism.

Fasting without Fasting?

In a homily preached on Easter, St. John Chrysostom gives us his interpretation of fasting. He uses the language of paradox, but his hearers must certainly have grasped the essential point he was making.

During the period when you were fasting, I told you it was possible not to fast while fasting; now I tell you it is possible to fast while not fasting! Is this a riddle? Let me put the truth to you more plainly. How is it possible not to fast while fasting? By abstaining from food but not from sin! And how is it possible to fast while not fasting? By enjoying food while having no taste for sin. This is a far better kind of fasting, and easier as well.[25]

We find the same thought and even some of the same language in St. Leo the Great: "During this time Christians should do with greater care and devotion what they should be doing at all times. Then the forty-day fast which we have from apostolic tradition will be marked not only by abstinence from food but also and especially by abstinence from sin."[26] St. Augustine uses the same language on several occasions: "If we are truly to fast, we must abstain, above all, from every sin."

Care of the Soul

Lent is, most basically, a time of care for the soul. Newcomers to the Catholic faith are not the only ones who must be concerned with the growth of their own soul; every Catholic, however long baptized, must have the same concern, since no one is assured of indefectibility. Speaking of those who are soon to be baptized and addressing himself to those already baptized, St. Leo points out the value and necessity for all of such concern for the soul:

The former [catechumens] need it [the fast] in order to receive what they do not have as yet; the latter [the baptized] need it in order to preserve what they have received. For the Apostle says: "Let anyone who thinks that he stands take heed lest he fall." . . . Let us therefore make good use, beloved, of this most propitious of seasons to polish the mirror of our hearts with greater care.[27]

Fasting consists first and foremost in abstaining from sin, but it is also to be noted that fasting, in turn, "rescues from sin those who fast and leads them to ineffable pleasures."[28]

In a homily on the first chapter of Genesis, St. John Chrysostom quotes St. Paul's Second Letter to the Corinthians—"although our outer self is wasting away, our inner self is being renewed day by day" (4:16)—and comments, "Fasting is the food of the soul. As bodily food makes the body fat, so fasting makes the soul healthier and makes its wings light so that it may be borne aloft and be capable of contemplating what is above."[29]

St. Augustine likewise tells us what he thinks the effects of Lenten abstinence on the soul are:

> When the soul is freed from the burden of excessive food and drink, it comes to know itself better. For, as people cannot tell from a dirty mirror what they really look like, so when they are dragged down by food and drink they think themselves to be other than they really are. But when the body is brought to a proper state through fasting, the soul comes to know itself and realizes how devotedly it should follow the Redeemer.[30]

In the last analysis, the essential purpose of fasting is that the soul may be more perfectly configured to the crucified Christ. Here we have the specific meaning of the Lenten fast. St. Augustine writes, "Let us also fast and humble our souls as we near the time when the Teacher of humility humbled himself and became obedient even to the point of dying on a Cross. Let us imitate him in his crucifixion by mastering our appetites and fixing them to the Cross with the nails of abstinence."[31]

St. Leo uses very similar language in expressing his view of the Lenten season: "The holy apostles, under the inspiration of the Holy Spirit, ordained that a greater fast should be observed during these days, in order that by a common sharing of Christ's Cross we may contribute something to what he has done for us, in accordance with the Apostle's words: 'If we have died with him, we shall also live with him.'"[32]

Fasting is thus a sharing in the suffering of Christ. This is why fasting means a relentless struggle of the kind Christ faced until the moment of his victory. For, "the tempter, always on the alert, attacks more intensely those he sees most careful to avoid sin. Who shall be exempt from his onslaughts, when he dared tempt even the Lord of majesty with his clever tricks?"[33]

There is no point in pushing our inquiry any further, since it will constantly lead us back to the same basic points. Fasting, as the Fathers think of it, belongs to every season and to every moment of life. Their main concern is to eliminate from the practice every taint of the fraudulent and the hypocritical. St. Augustine, for example, does not hesitate to assert that some people make Lent the occasion for sensuality and even abstain from wine for sensual motives:

> There are some who observe Lent more out of sensuality than religion, for they seek to cultivate new kinds of pleasure rather than to chastise their old appetites. They provide themselves with all kinds of abundant and costly fruits and delicacies in order to have a variety of tasty dishes. . . . There are some, too, who do not drink wine but replace it with liqueurs from the juice of other fruits.[34]

Fasting with the Entire Church

True Lenten observance has nothing to do with such practices as St. Augustine was rejecting. In fact, it is not even a matter of mere observances at all. The essence and purpose of Lent is, rather, for the Christian to become like the crucified Christ, to overcome the devil, and to reestablish a proper state of soul through union with God in prayer and with one's neighbor by means of a charity that leads to almsgiving and generous forgiveness.

In their pursuit of this Lenten asceticism, Christians are not cut off from others, nor is the fruit of their efforts to be found only in their own soul. The entire Church is involved in the struggle, with her attention focused on the catechumens who are preparing to renounce Satan and to put on Christ. In the conflict with the devil, the whole Christian army takes up its weapons and comes to grip with the enemy. "You know that this is the time when the devil rages throughout the world and the Christian army must do battle. If laziness has made some listless or worldly concerns have absorbed their attention, now is the time for them to don spiritual armor and be roused by the heavenly trumpet to enter the struggle."[35]

Completing the Temple of God

Thus, it is especially during the season of Lent that the hierarchy and each Catholic—in short, the entire Church—is summoned to cooperate in the redemptive work of the Head. We are "the temple of God, a temple whose foundation is the Founder himself." This place where God himself dwells must be built up in an honorable way:

> There is no doubt but that we cannot begin or complete the building unless its Architect helps us. Yet he who builds it has given us the ability

to make the building more perfect by our labors. For the material that God uses in constructing this temple is alive and endowed with reason, and the Spirit of grace inspires it to form, voluntarily, a single structure. . . . Since, then, each believer, and all believers together, form one and the same temple of God, the temple must be perfect not only in all together but in each.[36]

Consideration of fasting thus leads us eventually to the vision that should be our constant guide: the bringing of the Church to completion as the temple of God, "until we all attain . . . to the extent of the full stature of Christ" (Eph 4:13). This is the essential purpose of all our religious activity, be it ascetical, mystical, or liturgical. The ultimate purpose of fasting, then, is eschatological.

In the last analysis, fasting does its work in view of the last times. It is a remedy, but a remedy affecting eternal life. Jesus Christ, our Lord and our Head, instituted it for the purpose of healing, strengthening, purifying, and enlightening all in the unity of the one Church.

The Echo of Patristic Teaching

It is worth our while to inquire how the immediate successors of the Church fathers understood Christian asceticism. St. Benedict, whose Rule is steeped in patristic teaching and who often quotes the words of the fathers, is especially interesting in this respect. He is writing for a community of monks. He thinks of them, however, not as "specialists" in asceticism but simply as men who are to lead as thorough a Christian life as possible and to seek "the beginnings of perfection."

In chapter 49 of his Rule, St. Benedict deals with the observance of Lent. From the very opening words we can recognize not only the thinking but even some of the characteristic expressions of St. Leo the Great; the whole chapter is evidently inspired by his teaching. Those who have never made the acquaintance of the Rule of St. Benedict will profit by reading this beautiful chapter. It is simple and makes no display of theological learning, but it is certainly the fruit of profound experience in the search for God to the exclusion of all else.[37]

The life of a monk ought to be a continuous Lent. Since few, however, have the strength for this,[38] we urge the entire community during these days of Lent to keep its manner of life most pure and to wash away in this holy season the negligences of other times.[39] This we can do in a fitting manner by refusing to indulge evil habits and by devoting ourselves to prayer with tears, to reading, to compunction of heart and self-denial. During these days, therefore, we will add to the usual measure of our service[40] something by way of private prayer and abstinence from food or drink, so that each of us will have something above the assigned measure to offer God of his own will *with the joy of the Holy Spirit* (1 Thess 1:6). In other words, let each one deny himself some food, drink, sleep, needless talking and idle jesting, and look forward to holy Easter with joy and spiritual longing.

Everyone should, however, make known to the abbot what he intends to do, since it ought to be done with his prayer and approval. Whatever is undertaken without the permission of the spiritual father will be reckoned as presumption and vainglory, not deserving a reward. Therefore, everything must be done with the abbot's approval.

St. Benedict is envisaging Lent here, not in terms of the entire Church, but in terms only of the part of the Church that he directs and that is committed to living the complete Christian life. He does not touch on the needs of catechumens. One reason for this is that infant baptisms had become far more numerous by his time, but the chief reason is that monastic life, as he envisaged it, was not directly ordered to the apostolate. His emphasis is on asceticism, or more exactly (in the present passage) on a period when an asceticism that was exercised throughout the year was to be intensified. The point of the Lenten observance, therefore, was not to think up new practices but to do more perfectly and devoutly what was habitually being done at all times.

Even a superficial reading of the chapter will show the hierarchy of values that characterized religious life as established by St. Benedict, who was heir to the desert fathers and to such monastic lawgivers as Cassian, Pachomius, and Basil. In St. Benedict's view, Lent meant first and foremost a renewed dedication to prayer, reading, and compunction of heart—three essential aspects of monastic life that his Rule frequently emphasizes. Only after these three is abstinence mentioned.

St. Benedict also insists that Lent brings nothing new but only an intensification (in quantity but especially in quality) of what are constant elements of Christian life. As we have already indicated, the saint, in speaking of this point, repeats almost verbatim various statements of St. Leo the Great's Lenten sermons. In a similar way, St.

Ambrose advises virgins simply to intensify their habitual practices. For, in the last analysis, the important thing is not particular practices but the effort to reach God in detachment from self. The necessity of such detachment is what makes St. Benedict insist that nothing must be done without the abbot's approval.

On all these points, however, what St. Benedict says is hardly distinguishable from the commonplaces of spiritual writers generally. The special ethos of the chapter comes rather from the way in which he characterizes Lent as he wants his monks to live it. The point is made without special emphasis, yet it determines the character of the entire Lenten asceticism: "With the joy of spiritual desire he [the monk] may look forward to holy Easter."

For St. Benedict, as for the fathers generally and the liturgy, the mortification proper to Lent is part of the movement toward the day of the Lord's resurrection. Asceticism can have but one legitimate purpose: a liberation that consists, not in scorning the body, but in achieving a spiritual balance, a liberation for the sake of unconditional participation in the "great liberation" that is the Passover of the Lord. The purpose, then, is to die with Christ in order to arise with him.

As long as we live in this mortal dwelling, we must constantly strive for the needed balance, and that balance cannot be achieved and maintained without some asceticism. The asceticism must in turn be reinforced from time to time by making more intense demands on oneself. The only valid motive, however, for this Christian asceticism is to prepare oneself for Easter and for its eschatological fulfillment in the return of the Lord. This is why St. Benedict speaks of looking forward to Easter "with the joy of spiritual desire." An asceticism centered on the self cannot claim, without hypocrisy, to be permeated by authentic joy; the only joy it will experience is the transient, bitter joy that springs from satisfied pride in self-mastery. Only the expectation of Easter, and of the liberation of humanity and its world that Easter signifies, can beget genuine joy—that joy in the Holy Spirit of which St. Benedict speaks—amid the trials and difficulties of our present life.

In a preface for the Easter season, the Gelasian Sacramentary makes it clear that in the celebration of the paschal feast, what we should in the last analysis desire, prepare for, and await with joy is the final coming of Christ and our own "passage" to eternal life: "In your mercy grant, we pray you, that the more the faithful participate in the paschal sacraments and look forward with longing to your coming, the more may they be faithful to the mysteries by which they have been reborn, and be drawn into the new life that these mysteries make possible."[41]

3. THE CHURCH, PLACE OF DIVINIZATION

God's creation is something divine, and he has committed himself to restoring the world so that this divine character may once again be manifest in humankind and in the world itself. At the same time, however, he wills that humanity should be constantly living in quest of the divinization being offered. It was not enough to redeem humans; God also had to give them guidance. It was not enough that the Son should come into our world and die for us; he also had to remain in our world in some fashion or other. It was in order to meet both these needs that the Spirit was sent. The Spirit continues, in the Church, the action whereby God creates a divine reality. This means that the Church in turn is responsible for the divinization of humanity and of its world.

The Church must therefore have a twofold purpose in all she does. On the one hand, her task is to foster a new creation, a renewal in which death becomes simply a passage to a definitive life; this she does by calling people to faith in him who is the Resurrection and the Life. On the other hand, she must constantly endeavor to preserve and advance in the faith those who have already received the gift and have been trying to make it bear fruit in their lives.

Lent has a place in the achievement of both these purposes. It is a time when those who wish to receive baptism are prepared for the sacrament. It is also a time when the Church revitalizes and rejuvenates the faith of those already baptized and, if need be, restores life to those of the baptized who have been deadened by sin. Consequently, we find three organizational principles at work in the Lenten liturgy: (1) the liturgy is organized in terms of the catechumenate; (2) it is organized as a preparation for the reconciliation of penitents; (3) it is organized with a view to deepening the spiritual life of those faithful who wish to live more fully by faith and to advance in the concrete practice of the Christian life.

Turning to God

The Church's most important mission is to move people to *metanoia*, or conversion—that is, to bring them to travel a different road and to turn to God. Once the Church was not subject to persecution in the fourth century and was free to organize the forty days of Lent in a detailed way, she would engage in a sweeping revision of the cate-chumenate, traces of which can be seen at Rome in the third century, as reflected in St. Hippolytus's *Apostolic Tradition.**

It is clear that at this early period the entire local community was responsible for, and concerned about, the conversion of those who felt called to the faith. Hippolytus would die a martyr, for the period of persecution was not yet over, but the Church of Rome did not wait for persecution to end before showing her concern for those who were looking for the divinization for which they had been created. An individual catechesis did not seem adequate for this purpose; the whole ecclesial community had to assist in the recovery of the divine life lost by sin.

Nor was a merely intellectual conversion enough. More had to be done than to open the mind to new ideas, since the purpose of con-version was entry into a new people that regarded itself as chosen by God to be kings and priests, a people that proclaimed the advent of the final age of humankind and did not hesitate to think of itself as belonging to the "race" or "family" of God.

The rather detailed organization we see reflected in the *Apostolic Tradition* is itself a development of what we already know from Justin Martyr in his *First Apology*, which dates from about 150 and was ad-dressed to Emperor Antoninus Pius. Chapters 61 and 62 show the kind of preparation required of those who wished to join the Christian community. They had to believe what was taught to them and promise to live according to their new beliefs. They learned to pray and to seek forgiveness of their sins through fasting. Through all this the com-munity was very much concerned with those seeking admission to its ranks, and it prayed and fasted along with them during their time of preparation for baptism.

Meanwhile, there were also heretical sects that caused confusion of mind among those who wanted to cling to the true faith. The number of Christians was on the increase, but persecution inevitably caused defections. Tertullian worried as he saw Christians joining Gnostic sects, then returning to the Church, and finally rejoining the sects. Evidently a solid formation was needed.[1]

---

* The authorship and date of this work have been challenged since Nocent wrote this. See note on p. 128, vol. 1.

The *Apostolic Tradition* later gives us some detailed information on the state of a catechumenate that was already well organized. By this time catechumens were divided into two classes. The first of these classes consisted of catechumens in the proper sense of the term ("hearers" or "those being instructed"). When individuals sought to enter this group, they were questioned about their way of life and about the reasons why they wanted to enter the Church. Certain demands were made of them; for example, certain occupations had to be abandoned if the practitioners wanted to be accepted into this first stage of the catechumenate.

After this initial examination, those accepted were asked to come for instruction and were presented to the bishop by the members of the community who would be responsible for their detailed Christian education. The period of instruction lasted three years. After each lesson the catechumens prayed together; they did not join the faithful in prayer, nor did they give one another the kiss of peace. The instructor, whether a cleric or a layperson, prayed over them and imposed hands on them.

At the end of the three-year period, the catechumens were examined once again concerning their way of life and their practice of charity and good works. If their sponsors gave a favorable report about them, each was admitted to a new stage of the catechumenate and to the group known as the *phōtizomenoi* ("those being enlightened"). During this final period they listened to the Gospel and received a daily imposition of hands. As baptism became imminent, the bishop himself imposed hands on them. It is very likely that this episcopal laying on of hands took place on Holy Saturday morning,† while baptism would have been administered during the Easter Vigil, amid prayer and the reading of Scripture.[2]

How is all this related to Lent? The answer is that a good deal of the very substance of Lent is constituted by the prayer and fasting of the entire local community on behalf of those who will receive their divinization during the Easter Vigil. In the last analysis, Lent is organized in terms of this liberation and return to God.

At a later period the Gelasian Sacramentary gives a detailed idea of the organization of Lent and provides the prayers and the "scrutiny" celebrations proper to the season. The "scrutinies" were not

---

† "Very likely" may be too strong. The *Apostolic Tradition* never mentions the time of year.

inquiries into the intellectual or moral fitness of the candidates for baptism but exorcisms that gradually prepared them to become the dwelling place of the Spirit who would make them adoptive children of God. The celebrations of the scrutinies took place on Sundays; in these Masses, the prayers, readings, and parts of the Canon were slanted in favor of the catechumens and those in charge of them. As we go through the Sundays of Lent, we will have the opportunity to examine in greater detail the information contained in the Gelasian Sacramentary. In any case, extensive use has been made of this latter book in the current rite of adult baptism.

Clearly, then, Lent is, in the Church's view, not a time solely for personal meditation and asceticism; rather, it is a season that opens up wide vistas for the community that is celebrating it. It is a time of choice, when the community is summoned to return to God and to bring the world back to its real source. The entire Christian community prays and fasts for the true conversion of those who have entrusted themselves to it and are sincerely looking for the Lord. This is undoubtedly an aspect of Lent that was much neglected during the past century, with its emphasis on individual asceticism. When seen in its proper light, Lent is for the Church a period of great optimism, since it is a time when Christians recall the true meaning of human life, namely, that humanity is destined to enter into the realm of God himself through rebirth from water and the Spirit.

Metanoia, or Conversion

The Christian ideal of humanity's divinization is not an easy one to live up to. It is common knowledge that during the first seven centuries of the Church, Christians were so awed by what they had become in baptism that they were allowed only one opportunity throughout life to enter upon a regime of penitence that would reconcile them with God through the ministry of the Church. Only in the seventh century did Irish monks begin to give private absolution and to repeat it as needed.

We are rather taken aback by the severity of early Christian practice, since we like to emphasize the infinite mercy of God. The early Christians did not forget God's mercy; they were, however, keenly aware of the tremendous grace of divinization given to them in baptism and found it difficult to see how those who had reached this new life could fall back into sin.

The time for reconciliation was Lent. On Ash Wednesday the penitent entered the "order of penitents." (Later on, since every Christian
could rightly be regarded as a "sinner," the imposition of ashes was
universalized.) On Holy Thursday morning, after a period of expiation that might have lasted several years, the penitent was solemnly
reconciled to the Lord in the Church. Here again the Gelasian Sacramentary has preserved the texts for this Holy Thursday ceremony.
The celebration was somewhat amplified in the twelfth century; the
texts and rites were still to be found in the liturgical books until the
recent liturgical reform, but they had fallen into disuse. Holy Thursday thus marked the end of Lent. It was followed by an intra-paschal
fast that lasted from Good Friday to Communion during the Easter
Vigil.

We shall have the opportunity later in this book to present this
penitential ritual with its doctrinally rich texts and moving ceremonies. This will provide a new occasion for enlarging our conception
of Lent as a period when sinners are reconciled as the ecclesial community fasts and prays for them.

The Church Defines Lent in Her Prayers

Our earlier sampling of the writings of the fathers has shown us
the wider picture, of which fasting was only one part. It is equally
instructive to examine the texts of the liturgy, especially the prayers
and prefaces, for the Church's concept of fasting. Even if we were to
limit ourselves to the current Roman Missal, we would find a richly
detailed teaching; we must, however, go further and find in the chief
sacramentaries how the Church of a given age viewed fasting.

We must not, of course, expect to find in these various books a
teaching that is organized into a treatise. The liturgy, after all, is neither a handbook of ascetical theology nor a code of law. What we
find is something quite different. Like the catechumen who moves
forward to the light of Easter, we come into contact with the thinking
that is the basis of the Church's life during the forty days of Lent. The
catechumen does not receive a ready-made concept of fasting but
experiences the Church in her "state of fasting."

Those who seek entrance into the community of God's new people
are already aware that they encounter the Lord by means of and
through signs, and that in the process they come into an increasingly
closer union with the other members of the Church. Moreover, he

has already heard the Church herself called a "sacrament." The Church is not only an institution but also a sign. That is to say, she is not an institution exactly like the other institutions of this world; she is an institution that serves as a *sacramentum*, or sacred, effective sign. On the basis of Christ's incarnation, death, resurrection, and sending of the Spirit, the Church has been established as a "sign." In her, through her activity as Spouse of Christ and through her very nature, which is to be "Christ continued," we are efficaciously touched by the mysteries of Christ, that is, by all his salvific actions.

We have already seen how St. Leo the Great understood this *sacramentum*, this efficacious sacred sign or "sacrament." In his view, a sacrament is both an efficacious prolongation of Christ's salvific actions and, at the same time, an abiding reminder of his example. "The living faith of the Christian assembly not only draws on the well-spring of all perfection but at the same time discovers him who is the model of all perfection."[3]

We can readily apply this teaching to Lent and its fast. These too are sacraments and, as such, have an efficacy that derives from the salvific deeds of Christ. But they are also efficacious in that they render present to us the example of the Savior himself. When the Christian engages in the ascetical practice of fasting, it is impossible not to think of Christ fasting for forty days in the wilderness, battling with the demon, and emerging victorious. In fact, the account of Christ's fast in the wilderness is read on the First Sunday of Lent, which marks the beginning of the "sacrament of fasting" that will be effective in us both because of its institution by Christ and because of the encouraging example the Lord himself gives us.

We have also seen that Lent, like fasting, cannot be properly understood if the framework adopted is too narrow; it must be seen rather in the comprehensive perspective of the renewal of the world through the paschal mystery. There is, then, strictly speaking, no "sacrament of Lent and fasting" nor even any "sacrament of the resurrection." There is only a *sacramentum paschale*, a "paschal sacrament," that embraces Lent, the passion, the resurrection, the ascension, and the sending of the Holy Spirit.

These various points, which we have already met in the fathers and especially in St. Leo, recur in the Church's liturgical compositions. In these, fasting is part of the paschal sacrament. As such, it is a sign of a grace offered, that is, a sign of efficacious divine action; at the same time, it is a sign of and puts us into contact with the fasting, struggle, and victory of Christ.

The person who lives from day to day in the spirit of the Church and tries, without preconceived notions, to grasp in the liturgy the wealth of the Church's spirituality will conceive of fasting, not as the ascetical activity of an individual, but as a collective practice. Catechumens who have been enrolled for proximate baptism are not confronted with a requirement of individual asceticism and mortification; rather, they become part of an activity of the Church as a whole. The expression "collective practice" could indeed give rise to a false impression or lessen the esteem that the asceticism in question richly deserves. The danger can be avoided, however, by realizing that "practice" is not used here in the devotional sense. By "collective practice," as we have already indicated and as the Church's prayers during Lent show, we mean that fasting is a "sacrament" for the Church in its entirety and that its efficacy reaches to the whole people of God.

It is worthwhile to note the various descriptions given of Lent in the officially approved Latin edition of the revised Roman Missal. In the prayer over the offerings on the first Sunday, Lent is called a "venerable and sacred time" (*venerabilis sacramenti*), the beginning of which we celebrate on this day (the prayer comes from the Gelasian Sacramentary[4]). On other occasions, Lent is called an "exercise" or "observance." Thus the collect for the first Sunday speaks of the "observances of holy Lent" (*quadragesimalis exercitia sacramenti*), the phrase and indeed the whole prayer being taken from the Gelasian Sacramentary.[5] On Ash Wednesday the blessing of the ashes uses the words "Lenten observances" (*quadragesimalis exercitatio*), while the collect on Tuesday of the fourth week speaks of "the venerable exercises of holy devotion" (*exercitatio veneranda sanctae devotionis*).[6]

The term "observance" (*observantia*) is used elsewhere: "observance of Lent" (*quadragesimalis observantia*) occurs in the blessing of ashes on Ash Wednesday and again as "Lenten observance" in the prayer over the offerings on the Friday after Ash Wednesday and in the collect for Wednesday of the third week. Elsewhere we find the words: "Rejoicing in this annual celebration of our Lenten observance" (*observationis huius annua celebritate laetantes*).[7] Again, the Lord is asked to sanctify "our observance" (*observantiam nostram*).[8] Finally, in a phrase that reveals the true finality of the season as a whole, Lent is called "paschal observances" (*observatio paschalis*).[9]

God not only bids us observe a season of fasting; he also gives us the power to undertake it and to persevere in it: "Grant, O Lord, that we may begin with holy fasting this campaign of Christian service, so that, as we take up battle against spiritual evils, we may be armed with weapons of self-restraint."[10] It is to the Lord that we look for the ability to commit ourselves fully to the mortification that Lent imposes: "Grant, Lord, that we may observe the prescriptions with utter devotion."[11]

Our fasting is thus truly an action of God in us. It is this action that allows us to speak of Lent as a "sacrament" and also as a "mystery." This last term we find used in some older prayers, for example, "Almighty God, we pray you, be present in these holy mysteries of fasting."[12] Without the presence of the Lord, the solemn ecclesial act of fasting would have no power to sanctify but would simply be an outward performance.

It is easy to understand that because of this special presence of the Lord in his Church during Lent, the latter should be called "sacrament," "mystery," "solemnity," "feast." The Verona Sacramentary uses the same language in proclaiming the September fast: "Beloved, we are about to celebrate the annual feast of fasting."[13]

Festive Fasting

The name "feast" may well surprise us, since it is at least paradoxical to speak of a fast as a feast. Yet that is precisely how the fast has been seen, especially during the Easter Vigil. We must bear in mind that the vigil is thought of as a period of waiting for the return of Christ; it is the time when the praying Church awaits the return of her Spouse.

In the early Christian centuries the faithful thought that this return would take place during the night between Holy Saturday and Easter Sunday, since that night was the center of Christian life, being the anniversary of Christ's victory and the moment when that victory became present anew. The fast that marked the Vigil, and indeed the whole Lenten fast, is festive because it is leading up to the victory and return of the Spouse.

When Jesus was asked, "Why do we [the disciples of John the Baptist] and the Pharisees fast [much], but your disciples do not fast?" his reply was, "Can the wedding guests mourn as long as the bridegroom is with them? The days will come when the bridegroom is taken away from them, and then they will fast" (Matt 9:14-15; cf. Mark 2:19-20; Luke 5:34-35). We fast because the Spouse is absent. But he is coming back to us, since he has inaugurated the messianic age and will come again to assert his victory. The Church, therefore, can fast yet also celebrate in a festive way his imminent return. An old preface for the summer or post-Pentecostal Ember Days recalls the above passage from the Gospel: "Almighty, everlasting God, who . . . told the children of the Spouse that they were not to fast before his departure."[14]

The Christians of the first centuries thus took the passage as a prophetic instruction that would be valid for the whole time of the Church. The early Christians found it natural to be awaiting at every moment the return of Christ.

Fasting from Sin

The term "sacrament" is meaningfully applied to fasting only if the fasting sanctifies. The prayers of the liturgy show us the negative and positive aspects of this sanctification, the two often being presented as forming a single whole.

The extensive attention paid to the aspect of struggle and liberation should not surprise us. After all, Lent begins with the gospel account of Christ's struggle with Satan in the desert, thus putting the whole season under this sign.[15] Characteristic too is the collect for Ash Wednesday: "Grant, O Lord, that we may begin with holy fasting this campaign of Christian service, so that, as we take up battle against spiritual evils, we may be armed with weapons of self-restraint."[16]

The aspect of struggle, which thus comes to the fore at the very beginning of Lent, will be an underlying theme throughout the season. Fasting is intended to strengthen us against the enemy and is the source of new energy: "Grant, Lord, that our fasting may fill us with strength, and our abstinence make us invincible to all our enemies."[17]

Fasting is a powerful weapon in this struggle to the death against our foes. With its help and the help of our good deeds, we can win through to victory: "Grant, Lord, that by fasts and good works pleasing to you we may win your help and be able to overcome our enemies."[18]

Liberation from the "enemy" means liberation from sin. The movement here is, as it were, a circular one: our fasting would be illusory if it did not consist above all in avoiding sin, but, on the other hand, fasting is also a powerful help in de-energizing our evil inclinations.

The book of Isaiah, chapter 58—a postexilic document—presents an interiorized conception of religious practices. But at an earlier time Amos had already voiced the Lord's disgust with festivals and solemnities in which no interior attitude corresponded to the outward observances (Amos 5:21). The Church too is careful to keep reminding the faithful of what an authentic asceticism requires. A preface for the September Ember Days in the Verona Sacramentary reads as follows:

> But if amid our observances we do not abstain from what is harmful and forbidden, you assure us through the prophet that such fasting is not acceptable to you. For not only can bodily mortification not be profitable if the mind is enmeshed in evil thoughts; we are even worse off if the soul does not abstain from sin when its earthly condition has been rendered less burdensome.[19]

The Church is constantly on the alert lest the faithful delude themselves by practicing mortification without a corresponding complete detachment from sin. Such self-deception would be deadly for the Church as well as for the individual. We must be careful, of course, about calling the Church "sinful," but on the other hand we must certainly reckon with sin in the Church. Some twenty years ago this point was well expressed in this way:

> Sin does not arise from the nature of the Church but breaks into her from outside, through the power of the Evil One at work in humans. Sin does not belong to the nature of the Church but must be reckoned as part of the unnatural condition in which she is during her earthly pilgrimage. To put it in the way in which it is usually put: Sin in the Church is that failure in holiness caused by the power of the Evil Spirit through humans as members of the Church. Sin in the Church, as part of the Church (as indeed elsewhere), can only be seen as a dark, incomprehensible, ultimately meaningless paradox. But as such it must be taken seriously.[20]

Understanding the Mysteries of Christ

Purification, however, is not the ultimate purpose of the Church in its seasons of fasting; it is not an end in itself. To repent and to believe in the gospel (as the new formula for the imposition of ashes bids us do) means to make the effort required in order to understand the mysteries of Christ. The collect for the First Sunday of Lent expresses the deeper meaning these forty days should have for the catechumen, for the penitent, and indeed for every Christian: "Grant, almighty God, through the yearly observances of holy Lent, that we may grow in understanding of the riches hidden in Christ and by worthy conduct pursue their effects."[21]

"Growing in understanding," for the Christian as for biblical persons, is first of all a matter of contemplating the God who is Love, thanking him for the wonderful things he has done, and developing a capacity for admiration of his masterpieces in the world and in the human heart, especially of his extraordinary action in saving humanity. "Growing in understanding" also means entering into close communion with the mysteries of Christ that the Christian experiences through the sacraments. By thus gaining an experiential knowledge of Christ's mysteries—a knowledge fostered by fasting—we actively contemplate and become aware of the benefits we have already received from God, and we can appreciate their true value. At the same time, we come to realize our own need, and our devotion is deepened as we comprehend the benefits still in store for us. "For when we offer the homage of a suitable observance [i.e., fasting], we become grateful for the gifts we have received and still more grateful for gifts yet to come."[22]

Fasting thus proves enlightening to the spirit. We understand the secrets of the mystery of salvation. We become capable of appreciating the marvelous manifestation of good that the work of humanity's redemption represents. We acquire a clarity of spiritual vision, so that even amid our enthusiasm for the wealth bestowed on us, we do not lose sight of what we must still do to be perfect.

Yet, when confronted with such an outpouring of divine generosity, we feel a certain uneasiness. We are, after all, incapable of implementing by our own efforts such a vision of God, the world, and ourselves and of progressively making real in our lives the ideal we glimpse. How, then, are we to preserve intact what has been given to us? Indeed, the Church asks herself the same question, for she is well aware of how cowardly and weak the people are who make up her members, and she too feels a certain fear of the responsibility placed upon her to preserve what she has received.

It is precisely the asceticism involved in fasting that will help her guard the treasure bestowed on her. The Verona Sacramentary has a preface for the post-Pentecostal days of fast that reads as follows: "After the joyous days we spent honoring the Lord's resurrection from the dead and ascension into heaven, and after receiving the gift of the Holy Spirit, we are provided with this holy and necessary fast so that our purity of life may ensure the permanence of God's gifts to his Church."[23]

During Lent, the Lord gradually instructs "our minds by heavenly teaching."[24] He instills "the teachings of the Christian faith."[25]

We can glimpse in such prayers a reflection of the concern for catechumens that presided over the organization of Lent. The scrutinies celebrated for the catechumens have as their purpose a gradual assimilation to the faith, thus creating a pure dwelling in which the Spirit can enlighten those who seek the Lord.

Made Like to Christ

There is little reason to fear that catechumens or baptized Catholics will become proud on account of the divine life that fills them and the perfection such a life entails. For we know how asceticism will deepen their keen awareness of their own defects, which continue to be many.

But asceticism does more than this. Fasting also helps catechumens and Christians form their souls after the model of Christ himself.

Humility and submission to the Father's will, for example, are two traits to be found in the person who accepts the ascetical life of the Church. Individuals do not practice such asceticism in isolation or in whatever way they choose, for they have before them a model that the liturgy presents to the assembly of the faithful from the First Sunday of Lent. In their practice of fasting, catechumens and baptized believers are inspired by example; they become imitators of Christ. They develop this likeness first and foremost through a humility whose meaning is made clear to them in the asceticism of the Church: "God, you teach us, through fasting and prayer, what is meant by true humility in imitation of your only Son, our Lord."[26]

The same Christ taught an unconditioned submission to his Father's will. By creating in our souls an attitude of detachment, fasting leads us along this path of conformity to the divine will: "Grant, Lord, that through this holy fast we may become completely docile to you."[27]

Change Requires a Self-Conversion

This kind of change does not take place in us without our own cooperation. Unless we ourselves are profoundly committed to the task, God will not divinize us and refashion us in the likeness of his Son, nor will the Holy Spirit enable us to be imitators of Christ. In fact, our conversion is a task that is never finished and done with. That is why the prayer for conversion runs through the Lenten season in the new Roman Missal. Thus, the collect for the third Sunday lists the three activities needed if we are to improve our spiritual condition: "in fasting, prayer and almsgiving [you] have shown us a remedy for sin." This theme for the season as a whole is set by the liturgy for Ash Wednesday, in which the idea of conversion is central, as is faith, an essential element in conversion. As the new optional formula for the distribution of ashes puts it, echoing the gospel: "Repent, and believe in the Gospel" (cf. Mark 1:15). This, of course, cannot be accomplished without a struggle, for we must do battle with all that is evil in us.[28]

It may be that in the past too much stress was placed on corporal penance and fasting. No one would deny that modern life and the demands it makes of us constitute a penance that is often at least as hard as fasting. At the same time, however, we must face up to a permanent fact of our lives, namely, that the soul is so intimately bound up with the body that some training of the body will always be necessary. Doctors and psychologists are becoming more and more aware of this today. Is it not time for Catholics to do the same, with prudence indeed but for specifically gospel motives?

The new Roman Missal, it would seem, has been rather shy when it comes to prayers that speak of chastising the body in order to purify the soul. "O God, who have taught us to chasten our bodies for the healing of our souls."[29] "Grant, we pray, O Lord, that, preparing to celebrate the holy mysteries, we may bring before you as the fruit of bodily penance a joyful purity of heart."[30] The problem, in the last analysis, is an elementary one: to be convinced of our impoverished state and to free ourselves from the bonds of sins.[31] In fact, we should not even dignify with the name "problem" what is often only a simple weakness and a lack of courage in facing up to some proclivity of ours.

On the other hand, we must not stop with such considerations and think of our conversion as a narrowly individual matter. Our conversion is, in fact, connected with the conversion of the world, and if the celebration of the Eucharist can and does help us in our self-conversion, it is also the source of the world's conversion.[32]

Advancing toward the Paschal Mystery

The conversion of humanity and of the world in its entirety is possible only through participation in the paschal mystery of death and life. Lent is conceived precisely as a time of progress toward this mystery of liberation and renewal. Its purpose is that we should come with purified souls to the celebration of the paschal mystery.[33] The preface for the First Sunday of Lent turns our attention to Christ and reminds us that "By abstaining forty long days from earthly food, he consecrated through his fast the pattern of our Lenten observance and, by overturning all the snares of the ancient serpent, taught us to cast out the leaven of malice, so that, celebrating worthily the Paschal Mystery, we might pass over at last to the eternal paschal feast."

In the same vein, the prayer over the offerings on the second Sunday asks, "May this sacrifice, O Lord, we pray, cleanse us of our faults and sanctify your faithful in body and mind for the celebration of the paschal festivities." The collect for Thursday of the third week is a petition that "we may press forward all the more eagerly towards the worthy celebration of the Paschal Mystery," while the collect for the fourth Sunday urges us to "hasten toward the solemn celebrations to come."

Put off the Old Self and Put on the New

One of the most humiliating and discouraging things about life is that we tend to become spiritually decrepit, prisoners of habit and of the inclination to follow the path of least resistance. Individuals succumb to this tendency; so do whole groups. Many a community has been enthusiastic in its beginning but quickly yields to routine, which it regards as a simplification of life and sometimes even as a safeguard. Change always involves some risk and is never easy. We are not saying, of course, that we should have contempt for healthy tradition. The latter must not, however, be confused with the pious immobility that only destroys authentic tradition and renders it hateful.

Not only can people become prisoners of habit; they can even return to their sins that sap the soul's strength. We must have the courage to face up to this when it happens and to admit it in ourselves as we do in society at large and in the groups that people form to achieve high purposes.

Lent is a time for cleansing ourselves of any decrepitude and a time of renewal. The prayer after communion for Friday of the fourth week puts it thus: "Grant, we pray, O Lord, that, as we pass from old to new, so, with former ways left behind, we may be renewed in holiness of mind." Our whole aim should be "to pass from former ways to newness of life."[34] The Lord must "restore us anew" and cleanse us "of old ways."[35] It is he who must purify us of old earthly ways and renew us by growth in the heavenly life.[36]

The real source of renewal is, beyond any doubt, the Lord himself. The Church is very conscious of this fact and asks him to "increase in us grace of salvation and newness of life."[37]

The Sacraments Renew Us

It is basically and chiefly through his sacraments that the Lord effects his renewal in us. The preface for the fourth Sunday says: "By the mystery of the Incarnation, he has led the human race that walked in darkness into the radiance of the faith and has brought those born in slavery to ancient sin through the waters of regeneration to make them your adopted children." The prayer over the offerings for the Election or Enrollment of Names‡ makes the same point: "[you] restore us by the Sacrament of Baptism to eternal life as we confess your name," while the preface for the fifth Sunday speaks in more general terms: "[Christ] leads us by sacred mysteries to new life."

During this season the Lord communicates his strength both to those already baptized and to those who will soon be baptized during the Easter Vigil (see the collect, For the Election or Enrollment of Names).§[38]

---

‡ Nocent cited this as the prayer over the offerings for Saturday of the fifth week of Lent, but that prayer has been replaced with Ver. 895, newly added to the third edition of the Missal, so that this one appears only in the Rite of Election.

§ Nocent cited this as the collect for Saturday of the fifth week of Lent, but that prayer has been replaced with Gel. 480, newly added to the third edition of the Missal, so that this one appears only in the Rite of Election.

Renewal of Body and Soul

We would be mistaken to regard all that has been said as the expression of a spiritual vision that concerns only the soul. Let us not fall into that error! The liturgy, like the Bible before it, does not split a human being into two parts but thinks of renewal as affecting the whole person. The collect for Wednesday of the first week makes this quite clear and in the process gives a very apt expression of the body-soul interaction: "Look kindly, Lord, we pray, on the devotion of your people, that those who by self-denial are restrained in body may by the fruit of good works be renewed in mind."

The Eucharist purifies and renews us in soul, but it also gives strength to the body now and for eternity.[39] In the prayer over the offerings for the second Sunday, we pray that the Eucharist may sanctify us in body and mind and thus prepare us to celebrate the paschal festivities. The prayer after communion for Monday of the first week emphasizes the truth that one and the same salvation embraces body as well as soul: "We pray, O Lord, that in receiving your Sacrament, we may experience help in mind and body so that, kept safe in both, we may glory in the fullness of heavenly healing."[40]

Renewal for Eternal Life

The renewal we seek and ask of the Lord, while ourselves working to attain it, is for the sake of life in the world to come. Texts that express this point are numerous; we shall choose only a few of the more eloquent.

The prayer over the offerings on Tuesday of the fourth week is concise but clear: "may [these gifts] attest to your care as Creator for this our mortal life, and effect in us the healing that brings us immortality."[41] The collect for Monday of the fifth week spells out the requirements for such an entry into eternal life: "O God, by whose wondrous grace we are enriched with every blessing, grant us so to pass from former ways to newness of life, that we may be made ready for the glory of the heavenly Kingdom." The prayer after communion for the same day envisages us following Christ and hastening our steps upward toward God.

The Lord gives us pledges of this future life: "Grant, we pray, O Lord our God, that what you have given us as the pledge of immortality may work for our eternal salvation."[42] At the same time, however, even on earth we already possess, in a certain fashion, the blessings heaven has in store for us: "O God, who grant us by glorious healing remedies while still on earth to be partakers of the things of heaven."[43]

4. LENT AND THE MODERN CHRISTIAN

Disordered Humanity

Readers may have had the courage to read the preceding chapters with an unprejudiced mind and may have made the effort to understand them in the light of faith. But are they convinced now that the teaching expounded in these chapters can win a hearing from the people of our day and, specifically, from contemporary Christians? In other words, is it worth our while to try to enter more deeply into the biblico-liturgical theology of Lent, or must we rather regard it as unsuitable and therefore put an end to our study here and now?

Experience and the existential analyses it suggests do not make us especially optimistic about humanity and its possibilities. The human seems to be a radically disordered being. In fact, that is exactly how St. Paul viewed humanity when he set down in his letter to the Romans a number of brutally precise statements based on his experience of himself. He was humble enough to pass on to his readers this existential analysis—and how contemporary it sounds!

> We know that the law is spiritual; but I am carnal, sold into slavery to sin. What I do, I do not understand. For I do not do what I want, but I do what I hate. . . . So, then, I discover the principle that when I want to do right, evil is at hand. For I take delight in the law of God, in my inner self, but I see in my members another principle at war with the law of my mind, taking me captive to the law of sin that dwells in my members. (Rom 7:14-15, 21-23)

The Genesis story that is read at the beginning of Lent does not hide our real condition, and we have tried to assess that condition as objectively as possible. Thus far we have the impression that what Lent teaches is true to what we experience. To this extent, then, we may regard Lent as adapted to contemporary humanity.

Humanity Renewed

Lent, in brief, shows itself wholly bent on helping humans escape from their disordered state and regain union with God. But perhaps the means proposed to us seem inadequate? Perhaps the Church's demands seem too abstract, too unconnected with our real world?

As a matter of fact, given our situation, we may indeed be somewhat put off by the simplicity of the means offered us during Lent. We would prefer methods a bit more striking. We resemble to some extent Naaman the Syrian, who was angry to find that the only cure prescribed for his leprosy was a bath in the Jordan! We must be renewed and attain union with God once again. Fine! The Church, speaking in Christ's name, offers the catechumens a new life. Fine! But the means the Church proposes seem so modest; even the sacramental signs seem out of all proportion to what they are intended to produce.

More specifically, the activities of Lent seem too limited: prayer, almsgiving, mortification. Are these really calculated to suit the condition of modern humanity? No one doubts that people must change and be converted. But can the practices urged for Lent change the life of a drug addict? Can they calm lust and restore authentic love? Can they change hatred into harmony? Can they quench the fire of envy? Can they turn fidelity into heroism? No! All in all, experience seems to have demonstrated that the means urged on us by the Church are ineffective.

Such is the critique, but it is itself inadequate as a reflection of the real situation. Christians of today are very much concerned to recover for themselves the values of prayer. They will do so without perhaps making any grandiose claims, but they are well aware that they must indeed learn to pray. Contact with the young, from hippies to the members of "catechumenal" groups,* brings home to us their great thirst for prayer and the inner peace they look for in it and claim to find in it. Perhaps the young have not yet realized that what they are really pursuing is their own divinization. In any case, the numerous experiments with communal life and the increasing multiplication of houses of prayer show quite clearly that this means proposed by the Church is being accepted and appreciated and is gradually producing results.

Some individuals are doubtless striking out on the wrong paths. Not every quest is marked by the proper balance, and in some instances neo-romanticism or even neo-enlightenment is at work. But

---

* Hippies were better known in the United States when Nocent was writing. In France "catechumenal" groups were faith-sharing communities of young Christian seekers imitating some catechetical aspects of the catechumenate.

we must not overlook the good by concentrating on what is less good. The world seems to be praying again, and in so doing it is rediscovering what should be its primal activity; it is also rediscovering the divinization God intends for it. Through prayer it is getting the poison out of its system. It is slowly regaining a proper scale of values and overcoming its own confusion. Ideologies have less of a fascination for it, and it is beginning to realize that it has everything to gain by developing its contact with God and everything to lose by falling back into practical atheism.

Everyone is aware today of the phenomenon of prayer—even those who do not believe in it or who find it incomprehensible. It is a disconcerting phenomenon. Some people are afraid of it, for they see that its practitioners are no longer prisoners of our disordered world but are pursuing a union with God that demands a self-stripping for which not everyone has the courage.

Oddly enough, by God's grace the rediscovery of prayer has not caused its practitioners to turn in on themselves. On the contrary, through their prayer these people have regained the spirit of community. They have regained it through sharing with others, in the unity formed by the members of the Church as they follow the inspiration of the Spirit. Even more important, they pray together; they do not feel distracted by their neighbor but even require their "neighbor" as a visible embodiment and sign of the people that has been gathered again by the breath of the Spirit.

What I have been saying here is not wishful thinking. Everyone who is in contact with the youth of the Church or, more generally, with those who seek will bear witness to the same phenomenon.†

Those who have rediscovered prayer or are in the process of doing so are well aware that they cannot devote themselves to prayer to the exclusion of concern for others and without having developed a profound accord with them. We cannot evade or neglect the needs of our neighbor if we hope to enter into union with the Lord and to taste the fruits of prayer. St. Paul warned the Corinthians that they would not be able to recognize the eucharistic Body of Christ unless they were also intent on recognizing the Body of Christ that is the Church, and this in the person of their neighbor (1 Cor 11).

---

† Different movements for prayerful young people have evolved since Nocent was writing. Perhaps chief among them is World Youth Day and its regional derivatives.

Have people likewise rediscovered the need of mortification? Doctors have always taught us that the body must be mastered. Do Christians really believe this? It would be unjust, of course, to assert that they do not. Mortification has, to be sure, taken different forms than it had in other periods of history; people are less concerned with establishing records than with attaining the right measure. Asceticism is seen as a calculated discipline rather than as a total abstention in one or all areas of life. We can glimpse the ideal being pursued: to have and use what one has, but not to lose one's balance when one does not have it. Doesn't that represent an authentic conversion?

You may object that all this is rather idyllic and represents at best the outlook of a rather small elite. Well, the masses of people doubtless do not look at things in the way described. But then, can a more than superficial Christianity ever become the Christianity of the masses? I am not saying that Christ did not die for all. I am saying only that in some men and women the Spirit awakens the need for a deeper kind of Christian life. In this regard, our age has made its own a statement emphasized at the Second Vatican Council: that holiness is not linked exclusively to religious life but is an essential goal of the Church in its entirety. We are living today in a Church where many of the laity are seeking holiness and are rediscovering, even amid their human weakness, what it means to be divinized. Thus, there is evidently no basis for thinking or saying that the Church of today does not measure up to the Church of former times.

Whatever the state of the contemporary Church, there will always be room to enter more deeply into the meaning of the Lenten "sacrament" and to follow in faith the path the Church points out to us as leading to our ultimate renewal. It is not primarily with the help of medicine or psychoanalysis or other human arts and sciences that we will achieve this renewal. These things are important enough in themselves, but they are not, like Lent, a "sacrament" that produces divine effects in those who trustingly receive it. We must therefore cease to think of Lent first and foremost in terms of "practices"; we must experience it rather as a time in which we open ourselves to the divine life that God seeks to restore to us. If we do so, and if we bear in mind the various aspects of Lent—for example, the forgiveness of sins and the entry of the catechumens into the faith and the Church—Lent can indeed help us slake our thirst for transcendence.

Structure and Themes of
the Lenten Liturgy

5. LENT THEN AND NOW

Lent, a Time for Self-Enlightenment

The themes of the Lenten liturgy soon confront the Christian with a basic question, for they force the Church in its entirety to examine its conscience and rediscover what it truly is. Here is the Christian, a part of the new and ever-growing kingdom of God, but one has come to take for granted the sacred world in which one lives, moving at ease in it. Now one must ask oneself: By what right have secondary things become so important to me?

Christians must once again look closely at this world and its realities and realize anew that they have authentic meaning only because they have been inserted into a definitive, lasting, new world. They must also go back over the divine aids and instrumentalities they have received at the successive great moments of Christian life and examine their conscience on the use they have made of them in the past and the use they are to make of them in the future. Such is the fundamental activity of Christians in their "state of Lenten asceticism." This activity concerns their relation to God, to others, and to themselves.

Individuals soon discover that they cannot simply "live *their own* Lent" but must live it along with the rest of the Church so that the sinners who have destroyed themselves because they followed an illusory light but found only darkness may regain their place in the Church. They live Lent along with the Church in its entirety so that she may once again become truly one, shed all formalism, and regain the authentic life in Christ—so that she may grow and prove a welcoming mother to all who are looking for the true path. When Christians acquire this new perspective, this sense of community, they will discover a new side of Lent that they perhaps never suspected, for they will find themselves taking part in the Christian initiation of those who are preparing to put on the light of Christ and work for the building up of the Lord's Church.

If, however, we are to enter fully into the Church's liturgical life, then, not surprisingly, we are forced to acquire a better knowledge of how that life works and how it has evolved. We may at times regret the fact that the Church seems to carry with her so many vestigial organs. This does not justify us in failing to see that a great body like the Church has a history and that the framework of her institutions cannot change as quickly as the moods of our contemporaries. It can only enrich us to know how the Church's inner life has developed in the past. If, then, we are to enter fully into the spirituality of Lent, we must get a clear view of some indispensable points of reference in the complicated development of the Lenten season.

A Single Celebration

There is, in fact, but one theme that runs through Scripture, the liturgy, and the Church's life, and that theme is the death and resurrection of Christ in triumph over sin, Satan, and eternal damnation. Easter is the high point, the center of convergence, and the outcome or resolution that alone can provide human history with meaning. The Christians of the first centuries were fascinated by this indubitably real death and resurrection of the God who had come to restore everything in humanity and the universe. Consequently, they did not see the need for a special celebration of Christ's Passover—his death and resurrection—since the rite of the Last Supper, renewed each Sunday by the Savior's command, made that mystery of death and resurrection an ever-present reality.

Yet, people have a hankering for the unusual; repetition without inner renewal blunts their attention. Even the religious alertness of the soul is not exempt from the slackening that routine causes. Starting in the second century, therefore, the Christian people, for whom Easter was the central, towering event, began to celebrate an anniversary of the passion and resurrection of Christ with fasting and prayer. Now the year would have a center, and each Sunday, like a stream flowing from an inexhaustible fountain, would remind them of the Great Feast.

The Morrow of the Feast

We do not like to douse the lights, as it were, after a brilliant festival and return immediately to everyday life. Easter is a moment of such power, its spiritual resonances are so strong and its celebration so much a source of light, that we cannot fail to hear it echoing in our hearts and to see the sparks from its fire. As early as the third century, therefore, the celebration of Easter was prolonged for fifty days, with a final upsurge on the fiftieth day. Beginning in the fourth century, a new feast—Pentecost—focused attention on this final upsurge of the Easter spirit.

Going up for the Feast

The paschal festivities require preparation. The soul's joy becomes intense, after all, only when desire has been stimulated and an expectation created. From the very beginning, there was a fast (with a paradoxically festive quality to it) in preparation for the annual observance. Soon this fast became longer and longer and acquired a great importance. Meanwhile, in keeping with an intuition that was the fruit of the Spirit's working, baptism was increasingly reserved for Easter Vigil.

According to St. Paul, baptism means being conformed to Christ in his death and resurrection. It is because baptism makes real this mystery in the candidate that it incorporates each one into the Church, the great, ever-growing Body of Christ. This doctrine (Rom 6) quite naturally suggested that baptism should be administered amid the solemnity of the Easter Vigil. The time all Christians were to spend in preparation for the celebration of the paschal mystery also became the time of intensive preparation for the catechumens. The preparation for the baptism soon to be received was to be intellectual, moral, and, above all, spiritual.

Initial Organization

In the beginning, Christians celebrated a paschal Triduum that extended from Good Friday (the death of Christ), through Saturday (Christ in the tomb), to the Sunday of the resurrection. Soon the Triduum came to include Thursday (commemoration of the Last Supper), Friday, and Saturday (including the night before Sunday). The Saturday night celebration belongs both to the time when we celebrate the death of Christ and to the beginning of Sunday, when the Lord rises in glory. St. Augustine, for example, understood the liturgy of the Easter Vigil as a kind of hinge connecting the celebration of Christ's death and the celebration of his resurrection.

In the first stage, then, the preparation for the paschal festivities ended on Wednesday of Holy Week. It seems, however, though we cannot prove it, that very soon the whole week came to be directed toward the Easter Vigil and Resurrection Sunday. The week in its entirety was taken up with the passion of the Lord.

First Extensions

A week seemed quite inadequate as preparation for a solemnity that would last for fifty days. The first addition by way of preparation was three weeks of fasting. The liturgy of this new period was marked by a series of readings from the Gospel of St. John; traces of this are still to be seen.

Christians continued, however, to feel that there was still an imbalance between the time given over to the celebration of the paschal event and the time allowed to prepare for it. Consequently, from the end of the fourth century on, forty days were set aside for fasting; their beginning was marked by a Sunday whose very title bespeaks the length of the preparation for Easter: the first Sunday of the "quadragesimal" (forty-day) fast.

On Holy Thursday there was now not only the commemoration of the Last Supper but also the reconciliation of public penitents; the First Sunday of Lent became the day on which these individuals were enrolled for their time of penance. Later on, in order that there might be a full forty days of fasting, the Lenten season began on the Wednesday before the first Sunday, or Ash Wednesday (when sinners beginning their public penance had ashes placed on their heads). When the practice of public penance disappeared, all Christians began to receive the ashes on that day; at the end of the eleventh century, Pope Urban II extended this practice to the whole of Christendom.

During the forty days, the catechumens underwent a final, detailed, carefully organized preparation. In earlier times, there had first been a remote preparation that lasted at least three years;* this was the general catechumenate. This was succeeded by a period of proximate

---

* Research now shows that a three-year period was not universal.

preparation for those catechumens who were "chosen" and enrolled for baptism during the Easter Vigil.† At the beginning of the sixth century, the period of remote preparation was dropped. Adult baptisms were becoming infrequent, and the children presented for baptism were born into Christian families. As a result, the whole organization of the catechumenate changed.

Originally there were three "scrutinies." These consisted of exorcisms and instructions. Later on, in the second half of the sixth century, there would be seven of these scrutinies. The scrutinies were connected with the first part of the Mass and, in the time of the three scrutinies, were celebrated on the third, fourth, and fifth Sundays of Lent. At the later period, the scrutinies were first shifted to weekdays and finally separated entirely from the Lenten Masses.

This intense preparation of the catechumens and the organization of Lent for the purpose evidently shaped not only the Lenten liturgy but the Lenten spirit as well. The whole community fasted in union with both the public penitents and the catechumens soon to be baptized.

New Developments

At the beginning of the sixth century, the fast was extended to seven weeks and Quinquagesima Sunday made its appearance. Counting back from Easter day itself, Quinquagesima is the fiftieth day. The time after Easter and the time before Easter were now in perfect balance.

Things did not stop there. By the end of the sixth century, Sexagesima was being celebrated and, at the beginning of the seventh century, Septuagesima.

Enrichment within the Framework

Initially there were celebrations only on Sundays, Wednesdays, and Fridays; on the latter two days, however, this was simply a celebration of the word, without an accompanying Eucharist. Gradually, beginning in the fifth century, celebrations were established for Mondays, Tuesdays, and Saturdays, and from the sixth century on, all

---

† Similarly, a two-stage catechumenate was not universal in the early Church.

these celebrations included the Liturgy of the Eucharist as well as the Liturgy of the Word. Finally, formularies for the Thursdays of Lent were provided in the eighth century.

The liturgy of Lent was thus increasingly enriched. At Rome, with the pope presiding over congregations of clergy and faithful in the various basilicas of the city, the celebrations were called "stations." In the second century this word meant the fast on Wednesdays and Fridays. It soon came to signify the gatherings for common prayer. Each Lenten celebration took on its own well-defined character, since the formularies and readings were usually inspired both by peculiarities of the place chosen for the station and by the preparation of the catechumens or their sponsors.

Reorganizations and Profound Changes

As preparation for baptism gradually became less important and was separated from the Lenten liturgy, this liturgy inevitably took on a different character. The original choice of readings and chants had now become less suitable, since the preoccupation with baptism, which had dictated the choice, had faded. Meanwhile, there had already been a number of changes made—for example, in the liturgy of the third, fourth, and fifth Sundays as early as the beginning of the sixth century.

In any event, Lent became first and foremost a period in which Christians already baptized examined themselves in terms of their participation in the life of the Church. The thought of penitence and the catechumenate faded, and Lent took on a quite different character. The gradual suppression of the catechumenal rites meant that the season lost its orientation toward baptism; the theology of baptism no longer played a leading role.

The Recent Changes Initiated by the Second Vatican Council

The Second Vatican Council has restored to Lent the dimensions it originally had. It has not revived the reconciliation of penitents on Holy Thursday, but it has restored, at least in Year A, the readings and prayers for the five Sundays of Lent as celebrated in antiquity; the preparation of the catechumens has likewise been linked with these Sundays as in the past.

The Church has never thought that her catechumens required a merely intellectual and religious or doctrinal preparation. The efforts of these individuals to absorb the teaching given them and to observe the moral law could be but an imperfect preparation. God himself had to prepare the candidates in a progressive way by causing his grace to permeate their souls. That is precisely the significance of the exorcisms that the candidates underwent.

Undoubtedly, the exorcisms concentrate, at times in a rather dramatic way, on the expulsion of the devil, but it would be a mistake to consider this expulsion as their sole focus. The expelling of the demon is only the negative side of the rite and is a way of preparing the soul so that the light of faith may enter in. These exorcism rites were called "scrutinies," but "scrutiny" in this instance does not mean an inquiry into the doctrinal or moral fitness of the candidate. The ritual of the prebaptismal scrutinies is the vehicle for an important theology that has in large measure been revived in the new rite for adult baptism.

Until the beginning of the sixth century, three scrutinies were celebrated on the third, fourth, and fifth Sundays of Lent. In fact, the first five Sundays were all organized in terms of the catechumenate and, inseparably, in terms of a conversion of life for all Christians. The first Sunday, for which the gospel was that of Christ's temptation, was the Sunday for enrollment in the catechumenate. The enrollment was followed by three years of catechumenal preparation;[‡] the immediate preparation took the form of the three Sunday scrutinies. Once the candidate became associated with a Christian family, and especially if the candidate were a child, the enrollment on the First Sunday of Lent became enrollment for baptism during the coming Easter Vigil, that is, after the three Sunday scrutinies and a final scrutiny on Holy Saturday morning.

Why did the scrutinies not begin immediately, that is, on the Second Sunday of Lent? The answer is simple: The celebration of the Ember Days was introduced into the first week of Lent.[§] Now the Ember Saturday, with its six prophecies and its readings from the epistles

---

‡ Nocent is probably mistaken here. Enrollment was probably always associated with the proximate preparation for baptism, and there is scant evidence that a three-year catechumenate was required.

§ Ember Days marked the four seasons of the year with special prayers of penitence.

and the gospel, was celebrated during the night between Saturday and Sunday, and this meant the suppression of the Sunday celebration, a fact indicated in the old sacramentaries by the notation *Dominica vacat* ("the Sunday is empty or free," i.e., of a liturgical celebration). So the first scrutiny could not take place until the third Sunday.

The exorcisms were connected with the Liturgy of the Word, and the readings and prayers were chosen with a view to the catechumens. In addition, the catechumens were recommended to the Lord during the eucharistic prayer, in the formula that begins *Hanc igitur oblationem* ("Therefore, Lord, we pray, graciously accept this oblation"), while their sponsors were remembered in the *Memento* of the living.

From the fifth century on, there was also a ceremonial "handing over" (*traditio*) of the Creed. Each article was explained, and the catechumen was obliged to "hand it back" (*reddere, redditio*) at a later point; that is, each catechumen had to memorize and recite it. Subsequently, there were two further *traditiones*: of the Our Father (likewise explained, petition by petition) and, at the end of the sixth century, of the gospels; in the latter, a deacon read the beginning of each gospel and gave a brief commentary.

The formulas for the scrutinies in the Gelasian Sacramentary show that in most cases the Church was already dealing with infant baptisms. Once this situation became the rule, the three scrutinies, together with their readings and prayers, were transferred from Sundays to weekdays. The Sundays thus deprived took their gospel pericopes from the weekdays now occupied by the former Sunday scrutinies. Epistles were chosen that would be suitable to the now transformed third, fourth, and fifth Sundays.

It is evident that the features of Lent had now been radically altered; this became Lent as we knew it until the reform initiated by Vatican II. Since the children could not personally and actively answer to what was being done over them in the scrutinies, these were multiplied in a kind of compensatory spirit. The number was doubled to six; the final scrutiny on Holy Saturday morning made seven in all. Gradually the scrutinies became autonomous in relation to the Lenten Masses. *Ordo Romanus XI* already shows that the close links between the scrutinies and the Mass formularies had been abandoned.[1]

A word needs to be said on the role of St. John's gospel during Lent. Quite a few exegetes believe that the gospel was written for use as a baptismal catechesis. In any event, it was certainly used extensively during Lent, especially beginning with the third Sunday. The Roman liturgy has never lost sight of this tradition, and the recent reform has been careful to preserve it.

Since the liturgy of the Sunday scrutinies was to be restored (with adult catechumens in mind), and since the series of readings provided for the scrutinies constitutes a fine catechesis on the paschal mystery, it was decided to form Year A out of the readings formerly used on the scrutiny Sundays of Lent. These readings may be used every year in churches where there are catechumens, but it may also be used every year in other churches. When catechumens are present, the prayers written with them and their sponsors in mind should be used.

It was also decided, however, to provide Lent with two other sets of readings, Years B and C. These are less pastoral and in general less satisfactory. Furthermore, in order to form these sets, texts have been chosen that might usefully have been included in the weekday readings; at times the texts are not entirely suitable, simply because adequate material was lacking.

Given the special character of each year, especially Year A, we shall study each separately, referring the reader back to the commentary on Year A whenever the texts are similar. In order not to interrupt the succession of doctrinal themes proper to the Sundays, we shall study the weekdays, with their one-year cycle of readings, in a separate section. Similarly, we shall study Palm Sunday and the four following days as a separate unit (Lent ends on the morning of Holy Thursday).¶

Lent used to begin on the first Sunday. Only later was the beginning set on Ash Wednesday, a day originally geared to the public penitents who were to be reconciled on Holy Thursday morning. In order to give a more unified vision of Lent, we shall begin our discussion of it with the first Sunday. Ash Wednesday will be studied along with the weekdays of the season.** It will provide an opportunity for a summing up of the mentality with which the Church wishes us to approach Lent.

¶ More precisely, Lent ends before the Mass of the Lord's Supper on Holy Thursday.
** Apparently this project became too large. Nocent summarizes the themes of the Lenten weekdays in chapter 16 below.

Table of Readings in the Liturgy of the Hours (A Single-Year Cycle)		
First Sunday	Exod 5:1–6:1	The oppression of God's people
Second Sunday	Exod 13:17–14:9	The journey to the Red Sea
Third Sunday	Exod 22:20–23:9	The Covenant Code: The law concerning the orphan and the poor
Fourth Sunday	Lev 8:1-17; 9:22-24	The ordination of the priests
Fifth Sunday	Heb 1:1–2:4	The Son, heir of all things and exalted above the angels

6. FIRST AND SECOND SUNDAYS OF LENT (YEAR A): OUR VICTORY AND TRANSFORMATION IN CHRIST

Structure of Year A for the First Five Sundays			
Table of Readings in the Eucharistic Liturgy			
	Old Testament	Apostle	Gospel
First Sunday	Gen 2:7-9; 3:1-7 Creation and Fall	Rom 5:12-19 Sin and redemptive grace	Matt 4:1-11 Temptation of Christ
Second Sunday	Gen 12:1-4a Call of Abraham	2 Tim 1:8b-10 Our call to holiness	Matt 17:1-9 Transfiguration
Third Sunday	Exod 17:3-7 The thirst of Israel and the waters of despair	Rom 5:1-2, 5-8 God's love poured into our hearts	John 4:5-42 The Samaritan woman
Fourth Sunday	1 Sam 16:1b, 6-7, 10-13a The anointing of the king	Eph 5:8-14 Risen from the dead and enlightened	John 9:1-41 The man born blind
Fifth Sunday	Ezek 37:12-14 I will put my Spirit within you, and you shall live	Rom 8:8-11 The Spirit of him who raised Jesus dwells in you	John 11:1-45 Raising of Lazarus

Temptation of Christ, Temptation of Humankind

If we are to properly understand the liturgy of the first Sunday, we must go back in spirit to the period when the Christian community closed ranks around the catechumens and when each Christian could remember his or her own personal history of salvation. That situation is not, of course, to be found only in the distant past; Christian communities in many places can recognize in it their own concrete situation today. In any case, every Christian community must recover something of the same perspective and be united in it with all the other communities.

This opening day of the great catechesis shows the Church preoccupied with two main concerns. She has in mind the essential attitude that must be impressed on the souls of the catechumens; she also is attentive to the basic reactions that must be awakened in the souls of the faithful.

Earlier in this book we discussed the interpretation of the book of Genesis as read at the beginning of Lent. We return to those reflections now but shall be adding some new considerations.

The mission of Jesus began with a victorious struggle. It took place in the desert during his forty-day fast. The "forty days" evidently had something to do with the traditional choice of this reading to mark the opening of Lent, but Christ's victory over temptation also certainly played a part in the choice.

After his baptism in the Jordan and his official investiture as Messiah by the Holy Spirit, Christ was led into the desert by the same Spirit so that he might be tempted by the devil (Matt 3:13–4:11). Right from the beginning, then, the Spirit has a very specific activity. Just as he presided over the creation of the world, so he gives rise to the new creation and leads Christ into the desert in order to subject him to a conflict that, unlike that of Adam, will end in victory and be the prelude to the reconstruction and reunification of the world.

In St. Luke's gospel the succession of pericopes leads to a suggestive juxtaposition. In the latter part of chapter 3, the genealogy of Jesus traces his descent back to "the son of Adam, the son of God" (Luke 3:23-38). Immediately after this comes the account of how Jesus, "the son of Adam," confronts the devil. Ever since the confrontation in paradise, with all its implications for humanity, there had never been another decisive encounter between a human and Satan. Now, however, Jesus, "the son of Adam," takes his father's place and, in the name of humankind, confronts the devil once again. This time the conflict ends in a brilliant reversal of the original defeat.

Once this total victory has been achieved, Christ will henceforth be in constant open opposition to Satan. The many cures reported by the evangelists, as well as the expulsions of demons, point to the conflict in which Christ is engaged and are anticipations of his ultimate victory. He must also struggle against all whom the devil dominates. By expelling demons and curing all kinds of illness, Jesus intends to tell us that the reign of Satan is finished[1] and "the kingdom of God has come upon you" (Matt 12:28), but he tells us the same thing by his opposition to the "brood of vipers" (Matt 3:7) and to the real "children of Satan,"[2] namely, his proud and unbelieving hearers.

As we know, the Gospel of St. John develops two parallel themes: Jesus progressively reveals himself as Son of God and offers in proof signs that are more and more startling and unmistakable; at the same time, the refusal of the Jews to believe becomes daily more determined. The life of Jesus increasingly becomes a sign to be opposed, and the opposition will reach its climax in his crucifixion.

St. Luke, for his part, is fully aware of how the temptation in the wilderness is linked to the passion of Christ. At the end of his account of the temptation, he writes, "When the devil had finished every temptation, he departed from him *for a time*" (4:13). Later on, at the Supper, St. John emphasizes the fact that Satan is now entering the lists again: "The devil had already induced Judas, son of Simon the Iscariot, to hand him over" (13:2). Satan now "enters" the soul of Judas, as St. John points out (13:27). For St. Luke, the devil's possession of Judas (22:3) was the opportunity for which Satan had long been waiting. Jesus himself will several times speak of the devil as his passion draws near: "now the ruler of this world will be driven out" (John 12:31); "the ruler of the world is coming. He has no power over me" (John 14:30).

The activity of the "powers of evil" is constantly going on, but the victory of Christ is likewise ever present. His victory becomes ours in our baptism, which is our victory over death.

Victory of Christ, Victory of Humanity

The Fall in Genesis has its counterpart in the victory of Christ and in our victory as well. In the second reading for the First Sunday of Lent (Rom 5:12-19), that is the point St. Paul is making when he says that just as all became sinners because one man disobeyed, so all will become just, because one man obeyed. The parallel between the first Adam, natural father of the race, and Christ, Head of redeemed humankind, is dear to St. Paul and to the fathers.

In the Office of Readings, St. Augustine comments on Psalm 60 (61):2-3 and emphasizes the point that we who are tempted in Christ also conquer in Christ:

> [Christ] made us one with him when he chose to be tempted by Satan. We have heard in the gospel how the Lord Jesus Christ was tempted by the devil in the wilderness. Certainly Christ was tempted by the devil. In Christ you were tempted, for Christ received his flesh from

your nature, but by his own power gained salvation for you; he suffered death in your nature, but by his own power gained life for you; he suffered insults in your nature, but by his own power gained glory for you; therefore, he suffered temptation in your nature, but by his own power gained victory for you.

If in Christ we have been tempted, in him we overcome the devil.[3]

In the invitatory, or opening rite of each day's Office, we sing on this First Sunday of Lent: "Come, let us worship Christ the Lord, who for our sake endured temptation and suffering."

Where sin abounded, grace abounded still more—that is the optimistic vision St. Paul gives us in this reading from Romans. Our optimism is thus based on Christ's victory, which has become ours. It is not enough that the victory of Christ be real; it must also really become our own victory. What the victory means, as we enter upon the Christian life, is that we are unconditionally able, by the grace of God given to us, to regain the balance God intended for us. Victory does not mean that our life on earth will not be a life of conflict.

Saved in Hope

The person who receives baptism is rescued from the reign of darkness, this "present evil age" (Gal 1:4) that is ruled by Satan, "the god of this age [who] has blinded the minds of the unbelievers, so that they may not see the light of the gospel of the glory of Christ, who is the image of God" (2 Cor 4:4).

Christ frees the individual who through baptism is conformed to him in his death and resurrection. Before the Last Supper, Jesus spoke of the coming glorification that his death would bring: "Now is the time of judgment on this world; now the ruler of this world will be driven out. And when I am lifted up from the earth, I will draw everyone to myself" (John 12:31-32). In his first letter, St. John writes: "We know that . . . the whole world is under the power of the evil one" (1 John 5:19). Christ's resurrection, however, means that the baptized share in his victory: "the ruler of this world has been condemned" (John 16:11); "Indeed, the Son of God was revealed to destroy the works of the devil" (1 John 3:8).

It is possible for us, however, to lose sight of our real situation as St. Paul describes it: "we ourselves, who have the firstfruits of the

Spirit, we also groan within ourselves as we wait for adoption, the redemption of our bodies" (Rom 8:23). We have not regained the power to prevent the body from being autonomous and to subject it to the spirit. That is the hard fact behind the great human drama St. Paul describes when he speaks of the conflict he experiences within himself (Rom 7:14-25).

We are also forced to admit that even our spirit is not sufficiently subject to God's rule: "The spirit is not sufficiently penetrated by Christ, not united to Christ to the whole extent of its capacity, not yet entirely saturated by grace; and that is why, even after its effective redemption and prior to all personal sin, it still harbours virulent seeds of conflict."[4]

Christians are now "children of light" (cf. Eph 5:8). They live in the time of grace that precedes Christ's return. "And do this because you know the time; it is the hour now for you to awake from sleep. For our salvation is nearer now than when we first believed; the night is advanced, the day is at hand" (Rom 13:11-12).

We are already citizens of heaven, and from heaven we eagerly await the coming of the Lord Jesus Christ as our Savior (Phil 3:20). But that time of waiting is also a time of trial and temptation. Jesus in the wilderness shows us how we should conduct ourselves in the struggle.

We are a little "remnant," historical descendants of the little "remnant" that came back from captivity in the Old Testament. Like our Old Testament forebears, we are a remnant chosen by God in his gracious mercy. "But what is God's response to him [Elijah]? 'I have left for myself seven thousand men who have not knelt to Baal.' So also at the present time there is a remnant, chosen by grace" (Rom 11:4-5).

Like its Head, this little band must face temptation and trial. The Church was born from the Savior's side amid trial and suffering. The Christian's baptism, therefore, is not a promise of a placid life but a promise of the salvation that comes through toil and conflict. When James and John come to Jesus and ask that they might sit at his side in glory, he answers:

> "You do not know what you are asking. Can you drink the cup that I drink or be baptized with the baptism with which I am baptized?" They said to him, "We can." Jesus said to them, "The cup that I drink, you

will drink, and with the baptism with which I am baptized, you will be baptized; but to sit at my right or at my left is not mine to give but is for those for whom it has been prepared." (Mark 10:38-40)

Trials and testing, then, describe the condition of the Church as well as the condition of the baptized individual. The state of both, even on earth, is heavenly in principle, but both have many obstacles still to overcome. The Church is already saved and yet must face persecution and temptation: "I am coming quickly. Hold fast to what you have, so that no one may take your crown" (Rev 3:11).

Far from being surprised at trials, Christians who live in Christ should regard them as a sign that they indeed belong to Christ: "In fact, all who want to live religiously in Christ Jesus will be persecuted" (2 Tim 3:12). In fact, they are even more than a sign of belonging; they are necessary for the development of the Christian, who gains from them a new purity and solidity, like gold that is tried in the fire: "In this you rejoice, although now for a little while you may have to suffer through various trials, so that the genuineness of your faith, more precious than gold that is perishable even though tested by fire, may prove to be for praise, glory, and honor at the revelation of Jesus Christ" (1 Pet 1:6-7). In short, the Christian must expect to face trouble and suffering, but these are a path to the glory that lies ahead.

Like Christ, Christians will meet opposition from the world, but they look for the return of the Lord, and this vision determines their whole moral attitude. In 2 Corinthians, St. Paul lists some principles for our guidance: show yourselves servants of God and scandalize no one; be courageous in facing privations and difficulties, hunger and thirst; live a pure life that is guided by an enlightened faith; be patient, kind, and loving (6:1-10, the passage that used to be read on the First Sunday of Lent). "[T]he day is at hand. Let us then throw off the works of darkness [and] put on the armor of light; let us conduct ourselves properly as in the day" (Rom 13:12-13).

"You Can . . . Trample the Young Lion and the Dragon"

The warnings given to those who wish to become Christians and the stern reminder addressed to the faithful about the inevitable struggle with Satan may seem extremely harsh. The victory Christ has already won is indeed the basis for a Christian optimism, and every baptized person is aware that he already shares in that victory. Yet his situation in this world may seem somber enough.

Neither catechumen nor baptized Christian should be afraid. The entrance antiphon for the First Sunday of Lent is from Psalm 91 (a psalm also cited in today's gospel), which is a psalm expressing trust in the divine protection.

As the Liturgy of the Word gets underway, the Church wants to create an atmosphere of trust, for as Christians take their place in the army of Christ and face the struggle, their hearts should be filled with confidence in the divine protection: "When he calls on me, I will answer him; / I will be with him in distress; / I will deliver him, and give him glory"; "He who dwells in the shelter of the Most High, / and abides in the shade of the Almighty" (Ps 91:15, 1).

Those who engage in the struggle and persevere in it until the return of Christ are rescued from the fowler's snare and find a refuge under the Lord's wings. They need fear no arrow, for the Lord's fidelity is a buckler and a shield. The angels will watch over them and protect them from viper and lion and dragon. The psalm ends with a prophecy of paschal victory: "Since he clings to me in love, I will free him, / protect him, for he knows my name. / When he calls on me, . . . / I will be with him in distress; / I will deliver him, and give him glory. / With length of days I will content him; / I will show him my saving power" (vv. 14-16).

Thus the outcome of the struggle, from the midst of which the Christian cries out to the Lord, is not in doubt; its fruits are glorification and salvation. Commenting on Psalm 91, St. Jerome writes: "'He will cover you with his pinions.' He will be raised on the Cross, will extend his hands, and protect us. 'And under his wings you will find refuge,' that is, as you look upon his crucified hands, you will be healed should the serpent bite you."[5]

"Restore to Me the Gladness of Your Salvation"

Psalm 51, "Have mercy on me, O God, / according to your merciful love," has been chosen as the responsorial psalm after the first reading (Gen 2:7-9; 3:1-7). Its central theme is the sin that separates us from God in our earthly lives. The second reading, from Paul's Letter to the Romans, will show how Christ has rescued us from our sinful state.

The entire psalm takes the form of a confession that is both individual and communal. By the time the psalm was composed, Israel had developed to the point where each Israelite could recite it in private prayer as well as with the community in the liturgical celebration. The sin of which the psalm speaks consists in opposition to God: "Against you, you alone, have I sinned; / what is evil in your sight I have done." The point of this verse is that the sinner sees sin to be personal and acknowledges responsibility for it. The sinner asks to be purified of it, knowing that the Lord alone can accomplish this.

We find in this psalm the vocabulary for any penitential liturgy; read the psalm through and this will become clear. The verses chosen for the First Sunday of Lent emphasize the aspect of purification: "Create a pure heart for me, O God." They also ask for wisdom and strength: "renew a steadfast spirit within me. / Do not cast me away from your presence; / take not your holy spirit from me."

Such a purification will restore the special joy proper to being saved: "Restore in me the joy of your salvation." When the return to the Lord is effected, one cannot but break out into thanksgiving: "O Lord, open my lips / and my mouth shall proclaim your praise."

Psalm 51 proves extraordinarily powerful and stirs profound spiritual emotion not only when sung by the Church, with Christ, to the Father, but when addressed directly to Christ himself. If we use the psalm in this second manner, we immediately recapture a dimension of sin of which the New Testament was aware: sin is sin against Christ.

Transfiguration (Gospel, Second Sunday)

Those who make their decision and accept conflict are also destined to be transformed into the likeness of Christ.

Moses fasted for forty days, and later Elijah did the same; both ascended the holy mountain. In the Mass of the second Sunday they appear to the apostles in the company of the transfigured Christ: "he was transfigured before them; his face shone like the sun and his clothes became white as light. And behold, Moses and Elijah appeared to them, conversing with him" (Matt 17:2-3).

How significant that Moses and Elijah should be found in intimate conversation with Christ! During their life on earth they had already been invited to this intimacy with the Lord, and it was a fast of forty days that prepared each of them for their meeting with God.

After only a few days of Lent, catechumens and baptized alike have had the opportunity to see more deeply into the reality of Christian existence. On the first Sunday we have been present at the tempting of the Lord. Then the Church has shown us not only the attentive care of the Lord for his people but also the struggles, trials, and austerities they must embrace if they are to walk with him. Now we move on to the transfiguration, where we find Moses and Elijah with Christ.

The choice of this particular pericope is important, and we must dwell on it for a moment. Here the Church has her catechumens gathered before her. She has already introduced them to an austere life like that of Moses and Elijah. Now she takes them, along with the apostles, to the transfiguration. Christ will indeed be glorified, but he will reach that state by passing through suffering and death. The Church thus presents a program embracing the whole life of those who want to enter the baptismal font and model their life upon that of Christ.

Already we find ourselves at the heart of the paschal mystery, for this mystery can be summed up by saying that through his cross Christ entered into his glory. Observe that Peter, James, and John, who witness the transfiguration, will also see Christ in his agony. A further point to be noted is that this episode follows upon Peter's faith-inspired answer at Caesarea to Christ's question: "Who do people say that the Son of Man is? . . . But who do you say that I am?" (Matt 16:13, 15). At the transfiguration, Peter finds his profession of faith in Christ confirmed by the Father's words: "This is my beloved Son, with whom I am well pleased; listen to him" (Matt 17:5).

St. Luke's account of the transfiguration tells us what Christ was speaking of with Moses and Elijah: "[They] spoke of his exodus that he was to accomplish in Jerusalem" (Luke 9:31). More simply, they spoke of his passover. This is all the more striking in that the whole account of the transfiguration begins with the words "After six days" (Matt 17:1) or "About eight days after he said this" (Luke 9:28), that is, about six or eight days after Jesus had foretold his coming passion.

Once again, then, the transfiguration of the Lord focuses our attention wholly on the paschal mystery. But we are to attend to it in a more than narrowly contemplative manner, as if we were simply watching Jesus dying and rising and thus accomplishing "his" passover or passage. No, we are meant to approach it in an active way, as a mystery that involves us, a mystery that we are to accomplish with Christ. The Christian and the catechumen are to spend the forty days with Moses and Elijah in order to ascend the mountain with them. We must enter upon our own exodus, not simply contemplating the transfigured Christ, as the disciples did, but being transfigured with him.

St. Ambrose, commenting on the postbaptismal rite in which the newly baptized receive their white robe, writes, "Those who are baptized are purified according to the Gospel, because the garments of Christ were white as snow when he showed himself in the Gospel, in the glory proper to his resurrection. Those, therefore, whose sins are forgiven become whiter than snow."[6]

In the first volume of this series, when reflecting on Christ's baptism in the Jordan, we already discussed certain aspects of the transfiguration and especially the Father's words; we refer the reader to that discussion. Here we need only note that the transfiguration is connected with the accomplishment of the Father's will. In a sermon that is read in the Office of Readings for the Second Sunday of Lent, St. Leo the Great gives a fine commentary on the transfiguration and the profound significance it has for us:

> With no less forethought he was also providing a firm foundation for the hope of holy Church. The whole body of Christ was to understand the kind of transformation that it would receive as his gift. The members of that body were to look forward to a share in that glory which first blazed out in Christ their head.
>
> The Lord had himself spoken of this when he foretold the splendor of his coming: *Then the just will shine like the sun in the kingdom of their Father.* Saint Paul the apostle bore witness to this same truth when he said: *I consider that the sufferings of the present time are not to be compared with the future glory that is to be revealed in us.* In another place he says: *You are dead, and your life is hidden with Christ in God. When Christ, your life, is revealed, then you also will be revealed with him in glory.*[7]

Obey the Call

God's call of Abraham and his choice of Abraham's posterity (first reading, Second Sunday of Lent) has always had a profound significance for Christians, who see in it a prefiguration of their own call and the choice of the Church.

In this passage, as in many others, the text of Genesis shows the influence of three traditions concerning the event. The account nonetheless emerges as a unity, while the absence of anecdotal detail allows the figure of Abraham to stand out in all its religious splendor. He will forever be the man whom a loving God chose in order to bless him and entrust the divine promises to him. That is the way the Yahwist source wishes us to see him.

God's act of friendship, however, implies demands to be made on Abraham; the friendship must be returned. And the patriarch, amid the many trials and difficulties of his long life, does manifest a faith that people will always regard as an unparalleled model for their own faith. It is this moral stature of Abraham that the Elohist source wishes to bring home to us.

God's covenant with Abraham and his descendants must have its outward sign. The Priestly tradition, which is the third source for the narratives concerning Abraham, will emphasize the fact that God changes this man's name from Abram to Abraham, meaning "father of multitudes." He is chosen in order that he might be a "father." The sign of the covenant for his posterity will be their circumcision (Gen 17:4-14).

God chooses. It is impossible to read this account and not apply it to ourselves by asking whether God's choice extends to our own time and embraces anyone who seeks the truth. Do I see myself in this Abraham, who is the figure or model not only of Jesus Christ but of every person whom God calls? The whole history of salvation thus involves choice and call. We know the outcome of that history, and to us Abraham appears as the starting point of a divine action whose full extent we shall understand only at the end of time.

Suddenly God takes the initiative and speaks to Abraham. Abraham is now a man called, and immediately his life is changed. This man, a descendant of Shem, finds that he now belongs to God and must abandon his native land; he must depart from Ur. For God is a jealous God and sets apart anyone whom he chooses: "Go forth from the land of your kinsfolk and from your father's house to a land that I will show you. / "I will make of you a great nation" (Gen 12:1-2).

If we ask why it should be Abraham to whom these words were addressed, we will receive no answer. He is chosen from among many others, but not for any exceptional qualities we can discern in him. There is only one possible answer to our question: God chooses because he loves.

Abraham "went," for his going is the condition for receiving the fullness of God's gifts and becoming father of a posterity that will end in the new people of God of which the First Letter of Peter speaks (11:9). The road Abraham is to travel is unknown to him; he is in God's hands. The Letter to the Hebrews emphasizes this point: "he went out, not knowing where he was to go" (11:8).

Believe in Love

"He went out, not knowing where he was to go." Reliance on God presupposes faith in him and his love, and it implies a return of love. The person who is called accomplishes nothing great unless God helps accomplish it. Our own contribution is simply to grow in love. If we do, all else necessary will come from the God who anticipates us in our every action. The readings of the Lenten season will cast an indispensable light on the faith of Abraham and on the Christian imitation of that faith in daily life; this enlightenment will enable the Christian to avoid possible deviations.

Such deviations certainly can occur. The mere fact of being a descendant of Abraham gives one no guarantee that deviations will surely be avoided. No, the simple belonging must turn into a genuine giving of self to God. Jesus makes this point in an almost brutal way when speaking to the Jews: "I know that you are descendants of Abraham. But you are trying to kill me. . . . You belong to your father the devil and you willingly carry out your father's desires" (John 8:37, 44).

Those seeking the Catholic Church and those who belong to it both need to be reminded that juridical membership is not enough. We must not only belong to the stock of Abraham but be children of Abraham as well and do the works of the Father.

Even here, however, we can fall into a snare. To do the works of the Father in a formalistic way guarantees nothing, as Jesus points out on many occasions. In Christian life it is God who gives us the power to act, and to act out of love for him; the first and fundamental "observance" consists in charity. That is the point St. Paul is making in 1 Corinthians 13:1-13 (which used to be read on Quinquagesima Sunday).

The unconditional faith of Abraham is one of the best-known themes of the Old Testament and one of the most important for every one of us. The trials Abraham had to undergo show how God was taking the initiative in the work of salvation. Indeed, Abraham himself was fully aware that he had not been called because of any special merits or qualities of his own. The birth of Isaac brought home to him how God had a special destiny in mind for his posterity. Isaac was the fruit of an impossible conception, and Abraham saw in his birth a sign that God would indeed fulfill his promises (Gen 21:1-8).

According to a number of scholars, the account of the sacrifice of Isaac (Gen 22) was revised to some extent at a later time. In it we read that God ordered Abraham to offer up his own son in sacrifice. As a matter of fact, we know that the Canaanites did at times sacrifice children as part of their cult. In any case, the emphasis in the Genesis account is on two points. The first is that Abraham submits to God in faith and is ready to sacrifice his son: "[N]ow I know that you fear God, since you did not withhold from me your son, your only one" (Gen 22:12). Christian tradition will see in the sacrifice of Isaac a prefiguration of the sacrifice of God's only Son. The Church here is once again advising those who wish to become her members that their faith will have to be unconditional.

The second point stressed in the account (a point of less importance here) is that God intervenes to put an end to the practice of sacrificing children. The reediting of the account highlights this condemnation, one the prophets had often proclaimed. But this didactic aspect of the account in no way detracts from the faith of Abraham.

Under the covenant, God has the initiative to such an extent that even when it comes to offering him a sacrifice, he is the one who "will provide the sheep for the burnt offering" (Gen 22:8). Abraham himself makes this point, for after he has offered in Isaac's place a ram that had been trapped in a nearby thicket, the account tells us: "Abraham named that place Yahweh-yireh; hence people today say, 'On the mountain the LORD will provide'" (Gen 22:14).

The same principle applies to the sacrifice of Christ and his Church. God always provides the Victim, thus keeping the initiative in the work of salvation and making the liturgy his own. It is always the only Son who is offered, and it is always God who provides the Victim and hands him over for the salvation of the world.

God's Oath

There is an air of joy about Genesis when it tells us that "the LORD had blessed [Abraham] in every way" (Gen 24:1). Chapter 22 tells us of the oath God swore after he had intervened to save Isaac:

I swear by my very self—oracle of the LORD—that because you acted as you did in not withholding from me your son, your only one, I will bless you and make your descendants as countless as the stars of the sky and the sands of the seashore; your descendants will take possession of the gates of their enemies, and in your descendants all the nations of the earth will find blessing, because you obeyed my command. (Gen 22:16-18)

As we know, a single individual was to fulfill the promise and be *the* descendant of Abraham. The stock of Abraham proved unfaithful, and the history of the Old Testament is the history of its infidelities and of God's repeated efforts to bring it back to faith, love, and fidelity. His repeated efforts were failures. Thus, at first sight, God's blessing on Abraham seemed a failure. Its success becomes clear only when we move on to "the time of fulfillment."

The Church frequently speaks to us of "Abraham's bosom." The phrase comes from St. Luke's parable of Dives and Lazarus; the latter "was carried away by angels to the bosom of Abraham" (Luke 16:22). The Church wishes her children to end in the same way; our present liturgy for the dead prays that the soul of the deceased may be led "to Abraham's side."

The Christian of today is heir to the promise given to Abraham, but an heir through, and because of, Christ. In Christ alone was the promise completely fulfilled; he alone became the heir of the promise.

St. Paul speaks of these fundamental ideas in chapter 3 of his letter to the Galatians. His line of thought is quite clear. Abraham "believed God, and it was credited to him as righteousness" (3:6). In Abraham all nations were to be blessed, but only those that have faith would effectively be blessed along with Abraham, the man of faith (3:8-9). Observance of the law avails nothing, for "that no one is justified before God by the law is clear, for 'the one who is righteous by faith will live'" (3:11). Christ "ransomed us from the curse of the law by becoming a curse for us . . . that the blessing of Abraham might be extended to the Gentiles through Christ Jesus, so that we might receive the promise of the Spirit through faith" (3:13-14).

Clearly, then, the promise was fulfilled in a single individual. And yet God could rightly speak of a multitude of descendants because through Jesus Christ the many also become heirs of the promise. Christ adds that Abraham himself had a consoling vision of the complete fulfillment of the divine promise: "Abraham your father rejoiced to see my day; he saw it and was glad" (John 8:56).

All who are united to, and identified with, Christ are heirs to the promise with him: "For all of you who were baptized into Christ have clothed yourselves with Christ. There is neither Jew nor Greek, there is neither slave nor free person, there is not male and female; for you are all one in Christ Jesus. And if you belong to Christ, then you are Abraham's descendant, heirs according to the promise" (Gal 3:27-29).

Family of Abraham, Family of Christ

A suitable catechesis must bring home these points to those who seek to draw near to Christ and the Church. The baptism they wish to receive is the sacrament of faith. Once they have put on Christ, they will become children of the promise. Each of them will be "no longer a slave but a child, and if a child then also an heir" (Gal 4:7).

Here, once again, the liturgy offers the world a broad synthetic vision of the problem of salvation and the possibilities for its solution. The direction of the solution is clear and can be summed up in a phrase: the Lord's love. God loves, chooses, and calls. The appropriate response is unconditional faith, and the reward for such faith is the inheritance of the promise in Christ. God's love, which created humanity, still seeks to gather people into his kingdom, the kingdom that the heirs to the promise in Christ will possess.

Two Loves

Each Christian is the constant object of this divine love that makes one an heir to the promises and a child of the kingdom. But being a child and an heir presupposes, on the Christian's part, an unremitting effort to respond to the love that God pours out. Love alone gives meaning to the history of salvation, and love alone gives meaning and coherence to a Christian's life. First Corinthians 13, to which we alluded earlier, says this in an uncompromising way:

> If I speak in human and angelic tongues, but do not have love, I am a resounding gong or a clashing cymbal. And if I have the gift of prophecy and comprehend all mysteries and all knowledge; if I have faith, so as to move mountains, but do not have love, I am nothing. If I give away everything I own, and if I hand my body over so that I may boast but do not have love, I gain nothing. (1 Cor 13:1-3)

There can be no room for illusion here. Love is essential; nothing can avail without it, not even a faith powerful enough to move mountains. Love, or charity, then, is a comprehensive program for Christian life. It is, moreover, our answer to God's love that has been revealed in so many divine initiatives in the Old and New Testaments. God has always loved us first; he is the fountainhead of love. St. John explains this by telling us in the fourth chapter of his first letter just what love is: "In this way the love of God was revealed to us: God sent his only Son into the world so that we might have life through him. In this is love: not that we have loved God, but that he loved us and sent his Son as expiation for our sins" (1 John 4:9-10).

Love has been fully revealed to us in the person of Jesus and has reached its climactic expression in his death on the Cross. But Christ did not simply reveal to us the Father's love for us; he also showed us how we are to love the Father and one another.

In 1 Corinthians 13, St. Paul goes on to describe the specific qualities of love. He tells us that love for God is signified and expressed in love for our brothers and sisters:

> Love is patient, love is kind. It is not jealous, [love] is not pompous, it is not inflated, it is not rude, it does not seek its own interests, it is not quick-tempered, it does not brood over injury, it does not rejoice over wrongdoing but rejoices with the truth. It bears all things, believes all things, hopes all things, endures all things. (1 Cor 13:4-7)

Since we all belong to the one family of Abraham and have all clothed ourselves with Christ, this kind of charity is indeed a touchstone, as St. John insists: "Beloved, if God so loved us, we also must love one another" (1 John 4:11); "If any one says, 'I love God,' but hates his brother, he is a liar; for whoever does not love a brother whom he has seen cannot love God whom he has not seen. This is the commandment we have from him: whoever loves God must also love his brother" (1 John 4:20-21).

This basic law of Christianity allows no loopholes: we must love God and our neighbor. "This is how all will know that you are my disciples, if you have love for one another" (John 13:35).

The story of Abraham, which stands in such sharp contrast to the story of Adam, who is the very image of disobedience, points out the road the believer must travel: the road of faith, hope, and obedient love. Not only is there a contrast between Adam and Abraham; there is also a parallel between Abraham and Christ. The New Testament looks upon Christ as the fulfillment of the promise. Peter, in one of his sermons, tells his hearers that Christ belongs to Abraham's posterity: "You are the children of the prophets and of the covenant that God made with your ancestors when he said to Abraham, 'In your offspring all the families of the earth shall be blessed.' For you first, God raised up his servant and sent him to bless you by turning each of you from your evil ways" (Acts 3:25-26).

Our Holy Calling

"[O]ur savior Christ Jesus . . . destroyed death and brought life and immortality to light through the gospel" (2 Tim 1:10). Thus does St. Paul speak to us in the second reading for the second Sunday. In Christ, "[God] saved us and called us to a holy life" (2 Tim 1:9). This is important both for those preparing for baptism and for all the rest of us.

The first point about this calling that needs to be emphasized is that it is entirely free on God's part. If God has saved us and given us a call to holiness, it is not because of any merits of our own, says the Apostle. The idea of God's freely given call is a favorite of St. Paul; he speaks of us as being called to holiness (Rom 1:7; 1 Cor 1:2) and to charity (Gal 5:13). In all this, however, God has a plan that he is bent on carrying out, a plan that he reveals to us in his Son Jesus. In this context St. Paul speaks of "the mystery," meaning the divine plan that was hidden through the ages but has now been made known to all in Christ. And what is that plan? It is a plan to give humanity the victory over death and the gift of life and immortality—in short, the paschal victory.

We are called, then, to holiness, and if we respond to the call as Abraham and Jesus did, we shall eventually reach our triumphal transfiguration.

Such is the global vision of the history of salvation as presented in the readings for the first two Sundays of Lent. We were created that we might be holy and glorify the Father; we fell in Adam, and we succumbed to personal temptation. Now we are filled with the grace of Christ and called anew to holiness and to a glory that will be a sharing in the transfiguration of Christ himself. Baptism has given us the *rudimenta gloriae*, "the elements of our own future glorification," to use an expression from the Gelasian Sacramentary.[8]

The Entry into the Catechumenate

After a certain amount of pre-evangelization and a careful study of each adult who wishes to enter the Church, the local church celebrates in ritual the entry of the candidates into the catechumenate. The community that accepts responsibility for them is present, especially those individuals whose task it will be to guide and help them. The rite is connected with a Liturgy of the Word and may be followed by the Eucharist or held separately.[9]

The candidates are asked what they seek from the Church and then are given a brief exhortation in which they are told that the way of the Gospel is now opening before them, the way of faith that will lead them to love and eternal life. They are now asked whether they are ready to enter upon this way. Thereupon, the sponsors and the whole assembly are asked whether they are willing to help the catechumens. The celebrant offers a short prayer of thanksgiving, to which all respond with the words "We praise you, Lord, and we bless you."[10]

The signing of the catechumen's forehead with the cross belongs to the oldest part of the catechumenate ritual. The priest and the sponsors trace the sign, and the celebrant says: "N., receive the cross on your forehead. It is Christ himself who now strengthens you with this sign of his love. Learn now to know and follow him."[11]

This is followed by the (optional) signing of the catechumen's various senses: ears, eyes, lips, breast, and shoulders. This part of the ritual is then concluded by one or other of two prayers. The first is from the Gelasian Sacramentary: "Let us pray. Lord, we have signed these catechumens with the sign of Christ's cross. Protect them by its power, so that, faithful to the grace which has begun in them, they may keep your commandments and come to the glory of rebirth in baptism."[12]

The alternate prayer is of recent composition: "Almighty God, by the cross and resurrection of your Son you have given life to your people. Your servants have received the sign of the cross: make them living proof of its saving power and help them to persevere in the footsteps of Christ."[13]

If it be appropriate to do so, new names are given to the catechumens. Then they are conducted into the church, where a Liturgy of the Word is celebrated. After the homily (an innovation in relation to the tradition, which postpones the homily to a later point), the candidates are given the Book of the Gospels, and the congregation offers petitions for them. The celebrant then concludes the whole rite with a prayer. Two options are given. The first prayer suggested is again from the Gelasian Sacramentary, though it has been slightly revised: "[God of our fathers and] God of all creation, we ask you to look favorably on your servants N. and N.; make them fervent in spirit, joyful in hope, and always ready to serve your name. Lead them, Lord, to the baptism of new birth, so that, living a fruitful life in the company of your faithful, they may receive the eternal reward that you promise."[14]

The alternate prayer is one of recent composition: "Almighty God, source of all creation, you have made us in your image. Welcome with love those who come before you today. They have listened among us to the word of Christ; by its power renew them and by your grace refashion them, so that in time they may assume the full likeness of Christ."[15]

Even if the catechumens are then dismissed, the Liturgy of the Eucharist may be celebrated.

During the catechumenate and their period of instruction, the catechumens take part in further Liturgies of the Word that are celebrated specifically for them.

The priest, the deacon, and even the catechist may impose hands on the catechumens and pronounce "minor exorcisms" over them. The ritual provides a number of such prayers of exorcism, as well as formulas for blessing the catechumens.

The "handing over" or "presentation" (*traditio*) of the Creed and the Lord's Prayer may be anticipated. We shall speak of it, however, at the point where it should ordinarily be celebrated in accordance with the ancient tradition. It is also permissible to anoint the catechumens with blessed oil on the breast, on the hands, and even on other parts of the body if desirable.

After the period of the catechumenate comes the enrollment of the catechumens for their final preparation; this rite of election takes place at the beginning of the Lent immediately preceding their baptism. At this point the catechumenate in the strict sense is at an end, since the candidates cease to be simply "catechumens" (i.e., "hearers") and become "elect" (i.e., chosen for proximate baptism). (Thus the ancient tradition; we shall continue to use here the general term "catechumen.")

The priest or other person responsible for the initiation of the catechumens presents them to the community. The godparents are then questioned about the fitness of the candidates, and the catechumens are asked whether they indeed wish to be baptized at the next Easter Vigil. The community then offers petitions for them, and the celebrant ends the ceremony with a prayer. *

Two concluding prayers are provided, and again the first is from the Gelasian Sacramentary, while the alternate is of recent composition: "Lord God, you created the human race and are the author of its renewal. Bless all your adopted children and add these chosen ones to the harvest of your new covenant. As true children of the promise, may they rejoice in eternal life, won, not by the power of nature, but through the mystery of your grace";[16] "Father of love and power, it is your will to establish everything in Christ and to draw us into his all-embracing love. Guide the elect of your Church: strengthen them in their vocation, build them into the kingdom of your Son, and seal them with the Spirit of your promise."[17]

The "elect" are then dismissed and the Eucharist is celebrated.[†]

The enrollment for baptism was regarded in the past as highly important. The book of Exodus had spoken of heavenly books on which the names of God's elect were written (Exod 32:32-33). St. Gregory of Nyssa alludes to this when speaking of the catechumens enrolling for baptism: "Give me your names so that I may write them down in ink. But the Lord Himself will engrave them on incorruptible tablets, writing them with His own finger, as He once wrote the Law of the Hebrews."[18]

We will note that the catechumens and the elect are dismissed before the eucharistic liturgy begins. The point of the dismissal is not to keep the eucharistic celebration secret or simply to restore an

---

* Nocent does not call the celebrant "the bishop." The custom of having the bishop preside for the rite of election developed later. The English translation—more than the Latin—calls for the bishop to preside for this at the cathedral.

† In practice, most celebrations of the rite of election are liturgies of the word. Nocent correctly interprets the liturgical books, however, which presume that enrollment is being celebrated at Mass on the First Sunday of Lent.

ancient practice for its own sake. The intention is rather to emphasize the fact that normally one may not be present at the celebration of the eucharistic banquet unless one is worthy to eat of it. For this, one must be a baptized Catholic, and more.

Once enrolled, the catechumens begin a kind of retreat in preparation for baptism. In her *Diary of a Pilgrimage*, Egeria writes: "It is the custom here, throughout the forty days on which there is fasting, for those who are preparing for baptism to be exorcized by the clergy."[19] (Egeria was writing at the end of the fourth century and describing the liturgy at Jerusalem insofar as she could observe it.)

7. THIRD SUNDAY OF LENT (YEAR A): THE THIRST FOR THE WATER OF LIFE

Living Water

No better Scripture texts could have been chosen than those of this third Sunday for telling the catechumens how their thirst will be quenched. In these passages they meet the Lord as the Rock from which water flows forth in the desert (Exod 17:3-7), and they draw near to Christ, who is Living Water for those who believe in him (John 4:5-42).

The bitter water at Marah had earlier stirred the anger of God's people on their journey away from Egypt. On that occasion, a piece of wood thrown into the water had rendered it sweet (Exod 15:22-26). Now, a little while later, the lack of water is again being felt. The place is Massah and Meribah, two names given to Rephidim to mark it as the place where the people were tested and where they quarreled with Moses and their God.

The reading brings that tragic story home to the imagination and heart of the catechumens. The people of God are weary; they have been on the march for a long time, they are fatigued and have nothing, they have no sense of unity, no efficient organization. It is quite understandable, then, humanly speaking, that they should rebel. What is less understandable is that they should rebel against the God who has already done so much for them. They forget the past and the Lord's constant care for them and, with mindless violence, begin to complain and grow angry: "Give us water to drink" (Exod 17:2). Their cry, addressed to Moses and through him to God, might have been a confident appeal in time of trial, a request inspired by optimism and sure of a saving answer. In fact, it was a kind of curse uttered in despair.

Thus, the people of Israel were turning away from their God. Here was a crucial moment in their journey, and a sin of despair that would forever leave its mark on them. The psalms will remind Israel later on of this moment of infidelity: "Yet still they sinned against him, /

rebelled against the Most High in the desert. / In their heart they put God to the test / by demanding the food they craved. / They spoke against God and said: / 'Can God spread a table in the wilderness?'" (Ps 78:17-19).

The rock stands before the people, solid and inexorable. Apparently there is no human solution. Even Moses himself does not seem too sure of the Lord's omnipotence, and Aaron shares his uneasiness. And for this, both will be punished, as the parallel account in the book of Numbers tells us: "Because you did not have confidence in me, to acknowledge my holiness before the Israelites, therefore you shall not lead this assembly into the land I have given them" (20:12).

The power of the Lord does manifest itself, despite the weakness of Moses' faith: "Go over there in front of the people, along with some of the elders of Israel, holding in your hand, as you go, the staff with which you struck the river. I will be standing there in front of you on the rock in Horeb. Strike the rock, and the water will flow from it for the people to drink" (Exod 17:5-6). All trust must be in the Lord, but the trust is justified: "water came out in abundance" (Num 20:11).

The religious wonder roused by this event would last through the centuries: "He split the rocks in the desert. / He gave them plentiful drink, as from the deep. / He made streams flow out from the rock, / and made waters run down like rivers" (Ps 78:15-16). Isaiah speaks in the same tones: "They did not thirst / when he led them through dry lands; / Water from the rock he set flowing for them; / he cleft the rock, and waters welled forth" (Isa 48:21).

The water gushing from the rock was to play a key role in the life of Israel, for it was a sign of how much they were loved by that Lord who would henceforth be called the "Rock of salvation": "Come, let us ring out our joy to the LORD; / hail the rock who saves us" (Ps 95:1).

The fathers offer two different interpretations of this extremely important episode. Some see the water, taken in conjunction with the manna, as a prefiguration of the eucharistic wine. St. John Chrysostom interprets it this way when commenting on 1 Corinthians 10:4 and on the connection between the crossing of the Red Sea and baptism:

> After speaking of the sea, the cloud, and Moses, Paul adds: "And all ate the same supernatural food." He means: Just as you came up from the pool and ran to the table, so they came out of the sea and approached a new and miraculous table (I am referring to the manna). And just as you have a marvelous drink, the Savior's Blood, so they had a miracu-

lous drink. They found no springs or rivers, but they did receive abundant water from the hard, dry rock.[1]

St. Ambrose follows the same line of thought in his two catechetical works, *De sacramentis* and *De mysteriis*; for him too the water of Horeb prefigures the eucharistic wine. He expresses his thought quite clearly in *De sacramentis*:

> "They drank from the supernatural Rock which followed them, and the Rock was Christ." Drink, you too, that Christ may follow along with you. See the mystery! Moses is the prophet; his staff is God's word. The priest [Moses] touches the rock with the word of God and water flows, and the people drink. So, too, the priest [in the Eucharist] touches the chalice and water flows in the chalice and leaps up for eternal life.[2]

St. Augustine accepts the same parallelism.[3]

There is, however, another patristic interpretation that sees baptism prefigured in the water flowing from the rock at Horeb. While the first interpretation was based on St. Paul (1 Cor 10:4), this one appeals to St. John. St. Cyprian is one of the most important proponents of this interpretation:

> Every time that water alone is mentioned in the Holy Scripture, it refers to Baptism. God foretold through the Prophet [Isaiah] that while they were among pagan peoples and in dry places water would gush forth and fill the chosen people of God, that is, those who had been made his children by baptism. The Prophet says: "They thirsted not in the desert when he led them out: he brought forth water out of the rock for them, and he clove the rock, and the waters gushed out" (Isa 48:21). This was fulfilled in the gospel when the side of the Lord, who is the Rock, was pierced by a lance during his passion. He recalls what had been said of him by the Prophet when he exclaims: "If anyone thirst let him come to me and drink. He who believes in me, from his belly shall flow living waters." To emphasize that the Lord is speaking not of the chalice but of baptism, Scripture adds: "This he said of the Spirit, which they were to receive who believed in him" (John 7:37-39). And we receive the Spirit in baptism.[4]

"If You Knew the Gift of God"

It is an easy step from the account of the miraculous water in the book of Exodus to Jesus' words on the true "living water" in John's gospel (4:5-42). The meeting of Jesus and the Samaritan woman is fascinating indeed. Back in the book of Exodus we saw the Israelites full of complaints and standing before the Rock that would save them; we might, as we read, think ourselves transported to the dawn of creation, when God first encountered his fallen creatures. Here, in the Gospel of St. John, Christ meets one of his sinful creatures and, in her person, encounters humankind, which he intends to create anew.

St. Augustine has a fine commentary on the episode, as he describes the wearied Creator confronting the creature whom he is bent upon creating anew through his weariness and suffering:

> It was for you that Jesus was wearied from the journey. We find Jesus strong but also weak: a strong Jesus and a weak Jesus. Strong, because "in the beginning was the Word, and the Word was with God, and the Word was God. He was in the beginning with God." Would you know how strong this Son of God is? "All things were made through him, and without him was not anything made that was made," and all these things were made without effort. What can be stronger than him who made all things effortlessly?
>
> Do you want to see him weak? "The Word became flesh and dwelt among us." The strength of Christ created you; the weakness of Christ created you anew. The strength of Christ brought into existence what was not; the weakness of Christ prevented what was from perishing. He created us in his strength; he searched us out in his weakness.[5]

The baptismal typology in the story of the Samaritan woman is clear at several points. Thus: "whoever drinks the water I shall give will never thirst; the water I shall give will become in him a spring of water welling up to eternal life" (John 4:14). In other words, water by itself does not give life, but only water that has been transformed by Christ. The real "water from the well" is Christ.

We should bear in mind here one of the interpretations the fathers gave to the rock at Horeb. They saw in it the side of Christ that was opened to let water flow out (see the passage above from St. Ambrose).

St. Augustine, for his part, writes: "The rock is a prefiguration of Christ. . . . Moses struck the rock twice with his staff, and the two blows signify the two arms of the cross."[6] His interpretation looks to both baptism and the Eucharist, and enables us to better understand why John 4:13-14 should be chosen as a Communion antiphon for the Mass of the third Sunday: "For anyone who drinks it, says the Lord, the water I shall give will become in him a spring welling up to eternal life."

As even unbelievers can see when they meet Christians fervent in their faith, the latter do not hesitate, in whatever circumstances, to ask the Lord for "the sign of your favor, / that my foes may see to their shame / that you, O LORD, give me comfort and help" (Ps 86:17). When these Christians find themselves in the arid wastes, they feel no need to complain, as the Israelites did, but say simply: "Lord, give us water." And when they receive the Eucharist, they hear Christ say to them: "whoever drinks the water I shall give will never thirst."

The Christian is thus led to interpret the gift of water to the Samaritan woman in the same way as the gift of water to the Israelites at Horeb: It is a source of nourishment and strength. As the catechumens hear the gospel, it is as though they heard St. John himself telling them that the water the Lord gives is the water of rebirth.

The Mass for this third Sunday evidently has the catechumens very much in mind. If we but think of these readings and chants in the context of the scrutiny, with its special prayers for the Mass, we will have no difficulty in discerning the spirit in which the Mass formulary for the third Sunday was compiled. The catechumen, like the baptized Christian, is a human being who thirsts for God, a human being on a journey.

The prophet Isaiah links the episode of the rock at Horeb with the new exodus. The water that flowed from the rock becomes, in his eyes, a symbol of the salvation that God will give in the messianic age (see Isa 35:6; 41:18; 43:20; 48:21). At the well of Jacob, Jesus tells the Samaritan woman that the messianic age has come and that "I am he [the Messiah], the one speaking with you" (John 4:26).

The promises are now fulfilled. The Israelites had asked for water, and the Lord now gives it anew, but it is a mightier water than before. Now water will be the instrument of salvation, the source of life, a well out of which a person is reborn as one emerging with Christ from the tomb and entering upon a new life that is itself the pledge of eternal life. For baptism is not an end but a beginning, a rebirth leading to a struggle that will last until Christ returns. Water becomes a spiritual drink and is transformed into the blood of Christ that was poured out to ransom the multitude. Baptism and Eucharist together constitute a complete initiation into the life of God.

The Major Themes of the Conversation with the Samaritan Woman

It will be worth our while to review briefly the major themes of this gospel passage, which is certainly one of the most beautiful in the Fourth Gospel. This will also provide an opportunity to observe once again how the liturgy makes use of Scripture. If one were to approach the text purely as an exegete, it would be difficult to see in it any reference to the sacraments. And yet the Church, following the fathers, reads the text precisely in this way when she uses it on the Third Sunday of Lent, the day of the first scrutiny for those to be baptized. In such a reading, two sections are of special interest: the dialogue with the Samaritan woman (4:7-26) and the dialogue with the disciples (4:31-38).

In the first dialogue we find a favorite method of St. John at work: the conversation takes place on two levels, as it were, allowing two ways of understanding what is said. The Samaritan woman interprets the water and what is said of it as applying to a person's natural thirst, whereas Jesus sees in the water a sign. He promises a "living" water (vv. 7-15) that is God's gift. But the gift of living water is connected with the knowledge of Jesus, who, at a later point in this dialogue, will reveal himself to be the Messiah (v. 26, "I am he, the one speaking with you").

Water is an important theme throughout the Scriptures. In the prophetic books it is a symbol of the blessings the Messiah will bring (Zech 14:8; Joel 4:18). In the Wisdom literature water is equated with wisdom (Prov 13:14; etc.) or else it symbolizes the fruit derived from the study of the law (Sir 24:22-31), that is, wisdom from on high. In the New Testament, similarly, living water symbolizes the teaching of Christ.[7] In the dialogue with the Samaritan woman, then, when Jesus speaks of water, he is continuing the Jewish symbolism according to which water stands for wisdom. The wisdom now, however, is the wisdom of Christ.

At this point we pass to a new level. The water is the revelation that Jesus brings and is not given solely to the Samaritan woman. Rather, says Jesus, "whoever drinks the water I shall give will never thirst" (John 4:14). The Church, in her liturgy, sees in this water the sacramental water of baptism that associates a believer with the death and resurrection of Christ. In so doing, the Church is not distorting the meaning that the exegete finds in the text but is simply applying it to the life of the believer.

In this first dialogue with the Samaritan woman, Jesus also shows himself to be a prophet (vv. 16-19) and, most important, the Messiah (vv. 20-26). It is in this context that a statement is made that is very important both for the Christian's understanding of prayer and liturgical action and for the catechumen's ongoing education. Christ makes reference to a dispute over where people should worship. The Samaritans were convinced that people should worship on Mount Gerizim, where Noah had built an altar after the Flood and where Abraham too had offered sacrifice (Deut 27:4-8). The temple the Samaritans had built here was a rival of the temple at Jerusalem. No Israelite could accept that there should be two temples, and therefore the Samaritan woman's question was a relevant one: Where was true worship to be offered?

Jesus' answer is decisive: The time has come when worship will no longer be connected with a temple, since "true worshipers will worship the Father in Spirit and truth" (John 4:23). Does this mean that Christ is condemning all rites and all outward signs? Some people have so interpreted his words at certain critical moments when an exaggerated ritualism had cast its pall over Christian worship. The Reformers, for example, appealed to this text in order to condemn all external worship.

The key to the proper interpretation of the text is contained in the words "in Spirit." If the meaning is that authentic worship is to be purely spiritual, stripped of all material components, then any liturgy is to be condemned. In this reading of the text, Jesus is emphasizing the element of inwardness that all Christian prayer should have. In point of fact, however, when Jesus speaks of worship "in Spirit," he means prayer that the Holy Spirit prompts us to offer. He is saying what St. Paul says in his Letter to the Romans when he reminds his readers that the Spirit makes it possible for them to speak to God and call him "Father" (8:26-27).

We may also ask what Jesus means by worship "in truth." Does it mean genuine worship that replaces worship under the law, worship that was only a prefiguration of the real thing? To reach an answer, we must inquire into what "truth" means in the language of the Fourth Gospel. In this gospel, "truth" is the message that Jesus came to bring us. In fact, in the last analysis "truth" is Jesus himself, for he declares himself to be both Truth and Life. Authentic worship, then, is worship offered in and with Christ at the prompting of the Holy Spirit, who alone makes it possible.

The second dialogue is that of Jesus with his disciples, who return to the scene after Jesus' conversation with the woman (vv. 31-38). The first dialogue had made it clear what it means to be thirsty and to drink. The second will explain what it means to "eat." There is a food to be eaten of which the disciples are ignorant. In response to the disciples' question, Jesus launches upon a theme that is very prominent in St. John's gospel: doing the Father's will. "My food is to do the will of the one who sent me and to finish his work" (v. 34). When, contrary to prevailing prejudice, he spoke to the Samaritan woman and thus surprised and almost scandalized his own disciples, he was doing the Father's will and engaging in the work of salvation.

Another reason for the choice of this gospel pericope in today's Mass is the evangelist's summarizing statement: "Many of the Samaritans of that town began to believe in him because of the word of the woman. . . . Many more began to believe in him because of his word, and they said to the woman, 'We no longer believe because of your word; for we have heard for ourselves, and we know that this is truly the savior of the world'" (vv. 39-42). These verses are important because they emphasize the universality of Jesus' work and of the work of the Church and thus reassure those who are coming to the faith.

God's Love Poured into Our Hearts

The second reading in the Mass of the third Sunday brings out the full spiritual meaning of the gospel pericope. The latter speaks of the water that leaps up to provide eternal life, while the first reading had shown us the thirsty Israelites despairing and rebelling. With St. Paul we are caught up by hope (Rom 5:1-2, 5-8). "And hope does not disappoint," he tells us, "because the love of God has been poured out into our hearts through the Holy Spirit who has been given to us" (v. 5). In other words, we have within us the wellspring from which the life-giving water flows, and it—he!—justifies us through faith. This is, of course, a mystery of love that we really cannot comprehend. Paul underscores the incomprehensibility: "Indeed, only with difficulty does one die for a just person, though perhaps for a good person one might even find courage to die. But God proves his love for us in that while we were still sinners Christ died for us" (vv. 7-8).

This Sunday of the first scrutiny thus focuses on the gift of the love that quenches our thirst. It is indeed a "sacramental Sunday." That is doubtless how the Church thinks of it, without in any way distorting the objective meaning of the texts she has us read. Water is a sign of a gift, and the gift is the love that justifies us through the action of the Spirit. How could the Church fail to link this water with the sacramental water of baptism?

The First Scrutiny

As we pointed out earlier, the scrutinies began on the Third Sunday of Lent. "Scrutiny," let us remember, does not here mean an inquiry; it means an exorcism that prepares the catechumen to receive the Spirit in baptism. The new rite for adult baptism has restored the scrutinies. When catechumens are actually present and a scrutiny is to be held, the collect of the Mass is for the catechumens: "Grant, we pray, O Lord, that these chosen ones may come worthily and wisely to the confession of your praise, so that in accordance with that first dignity which they lost by original sin they may be fashioned anew through your glory."[8]

The readings and chants are those of Year A.[*] After the homily the catechumens and their godparents come before the celebrant; he invites the assembly to pray silently for the catechumens and then asks the catechumens likewise to pray silently; they bow or kneel to show their repentance. This period of silent prayer is followed by intercessions for the catechumens and by the exorcism.

The exorcism has been completely rewritten. The exorcism given in the Gelasian Sacramentary and in the baptismal rite for both adults and children down to our own time could hardly have been taken over into a revised rite, given its rather medieval emphasis on the power of the demon. That power is indeed not to be underestimated, but it can be presented in ways that would only antagonize our contemporaries. Let us look first at the old formulas; we will then be in

---

[*] Actually, even when Nocent was writing, the entrance and communion antiphons were taken from the scrutiny Masses in the RCIA and the Missal. In the third edition of the Missal, the same three communion antiphons reappear, but two entrance antiphons have been added to complement the single one used for all three Masses in previous editions.

a position to appreciate the adaptation that has been deemed necessary. The older rite contained a prayer followed by an exorcism proper; there were separate prayers for men and women. At the end the priest added a closing prayer.

Prayer over Men: "O God of Abraham, God of Isaac, God of Jacob, you appeared on Mount Sinai to your servant, Moses; you led the children of Israel out of Egypt, graciously appointing an angel to guard them day and night. We ask you, Lord, to send your holy angel from heaven to guard in the same way your servants, N. and N., and to lead them to the grace of your baptism. Through Christ our Lord. Amen."[9]

Exorcism of Men: "Therefore, accursed devil, acknowledge your condemnation, and pay homage to the living and true God; pay homage to Jesus Christ, his Son, and to the Holy Spirit, and keep far from these servants of God, N. and N., for Jesus Christ, our God and Lord, has called them to his holy grace and to the font of baptism. Accursed devil, never dare to desecrate this sign of the holy cross which we are tracing upon their foreheads. Through the same Jesus Christ our Lord, who is to come to judge the living and the dead and the world by fire. Amen."[10]

Prayer over Women: "O God of the heavens and the earth, God of the angels and the archangels, God of the patriarchs and of the prophets, God of the apostles and of the martyrs, God of the confessors and of the virgins, God of all who live holy lives, God to whom every knee bends of those in heaven, on earth, and under the earth: I beg you, Lord, to protect these your servants, N. and N., and to lead them to the grace of your baptism. Through Christ our Lord. Amen."[11]

Exorcism of Women: "Therefore, accursed devil . . ." (same as exorcism of men).

Concluding Prayer: "Lord, holy Father, almighty and eternal God, source of all light and truth, I humbly beg your never-ending and most holy mercy upon these servants of yours, N. and N. May it please you to grant them the light of your own wisdom. Cleanse them and make them holy. Give them true knowledge, so that they may be made worthy to come to the grace of your baptism. May they maintain firm hope, sound judgment, and a grasp of holy doctrine, so that they may be able to receive your grace. Through Christ our Lord. Amen."[12]

Here now are the formulas in the new rite. It can be said that they are derived from the old prayers, but they have been adapted to a new and different audience of Christians and candidates for baptism. It will be noted, too, that they make explicit reference to the three readings of the Mass.

After the intercessions for the catechumens, the celebrant turns to the latter and says:

> God of power, you sent your Son to be our Savior. Grant that these catechumens, who, like the woman of Samaria, thirst for living water, may turn to the Lord as they hear his word and acknowledge the sins and weaknesses that weigh them down. Protect them from vain reliance on self and defend them from the power of Satan. Free them from the spirit of deceit, so that, admitting the wrong they have done, they may attain purity of heart and advance on the way to salvation. We ask this through Christ our Lord. Amen.

He then extends his hands over the candidates and continues:

> Lord Jesus, you are the fountain for which they thirst, you are the Master whom they seek. In your presence they dare not claim to be without sin, for you alone are the Holy One of God. They open their hearts to you in faith, they confess their faults and lay bare their hidden wounds. In your love free them from their infirmities, heal their sickness, quench their thirst, and give them peace. In the power of your name, which we call upon in faith, stand by them now and heal them. Rule over that spirit of evil, conquered by your rising from the dead. Show your elect the way of salvation in the Holy Spirit that they may come to worship the Father in truth, for you live and reign for ever and ever. Amen.[13]

After the scrutiny the candidates leave the assembly, and the eucharistic liturgy begins. But even though the catechumens have left, the community continues to pray for them and their godparents. The following are the special prayers for the third Sunday when a scrutiny is celebrated at the Mass.[14]

Prayer over the Offerings: "May your merciful grace prepare your servants, O Lord, for the worthy celebration of these mysteries and lead them to it by a devout way of life."

During the Eucharistic Prayer (when Eucharistic Prayer I is used, special forms of the *Memento* of the living and of the *Hanc igitur* are used): "Remember, Lord, your servants who are to present your chosen ones for the holy grace of your Baptism [Here the names of the godparents are read out], and all gathered here. . . . Therefore,

Lord, we pray: graciously accept this oblation which we make to you for your servants, whom you have been pleased to enroll, choose and call for eternal life and for the blessed gift of your grace."[†]

Prayer after Communion: "Give help, O Lord, we pray, by the grace of your redemption and be pleased to protect and prepare those you are to initiate through the Sacraments of eternal life."

The theology of these prayers (which include the collect cited earlier) is simple but substantial. The collect summarizes very briefly the effects of the baptism for which the candidates are preparing: They will be reborn and have restored to them their original dignity (lost by original sin). Such a change is evidently a work possible only to God. When people are born into the world, they are in connivance, as it were, with evil as well as with good. They are incapable, by their own powers, of changing these relationships to the milieu into which they are born; only God can dissolve this solidarity with evil.

In thus changing people, God restores them to their true dignity and bestows true wisdom upon them. "Wisdom" here has nothing to do with the wisdom of the philosophers but is specifically Christian, being identical with the personal experience of God in and through the community. Humanity's restoration to the state that God originally intended has but one ultimate purpose, namely, the praise of God's glory.

The prayer over the offerings likewise shows God taking the initiative in the transformation that the catechumen will undergo. Catechumens must indeed have faith and love, but it is God who invites them to share in the Eucharist and gives them the sacraments of baptism and confirmation as the way by which they gain full access to the Lord's Supper.

The special inserts in the eucharistic prayers are indicative of the importance the Church attributes to the work of the godparents. Their names are read out in the *Memento* of the living, since they will not only present the candidates for baptism but also have a responsibility for them once they are baptized. At the same time, the Church bids the whole community play its part in the great task of giving divine life to others.

---

† The third edition of the Missal now includes similar inserts for Eucharistic Prayers II and III.

It is evident that when the Church administers a sacrament, she does not think of herself as simply entrusted with powers whose use she supervises. She does not think of the sacrament as merely a tool she uses and whose application she regulates while herself remaining, as it were, completely external to it. For when the Church administers a sacrament, she can only do so as the Body of Christ; this means that her role in the sacrament is literally a vital, that is, life-giving, role. She is fully aware of this fact, and the way in which she associates the whole community with the baptism shortly to be administered is a stirring proof of it.

The prayer for those to be baptized, in the *Hanc igitur*, supposes that their names too have been mentioned.‡ In this prayer the typical biblical word "call" indicates both God's initiative in salvation and the situation of the Christian over against the world. Christians live in the world, but they live there as people set apart because they have been chosen and called.[15]

---

‡ Actually, it doesn't. The Roman Canon does not include the names of catechumens or non-Christians.

8. FOURTH SUNDAY OF LENT (YEAR A):
THE LIGHT OF TRUTH

Finding the Light

The gospel for the fourth Sunday (John 9:1-41) is a deeply moving one, and its teaching is rich in meaning for each of us. In general terms, here is what it tells us. All of us have been born blind, and the catechumens, despite their desire to attain to the truth, are still blind. But now the Lord tells them: "While I am in the world, I am the light of the world" (John 9:5). On our own, we can do nothing, for, as Jesus says, "I came into this world for judgment, so that those who do not see might see, and those who do see might become blind" (John 9:39). He alone is the Light, and he alone can give light because he alone has been sent by the Father to do so. Is there anything we can do? Yes, "Go wash in the Pool of Siloam" (v. 7). Then our eyes are opened, and we who were born blind can see. This is the Lord's doing.

In his catecheses, St. Ambrose gives an enthusiastic comment on this passage from the Fourth Gospel. His words are addressed to Christians recently baptized, but they also show us how the saint preferred to approach baptism.

> When you had yourself registered, he [Jesus] took some clay and spread it on your eyes. What does that mean? It means that you were forced to acknowledge your sin, examine your conscience, do penance for your faults—in short, you had to admit to the state that the whole human race shares. For although the people approaching baptism make no confession of sins, they do nonetheless admit their sins by asking for the baptism that justifies and by asking to pass from sin to grace.
>
> Do not think that this act is useless. There are those—I know at least one, who, when we told him: "At your age you have a greater obligation to be baptized," replied: "Why should I be baptized? I have no sins. I have never committed a sin, have I?" Such a man had no clay, because Christ had not spread it on his eyes; which is to say that Christ had not opened his eyes. For, in fact, no one is without sin.
>
> Consequently, those who take refuge in baptism acknowledge that they are but human. Christ, then, put mud on you, that is, he gave you

a reverential fear, prudence, and a consciousness of your own weakness, and he said to you: "Go to Siloam." What is "Siloam"? It means (says the evangelist) "Sent." In other words, then: Go to the fountain where they preach the Cross of Christ the Lord; go to the fountain in which Christ has paid the ransom for the sins of all.

You went, you washed, you came to the altar, you began to see what you had not seen before. In short, your eyes were opened in the fountain of the Lord and by the preaching of the Lord's Passion. You seemed previously to be blind of heart; now you began to see the light.[1]

In his forty-fourth discourse on the Fourth Gospel, St. Augustine offers this commentary:

If, then, we reflect on the meaning of this miracle, we will see that the blind man is the human race. The blindness struck the first man because of sin, and he became for us the source not only of death but of sin as well. . . . The evangelist makes a point of telling us the name of the pool, and the fact that the name means "Sent." You already know, of course, who the "One sent" is. Unless he had been sent, none of us would have been freed of sin. . . .

Ask a man, "Are you a Christian?" If he is a pagan or a Jew, he will answer, "I am not." But if he says, "I am," then ask him, "A catechumen or one of the faithful?" If he says, "A catechumen," then he has been anointed but not washed. But how did he get anointed? Ask him and he will tell you. Ask him in whom he believes, and because he is a catechumen he will say, "In Christ." Now, I am speaking, of course, to both faithful and catechumens. What did I say of the spittle and mud? That the Word became flesh. That is what the catechumens learn. But it is not enough for them to have been anointed; let them hasten on to the font if they seek the Light.[2]

The second reading in the Office of Readings for this day is from this same commentary on St. John. Part of the passage reads as follows:

[Brothers and sisters], that light shines on us now, for we have had our eyes anointed with the eye-salve of faith. His saliva was mixed with earth to anoint the man born blind. We are of Adam's stock, blind from our birth; we need him to give us light. . . . We shall be in possession of the truth when we see face to face. This is his promise to us. . . . You are not told: Strive to find the way so that you may reach the truth and the life. That is not what you are told! Rise up from your laziness! The way itself has come to you and roused you from your sleep... rise, therefore, and walk![3]

The Man Called Jesus

How clear and simple is the answer the man born blind gives to the Pharisees when they asked about his cure: "The man called Jesus made clay and anointed my eyes and told me, 'Go to Siloam and wash.' So I went there and washed and was able to see" (John 9:11). But the man himself was not the only one to know what had happened; the crowd saw and was amazed that the man born blind could now see (vv. 8-13). Evidently, he who worked this wonder must have been a prophet or even the Messiah (vv. 40-43). The people were disturbed, for they could not come to a clear judgment on just who the man Jesus was.

The authorities of the synagogue refused to see anything at all. Their reaction is entirely juridical in character: We are disciples of Moses; this man Jesus is a sinner, since he has not observed the laws governing the Sabbath, and God does not listen to sinners. In the end they can only assert, "we do not know where this one is from" (v. 29). The blind man, on the other hand, is quite logical in his thinking: "If this man were not from God, he would not be able to do anything" (v. 33). As a result, he is expelled from the synagogue as a sinner and a rude mocker.

The Son of Man, Light of the World

By healing the man born blind, Jesus shows himself to be Son of Man and Light of the world. The very purpose of the sign, indeed, is to show others what he really is. He is the Light of the world, the Light that enlightens everyone (John 1:9). The works that he does and that prove him to be the Light are nothing but the carrying out of the Father's will. We must even say that they are God's own works rendered visible through signs.

The main point of the whole narrative, then, is to show that Jesus is the Son of the Father and the Light of the world and that he has been sent to carry out the Father's plan of salvation.

Here, once again, we see the difference between a purely exegetical reading and a liturgical reading. From the purely exegetical viewpoint, the aim of the passage is to show the divinity of Christ through a sign that he has given. The liturgical reading of the passage does not deny this first aspect, but it focuses on something else. The mention of the pool of Siloam and the fact that a man is cured of blindness resulted in the account being used, from a very early period, as a baptismal catechesis. The liturgy thus emphasizes not only the revelation of Jesus' person but also the sign itself, with its relation to baptism, and the effect the sign had, that is, the curing of blindness. Because the sacrament does have this effect, the baptized are described as "the enlightened."

Christ Will Give You Light

The liturgical significance of the gospel pericope determined the choice of the second reading, the passage from the Letter to the Ephesians in which St. Paul tells the faithful that they were once darkness but are now light in the Lord and that consequently they must live as children of the light (Eph 5:8-14).

Christians have become light; that is, they have been wakened from the dead and enlightened by Christ. The statement is not vaguely poetic; it is real and a source of joy, but it also brings serious obligations. It is no easy matter to be, with Christ, a light for the world. Yet such is the responsibility of the entire Church and in a special way of all those in the Church who continue the work of the apostles. This second group must not, however, be made to bear the whole burden. Each of us is in our own way a light; that is what our baptism means.

St. Paul contrasts the time of darkness, before baptism, and the time of light that follows and results from baptism. In this time of light we must bear the "fruit of light," which "produces every kind of goodness and righteousness and truth" (v. 9).

The Lord Chooses His Anointed One

The first reading for the fourth Sunday (1 Sam 16:1b, 6-7, 10-13a) brings out once again the fact that in the gospel reading the Church has a special interest in the cure of the blind man as a sign of baptism. It is impossible to establish any concrete link between the first reading and the other two, and yet a broadly conceived but coherent connection does exist.

The first reading emphasizes the fact that God chooses those whom he wills to draw to himself and consecrate. There is evidently an allusion here, in the liturgical context, to the gift of faith that God freely gives to the catechumens. His choices are manifested in a very personal way; that is, God has his own way of choosing and judging, and his judgments are not superficial, like those of humans, who can only judge by externals. Those chosen for the gift of faith are not chosen because of any merits on their part; in fact, the gift is often a thorough surprise to others looking on and even baffles them completely.

This element of free choice is the point to be emphasized in this reading, as I see it. At the same time, we cannot forget the anointing, which can be related to the anointing of the eyes of the man born blind. Such a parallel may seem forced, however, and we need not insist on it.

The prayer after Communion tells us in a few words what our prayer should be: "O God, who enlighten everyone who comes into this world, illuminate our hearts, we pray, with the splendor of your grace, that we may always ponder what is worthy and pleasing to your majesty and love you in all sincerity."

The Second Scrutiny

The Gelasian Sacramentary (and the older baptismal liturgy) supplies us with the rite for the second scrutiny, which was celebrated on this Fourth Sunday of Lent. Here is the exorcism proper:

> Hear, accursed Satan, I adjure you by the name of the eternal God and of our Savior Jesus Christ, depart with your envy, conquered, trembling, and groaning. May you have no part in these servants of God, N. and N., who already have thoughts of heaven and who are about to renounce you and your world and achieve a blessed immortality. Therefore give honor to the Holy Spirit who, descending from the high throne of heaven, comes to upset your wiles and to make perfect the hearts cleansed at the divine fountain, temples, and dwelling places dedicated to God. And thus entirely freed from the harmful effects of past sins, may these servants of God give thanks always to the eternal God, and bless his holy name forever and ever. Amen.[4]

In the Gelasian Sacramentary the exorcism of women was preceded by the following prayer: "God of Abraham, God of Isaac, God of Jacob, God who instructed the tribes of Israel and freed Susanna from a false accusation, I humbly pray you to free these your servants and in your mercy lead them to the grace of your baptism."[5] To be noted here is the reference to Susanna; her story had been read on the preceding day, Saturday of the third week.

In the new rite for adult initiation, the scrutiny is celebrated according to the same pattern as the first (on the third Sunday). The two prayers of exorcism are notable both for clarity and for wealth of teaching. The celebrant turns to the candidates and with hands joined says: "Father of mercy, you led the man born blind to the kingdom of light through the gift of faith in your Son. Free these elect from the false values that surround and blind them. Set them firmly in your truth, children of the light for ever."

With hands extended over the candidates, he continues: "Lord Jesus, you are the true light that enlightens the world. Through your Spirit of truth, free those who are enslaved by the father of lies. Stir up the desire for good in these elect, whom you have chosen for your sacraments. Let them rejoice in your light, that they may see, and, like the man born blind whose sight you restored, let them prove to be staunch and fearless witnesses to the faith, for you are Lord for ever and ever. Amen."[6]

9. FIFTH SUNDAY OF LENT (YEAR A): ARISE AND LIVE

"Your Brother Will Rise"

Christ is still saying to us: "Your brother will rise." But he does not now say it to the members of the Church in the same way that he once said it to the sisters of Lazarus. The latter were indeed trustful as they listened to the Lord, but they were also forced to be passive; they could only await what sign the Lord might give. Now, however, Christ speaks his words to the Church, and it is with the entire Church and each of her members that he raises his voice in prayer to the Father. On the day of baptism the Church says to the catechumen, as she does also to the Christian who has fallen into sin: "Lazarus, come out!" Christ and the Church together say, "Untie him and let him go," and the bonds of sin fall away at the words of Christ and his Church.

Christ is the Light of the world (John 11:9-10), and now, through the Church, he is also the Resurrection and Life of the world (vv. 25-26). Along with Christ, the Church is "deeply troubled" before the tomb of Lazarus the sinner, and her prayer unties the fetters of sin and restores Lazarus to life.

When we read that Christ was "perturbed and deeply troubled" at Lazarus's tomb, and when we hear it asserted that the Church is troubled along with him, we should not see in the phrase merely the expression of profound human and spiritual love and concern. The deep sorrow of Christ, the Incarnate God, is a sorrow at what sin has done to humanity. In Christ, God is recalling the Adam he once made in his own image, a creature radiant with life and beauty of body and spirit. Now Christ finds himself confronted with the failure of that first creation, and the Church must always experience the same disturbance of soul as she sees what that initial disaster has done to humankind. She can see these evil effects at every moment, for she need only look at the pagan world and at her own members, since they too are less than fully alive because of sin.

In his forty-ninth discourse on the Fourth Gospel, St. Augustine comments on the raising of Lazarus. In Lazarus he sees a great sinner and emphasizes the fact that the man has now been buried for four days. Why this emphasis? Because for Augustine the four days represent original sin, sin against the natural law, sin against the law of Moses, and sin against the law set down in the gospel.[1] "This interpretation will leave its mark on numerous texts of the liturgy. For example, the preface for the consecration of cemeteries speaks of 'the fourfold weight of sin.' "[2] An old preface for the fifth Sunday uses similar language: "Being a weak human like us, Jesus wept for Lazarus. Then by the power of his divinity he restored the man to life and raised humanity up when it was buried under the fourfold weight of sin."[3]

In the discourse already mentioned, St. Augustine highlights something that is quite important, namely, the necessity of faith if we are to have and preserve the life that Christ gives. The gospel about the raising of Lazarus (John 11:1-45), which is read on the Fifth Sunday of Lent, develops this point quite forcefully. No life without faith—faith is an indispensable condition, but on the other hand its effect is sure: "everyone who lives and believes in me will never die" (John 11:26).

St. Augustine asks, and answers, another question:

> Someone may say, "How can Lazarus be a symbol of the sinner and yet be so loved by the Lord?" Let the questioner listen to the Lord: "I came not to call the righteous, but sinners!" If God did not love sinners, he would not have come to earth.
>
> On hearing of Lazarus's illness, Jesus said: "This illness is not unto death; it is for the glory of God, so that the Son of God may be glorified by means of it." Such a glorification of the Son of God did not really increase his glory, but it was useful to us. He says, then, "This illness is not unto death." The reason is that even the death of Lazarus was not unto death but happened for the sake of the miracle, the performance of which would lead people to believe in Christ and so avoid real death. Consider here how the Lord indirectly calls himself God, having in mind those who deny that he is God.[4]

In his commentary St. Augustine stresses the glorification of the Son. Jesus tells Martha: "Did I not tell you that if you believe you would see the glory of God?" (v. 40). We are reminded here of the familiar yet always inspiring words of St. Irenaeus: "A person fully alive is the glory God seeks" (*Gloria Dei, vivens homo*). For when a person is fully alive, the covenant and the second creation are a success. It is to that success that the raising of Lazarus points.

Jesus is "perturbed and deeply troubled" at the sight of God's first creation fallen into disorder, death, and destruction. His own glory, on the other hand, will shine out most fully in the passion, when he shows himself Master of death and Master of life and does so at the time and place he himself has decided on. The miracle of the raising of Lazarus presupposes the whole work, past and yet to come, of Jesus and is a sign of it. Now catechumens are urged to see their own glory as implied in the glory of Jesus and of the Church. The glorification of Christ is completed in the glorification of Christians: "I have been glorified in them," says Jesus in his priestly prayer (John 17:10). The raising of Lazarus is a sign of the restoration of creation to its original splendor.

When Christians receive the Body of Christ, they sing of their own resurrection, for of that the Eucharist is their pledge. "When Jesus saw her [Mary] weeping and the Jews who had come with her weeping, he became perturbed and deeply troubled. . . . Jesus wept. . . . [H]e cried out in a loud voice, 'Lazarus, come out!' The dead man came out, tied hand and foot with burial bands, and his face was wrapped in a cloth" (John 11:33, 35, 43, 44).

That You May Believe

The choice of this gospel for the fifth Sunday was motivated by the desire to give prominence to an important form of baptismal typology: the resurrection of Lazarus as a figure and type of the resurrection of Jesus and of our twofold resurrection (our resurrection to divine life in baptism and our later, definitive resurrection at the end). The sign of Lazarus is a good example of how St. John conceives of such signs. The sign is done in response to faith and for the glory of God. With regard to faith, the sign not only is a response but also moves individuals to a still deeper faith, as Christ's own words bring out (11:11-26). As a matter of fact, John's entire gospel is written for the purpose of rousing faith (see 20:31).

Martha's faith is implied in her regretful words, "Lord, if you had been here, my brother would not have died" (v. 21). She believes in the power and presence of Jesus; when he is there, we may hope for anything and everything. In fact, even now her words show that her hope is still alive, for cannot Jesus do anything he wishes? It is at this point that Jesus begins his catechesis; as so often in John, the Lord uses for his point of departure a misunderstanding he himself has deliberately allowed his interlocutor to fall into. He thus leads Martha from belief in the resurrection on the last day (which Jews accepted and to which Jesus himself seemed to be referring) to a belief in himself as the Resurrection and Life of all who believe in him (11:25-26).

The resurrection of Jesus, prefigured in the raising of Lazarus, is a sign of our own resurrection. Martha moves from faith in a Christ who can work miracles to a faith in the word of him whom the Father has sent. This is the act of faith that every person makes at baptism: each one believes in the Word, the Christ who died and was raised from the dead. The second reading (Rom 8:8-11) emphasizes this faith in the power of the Spirit of the risen Christ, the Spirit who dwells in us and will cause us likewise to rise from the dead.

Mary's faith is like that of her sister Martha. When she leaves the house on hearing of Jesus' arrival, she goes not to weep at her brother's tomb, as the Jews believe, but to meet Jesus, and she falls at his feet. Then we hear from her the same profession of implicit faith as her sister had uttered: "Lord, if you had been here, my brother would not have died" (v. 32).

It is at this point that the evangelist shows us a Christ who is troubled and deeply moved both by the sorrow of his friends and by their profession of faith.

Jesus and Death

It is important to observe how Jesus the human acts in the face of death. We are told that he is moved by deep emotions and that he weeps (vv. 33-35). Despite this, when he raises Lazarus, he does so in order that God may be glorified. If Martha has faith, she will see this glory of God (v. 40). He also raises Lazarus in order to move people to faith and to draw them gradually to a belief in his own resurrection, which is a sign of our final resurrection that will give death a new meaning for the Christian.

The fact, however, that death will have, and indeed already has, a new meaning in no way lessens the human compassion of Jesus in the face of the brutal reality of death. This is not the place for a disquisition on how Jesus viewed death; that is not why this gospel was chosen. The important thing here is how Jesus relates death to what will follow it, namely, the resurrection that will give glory to God. To the Christian, death is a passage to a new life, a passage from a bodily, material life to a spiritual life, a passage that takes place in Jesus, by the power of his Spirit. This, as we said above, is the point being made in the second reading.

The Spirit and Life

The first reading has already focused our attention on God's will to bestow life on people (Ezek 37:12-14). St. Jerome points out that the prophet's image shows a belief in the future resurrection and that the Church's use of the passage shows her sharing this belief: "The image of the resurrection would never have been used to signify the restoration of the Israelite people unless there was indeed a resurrection and unless people believed that it would come to pass, for no one proves the uncertain by the nonexistent."[5]

The words "I will put my spirit in you that you may live" (Ezek 37:14) immediately bring to mind the passage of Romans (8:8-11) that has been selected as the second reading. Both passages speak of a gift and an activity of the Spirit who makes alive. We have Christ living in us; consequently, though our bodies are condemned to death because of sin, the Spirit is our true Life, now that we have been justified and sanctified. He who raised Jesus from the dead will also restore life to our mortal bodies by the power of his Spirit who dwells in us.

The passage from Romans provides the clearest and most complete commentary on the entire liturgy of the fifth Sunday: Once we are baptized, the Spirit of Jesus dwells in us and we have the pledge of resurrection and life. That says everything, and if we really want to understand the attitude of Jesus toward death, we must approach it in the light of St. Paul's words in Romans 8. The Christian does not look upon death as other people do; for Christians, death means the beginning of a new life or, more accurately, the further unfolding of a life that is already theirs, once they have been justified by baptism and have Christ living in them.

The Third Scrutiny

On this Sunday the Church continues her proximate preparation of catechumens for baptism. The celebration of this third scrutiny follows the same format as that of the first two scrutinies on the two preceding Sundays.

After the intercessions for catechumens, the celebrant turns to them and prays:

> Father of life and God not of the dead but of the living, you sent your Son to proclaim life, to snatch us from the realm of death, and to lead us to the resurrection. Free these elect from the death-dealing power of the spirit of evil, so that they may bear witness to their new life in the risen Christ, for he lives and reigns for ever and ever.

Then, having silently laid hands on each catechumen, he extends his hands over them all and says:

> Lord Jesus, by raising Lazarus from the dead you showed that you came that we might have life and have it more abundantly. Free from the grasp of death those who await your life-giving sacraments and deliver them from the spirit of corruption. Through your Spirit, who gives life, fill them with faith, hope, and charity, that they may live with you always in the glory of your resurrection, for you are Lord for ever and ever.[6]

The "Presentations"

It was in connection with the celebrations on these Sundays and during the weeks of Lent that the Church introduced and gradually organized what were called the "presentations" (*traditiones*): of the Creed, or profession of faith; of the Lord's Prayer; and of the gospels. These were celebrations in which these texts were read to the catechumens and some commentary on them was given. The new rite of Christian initiation of adults has restored the practice of the presentations, though in a simplified form. We think it worthwhile to provide the reader here with the text of these ceremonies in their ancient form.

Presentation of the Creed

> *Here begins the presentation of the Creed to the candidates. Before reciting the Creed, address them as follows:*
> Dear sons and daughters, you are about to receive the sacrament of baptism and to be begotten as new creatures of the Holy Spirit. Welcome

wholeheartedly the statement of the faith that will justify you if you truly believe. With your souls now changed by a true conversion, draw near to God who enlightens our minds, and receive the sacrament of the evangelical Creed that the Lord inspired and the apostles established. Its words are few, but it contains great mysteries. For the Holy Spirit, by dictating these truths to the teachers of the Church, created so concise and eloquent a statement of our saving faith that what you are to believe and constantly pay heed to cannot be too much for your understanding or your memory.

Exert yourselves, then, to learn the Creed. What we ourselves have received we hand on to you. Write it down, not on a material substance that can decay, but on the pages of your heart. This, then, is how the confession of the faith you have received begins. . . .[7]

When this has been done [when the acolyte, with his hand on the catechumen's head, has recited the Creed], *the priest continues:*

That is the summary of our faith, dear sons and daughters; those are the words of the Creed that are not the fruit of human wisdom but are true and divinely ordered. No one is incapable of understanding and observing them. According to this Creed, the power of God the Father and the power of God the Son is one and equal. It tells us that the only-begotten Son of God was born, according to the flesh, from the Virgin Mary and the Holy Spirit; that he was crucified and buried and that he rose on the third day; that he ascended into heaven and is seated at the right hand of the Father's majesty, and will come to judge the living and the dead. In this Creed we acknowledge that the Holy Spirit possesses, inseparably, the same divine nature as the Father and the Son. And finally we confess the calling into being of the Church, the forgiveness of sins, and the resurrection of the flesh.

Now, beloved, you are being changed from your old self to a new self; you are beginning to be no longer carnal but spiritual, no longer earthly but heavenly. Believe with constant assurance that the resurrection accomplished in Christ will be accomplished in all of us as well, and that what the Head first experienced, the whole Body will experience later on. The very sacrament of baptism that you are soon to receive gives expression to that hope, for in baptism we celebrate a death and a resurrection, as the old self is laid aside and a new one received. A sinner enters the waters, a person justified comes forth from them. We reject him who brought us to death and accept him who brings us back to life and through whose grace you become children of God, begotten now not by the desire of the flesh but by the power of the Holy Spirit.

You must adhere with all your heart to this very brief yet very full confession so that you may use it as a safeguard at all times. It is a weapon whose power is always invincible and will help us to be good soldiers of Christ despite any ambush the enemy may lay. Let the devil, who never ceases to tempt a person, find you always shielded by this confession of faith. Then you will overcome the enemy you renounce, and, under the protection of him whom you confess, you will preserve the grace of the Lord incorrupt and stainless until the end. Finally, in him from whom you receive the forgiveness of your sins, you will also attain to the glorious resurrection.

Beloved, you now know the Catholic Creed that has been presented to you; go and be obedient to its teaching, without changing a single word of it. For the merciful God is mighty. May he guide you as you advance to the baptismal faith, and may he bring us, who hand the mysteries on to you, to the kingdom of heaven in your company, through the same Jesus Christ, our Lord, who lives and reigns for ever and ever. Amen.[8]

Presentation of the Lord's Prayer

Presentation of the Lord's Prayer. The deacon exhorts the candidates:

In addition to other salutary instructions, our Lord and Savior Jesus Christ gave his disciples a formula of prayer when they asked him how they should pray. The reading we just heard has made you more fully cognizant of this prayer. Listen now, beloved, to how the Lord teaches his disciples to pray to God, the almighty Father: "When you pray, go into your room and shut the door and pray to your Father who is in secret." "Room" does not refer to a hidden part of the house but reminds us that the recesses of our heart are known to God alone. To shut the door in order to worship God means to turn a mystical key and exclude evil thoughts from our minds, and to speak to God with closed mouth and pure heart. Our God listens to our faith, not to our words. We must therefore use the key of faith to close our hearts to the snares of the enemy and open them to God alone, whose temple they are, so that he who dwells in us may be our Advocate as we pray.

Christ, our Lord, who is the Word of God and the Wisdom of God, has taught us this prayer. Here, then, is how we should pray:

Here you are to comment on the Lord's Prayer:

Our Father, who art in heaven. These are the words of a person free and full of confidence. You are to live in such a way that you may indeed be children of God and brothers and sisters of Christ. For who would be rash enough to address God as Father while failing to do God's will? Beloved, show yourselves worthy of adoption by God, for it is written: "To all who received him, who believed in his name, he gave power to become children of God."

Hallowed be thy name. The meaning is not that our prayers make God holy, for he is always holy. Rather do we ask that his name be made holy in us so that, after being sanctified in his baptism, we may continue as we have begun.

Thy kingdom come. But when does our God not reign, since his reign is unending? Therefore, when we say "Thy kingdom come," we are asking that our kingdom may come; the kingdom promised us by God and won for us by the blood and suffering of Christ.

Thy will be done on earth as it is in heaven. Your will be done in the sense that what you will in heaven, we who dwell on earth may accomplish in an irreproachable way.

Give us this day our daily bread. The "bread" here is to be understood as spiritual bread. Our real bread is Christ, who said: "I am the bread that came down from heaven." We speak of it as "daily" because we must always be asking to be preserved from sin so that we may be worthy of heavenly food.

And forgive us our trespasses as we forgive those who trespass against us. The sense of this petition is that we cannot win forgiveness of our sins unless we first forgive those who have offended us. As the Lord says in the Gospel: "If you do not forgive others their trespasses, neither will your Father forgive your trespasses."

And lead us not into temptation. That is, do not let us be led into temptation by the tempter, who is the source of all corruption. For, as the Scriptures tell us, "God . . . tempts no one." The devil is the real tempter. So that we may overcome him, the Lord tells us: "Watch and pray that you may not enter into temptation."

But deliver us from evil. He says this because, as the Apostle remarks, "We do not know how to pray as we ought." We must so pray to the one all-powerful God that in his mercy he would grant us the power to overcome the evil that human weakness is powerless to guard against and avoid. This we ask of Jesus Christ our Lord, who lives and reigns as God in the unity of the Holy Spirit, for ever and ever.

Then the deacon exhorts the catechumens: Remain in order and silence, and listen attentively. You have heard, beloved, the holy mysteries of the Lord's Prayer. When you depart from here, renew them in your heart so that, as men and women who are perfect in Christ, you may be able to ask and receive the merciful favor of God. For God our Lord has power to lead you, runners toward the faith, to the waters of rebirth, and to bring us, who have handed on to you the mystery of the Catholic faith, into the kingdom of heaven along with you—he who lives and reigns with God the Father in the unity of the Holy Spirit, for ever and ever.[9]

The new rite of Christian initiation suggests readings for each of the two presentations. Each ends with a prayer over the candidates. The prayer at the end of the presentation of the Creed is as follows: "Lord, eternal source of light, justice, and truth, take under your tender care your servants N. and N. Purify them and make them holy; give them true knowledge, sure hope, and sound understanding, and make them worthy to receive the grace of baptism. We ask this through Christ our Lord."[10]

In that earlier time, the presentation of the Creed took place on Wednesday of the fourth week of Lent. The readings for the Mass during which the presentation was made were Ezekiel 36:23-28; Isaiah 1:16-19; and John 9:1-38. If we bear in mind the theme of the first two readings (the renewal, through baptism, of the person who obeys the Lord's commands) and if we take the trouble at this point to reread the gospel, especially the end of it, we will be struck by the unity between the Mass proper and the presentation of the Creed. The end of the gospel is especially appropriate. Jesus hears that the blind man whom he cured has been expelled from the synagogue; he seeks the man out, and the following dialogue takes place: " 'Do you believe in the Son of Man?' He answered and said, 'Who is he, sir, that I may believe in him?' Jesus said to him, 'You have seen him and the one speaking with you is he.' He said, I do believe, Lord' " (John 9:35-38).

Note the question Christ asks, and also his statement: "You have seen him." The text is evidently appropriate also in relation to the scrutiny (celebrated at this same Mass), in which the community prayed that the candidates' minds and hearts might be opened to the light of faith. At the beginning of the gospel, Jesus says: "I am the light of the world" (John 9:5). The catechumens can glimpse the light dawning for them and continue on their way to full enlightenment.[11]

The presentation of the Lord's Prayer seems to have taken place on Saturday of the fourth week of Lent. This conclusion is suggested by the readings once assigned to that day. The new Rite of Christian Initiation of Adults has revived the presentation of the Lord's Prayer while adapting it to our day. A Liturgy of the Word precedes the ceremony of the presentation of the Lord's Prayer. The deacon then reads the passage from St. Matthew's gospel (6:9-13) in which Christ teaches his disciples the Our Father, and the celebrant gives a homily explaining the meaning and importance of the prayer. The ceremony concludes with a prayer: "Almighty and eternal God, you continually enlarge the family of your Church. Deepen the faith and understanding of these elect, chosen for baptism. Give them new birth in your living waters, so that they may be numbered among your adopted children. We ask this through Christ our Lord."[12]

Presentation of the Gospels

This was the last of the presentations to be introduced into the liturgy. Here is how the ceremony was conducted during the period when the Gelasian Sacramentary was in use:

Here begins the explanation of the Gospels to the candidates so that their ears may be opened.

First, four deacons emerge from the sacristy, preceded by candle-bearers and censer-bearers and carrying the four Gospels; these they place on the four corners of the altar. Then, before any of the deacons reads, the priest speaks as follows:

Dear sons and daughters, we are about to open to you the Gospels, that is, the acts of God. First, however, we must tell you in an orderly way what a Gospel is, where it comes from, whose words it contains, why four men wrote of these acts, and who the four are whom the Holy Spirit appointed in accordance with prophecy. For if we do not proceed in an orderly fashion, we may leave you confused. You came here that your ears might be opened; we must not begin by blunting your minds.

A Gospel is literally "good news." Specifically, it is the good news of Jesus Christ our Lord. It is called "good news" because it proclaims and manifests the coming in the flesh of him who spoke through the prophets and foretold: "In that day they shall know that it is I who speak; here am I." That, briefly, is what a Gospel is. As we explain now who the four were whom the prophet had foretold, we shall link their names to the symbols the prophet used for them. The prophet Ezekiel says: "Each had the face of a man in front; the four had the face of a lion on the right side, the four had the face of an ox on the left side, and the four had the face of an eagle at the back." There can be no doubt that these four figures are the evangelists. The names of those who wrote the Gospels are Matthew, Mark, Luke, and John.

A deacon then proclaims: Remain silent and listen attentively.

He then starts the reading of Matthew and reads from the beginning to the words: "He will save his people from their sins."

After the reading, the priest comments thus: Dear sons and daughters, lest we keep you too long in suspense, we shall explain to you the reason for the symbol assigned to each evangelist, and why Matthew has the face of a man. The reason is that at the beginning of his Gospel he gives the full genealogy of the Savior and tells us of his birth. His Gospel begins with the words: "The book of the genealogy of Jesus Christ, the son of David, the son of Abraham." You see, there is reason for making a man the symbol of Matthew, since he begins with the birth of a man, and for identifying Matthew with the symbol of the prophet.

Another deacon then proclaims, as before: Remain silent and listen attentively.

He then reads the beginning of the Gospel according to Mark, down to the words: "I have baptized you with water; but he will baptize you with the Holy Spirit."

Then the priest continues: Mark the evangelist, who is represented by a lion, begins in the desert, for he says: "The voice of one crying out in the wilderness: Prepare the way of the Lord!" An added reason is that the lion reigns unconquered in the desert. We find many examples of this lion, so that this prophecy, for instance, is not without meaning: "Judah is a lion's whelp; from the prey, my son, you have gone up. He stooped down, he couched as a lion, and as a lioness; who dares rouse him up?"

A third deacon makes the same proclamation as before. Then he reads the beginning of the Gospel according to Luke, down to the words: "To make ready for the Lord a people prepared."

Then the priest continues: Luke the evangelist has the features of the ox, to which our Savior in his sacrifice is to be compared. In reporting the good news of Christ, Luke begins with Zechariah and Elizabeth, the elderly parents of whom John the Baptist was born. Luke is compared to an ox because in him we can see two horns, that is, the two Testaments, and, in a nascent state, young and vigorous, the four hooves which are the four Gospels.

The fourth deacon makes the same proclamation as before. He then reads the beginning of the Gospel according to St. John, down to the words: "Full of grace and truth."

The priest then continues: John is like an eagle because he seeks great heights. Does he not say: "In the beginning was the Word, and the Word was with God, and the Word was God. He was in the beginning with God"? Then, too, David says of Christ: "Your youth is renewed like the eagle's," that is, the youthfulness of Jesus Christ who rose from the dead and ascended into heaven.

Having conceived you, the Church that bears you in her womb rejoices that the celebration of her liturgy is leading to new beginnings for Christianity. As the holy day of Easter approaches, may you be reborn in the bath of baptism, and merit, like all the saints, to receive the incorruptible gift of adoption from Christ our Lord, who lives and reigns for ever and ever.[13]

10. FIRST SUNDAY OF LENT (YEAR B): THE FLOOD AND THE COVENANT

Year B is not as carefully constructed as Year A. On the first two Sundays the classical themes of the temptation and transfiguration of Jesus have been kept, as they have been in Year A and will be again in Year C. In Year B the pertinent passages are from the Gospel of Mark.

Structure of Year B for the First Five Sundays			
Table of Readings in the Eucharistic Liturgy			
	Old Testament	Apostle	Gospel
First Sunday	Gen 9:8-15 Flood and covenant	1 Pet 3:18-22 Flood, an image of saving baptism	Mark 1:12-15 Temptation of Jesus
Second Sunday	Gen 22:1-2, 9, 10-13, 15-18 Sacrifice of Abraham	Rom 8:31b-34 God gave his Son for our sake	Mark 9:2-10 This is my beloved Son
Third Sunday	Exod 20:1-17 The law given by Moses	1 Cor 1:22-25 The crucified Messiah, wisdom, yet a stumbling block	John 2:13-25 Destroy this temple, and in three days I will raise it up
Fourth Sunday	2 Chr 36:14-16, 19-23 Exile and liberation; God's anger and mercy	Eph 2:4-10 Dead through sin, raised up by grace	John 3:14-21 The Son sent to save the world
Fifth Sunday	Jer 31:31-34 The new covenant with forgiveness of past sins	Heb 5:7-9 Christ's obedience, cause of eternal salvation	John 12:20-33 The grain of wheat that dies bears fruit

The Waters of Destruction

When the LORD saw how great the wickedness of human beings was on earth, and how every desire that their heart conceived was always nothing but evil, the LORD regretted making human beings on the earth, and his heart was grieved.

So the LORD said, I will wipe out from the earth the human beings I have created, and not only the human beings, but also the animals and the crawling things and the birds of the air, for I regret that I made them. (Gen 6:5-7)

So widespread has corruption become that Yahweh regrets ever having created humanity and its world! Note how the account sees not only human but subhuman creatures too as a single object of God's intention to destroy. We saw earlier that Adam in paradise was a person with links to the entire cosmos, that he was not created to be an isolated individual but the ancestor of a race and steward in charge of the subhuman world. Sin causes a radical upheaval of the unity proper to creation; consequently, God's intention to destroy his creature embraces not only humanity itself but all that is connected with it.

The Flood is, in fact, the second destructive act and, like the first, is a response to the disorder in humanity. The first resulted from Adam's disobedience, the second from the deepening corruption of his posterity.

Although the Lord tells Noah that "never again shall all bodily creatures be destroyed by the waters of a flood" (Gen 9:11), he will continue to use water as a means of punishing. At the time of the Exodus, for example, water will engulf the soldiers of Pharaoh (Deut 11:14; Ps 106:11; Wis 18:5). Indeed, punishment by water will be the habitual way for God to exercise a just vengeance: "The flood shall sweep away his house, / torrents in the day of God's anger" (Job 20:28).

There will, moreover, be another deluge. At least, that is how Isaiah describes the invasion by the Assyrians, who come from the region of the Euphrates and punish Israel for its lack of faith:

> Because this people has rejected
>   the waters of Shiloah that flow gently,
> And melts with fear at the display of Rezin's and Remaliah's son,
> Therefore, the Lord is bringing up against them
>   the waters of the River, great and mighty,
>   the king of Assyria and all his glory.
> It shall rise above all its channels,
>   and overflow all its banks.
> It shall roll on into Judah,
>   it shall rage and pass on—
>   up to the neck it shall reach.
> But his outspread wings will fill
>   the width of your land, Emmanuel! (Isa 8:6-8)

Water, then, is the instrument God uses when he turns in wrath upon a corrupt world. This does not mean that water does away with human wickedness. Wickedness constantly springs up anew; the world's situation can be described in images of the Tower of Babel, the confusion of tongues, and the dispersal of the peoples, for all these are consequences of original sin that destroyed the world's unity and so frustrated God's plan.

The Waters of Salvation

We noted earlier that the liturgy never bids the faithful meditate on sin without reminding them that sin is also the starting point of redemption. The attitude of the Church in her liturgy is always that expressed in the *felix culpa* of the Easter Proclamation. This does not mean that corruption is ever glossed over. Those people who wish to draw near to God and to achieve the conversion that will turn them to the Lord must be aware of the world's, and their own, corruption. When candidates prepare to enter the intensive forty-day catechumenate of Lent, the Church does her duty and forces them to face the reality of the world's sinfulness. At the same time, however, she always emphasizes what the Lord has done and is still doing in order to eliminate evil.

The Church takes the same view of the Flood. Just as sin is always seen in the perspective of healing, so punishment is always seen as part of the process of rebuilding.

Throughout Lent, and especially during the Easter Vigil, the liturgy gives prominence to the theme of the "waters that save." From the beginning of this season, the Church offers a synthetic view of the history of salvation both to those who are preparing for baptism and to the rest of us who have already received the sacrament.

Water can destroy, but life always emerges from the punishments that God inflicts. Only humans experience the sad necessity of inflicting a punishment that leads only to death. That is not God's way. Water can indeed destroy, for like every other creature it is entirely at God's service: "He holds back the waters and there is drought; / he sends them forth and they overwhelm the land" (Job 12:15); "He roars at the sea and leaves it dry, / and all the rivers he dries up" (Nah 1:4). But water can also save, and the Flood, as it turns out, sets a pattern that recurs throughout the history of salvation: Humans sin; God punishes and destroys the world, but he also leaves a "little remnant" that will be the nucleus of a new people. In saying that the Flood sets a pattern, we are not denying, of course, that the account in Genesis underwent revisions that were intended precisely to bring out the pattern that would recur later on.

In Sirach, Noah is quite clearly presented as a "remnant": "NOAH, found just and perfect, / renewed the race in the time of devastation. / Because of his worth, there were survivors, / and with a sign to him the deluge ended. / A lasting covenant was made with him, / that never again would all flesh be destroyed" (Sir 44:17-18).[1]

The New Testament and the fathers' commentaries on it see the Flood as prefiguring baptism and salvation. The account of the Flood, which presents in an exemplary form the divine ways of bringing humanity to salvation, is a special favorite of the fathers because it serves the catechumens both as a doctrinal summary and as an image of Lent itself. For, like Lent, the purifying Flood lasted forty days: "For forty days and forty nights heavy rain poured down on the earth" (Gen 7:12); "The flood continued upon the earth for forty days" (Gen 7:17); "At the end of forty days Noah opened the hatch of the ark that he had made" (Gen 8:6).

Once again, then, Scripture itself tells us how we are to understand Scripture.

Flood and Baptism

As the reader may be aware, many exegetes regard the First Letter of Peter as a baptismal catechesis. In chapter 3 we find a reference to the close connection between the Flood and baptism. After recalling the ark in which "a few persons, eight in all, were saved through water" (v. 20), the writer goes on to say: "This prefigured baptism, which saves you now" (v. 21). We must not overlook the phrase "saved through water": the same water that destroys sinners is a source of salvation for the little remnant.

The letter stresses the correspondence between the Flood and baptism. In this correspondence, the Flood is the "type." We must, however, be on guard against a simplistic view of types, as though they were mere examples or illustrations. A type, for the Bible, is the beginning of a historical process, of a saving action that is still going on. The connection between the Flood and baptism is more than that between an image in the past and something we see now occurring. Baptism is in close continuity with the Flood; the former is truly and effectively what the latter was. In fact, baptism is the full realization of all that the Flood was, so that now baptism is the true Flood. If, then, there is evidently a distinction and a contrast between type and reality, we must nonetheless see in the type more than a mere image, for the type contains the seed of a reality that will someday achieve its full stature.

It is easy enough to see the correspondences between the Flood and baptism. At the same time, however, we should not press details of the relation between type and reality. It should be enough, from the standpoint of a spirituality of baptism, to see how anticipations of baptism existed millennia ago. If we push the correspondences too far, we may end up with unreliable and contrived conclusions. The fathers did not always avoid moving in this direction. St. Justin, for example, sees in the explicit mention of eight people being saved a symbol of the eighth day, the day of the resurrection. The person who descends into death with Christ in baptism also rises with Christ. "St. Justin gave this symbolism definitive form. Noah with his wife, his three sons and the wives of his sons form the number eight and provide the symbol of the eighth day, the day of the manifestation of the resurrection."[2]

We must not, however, be too hard on St. Justin. This same passage from his writings provides a very interesting commentary: "In the Flood was revealed the mystery of human salvation." Evidently Justin understands the true status of a biblical type. "Christ, as the First-born of every creature, became the Head of a new race to which he gave birth through water, faith, and the wood that contains the mystery of the Cross, just as Noah was saved by wood and carried on the waters with his family."[3]

The Flood as type of baptism, the ark as type of the Church, the dove as symbolizing the Holy Spirit—these are constant themes in the fathers. Here we need cite only two classic texts. The first is from Tertullian's treatise on baptism:

> After the waters of the Flood had cleansed away the ancient iniquity and thus baptized the world, as it were, a dove was sent from the ark and returned with an olive branch. Even the pagans regard this as a symbol of peace. Thus it heralded the appeasement of heaven's wrath.

By a similar ordinance aiming at a wholly spiritual effect, the Dove that is the Holy Spirit is sent from heaven, where the Church (prefigured by the ark) dwells, and flies down to bring God's peace to earth, that is, to our fleshly nature as we emerge from the bath after being cleansed from our old sins.[4]

We should note Tertullian's emphasis on the dove as a symbol of the Spirit and on the ark as a figure of the Church. Scripture itself, of course, offers us no commentary on either the dove or the ark. Yet patristic tradition is of one mind in developing this typology, especially as it concerns the ark, and the liturgy took it over at an early date.[5] The typology is evidently an attractive one and expresses something that remains true for us today.

The second classic commentary is from the pen of St. Ambrose. This father wrote a treatise on Noah and the ark,[6] a passage of which was read at Matins in the monastic breviary on what used to be Sexagesima Sunday. But it is in the two little works *De sacramentis* and *De mysteriis* that we find the most interesting and best-known passages.[7]

In *De sacramentis*, we read:

In the Flood, too, there was already a prefiguration of baptism. We were just beginning to explain this yesterday.[8] What is the Flood, after all, but a means of preserving the just one in order to propagate justice, and of destroying sin? That is why the Lord, seeing the sins of humanity being multiplied, spared but a single just man, along with his children, and commanded the waters to rise over the mountains. In the Flood, then, all fleshly corruption perished, and only the race and example of the just one survived. Does the Flood, then, not resemble that other flood that is baptism, in which all sins are wiped away, while only the soul and grace of the just one are raised to life?[9]

Ambrose is evidently adopting the basic theology of the First Letter of Peter, without reading into it anything more than it says. In both the Flood and baptism he sees water at work destroying corruption and at the same time preserving "the race and example of the just one."

In *De mysteriis*, Ambrose repeats some of Tertullian's favorite themes:

Here is another testimony. All flesh had become corrupt because of its sin, and so the Lord said: "My spirit shall not abide in humans for ever, for they are flesh." He thus shows that fleshly uncleanness and the stain of more serious sins are a bar to spiritual grace. Wishing to restore what he had originally given, God therefore caused a Flood and bade Noah, a just man, to enter the ark. When the Flood had ceased, Noah released a crow, which did not return; then he released a dove, which did return, carrying, we are told, an olive branch. You see the water, the wood, and the dove. Can you have any doubt of the mystery they contain?

The water is that in which the flesh is immersed so that all fleshly sin may be washed away; in the water all sin is buried. The wood is that to which the Lord Jesus was nailed when he suffered for us. The dove is the one in whose likeness the Holy Spirit descended (as you learn from the New Testament) in order to instill in you peace of soul and tranquility of heart. The crow is a figure of sin, which departs and does not return, provided you imitate the observance and example of the just one.[10]

Water and the End of Time

There is another point in the Genesis story that the First Letter of Peter especially emphasizes: the divine patience that made God wait before imposing sentence. "God patiently waited in the days of Noah during the building of the ark" (1 Pet 3:20). The Second Letter of Peter makes the same point:

> Know this first of all, that in the last days scoffers will come [to] scoff, living according to their own desires and saying, "Where is the promise of his coming? From the time when our ancestors fell asleep, everything has remained as it was from the beginning of creation." They deliberately ignore the fact that the heavens existed of old and earth was formed out of water and through water by the word of God; through these the world that then existed was destroyed, deluged with water. The present heavens and earth have been reserved by the same word for fire, kept for the day of judgment and of destruction of the godless.
>
> But do not ignore this one fact, beloved, that with the Lord one day is like a thousand years and a thousand years like one day. (2 Pet 3:3-8)

This passage is, in fact, repeating Jesus' own commentary on the "patience of God": "In [those] days before the flood, they were eating and drinking, marrying and giving in marriage, up to the day that Noah entered the ark. They did not know until the flood came and carried them all away. So will it be [also] at the coming of the Son of Man" (Matt 24:38-39).

The Flood, then, in both the New Testament and the fathers, has an eschatological dimension. The Second Letter of Peter indicates a parallel between the time before the Flood and the time still separating us from the final judgment. The delay that God in his patience provides has for its purpose to bring us to repentance: "The Lord . . . is patient with you, not wishing that any should perish but that all should come to repentance" (2 Pet 3:9).

We must observe, however, that if in the eyes of the fathers the Flood has an eschatological meaning and is a preparation for the coming judgment, baptism has the same significance. It too prepares for and prefigures the judgment at the end of time. Origen writes: "In rebirth through the bath of water we were buried with Christ. . . . Through the regeneration effected by that bath, in which fire and Spirit are at work, we become like the glorious Christ as he sits upon his throne of glory, and we too sit upon twelve thrones with him."[11]

The Obstacles to Salvation

Evidently the plan of salvation meets with difficulties; there are obstacles to the fulfillment of the purposes God has in his work. The evil powers and the spirit of the world combine to try to frustrate him.

The catechumen who is seeking to reach the Light has been presented in the liturgy with a synthesis of the mystery and history of salvation. The need, for catechumens and for all Christians, is to enter into, and become part of, the mystery that concerns them so intimately. For only the just one will be saved, that is, the one found worthy to enter the ark; all others will be destroyed. In principle, of course, the baptized have entered the ark, which is the Church; they continue, however, to be human and subject to the human condition. St. Augustine brings out the tragic character of humanity's paradoxical condition:

> Now we begin already to be *like to God*, since we have the firstfruits of the Spirit; and yet we are *still unlike* because the old Adam is still with us. . . . Now we have the firstfruits of the Spirit, and so have already really become the children of God. For the rest, it is in hope that we are saved, and renewed, and, in the same way, become children of God:

because we are not yet saved in all reality, we are not yet fully renewed, not yet even children of God, but children of this world. . . . Let all then be consumed that keeps us still children of the flesh and of the world, and let all be perfected that makes us children of God and renewed in the Spirit.[12]

On this First Sunday of Lent, both the seeker of light and the baptized are confronted once again with the mystery of salvation. This salvation is a gift of rebirth, but its completion comes after a long process of maturation during which God patiently waits for us to manifest our active goodwill. Gregory of Nyssa points out: "Each human being is born by his or her own choice. Thus we are to some extent our own fathers and mothers, because we freely conceive ourselves as we wish to be."[13]

Covenant and Sacrifice

The global vision of the mystery of salvation offered us would have a serious lacuna if nothing were said of covenant and sacrifice. After all, the reason why God exercises patience is that he may eventually be reunited to humanity and bring it into a covenant whose sign is sacrifice. On this point, once again, the account in Genesis has been reedited, and the covenant that is really to begin in its full form with Abraham has been projected back and connected with the salvation offered to Noah and his posterity.

The account of the Flood in Genesis shows us a Noah who, after the forty days, is a new person; he is the father of a new race, and thus he is a new Adam and a figure of Christ. The Church delights in showing to her faithful and to all who seek the light this figure of a person renewed. At the same time, she emphasizes the fact that the covenant is sealed by a sacrifice: "Then Noah built an altar to the LORD, and choosing from every clean animal and every clean bird, he offered burnt offerings on the altar. When the LORD smelled the sweet odor, the LORD said to himself: Never again will I curse the ground because of human beings" (Gen. 8:20-21).

The sacrifice brings the covenant into existence, for by sacrifice creation pays homage to the God who takes the initiative. God accepts the sacrifice, and the covenant is concluded:

God said to Noah and to his sons with him: "See, I am now establishing my covenant with you and your descendants after you and with every living creature that was with you: all the birds and the various tame and wild animals that were with you and came out of the ark. I will establish my covenant with you, that never again shall all bodily creatures be destroyed by the waters of a flood; there shall not be another flood to devastate the earth." God added: "This is the sign that I am giving for all ages to come, of the covenant between me and you and every living creature with you: I set my bow in the clouds to serve as a sign of the covenant between me and the earth." (Gen 9:8-13)

11. SECOND AND THIRD SUNDAYS OF LENT (YEAR B): GOD HAS HANDED OVER HIS SON FOR US

"This Is My Beloved Son"

These words of the Father in the story of the transfiguration are full of meaning for us. The same words were spoken at the Epiphany, and our study of the Epiphany liturgy has already given us the opportunity to discuss certain aspects of them.

We can hear in the words an echo of Abraham's words as he offers the Father his only son. In the case of Christ, the Son has come and offered himself, but he has done so out of obedience and the desire to do the Father's will, thus counteracting the disobedience of Adam. For his obedience Christ is rewarded with the transfiguration; the latter then becomes the sign of the transfiguration of every person who chooses to walk the paths of God and do the Father's will.

The account of the transfiguration raises a number of problems, but these are not our concern here since we intend to be faithful to our purpose, which is the liturgical reading of the Scriptures. In Year A the transfiguration was seen as resulting from the response to a call. On this second Sunday of Year B, the theme is somewhat different: now the transfiguration crowns the response to a call, but a response that includes the offering of sacrifice. This is the theme of the first reading, on the sacrifice of Abraham. It is also the theme of the second reading, in which St. Paul reminds us that God has handed over his own Son for our salvation. It is Christ's willingness to sacrifice himself that gives full meaning to the words, "This is my beloved Son."

There is a point I would like to raise here concerning the gospel pericope, although it is not a point that determined the choice of the gospel for the Second Sunday of Lent. I am referring to the secrecy that Christ imposed on his disciples after the transfiguration (Mark 9:9-10). This is not the only occasion, of course, on which Christ imposes secrecy on the witnesses of his miracles, his exorcisms, and

124

even his parables. St. Mark has his special way of dealing with this whole matter. He emphasizes the secrecy and notes, on this particular occasion, that the witnesses do observe the secrecy, though they do not understand "what rising from the dead meant" (v. 10).

Perhaps Christ's intention in ordering secrecy is to make a slow initiation possible. His action would then be part of a catechetical and pastoral method. The truth is admittedly one, but there are degrees of fullness in presenting it. We see Jesus acting and speaking in one way with a small group of disciples, in another with a larger group of followers, and in still another with the crowd. He chooses to reveal his messiahship in varying degrees.

By emphasizing this aspect of Jesus' method, St. Mark and the early Church reply to the accusation that Jesus manifested nothing of the glory and splendor that should surround the coming and work of the Messiah. Their answer is that Jesus did indeed manifest his glory, and in several degrees, but that he also did not want all to know of this glory.

The gospel itself can be read with varying degrees of comprehension. Christ, then, provides us with the example of a prudent catechesis that respects the pace each hearer keeps in attaining full understanding of Christian teaching or of the inspired word of God.

The Sacrifice of Abraham

In the story of Abraham preparing to sacrifice his son, there is a striking sentence that prepares us for the second reading, in which we will hear of the Son sent to save us: "God will provide the sheep for the burnt offering" (Gen. 22:8). Abraham went ahead with the preparation that would lead to the sacrifice of his son because he believed in God's promise, even though everything seemed to be preventing its fulfillment.

The sacrifice of Abraham became a theme in the eucharistic liturgy; the eucharistic prayers, especially the Roman Canon (the first of our present four eucharistic prayers), often mention it.* The *De sacramentis* of St. Ambrose contains the nucleus of the Roman Canon, and there we already find reference to Abraham and his sacrifice:

---

* Within a few years after Nocent wrote this, six more eucharistic prayers were added to the Roman Missal.

And the priest says: "Mindful, therefore, of his most glorious Passion and his resurrection from the dead and his ascension into heaven, we offer you this spotless Victim, this spiritual Victim, this unbloody Victim, this holy bread and chalice of eternal life, and we ask and pray that you would accept this offering on your altar on high, through the hands of your angels, as you deigned to accept the gifts of your just servant Abel, the sacrifice of our father Abraham, and the offering your high priest Melchizedek made to you."[1]

This prayer is plainly very close to the passage that follows immediately upon the consecration in the Roman Canon. The only real difference is that the reference to the angel(s) and the altar on high now comes after the mention of Abel, Abraham, and Melchizedek.

The Son Handed over for Us

St. Paul in this passage (Rom 8:31-34) simply mentions the gift of the Son to us without discussing it. He sees it as part of God's saving plan and a sign of the Father's love for us. God sacrifices his own Son as part of his plan for the reconstruction and reunification of the world (see Rom 16:25-26). From our creaturely point of view, the Father's gift of his Son to us is a revelation of the "mystery," that is, the secret plan of salvation that has been hidden in God from eternity.

The purpose God has in giving us his Son is to make us likewise his children after the image of the only-begotten Son. That is why the Word takes to himself a human nature like ours (see Rom 8:3). God handed his Son over to death for the sake of us all. Consequently, there can be no further accusation against us: "If God is for us, who can be against us? . . . Who will bring a charge against God's chosen ones? . . . [W]ho will condemn?" (Rom 8:31-34). Jesus, after all, has died for us; more than that, he rose to life for us and is now seated at God's right hand. Here we are prepared for the gospel of Jesus' transfiguration and prediction of his resurrection.

Psalm 116, the responsorial psalm for the second Sunday, expresses very well the sentiments of Abraham and Christ and our own sentiments too: "Your servant, LORD, your servant am I, / the son of your handmaid; / you have loosened my bonds. / A thanksgiving sacrifice I make; / I will call on the name of the LORD" (vv. 16-17).

Jesus Crucified, a Stumbling Block for the World

It is not easy to discern the unity of the three readings for the third Sunday in Year B, and we must not try to force them into a pattern.

The second reading (1 Cor 1:22-25) brings out the power inherent in Christian witness, but it also emphasizes the great obstacle: Christ is seen by many as foolishness and a stumbling block. The Apostle is not saying that the Christian should love what makes no sense; we cannot imagine God requiring his followers to be stupid. The thing that eludes human comprehension is that God should love us to the point of sending his Son to save us.

St. Paul confronts us with a fact: "Jews demand signs and Greeks look for wisdom, but we proclaim Christ crucified" (vv. 22-23). The Church's message is that Christ was crucified for our salvation, and she will keep on preaching that message to the end of time as her dearest possession, even though it is a message that does not always win her sympathy. On the other hand, "to those who are called, Jews and Greeks alike, Christ [is] the power of God and the wisdom of God. For the foolishness of God is wiser than human wisdom, and the weakness of God is stronger than human strength" (vv. 24-25).

The language of this last sentence is strong and will not let us slip by inattentively. The message and the reality to which it points condition our lives; we cannot ignore them. This, after all, is the only message we really have for humanity, and what a demanding message it is! All who believe in Christ must also walk in his steps, but this means that they will be in conflict and that a radical detachment will be required of them. The foolishness of God must become our foolishness. It is evidently impossible to maintain such an attitude unless we believe unconditionally in the resurrection of Christ. Consequently, when St. Paul writes in his Letter to the Romans, "[I]f you confess with your mouth that Jesus is Lord and believe in your heart that God raised him from the dead, you will be saved" (Rom 10:9), he is but repeating an ancient confessional formula and expressing the basic belief without which Christianity would simply not exist.

Belief in and knowledge of the risen Christ are the reason why the gospels can present the life, work, suffering, and death of Jesus as still real and operative. The crucifixion has always been a stumbling block; today the resurrection is too. This is not the place to raise problems proper to Easter day, but we must at least ask ourselves how real the resurrection is and whether it makes any difference in our lives. Only on condition that the resurrection is real in every possible sense of the word can we proclaim Christ crucified and sacrificed, in accordance with the Father's will, for the sake of our salvation.

The Sign of the Temple

It is because of the key importance of the resurrection that the liturgy proposes to us as a gospel reading for the third Sunday a passage in which Christ foretells his own resurrection (John 2:13-25). In dealing with this passage, we must, once again, not get overly involved in details of historical exegesis. The point is not that these details are negligible but that our purpose is rather to discern the point of view the liturgy takes in proposing this reading for the Third Sunday of Lent.

The main reason why the reading has been chosen is Jesus' prophecy of his resurrection: "Destroy this temple and in three days I will raise it up" (v. 19). Later on, Jesus would be accused of wanting to tear down the temple in Jerusalem (Matt 25:61; Mark 14:58). To make clear what Jesus really meant, St. Mark expands Jesus' words: "We heard him say, 'I will destroy this temple made with hands and within three days I will build another not made with hands'" (Mark 14:58). Jesus is evidently referring to the building of a new eschatological temple.

St. John, who always chooses words that are more exact and richer in meaning, uses here not the Greek word *oikodoman*, "to build" (as in Mark), but the verb *egeirein*, "to awaken, to raise up," which can refer both to the material reconstruction of the temple building and to the raising of his own body from death. Christ's hearers do not understand and begin to mock him: "This temple has been under construction for forty-six years, and you will raise it up in three days?" (v. 20).

St. John himself explains what Jesus meant: "But he was speaking about the temple of his body" (v. 21). This does not mean that the apostles immediately understood at the time the meaning of Jesus' words. We have every reason for thinking that they understood only after Jesus had risen from the dead and they themselves had been enlightened by the Holy Spirit.

The body of the risen Jesus will be the new temple, the spiritual temple in which people will worship in Spirit and truth (John 4:21). St. John was the first to understand that the new temple was the risen body of Jesus, but the entire New Testament, especially St. Paul when speaking of the Church (Eph 2:19-21; etc.), uses the symbol of the temple.

St. John emphasizes the faith of those who see the signs Jesus gives. As everyone is aware, in his writings generally and especially in his gospel, St. John develops a theology of the place of such signs in Christian life. The sign is given either in response to faith or in order to rouse faith. The faith thus roused may be full and perfect, or it may be still unsure. It is to a still imperfect faith that John is referring when he says: "[M]any began to believe in his name when they saw the signs he was doing. But Jesus would not trust himself to them because he knew them all" (John 2:23-24). We must speak, then, of a faith that is roused by the word and a faith that is roused by signs.

The Law That Frees

St. Paul speaks of the law as a yoke: "[W]e were held in custody under law, confined for the faith that was to be revealed" (Gal 3:23). The law, however (that is, the law proper to the old covenant), "has only a shadow of the good things to come" (Heb 10:1). We know how Paul likes to contrast the law and faith: We are no longer under the law (Rom 6:14) but are dead to the law (Rom 7:4) so that we may live for God (Gal 2:19); Christ has redeemed us from the curse of the law (Gal 3:13), having in his own flesh abolished the law (Eph 2:15). Paul writes of the Christian in confrontation with the law (Rom 7) and of our salvation as coming through faith, not through the law (Gal 3). For his part, St. John tells us that the law came through Moses but that grace came through Jesus Christ (John 1:16-17).

In contrast to these various New Testament approaches, the passage read from Exodus on this third Sunday speaks of the law as something that liberates, as a road leading God's people to freedom. The Old Testament contains several codes of law, but the one in Exodus 20 is the most important. We will recall that Jesus himself quotes passages from it to the rich young man who asks him what must be done to attain eternal life (Mark 10:17-25).[2]

The Ten Commandments are, in fact, signs of God's love and a means of liberation. Psalm 81 recalls the Decalogue in the context of Israel's birth into freedom (Ps 81:7). In a similar way, today's reading from Exodus begins by reminding us, "I, the LORD, am your God, who brought you out of the land of Egypt" (v. 2). The law that the Lord promulgates gives life and brings the people of God into existence.

In the light of the last statement, we can grasp the connection between this reading and the other readings for this Sunday, although we shall not be emphasizing the connection. The law is an intermediate, transitional stage; it cannot give life or the justice that is God's gift (Gal 3:21). It was given, therefore, to call attention to sin and to prevent it. Being concerned only with transgressions, the law is imperfect. On the other hand, Christ came to fulfill the law by making its purpose possible, namely, radical intimacy with God; we must therefore acknowledge that the law led to Christ. The goal of the law is Christ, through whom comes the justice (forgiveness of sins, holiness) that is promised to everyone who believes (Rom 10:4). But Christ also puts an end to the law by fulfilling all of its precepts in his great act of obedience (Gal 3:13). Christ became a human among the Jews so that he might submit to their law and thereby ransom them from their slavery (Gal 4:4-5).

The responsorial psalm that follows this first reading glorifies the law as perfect, trustworthy, and a source of wisdom for the simple (Ps 19:8). A passage from Origen shows us that if we are to have a true knowledge of the Decalogue, we must already have reached a certain level of holiness:

> Of all who have learned to scorn the present world ("Egypt" in figurative language) and have been carried up (to use the scriptural term) by the word of God so that they are no longer to be found here because they are hastening toward the world to come—of every such soul the Lord says: "I am the Lord your God, who brought you out of the land of Egypt, out of the house of bondage." These words, therefore, are not directed solely to those who once came out of Egypt. Much more does the Lord say to you who hear them now, provided you have indeed left Egypt and no longer serve the Egyptians: "I am the Lord your God, who brought you out of the land of Egypt, out of the house of bondage." Consider: Are not worldly affairs and fleshly deeds a house of bondage? On the other hand, are not the abandonment of worldly concerns and a life according to God a house of freedom? The Lord tells us so in the Gospel: "If you continue in my word, you are truly my disciples, and you will know the truth, and the truth will make you free."[3]

12. FOURTH AND FIFTH SUNDAYS OF LENT (YEAR B): THE SALVATION OF THE WORLD

The Son Sent to Save the World

This theme, which is elaborated in the gospel for the fourth Sunday (John 3:14-21), was already broached and developed in the readings for the second Sunday, especially the first (Gen 22:1-2, 9, 10-13, 15-18) and second (Rom 8:31b-34). Today's gospel reading has its problems, but these are of only remote concern to its use in the liturgy.

For example, when we read chapter 3 of the Fourth Gospel, we easily see a notable difference of style between verses 1-12 and verses 13-21. In this second section, which we read today, there *is* still question of humanity achieving rebirth through the death and resurrection of Jesus. But the style is different. The speaker is now "we" rather than "I": "you people do not accept our testimony" (v. 11). From verse 13 on, Jesus no longer converses with Nicodemus but speaks of himself in the third person. Moreover, there is an emphasis on the exaltation of the Son of Man that has only a vague connection with the first part of the chapter.

The passage suggests, then, that these verses are a catechesis of John himself and that he has composed them. This is a position taken in German exegesis and represented by a number of authors whom we need not cite here. It does seem that John has at least rewritten the passage, although we cannot hope to determine just which words were spoken by Jesus and what John himself added—all under the inspiration of the Holy Spirit. This is a problem that runs throughout the Fourth Gospel. I do not mean that John introduces his personal fantasies (the contrary has often been shown) but that, under the guidance of the Spirit, he goes back over the words and deeds of Jesus in order to shape them into a catechesis that will stimulate faith. That is what has happened in the passage with which we are dealing now.

The basic theme of today's liturgy is the rebirth of humanity, a rebirth that depends on the sending and coming of the Son and on his exaltation, that is, his crucifixion and triumphant resurrection. Such is God's love-inspired plan for humankind. The love that God has for us is the starting point of the entire work of salvation. Yet the salvation must also be accepted—and when the light came, people preferred the darkness! This response, elicited by Christ's coming, turns into a condemnation of the world. People condemn themselves because, in their desire to continue in their evil ways, they refuse the light.

Rebirth, therefore, requires certain attitudes in a person; the renewal offered us does not take place mechanically. Christ came to give life, but the gift must be accepted or it will turn into a condemnation. We must act according to the truth if we want to reach the light. But what does it mean to "act according to the truth"? "Truth" is a favorite word of St. John. But how are we to interpret it, since in the Greek text *alētheia*, "truth" in the intellectual sense, was used to translate the Hebrew *'emet*, which means "truth" in a moral sense. Which of the two does St. John have in mind?

Take verse 21: "whoever lives the truth comes to the light." We might rephrase this and say: "whoever acts well [*or:* uprightly] comes to the light." Then we are choosing the Hebrew meaning of *'emet*, "fidelity," of which the Old Testament provides so many examples (see Gen 32:10; 47:29; etc.), and we are restricting "truth" to its moral meaning. Does such a limitation fit in with the mentality St. John shows throughout his gospel? When he writes, "when he comes, the Spirit of truth, he will guide you to all truth" (John 16:13), John means precisely truth, not fidelity; that is, he means knowledge of the reality Jesus has made accessible to us, the eternal reality he has revealed to humanity. In fact, Christ does not simply reveal this reality to us; he himself *is* this reality in its definitive form (see John 14:10).

The Son has thus brought the truth to the world, and this action produces light (a light which, again, he himself is in its definitive form: the "true" light). We must live and act in accordance with this truth if we are to reach the light and be reborn. We can see how important such a text is with regard to the sacraments: A sacramental sign is not a magical gesture but always supposes the recipient's faith and acceptance of truth in the light.

"God So Loved the World"

In this same passage from the Fourth Gospel there is a short sentence that leaps out from the page when the people of our day read it: "God so loved the world." No one has ever denied what the sentence says, but there has always been, and still is, a spirituality that puts more emphasis on the fact that we must love God than on the fact that we are loved by him. Yet John frequently stresses God's love for us, as revealed in the salvific activity of his Son. He writes, for example, "In this way the love of God was revealed to us: God sent his only Son into the world so that we might have life through him. In this is love: not that we have loved God, but that he loved us and sent his Son as expiation for our sins" (1 John 4:9-10).

The priority of God's love for us is one of the most deeply moving truths Christianity preaches, for it presupposes that God is full of mercy toward weak and sinful humanity. John does not tire of preaching this love: "The way we came to know love was that he laid down his life for us" (1 John 3:16). Recognition of God's freely given love becomes characteristic of the believing Christian: "We have come to know and to believe in the love God has for us" (1 John 4:16). This awareness on the part of the Christian is not a fleeting thing but a necessary and constant part of one's make-up: "God is love, and whoever remains in love remains in God and God in him" (1 John 4:16).

Whoever, on the other hand, does not believe is already condemned for not accepting the Son (John 3:18). The reason for the condemnation is clear: the Light came into the world, but people loved the darkness more (John 3:19).

The struggle between light and darkness, a favorite theme of the Fourth Gospel, reveals the drama in every Christian's life. The Christian is faced with an inescapable choice.

The Wrath and Mercy of God

The account read in the first reading for this fourth Sunday shows us the unfaithfulness of Israel: "In those days, all the princes of Judah, the priests, and the people added infidelity to infidelity" (2 Chr 36:14). The passage also tells us that all scorned the messengers that God sent and mocked the prophets. The passage thus illustrates what the gospel will say: People refused the light because they loved the darkness. God's wrath at Israel's infidelity will lead to the destruction of the temple and the deportation to Babylon of those who had escaped the slaughter.

But the Lord is also a God of love, and the passage from Chronicles alludes to the way in which his love would later gain the upper hand over his wrath (vv. 22-23). Seventy years later, Cyrus, king of Persia, would rebuild the temple and permit the people of God to return to Jerusalem.

The responsorial psalm for this reading gives admirable expression to the sentiments of the Israelites in exile; it can be the expression of our own sentiments as well: "O how could we sing / the song of the LORD / on foreign soil? / If I forget you, Jerusalem, / let my right hand wither!" (Ps 137:4-5).

Awareness of not having acted toward God as truth requires, along with suffering and expiation—these make it possible to return to the good graces so characteristic of the God of the Old Testament and the New, for he is a God who pardons and raises up. This is the point emphasized in the second reading (Eph 2:4-10) for this fourth Sunday.

Dead through Sin, Raised up by Grace

In his Letter to the Ephesians, St. Paul uses strong language: "God, who is rich in mercy, because of the great love he had for us, even when we were dead in our transgressions, brought us to life with Christ—by grace you have been saved—, raised us up with him, and seated us with him in the heavens in Christ Jesus" (2:4-6).

Here is the full reality and effectiveness of that divine love of which the gospel speaks. As the Letter to the Romans puts it: "God proves his love for us in that while we were still sinners Christ died for us" (Rom 5:8). We know what Paul's own experience had been, and we can glimpse something of his profound feeling when he writes, in the verses immediately preceding the verse just quoted, "Christ, while we were still helpless, yet died at the appointed time for the ungodly. Indeed, only with difficulty does one die for a just person, though perhaps for a good person one will even find courage to die" (Rom 5:6-7).

We are now alive, and alive with Christ: "[God,] even when we were dead in our transgressions, brought us to life with Christ" (Eph 2:5). Elsewhere Paul expands that statement: "You were buried with him [Christ] in baptism, in which you were also raised with him through faith in the power of God, who raised him from the dead" (Col 2:12). Not only are we risen with Christ but we also experience our ascension with him: "[He] raised us up with him, and seated us with him in the heavens in Christ Jesus" (Eph 2:6). For St. Paul, the ascension is the sign of Christ's glorious state after the act of obedience that brought him to death (Phil 2:9). But Christ's ascension is also ours, not only as an encouraging promise that will be fulfilled at the end of our life, but as a reality that has already begun. Baptism is the beginning of our ascension, because in baptism we rise with Christ.

On this fourth Sunday, then, we contemplate the superabundant grace the Father has bestowed on us. We are saved by grace; this grace is inexhaustibly rich and makes our actions good in God's sight.

Such is the wealth of teaching given on this Fourth Sunday of Lent. As we contemplate it, we must grasp the marvelous coherence of God's plan of salvation, but, more than that, we must ask ourselves how we are to live out the mystery in our everyday lives.

The Seed That Dies When Its "Hour" Comes

The fifth Sunday continues to spell out the work of salvation in which we are participating. The grain dies and bears fruit, and the fruit, cultivated by obedience, is eternal salvation, a new covenant based on God's forgetfulness of our past sins. In this or a similar way we can sum up the message of the fifth Sunday.

The theme of the seed that is buried in the ground and then bears fruit is found in the Synoptics as well as in John. But John here gives the parable a special twist: the seed is Jesus himself, who by dying will give life to humanity. We would therefore lessen or even destroy the meaning John gives the image if we were to draw from it only a moral lesson, seeing in it simply a call to humble and mortify ourselves so that we may bear fruits of holiness. That would indeed be a profound misinterpretation, for what the image conveys in John is a Christology.

The Synoptics have parables dealing with seed and use them chiefly because of the development a seed undergoes; see, for example, the parable of the mustard seed in Mark 4:30-32 (see other parables in Mark 4:1-9 and 26-29, with the parallels in the other Synoptics). John, however, emphasizes chiefly the death and burial of the seed, that is, of Christ, and the fruit that springs from this self-giving of the Lord. Here the seed is a Person.

We would even be mistaken if we gave a merely moralistic interpretation to such words as these: "Whoever serves me must follow me, and where I am, there also will my servant be. The Father will honor whoever serves me" (John 12:26). The real point in this whole section of the gospel is the journey taken not only by Christ but by the Christian after him. The catechumens' baptism imprints on them the image of Jesus in the Spirit, so that it is now natural and inevitable for them too to pass through death in order to reach resurrection.

We should note, at the beginning of the passage, the desire of the Greeks "to see Jesus." They mean simply that they want to see a man who draws crowds and enjoys a certain success. Jesus' answer, however, clearly summons the Greeks to advance to a new level, for he tells them that he is one who dies, rises, and is glorified and that to follow him means traveling the same road.

The petition of the Greeks draws from Jesus the mention of another favorite theme of St. John: the "hour" that is coming and is already at hand. The presence of this theme gives the parable of the dying seed a special tonality.[1]

The "hour" is here linked with the "glorification," a term that, as John uses it, includes the passion, death, resurrection, and ascension of Jesus. Verse 23 of the passage brings the two terms together: "The hour has come for the Son of Man to be glorified."

John's gospel traces the stages within this "hour." At the marriage feast of Cana, Jesus says that his "hour" has not yet come (2:4). Chapter 7 contains three mentions of this hour that has not yet come (vv. 6, 8, 30). Chapter 8 repeats the theme: "But no one arrested him, because his hour had not yet come" (v. 20). Now, at last, the hour has come, and it is the hour of Jesus' glorification, this last term having the various complementary meanings John assigns to it. Christ has come to this hour so that now the Father may glorify his own name through him.

It is important to emphasize the connection between the "hour" and the glorification. Several passages of John bring the two terms together: "The hour has come for the Son of Man to be glorified" (12:23); "When he [Judas] had left, Jesus said, 'Now is the Son of Man glorified, and God is glorified in him'" (13:31); "Father, the hour has come. Give glory to your son, so that your son may glorify you" (17:1). In these passages the hour and the glorification are connected, and the glorification refers to the mystery of Christ's death and resurrection.

The voice of the Father that is heard in the pericope we are discussing foretells the glorious passion of the Son. Immediately after the Father's words, Jesus proclaims judgment upon the world—judgment through the cross, which will be victorious over evil. When Jesus is "lifted up" (and John is careful to explain what being "lifted up" means: it refers to the manner of his death), he will draw everyone to himself.

What more explicit statement than this could we want to prove that God indeed wills to save everyone? The seed, then, that dies when its hour comes saves the world and all humankind.

Christ Saves Everyone by His Obedience

This universal salvation was made possible, however, only because the Son obeyed to the point of dying. This theme has been the subject of so much commentary that there seems to be no point in dwelling on it here, and yet it is a theme that situates us at the very center of the history of salvation. The fathers saw in Christ's obedience the counterweight to Adam's disobedience. We have already discussed the parallel and contrast that St. Paul emphasizes so heavily: by one man sin entered the world, and by one man grace renewed the world.

The Letter to the Hebrews may surprise us with the statements it makes in the passage read on the fifth Sunday. We read, for example: "Son though he was, he learned obedience from what he suffered; and when he was made perfect, he became the source of eternal salvation for all who obey him" (5:8-9). The author of the letter sees further perfection possible for Christ in the line of obedience. The Christ shown us here is the Christ who, though Son, shared our human nature in all things except sin; consequently, he was called to the experience of suffering and obedience. This is not an abstract Jesus. At the same time, however, the author is careful to stress the harmony that existed between the attitudes of the transcendent Christ and those of the Christ visible to us in the gospel. The author can therefore assert that all who obey the Christ visible among us will have eternal salvation through the Christ who was obedient unto death.

"I Will Remember Their Sin No More"

Infidelity, divine wrath, establishment (or renewal) of a covenant—here is a pattern that runs through the entire Old Testament. Now, in the New Testament, there is question again of a covenant, but now it is a "new" covenant.

The new covenant is described for us by Jeremiah in the first reading for the fifth Sunday: "I will be their God, and they shall be my people" (31:33). The theme is one that would be taken up by later prophets (Ezek 11:20; 14:11; 36:28; 37:23-27; Zech 8:8), and it occurs a number of times in Jeremiah himself (24:7; 30:22; 31:1; 32:28). Here the relationship between the Lord and Israel are clearly defined. We have already seen how the prophet Hosea expresses the relationship between the Lord and his people through the image of betrothal and marriage or the image of a father's dealings with his son (Hos 2:2; 3:1; 3:4; 11:1-4). In Jeremiah the covenant is also connected with knowledge of the Lord: "All, from least to greatest, shall know me" (v. 34).

But what is "new" about this covenant? It is new because the covenant will be written in people's hearts, and this makes it notably different from the old covenant. In the latter, God's will was expressed from outside, as it were; here, each person will carry the Lord's law in his or her heart. In consequence, knowledge of and union with the Lord will no longer be reserved to an elite, especially the prophets, but will be accessible to all. "All, from least to greatest, shall know me"; recall here what the gospel says about Jesus drawing all people to himself. The new covenant will also bring the forgiveness of sins: "I will . . . remember their sin no more" (v. 34).

To this last-quoted text Psalm 51 responds with a prayer: "Wash me completely from my iniquity, / and cleanse me from my sin. . . . / Create a pure heart for me, O God; . . . / Restore in me the joy of your salvation" (vv. 4, 12, 14).

The grain of wheat is buried in the ground when its hour comes, and it then bears its fruit. So the obedience of Christ gives his followers access to eternal life, and in his new covenant God remembers past sins no more.

13. FIRST AND SECOND SUNDAYS OF LENT (YEAR C): THE FAITH THAT TRANSFORMS

Structure of Year C for the First Five Sundays			
Table of Readings in the Eucharistic Liturgy			
	Old Testament	Apostle	Gospel
First Sunday	Deut 26:4-10 Faith of the people of Israel	Rom 10:8-13 Faith in Christ	Luke 4:1 13 Temptation of Christ
Second Sunday	Gen 15:5-12, 17-18 Abraham's faith and the covenant	Phil 3:17–4:1 Our transfigured bodies	Luke 9:28-36 Transfiguration of Christ
Third Sunday	Exod 3:1-8a, 13-15 The Lord rescues his people	1 Cor 10:1-6, 10-12 The desert journey, an example for us	Luke 13:1-9 Be converted or perish
Fourth Sunday	Josh 5:9a, 10-12 The Passover celebrated in the promised land	2 Cor 5:17-21 Reconciled to God in Christ	Luke 15:1-3, 11-32 The prodigal son
Fifth Sunday	Isa 43:16-21 Dream not of the past; a new world is here	Phil 3:8-14 Rising with Christ	John 8:1-11 The woman taken in adultery

Tempted but Victorious through Faith

As in the other two years, we read the account of the temptation of the Lord on the first Sunday of Lent in Year C. Here the temptation acquires a special meaning, inasmuch as the trial that Christ undergoes ends in a victory, a victory of confidence in the Father and of the will to do what the Father has determined. One does not live on material bread alone; in fact, the important bread, which one absolutely must eat, is the Father's will as made known through his living word (Isa 55:1). For Jesus, the word of God is a bread we must eat daily (Matt 4:4); to that word we must commit ourselves in faith (John 6:35-47), for we must worship the one God by doing his will, without asking him to explain himself to us.

This kind of faith in God turned Israel into a great nation. Even when the nation had been reduced to slavery, Israel's God listened to his people, rescued them, and led them into a land flowing with milk and honey. The first reading for today tells us of Israel's faith and how the nation was saved through tribulation (Deut 26:4-10). Psalm 91 serves as a response to this reading, and in it we hear the triumphant cry of a nation that has been tried and led into slavery: "says to the LORD, 'My refuge, / my stronghold, my God in whom I trust!'" (Ps 91:2). The psalm also gives us God's response in turn: "Since he clings to me in love, I will free him, / protect him, for he knows my name. When he calls on me, I will answer him; / I will be with him in distress; / I will deliver him, and give him glory. / With length of days I will content him; / I will show him my saving power" (vv. 14-16).

Those who believe in Christ should be animated by a similar confidence. In the second reading St. Paul encourages us against times of trial and suffering: *"The word is near you, / in your mouth and in your heart"* (Rom 10:8; cf. Deut 30:14). The entire passage, in fact, is a cry of trust and of certainty that deliverance will come: "if you confess with your mouth that Jesus is Lord and believe in your heart that God raised him from the dead, you will be saved. For one believes with the heart and so is justified, and one confesses with the mouth and so is saved" (Rom 10:9-10).

Paul's words of encouragement touch us in the details of our everyday life. There is no single moment at which we cannot be sure of our salvation, provided that we believe and call upon the name of the Lord, who is generous to all who invoke him.

The central thought of this first Sunday is "salvation" through faith; faith and salvation are the two dominant themes. We must be careful, however, to note that the message is addressed to all people: "there is no distinction between Jew and Greek; the same Lord is Lord of all, enriching all who call upon him. For 'everyone who calls on the name of the Lord will be saved'" (Rom 10:12-13, citing Joel 3:5). Salvation is not reserved to a single people or to a single race; it is not reserved even to the people of the promise. Christ shows us a far vaster and deeper conception of the economy of salvation than the one with which Abraham, Moses, and Israel were familiar.

In verses 5 and 6 of chapter 10, which are not included in today's reading from Romans, St. Paul contrasts the justice that comes from the law with the justice that comes from faith. The law proved incapable of really saving those who tried to achieve salvation through their own works (Rom 10:3; see also Rom 9:32). In faith, on the other hand, one entrusts oneself to God and does not attempt the impossible, namely, to win salvation through one's own uprightness. The law simply points out what is sinful (Rom 3:20), whereas faith brings the power of the Spirit who sanctifies (Rom 1:4; 8:11); faith thus gives salvation.

In obeying the law, Israelites were seeking to satisfy their legitimate desire for a plenitude of life; the way of faith, however, leads to the salvation that God alone can give. Faith, moreover, gives a salvation that is something present now yet also reserved for the future: "one confesses with the mouth and so is saved" (Rom 10:10), and when life is over, and people are judged, no one who thus confessed faith will be put to shame, but "everyone who calls on the name of the Lord will be saved" (Rom 10:13).

The first reading, from Deuteronomy, connects the profession of faith (26:5-9) with a ritual in which the firstfruits of the harvest are offered to the Lord (vv. 4, 10). The exegetes see in this passage the desire to transform the agrarian cults into the worship of Yahweh. The gifts of the earth thus become a present embodiment of salvation and show that God indeed intends to save his people, provided that they have trust in him. Evidently the first and second readings are linked together, with the second presenting the full Christian reality that is only distantly anticipated in the first.

In the gospel of the temptation, the chief thing to be emphasized is trust in, and worship of, the one true God. The text provides us with another occasion to point out how one and the same text will be differently interpreted in different liturgies, depending on the other texts being read at the same time. The gospel of the temptation is read on the first Sunday in all three years, but it calls for comment in each year from a viewpoint that is determined by the other two readings.

Our Transfigured Bodies

Once again, the gospel pericope for the second Sunday is the same as in the other two years, and once again our reading of it must take account of the two readings that accompany it.

The first reading tells us of Abraham's faith and the covenant (Gen 15:5-12, 17-18). It recounts an awesome theophany in which the Lord makes a promise that is connected with a sacrificial rite. The first part of the account speaks of Abraham's faith in the Lord's promises; in the second part, immediately after the sacrifice and by way of recompense to Abraham for his faith, the Lord concludes his covenant. The narrative moves swiftly, and the elimination of some verses in the pericope as found in the liturgy makes the narrative even more succinct, perhaps even oversimplifies it a bit. We have the Lord's promise and Abraham's faith, and these are immediately followed by the fulfillment of the promise in the form of a covenant.

The responsorial psalm, Psalm 27, fits in nicely with the theophany in the reading: "It is your face, O LORD, that I seek; / hide not your face from me. / Dismiss not your servant in anger; / . . . I believe I shall see the LORD's goodness / in the land of the living. / Wait for the LORD; be strong; / be stouthearted, and wait for the LORD!" (vv. 8-9, 13-14).

The first reading and the responsorial psalm indicate to us that obedience and unlimited trust provide the perspective in which we are to read the gospel of the transfiguration. In Luke's version, as compared with those of Matthew and Mark, the account has a more pronounced paschal orientation. Not only does Christ appear in his glory, but Moses and Elijah are present as witnesses to his passion; they seem to be helping Jesus to face the trial that awaits him in Jerusalem. Christ's death is seen as a kind of baptism (his "departure"); in another context, the image of "baptism" for his passion is accompanied by the image of the "cup," and the latter image recurs in Christ's words during the agony in the garden.

In chapter 24 of Luke's gospel we find a typology of the paschal mystery: entry of Christ into the world, departure from this world, and entry into glory. This pattern is connected with Moses, and Jesus accomplishes in its perfect form the work that the Hebrew leader had done long before, since Jesus crosses the waters of death in order to save his people and lead them into the eternal kingdom of his Father. Jesus is thus the Moses of the new Exodus. He is also, however, the new Elijah who has "come to set the earth on fire" (Luke 12:49).

As in the other accounts of the transfiguration, so in Luke's narrative the Father's voice tells us, in the presence of the Spirit, who Jesus is: "This is my chosen Son." We have already pointed out the fullness of meaning attached to these words.

The reason, then, why Jesus is gloriously transfigured is his trustful, unconditional obedience to the Father's will. That obedience will motivate him in his passage through death to life. With him he will take all his followers, leading them along the way of salvation that culminates in glory.

In the second reading (Phil 3:17–4:1), St. Paul develops the thought that all who are baptized will share in the glory of the transfigured Christ. He urges the Philippians to follow his own example and not let their hearts become attached to earthly things. They are already citizens of heaven. How, then, could they glory in what is really a cause for shame or make anything earthly the goal of their life?

Christians are constantly confronted with choices they cannot evade. They must choose, and they must keep on choosing, since, though already citizens of heaven, they still live in that "form of a slave" that Christ himself assumed and in which he was humbled even to the point of dying (Phil 2:6-11). But the day of the Lord's return will be the day when their fidelity will be rewarded: They will be transformed and become like the glorious Christ.

This, then, is the lesson of the Second Sunday of Lent as it seeks to bring about our conversion: We must change our ways; we must choose and follow the Apostle; that is, in the last analysis we must follow Christ on his paschal journey so that with him we may finally rise transformed and glorious.

14. THIRD AND FOURTH SUNDAYS OF LENT (YEAR C): BE CONVERTED AND RECONCILED IN ORDER TO RISE NEW WITH CHRIST

Be Converted or Perish

The last three Sundays of Lent focus on conversion and on the new life of the convert. It is of some interest to observe how the first emphasis in the Lenten renewal is on conversion. The gospel of the third Sunday is significant in this regard, as the problem of conversion is raised against the background of two somewhat unusual events: Pilate had some Galileans slaughtered while they were offering sacrifice, and in Siloam a falling tower killed eighteen people. Jesus asserts that these people were not greater sinners than the other inhabitants of Galilee or Jerusalem. He insists that conversion is an urgent need for all without exception: "if you do not repent, you will all perish as they did!" (Luke 13:5). At the same time, however, the Lord is patient as he waits for conversion.

God's patience is the subject of the second part of the pericope, the parable of the barren fig tree, in which the vinedresser says to the impatient landowner: "Sir, leave it [the fig tree] for this year also, and I shall cultivate the ground around it and fertilize it; it may bear fruit in the future. If not you can cut it down" (vv. 8-9).

Let us analyze this passage a little more closely. To begin with, Jesus nowhere tells us that those who were victims of Pilate and of the falling tower were being punished for their sins. In fact, he tells us elsewhere that accidents of this kind are not always due to the victims' moral faults. Thus, in the case of the man born blind, Jesus says that his blindness was not due either to his own or his parents' sins (John 9:3). Similarly, in today's gospel he insists that the victims were no more sinful than the people who survived.

Christ does, however, draw a practical lesson from the two events: "if you do not repent, you will all perish as they did!" (Luke 13:5). He rejects a certain idea of punishment in time and chastisement on earth and sees in the events, rather, a warning about the punishment that will indeed come at the end of time. All of us are sinners and deserve to be rejected by God; therefore, we must repent in anticipation of the judgment. The second part of the pericope is especially interesting and has profound scriptural resonances. Israel is the Lord's vineyard (Isa 5:1-4; Jer 2:21; Ezek 17:6; 19:10-11; Ps 80:9-17). When the vineyard fails and becomes barren, the avenging hand of God is felt (Isa 5:5-6; Jer 5:10; 6:9; 12:10; Ezek 15:6; 17:10; 19:12-14).

Nonetheless, toward sin and sinner God is patient in a way that deeply moves us and stimulates us not to procrastinate but to begin our conversion today and to put all our energies into it. In the last analysis, this patient mercy of God seems to be the most important point made in this passage from Luke's gospel.

The first reading confirms this impression. Both the theophany in the form of fire and the conversation between the Lord thus present and Moses emphasize the Lord's boundless mercy: "I have witnessed the affliction of my people in Egypt. . . . I know well what they are suffering. Therefore I have come down to rescue them from the hands of the Egyptians" (Exod 3:7-8). So great is his compassion for his suffering people that he reveals himself once and for all, as the God of Abraham, the God of Isaac, and the God of Jacob; it is as such that he wishes to be celebrated forevermore. *That* is the lesson of this reading from the book of Exodus.

The responsorial psalm, Psalm 103, picks up this last theme and sings of the tender love of this God: "The LORD is compassionate and gracious, / slow to anger and rich in mercy" (Ps 103:8).

The passage from St. Paul's First Letter to the Corinthians (10:1-6, 10-12) continues with the thought of what God did at the Exodus. Paul speaks of the journey through the desert and of the varied fates of those who journeyed. All, indeed, had crossed the Red Sea and had been united to Moses as though by a baptism in cloud and sea; all ate of the same spiritual food. Yet many of them died on the way; they perished in the desert because they were not pleasing to God.

This is a grim warning to each of us that we must not slip into the kind of sacramental spirituality that excuses us from living in love and from respect for God's will. The really important thing to remember is that baptism in itself and alone is not enough. As such, baptism does not prevent spiritual death; the baptized person must persevere in love and in obedience to God's holy will.

The Return to the Father

We all know the story of the prodigal son that is told in the gospel of the fourth Sunday (Luke 15:1-3, 11-32). We shall simply note two important points in the account. One is the movement of conversion that the prodigal son voices: "I shall get up and go to my father and I shall say to him, 'Father, I have sinned against heaven and against you'" (v. 18). The other is the father's words to the older son: "your brother was dead and has come to life again" (v. 32).

At the end of the parable we are pervaded by the spirit of unrestrained paschal joy that finds expression in a banquet: "now we must celebrate and rejoice, because your brother was dead and has come to life again; he was lost and has been found" (v. 32).

In this account the older brother evidently believes his father to be unjust, and he resents this. He has been faithful and observant; he has never neglected the smallest duty; he has been constantly at his father's side and has been scrupulous in helping him in his work. By thus giving us a picture of the elder brother as well as of the younger, the parable brings out the full character of God's mercy. He relies lovingly on the person who is faithful to him, but he cannot therefore be insensible of the person who strays, repents, and returns. Rather, his inner feelings burst forth and show us the infinite love God has for anyone who takes even a single step toward him. The Lord not only waits hopefully for this step but even tries to get people to take it. Such is the full depth of God's tender love for the sinner.

The Banquet in the Father's House

The first reading for this fourth Sunday shows the approach we are to take to the gospel, for it is a reading about a banquet and a table to which sinners are invited (Josh 5:9a, 10-12). What chiefly concerns the author of the passage is not so much the ritual followed in celebrating the Passover but the fact of entry into the promised land and of partaking of its food. (How can we fail, as we read, to think of the feast prepared for the prodigal son, a feast at which he will eat the food proper to his father's house?) The banquet Joshua describes takes place at the end of the very difficult years in the desert and marks the beginning of a new way of life. The manna ceases to fall, for, while a nourishment, it was also a test, inasmuch as many died because they murmured as they ate and refused to accept their circumstances as willed by God. Moreover, the manna pointed forward to the true food that Jesus alone will someday give.

It is, after all, only in Christ that we are truly reconciled to God. This is the theme of the second reading (2 Cor 5:17-21). The reconciliation of all people in Christ is, St. Paul tells us, the basic purpose of the apostolic ministry. For, as a result of Christ's death and resurrection, we are a new creation; the old order has passed away, and a new order has already been born. God has reconciled us to himself through Christ. How poignantly relevant the urging of the Apostle is, today as in the past: "We implore you on behalf of Christ, be reconciled to God" (2 Cor 5:20).

Do we perhaps answer him despairingly: "We would like to be reconciled, but we feel incapable of it. We are so full of evil tendencies, so full of desires for this world and its pleasures that we cannot overcome them"? But Paul in turn replies, "For our sake he made him to be sin who did not know sin, so that we might become the righteousness of God in him" (2 Cor 5:21). It is by the power of Christ who made our human nature his own that we can be reconciled. In fact, he has already reconciled us through his sacrifice; now we have the power to share in the holiness of God himself.

These are real possibilities for us, and our attitude must be one of desire to return to the Father and share in the banquet set for sinners and, to this end, to be reconciled in Christ Jesus. Psalm 34, the responsorial psalm, becomes, in this context, a eucharistic song, expressing the gratitude of all who experience God and know that he hears them as soon as they turn to him in their distress. In responding to the account of the Passover in the reading from the book of Joshua, the psalm also becomes the song of those who have been reconciled through Christ and have returned to their Father's house and who now, in the Eucharist (which is a sign of the definitive banquet at the end of time), share in a joyous feast to celebrate their homecoming.

15. FIFTH SUNDAY OF LENT (YEAR C): LIVE AGAIN AND REGAIN YOUR TRUE DIGNITY IN A NEW LIFE

Today's gospel is a familiar one (John 8:1-11). At times it has been misinterpreted to mean that Christ is indulgent toward sins of the flesh. And yet the last words of the passage are clear enough: "Neither do I condemn you. Go, and from now on do not sin any more" (v. 11). One of the suggested verses before the Gospel brings out the same point: "As I live—oracle of the LORD God—I swear I take no pleasure in the death of the wicked, but rather that they turn from their ways and live" (Ezek 33:11). It would be a distortion, therefore, either to use the passage as a basis for moralizing or, on the other hand, to draw false inferences in favor of the weaknesses of the flesh.

The real meaning of the passage lies in quite another direction, for the point being made is that the Lord's mercy is inexhaustible and that he does not condemn people but wants them to live, though they must repent if they are to do so. As soon as people repent, God renews them and restores them to their true dignity. We can see this happening in the case of the adulterous woman. Once she has repented, she regains her dignity as a woman whom no one is now willing to condemn and who is determined henceforth to lead a new life.

The first reading (Isa 43:16-21) focuses on the same theme: "Remember not the events of the past, / the things of long ago consider not; / see, I am doing something new! / Now it springs forth, do you not perceive it? / . . . [T]he people whom I formed for myself, / that they might announce my praise" (Isa 43:18-21). The Christian who has sinned but then repented has no past any longer. Once converted, the Christian is a new person in a new world and is able to engage in the activity proper to the redeemed: the praise of God.

Our conversion and return to our dignity as children of God is the greatest of God's "wonderful deeds." Thereby he leads us out of captivity, as he did his people of old. "What great deeds the LORD worked for us! / Indeed, we were glad," says Psalm 126:3, the responsorial psalm.

The hope of every Christian originates in the new life that is given with the risen Christ. St. Paul, who experienced this new life, believed that the most important element in it is the knowledge of Christ (Phil 3:8-14). There is only one goal worthy of the Christian's striving, he says, and that goal is to find Christ, in whom God acknowledges us as upright. Our aim, then, must be to know Christ through faith and to experience the power of his resurrection by sharing in his sufferings and by reproducing his death in ourselves, in the hope of rising with him from the dead. We must forget what lies behind and push forward so as to obtain the prize to which God calls us on high in Christ Jesus.

As soon as we seek Christ in faith, we who are sinners regain our original dignity. All things become new for us, and we come to know a God who, in his Son, summons us to resurrection.

16. THE MAIN THEMES OF THE LENTEN WEEKDAY CELEBRATIONS

Structure of the Weekdays of Lent		
Table of Readings in the Eucharistic Liturgy		
Week of Ash Wednesday		
A Spiritual Fast; Interior Conversion and Sharing		
Ash Wednesday	1	Interior conversion; Joel 2:12-18
	2	Now is the acceptable time; 2 Cor 5:20–6:2
	3	Prayer and good works, in secret; Matt 6:1-6, 16-18
Thursday	4	Choose the way of God; Deut 30:15-20
	5	Lose your life to save it; Luke 9:22-25
Friday	6	Fasting means sharing; Isa 58:1-9a
	7	Fast when the Spouse is absent; Matt 9:14-15
Saturday	8	Give your bread and live in the light; Isa 58:9-14
	9	The call of sinners to conversion; Luke 5:27-32
First Week of Lent		
Love of Neighbor and Conversion		
Monday	10	Justice to your neighbor; Lev 19:1-2, 11-18
	11	What you do to one of my brothers . . . ; Matt 25:31-46
Tuesday	12	The word of God accomplishes the conversion he wills; Isa 55:10-11
	13	The Our Father: God's will be done; forgive us as we forgive others; Matt 6:7-15
Wednesday	14	The sign of Jonah and the conversion of the Ninevites; Jonah 3:1-10
	15	The sign of the Son of Man; Luke 11:29-32
Thursday	16	The Lord is our sole help; Esth 14:1, 3-5, 12-15a
	17	Ask and you shall receive; Matt 7:7-12
Friday	18	The Lord wants the sinner's conversion; Ezek 18:21-28
	19	Conversion supposes reconciliation with our brother; Matt 5:20-26

Saturday	20	Be a holy people for the Lord; Deut 26:16-19
	21	Be perfect like your heavenly Father, and forgive; Matt 5:43-48

Second Week

Forgiveness of Sins (Monday, Tuesday, Saturday); Inwardness and True Values (Thursday); Prediction of the Passion (Wednesday, Friday)

Monday	22	We have sinned; Dan 9:4b-10
	23	Forgive, and you will be forgiven; Luke 6:36-38
Tuesday	24	Cease to do evil; become pure; Isa 1:10, 16-20
	25	Practice what you preach; Matt 23:1-12
Wednesday	26	Strike down the prophet; Jer 18:18-20
	27	Plotting Jesus' death; Matt 20:17-28
Thursday	28	Trust in the Lord; Jer 17:5-10
	29	Happiness now or in heaven? Luke 16:19-31
Friday	30	Joseph the dreamer: kill him! Gen 37:3-4, 12-13a, 17b-28
	31	He is the heir: kill him! Matt 21:33-43, 45-46
Saturday	32	Cast all our sins into the sea; Mic 7:14-15, 18-20
	33	Your brother was dead and has come back to life; Luke 15:1-3, 11-32

Third Week

Listen to the One Lord (Wednesday, Thursday, Friday); He Saves All People (Monday); Forgive Others (Tuesday); Interior Worship (Saturday)

Monday	34	Naaman the Syrian is healed; 2 Kgs 5:1-15a
	35	Jesus has been sent to all humanity; Luke 4:24-30
Tuesday	36	Receive us with humble and contrite hearts; Dan 3:2, 11-20
	37	Forgive if you would be forgiven; Matt 18:21-35
Wednesday	38	Keep the commandments; Deut 4:1, 5-9
	39	The kingdom belongs to those who keep the commandments; Matt 5:17-19
Thursday	40	They did not listen; Jer 7:23-28
	41	With me or against me; Luke 11:14-23
Friday	42	God is the sole source of happiness; Hos 14:1-9
	43	The Lord is the only Lord; love him! Mark 12:28b-34
Saturday	44	Love and not sacrifice; Hos 5:15c–6:6
	45	Interior worship; Luke 18:9-14

Fourth Week		
Life through a New Covenant (Monday, Tuesday, Wednesday); Unbelief and Attempts to Kill Christ (Thursday, Friday, Saturday)		
Monday	46	A new earth and long life; Isa 65:17-21
	47	Go, your son lives; John 4:41-54
Tuesday	48	Saved by the water from the temple; Ezek 47:1-9, 12
	49	The paralytic at the pool of Bethesda; John 5:1-3, 5-16
Wednesday	50	The Lord's love for his people; Isa 49:8-15
	51	The Son gives life to those he chooses; John 5:17-30
Thursday	52	Moses intercedes and allays the Lord's wrath; Exod 32:7-14
	53	Moses will accuse the Jews because they did not listen to God's word; John 5:31-47
Friday	54	Condemn the just person to a shameful death; Wis 2:1a, 12-22
	55	They sought to arrest Jesus; John 7:1-2, 10, 25-30
Saturday	56	Like a lamb led to slaughter; Jer 11:18-20
	57	Arrest Jesus and condemn him; John 7:40-53
Fifth Week		
The Power of the Lord Who by His Death Saves People and Gathers Them into Unity		
Monday	58	Susanna falsely accused but rescued; Dan 13:1-9, 15-17, 19-30, 33-62
	59	The adulterous woman forgiven; John 8:1-11; *or* Christ, the Light of the world; John 8:12-20
Tuesday	60	The serpent raised up and healing people; Num 21:4-9
	61	The Son of Man lifted up on the cross; John 8:21-30
Wednesday	62	The three young men saved from the fire; Dan 3:14-20, 24-25, 28
	63	The truth will set you free; John 8:31-42
Thursday	64	Abraham receives the covenant and becomes the father of many peoples; Gen 17:3-9
	65	Before Abraham was, I am; he who keeps my words will never die; John 8:51-59
Friday	66	Jeremiah is persecuted but the Lord is with him; Jer 20:10-13
	67	Jesus escapes from the hands of the Jews; John 10:31-42
Saturday	68	I will make one nation of them; Ezek 37:21-28
	69	Jesus must die in order to gather the scattered children of God; John 11:45-57

It is not feasible for us to comment on each weekday of Lent. Nor would a commentary be very useful, since the choice of readings and their meanings are often clear enough and need no further explanation. More than that, a detailed commentary might well make us lose sight of the essential thing, which is the series of Sundays that provide the basic framework of Lent. We shall therefore try rather to reinforce what we have been saying about the Sundays by concentrating here on the main themes of the Lenten weekday liturgies. In order not to overload our text with quotations, we have assigned each reading in the foregoing list a number in square brackets; in the next few pages we shall use these numbers in referring to the readings.

Three major themes are developed in the weekday liturgies: conversion and interior worship; forgiveness for ourselves as conditioned by our forgiveness of others; renewal and the gift of life through the passion of Christ.

Conversion and Interior Worship

The readings on Ash Wednesday tell us the authentic spirit that must characterize Lent: rend your hearts and not your garments [1]. We must struggle against the spirit of evil (collect for Ash Wednesday) and—to look at the positive side—have a pure heart that has been renewed by the Lord (Ps 51, responsorial psalm for Ash Wednesday). The new optional formula for the imposition of ashes is meaningful in this context: "Repent and believe in the gospel" (Mark 1:15), as are the antiphons to be sung while the ashes are being imposed: "Let us change our garments to sackcloth and ashes" (first antiphon); "Blot out my transgressions, O Lord" (third antiphon); and "Let the priests, the ministers of the Lord . . . weep and cry out: Spare, O Lord, spare your people" (second antiphon). We must indeed be cleansed of our sins if we are to celebrate more effectively the passion of Christ (prayer over the offerings, Ash Wednesday). But when we pray, it should be in secret, just as we should do our good works in secret [3].

The Lord desires the sinner's conversion [18]; he wants us to become a holy people [20] and to be perfect as he is perfect [21]. We must therefore cease doing evil and cleanse ourselves [24]; we must once again learn a proper scale of values [28]. All this has to be more than a mere abstraction; we must practice what we preach [25, 38–39]. Such a conversion supposes that we have listened to the word that effects whatever God wills [12]. If the Jews are to be accused by Moses at the judgment, it is because they have not listened to the word [53, 40].

The kind of conversion Christ preaches requires of us a deep inwardness: we must choose to follow God's way [4], be willing to lose our life in order to save it [5], be always attentive to God's will [13], and take advantage of the acceptable time [2]; in short, we must be either with Christ or against him [41]. The Lord is our only source of help [16] and of happiness [42]; he alone must be loved [43] and to him we must pray. What wins his goodwill toward us, however, is not outward rites but charity [44] and interior worship [45].

Such is the vision given us in the weekday liturgies of the conversion to which we are called [9].

Forgiveness for Us Conditioned by Our Forgiveness of Others

Conversion on our part elicits forgiveness of our sins by God. But his forgiveness is also conditioned by the forgiveness we ourselves give to others.

It is worth our while to go through the list of readings and see what great emphasis is placed on our forgiveness of neighbor. Forgiveness, moreover, includes in this context our love of and sharing with our neighbor.

From the very beginning of Lent, we are shown that fasting is a form of sharing [6]. Give your bread and live in the light—that is Isaiah's program for us [8]. The first week of Lent focuses almost exclusively on the fact that conversion necessarily involves our relationship with our neighbor.

Love of neighbors consists first of all in being just toward them [10]. Justice is a first stage of love; this is so evident that it hardly seems to warrant mention. But experience of the world quickly shows us that justice to the neighbor is a far from easy thing and that people die and kill in the process of restoring or gaining justice. In fact, the whole drama of humanity is concentrated in the problem of justice to the neighbor.

What does "being just" mean? It is impossible for an unenlightened person to be just, and people cannot be enlightened until they have been forgiven by God. God's pardon, however, is obtained only by pardoning our neighbor: "[F]orgive us our trespasses, / as we forgive those who trespass against us" [13]. Every conversion supposes a reconciliation with our neighbors [19], and we must forgive if we are to be forgiven [23, 37]. Conversion supposes that we see the Lord himself in our neighbor, so much so that what we do to our neighbor we do to God himself [11]. In this way we determine the measure of the pardon we ourselves will receive from God; the forgiveness of our own sins is conditioned by the forgiveness we bestow upon others, and our conversion is necessarily bound up with our generosity to others.

Such are the conditions we must fulfill if we are to be converted and have God forgive our sins. The conditions are simple enough but very difficult to put into practice.

Renewal and the Gift of Life through the Passion of Christ

Interior conversion and loving awareness of others are attitudes that lead to renewal and new life. Lent is the acceptable time for developing these attitudes [2]. In fact, we must say that, for us Christians, Lent is a sign we must obey if we are to be saved from destruction and that no other sign will be given to us [14, 15]. Lent is the time when we turn our attention more fully to the mystery of Christ, who gave himself that we might have life.

From the second week on, especially on Wednesdays and Fridays, the readings remind us of the opposition, to the point of death, that the Lord endured for our liberation. His words anger the Jews, and as they once persecuted Jeremiah [26], so now they plot to kill Jesus [27]. They do not accept the Son whom the Father has sent: "Here comes that master dreamer! Come on, let us kill him" [30]; "This is the heir. Come, let us kill him" [31]. The just one is threatened with a shameful death, and Jesus' enemies are constantly on the watch to get rid of him [54, 55]. When arrested and sentenced [57], he will be like a lamb led to slaughter [56]. And yet, it is of his own free will that Jesus will hand himself over to the Jews when his "hour" has come. He is persecuted, but the Lord is with him [66], and he eludes the hands of the Jews [67] until such time as he decides to surrender to them.

During this period the whole history of salvation reaches its climax and center. Christ shows that he has been sent for the sake of all humanity [34, 35]. He gives signs that accredit him and through his miracles proclaims a new life [46]. He cures people of paralysis and thus prefigures the renewal effected by baptism [48, 49]. He brings the truth that frees people [63], and for the sake of that truth and for the liberation of the world every Christian must, like Christ, suffer even martyrdom [62]. The powers of evil seek to destroy the just one [58], but Jesus raises up the fallen and the scorned [59]. He gives life [47], and those who keep his word will never die [65]. Those who look upon him when he is lifted up on the cross find everlasting life [60, 61], but the Son gives this life to whomever he wishes [51].

The entire work of salvation that is described in these readings leads to the restoration of the world that God had created in unity. The Lord wills to make his people a single nation [68], and Jesus responds to this divine will by dying so that the scattered children of God may be gathered and united [69].

This short synthesis may give the reader a first idea of the riches contained in the weekday lectionary. Our summary is elementary and incomplete, but it may at least serve to situate the various readings in a broader context and enable the reader to link them to each other, both within each celebration and from celebration to celebration. Use of the list we have given will help readers find where they are and give them a sense of direction so that they may fruitfully read and listen to the word of God.

The Journey of the People of Israel

Table of Readings for Weekdays in the Liturgy of the Hours	
Week of Ash Wednesday	
Ash Wednesday	The fast that pleases God; Isa 58:1-2
Thursday	Israel oppressed; Exod 1:1-22
Friday	Birth and flight of Moses; Exod 2:1-22; 18:4
Saturday	Call of Moses and revelation of the Lord's name; Exod 3:1-20
First Week of Lent	
Monday	Call of Moses; Exod 6:2-13
Tuesday	First plague sent on Egypt; Exod 6:29–7:25
Wednesday	Plague of darkness and warning of the death of the firstborn; Exod 10:21–11:10
Thursday	Passover and unleavened bread; Exod 12:1-20
Friday	Death of the firstborn; Exod 12:21-36
Saturday	Departure of the Hebrews; Exod 12:37-49; 13:11-16

Second Week	
Monday	Crossing of the Red Sea; Exod 14:10-31
Tuesday	The manna; Exod 16:1-18, 35
Wednesday	The water from the rock at Horeb; Exod 17:1-16
Thursday	Appointment of the judges; Exod 18:13-27
Friday	Promise of the covenant; the Lord appears on Sinai; Exod 19:1-19; 20:18-21
Saturday	The law is given on Sinai; Exod 20:1-17
Third Week	
Monday	The covenant is ratified on Sinai; Exod 24:1-18
Tuesday	The golden calf; Exod 32:1-20
Wednesday	Revelation of the Lord to Moses; Exod 33:7-11, 18-23; 34:5-9, 29-35
Thursday	The book of the covenant; Exod 34:10-28
Friday	The sanctuary and the ark; Exod 35:30–36:1; 37:1-9
Saturday	The tabernacle and the cloud; Exod 40:16-38
Fourth Week	
Monday	The day of atonement; Lev 16:2-28
Tuesday	Commandments concerning the neighbor; Lev 19:1-18, 31-37
Wednesday	The spirit poured out on Joshua and the elders; Num 11:4-6, 10-30
Thursday	Scouts sent into Canaan; Num 12:16–13:3, 17-33
Friday	Murmuring of the people and intervention of Moses; Num 14:1-25
Saturday	The waters of Meribah; the bronze serpent; Num 20:1-13; 21:4-9
Fifth Week	
Monday	Jesus, Author of salvation, likes his brothers in every way; Heb 2:5-18
Tuesday	Jesus, Apostle of our faith; Heb 3:1-19
Wednesday	God's fidelity is our hope; Heb 6:9-20
Thursday	Melchizedek, type of the perfect priest; Heb 7:1-10
Friday	The eternal priesthood of Christ; Heb 7:11-28
Saturday	The priesthood of Christ in the new covenant; Heb 8:1-13

Meanwhile, in the weekday Office of Lent, the readings take us through the great moments of the history of Israel down to the great new Passover of Christ.

We shall not offer a commentary on these texts of the weekday Office. We shall, however, supply a list of the readings, along with titles that will enable the reader to follow the historical and spiritual journey of Israel. We make that journey our own during Lent; along with Israel, we go up to Jerusalem.

Those who do not possess the *Liturgy of the Hours* can use the table for selecting readings for communal celebrations or for private reading during Lent.

It will be clear from the list that in the Liturgy of the Hours the last week of Lent is entirely focused on Christ and his priestly action as being the final act in the history of salvation.

17. PALM SUNDAY, MONDAY, TUESDAY, AND WEDNESDAY OF HOLY WEEK: TOWARD THE MOUNT OF OLIVES

The Celebration of These Days in the Past

Devotion to the paschal mystery is not optional, any more than its celebration is something exceptional in our liturgy. Rather, the paschal mystery exemplifies and prescribes the law that must govern our lives: the law of death and of life coming through and by means of death. So too, the paschal mystery is really the very heart of the liturgy, and the entire liturgical year grows out of it.

The early generations of Christians were very conscious of the primordial place of the paschal mystery. They celebrated only the night of the "Pasch," which they understood as a "passage" through death to authentic life.

Even today the holy days are celebrated with great simplicity in some of the rites. In the Coptic Rite, for example, the celebration consists entirely of readings from the Old and New Testaments that enlighten us on the meaning of the paschal mystery, praise the Lord for it, render it present, and prepare the faithful for his return. This liturgy, with its monastic simplicity and essentially contemplative character, is especially notable during the Easter Vigil, where, once again, it consists entirely of readings.

At Rome the focus of celebration was the Easter Vigil that ended with the eucharistic sacrifice and soon came to include the administration of baptism as well. This primitive nucleus was quickly expanded. In fifth-century Africa, when St. Augustine speaks of the paschal celebration, he calls it "the triduum of Christ crucified, buried, and risen" and is referring to Good Friday, Holy Saturday, and Easter Sunday.* The climax of the three days was the single eucharistic celebration during the night between Saturday and Sunday.

---

* Augustine may be referring to the historical three days in the life of Christ, not their liturgical observance.

The Last Days of Lent		
Readings in the Eucharistic Liturgy		
Palm Sunday Procession	Blessed be he who comes in the name of the Lord!	A: Matt 21:1-11; B: Mark 11:1-10 *or* John 12:12-16; C: Luke 19:28-40
Palm Sunday Mass	I gave my back to those who beat me; I am not disgraced	Isa 50:4-7
	Christ humbled himself, therefore God exalted him	Phil 2:6-11
	Passion of our Lord Jesus Christ	A: Matt 26:14–27:66; B: Mark 14–15:47; C: Luke 22:14–23:56
Monday	Here is my servant whom I uphold	Isa 42:1-7
	Let her keep this perfume for the day of my burial	John 12:1-11
Tuesday	I will make my salvation reach to the ends of the earth	Isa 49:1-6
	One of you will betray me	John 13:21-33, 33-38
Wednesday	I did not cover my face against insults and spittle	Isa 50:4-9a
	Woe to that person by whom the Son of Man is betrayed	Matt 26:14-25
Readings in the Liturgy of the Hours		
Palm Sunday	We are sanctified through Christ's offering	Heb 10:1-18
Monday	Perseverance in faith; waiting for God's judgment	Heb 10:19-39
Tuesday	Let us go forth to the struggle with Christ as our Leader	Heb 12:1-13
Wednesday	Let us ascend the mountain of the living God	Heb 12:14-29
Thursday	Christ, our High Priest	Heb 4:14–5:10

At Jerusalem, however, where it was easier than elsewhere to follow the historical unfolding of the paschal mystery by visiting the holy places, the liturgy was already quite extensively developed. The travel diary of Egeria, a fourth-century widow, provides us with a detailed description of the Jerusalem liturgy, beginning with Palm Sunday.[1] The liturgy took the form of a deliberately accurate reconstruction of the final actions of Jesus' life; yet the liturgy celebrated the whole of the paschal mystery and did not break it up, even if each day was given over to one particular aspect of it.

In order to copy what was done at Jerusalem and to bring to life the details afforded by the evangelists, the Western liturgy expanded. A detailed celebration took up the whole of what we now call Holy Week, although the main concentration was on the last days of the week and on Easter Sunday.

The danger of such a detailed and anecdotal reconstruction of the sacred actions that make up the paschal mystery was that the faithful might break up the mystery into unconnected parts and might separate the celebration of Jesus' death too much from the celebration of his resurrection. The danger of fragmentation, of turning the whole into disparate aspects not seen in the context of the paschal mystery, was not always successfully avoided. In the Middle Ages, Holy Week was referred to as the "Week of Sorrow," thus emphasizing the suffering of Jesus and the loving compassion of Christians for him but insufficiently adverting to the aspect of triumph and victory.

The tendency to an anecdotal reading of the gospel had important consequences, some of which are still with us. Toward the middle or end of the seventh century, a commemoration of the Last Supper was introduced at Rome, where Holy Thursday had hitherto been chiefly the day for the reconciliation of penitents. This caused a displacement: The paschal Triduum now meant Holy Thursday, Good Friday, and Holy Saturday. We shall return to this later. The point to be made here is that this new Triduum could turn the minds of the faithful from the full meaning of the paschal mystery, inasmuch as what we now call "the three holy days" do not perfectly coincide with what the Church of St. Augustine's time called the Holy Triduum. For Augustine, the three days were Friday, Saturday, and Sunday; for us, they are Thursday, Friday, and Saturday.

The intention of people at that time was evidently to lend the liturgy a dramatic quality, but the quality was somewhat contrived; it could also be, and has in fact often been, misunderstood. The liturgy, after all, is not simply a play. We do not take part in the liturgy in order to recall past events in an atmosphere of spiritual emotion. We take part in it in order to celebrate a mystery that the liturgy itself renders present. The liturgical celebration makes present the spiritual efficacy of a moment that in its material, anecdotal form is historically past. The historical event was complete in itself. For this reason it does not have to be repeated; what we want is that it should be present to each moment of history as a source of value.

We must keep these basic considerations in mind, for they are essential to the celebration of Holy Week, and indeed to every liturgical celebration.

The Messianic Entry into Jerusalem

It was at Jerusalem, around the year 400, that an attempt was made to reenact in all possible detail the Lord's entry into Jerusalem. As we noted above, from this Sunday on, Christians were very anxious to follow in the footsteps of Christ, incident by incident, through Holy Week.

Egeria the pilgrim describes the Palm Sunday procession as it was celebrated at Jerusalem toward the end of the fourth century:

> As the eleventh hour [five o'clock in the afternoon] draws near, that particular passage from Scripture is read in which the children bearing palms and branches came forth to meet the Lord, saying: *Blessed is He who comes in the name of the Lord.* The bishop and all the people rise immediately, and then everyone walks down from the top of the Mount of Olives, with the people preceding the bishop and responding continually with *Blessed is He who comes in the name of the Lord* to the hymns and antiphons. All the children who are present here, including those who are not able to walk because they are too young and therefore are carried on their parents' shoulders, all of them bear branches, some carrying palms, others, olive branches. And the bishop is led in the same manner as the Lord once was led. From the top of the mountain as far as the city, and from there through the entire city as far as the Anastasis, everyone accompanies the bishop the whole way on foot, and this includes distinguished ladies and men of consequence, reciting the responses all the while; and they move very slowly so that the people will not tire. By the time they arrive at the Anastasis, it is already evening. Once they have arrived there, even though it is evening, vespers is celebrated; then a prayer is said at the cross and the people are dismissed.[2]

Egeria notes the presence of little children in the procession, whereas the evangelists say nothing about them. St. Matthew does say that children, observing the wonders Jesus had just accomplished, were shouting in the temple precincts, "Hosanna to the Son of David" (21:15). Jesus comments on their action by citing Psalm 8:3: "Out of the mouths of infants and nurslings you have brought forth praise"

(Matt 21:16). At Jerusalem later on, the Palm Sunday procession was turned into a kind of children's feast. This may in turn have given rise to the antiphon "The children of Jerusalem . . ." and the hymn "All Glory, Laud, and Honor," which are still used for the Palm Sunday procession in the Roman liturgy; both of these speak of children praising Christ with hosannas.[3]

This kind of procession could not but be extremely successful and popular, so much so that in the East this Sunday concentrates entirely on the theme of Jesus' entry into Jerusalem, with both the Mass and the Office developing it fully. Naturally, dramatic touches were added to the celebration as time went on. Thus, while in Egypt the cross was carried in triumph on Palm Sunday, in Jerusalem the bishop representing Christ rode on an ass in the procession.[4]

As happened so often in the history of the liturgy, these customs passed from the East to Spain and Gaul. We should note that in Spain on this Sunday before Easter the *Ephphetha*, or rite of expulsion of the devil, took place in the morning, while the Mass contained the presentation of the Creed.[5] The *Liber ordinum* (beginning of the seventh century) gives us the readings for this Mass; only the gospel deals with the entry of Jesus into Jerusalem. The *Liber ordinum* speaks of the procession with the palms, preceded by the blessing of the palms at the altar and the blessing of the people; there is, however, no description of the procession itself.[6]

In Gaul, Palm Sunday began to be celebrated toward the end of the seventh century. The liturgical books of the period describe a blessing of palms at the altar on Palm Sunday, but they say nothing about a procession. By the ninth century, however, the procession is clearly attested; it was for this that Theodulf of Orléans composed the hymn "All Glory, Laud, and Honor."

At Rome, meanwhile, the passion narrative was read on Palm Sunday. The nineteen sermons of Pope St. Leo the Great on the Lord's passion make it clear that in the Rome of his day attention was focused on the passion. Seven of these homilies were given on the Sunday itself; the theme was then taken up again on Wednesday. At the end of his third sermon, St. Leo makes it clear that the reading of the passion will begin anew on Wednesday.[7]

For the Romans, then, this Sunday before Easter is the "Sunday of the Lord's Passion." At the end of the seventh century, however, and during the eighth, we find the title "Palm Sunday" given to this day.[8]

But it is only when the Romano-Germanic Pontifical (tenth century) reaches Rome in the eleventh century that the procession of the palms becomes a Roman custom.[9] The ceremony as described in this Pontifical is quite complex, being practically the same as what we used to have in the Roman Missal, before the reform of 1955, for the blessing and procession of palms. In other words, it was a kind of fore-Mass with a reading of the epistle and gospel and several prayers for the blessing of the palms.[10] The procession proper came into use at Rome beginning in the twelfth century.

The Romano-Germanic Pontifical of the twelfth century describes the practice in Gaul or at Mainz at that time. While the churches of Rome were generally receptive to an elaborate blessing of palms and an elaborate procession, the papal church of the Lateran was not. The twelfth-century Pontifical shows that the papal liturgy of the palms was very modest. The pope distributed the palms that were blessed in a chapel of his palace; then the papal retinue went to the Lateran Basilica for the celebration of Mass. Those in the procession carried palms in their hands and sang antiphons; the hymn "All Glory, Laud, and Honor" was sung before the closed door of the Lateran, and when it was opened, the procession entered singing the response "When the people heard that Jesus was entering Jerusalem."[11]

We can see, then, that Rome, or at least the papal liturgy, was reserved with regard to the procession of the palms. The reason is that at Rome there was a greater preoccupation with the passion of Christ.[12]

The Celebration Today

The oldest Roman tradition makes the Sunday before Easter a day for commemorating the passion of the Lord. In the second half of the seventh century, the name "Passion Sunday" was transferred to the Fifth Sunday of Lent, previously known as "Lazarus Sunday," and the Sixth Sunday of Lent came to be called "Palm Sunday" in the seventh and eighth centuries. The recent reform has changed the first five Sundays of Lent once again into a continuous preparation for the paschal mystery of Christ's death and resurrection. The fifth Sunday is no longer "Passion Sunday" and has become again a Sunday that points ahead to the resurrection (Lazarus). Palm Sunday has become once again the Sunday of the passion of the Lord.

The tendency to extend a seasonal liturgy (that of the passion, for example) back into the time preceding that season has affected the whole of Lent. Due to various influences, this penitential season became longer and longer, finally reaching back as far as Septuagesima Sunday, with Lent proper beginning on Ash Wednesday. The liturgical form has now imposed due limits on Lent. The reformers could have gone all the way and had Lent begin, as of old, on the First Sunday of Lent. The difficulty, however, was that everyone, even nonbelievers, had gotten used to Ash Wednesday as a day when all Christians acknowledged themselves to be sinners; it was no longer a day reserved for those obligated to public penance and public reconciliation.

The celebration of the liturgy of the palms has now been restored to a greater simplicity and can, moreover, be carried out in various ways, depending on available resources and the character of the place where the liturgy is being celebrated. The emphasis is on the messianic entry of the Lord into Jerusalem, and the blessing of the palms is quite secondary.

The custom of veiling the cross has now become optional (the origins of the custom were in any case obscure and debated). Since the thought of the cross dominates the entire week, there is no longer any requirement for veiling the cross.

Formerly, the passion of Christ was read on Palm Sunday and on Tuesday and Wednesday of Holy Week. Now it is read only on Palm Sunday (a different synoptic account in each year of the three-year cycle), while the account in St. John's gospel is read every year on Good Friday.

We shall end our discussion of these first days of Holy Week with the penitential celebration on Holy Thursday (below, chap. 19). The reconciliation of penitents, in fact, puts an end to Lent proper. The penitential fast ends on Thursday. The fast on Good Friday (the first day of the Triduum of the dead, buried, and risen Christ) is actually a festive fast; it takes place within the paschal mystery, and the dominant mood is expectation of the Lord's glorious resurrection.

18. TOWARD THE GLORIOUS PASSION OF THE LORD

He Who Comes in the Name of the Lord

As we have seen, the procession with palms was introduced in Rome at a relatively late date. Once it was introduced there, however, the folkloric spirit influenced it just as much as elsewhere. The amount of space that the Romano-Germanic Pontifical of the tenth century gives to the blessing and procession of the palms shows that the people of the day were enamored of these ceremonies, with their dramatic evocation of incidents in the gospel.[1]

The people gather outside the city. There the priest blesses salt and water as the *Hosanna* is intoned; the priest then reads a prayer. Exodus 15:27 and 16:1-10 are read, and the response "The princes of the peoples are gathered together" is sung. The gospel of the entry into Jerusalem is then proclaimed, either from Matthew 21:1-9 or Mark 11:1-10. The priest then blesses the branches, using any one of ten or so prayers, depending on whether the material is palms, boughs of trees, olive branches, etc. When olive branches are used, the blessing expands into a preface.

The palms are sprinkled and incensed, another prayer is said, the palms are distributed, and the procession begins. During the procession those present sing antiphons. When the procession reaches a place where a cross has been set up, the children approach it, spread their coats on the ground, prostrate themselves, and adore the cross while the antiphon "The children of the Hebrews spread their cloaks" is sung. Another group of children follows them and sings *Kyrie eleison* while throwing palms down before the cross; they then prostrate themselves while others sing, "The children of the Hebrews carried branches." At this point, all sing the hymn to Christ the King, "All Glory, Laud, and Honor," composed by Theodulf of Orléans. Psalm 147B (= Ps 147:12-20), "O Jerusalem, glorify the LORD!" is then sung, and the faithful throw flowers and leaves. The bishop prostrates himself before the cross and then sings a prayer, and finally the procession moves on. When it reaches the gates of the city, the faithful sing *Kyrie eleison,* and the antiphon "As the Lord entered the holy city" is intoned. The procession is followed by Mass, during which the clergy and people hold the palms in their hand.

The whole ceremony was evidently conceived as an act of homage to Christ the King, one that we today might find a bit on the boisterous side. It might seem, too, that when this ceremony was introduced into the Roman liturgy, it would push into the background the theme of the glorious passion of Christ. Yet that did not happen.

The reformed liturgy has not hesitated to highlight the procession in honor of Christ the King. The rite for blessing the palms has been much simplified, for the important thing is not the palms themselves but the procession in which the palms are carried. It is worth noting that the new liturgy has kept the custom of gathering for the procession outside the church, where this is feasible. As the faithful hold their palm branches, an antiphon strikes the keynote of the celebration that will follow: "Hosanna to the Son of David; blessed is he who comes in the name of the Lord, the King of Israel. Hosanna in the highest."

The priest then greets the people and gives a short introduction. After a prayer, the palm branches are sprinkled with blessed water in silence. The gospel of Jesus' entry into Jerusalem is then read. Then, to illustrate the gospel, all present walk in procession to the church where Mass will be celebrated. During the procession, an antiphon is sung: "The children of the Hebrews, carrying olive branches," followed by Psalm 24. Thereupon another antiphon is sung: "The children of the Hebrews spread their garments on the road," followed by Psalm 47.

During the procession the following hymn in honor of Christ the King or another suitable hymn is sung:

> Glory and honor and praise be to you, Christ, King and Redeemer,
> to whom young children cried out loving Hosannas with joy.
> Israel's King are you, King David's magnificent offspring;
> you are the ruler who come blest in the name of the Lord.
> Heavenly hosts on high unite in singing your praises;
> men and women on earth and all creation join in.
> Bearing branches of palm, Hebrews came crowding to greet you;
> see how with prayers and hymns we come to pay you our vows.
> They offered gifts of praise to you, so near to your Passion;
> see how we sing this song now to you reigning on high.
> Those you were pleased to accept; now accept our gifts of devotion,
> good and merciful King, lover of all that is good.

In this procession we are to see much more than a mimetic reminder; we are to see the ascent of God's people, and our own ascent, with Jesus to the sacrifice. Moreover, although the procession recalls Christ's triumph at Jerusalem, it leads us here and now to the sacrifice of the cross, as rendered present in the sacrifice of the Mass that is soon to be celebrated. If we were to see in the procession only a crowd waving palms and singing joyous songs, we would miss its real significance in the Roman liturgy. That liturgy looks upon the procession not simply as a commemoration of Christ's entry into Jerusalem or simply as a triumphal march but rather as Christ's journey, together with his people, to Calvary and the great central act of redemption.

Palm Sunday, the first act of Holy Week, is perhaps the part of Holy Week that most sticks in the minds of ordinary people; sometimes there is even a certain amount of superstition mixed in with the celebration. Yet the rich content of the texts, and the frequent opportunities the pastor has of explaining them, can offset errors, and the faithful can be brought to a proper understanding of the paschal mystery that is now to be celebrated for us once again in a solemn manner.

The Glorious Passion for the Sake of the Covenant

On Palm Sunday the account of the passion is read, with the text taken from a different Synoptic Gospel in each year of the three-year cycle.

Some exegetes stress that the Gospel of St. Matthew is to be read against the background of, and with reference to, the story of Moses. They have found so many points of contact with the latter that they believe St. Matthew is deliberately presenting Jesus to us as the new Moses.[2] Now, it is doubtless the case that the choice of St. Matthew's account for Palm Sunday was not motivated by the parallel with Moses and the desire to show Christ as the Person of the new covenant or to bring out the close connection between covenant and passion. The liturgical reformers simply followed the traditional order of the four gospels and had no theological thesis in mind when they assigned Matthew to Palm Sunday. We can nevertheless make use of the Christ-Moses parallel.

The connection between Moses and Christ is already present in the gospel narrative of Christ's entry into Jerusalem. The Midrash Rabbah (Great Midrash) on Qoheleth says: "As the first redeemer, so the last redeemer. As it is said of the first redeemer: And Moses took his wife and his sons and had them ride on an ass (Exod. 4:20), so the last redeemer, for it is said: Lowly and riding on an ass (Zech. 9:9)."[3]

It will be enough for our purpose here to cite the following passage that brings out the clear parallel drawn in Matthew's gospel between Christ and Moses:

> Certain incidents in the passion should be noted. We should mention first the few details given us concerning the betrayal by Judas. Matthew twice (26:14-16; 27:3-10) refers to Zechariah 11:11-13. The prophet had symbolically taken the place of Yahweh, the Shepherd of Israel (11:4) but when confronted with the bad will of the people, he broke off the covenant (11:10). The ruling class (the high priests) valued his efforts— and thus the pastoral action of Yahweh himself— at thirty pieces of silver, which was the price of a slave (see Exod 21:32).
>
> In Jesus this story finds its fulfillment, for he too, though he was the Shepherd of Israel, was valued at thirty pieces of silver. But Judas was stricken with remorse and threw the coins into the sanctuary before going out and hanging himself (Matt 27:5); the high priests then collected the blood-money (Matt 27:6). The passion of Christ, in which the blood so undervalued by the Jews was shed, put an end to the old covenant. . . .
>
> We should also note the numerous references to Psalm 22 in Matthew's account of the passion (cf. 27:35, 39, 43, 46). The psalm ends with the promise that God's rule will extend to the entire universe, in consequence of the sufferings and preaching of the faithful Servant. The connection between the death of Jesus and the transition to a new covenant is brought out in many other ways too. Thus, Jesus is condemned to death and executed because he had predicted the coming of a new temple, which meant the end of the Sinai legislation concerning worship (Matt 26:61; 27:40).[4]

The Church is well aware that she is the people of the new covenant. That is why she has us read from the Letter to the Philippians in the second reading for the Palm Sunday Mass: "Christ Jesus, though he was in the form of God, / did not regard equality with God / something to be grasped. / Rather, he emptied himself, / taking the form of a slave, / coming in human likeness; / and found in human appearance, / he humbled himself, / becoming obedient to the point of death, / even death on a cross" (Phil 2:6-8).

This vision of Christ's passion, which will soon be rendered present anew in our midst, moves the Church deeply. For she knows that

God has supremely exalted this Man who humbled himself in obedience to the point of dying on the cross. God has given him the name that is above every name.

The acclamation before the gospel repeats Philippians 2:8-9. This Christ is truly the Christ of the new covenant. In the acclamation, therefore, we greet this God who came and suffered in order to save us; who bowed in defeat, but in order to be triumphant; who died, but in order to give us eternal life. St. Leo the Great writes as follows in his eleventh sermon on the passion: "What the false witnesses, bloodthirsty leaders, and wicked priests inflicted on the Lord Jesus Christ with the help of a cowardly procurator and an ignorant cohort is something every age must both detest and embrace. For the cross of the Lord was not only cruel in the intention of the Jews, but admirable because of the power of the Crucified."[5]

The Church knows the price her Lord paid for the glory of the resurrection. In the first reading of the Palm Sunday Mass (Isa 50:4-7), she shows us the Christ who did not defend himself against insults. The response to this reading is from Psalm 22 and shows us still another aspect of Christ's suffering as he cries out on the cross: "My God, my God, why have you forsaken me?"

How fitting, then, that Christians should sing, as they approach the communion table, the words, "Father, if this chalice cannot pass without my drinking it, your will be done" (Matt 26:42). For to drink the blood of the new covenant is to accept the Lord's passion in a fully real and concrete way so that we may also share his triumph with him.

The passion according to St. Matthew implicitly compares the mystery of the new covenant and of Christ, its Leader, with the old covenant that Moses had concluded. St. Mark, for his part, tells the story of the passion in a very concrete manner and in a spirit of tragic realism. The Christian feels overwhelmed by the suffering Christ, who remains silent throughout and dies alone and abandoned by the Father. At this moment every Christian, indeed every human being, becomes aware that in one's own earthly life one must meet the same fate: like the Son of Man, one must also go up from Galilee to Jerusalem, ascend the cross, and go down into death. It is the penitential journey that fallen humanity must make, but Christ determined to make it for us all. He made the journey, but it led him to resurrection and to glory at the Father's side. He thus became our Way that leads to salvation and life. His suffering won the forgiveness of our sins, and he showed us the way we must travel in imitation of him in order to make that forgiveness our own.

St. Luke, in his account of the passion, emphasizes the cross as a cause of conversion. He has no hesitation about departing from the Markan scheme. When, for example, he introduces Simon of Cyrene and the women whom Jesus meets along the way of the cross and the other women whom we find on Calvary, he does so because he wants witnesses to the events but much more because he wants the Christian to become more intimately associated with the cross of Christ. Simon carries the cross after Jesus, and every Christian should want to do the same. Luke mentions several groups of nameless devout women: those who weep for Jesus along the way to Calvary (Luke 23:27) and those who had followed Jesus during his ministry and now stand at a distance watching everything (Luke 23:49).

As for the power of the cross, Luke notes that "When all the people who had gathered for this spectacle saw what had happened, they returned home beating their breasts" (Luke 23:48). One of the two criminals crucified with Jesus repents and is saved: "Amen, I say to you, today you will be with me in Paradise" (Luke 23:43). When Jesus dies, the centurion is struck by the accompanying phenomena and says, "This man was innocent beyond doubt" (Luke 23:47).

We may sum up our observations on the various accounts of the passion by saying that St. Matthew presents Christ as seen in the light of faith and in his relation to the Church; St. Mark emphasizes the revolution produced by the events involving Jesus and his disciples; and St. Luke insists on the bond that links the disciples as followers of Jesus and his cross.

The first of the readings at Mass is from the third of the Servant Songs of Isaiah (50:4-7). The words are those of the Servant who listens to the word morning after morning and does not rebel against it but opens his heart to it. Hearing the word means accepting events as they come. Therefore, the Servant submits to being struck on his back and cheek and to having his beard pulled. He does not protect his face against insult and spittle. How can we help seeing in this poem the very story of the Lord's passion? But God comes to the aid of his obedient Servant and does not let him end in disgrace.

Psalm 22, chosen as the responsorial psalm for this Sunday, was on Christ's lips as he hung on the cross: "My God, my God, why have you forsaken me?" The New Testament rightly saw in it the psalm that was supremely transformed by Christ's application of it to himself. The Christian community realized how closely the psalmist's prayer corresponded to what Jesus suffered, and the evangelists made use of the correspondence.

What does Christ's passion mean for us? It must be admitted that, in reflecting on it, devout Christians have often had eyes exclusively for Christ's sufferings. It is true enough, of course, that the prophecies describe Christ as a man of sorrows. It is also undoubtedly very important not to forget that Christ endured suffering and opposition from the world and that he was a suffering witness and martyr. His purpose, after all, in suffering and dying was to establish the reign of God among liberated human beings and to bring into the kingdom a race all of whose wretchedness he had shared, except the wretchedness of sin.

If, however, we look only at the painful side, we shall not understand the passion. The danger here is to have eyes only for details and incidents; it is a danger that the Good Friday liturgy has managed to overcome in the Roman Rite. Surely it is a striking fact that the evangelists, being witnesses also of the resurrection, cannot present the passion to us in terms solely of suffering. They see and understand the passion in the light of the glorious vision of the risen Christ whom they had seen ascend into glory. Their outlook is summed up for us in the words of the Acts of the Apostles: "God has made him both Lord and Messiah, this Jesus whom you crucified" (2:36).

The best means of avoiding a one-sided emphasis on suffering in our approach to the passion is given us in the second reading for Palm Sunday. In it St. Paul tells the Philippians of the self-humbling of Christ, who adopted the rank of a slave, became like other humans, and carried obedience to the length of dying on a cross. But Paul immediately adds, "Because of this, God greatly exalted him" (Phil 2:9). In consequence, at his name all beings in heaven and earth bend their knee, and every tongue proclaims that Jesus is Lord, to the glory of God the Father.

The Palm Sunday liturgy thus gives a complete and rounded theological vision of the mystery of Christ. It tells that this mystery is not a mystery of death alone but a mystery of life that triumphs over death. This vision is important for a proper conception of the spiritual life.

The Day of Jesus' Glorious Death Is Coming

The liturgical celebrations of Monday, Tuesday, and Wednesday continue to show Christ to us as the obedient, suffering Servant but also as the Servant who dies only to be victorious in the end.

On Monday, Tuesday, and Wednesday, the first reading is one of the first three Servant Songs (Isa 42:1-7; 49:1-6; 50:4-9a). All three show a close connection between the Servant's sufferings and experience of abandonment and what happens to Christ. The Christian community understandably had a high regard for these poems.

Each of the poems, however, offers its own particular insight. On Monday, we see Christ as the chosen Servant on whom the Lord makes his Spirit rest (Isa 42:1-7). The Servant's characteristics are carefully described: He will not quench the smoldering wick; he will establish justice in the land, so that the coastlands will wait for his teaching. The Lord has made of him a covenant of the people and a light for the nations. Moreover, as a sign that the kingdom is now present, he will open the eyes of the blind, bring prisoners from their cells, and deliver those who live in darkness from their dungeons. The responsorial psalm for this reading, Psalm 27, applies the theme of light to this Servant who need not fear even if the wicked come at him, because the Lord is his light and salvation and his life's refuge.

The second poem (Isa 49:1-6), which is read on Tuesday, hails the appointment of the Servant by God: "You are my servant, / . . . Israel, through whom I show my glory" (Isa 49:3). The poem also continues a theme of the first song: "It is too little, he says, for you to be my servant, / . . . I will make you a light to the nations, / that my salvation may reach to the ends of the earth" (v. 6). The responsorial psalm, Psalm 71, reasserts the confidence of the Servant, whose God is rock and fortress, a God who in his fidelity hears and saves.

The third poem (Isa 50:4-9a) is read on Wednesday. This is the supreme poem of the passion, in the sense that it describes Christ's suffering in such detail. The responsorial psalm, Psalm 69, speaks of the Christ who is insulted and whose face is covered with shame, but who endures it all in order to praise God. His food is bitter, vinegar is his drink, but the Lord hears his prayer.

The gospel pericopes for these first three days of Holy Week are a preparation for the death of Jesus. The first announces his forthcoming embalmment in the well-known story from John 12:1-11. John tells us how during a meal in the home of Lazarus, the latter's sister Mary anoints the feet of Jesus with perfume. John also reports Judas's criticism; more than that, he emphasizes it and lays bare its motivation. Judas did not suddenly turn into a traitor on this day; there had been a long preparation for the final act, which was but the end result of a deliberately adopted attitude.

Judas's words provide Christ with an opportunity to foretell his own death. The fact that the meal is being taken in Lazarus's home permits John to speak of the attitude of the Jews toward Lazarus. The raising of Lazarus had stupefied the Jews. It was impossible to deny the power Christ had shown in raising this man from the dead and impossible also not to ask some earthshaking questions about the event. Was not the raising of a dead person a sign that the coming kingdom and the coming Messiah were already present? The raising of Lazarus was a prediction that Jesus too would be raised up. The Jews therefore decided to put to death not only Jesus but Lazarus as well.

The gospel for Tuesday (John 13:21-33, 36-38) foretells betrayal, in fact, a twofold betrayal—not only the treachery of Judas, but the inexplicable weakness of Peter: "Amen, amen, I say to you, the cock will not crow before you deny me three times" (v. 38). We should not overlook how this passage links the Supper, the treachery of Judas, and the glorification predicted by Christ (the glorification of both the Son of Man and the Father). Here is summed up the whole meaning of Calvary but also the whole meaning of the Supper that makes Calvary present for the glorification of Father and Son. The passage shows clearly the perspective of the glorious passion; the sufferings of Christ bring glory to the Father and to himself.

The gospel for Wednesday is from St. Matthew (26:14-25). The theme is the same as in Tuesday's gospel, but there is a greater emphasis on the treachery and the curse it brings upon the betrayer.

The prayers of these three days focus on the imitation of Christ in our lives. The passion of Christ that we celebrate should be a source of strength for us (collect, Monday); it should be a wellspring of forgiveness (collect, Tuesday); and it will rescue us from Satan's power and lead us to share in the resurrection (collect, Wednesday).

19. RECONCILIATION

The term "public penance" has frequently led to two misunderstandings. First of all, despite what people may think, public confession of sins has never been the rule in the Church; sins were confessed privately to the bishop, and this confession was always obligatory. History does indeed record examples of public confession, but such confessions were entirely a matter of personal initiative, special signs of profound repentance; they were not an obligatory part of the ancient penitential discipline.

Second, we should not think that alongside this "public" penance there existed another kind of sacramental penance that was private. Except in Ireland from the seventh century on, there was no private, repeated sacramental penance in the Church before the ninth century. Confession was private, but only the penance was public (the reason for it being known to the confessor alone). The distinction between sins in terms of relative seriousness arose less from an analysis of the sin in itself than from the way it was expiated. A sin was serious or mortal when it required canonical penance, a penance that presupposed the intervention of the Church in the process of reconciliation. A sin was venial or light when it could be expiated by private mortifications.[1]

From the end of the first century on, a kind of penitential discipline can be seen taking shape. The person who sinned seriously was, above all else, deprived of the Eucharist. The leaders of the community determined the extent of this excommunication.[2] In the third century, penitential practice became more specific due to social changes. The reconciliation of sinners who were guilty of adultery, fornication, or, above all, apostasy led to controversies that in turn caused the gradual elaboration of a penitential doctrine.

Tertullian (d. 220) exercised a major influence in the controversies. In his treatise on penance[3] he provides a fairly detailed description of the penitential customs of his day. In order to win the forgiveness of serious sins, a person had to spend a period in rather harsh expiation. A confession of sins and a total interior conversion were presupposed; the inner conversion included sorrow and the resolution to amend one's life. The confession itself was not public, but the outward penitential practices required let everyone know that the person was indeed a sinner. Penitents prayed, prostrate and with ashes on their heads, first outside the church, then within it, for a period determined by the bishop, down to the day of reconciliation. This public penance could not be repeated—an extremely harsh practice that lasted until the seventh century. The penitent who sinned again was left to the mercy of God; the Church did not intervene a second time to reconcile.

We observe a decline in the ancient penitential practice from the fourth to the sixth centuries. Yet the ancient discipline that decreed that serious sin required ecclesiastical penance remained in force. The difficulty arose with the principles for classifying the sins that required such penance, as distinct from sins that could be expiated by good works.

In the seventh and eighth centuries, people hardly ever sought reconciliation until they were dying. Canonical penance had become too severe for these later generations and no longer had any place in the life of Christians. In the seventh century, therefore, the Celts and Anglo-Saxons started something new: a kind of penance that could be repeated. Beginning in the eighth century we find in use a book of penances that a priest or bishop could consult in assigning a predetermined penance for various sins. In this new situation, the working principle was that serious but private sins were expiated according to a list in the book of penances; public serious sins still required public penance. In fact, public sinners were also subject to imprisonment.

The Gelasian Sacramentary contains a ritual for reconciliation, and some of its prayers are very beautiful. In brief outline, the ceremonies connected with reconciliation were as follows. On Ash Wednesday, before Mass, the bishop received the penitents and gave them the sackcloth they were to wear; after a series of prayers, the penitents were expelled from the church and locked out until Holy Thursday.[4] On Holy Thursday, they were free to come to the church, where they prostrated themselves at the door. The deacon then asked the bishop to reconcile them. The bishop exhorted the penitents and then spoke the very beautiful prayers of reconciliation.[5]

In the tenth century (950), the Romano-Germanic Pontifical took over the Gelasian ritual and made it more showy and expansive.[6] Later on, at the end of the thirteenth century, William Durand, bishop of Mende, composed a Pontifical containing a ritual of reconciliation that has come down to us only slightly modified in later pontificals.[7] It was this ritual that the modern Pontifical still preserved down to the post–Vatican II reform. The following is a description of the ceremony along with the prayers in it.[8]

The reconciliation of penitents takes place on Holy Thursday. At the beginning of Lent the Church has segregated the penitents from the rest of the community and assigned them a solemn penance. Now, on the day of reconciliation, the bishop comes, surrounded by his clergy, and kneels at the faldstool before the altar while the Litany of the Saints is sung. Meanwhile, the penitents, barefooted, are kneeling at the door of the church, carrying unlit candles in their hands.

When the invocation "All you holy patriarchs and prophets, pray for us" has been sung and the choir has repeated it, there is a pause. The bishop then sends out to the penitents two subdeacons who carry lighted candles and sing, "As I live, says the Lord, I want the sinner not to die but to be converted and live." When the antiphon is finished, they extinguish their candles and return to their place as the litany continues.

When the invocation "All you holy martyrs, pray for us" has been sung and the choir has repeated it, there is another pause, and the bishop once again sends out to the penitents two subdeacons with lighted candles. The subdeacons stand at the door of the church and sing the antiphon "The Lord says: Do penance, for the kingdom of God is at hand." They extinguish their candles, and the penitents return to their former position. The litany then continues down to Lamb of God (exclusively).

The bishop now sends out to the penitents a single elderly deacon holding a tall lighted candle. He stands at the door of the church and sings the antiphon "Lift up your heads, for your redemption is at hand." The penitents then light their candles from the deacon's, and the deacon returns with his candle still lit. The Lamb of God and other invocations are then sung to the end of the litany.

The bishop stands up; the clergy and ministers also stand and process before the bishop with cross, censer, and candles, and the whole procession leaves the choir. A kind of throne has been set up at the center of the church; the clergy line up along both sides of the nave, facing the door. Then the archdeacon, at the threshold, says aloud, in a reading tone, to the penitents standing before the door, "Be silent and listen attentively." Then, turning to the bishop, he says, still in a reading tone:

> Venerable Pontiff, the acceptable time is at hand, the day of God's mercy and humanity's salvation, when death is destroyed and eternal life begins; the day when new shoots are to be planted in the vineyard of the Lord of Hosts so that the ancient curse may be removed. For, although there is no moment when God's goodness and love are absent, now in his mercy his forgiveness of sins is more abundant, and he more effectively raises up those who are reborn through grace. Now our community is increased by the reborn, our numbers augmented by those returning. The waters cleanse and so do tears; therefore we rejoice at those who are now being called, and our joy is great when sinners are forgiven. Your servants have fallen into various sins through neglect of the heavenly commandments and through transgression of approved ways. Now, humbled and prostrate before you, they cry out to you with the prophet, "Like our fathers we have sinned, we have acted wickedly; have mercy on us, Lord, have mercy on us!"
>
> Not in vain have they heard the words of the gospel, "Blessed are those who mourn, for they shall be comforted." As Scripture bids them, they have eaten the bread of sorrow and dampened their pillow with tears; they have afflicted their hearts with grief, their bodies with fasting, so that they might regain their lost health of soul. Penance is the extraordinary remedy that is useful to each individual and helpful to the community.

The bishop with his ministers now goes to the door of the church (the choir of the clergy stay where they are). Standing in the doorway, the bishop addresses the penitents in a brief exhortation on God's mercy and his promise of forgiveness; he tells them how they will soon be brought back into the Church and how they must live therein. Then he sings the antiphon "Come, come, come, children, listen to me and I will teach you the fear of the Lord." Then the deacon takes his place beside the penitents and says in their name, "Let us kneel," and "Let us stand." The bishop sings the same antiphon three times in all, the deacon following it each time with "Let us kneel" and "Let us stand."

The bishop enters the church and stands at a suitable distance from the door. The archdeacon intones an antiphon, and the choir finishes it: "Look to him, and be radiant; so your faces shall never be ashamed," and adds Psalm 34 (33), "I will bless the LORD at all times."

The penitents meanwhile enter the church and kneel before the bishop; they remain there until the psalm and antiphon are finished. The archpresbyter then says in a reading tone:

Bishop and successor of the apostles, restore to these people what was corrupted under the devil's influence. With the help of your prayers and through the grace of divine reconciliation, draw them close to God so that while earlier they displeased him by their perverse actions, they may now happily please him in the land of the living, once he who caused their death has been overcome.

The bishop asks the archpresbyter, "Do you believe them worthy of reconciliation?" He replies, "I know and attest that they are worthy." Another deacon then says to the penitents, "Stand." They stand up, and the bishop takes the hand of one of them, while all the others link hands to form a chain.

The archpresbyter says in a loud voice, "I know my iniquities. *R.:* And my sins are always before me. *V.:* Turn your gaze from my sins. *R.:* And wipe away all my iniquities. *V.:* Give me again the joy of your salvation. *R.:* And strengthen in me your spirit that makes me holy."

The bishop then intones an antiphon, which is taken up by the choir: "I tell you, the angels of God rejoice over a single sinner who repents." Now he draws the person whose hand he is holding (and he in turn the others) and leads him to the throne that is set up at the center of the church. There he stops and, turning to the penitents, who kneel down, begins the antiphon "My son, you should rejoice because your brother was dead and is alive again, was lost and has been found."

He then prays: "May the almighty and eternal God absolve you from every bond of sin so that you may have eternal life and live: through Jesus Christ our Lord." Then, joining his hands at his breast, he continues in a lower tone:

It is truly right . . . to praise you, Lord, through Jesus Christ, your Son, whom you, almighty Father, willed should be born in a mysterious way so that he might pay the debt Adam owed to you, eternal Father, and that he might destroy our death by his own, bear our wounds in his own body, and wash away our stains with his blood. Thus we who had been laid low by the hatred of the ancient enemy might be raised up by your Son's mercy. Through him, Lord, we humbly ask and beseech you to hear our prayers for the sins of others, since we cannot adequately petition you for our own. Therefore, most merciful Lord, in your wonted kindness call back to yourself these servants of yours whom sin has separated from you. You did not scorn the guilty Ahab when he humbled himself, but remitted the punishment he deserved. You accepted Peter's tears and afterward gave him the keys of the heavenly kingdom. When the thief confessed his guilt, you promised him the rewards of the kingdom. Therefore, merciful Lord, accept these men and women for whom we pray, and restore them to the bosom of the Church so that the enemy may not triumph over them. Let your Son, who is equal to you, reconcile them to you, cleanse them of all their sins, admit them to his holy Supper, and so strengthen them with his Flesh and Blood that he may lead them into the heavenly kingdom when this present life has run its course: Jesus Christ, your Son and our Lord.

When the preface is finished, the bishop prostrates himself at his place, the ministers on the carpet, the clergy and people on the floor, while the cantor begins the antiphon, and the choir finishes it and adds the psalms. "Create a pure heart for me, O God; / renew a steadfast spirit within me" (Ps 51:12). The psalms are Psalms 51, 56, and 57. The bishop now stands and turns to the penitents, praying, "Lord, have mercy on us. Christ, have mercy on us. Lord, have mercy. Our Father . . . " Then, after the introductory versicles, he says a series of prayers:

Let us pray. Hear our prayers, Lord, and in your mercy listen to me, though I am the first to need your forgiveness, for through no merits of my own but solely through your grace I have been appointed minister of this reconciliation. Grant me confidence in carrying out your work, and do you, through my ministry, accomplish your loving will. Through Jesus Christ . . .

Let us pray. Lord, grant that these servants of yours may produce worthy fruits of repentance so that after departing through sin from the purity of your Church, they may be forgiven and restored. Through Jesus Christ . . .

Let us pray. Lord, I implore you, by the mercy proper to your Majesty and your Name, that you would pardon these your servants who confess their sins and misdeeds, and that you would release them from the bonds of their past sins. You carried the lost sheep back to the fold on your shoulder; you were pleased by the tax collector's confession and listened to his prayer. Lord, do you also have mercy on these servants of yours and in your goodness hear their prayers so that they may continue to weep and confess their sins, and may quickly experience your mercy. Then, given access again to your holy altar, they may be renewed in hope of eternal glory in heaven: you who live and reign . . .

Let us pray. Lord, in your goodness you created the human race and in your mercy you created it anew. When humanity was cast forth from eternal life by the trickery of Satan, you redeemed it with the blood of your only Son. Give life now to these servants of yours, whom you do not wish to see dead. You let them go when they strayed; take them back now that they have changed their ways. Let their tearful sighs move you to mercy, Lord; heal their wounds, reach out your saving hand to them as they lie downcast, lest your Church be deprived of any part of its Body and your flock suffer any loss, and lest the enemy boast of a loss to your family or the second death take possession of those who had been reborn in the bath of salvation. To you, then, Lord, do we humbly pour out our prayers and tears. Spare those who confess to you, and grant that they may weep for their sins during this mortal life so that on the day of fearful judgment they may not receive the sentence of eternal damnation nor experience the terrible darkness and the whistling flames. Let them turn from error to the true path. Let them be wounded no more but retain forever in its fullness the gift of your grace and the renewal your mercy brings: through Jesus Christ . . .

Let us pray. Kind and merciful God, in your great goodness you wipe away the sins of the repentant and forgive their past misdeeds. Look now upon these servants of yours and hear their prayer as they ask with sincere hearts for the forgiveness of all their sins. Loving Father, make new in them what their earthbound weakness has corrupted or Satan's trickery has profaned. Restore them through complete forgiveness to the unity of your Church's Body. Have mercy, Lord, on their groans; have mercy on their tears. Admit to the sacrament of reconciliation these servants who trust only in your mercy: through Jesus Christ . . .

Let us pray. We humbly implore your divine Majesty, almighty, ever-living God, to bestow the grace of forgiveness on these servants, who are worn out from long and difficult penance. Let them put on the wedding garment and be admitted once again to the royal table from which they were excluded for their sins: through Jesus Christ . . .

[Absolution] Let us pray. May our Lord Jesus Christ, who wiped away the sins of the whole world by handing himself over and shedding his pure blood, and who said to his disciples: "Whatever you shall bind on earth will be bound also in heaven, and whatever you loose on earth will be loosed also in heaven," and who willed that I, unworthy and sinful though I am, should be one of these disciples and his minister—may he, through the intercession of Mary the Mother of God, St. Michael the Archangel, St. Peter the Apostle, who received the power to bind and loose, and all the saints, absolve you, by the power of his sacred blood that was shed for the forgiveness of sins, and through my ministry, from all your sins of negligent thought, word, and action, and may he lead you, freed from the bonds of your sins, to the kingdom of heaven: through the same Jesus Christ . . .

Then the bishop sprinkles the penitents with holy water and incenses them, saying, "Rise up, sleeper! Rise from the dead, and Christ will enlighten you!"

Finally, he grants them forgiveness. Then, with hands raised and extended over them, he says, "By the prayers and merits of Blessed Mary ever Virgin, St. Michael the Archangel, St. John the Baptist, the holy apostles Peter and Paul, and all the saints, may almighty God have mercy on you, forgive you your sins, and bring you to everlasting life. R. Amen.

"May the almighty and merciful Lord grant you pardon, absolution, and remission of all your sins. R. Amen."

At the end he blesses them: "May almighty God bless you, the Father and the Son and the Holy Spirit. R. Amen."

This ritual of reconciliation is unknown to most Christians, and yet it can help us to grasp what the sacrament of penance really is. As a way of pulling together the elements of the ceremony, we need only sum up the rich insights provided by the prayers.

The bishop prays for himself as minister of this sacrament, being fully aware that he who acts as God's instrument is himself a sinner and that he is subject to weakness like the others whose misdeeds he forgives (first in the final series of prayers). The second prayer is more general in character, asking for the restoration to the Church of those whose sins had excluded them from the company of the faithful. The confession of sin leads to pardon, and pardon in turn gives sinners access to the holy altar and allows them to hope for eternal glory in heaven (third prayer).

Forgiveness, then, is life giving. The Lord has not, in fact, abandoned sinners even for a moment. The Church is not to be deprived of one of her members, nor is the second death to lay hold of those who have been reborn. Confession, followed by forgiveness that is intended to be definitive, rescues sinners from a final condemnation (fourth prayer). This pardon will make them once again full members of the ecclesial body (fifth prayer). They will don again the wedding garment and be readmitted to the royal table from which they had been excluded (sixth prayer).

Notable throughout is the emphasis on the community aspect of reconciliation. Sin is an attack on the flock of Christ; reconciliation, on the contrary, means growth for the Church. Penance is seen as closely connected with the paschal mystery of death and resurrection, light and life. The prayers, scriptural in their inspiration, also point out the parallelism between baptism and penance. The role of bishop or priest is carefully indicated, especially that of the bishop, who stands for Christ and the apostles and who in the name of the Lord welcomes sinners back after first urging them to return to the Church. Above all, penance allows the forgiven sinners to take their place once more at the eucharistic banquet, in which the Body of Christ renews and restores them and gives them once again the pledge of eternal life.

A careful and meditative reading of this ceremony (once we clear away the secondary bits of theatricality that it picked up over the centuries) would enable many Christians of our day to acquire a more accurate understanding of penance. The ceremony could also serve as the basis for penance services of a kind that might well fill in for the former Holy Thursday usage. Such services would bring out the fact that confession of sins and absolution from them restore people to their state of new birth or establish them more firmly in it if it had not been entirely lost. We would realize more fully that the new birth of baptism gives us the right to sit at the common table of the eucharistic banquet and that absolution restores us to our full place in the people of God. These truths are essential elements in the paschal mystery as applied to us, and they were brought home to Christians in an especially striking way in the ancient Holy Thursday ritual of reconciliation.

It is because of Christ's death and triumph over death that we can constantly renew the new covenant with the Father, through the Son. We can, at the climactic moment of the Easter Vigil, eat the Bread and drink the Blood of the new and eternal covenant. Not only does the sacrament of penance derive its efficacy from the blood of the Lord; it also gives us renewed access to the eucharistic table, where the feast of victory and resurrection is celebrated. Penance is thus closely connected with the painful yet triumphant paschal mystery; it is indissolubly linked to baptism and the Eucharist; it renews the Christian people and strengthens the structure of God's people as realized in the Church.

Penance, then, is to be seen first and foremost as bound up with the presence of the risen Christ. All the actions that make up the sacrament of penance have as their focal point the Christ who "lives forever to make intercession" for us (Heb 7:25), the Christ who is always present with and praying for his Church. The repentant Christian stands before the Christ who is at the Father's right hand. It is in his presence that Christians should speak of sin and repentance, and it is in his presence that the Lenten liturgy speaks of it. Sinners must undergo conversion; that is, they must "lose their self-centeredness and [must] focus on God in Jesus Christ. Conversion is one's entrance into the mystery of Christ's death and Resurrection, because it is God in Jesus Christ who enables one to repent, to reunite with him, to surrender oneself and to plunge anew into eternal life."[9]

All genuine repentance implies an intense desire to enter into a full and unreserved dialogue with God. This dialogue once involved God and Christ; now it involves God and the Church, with each Christian sharing in the dialogue in and through the Church. The penitential outlook, then, is not solely an entering into oneself; it also supposes another speaker, someone who listens, answers, and forgives. Repentant sinners engage in a dialogue. The dialogue in turn helps them face the struggle that characterizes the whole period between the resurrection of Christ, in whom we are certain that salvation has been won for us once and for all, and the return of Christ, when the salvation thus won will become definitively ours.

"[Y]ou know the time," says St. Paul (Rom 13:11). We have been saved in hope; we have the root of salvation in us through baptism into the death of Christ; but we still live in a period of conflict. The whole of the Lenten liturgy insists on this last fact and endeavors to help us understand it more fully. The activity of repentance is, however, also linked in the liturgy with the eschatological period and the promised return of Christ that is the foundation of our hope for salvation. We should recall here how the entire fourth week of Lent looks forward to the return of Christ and to the heavenly Jerusalem. In her expressions of repentance, the Church always looks to this return of the Lord and to the coming of the new Jerusalem.

It is against this eschatological background that we can discern the real mind of the Church concerning penance, as reflected in the seasonal liturgy of Lent.

Repentance always takes place in the Church and with reference to the risen Christ seated at the Father's right hand and present here and now with his Church. Penitents stand before this Christ, but they do so in the Church and in the consciousness of Christ's infinite power of intercession. The aim of the penitent is to turn away from sin, to struggle with it, and to be converted. The Good Shepherd cannot resist the sinner's sincere and humble faith, and he grants his forgiveness. Penance is not a static thing but an onward journey

toward the heavenly Jerusalem, where the penitent will be transformed by the glory of the risen Christ.

In his commentary on the gospel of the widow of Naim, St. Ambrose writes:

> Even if there be serious sin that you cannot wash away yourself by tears
> of repentance, let Mother Church weep for you, for she intercedes for
> each individual like a widowed mother for her only son. . . . Let this
> devoted mother mourn, then, and let the crowd stand by. . . . Presently
> you will rise up from the dead; presently you will be liberated from the
> tomb.[10]

It is possible to use at least some of the texts from this Holy Thursday ritual of reconciliation by taking their themes and adapting
them to our mentality. In any case, it seemed important, at the end
of our reflections on Lent, to show how the Church saw the sacrament of penance as the climax of the season's asceticism in its
various aspects.

20. THE ONGOING RENEWAL OF CREATION

The Chrism of Salvation

It seems that in Gaul, until the end of the seventh century, the blessing of the holy oils took place during Lent rather than on Holy Thursday. The blessing appears in the Gelasian Sacramentary toward the end of the seventh century, but the section in which it appears was redacted in Gaul.[1] Yet, despite the clear influence of Gallican custom, the blessing of the holy oils and of chrism is originally Roman.

From the theological point of view, the blessing of the holy oils and the consecration of the chrism can be linked to the Eucharist. This interesting theology, which makes all the sacraments depend on the Eucharist, cannot, however, be regarded as the reason why the blessing of the oils and chrism was put on Holy Thursday. It seems, rather, that the reason was purely practical: the oils and chrism would be needed for baptism and confirmation during the Easter Vigil; therefore, there had to be a ceremony of blessing.

The Holy Week reform of 1955 restored the chrism Mass. The origin of the various formularies that make it up is not clear. Some scholars claim the prayers cannot have originated in Rome;[2] others maintain that some, at least, may have been Roman.[3] Moreover, the chrism Mass originally had no Liturgy of the Word, but the reason for this is again not clear. Perhaps the liturgy of reconciliation preceded this eucharistic celebration and took the place of the Liturgy of the Word. Perhaps what we have is a vestige of the ancient discipline according to which there was neither a Liturgy of the Word nor a eucharistic liturgy on Thursdays; when, finally, the Eucharist began to be celebrated on Holy Thursday, no one thought of beginning it with a Liturgy of the Word.

Before the reform of 1955, the blessing of the oils and the consecration of the chrism took place apart from Mass.

The reform initiated by the Second Vatican Council permits putting the blessing of oils and consecration of chrism before the preparation of the gifts and after the renewal by priests of their commitment to service. Here we glimpse a novelty introduced in the present reform: The blessing of oils and consecration of chrism are an occasion for bringing all the clergy together with their bishop and for introducing into the ceremony a renewal of priestly promises. The eucharistic celebration in the evening will again highlight the unity of the priesthood.

The new chrism Mass emphasizes this "feast of priesthood" element;[*] the texts selected for the readings bring out the traits of one who has been chosen to exercise priestly functions. The texts are easily grasped, and, in addition, we have met some of them already. The first reading is from Isaiah (61:1-3a, 6a, 8b-9). The theme is familiar and quite suited to the present celebration as now conceived: "The Spirit of the Lord GOD is upon me, / because the LORD has anointed me; / He has sent me to bring glad tidings to the lowly / . . . To give them oil of gladness." The gospel pericope fits in perfectly with this first reading, because in it Christ reads this very passage from Isaiah in the synagogue at Nazareth and claims that it refers to himself (Luke 4:16-21). The responsorial psalm, Psalm 89, sings of the anointing of David, God's servant. The second reading, from the Revelation of St. John (1:5-8), is the one most explicitly focused on the object of the celebration: Christ has "made us into a Kingdom, priests for his God and Father."

The renewal of priestly promises provides an opportunity for recalling the theology of priesthood. Ordination was accepted out of love for Christ and in order to serve the Church. Priests are stewards of the mysteries of God and exercise their stewardship by preaching the word and celebrating the Eucharist and other sacraments. The bishop's office is that of the apostles; amid priests and faithful he holds the place of Christ, who is Priest, Good Shepherd, Teacher, and Servant of all.

When it is time to bless the oils and chrism, the bishop blesses the oil of the sick and then the oil of catechumens, and finally he consecrates the chrism.

---

[*] Nocent's interpretation is overly influenced by the renewal of priestly promises. All the text he cites have more to do with oil than priesthood.

Sacred Signs

The blessings of elements that are to serve humanity in a new way for the glory of God are a manifestation of the fact that Christ's work in this world has been effective. God is constantly acting through elements made for humanity; through them he is accomplishing the salvation, not of our soul alone, but of soul and body together, of the whole human person. Our entire being is gradually being transformed and re-created according to the image God dreamed of when he first created the world. We are becoming once again the kings of the created world. We are once again becoming prophets and priests, spreading the Good News of Christ's death and resurrection throughout a world that is still undergoing its reconstruction, still acquiring its true meaning. Because of the death and resurrection of Christ, these created elements can now be a means of communicating to us the grace of the Holy Spirit, whom the heavenly Christ is constantly sending to us.

We are now caught up into the mighty action of the Three Persons: the Father who created us and loved us enough to send his Son to us; the Son whose brothers and sisters we now are, because we are adopted of his Father; and the Spirit who is sent to us by the Son and constantly makes us grow into a more perfect likeness to the Father. Not we alone, but the whole of creation is being reformed and brought to fulfillment; the holy oils manifest the extent to which this reformation has already succeeded. Created elements now serve God's glory by contributing to the life of humanity and to its transformation into a monarch who is invited to sit at the banquet table on the last day.

All this is possible because of Christ's sacrifice. Subhuman creatures have had their original power restored to them, and they now act upon our bodies, which have been corrupted by sin and have become the dwelling place of evil powers bent on destroying the body's true being. These elements, by the power that the Spirit communicates to them, act upon our persons, and we gradually recover our true powers; we see that we can become masters of ourselves and regain the balance that should be ours. We are healed and capable of living in God.

Our soul and body are not two separate, isolated spheres. Our body became mortal because our soul was fatally wounded by sin. The sacrament of chrism consolidates the union and unity of soul and body. In this sacrament a created substance becomes capable once again, through the power of the Spirit, of exercising its true role, which is to serve humans and to do so by touching them and healing them in body and soul. More accurately, it is by touching the soul through the body that it heals the soul and thereby the body as well.

We should reread the texts for the blessing of the oils. They are rich in content and can bring home to us a truth that is a source of intense joy: the truth, the certainty, that salvation is ours even now.

21. LENT IN THE LITURGIES OF THE PAST

In accordance with our usual plan, we shall here look briefly at the Lenten liturgy as we find it in the early Roman liturgy and in some of the non-Roman liturgies. We emphasize again that our purpose is neither idle curiosity nor the study of the past for its own sake but to indicate texts that may prove helpful and for the knowledge of other viewpoints.

1. Lent in the Roman Tradition

We have chosen to reproduce in the table only the most characteristic lists; to give a list for all the divergent lectionaries would occupy far too much space and would not be in keeping with our purpose here.

As the list makes clear, a well-established tradition was reflected in these various lectionaries. The older books show the absence of a Thursday liturgy, which began to be celebrated only in the eighth century. These older books likewise show no liturgy for the Second Sunday of Lent; the reason for this is that the Ember Day Mass was celebrated during the night between Saturday and Sunday, and consequently there was no further celebration on Sunday.

We can see that the gospel pericopes found in the Roman Missal that was in use until recently were already present in the Würzburg Evangeliary and passed from there to the Murbach Lectionary and the Roman Missal of 1570. By the time of the Würzburg Evangeliary (ca. 645), the celebration of the scrutinies had already been shifted to weekdays.

		Würzburg Epistolary[1]	*Würzburg Evangeliary*[2]	*Murbach Lectionary*[3]	*Roman Missal of 1570*
	Ash Wednesday	Joel 2:12-13		Joel 2:12-13	Joel 2:12-19
			Matt 6:16-21	Matt 6:16-21	Matt 6:16-21
	Thursday			Isa 38:1-6	Isa 38:1-6
				Matt 8:5-13	Matt 8:5-13
	Friday	Isa 58:1-9		Isa 58:1-9	Isa 58:1-9
			Matt 5:43–6:4	Matt 5:43–6:4	Matt 5:43–6:4
	Saturday			Isa 58:9-14	Isa 58:9-14
				Mark 6:47-56	Mark 6:47 56
First Week	Sunday	2 Cor 6:1-10		2 Cor 6:1-10	2 Cor 6:1-10
			Matt 4:1-11	Matt 4:1-11	Matt 4:1-11
	Monday	Ezek 34:11-16		Ezek 34:11-16	Ezek 34:11-16
			Matt 25:37-46	Matt 25:37-46	Matt 25:31-46
	Tuesday	Isa 55:6-11		Isa 55:6-11	Isa 55:6-11
			Matt 21:10-17	Matt 21:10-17	Matt 21:10-17
	Wednesday (Ember Day)	Exod 24:12-18		Exod 24:12-18	Exod 24:12-18
		1 Kgs 19:3-8		1 Kgs 19:3-8	1 Kgs 19:3-8
			Matt 12:18-50	Matt 12:18-50	Matt 12:18-50
	Thursday			Ezek 18:1-9	Ezek 18:1-9
				John 8:31-47	John 8:31-47
	Friday (Ember Day)	Ezek 18:20-28		Ezek 18:20-28	Ezek 18:20-28
			John 5:1-15	John 5:1-15	John 5:1-15
	Saturday (Ember Day)				Deut 26:12-19
					Deut 11:22-25
					Sir 36:1-10
					Dan 3:47-51
					1 Thess 5:14-23
			Matt 17:1-9	Matt 17:1-9	Matt 17:1-9

Second Week	Sunday	1 Thess 4:1-7		1 Thess 4:1-7	1 Thess 4:1-7
				Mark 1:40-45	Matt 17:1-9
	Monday	Dan 9:15-19		Dan 9:15-19	Dan 9:15-19
			John 8:21-29	John 8:21-29	John 8:21-29
	Tuesday	1 Kgs 17:8-16		1 Kgs 17:8-16	1 Kgs 17:8-16
			Matt 23:1-12	Matt 23:1-12	Matt 23:1-12
	Wednesday	Esth 13:9-17		Esth 13:8-17	Esth 13:8-11, 15-17
			Matt 20:17-28	Matt 20:17-28	Matt 20:17-28
	Thursday			Jer 17:5-10	Jer 17:5-10
				John 5:30-47	Luke 16:19-31
	Friday	Gen 37:6-22		Gen 37:6-22	Gen 37:6-22
			Matt 21:33-46	Matt 21:33-46	Matt 21:33-46
	Saturday	Gen 27:6-39		Gen 27:6-39	Gen 27:6-40
			Luke 15:11-32	Luke 15:11-32	Luke 15:11-32
Third Week	Sunday	Eph 5:1-9		Eph 5:1-9	Eph 5:1-9
			Luke 11:14-28	Luke 11:14-28	Luke 11:14-28
	Monday	2 Kgs 5:1-15		2 Kgs 5:1-15	2 Kgs 5:1-15
			Luke 4:23-30	Luke 4:23-30	Luke 4:23-30
	Tuesday	2 Kgs 4:1-7		2 Kgs 4:1-7	2 Kgs 4:1-7
			Matt 18:15-22	Matt 18:15-22	Matt 18:15-22
	Wednesday	Exod 20:12-24		Exod 20:12-24	Exod 20:12-24
			Matt 15:1-20	Matt 15:1-20	Matt 15:1-20
	Thursday			Jer 7:1-17	Jer 7:1-17
				John 6:27-35	John 6:27-35
	Friday	Num 20:1-13		Num 20:1-13	Num 20:1-3, 6-13
			John 4:6-42	John 4:6-42	John 4:5-42
	Saturday	Dan 13:1-62		Dan 13:1-62	Dan 13:1-9, 15-17
			John 8:1-11	John 8:1-11	John 8:1-11

Fourth Week	Sunday	Gal 4:22-31			Gal 4:22-31	Gal 4:22-31
			John 6:1-15		John 6:1-15	John 6:1-15
	Monday	1 Kgs 3:16-28			1 Kgs 3:16-28	1 Kgs 3:16-28
			John 2:13-25		John 2:13-25	John 2:13-25
	Tuesday	Exod 32:7-14			Exod 32:7-14	Exod 32:7-14
			John 7:14-31		John 7:14-31	John 7:14-31
	Wednesday	Ezek 36:23-28			Ezek 36:23-28	Ezek 36:23-28
		Isa 1:16-19			Isa 1:16-39	Isa 1:16-19
			John 9:1-38		John 9:1-38	John 9:1-38
	Thursday				2 Kgs 4:25-38	2 Kgs 4:25-38
					John 5:17-39	John 5:17-39
	Friday	1 Kgs 17:17-24			1 Kgs 17:17-24	1 Kgs 17:17-24
			John 11:1-45		John 11:1-45	John 11:1-45
	Saturday	Isa 49:8-15			Isa 49:8-15	Isa 49:8-15
		Isa 55:1-11			Isa 55:1-11	
			John 8:12-20		John 8:12-20	John 8:46-59
Fifth Week	Sunday	Heb 9:11-15			Heb 9:11-15	Heb 9:11-15
			John 8:46-59		John 8:46-59	John 8:46-59
	Monday	Jonah 3:1-10			Jonah 3:1-10	Jonah 3:1-10
			John 7:32-39		John 7:32-39	John 7:32-39
	Tuesday	Dan 14:27-42			Dan 14:27-42	Dan 14:27-42
			John 7:1-13		John 7:1-13	John 7:1-13
	Wednesday	Lev 19:11-19			Lev 19:11-19	Lev 19:1-2, 11-19, 25
			John 10:22-38		John 10:23-38	John 10:22-38
	Thursday				Dan 3:34-45	Dan 3:25, 34-45
					John 7:40-53	Luke 7:36-50
	Friday	Jer 17:13-18			Jer 17:13-18	Jer 17:13-18
			John 11:17-54		John 11:17-54	John 11:47-54
	Saturday				Jer 18:18-23	Jer 18:18-23
					John 6:53-71	John 12:10

Holy Week	Palm Sunday				Matt 21:1-9
		Phil 2:5-11		Phil 2:5-11	Phil 2:5-11
			Matt 26:2–27:66	Matt 26:2–27:66	Matt 26:2–27:60
	Monday	Isa 50:5-10		Isa 50:5-10	Isa 50:5-10
				Zech 11:12-13, 10-11a; 13:6-9	
			John 12:1-36	John 12:1-23	John 2:1-9
	Tuesday	Jer 11:18-20		Jer 11:18-20	Jer 11:18-20
		Wis 2:12-22		Wis 2:12-22	
			John 13:1-32	John 12:24-43	Mark 14:32–15:46
	Wednesday	Isa 62:11–63:7		Isa 62:11–63:7	Isa 62:11–63:7
		Isa 53:1-12		Isa 53:1-12	Isa 53:1-12
			Luke 22:1–23:53	Luke 22:1–23:53	Luke 22:39–23:53

	Northern Italy Aquileia Evangeliary[4]	Southern Italy Beneventan Liturgy [5]
First Sunday	Temptation of Christ; Matt 4:1-11	
Second Sunday	Sell your possessions, give alms, be ready; Luke 12:32-34	The Samaritan woman; John 4:5-42
Third Sunday	Jesus, Light of the world; before Abraham; John 8:12-59	John 8:12-59
Fourth Sunday	The man born blind; John 9:1	John 9:1-38
Fifth Sunday	Raising of Lazarus; John 11:1	John 11:1-45

2. Lent Elsewhere in Italy

Other Italian traditions show different readings that had probably been used at Rome before the time of the Würzburg Lectionary and Evangeliary. We shall pause for a moment only on two sections of the country and limit our examples to the Sundays (see chart, above).

It should be noted that in the Beneventan liturgy, the gospel of the Samaritan woman is read on the second Sunday, while on the third the gospel is the rather long passage on Jesus as the Light of the world who is before Abraham was. The introduction of the Ember Days, however, doubtless caused the gospel of the second Sunday to be suppressed, since the Ember Day liturgy was celebrated during Saturday night, and the Sunday had no liturgy of its own.

3. Lent at Milan

The only witnesses to the Ambrosian liturgy that we shall call upon here are the Sacramentary of Bergamo[6] and the Ambrosian Missal.[7] Once again, we shall limit ourselves to the Sundays. For the most part, the Bergamo Sacramentary repeats the readings used in the earlier liturgical books of the Milanese rite.

Readings

	Sacramentary of Bergamo	*Ambrosian Missal*
First Sunday		Isa 57:21–58:12
	2 Cor 6:1-10	2 Cor 6:1-10
	Matt 4:1-11; Temptation of Christ	Matt 4:1-11
Second Sunday		Exod 20:1-24
	Eph 1:15-23	Eph 1:15-23
	John 4:5-42; Samaritan woman	John 4:5-42
Third Sunday	1 Thess 2:20–3:8	1 Thess 2:20–3:8
		Exod 34:1-10
	John 8:31-59; Jesus and Abraham	John 8:31-59
Fourth Sunday		Exod 34:23–35:1
	1 Thess 4:1-12	1 Thess 4:1-11
	John 9:1-38; Man born blind	John 9:1-38
Fifth Sunday		Exod 14:15-31
	Eph 5:15-22	Eph 5:15-22
	John 11:1-45; Lazarus	John 11:1-45
Palm Sunday		Isa 53:1-12
	2 Thess 2:15–3:5	2 Thess 2:14–3:5
	John 11:55–12:11; Anointing at Bethany	John 11:55–12:11

Prayers

The Milanese liturgy offers us some fine prefaces. Here is the one in the Bergamo Sacramentary for the First Sunday of Lent:

> Through Christ our Lord, who nourishes the faith, deepens the hope, and intensifies the love of those who fast. For he is the true and life-giving Bread, being the substance of eternity and the food of virtue. Your Word, through whom all things were made, is the Bread not only of human souls but of the very angels themselves. Sustained by this Bread, your servant Moses, when about to receive the Law, fasted forty days and nights, abstaining from earthly food so that he might be better able to taste your sweetness. That is why he did not feel bodily hunger, but forgot about material food. The sight of your glory enlightened him, and under the influence of the Spirit of God your word nourished him. You never cease to give us this same Bread, Jesus Christ, and you exhort us to hunger for it constantly.[8]

Each day of Lent has its own special preface, and it is often quite rich in content. Let us look at the preface for the second Sunday, a day on which, in this liturgy, the gospel of the Samaritan woman was read: "Through Christ our Lord, who, in order to help us grasp the mystery of his humility, sat wearied by the well. There he who had bestowed faith on the Samaritan woman asked her for a drink of water."[9]

The preface for Tuesday of the third week reads as follows: "You do not want souls to perish, nor do you always pass judgment straightway on sinners and their misdeeds, but you move them to repentance and wait for them. Turn away from us the wrath we deserve, and pour out upon us the mercy we ask. May we be purified by the holy fast and joined to the assembly of your chosen ones."[10]

4. Lent in Gaul

For the Gallican tradition our table lists the collections whose data are the most valuable to us. We have not listed the Lectionary of Luxeuil because its data are too sparse; the lectionary is fragmentary and gives only a few pericopes. The same holds for the Wolfenbüttel palimpsest, which gives the readings only for the first Sunday and four weekdays.

To be noted especially is the originality of a number of choices in these lectionaries from Merovingian Gaul. The variety is most interesting. On the other hand, the connection of these readings with the Lenten season is not always evident at first sight. Not to be overlooked is the reading from the discourse on the bread of life (John 6) in the Evangeliary of Trier.

5. Lent in Spain

Readings

The liturgical books provide abundant information on the readings in the Lenten liturgy of Spain. For the most part, the lectionaries copy and repeat one another. Nonetheless, for the sake of the reader who has no access to these sources, we list the readings from several of the lectionaries, just as we did above for the early Roman liturgy. We list only the readings for the Sundays.

Other manuscripts, such as the *Liber commicus* of Carcassone (800) or the Madrid Bible (ninth to tenth centuries), list the readings only for weekdays.

	Bobbio Epistolary[11]	Bobbio Missal[12]	Sélestat Lectionary[13]		Evangeliary of St. Kilian[14]	Evangeliary of Trier[15]
			I	II		
First Sunday	2 Cor 6:2-10	1 Kgs 19:3-15		1 Cor 2:11-14		
	2 Cor 12:12	2 Cor 6:2-10		2 Cor 6:2-10		
		Matt 6:1-8			Matt 7:12	Matt 6:1-8
		Matt 4:1-11			Luke 15:20	
Second Sunday			Prov 3:19-34			
	Eph 4:23			1 Thess 3:6-8		
		Luke 15:11-24			Luke 15:11-32	Luke 15:11-32
Third Sunday			Isa 58:1-8			
	Col 2:4					
		John 6:28-54			John 8:12-54	John 6:30

Fourth Sunday			Zech 8:19-23		
	Gal 1:4				
				Luke 20:1-19	John 6:71
Fifth Sunday		Jer 18:13-23			
	Rom 6:17				
					John 11:47
Palm Sunday		Isa 57:1-4, 13	Zech 9:7-17		
	Rom 13:12	1 Pet 2:21-25			John 12:1-50
		John 12:1-16		John 11:47–12:8	John 17:1-26

	Toledo Missal[16]	*Toledo Lectionary*[17]	*Silos Lectionary*[18]	*San Millàn Lectionary*[19]
First Sunday	Prov 1:23-32	1 Kgs 19:3-15	1 Kgs 19:3-15	1 Kgs 19:3-15
		2 Cor 6:2-10	2 Cor 6:2-10	2 Cor 6:2-10
	John 4:5-42	Matt 4:1-11	Matt 4:1-11	Matt 4:1-11
Second Sunday	Prov 14:33–15:8	Hos 14:2-10	Hos 14:2-10	Hos 14:2-10
	Gen 41:1-45	Dan 2	Dan 2	Dan 2
	Jas 2:14-23	Jas 2:21–3:13	Jas 2:21–3:13	Jas 2:21–3:13
		1 Pet 3:5-9	1 Pet 3:5-9	1 Pet 3:5-9
		John 6:28-40	John 6:28-35	John 6:28-35
	John 9:1-36	John 4:5-42	John 4:5-42	John 4:5-42
Third Sunday	(Num 12:3–14:24)	Dan 4	Dan 4	Dan 4
	Prov 20:7-28			
	Num 22:2–23:11			
	1 Pet 1:1-2	1 John 1:5–2:2	1 John 1:6-9	1 John 1:5-9
	John 11:1-53	John 9:1-38	John 9:1-38	John 9:1-38

Fourth Sunday			Dan 13:1-64	Dan 13:1-65
			Jas 4:1-16	Jas 4:1-16
			John 8:15-20	John 8:15-20
	Sir 15:11-22		Dan 10:1–11:2	Dan 10:1–11:2; 12:1-13
	1 Kgs 1:1-21			
	2 Pet 1:1-12		Jas 3:14-18	Jas 3:14-18
	John 7:2-15		John 7:14-20	John 7:14-20
Fifth Sunday	1 Kgs 26:1-25		Lev 23:5-8, 23-28, 39-41	Lev 23:5-8, 23-28, 39-41
	Sir 47:24-30, 21-23			
	1 John 1:1-8		1 John 5:16-20	1 John 5:16-20
	John 10:1-17		John 11:1-52	John 11:1-52
Palm Sunday			Isa 49:22-26	Isa 49:22-26
			1 Pet 1:25–2:10	1 Pet 1:25–2:10
			Mark 7:31-37	Mark 7:31-37
			Exod 19:4-5 + Deut 5:32-33 + 6:2-3 + 10:17-21 + 11:16-22 + 30:3-5 + 28:10-11	
			1 John 2:9-17	
	John 11:55–12:13		John 11:55–12:13	

Prayers

The *Liber mozarabicus sacramentorum* is very rich in prayers for Lent.[20] As is usual in this liturgy, the formularies are quite lengthy; they are also full of images and endeavor to give a current application to the events related in the gospel of the day.

The Sunday Masses are as follows: second Sunday, Mass of the Samaritan woman; third Sunday, Mass of the man born blind (but the title reads: "Mass to be said on the second Sunday of Lent"); fourth Sunday, Mass of mid-Lent (twentieth day of Lent); fifth Sunday, Mass of Lazarus.[21] The following are some examples of the prayers in the Spanish Lenten liturgy.

Therefore, though wearied in the flesh, he did not let us grow weak in his weakness. For his very weakness is stronger than ours. Consequently, when he came in lowliness to rescue the world from the power of darkness, he sat and thirsted and asked for water. He was humbled in his flesh when he sat at the well and conversed with the woman. He thirsted for water and asked her to believe. But he himself created in this woman the faith he sought and asked for. When his disciples returned, he said of that faith: "I have food to eat of which you do not know." He who had already bestowed upon her the gift of faith asked her for a drink; he who was burning her in the flame of love for him asked her for the cup that would slake his thirst.[22]

Here is another example of liturgical theology, this time in relation to the man born blind:

He [Christ] dispelled the world's darkness by the light of faith in himself and turned those who were prisoners by sentence of the law into children of grace. He came to judge the world so that the blind might see and the seeing might become blind; that those who admit they are in darkness might receive the eternal light and emerge from the darkness of sin, while those who boasted that by their merits they possessed the light of justice might find themselves in darkness, being puffed up with pride and trusting in their own righteousness. They did not seek the Physician who could heal them.[23]

On Lazarus Sunday, a post-*Sanctus* prayer says:

His grace freed us from the burden of the law and made us adopted children. When he came to raise Lazarus, he cried out, "Take away the stone," so that the weight of damnation might be removed from this man who already stank from the dreadful action of the grave. "Take from him," Jesus said, "the weight of the law which has forced him down into death so that the grace of my voice may come to his aid." For it is a grace of God when we hear his voice and, with Lazarus, follow Christ by walking in right paths.[24]

These texts, the flavor of which is so difficult to capture in translation, show us how the eucharistic liturgy in Spain attempted to "sacramentalize" the readings in the Liturgy of the Word. Indeed, it is one of the characteristics of this liturgy that throughout the Mass it continues to develop the main theme in the celebration of the word. It does this at times in ways that are not always adapted to our modern mentality, but the Spanish liturgy nonetheless remains a rich source of "sacramentalist" meditation on the word of God.

The Lenten season proves to be an inexhaustible source from which each of us can draw what we need. We have seen that, far from being a somber period of negative asceticism, it is rather a starting point for the development in which we rise above ourselves and contribute to the authentic reconstruction of a world whose values can certainly be useful if approached in a prudent, balanced way. Living through these weeks in depth can help us Christians toward the unconditional that is the goal of our life. The true Christian attitude is not one of contempt for human beings and material things; the Christian is rather one who loves human beings and material things but allows none of them to be a master. When the liturgy is fervently celebrated, it helps us to develop such an attitude.

The Sacred Paschal Triduum

Biblico-Liturgical Reflections on the Sacred Paschal Triduum

22. A CRUCIFIED GOD

Three Basic Questions

The three holy days raise three closely related problems that are basic for Christian life and indeed for the life of the world at large: the problem of a crucified God, the problem of his resurrection, and the problem of the Eucharist as a sign that renders the other two saving events present and active in our midst.

We must repeat here what we had occasion to say in the previous volume of this series, namely, that anyone who does not believe in the reality of this crucified God, his resurrection, and the Eucharist will be unable to accept or understand what follows upon them. At the same time, however, even if we do believe in them, we should ask ourselves what kind of faith we have in them and how they affect modern life and the difficulties we face. To ask these questions is not to enter into apologetics. Our aim is more modest. We want simply to discover or rediscover these three realities. They are so basic that if the Church were no longer to acknowledge them as real, she would cease to exist.

Albert Camus wrote the following lines, which are truly fine, even if they are open to some valid criticism:

> Christ came to solve two problems: evil and death, both of which are problems of rebellion. His solution first consisted in taking them on himself. The God-man also suffers, and does so with patience. Evil cannot be as fully ascribed to him as death, as he too is shattered and dies. The night of Golgotha only has so much significance for man because in its darkness the Godhead, visibly renouncing all inherited privileges, endures to the end the anguish of death, including the depths of despair. This is the explanation of the *Lama sabachthani* and Christ's gruesome doubt in agony. The agony would have been easy if it could have been supported by eternal hope. But for God to be man, he had to despair.[1]

Jürgen Moltmann, who quotes these lines from Camus, offers his own reflections on them. As he reads Camus, the latter does not really think that Christ has resolved evil and death as problems of rebellion.[2] We must not let ourselves be fooled by the excellence of Camus's writing here. He does emphasize the importance of what Christ did in accepting crucifixion; the crucifixion is asserted to be a solution for the world's problems; there is no denying that Christ experienced agony and abandonment on the cross, as the evangelists insist. Nonetheless, there is something essential lacking in Camus's reflections. Moltmann puts his finger on it quite accurately: "He [Camus] saw God vanish on the cross, but he did not see Christ's death or the cross taken up into God. Yet only this change of perspective indicates why the night of Golgotha gained so much significance for mankind."[3]

We may recall here the simplicity and grandeur with which St. Paul describes this same change of perspective:

> and found human in appearance,
> he humbled himself,
> becoming obedient to death,
>   even death on a cross.
> Because of this, God greatly exalted him
> and bestowed on him the name
> that is above every name. (Phil. 2:7-9)

Camus's words undoubtedly could serve as a starting point for theological reflection, but it would be reflection closely allied to humanism and congenial to a contemporary vision of anthropology. Our concern, on the contrary, is with God's approach to reality. How does Scripture envisage the "crucified God"? If we want to understand the cross and its efficacy, we must take as our starting point, not ourselves nor our rebellions in the face of suffering and death nor our ideas about God, but God's own plan as expressed in the Scriptures and in the Church's understanding of the Scriptures.

Jesus and His Cross

Let us begin by asking Jesus himself about the meaning and efficacy of the cross. Who better than he can show us the way to a true understanding?

Christ draws his disciples' attention to this very same question: "how is it written regarding the Son of Man that he must suffer greatly and be treated with contempt?" (Mark 9:12). He does not provide them with a direct answer to the question, but if we continue to search through the gospels, we may be able to find an answer.

In many passages Jesus foretells his own violent death. St. Matthew records these significant words: "so will the Son of Man be in the heart of the earth three days and three nights" (12:40). According to St. John, Christ says: "Destroy this temple and in three days I will raise it up" (2:19). And there comes a point when Jesus begins to tell his disciples frequently that he must go up to Jerusalem and be put to death (Matt 16:21, with the parallels in Mark 8:31; Luke 9:22; Mark 9:31; 10:32-34).

Later on, Jesus speaks of the "hour," which indicates not so much a point of time as his personal, free self-offering as obedient Victim to the Father. Thus, at the moment when Jesus' arrest is imminent, he says, "Behold, the hour is at hand when the Son of Man is to be handed over to sinners" (Matt 26:45). This idea of being "handed over" occurs frequently not only in Matthew but in the other Synoptics as well: "The Son of Man will be handed over to the chief priests and the scribes" (Matt 20:18; Mark 10:33; cf. Luke 18:31). In Matthew's gospel, Jesus continues the sentence just quoted: ". . . the chief priests and the scribes, and they will condemn him to death, and hand him over to the Gentiles to be mocked and scourged and crucified" (Matt 20:18-19). Yet the true disciple must share that death with Jesus: "Whoever loses his life for my sake will find it" (Matt 10:39).

In St. Mark's gospel, as we have already seen, Jesus makes the same prediction in the form of a question: "how is it written regarding the Son of Man that he must suffer greatly and be treated with contempt?" (9:12). A little earlier, Mark reports the following incident:

> He began to teach them that the Son of Man must suffer greatly and be rejected by the elders, the chief priests, and the scribes, and be killed, and rise after three days. He spoke this openly. Then Peter took him aside and began to rebuke him. At this he turned around and, looking at his disciples, rebuked Peter and said, "Get behind me, Satan. You are thinking not as God does, but as human beings do." (8:31-33)

Christ is not giving the disciples an answer to his question, "Why the cross?" but he does make the cross something necessary, something the Father wills. The cross is his response and justifies the words the Father spoke at the transfiguration: "This is my beloved Son. Listen to him" (Mark 9:7).

And yet Jesus did feel a certain inward rebellion against what the Father was asking, for we see him praying that, if possible, this "hour" might pass him by (Mark 14:35; Matt 26:39; Luke 22:42; John 12:27).

St. Luke develops the same themes as Matthew and Mark, and there is no point in going over all of them again. According to Luke, Jesus, in predicting his death, uses the image of baptism: "There is a baptism with which I must be baptized" (12:50). A little later, he says, "on the third day I accomplish my purpose" (13:32). Not only does Jesus foretell his death (18:33; cf. Matt 20:19; Mark 10:34), but the evangelist, speaking in his own name, says, "When the days for his being taken up were fulfilled . . ." (9:51).

A Glorious Cross

In St. John's gospel we find a more theological kind of reflection on the death of Jesus. As the reader is aware, the Synoptics supply historical details of the passion that are not to be found in St. John. St. John, on the other hand, develops aspects of the passion that in some instances are present in rudimentary form in the other gospels but are not spelled out as they are in the Fourth Gospel. We have in mind especially the voluntary aspect of Christ's death. Jesus hands himself over and does so with great dignity and on condition that his disciples are allowed to go free (John 18:6-8). Elsewhere, he himself chooses the "hour" when he will surrender to his executioners.

The theme of the "hour" is quite extensively developed in St. John. Christ uses the word himself: "My hour has not yet come" (2:4); "My time is not yet here" (7:6); "I have told you this in figures of speech. The hour is coming when I will no longer speak to you in figures" (16:25); "Behold, the hour is coming and has arrived when each of you will be scattered" (16:32). In two passages Jesus' use of the word is connected with a theology of his passion and death: "The hour has come for the Son of Man to be glorified" (12:23). But the glorification in no way lessens his burden of anguish: "'I am troubled now. Yet what should I say? "Father, save me from this hour"? But it was for this purpose that I came to this hour. Father, glorify your name.' Then a voice came from heaven, 'I have glorified it, and I will glorify it again'" (12:27-28).

For St. John, then, Christ's cross and death are unintelligible unless they are seen as a sign of his glorification and exaltation. In this context, the evangelist twice uses the verb "lift up" with a double meaning. "Now is the time of judgment on this world; now the ruler of this world will be driven out. And when I am lifted up from the earth, I will draw everyone to myself" (12:31-32). John then adds an explanation: "He said this indicating the kind of death he would die" (12:33). The cross thus effects both Christ's own glorification and the unification of humanity.

As St. John sees it, the sacrifice of the cross changed the course of history. The crucifixion is indeed a sign, but not a sign of death alone; it is also a sign of exaltation to glory. If Christ had simply died, history would only have witnessed one more person laid low. But Christ also rose from the dead; his resurrection is inseparable from his death and is but the other side of it.

Here John seems to be making his own a tradition that was already a vital one since the very first days of the Church. Thus he insists several times on the reality of Christ's resurrection. Inevitably, then, the cross points not only to death but to glory and is therefore an event that has forever changed the meaning of human life in this world. It would doubtless be an exaggeration to say that the other New Testament writings present Jesus' death as a humiliation and then bring in the resurrection as the great corrective to the humiliation. But at least we must say that in St. John's gospel, the cross itself is presented as resurrection and glory no less than as death. John certainly depicts the crucifixion as a visible, sensibly real event, but he also insists that it be seen as a sign that contains what it signifies, namely, Christ's glorification. When Christ is dying, he is already going back to the Father (16:17; cf. 14:28; 16:10). We shall have further occasion to emphasize this point, which is so dear to John.[4]

The Death-Resurrection

It is impossible for us to present here the whole Johannine theology of Christ's death. Let us therefore pass on to the theology of St. Paul and recall its main characteristic lines.

As with John, so with Paul we must see death and resurrection as closely related if we are to understand the meaning and importance of the death itself. At the same time, however, it is legitimate for us to ask what the death on the cross meant, as such, to St. Paul.

Again as with John, we find developed to some degree a theology of the cross. In this regard Paul is aware of having inherited a firm tradition, as the First Letter to the Corinthians shows. He tells us there that the death and resurrection of Jesus are the principal object of Christian preaching and that if one is converted to the faith, one's belief in the death-resurrection of the Lord is decisive (1 Cor 15:1-11).

There is also a close link between the Eucharist and the death-resurrection of Christ. Thus we see Paul, in the First Letter to the Corinthians, telling us how a very summary account of the death of Christ is part of the eucharistic celebration (11:23-25). In this he is but following a tradition he himself has received. The Supper also contains the true theology of the cross. When Christ celebrates the Supper, he does so in order that the memorial of his covenant sacrifice may be celebrated, that is, rendered always present and active. The death thus rendered present is the new covenant in Christ's blood; it is his death for the forgiveness of sins.

The Cross and Love

When Paul speaks of the death of Christ, the factor on which he lays the greatest emphasis is love. Theologians have often tended to see in the cross of Christ a kind of divine vengeance, with Christ as the necessary Victim. What Paul sees in it is above all a proof of love: Christ's love for humanity, and the Father's love for Christ and for humanity. It is out of love that Christ handed himself over to death (1 Cor 8:11-13; Rom 14:15; Gal 11:20; Eph 5:1-2, 25). St. John says the same (13:1). But in Christ's love for human beings we glimpse the Father's love for them too, and we can grasp something of the depth of the Father's love for us precisely from the fact that when we were still sinners, Christ died for us (Rom 5:8). God did not spare his own Son but handed him over for us (Rom 8:32).

The Cross and Sin

The death of Christ must also be seen in relation to sin. It is a central motif of the letters of Paul that Christ died for our sins: "[Jesus] was handed over for our transgressions" (Rom 4:25); "[Christ] died for us" (1 Thess 5:10); "one died for all" (2 Cor 5:14); "Christ, while we were still helpless, yet died at the appointed time for the ungodly" (Rom 5:6); "while we were still sinners Christ died for us" (Rom 5:8); "Do not destroy [your brother] for whom Christ died" (Rom 14:15; cf. 1 Cor 8:11). We should note, too, that Paul often speaks of "sin" rather than "sins." In other words, he concentrates on an attitude taken by humanity rather than on the many actions that flow from the basic attitude that is "sin."

The death of Christ liberates from this state of sin. St. Paul likes antitheses, especially the antithesis of slavery and freedom. On the one hand, "you were slaves of sin" (Rom 6:20; cf. 6:6, 16); "taking me captive to the law of sin that dwells in my members" (Rom 7:23); "as sin reigned in death" (Rom 5:21; cf. 6:14); "Jews and Greeks alike . . . are all under the domination of sin" (Rom 3:9). On the other hand, "we . . . died to sin" (Rom 6:2); "our old self was crucified with him, so that our sinful body might be done away with, that we might no longer be in slavery to sin" (Rom 6:6); "now . . . you have been freed from sin" (Rom 6:22); "For the law of the Spirit of life in Christ Jesus has freed you from the law of sin and death" (Rom 8:2).

The death of Christ ransoms us—although there is no need, when we use a word like "ransom," to insist on the metaphor; the real point is that his death makes us free. We were "sold" to sin (Rom 7:14), but now we have been bought back at a great price (1 Cor 6:20; 7:23); we have been ransomed from the curse of the law (Gal 3:13). Our liberation was effected by the cross: "Christ ransomed us from the curse of the law by becoming a curse for us, for it is written, 'Cursed be everyone who hangs on a tree,' that the blessing of Abraham might be extended to the Gentiles through Christ Jesus, so that we might receive the promise of the Spirit through faith" (Gal 3:13-14). We are now justified by the redemption wrought for us in Christ Jesus (Rom 3:24-25); he is our ransom (1 Cor 1:30). "In him we have redemption by his blood, the forgiveness of transgressions, in accord with the riches of his grace that he lavished upon us" (Eph 1:7-8).

To be freed from sin is simultaneously to be reunited to God: "Indeed, if, while we were enemies, we were reconciled to God by the death of his Son, how much more, once reconciled, will we be saved by his life" (Rom 5:10); "[that he] might reconcile both with God, in one body, through the cross, putting that enmity to death by it" (Eph 2:16; cf. Col 1:21-22). The initiative in this reconciliation comes from God himself: "all this is from God, who has reconciled us to himself through Christ and given us the ministry of reconciliation, namely, God was reconciling the world to himself in Christ, not counting their trespasses against them and entrusting to us the message of reconciliation" (2 Cor 5:18-19).[5]

The Cross, a Sacrifice of Expiation

The cross also brings us forgiveness. When dealing with this aspect of redemption, St. Paul often cites texts from the Old Testament, as in Romans 4:7-8, where he cites Psalm 32:1-2: "Blessed is he whose transgression is forgiven, whose sin is covered. Blessed is the man to whom the LORD imputes no guilt, in whose spirit is no guile." We obtain redemption, the forgiveness of our sins, through the Son (Col 1:13).

Furthermore, Paul thinks of the cross of Christ as being a sacrifice; it is as a sacrifice that it forgives sins. He writes, in his Letter to the Romans: "all have sinned and are deprived of the glory of God. They are justified freely by his grace through the redemption in Christ Jesus, whom God has set forth as an expiation, through faith, by his blood" (3:23-25). If we are now able to "enter" the promised land, we can do so thanks to the Lamb who was sacrificed: "our paschal lamb, Christ, has been sacrificed" (1 Cor 5:7). Jesus offered himself as a sacrifice for us: "Christ loved us and handed himself over for us as a sacrificial offering to God for a fragrant aroma" (Eph 5:2). We must bear in mind, however, that Christ redeemed not only us but the entire world through his cross: "despoiling the principalities and the powers, [God] made a public spectacle of them, leading them away in triumph by [the cross]" (Col 2:15).

St. Paul, like the rest of us, finds it difficult to describe, in the terms elaborated by human wisdom, the meaning of the Son's death. In fact, for us that death is foolishness; only God could have imagined saving humanity through the cross. The First Letter to the Corinthians is quite hard on those who attempt to explain this extraordinary action of the Father and the Son by human reasoning (1 Cor 1:17-25). All we can really do is grasp the fact, without fully understanding it: "[Christ Jesus], though he was in the form of God, did not regard equality with God something to be grasped. Rather, he emptied himself, taking the form of a slave, coming in human likeness; and found human in appearance, he humbled himself, becoming obedient to death, even death on a cross" (Phil 2:6-8). There can be no explanation in human terms for such a gesture. The only hint given us is this: "Because of this, God greatly exalted him" (Phil 2:9).

Knowing God through the Cross

"The new converging trends in theological thought today concentrate the question and the knowledge of God on the death of Christ on the cross, and attempt to understand God's being from the death of Jesus."[6] Only the study of Scripture can get us anywhere in this area. If we do look into the Scriptures, we find that they see Christ as the sign of encounter with God. In fact, "the scriptural basis for Christian belief in the triune God is . . . the thoroughgoing, unitary testimony of the cross; and the shortest expression of the Trinity is the divine act of the cross, in which the Father allows the Son to sacrifice himself through the Spirit."[7]

Some years back, a Jewish writer spoke of the problem of God. The way in which he does so brings home to us the problem of the cross:

> The SS hanged two Jewish men and a youth in front of the whole camp. The men died quickly, but the death throes of the youth lasted for half an hour. "Where is God? Where is he?" someone asked behind me. As the youth still hung in torment in the noose after a long time, I heard the man call again, "Where is God now?" And I heard a voice in myself answer: "Where is he? He is here. He is hanging there on the gallows."[8]

Carrying the cross of Christ is not something reducible to mere metaphor. Yet, heavy though the cross is, God carries it with us, although this is a fact that faith alone can grasp. The Church preaches the cross no less than she preaches the resurrection. We can and must affirm that the cross was raised for our sake and that it manifests God's love for us, now and always. How can God suffer? How could Christ, fully God as well as fully human, suffer? These are questions we shall not tackle, important though they are. They contain a mystery that St. Paul says is foolishness to humans and defies their wisdom.

23. THE GLORIOUS CHRIST, VICTOR OVER DEATH

Reality of the Resurrection

It is a notable fact that the Church has never celebrated the death of Christ without at the same time celebrating his resurrection. This conjunction is exceptionally important. It means that the living tradition of the Church has always kept in view the ultimate purpose of the cross, namely, a life that lasts until, and beyond, the reconstruction of the created world and the parousia of Christ. Despite interpretations claiming the contrary, at no time or place in her history has the Church ever celebrated the death of Christ in isolation; at all times that death is linked to his resurrection. It could not be otherwise, since the Scriptures look at the death and resurrection as one complete action.

It is common knowledge that the objective reality of the resurrection is under attack today. But

> to reduce the fact of the Resurrection to nothing but the birth of the Apostles' *faith* is . . . to contradict the Gospel, by presenting their *evidence* on the Resurrection as the *only* historically certain *content* of the Resurrection. What the Apostles intended to bear witness to was not a faith which governed the existence of a fact, but rather a fact which gave birth to their faith.[1]

The anthropology of the resurrection has to be studied first of all in Scripture. We cannot expect to find there a theological reflection on the resurrection, nor shall we attempt to supply for the lack, but we do find a concrete experience of the resurrection. The apostles experienced it, or, more accurately, "in the *Risen [One]* they . . . as it were grasped the ungraspable character of the *Resurrection*." Yet, the fact and objective reality of the resurrection are not reducible to the faith and experience of the apostles, because their experience "is not for us the *only reality* of that resurrection; it is the *historical* approach to that supreme event, which cannot be reduced to the experience;

for what the Apostles *experienced* concerns *something in existence,* which, now that it exists, is *binding* on us."[2]

The evangelists are very discreet when it comes to the resurrection, so much so that we are tempted to think they could have dwelt a good deal more on it. After all, would not the resurrection have provided an extraordinarily effective apologetic argument for the divinity of Christ and the redemptive value of his activity? In answer, we must point out that, unlike those theologians who have a rather narrow view of the resurrection, the evangelists never thought of it in apologetic terms but as a sign of life's victory over death, a victory now shared by all believers. Once we start looking for the passages concerning the resurrection, we find that they are relatively few in the gospels. Matthew speaks of it in four places (12:39-41; 17:22-23; 26:32; 28:2); Mark in three (8:31; 9:31; 16:1-20); Luke in six (9:22; 11:30; 18:33; 24:1-52 [vv. 5, 24, 31]). John dwells on it more often and in a more "theological" fashion (seven places: 2:19; 7:33-34; 7:39; 12:16; 13:31-32; 14:18-19; 20:1-10).

If we summarize what we are told in these passages, we are left with three points: the assertion of the resurrection on the third day; the empty tomb; the glorification of Christ and the action of the Spirit. None of the evangelists is interested in the "how" of the resurrection; they simply describe a fact: the empty tomb. But, given that fact, they—especially St. John—dwell on the reality of Christ's human body after his resurrection, despite the fact that some great change has also taken place in his body. This is why the accounts of the apparitions are so important.

Christ behaves quite differently from how he did before his death: he suddenly appears and disappears; he is no longer subject to the restrictions of space and the resistances of matter; he enters rooms even while the doors are, and remain, locked. And yet it is indeed he; his body is truly his body, for he eats like other people. Again, we are not given theological reflections on the nature of a glorified body; what the evangelists, especially St. John, want to communicate to us is their experience of Christ's glorified body. The faith of the apostles is built on facts, and what they want us to share is not a theology of the resurrection but their own experience of the fact. The risen Christ appears within historical time after his death. He is evidently no longer subject to the conditions of space and time, and yet, though no longer the same, he continues to be the same Jesus. *That* is the point of the apparition stories; no explanation of any kind is being offered.

The Glory of the Resurrection

The difficulties we have in adapting ourselves to the evangelists' approach are due entirely to our modern mentality. The fact of the resurrection stirs what we might call our "medical" curiosity. But such is not the apostles' viewpoint. They feel no need of knowing how it all happened. They know for a fact that they laid Jesus' body in the tomb, that the tomb is now empty, and that everyone saw Jesus later. That is enough for them.

We, on the contrary, find it difficult not to wonder about how all this happened. How can a corpse come back to life? The apostolic writings will not satisfy our curiosity. Their only concern is that Christ was crucified and died and is now in his glory, that he sends us the Spirit who raised him up, and thereby gives us a share in his glorified life. Since that is their only concern, the evangelists leave us with a kind of negative vision: the empty tomb, and a distinct positive vision: the apparitions and the apostolic experience of the real but glorified body of Christ.

Let us dwell for a moment on St. John's presentation of the mystery. In the farewell discourse of Christ we find a dialogue on the departure and return of the Lord (13:31–14:31). The whole passage speaks simply of departure and return, but it is not difficult to see that Christ is telling the disciples of his death and resurrection. The dialogue begins with a vision of glory: "Now is the Son of Man glorified, and God is glorified in him. [If God is glorified in him,] God will also glorify him in himself, and he will glorify him at once" (13:31-32). The disciples cannot understand this, so Jesus repeats it in more concrete terms: "I will be with you only a little while longer. . . . 'Where I go you cannot come'" (13:33).

The glory that Jesus already has and will increasingly have is going to be shared by others. That sharing is the purpose of his death and resurrection: "And if I go and prepare a place for you, I will come back again and take you to myself, so that where I am you also may be. Where [I] am going you know the way" (14:3-4).

All of this will take place in order to transform the disciples' lives. Here Christ grows more specific. If the disciple keeps Christ's word, "my Father will love him, and we will come to him and make our dwelling with him" (14:23). Jesus tells them this while he is still with them, and they must believe. The Holy Spirit whom the Father will send in Jesus' name will instruct them fully and remind them of everything Jesus had said (14:25-26). Finally, Jesus returns to his opening theme: "You heard me tell you, 'I am going away, and I will come back to you.' . . . And now I have told you this before it happens, so that when it happens, you may believe" (14:28-29).

Chapters 15 and 16 go back over the same themes but add new revelations that are extremely important for the life of the disciples and the future Church. In 15:1-17 Jesus speaks of the union between Father, Son, and Church (that is, the first disciples who were to spread the Church throughout the world). A deeply moved Christ uses the language of love for these disciples whom he himself has chosen and who are now his friends. He is going to give his life for them; they must abide in his love and must love one another. In 15:1–16:33 the disciples see themselves confronting a world that does not understand them. But the Spirit will come and lead them to the truth, despite all opposition.

In these chapters we see how John thinks of the death and resurrection of Jesus. He does not think in our categories, nor do the difficulties felt by our contemporaries occur to him. For him, all difficulties are lost from sight in the glory of the *Kyrios* and his close union with his Church, which he now protects and which the Spirit guides.

The Experience of St. Paul

St. Paul too tells us of his experience of Christ as risen. In fact, his very first Christian experience is a vision of the risen Christ, given him at the moment of his conversion. He takes this vision as comparable to that enjoyed by the apostles; like them, he has seen the risen Christ and is a witness to him:

> For I handed on to you as of first importance what I also received: that Christ died for our sins in accordance with the scriptures; that he was buried; that he was raised on the third day in accordance with the scriptures; that he appeared to Cephas, then to the Twelve. After that, he appeared to more than five hundred brothers at once, most of whom are still living, though some have fallen asleep. After that he appeared

to James, then to all the apostles. Last of all, as to one born abnormally, he appeared to me. (1 Cor 15:3-8)

Since he has seen the risen Christ, Paul is an apostle: "Am I not an apostle? Have I not seen Jesus our Lord?" (1 Cor 9:1).

We must turn to Paul's discourse at Antioch in Pisidia (Acts 13:16-41) if we want to see how, in writing about the resurrection, he refers to the Scriptures and to the way the Christian community thought of the event. In his discourse Paul recalls Old Testament history down to the sending of Jesus. Then, after reminding his hearers of Jesus' death and descent into the tomb, in accordance with the Scriptures, Paul says, "But God raised him from the dead, and for many days he appeared to those who had come up with him from Galilee to Jerusalem. These are [now] his witnesses before the people" (Acts 13:30-31).

Finally, Paul comes to the essential point in his message:

We ourselves are proclaiming this good news to you that what God promised our ancestors he had brought to fulfillment for us, (their) children, by raising up Jesus, as it is written in the second psalm, "You are my son; this day I have begotten you." And that he raised him from the dead never to return to corruption he declared in this way, "I shall give you the benefits assured to David." That is why he also says in another psalm, "You will not suffer your holy one to see corruption." (Acts 13:32-35)

Paul goes on to point to the effect of Christ's death and resurrection: "Through him forgiveness of sins is being proclaimed to you" (v. 38).

Elsewhere, though less extensively, Paul continues to rely on the Scriptures. He tells us that the prophets had proclaimed Christ's resurrection (Rom 1:2-4) and that Psalm 110, which sings of exaltation at God's right hand, was already foretelling Christ's glorification (Eph 1:20; Col 3:1).

Resurrection: Revival of a Dead Man?

Objections to the resurrection existed even in St. Paul's day. Since the Greek philosophers regarded the body as a burden upon the soul, they hoped the day would come when the soul would be completely freed of the material body. Why raise the body? An all-powerful God can undoubtedly restore life to a corpse, but why should he do so?

Why should he restore life to that which is inferior and only brings humiliation on a person?[3]

In answer, Paul repeats, but in more precise and concrete terms, what he had already taught in this First Letter to the Thessalonians. In the First Letter to the Corinthians he writes: "It is sown corruptible; it is raised incorruptible. It is sown dishonorable; it is raised glorious. It is sown weak; it is raised powerful. It is sown a natural body; it is raised a spiritual body" (1 Cor 15:42-44). The Apostle is here attempting to give a kind of definition of a glorified body; its qualities, such as they are, are possessed in a supreme degree by the body of the risen Christ.

Flesh and blood, then, cannot possess the kingdom of God. The Christ, the Lord of glory, does possess a risen body, but it is heavenly and incorruptible. Christ is one and the same; he whom the apostles saw and touched before his death is the one whom they saw and whom Thomas touched after the resurrection. The body they saw and touched after the resurrection is, however, a glorious body that is no longer subject to space and time or to the material condition proper to things of our world.

Risen in Christ

The resurrection of Christ has two consequences for us, or rather a single consequence that can be seen as possessing two stages: Christ's resurrection guarantees ours, and ours has in a way already begun. That is a legitimate way of summing up St. Paul's thought on the matter. In his view, there is not only the resurrection at the parousia but also a kind of resurrection that is already ours and marks, as it were, the beginning of the parousia. If we believe in the final resurrection of each of us, in virtue of Christ's resurrection, then we ought also to believe that this resurrection has already begun for each of us.

The resurrection is linked to the *eschaton*, the messianic age. Numerous texts thus connect our resurrection at the end of time with the resurrection of Christ—"For since death came through a human being, the resurrection of the dead came also from a human being. For just as in Adam all die, so too in Christ shall all be brought to life" (1 Cor 15:21-22)—and our resurrection will make us like the risen Christ (1 Cor 15:49). Earlier in this same letter Paul writes, "God raised the Lord and will also raise us up by his power" (1 Cor 6:14).

This change in us will not have its source totally outside us: "Indeed, if, while we were enemies, we were reconciled to God by the death of his Son, how much more, once reconciled, will we be saved by his life. Not only that, but we also boast of God through our Lord Jesus Christ, through whom we have now received reconciliation" (Rom 5:10-11). We are truly assimilated to Christ in his risen state (Rom 6:8) and truly share in his glory (Rom 8:17), and the agent of this resurrection is the Spirit who now dwells within us: "If the Spirit of the one who raised Jesus from the dead dwells in you, the one who raised Christ from the dead will give life to your mortal bodies also, through his Spirit that dwells in you" (Rom 8:11).

More than this, we have already in a way been raised from the dead, and our bodies already possess a certain glory, since they are the temple of the Spirit (1 Cor 6:19). We experience the presence of the Spirit in us (2 Cor 5:1-19); we already possess the riches of heaven (1 Cor 4:8). The risen Christ is thus the source of all life (Rom 1:4; 1 Cor 15:45).

We shall find that all these consequences of the resurrection are given concrete expression in the celebrations of the holy days.[4]

24. THE RESURRECTION AND THE EUCHARIST

As we shall be asserting again later on, the most important eucharistic celebration in this last part of Holy Week is not that of Holy Thursday, which is rather commemorative in character, but that of the Easter Vigil. The celebration during the Vigil is the culmination of all the celebrations during Holy Week, and the latter should be steps toward this climax.

The central importance of the Vigil Eucharist is not yet fully understood by many people. In a good number of locales, people set a higher value on the Christmas Midnight Mass, with its folklore and familial spirit, than on the Easter Vigil. As a result, we find them tending to push the Vigil service back into the early evening of Saturday.

The ceremonies of the Vigil, moreover, are strange to people and a bit complicated. The attention of the faithful thus tends to be drawn to what is, in fact, peripheral rather than to what is the real heart of the celebration, namely, the Eucharist of the risen Christ.

For these various reasons, we must stop for a moment and show at least in broad outline the connection between the resurrection and the Eucharist.

During his earthly life, Jesus was the instrument of our salvation because in him we could touch and see the Father. Christ says as much in his rather impatient answer to Philip's request, "show us the Father": "[Philip], whoever has seen me has seen the Father" (John 14:8-9). Conversely, the reason why the Father sent Jesus was that in Jesus we might encounter the Father. For in encountering the human Jesus in a personal way, every human has access to the Father, the one who determined that the Son should be his instrument in saving the world.

At this point, however, a difficulty arises, for the post-resurrection situation of Christ seems to contradict the Father's plan. The Father sent his Son in human form in order that we might see his real bodily self and thus be in contact with a person who, though divine, is also truly human. Yet now Jesus tells us, "It is better for you that I go" (John 16:7)! How can this be so, since it means that during the time between the Passover and resurrection of the Lord at one end and his parousia or return at the other we shall no longer be able to be in contact with the instrument of our salvation, the very one whom the Father sent that he might save us and reunite us with the Sender. Are we then to encounter Christ only through memory, by recalling what he did, as we recall the deeds of the human beings who gave us life and helped us on our earthly journey?

But there is another side to the same problem, and it provides us with an answer. We can get at this other side by recalling what John and Paul and early Christian tradition thought about the resurrection of Christ. What good would the incarnation have been if it had ended with the expiatory death of Jesus on the cross? Such a death would indeed have been a great and magnificent thing, but if it had also marked the end of Christ's incarnation, we would be left with a highly juridical view of his coming, as though his whole purpose was to pay a debt that humanity owed. That aspect of it is part of the picture, but is it the whole picture? Must we not look beyond the death to the glorification and the glorified body if we want to see the full meaning and scope of the incarnation? The risen Christ has a glorified body that is not subject to the conditions of time and space. Cannot this body be in contact with us through signs?

It can indeed, and this is exactly what happens through the mediation of the Church and its sacraments, each of which can be regarded as being in its own way an earthly extension of the glorified body of Christ. Now the condition for such a possible contact with Christ, the absolutely necessary condition of his further presence to us as incarnate, was his resurrection in a glorified body and his departure. Once he was risen and had withdrawn his visible presence, he could send the Spirit who gives life. The flesh of itself has no value here. The Spirit enables us to be always and everywhere in contact with the glorified body of the risen Lord.

Christ's presence among us is thus in no sense something abstract. Through faith we can touch him by touching the Church and celebrating the sacraments. We understand the word "sacraments" here in a broad sense, since we also touch Christ present among us by listening to his word and by contact with the Church in our various dealings with her.

Christ, then, wanted to retain the possibility of encountering us as a human. This possibility he has by reason of his glorified body. On our side, our possibility of having some concrete contact with him depends on the incarnation being prolonged somehow in our midst; in other words, the heavenly body of Christ has to be made visible here on earth. Christ creates this visibility through earthly realities that function as signs. A sacrament makes it possible for us to enter into contact, through visible things, with the invisible but real, glorified body of Christ. The sacraments are thus earthly extensions of the glorified humanity of Christ, and each sacramental action embodies his presence when and where it is celebrated.

This presence has its highest form in the Eucharist. By virtue of transubstantiation, Christ is really present (he is also really present in the other sacraments) and in a special way that involves changing the very substance of the sign that points to his presence. He is present in the Eucharist both as sacrificing Priest and as Victim. Consequently, through the eucharistic sign he is in contact with today's world just as he was in contact with the world of his time on earth.

It would have been impossible, however, to repeat the Supper as anything more than an outward gesture if Christ had not been raised from the dead and given the glorified body that is now in contact with us through the eucharistic sign.[1] He touches us, therefore, as the Lord who is Master of death. The entire world is now "changed" and "assumed" by the glorified Christ; it is in contact with his person. When he appeared to people after his resurrection, he appeared in his visible body. In the eucharistic sign the presence is the same but the manner is not. Christ remains invisible, and we touch him through the sign that is truly life giving by reason of the resurrection and ascension of Christ and the sending of the Spirit. We possess what we love but we do not see it, and we wait for the time of signs to end so that we may enter into direct contact with the Christ of glory.

The resurrection of Christ, therefore, is essential if the Church is to have her deeper meaning as sacrament and as basis for all the individual sacraments, especially the Eucharist. How could we speak of the "real" eucharistic presence if Christ were not risen and in possession of a real, glorified body? Evidently, then, the life of every Christian is centered on the resurrection and glorious body of the Lord.

At the same time, however, every celebration of the Eucharist looks forward to the day when Christ returns to do away with signs and we can see him directly, as the apostles did when he appeared in their midst. To celebrate the Eucharist, then, is to celebrate our own resurrection and to wait with active hope and love for the day when our own bodies will be made glorious like that of the Lord whom we "put on" in baptism.

Structure and Themes of the Three Holy Days

Thursday of the Lord's Supper, at the Evening Mass

25. CELEBRATIONS ANCIENT AND MODERN

The Christian faith has always found its essential statement in the affirmation: "On the third day he rose again from the dead." Two fourth-century fathers of the Church tell us in straightforward language what they consider to be the meaning of the paschal Triduum. St. Ambrose, bishop of Milan, writes:

> We must observe not only the day of the passion but the day of the resurrection as well. Thus we will have a day of bitterness and a day of joy; on the one, let us fast, on the other let us seek refreshment. . . . During this sacred Triduum. . . . [Christ] suffered, rested, and rose from the dead. Of that three-day period he himself says: "Destroy this temple, and in three days I will raise it up."[1]

St. Ambrose here bases his argument on the biblical typology of the temple that is destroyed and then rebuilt in three days. Christ's words also show that his death and his resurrection are inseparable from each other:

> It is one and the same temple that is destroyed and then raised up in three days' time, one and the same Lord who dies and then is raised up in the mystery of a single Pasch [Passover], that is, his passage from this world to the Father. St. Ambrose emphasizes the fact that this Pasch or passage of the dead and risen Christ is celebrated by the Church in a single process that includes the fasting and mourning of Friday and Saturday and the joy of the eucharistic celebration during the Easter Vigil. The fasting stands in contrast to the joy, yet it also prepares for it and forms with it a single whole. The three-day celebration of the Pasch

means for the Church a passage from repentance to joy, from mourning to new life.[2]

The other fourth-century father to whom we refer is St. Augustine. He concentrates especially on the typology of Jonah and its application to Christ and on Jesus' words in speaking of his resurrection on the third day. Thus, Augustine speaks of "the Triduum in which the Lord died and rose"[3] and of "the most holy Triduum of the crucified, buried, and risen [Lord]."[4]

There can be no doubt that the Triduum* of which Augustine and Ambrose speak begins on Friday and ends on Easter Sunday evening.

> The paschal mystery includes both the passion and the resurrection of Jesus Christ, the two being inseparable. Not only is the resurrection inseparably connected with the passion, but it also springs from the passion as it were: life springs from death, and redemption from sin has its roots in the suffering that is the consequence of sin.[5]

This is not the place to explain at length what the paschal mystery is. In any case, we can best come to understand this mystery by living through these holy days. What we have been saying will be enough to show that the early Church, by celebrating the paschal triduum from Good Friday to Easter Sunday evening, was really respecting the true theological nature of the mystery. In view of the new grasp that the Christian people have of the value and meaning of the paschal mystery, the liturgical reform, especially since Vatican II, might well have returned to ancient practice by celebrating a paschal Triduum that runs from Friday morning to Sunday evening.

If we adopt the ancient perspective, Holy Thursday marks the end of the Lenten fast. The day begins with the reconciliation of penitents, who are thereby readmitted to the eucharistic table; then, in the evening, the Church solemnly celebrates the institution of the Eucharist as something intimately linked to the paschal mystery.

In the Roman Church down to the seventh century, Holy Thursday was simply the day for the reconciliation of penitents; there was no trace of a commemoration of the Last Supper. The Eucharist to which

---

* They are probably not, however, speaking of a liturgically developed Triduum, which came later.

the penitents were readmitted was the paschal Eucharist that was celebrated during the Easter Vigil as the climax of the whole liturgical year.

In the middle of the sixth century we find two Masses being celebrated on Holy Thursday, one in the morning, the other in the evening.[6] At Rome, however, we find no eucharistic celebration on Holy Thursday during this period; as we just said, Holy Thursday at Rome was given over to the reconciliation of penitents. We have plenty of evidence for this. For example, in a letter to Bishop Decentius of Gubbio (beginning of the fifth century), Pope Innocent I says that the Roman custom is to reconcile penitents on the Thursday before Easter.[7] Various Church writers have left us descriptions of public penance and of the reconciliation of sinners on Holy Thursday. St. Jerome, for example, describes the penance that Fabiola had undergone fifteen or twenty years earlier at the Lateran Basilica, prior to Easter.[8]

Elsewhere, the Council of Carthage in 397 shows that the Eucharist was being celebrated on Holy Thursday.[9] From a well-known letter of St. Augustine to Januarius, we can see that the Eucharist might be celebrated twice on that day—once in the morning for those who wanted to end their fast sooner, the other in the evening.[10]

According to Egeria's travel diary, the same custom was followed at Jerusalem:

> When all the people have assembled [at the eighth hour], the prescribed rites are celebrated. On that day the sacrifice is offered at the Martyrium, and the dismissal from there is given around the tenth hour. Before the dismissal is given, however, the archdeacon raises his voice, saying: "At the first hour of the night [7 p.m.] let us assemble at the church which is on the Eleona, for much toil lies ahead of us on this day's night." Following the dismissal from the Martyrium everyone proceeds behind the cross, where, after a hymn is sung and a prayer is said, the bishop offers the sacrifice and everyone receives Communion.[11]

It is possible to follow the development of the Roman liturgy for Holy Thursday from the seventh century on, although the liturgists do not agree on all points of historical interpretation.[12] It seems that beginning at that time there were three Masses at Rome—one in the morning; a second at midday, at which the holy oils were consecrated; and a third in the evening. The Mass for the consecration of the oils and the Mass in the evening contained no Liturgy of the Word but began immediately with the offertory. The absence of a Liturgy of the Word, though unusual in the seventh century, was nothing new in the Roman liturgy. We know, for example, from St. Justin's description of the baptismal Mass in 150, that when baptisms were held, the Mass after them began directly with the offertory.[†13] Later, in 215, the *Apostolic Tradition* of St. Hippolytus of Rome[‡] shows that the same practice was followed in the Mass after a baptism and in the Mass for the consecration of a bishop.[14]

As we have already insisted, Holy Thursday at Rome was first and foremost the day for the reconciliation of penitents.

The *mandatum*, or washing of feet, was already part of the ritual at Jerusalem in the middle of the fifth century.[15] The rite then spread throughout the East and from there into the West.

The Romano-Germanic Pontifical of the tenth century shows only the chrism Mass in the morning and the evening Mass.[16] The first morning Mass, therefore, was no longer being celebrated; on the other hand, the evening Mass now contained a Liturgy of the Word.

The Holy Thursday liturgy later received two further additions. The first was the solemn transfer of the reserved Sacrament to the repository, where it awaited the ceremonies of Good Friday. This rite developed during the period from the thirteenth to the fifteenth centuries; we shall come back to it later and see the different stages of this development.

The other addition was the stripping of the altars. In the seventh century this was still a simple utilitarian action, since the cloths were left on the altars only for the celebration of the Eucharist, but with the passage of time the rite came to symbolize the stripping of Christ for his crucifixion.

In the post–Vatican II liturgical reform, the Holy Thursday celebrations have been restored to their original, very simple forms. It might perhaps have been preferable to leave Holy Thursday outside the paschal Triduum, thus returning to the early tradition as found

---

† Nocent's use of the word "Mass" is anachronistic. Justin does not mention the readings in chapter 65, but that does not necessarily mean that there were none.

‡ As indicated in vol. 1, p. 128, the authorship and date of this work is much disputed. Similarly, the absence of a reference to readings does not mean that none were heard.

in the fathers.§ Such a move, however, would probably have been an exercise in archaism and would have disturbed many of the faithful. In any event, there is a danger of expending greater attention and devotion on the Holy Thursday Eucharist than on the Eucharist during the Easter Vigil, the Eucharist that is the climax of the Triduum.

The Church of today wants the Holy Thursday chrism Mass to be for priests a celebration and commemoration of their priesthood and of their union with their bishop. Moreover, concelebration is strongly recommended on this day. In this regard, we should note that the Church in our day has courageously adapted to new situations. The fifth-century Church at Rome would doubtless never have even thought of concelebration; she saw Christ in the bishop and preferred to have him be the sole celebrant on this day of days when the institution of the Eucharist is commemorated. The Church in our day sees the chrism Mass of Holy Thursday as commemorating rather the priesthood shared by every priest in union with his bishop.

The ritual for the Evening Mass has been very much simplified, and secondary matters have been put in their proper place. For example, anything suggesting sadness or sorrow has been eliminated from the celebration of the Eucharist; the procession to the repository has, like the repository itself, been simplified; the stripping of the altar is done in a discreet manner. The washing of the feet has been retained but is not obligatory; it is left to the discretion of the one responsible for the community in which it is to be celebrated,¶ and he must judge whether or not the gesture will have the ring of authenticity.

Scripture Readings in the Liturgy of the Hours		
Holy Thursday	Jesus, the High Priest	Heb 4:14–5:10
Good Friday	Jesus enters the sanctuary	Heb 9:11-28
Holy Saturday	The Lord's rest	Heb 4:1-13

§ Again, it is unlikely that the fathers were referring to liturgical celebrations when they spoke of the Triduum. Since Nocent wrote these books, the inclusion of Holy Thursday's evening Mass into the Triduum has not been seriously challenged.

¶ Actually, the rubrics call for the washing of the feet "where a pastoral reason suggests it." In reality, the decision will probably be made by the one responsible for the community, but the rubric is not so specific.

Readings in the Eucharistic Liturgy			
	Old Testament	*Apostle*	*Gospel*
Holy Thursday	The Passover of the Jews; Exod 12:1-8, 11-14	Proclaim the Lord's death by eating the bread and drinking the cup; 1 Cor 11:23-26	Love that is faithful even to death; John 13:1-15
Good Friday	The Servant mistreated because of our sins; Isa 52:13–53:12	The obedient Jesus, cause of our salvation; Heb 4:14-16; 5:7-9	Passion of the Lord; John 18:1–19:42
Easter Vigil	Creation; Gen 1:1–2:2		
	Sacrifice of Isaac; Gen 22:1-18		
	Crossing of the Red Sea; Exod 14:15–15:1		
	The new Jerusalem; Isa 54:5-14		
	An eternal covenant; Isa 55:1-11		
	Wisdom has come to earth; Bar 3:9-15, 32–4:4		
	A new heart; Ezek 36:16-17a, 18-28	The risen Christ dies no more; Rom 6:3-11	Christ is risen; A: Matt 28:1-10; B: Mark 16:1-8; C: Luke 24:1-12

26. THE PASCH THAT GATHERS

Glorying in the Cross of the Lord

In anticipation of the eucharistic celebration that will be the climax of the Easter Vigil, the Church reminds us on Holy Thursday evening of the institution of the Eucharist at the Last Supper.

Even in the entrance antiphon of the Mass, as the Church invites us to share in the meal, she also lets us know what the meal really means: "We should glory in the Cross of our Lord Jesus Christ, in whom is our salvation, life and resurrection, through whom we are saved and delivered."

When we hear the word "glory," and when we recall what was said earlier about the true meaning of the cross, especially in St. John's gospel, namely, that the cross glorifies the risen Christ and glorifies us as well, we may well be inclined to ask: Should we not rather say in the antiphon that we are glorified by the cross of Christ? Christ and his cross, after all, are the source of our salvation, life, and resurrection. Biblically and theologically, such a rephrasing would say a great deal more than is expressed in the simple statement that "We should glory in the Cross." When we repeatedly celebrate the sign of the Supper, we make really present in time and space the one sacrifice of Christ on Calvary and the victory over death that brought him to his glory. We then share in that sacrifice, and, in consequence, some of Christ's glory is reflected in us.

The collect of the Mass is a brief recall of what the rite that we are about to celebrate means: "O God, who have called us to participate in this most sacred Supper, in which your Only Begotten Son, when about to hand himself over to death, entrusted to the Church a sacrifice new for all eternity, the banquet of his love, grant, we pray, that we may draw from so great a mystery, the fullness of charity and of life."

One phrase in the prayer creates a problem. It is the phrase "when about to hand himself over to death," which is paralleled by another in the words of consecration: the blood that "will be poured out" (*effundetur*). Both verbs refer to the future and confront us with something very mysterious. Christ is already celebrating, at the Last Supper, something that will take place only later on. Does the celebration, then, have a real content, or does it simply image forth what will be in the future?

By reason of our faith, we believe that the Supper was truly a rendering present of what was going to happen later on. We should note, moreover, that the Greek text of the words of consecration uses a participle that functions with either a present or a future sense, "which is *or* will be poured out," while the Vulgate translation in Latin uses a simple future, "which will be poured out"; we are therefore dealing with words whose exact meaning must be carefully established. In any event, what Christ does at the Supper is an actualization of something that, as a historical event, will take place the next day, Good Friday.

On the other hand, what we do at Mass and what Christ has entrusted his Church with doing is to repeat the Supper and thereby actualize that same Good Friday event, an event that is now past and no longer in the future, as it was at the Last Supper. Thus, the Last Supper and our celebration of the Eucharist are alike in that they actualize the Good Friday event; they differ in that the Supper actualized what was yet to come while our Eucharist actualizes an event now past.

Can we not go a step further and lift at least a corner of the veil that hides the mystery? The actualization of a historical event, whether future or past, is possible because Jesus is both God and human. As a human, Christ was subject to the limitations of space and time; as God, however, he exists outside the conditions of time and space. He can, as God, anticipate his human death and the glorification of his body, can render present the coming sacrifice, and can establish a sign of his glorified body. Similarly, he can entrust to the Church the command to celebrate the Supper again and render present the now-past sacrifice, using the sign of the presence of his glorified body. In this sense, we may say that the Church "renews" the sacrifice of the cross. The statement does not mean that the sacrifice is repeated in its historical reality; it was a once-and-for-all sacrifice and cannot be repeated. It can, however, be rendered present and be a here-and-now offering that Christ, as Head of the Church, makes to the Father's glory for the forgiveness of sins.

The Exodus Meal

The first reading at the Holy Thursday evening Mass brings us back to the preparation of the Jewish Passover meal. The reading is very appropriate and should remind us that Jesus had a reason for instituting his Eucharist in the context of a meal that commemorated the Exodus. In fact, if we look closely, we will find that chapter 6 of St. John's gospel, the account of the multiplication of the loaves (a prefiguration of the Eucharist), is developed in a manner strikingly parallel to the account in the book of Exodus. In the present reading, however, the emphasis is on the ritual and its meaning as a memorial.

Without going into too much detail, we think it useful to give here some information on the ritual according to which the Jews celebrated the Passover. The ritual used today has undoubtedly been often revised since the time of Christ, and yet it may also be said to have preserved a substantial identity. We should note, to begin with, that the celebration of Passover is a domestic affair; it takes place in a family's home, with the head of the house presiding, and not in the temple or synagogue.

The *Seder*, or supper service, for the first two evenings of Passover goes back to the time of the Exodus from Egypt. The Torah (Exod 12:8) prescribes that at the beginning of the fifteenth day of Nisan the Jews are to eat the *Korban pesah*, the lamb slain earlier that afternoon; with it they are to eat unleavened bread and bitter herbs. The same passage orders that the children of the family are to be told of the events being commemorated. This part of the ceremony is so important that the verb *hagged*, "to narrate," has given rise to the noun *haggadah*, the commemorative story told during the meal. Since the destruction of Jerusalem and the temple, the lamb cannot, of course, be sacrificed. The Jews have continued, however, to eat the bitter herbs, the unleavened bread, and a substitute leg of lamb; they also continue to tell the story of the Exodus. Here are the general components of the service:

A. First, there are prayers and blessings taken from the psalms used in the synagogal liturgy or in the domestic liturgy for weekdays. Among these prayers we find the *Kiddush* (introductory prayers); the *Hallel*, consisting of Psalms 112 and 113; the *Birkat ha-mazon*, or thanksgiving prayers for the liberation from Egypt; the *Hallel ha-gadol*, or Psalms 114–17 and, in some communities, Psalm 135; the *Nismat* or *Birkat ha-shir*, which are the concluding prayers.

B. Second, there is the *haggadah*, or story of the Exodus: the persecutions, the punishment of the Egyptians, and the liberation. This story is meant for the children of the family.

C. In a sort of appendix come hymns of more recent origin; some of these have a liturgical character; others are of a more popular kind.

We have no intention of describing the ritual in all its detail, but it is important for us to be aware at least of its broad outline.[1]

1) The Kiddush is recited over a first cup of wine; the blessing varies according to whether or not the feast falls on a Sabbath.

2) The guests wash their hands in silence.

3) The master of the house dips the bitter herbs in vinegar and distributes them; before eating them, all recite a blessing: "Blessed art Thou, Eternal our God, Ruler of the universe, Creator of the fruit of the earth."

4) On the table before the master of the house are three matzoth; he breaks the middle one of the three and puts one half aside to be eaten after the supper, while the other half he places between the two unbroken matzoth.

5) He uncovers the matzoth and lifts up the plate for all to see; he then begins the recital of the haggadah with these words: "This is the bread of affliction which our forefathers ate in the land of Egypt. All who are hungry—let them come and eat. All who are needy—let them come and celebrate the Passover with us. Now we are here; next year may we be in the land of Israel. Now we are slaves; next year may we be free men." He then puts down the plate and covers the matzoth; the second cup of wine is filled.

6) The youngest present asks the four questions about why this night is different from all others; the rest of the haggadah is a response to these questions. It recounts the sufferings of the Israelites in Egypt and the punishments the Lord inflicted on the Egyptians, the way the Lord rescued them from Egypt and the reason why the Passover lamb is eaten. (See the reading from the book of Exodus, chapter 12, in the Holy Thursday evening Mass.)

7) The narrator points to the matzoth and explains its meaning (Exod 12:39).

8) He points to the bitter herbs and explains their meaning (Exod 12:14).

9) He then sings the first part of the Hallel (Pss 113–14); he raises the cup of wine and says:

> Blessed art Thou, Eternal our God, Ruler of the universe, Who redeemed us and redeemed our forefathers from Egypt, and brought us to this night to eat thereon matzah and bitter herbs. Thus may the Eternal our God and God of our fathers bring us to future feasts and festivals in peace; and to the upbuilding of Your city Jerusalem, and to the happiness of Your service, so that we may partake there of the ancient offerings. We shall then offer unto You a new song for our redemption and salvation. Blessed art Thou, Eternal, Who redeemed Israel.
>
> Blessed art Thou, Eternal our God, Ruler of the universe, Creator of the fruit of the vine.

Those present drink the second cup of wine.

10) The guests wash their hands to the accompaniment of a blessing.

11) The master of the house then says the two blessings over the matzoth: "Blessed art Thou, Eternal our God, Ruler of the universe, Who brings forth bread from the earth," and, "Blessed art Thou, Eternal our God, Ruler of the universe, Who made us holy with his commandments, and commanded us concerning the eating of matzoth." The matzoth are eaten.

12) The bitter herbs are dipped in the *haroseth* (a compote of nuts, fruit, and wine) to the accompaniment of a blessing, and are then eaten.

13) The festival meal begins.

14) After the meal, the *afikoman*, or half of a matzoth that was set aside at the beginning of the meal, is distributed and eaten.

15) The third cup of wine is poured; this is the "cup of blessing" or thanksgiving. Psalms are sung and prayers are said; these may differ from country to country, but all strike the note of thanksgiving. The third cup is drunk.

16) The fourth cup is poured and drunk to the accompaniment of a blessing:

> Blessed art Thou, Eternal our God, Ruler of the Universe, for the vine, and for the fruit of the vine, for the produce of the field and for that

precious, good and spacious land which You gave to our ancestors, to eat of its fruit, and to enjoy its goodness. Have compassion, O Eternal our God, upon us, upon Israel your people, upon Jerusalem your city, on Zion the abode of Your glory, and upon Your altar and Your temple. Rebuild Jerusalem, Your holy city, speedily in our days. Bring us there, and cheer us with her rebuilding; may we eat of her fruit and enjoy her blessings; and we will bless you for this in holiness and purity. Grant us joy on this Festival of Matzoth, for You, O God, are good and beneficent to all; and we therefore give thanks unto You for the land and the fruit of the vine. Blessed art Thou, Eternal, for the land and the fruit of the vine.

After the rest of the Hallel (Pss 115–18) has been sung, other hymns may be added that differ according to country.

The New Testament and the Jewish Passover Ritual

The ritual whose broad outline we have just sketched can help us understand the actions of Christ at the Last Supper. Though the ritual has developed over the centuries, its main lines have remained the same. We can see from the accounts given us in the gospels that the narrators present what they actually experienced, even if their descriptions of the Supper also reflect the liturgy of the very early Church.

With the Jewish Passover ritual in mind, we will be struck by a word that both Matthew and Mark use in describing Jesus' consecration of the bread. Just as a prayer of "blessing" is said over the bread in the Passover meal, so, according to these two evangelists, Jesus "says a prayer of blessing" before he breaks the bread. Similarly, and still with the Passover ritual as a point of reference, they tell us that when Jesus took the cup, he "said a prayer of thanks" before passing it around. In the Passover ritual, as described above, there is a similar distinction between the prayer of blessing over the bread and the prayer of thanksgiving over the cup at the end of the meal (*eulogēsas* in Matt 26:26 and Mark 14:22; *eucharistēsas* in Matt 26:27 and Mark 14:23).

St. Luke and St. Paul likewise tell us that when the meal was finished, Christ gave thanks over the cup (Luke 22:20; 1 Cor 11:25). What we have, therefore, in all these writings is a liturgical narrative relating to the Supper. The Passover context is still discernible, but now the meal proper has been eliminated, and the liturgical account brings into immediate proximity the two key moments of the "consecration" of the bread and the wine.

A Sacrificial Meal

The second reading of the Holy Thursday evening Mass brings us to the heart of today's celebration. St. Paul avoids any possible confusion at the very outset by telling us that the Eucharist is not an ordinary meal but a commemoration of something very special:

> [T]he Lord Jesus, on the night he was handed over, took bread, and, after he had given thanks, broke it and said, "This is my body that is for you. Do this in remembrance of me." In the same way also the cup, after supper, saying, "This cup is the new covenant in my blood. Do this, as often as you drink it, in remembrance of me." For as often as you eat this bread and drink the cup, you proclaim the death of the Lord until he comes. (1 Cor 11:23-26)

This meal is inseparably connected with the Lord's cross and is therefore a sacrificial meal and the sign of the new covenant.

Many writers have reminded us of the fact in the past, but we must remind ourselves once again that the Lord's Supper was a Jewish meal in the course of which a prayer of blessing was spoken. It is important for us to realize that our Lord, consistently applying a pedagogy dear to him, did not introduce strange new practices into the world. He was anxious to meet humanity on familiar ground, and so he tried to convey the realities of salvation in the form of practices already in use. For this reason we will be unable to understand the Mass unless we start with the everyday sign Christ used: the meal.

Recent books on the date of the Last Supper have given us some new information but have not dissipated all obscurity. The problem is too complicated for us to go into it here, and, in any case, such a discussion would be out of place for us.[2]

Christ's words, "Do this in memory of me" (Luke 22:19; cf. 1 Cor 11:24-25), invite us to inquire into the nature of this memorial meal. As soon as we ask the question, we see that the Last Supper is no ordinary meal but stands apart. The material elements are those of the usual repast, but the meal as such is not an everyday affair.

The book of Leviticus, in describing how the showbread is to be made, uses the term "memorial":

> And you shall take bran flour and bake it into twelve cakes, using two tenths of an ephah of flour for each cake. These you shall place in two piles, six in each pile, on the pure gold table before the LORD. With each pile put some pure frankincense, which shall serve as an oblation to the LORD, a token of the bread offering. Regularly on each sabbath day the bread shall be set out before the LORD on behalf of the Israelites by an everlasting covenant. It shall belong to Aaron and his sons, who must eat it in a sacred place, since it is most sacred, his as a perpetual due from the oblations to the LORD. (Lev 24:5-9)

This text speaks of three things that are evidently related: the show-bread, the memorial, and the covenant. The meaning is quite clear. The showbread recalls the covenant between God and his people, and the offering of it reminds God that he has bound himself to the nation of Israel. There is no slightest doubt of Yahweh's fidelity; nonetheless, the people need to persuade themselves that he cannot forget, that, in fact, he does not forget, and that whenever he remembers, that is, at every point of time, he acts in their behalf.

By this cultic action, then, the people voice their persuasion that Yahweh keeps his promises with utmost fidelity. It is by no means unusual in the Old Testament to find people offering prayers or other cultic actions as a reminder to the Lord of his covenant with them. Even things that are quite external can recall the fidelity of God, for example, the adornments of the high priest (Exod 28:6-14; 39:2-7; 28:29, 35) or the feast of Passover (Exod 12:14) or an offering (Lev 2:1-2).[3] But we already have a good example from the time of the Exodus itself, and what we are told of the sacrifice offered at Sinai is extremely valuable to us.

> Then, having sent young men of the Israelites to offer burnt offerings and sacrifice young bulls as communion offerings to the LORD, Moses took half of the blood and put it in large bowls; the other half he splashed on the altar. Taking the book of the covenant, he read it aloud to the people, who answered, "All that the LORD has said, we will hear and do." Then he took the blood and splashed it on the people, saying, "This is the blood of the covenant which the LORD has made with you according to all these words." (Exod 24:5-8)

The book of Leviticus (2:1) shows that part of the sacrifice was offered to Yahweh while the rest was eaten.

When St. Paul relates Christ's words, "Do this . . . in remembrance of me" (1 Cor. 11:24-25), he could not have failed to remember, any more than Christ himself could have, the scene in Exodus. In reporting the Lord's words, then, Paul knows that he is describing a covenant rite that reminds God to be faithful. Paul's remarks to the Corinthians make it clear enough that this covenant rite involved eating part of the offering as a sign of the union between God and his people. There is, however, an essential difference between the rite in Exodus and the rite at the Last Supper. It is indicated by Christ's words, "This is my body. . . . This is my blood." Christ himself is the Victim of sacrifice, which is now eaten by all. This in turn presupposes, not a new immolation, but the presence throughout time and space of the one sacrifice of the Lord upon the cross of Calvary.

The Passover meal was itself a memorial meal. But how did the Jews conceive of this memorial?

> In the course of the commemorations of events now past, the Jewish people voice their view, their belief, that they are contemporaries of what once was. To commemorate is not to stand off from what had once taken place; on the contrary, it means eliminating the distance that separates. It means bringing the past to life again; it means thinking that each and all of us are contemporaries of the historical events whose consequences we still endure or whose effects are still real in us. Nothing could be more illuminating in this respect than something that is said during the Jewish Passover meal, which commemorates the departure from Egypt; a verse in the Haggadah for the Seder says that on this feastday all Jews must think of themselves as having been personally brought out of Egypt. What is meant is not a symbolical or allegorical liberation, not a liberation whose reality would be an idea or a burst of feeling. By the fact that our forebears were liberated from Egypt, we ourselves will be liberated from all the new Egypts that can exist either within our hearts or around our religious community.[4]

Here we have the spiritual context within which Christ could institute his own memorial meal—a memorial within a memorial! The Passover ritual has often been described. We would like here to concentrate for a moment on the prayers said during the meal as an accompaniment to the ritual action. They are a type of prayer that goes back to the earliest times depicted in the Bible.[5]

In Genesis 24 we are told how the servant of Abraham returns to Nahor in Aram Naharaim looking for a wife for his master's son. In the account, we are given an example of the characteristic Jewish prayer, the "blessing." The servant, not knowing how to proceed, asks the Lord for a sign. When he receives the sign, he bows in worship and says, "Blessed be the LORD, the God of my master Abraham, who has not let his kindness and fidelity toward my master fail" (Gen 24:27). The prayer is not a liturgical prayer, but how well and spontaneously it expresses what the moment calls for! First there is an exclamation of praise, then a statement of the reason for the exclamation. This kind of prayer, so dear to the Jewish people, must early have become a liturgical form, a function for which it was well suited. In private prayer we find it still being used in the New Testament; recall the *Benedictus*, "Blessed be the Lord, the God of Israel, for he has visited and brought redemption to his people" (Luke 1:68), and the *Magnificat*, "My soul proclaims the greatness of the Lord, . . . for he has looked upon his handmaid's lowliness" (Luke 1:46-48).

In its liturgical use, the statement of the motives for the exclamation "Blessed be you, Yahweh" was quite naturally expanded; the result was the special literary genre of the "anamnesis."[6] At the end of a sometimes lengthy list of motives, there would be a return to the initial exclamation of praise, in the form of a doxology, for example, "To you be glory through the ages. Amen."

The Jewish blessing clearly influenced Judeo-Christian prayer. A good example of the latter is the prayers found in the *Didache*, a document that dates perhaps from the end of the first century AD. In these prayers we will note that after recalling what the Lord has done, the one praying makes God's past goodness the basis for petitions regarding the future. This element must also have been present in the Jewish blessing.

What we have, then, is a blessing or prayer with four parts: an exclamation to the Lord, "Blessed be you, Yahweh"; the enumeration of motives for the exclamation; a petition inspired by God's past manifestations of his power and goodness; a final brief hymn of praise, or doxology. Not all four elements are present in every instance, nor is the order of components always the same; sometimes a petition is enclosed between two doxologies. Here is a passage from the *Didache*:

> After you have eaten enough, give thanks thus: "We thank you, holy Father, for your holy name which you have made to dwell in our hearts,

and for the knowledge and faith and immortality you have revealed to us through Jesus your Servant. Glory be yours through all ages! Amen. All-powerful Master, you created all things for your name's sake, and you gave food and drink to human children for their enjoyment so that they might thank you. On us, however, you have bestowed a spiritual food and drink that leads to eternal life, through Jesus your Servant. Above all, we thank you because you are mighty. Glory be yours through all ages! Amen. Remember, Lord, your Church and deliver it from all evil; make it perfect in love of you, and gather it from the four winds, this sanctified Church, into your kingdom which you have prepared for it, for power and glory is yours through all ages. Amen."[7]

At the Last Supper, then, Christ was using a traditional prayer formula when he spoke his "blessing." After "blessing" the Father, he enumerated all the extraordinary things the Father had done in saving Israel, especially the liberation from Egypt and the crossing of the Red Sea. But then he went on and added a remembrance or anamnesis of his own sacrifice: "Here is the body broken for you; here is the blood shed for you." This anamnesis rendered present the one all-important sacrifice of the new covenant. Having mentioned the various covenants that God had made with Israel, Christ designated the sacrifice he was rendering present as the sacrifice of the new and eternal covenant in his blood.

Here the memorial embodied in the Supper departed radically from the memorial proper to the Old Testament. At the Supper a sacrifice offered once and for all is made present, and the very Victim of that sacrifice is eaten by the guests as a sign that they accept the Lord's covenant. The fathers of the Church liked to apply Psalm 111:5 to the Supper: "He gives food to those who fear him; / keeps his covenant ever in mind."

By sharing in the meal as a sign, we enter into the mystery of the eucharistic celebration. For in this sacrificial meal, which can be repeated over and over, the one sacrifice offered by Christ alone is made present. Consequently, in the Mass the whole Church can associate itself with the action that brought the new covenant into being. Before his passion, Christ celebrated the Supper as an anticipatory sacrifice. Now that the cross is in the past, the sacrifice of the cross is made present. It cannot be repeated, for it was a historical action; it need not be repeated, for it was of infinite value. It is, however, made present, and the Church now joins Christ in offering it.

Proclaiming the Death of the Lord

To recall the "wonderful deeds" the Lord has done is to proclaim his power and work. So too, when the Church gives thanks and in her anamnesis mentions the death, resurrection, and glorious ascension of Christ, she proclaims these to the world. This proclaiming is the basic form her message takes, and it is also the basic form of Christian witnessing, an effective witness given by the entire Church as it gathers and proclaims the death of the Lord by eating the bread and drinking the cup. Thus, in the great prayer of blessing that is called the eucharistic prayer in the Roman Latin liturgy, the Church is constantly recalling and proclaiming the Lord's death. She does so and will continue to do so until the Lord returns, for the Supper is only a prefigurement of the covenant meal at the end of time. Christ himself says that a day will come when he will drink new wine with his disciples (Luke 22:18; Mark 14:25; Matt 26:29).

The Unity of God's People

What the gospel for Holy Thursday has to tell us is closely connected with St. Paul's teaching on the Eucharist. According to Paul, Christ has given us a double gift: he handed himself over to be slain for our salvation, and he gave us the rite wherein we celebrate the mystery of his Body and Blood. Love was evidently the motive that led to this twofold gift, and love plays an essential role in the Holy Thursday liturgy, as indeed it does in every liturgy. It was love that Christ came to reveal to the world: the love of the Father in which we all share, having received it from Christ, and which we must pass on to others. For this reason the Church at an early date introduced into the Holy Thursday liturgy a solemn and moving rite in which she imitates the action of Jesus as recorded in the gospel.

In the time of St. Augustine, the washing of feet in imitation of Christ was a common Holy Thursday practice.[8] In monasteries (in St. Benedict's time, for example) it was the custom to wash the feet of a guest simply as a sign of hospitality.[9] In addition, those assigned to serve table for the week washed the feet of their brothers as a sign of humility when their period of service ended on Saturday.[10] At Rome, in the seventh century, the pope washed his chamberlains' feet on Holy Thursday.[11]

The third canon of the seventeenth Council of Toledo speaks of the washing of feet and offers some instruction on it; we are now in the year 694. The washing of feet on Holy Thursday became increasingly widespread in the Carolingian period. It was practiced in cathedrals, where a distinction was made between the washing of the clerics' feet and the washing of the feet of the poor; it was also practiced in monasteries, where, again, there were two distinct ceremonies. From the end of the Middle Ages on, only the washing of the feet of the clerics or monks was practiced in cathedrals and monasteries.

The *mandatum* is to be found on Holy Thursday at Jerusalem as early as the fifth century.[12] In many regions, the feet of the newly baptized were also washed as they came from the font. For St. Caesarius, in Gaul, this was a gesture of welcome and hospitality. For St. Ambrose, at Milan, it was more than a simple act of humility; it brought with it a special grace, and he calls it a "sanctifying" action.[13] A number of exegetes have asked "whether we should not relate the Gospel account of the washing of the feet to baptism or the Eucharist."[14]

In the Syrian and Byzantine Rites the washing of the feet comes during the gospel, not after it.[15] This ceremony, however, takes place after the celebration of the Eucharist, as it did in the Roman liturgy down to the reform of 1955. In fact, the rite was not used at all except after the morning Mass on Holy Thursday. The recent reform has followed the Coptic usage and put the washing of the feet before the Liturgy of the Eucharist in the Mass.[16]

The Byzantine practice of washing the feet during the reading of the *mandatum* gospel after the Mass offers us the example of an Eastern Rite celebration. Several personages take part in it: the priest, who reads the gospel; the superior of the monastery, who represents Christ; the porter, who plays Judas; and the steward of the house, who plays Peter.

The superior rises and prepares to imitate the actions of the Lord as each is told in the gospel (John 13:2-10):

> So, during supper, fully aware that the Father had put everything into his power and that he had come from God and was returning to God, [Jesus] rose from supper and took off his outer garments [*the superior lays aside his mandhyas*[17]]. He took a towel and tied it around his waist [the superior puts on a *savvanon*[18]]. Then he poured water into a basin [*the superior pours warm water into a basin*] and began to wash the disciples' feet and dry them with the towel around his waist [*the superior*

begins to wash the feet of the assigned brothers, who are seated on benches on both sides; he begins with the porter, who represents Judas, and comes finally to the steward, who represents Peter. He dries and kisses the feet of each. Meanwhile the priest repeats the relevant words of the sacred text as often as is needed—eleven times in fact. When the superior comes to the steward, the reader continues with the sacred text. The superior speaks the words of Christ, the steward those of Peter, and the priest the connecting narrative]. He came to Simon Peter, who said to him, "Master, are you going to wash my feet?" Jesus answered and said to him, "What I am doing, you do not understand now, but you will understand later." Peter said to him, "You will never wash my feet." Jesus answered him, "Unless I wash you, you will have no inheritance with me." Simon Peter said to him, "Master, then not only my feet, but my hands and head as well." Jesus said to him, "Whoever has bathed has no need except to have his feet washed, for he is clean all over; so you are clean, but not all." [*As the superior says these words, he turns slightly toward the porter or even points to him. Then he washes the steward's feet. Meanwhile the priest finishes the reading of the Gospel.*][19]

Modern exegetes have seen in the washing of the feet more than a simple gesture of humility. When Christ thus took the part of a servant, he must inevitably have reminded his disciples of the prophecy concerning the Servant of Yahweh in the book of Isaiah: "Because of his anguish . . . my servant, the just one, shall justify the many, their iniquity he shall bear" (53:11). Against this background, the gesture of washing the feet can be seen to be rich in teaching concerning salvation: concerning the blood of the covenant, the union of love between all the redeemed, the significance of mutual loving service. What real meaning does baptism have, after all, if it is not ordered (together with confirmation, which brings out all the priestly implications of baptism) to the celebration of the Eucharist within the unity of a new people?

When the *Asperges* was introduced into the Sunday service in the West (about the ninth century), it carried many of the same overtones. The verse (9) from Psalm 51, "Cleanse me with hyssop, and I shall be pure; / wash me, and I shall be whiter than snow," was soon taken as alluding to baptism. It has been pointed out, moreover, that this verse at times showed an interesting variant: "You will sprinkle me with hyssop through the blood of the Cross."[20] During Easter time the antiphon for the *Asperges* was taken from Ezekiel (47:1); it sang of the water that flowed from the right side of the temple. It is thought that the application of this verse to Christ is what led some artists to paint the crucified Christ with the wound from the lance in his right side rather than in his left.[21]

The passage from St. Paul that is read at this Holy Thursday evening Mass (1 Cor 11:23-26) reminds the Christians of Corinth that they must be united in love, especially at the celebration of the Supper. The eucharistic celebration presupposes unity; the Church has always taken this as obvious, since the Lord himself had given very pointed instructions on the matter: "Therefore, if you bring your gift to the altar, and there recall that your brother has anything against you, leave your gift there at the altar, go first and be reconciled with your brother, and then come and offer your gift" (Matt 5:23-24).

St. Paul insists on this necessary union of the members of the community, although he is well aware how difficult it is to maintain: "Because the loaf of bread is one, we, though many, are one body, for we all partake of the one loaf" (1 Cor 10:17).

In the Letter of St. James we find the same concern for the character of the Christian assembly; the concern is given more concrete expression than in St. Paul:

> My brothers, show no partiality as you adhere to the faith in our glorious Lord Jesus Christ. For if a man with gold rings on his fingers and in fine clothes comes into your assembly, and a poor person in shabby clothes also comes in, and you pay attention to the one wearing the fine clothes and say, "Sit here, please," while you say to the poor one, "Stand there," or, "Sit at my feet," have you not made distinctions among yourselves and become judges with evil designs? (Jas 2:1-4)

The third-century *Didascalia Apostolorum* (a Greek original that we now have only in a Syriac and a fragmentary Latin version) gives very clear instructions on the point St. James raised. The instructions are all the more notable in that they are directed to the bishop himself, in whom the *Didascalia* sees Christ. We read in chapter 12:

> But if, as you are sitting, someone else should come, whether a man or a woman, who has some worldly honor, either of the same district or of another congregation: you, O bishop, if you are speaking the word of God, or hearing, or reading, shall not respect [mere] persons and leave the ministry of your word and appoint them a place; but remain as you are and do not interrupt your word, and let others in the community receive them. And if there be no place, let one of the others who is full of charity and loves his or her neighbor, and is one fitted to do

an honor, rise and give them place, and stand up. . . . But if a poor man or woman should come, whether of the same district or of another congregation, and especially if they are stricken in years, and there be no place for such, O bishop, with all your heart provide a place for them, even if you have to sit upon the ground; that you be not as one who respects the persons of [mere] people, but that your ministry may be acceptable to God.[22]

The Church is thus strong on the concrete manifestation of Christian charity, especially in the celebration of the Eucharist. St. John has preserved for us the marvelous discourses of the Savior after the Last Supper, and it is from his thirteenth chapter, in which the Lord gives his disciples a "new commandment" (*mandatum novum*) that we derive the ritual of the washing of feet, which is a gesture pointing to the love that is at the core of all Christian action. The rite itself was given the name *mandatum* in the Church, for it symbolizes that new commandment that is to be a distinctive sign of the Christian. "This is how all will know that you are my disciples, if you have love for one another" (John 13:35). To obey this new commandment is simply to imitate the loving Christ: "love one another. As I have loved you, so you also should love one another" (John 13:34).

The antiphons sung during the washing of the feet repeat these last two texts, along with others from the gospel of the Mass. During the procession that follows upon the *mandatum*, a song is sung that combines texts from St. Paul with other texts:

Where true charity is dwelling, God is present there. By the love of Christ we have been brought together: let us find in him our gladness and our pleasure; may we love him and revere him, God the living; and in love respect each other with sincere hearts.

Where true charity is dwelling, God is present there. So when we are gathered all together, let us strive to keep our minds free of division; may there be an end to malice, strife and quarrels, and let Christ our God be dwelling here among us.

The seventh of the antiphons sung during the *mandatum* recalls the three theological virtues and reminds us that charity is the first and most important of them: "Let faith, hope, and charity, these three, remain among you, but the greatest of these is charity" (1 Cor 13:13).

27. THE LORD'S SUPPER

The Lord's Twofold Gift of Himself

The eucharistic celebration on Holy Thursday evening, and indeed every eucharistic celebration, is a memorial of the Lord's twofold gift of himself: his death for our salvation and his institution of the Eucharist. The first preface of the Holy Eucharist brings out the double gift: "For he is the true and eternal Priest, who instituted the pattern of an everlasting sacrifice and was the first to offer himself as the saving Victim, commanding us to make this offering as his memorial."

The "night he was handed over" (1 Cor 11:23) is what the Church is commemorating on this day. She has already been commemorating it in the Liturgy of the Word, where a number of read or sung texts recall this "handing over" of the Lord to his death. By means of these texts in the Liturgy of the Word, the Church has already been celebrating a genuine "memorial." We should not think of the songs and readings as simply an exhortation or a reminder of the great moment in the Lord's life when he seals his covenant and becomes a part of people's lives. No, the proclamation is already an "objective memorial" of God's acts, and a way of making the Savior and his saving actions present again in his Church. As the Constitution on the Sacred Liturgy (no. 7) says: "Christ is always present in his Church, especially in liturgical celebrations. . . . He is present in his word since it is he himself who speaks when the holy scriptures are read in the Church."[1]

Just as the readings are not simply a record of the past, neither is the celebration of the Eucharist intended merely to remind us of past events. The eucharistic action is a present action of Christ, although one that depends for its redemptive value on a past action of Christ that was accomplished once and for all.

It is that past action of the Christ who was handed over and who gave himself to his Father that we commemorate by rendering it present. In the Garden of Gethsemane, Christ—and we—become aware of the dramatic conflict that the Gospel of Mark sums up in a few words: "but not what I will, but what you will" (14:36). The outcome of the struggle in Christ is completely in keeping with his mission, for he, the completely just one, came into the world to do God's will (see Heb 10:5-9). In the Acts of the Apostles, St. Paul quotes Psalm 89:21, which refers to David but is far more applicable to Christ: "I have found David, son of Jesse, a man after my own heart; he will carry out my every wish" (Acts 13:22).

Christ was handed over to death, yet there is no contradiction when we sing in the entrance antiphon of the Holy Thursday evening Mass: "We should glory in the Cross of our Lord Jesus Christ, in whom is our salvation, life and resurrection, through whom we are saved and delivered." Why is there no contradiction? Because while Christ was indeed handed over, this happened because he himself freely chose that it should be so. We have adverted to this truth already in saying that Christ's "hour" designates not so much a point of time but an action deliberately taken. The hour in which Jesus is handed over and that seems to mark the victory of his enemies is also the hour when Jesus asks the Father to glorify him: "Father, the hour has come. Give glory to your son, so that your son may glorify you" (John 17:1). Elsewhere, Jesus is careful to point out that his "being handed over" is, in fact, his own voluntary giving of his life to the Father for the sake of those whom he loves: "This is why the Father loves me, because I lay down my life in order to take it up again. No one takes it from me, but I lay it down of my own. I have power to lay it down, and power to take it again. This command I have received from my Father" (John 10:17-18).

Later on, when he is being questioned, Jesus says to Pilate, "You would have no power over me if it had not been given you from above" (John 19:11).

The heart of Christ's redemptive act is the voluntary offering he makes of himself and of the human race he represents. What effects our redemption is not strictly the death of Christ nor the shedding of his blood but the interior act that these signify, that is, the voluntary and total gift Jesus makes of himself to his Father. But we must properly understand this statement.

The philosophies to which we are accustomed distinguish between a sign and the reality it signifies. Semites typically deemphasize any distinction of this kind; for them, the sign already contains in a way the reality signified. From the Semite's point of view, then, we can rightly say that the bloodshed and death of Christ redeem us. These signs, in the Semite's view, contain, and cannot but contain, the reality to which they point, namely, Christ's unreserved gift of himself to his Father, an act that more than makes up for the first human's refusal to serve.

If, moreover, it is accurate to say that Christ's shedding of blood and his death could not, simply by themselves, have redeemed us, it is also accurate to say that we could not have been redeemed without them, that is, if his self-giving had not involved the shedding of his blood and his death. The reason is that the sign is closely bound up with the reality it signifies. In addition, we who are creatures composed of body and soul need a sensible sign through which we can touch the realities of our salvation.

It is this voluntary self-giving of Christ to his Father that the eucharistic celebration makes present to us. When Christ says, "This is my body that is for you" (1 Cor 11:24, with variant reading), the substance of the bread is no longer there, and we are in the presence of his body. We are thereby also in the presence of all the mysteries of Christ and are even in a position to relive them with him for the rebuilding of the world. The past mysteries of Christ thus become truly present in the liturgy. It is now that Christ is handed over for our sake; were this not so, the Mass would be almost emptied of meaning.

At the same time, however, we cannot believe that the past begins all over again. St. Leo writes: "This state of infancy, which the Son of God did not judge unworthy of his majesty, matured. . . . Once he had achieved the victory of his suffering and resurrection, all the actions he did for us in lowliness passed away."[2] But the saint also writes: "All that the Son of God did and taught for the reconciliation of the world we not only know from the history of the past but we experience in virtue of his present works."[3]

The singleness of Christ's redemptive sacrifice is taught clearly in the Letter to the Hebrews: "[He offered sacrifice] once for all when he offered himself" (7:27). St. Paul says the same: "We know that Christ, raised from the dead, dies no more; death no longer has power over him. As to his death, he died to sin once and for all; as to his life, he lives for God" (Rom 6:9-10).

Despite this undeniable truth, we must admit that the Christ who is really present in the Eucharist brings with him the real presence of all his mysteries. These mysteries are not repeated, any more than his death is, but they are made present so that we can actively participate in them. We cannot claim that the mysteries of the Lord continue to act on us and that we have an obligation of participating in them with him unless they are in some way rendered present. The Mass, then, makes present the self-giving of Christ to his Father and draws us to give ourselves along with our Head.

Christ, then, was given over to death, but he also gave us the mysteries of his Body and Blood. The Holy Thursday evening Mass says as much in the *Hanc igitur* prayer: "Therefore, Lord, we pray: graciously accept this oblation of our service, that of your whole family, which we make to you as we observe the day on which our Lord Jesus Christ handed on the mysteries of his Body and Blood for his disciples to celebrate."

All this means that the Eucharist offered by any priest must be regarded as the Eucharist offered by Christ himself. What is the Eucharist, after all? If we examine it closely, we see that it is simply a response of individuals to God's plan for them and for humanity. It is thanksgiving, in response to the God who calls and who distributes to people the wonders of his salvation. Yet this response was, in fact, impossible for humans, and it would continue to be impossible if Christ himself were not making that response by celebrating the Eucharist through a priest's agency. No longer is the response made to God by an isolated Christ; it is made by Christ and the Church that he won as his Spouse through the cross. This brings us back once again to the need of unity as a condition for properly celebrating the eucharistic mystery, since it is on the mystery of unity that the possibility of a genuine response to God depends, both for the individual and for the people of God as a whole.

Christ's prayer after the Supper tells us why this unity is so basic:

> I pray not only for them, but also for those who will believe in me
> through their word, so that they may all be one, as you, Father, are in
> me and I in you, that they also may be in us, that the world may believe
> that you sent me. And I have given them the glory you gave me, so that
> they may be one, as we are one, I in them and you in me, that they may
> be brought to perfection as one, that the world may know that you sent
> me, and that you loved them even as you loved me. (John 17:20-23)

What Jesus' sacrifice effected was his own perfect unity with the Father. We can share in that mysterious unity only if we are completely one with Christ. All of us, therefore, must be caught up in the one Eucharist that Christ offers. That, in turn, is possible, however, only if Christ continues unceasingly to celebrate for us his one Eucharist that makes the entire Church one. It was to this end that Christ "handed on the mysteries of his Body and Blood for his disciples to celebrate." Not any and every individual can thus render present the Lord's one Eucharist (to say so would be to think in terms of magic), but only those to whom the Lord handed over the mysteries of his Body and Blood.

When the Second Vatican Council voted to restore eucharistic con-celebration in the modern Latin Church, it proposed Holy Thursday as one occasion for it.[4] Concelebration makes manifest the point we have just been emphasizing about Christ's one Eucharist, namely, that there is really only one celebrant, Christ himself. So true is this that the multiplication of celebrations does not mean a multiplication of Christ's Eucharist or thanksgiving. In all the Eucharists of all the earthly priests, there is but a single Eucharist: that which Christ is offering through the mediation of those whom he appoints and to whom he has entrusted the mysteries of his Body and Blood. Thus, when new priests celebrate the Eucharist on the day of their ordina-tion with the bishop who has just ordained them, there is really only a single celebration.

It seems we must say that concelebration as practiced today, in which all the priests pronounce at least the words of consecration, was not the practice of the early Church. Since there is in reality only one celebrant, namely, Christ who offers his Eucharist through his Church, we can understand why, in the early Church, only the bishop spoke the eucharistic prayer, while the other priests shared in the celebration simply by receiving the consecrated bread and wine. That was their way of concelebrating.

In the Roman Church, as far back as we can go, we find concelebra-tion in the modern manner in only two cases. One was the consecra-tion of a bishop; on this occasion the consecrating bishops all joined the newly consecrated bishop in imposing hands on the offerings.[5] The other was the ordination of priests, who concelebrated with the bishop who ordained them. The point in both cases was to emphasize the sharing of power and to bring out a kind of collegiality.

Apart from these cases, a priest celebrated the Eucharist (i.e., pro-nounced the prayers of the liturgy) only in the service of a community and when the bishop could not be there to do it himself. On these occasions, he celebrated the Eucharist as the bishop's delegate, a fact brought out by means of the *fermentum* (literally, "leaven"). The *fermentum* was a piece of consecrated bread that the bishop sent from his altar to a priest whom he had appointed to celebrate the Eucharist elsewhere. The priest showed that he was celebrating only as a delegate, and in union with the bishop, by putting the *fermentum* in his own chalice. There was therefore, at the human level, only one celebrant, in a sense; this oneness pointed in turn to the one Christ who celebrates his Eucharist in every earthly Eucharist.

From this we can see that concelebration should not be thought of simply as a pragmatic way of easing the burden of a sacristan when "private" Masses are multiplied. Nor is it meant merely to satisfy the desire of the individual priest not to have to say Mass by himself. Concelebration of the modern type should be reserved for certain occasions when it is desirable to manifest the unity of priesthood and Eucharist. We are not saying, of course, that the "private" Mass is invalid; we do say, however, that its meaningfulness is lessened by the absence of a congregation.* The early Church thought of the Mass in terms of a service to the Christian community; it was in the service of the community that a priest, representing Christ in his one sacrifice, repeated the gestures and words of the Supper.

Until the recent reform, a single priest said the eucharistic prayer at the Holy Thursday Mass; other priests associated themselves with the rite by receiving Communion. Such was the normal practice of the Latin Church in the first centuries, except on days of episcopal consecration or priestly ordination. The practice highlighted the unicity of the priest, namely, of Christ. The modern practice of having all the priests say the eucharistic prayer together emphasizes something else, namely, the unity of the priesthood, and was hitherto reserved, as we have indicated, for two occasions: episcopal consecration and ordination to the priesthood.

The Second Vatican Council has opened the way for more frequent concelebration (in the modern form), and there is no reason for renouncing the possibility. Moreover, there exists the alternative, for those priests who wish it and who have no obligation to celebrate

* This Mass, formerly called "Order of Mass without a Congregation," is now called, "Order of Mass, with the Participation of a Single Minister."

for a community, of participating in the Sacrifice by receiving under both species.

They Recognized Him in the Breaking of the Bread

The phrase "breaking of bread" was for a long time an accepted synonym for "celebrating the Eucharist," in accordance with the well-known text in St. Luke: "Then the two recounted . . . how he was made known to them in the breaking of the bread" (Luke 24:35).[6] Full participation in the covenant requires the eating of the bread, since the covenant rite consists in the eating of a sacrificial meal. As we observed earlier, there is something strikingly new about the covenant meal of Christ: that what we eat is not simply bread but the very Victim of the historical sacrifice offered once and for all for the world's redemption.

Communion is not, however, to be thought of as being simply an extension of the sacrifice. The distinction between the priestly consecratory prayer and the Communion is required in exposition because our minds cannot grasp and express wholes all at once. As a matter of fact, we cannot conceive of the Eucharist apart from the eating that is required under pain of eliminating its character as a covenant sign and thus entirely destroying it. We must be fully incorporated into Christ if we are to share in his covenant, and we must therefore eat the bread if full expression is to be given to our solidarity with him and our entry into the unity with the Father that he has restored.

Given this truth, we can see why we really offer nothing (ritually) in the sacrifice of the Mass; instead, Christ takes our gifts, offers them himself to the Father, and then gives us a share in the covenant unity established by his blood. This is why the word "offertory" as a description of the preparation of the matter for the sacrifice in the Roman liturgy is so ill chosen. There are not two moments of "offering" in the Mass—one when the faithful come with their gifts, the other when Christ offers himself to the Father. No, there is only one real offerer, Christ; with him we are closely associated, to the point of sharing in his Body and Blood.

The sharing in the body of Christ and in the covenant sealed by his blood is our pledge of eternal life. To understand this, we need only read St. John's gospel, chapter 6, and meditate on the Lord's words:

I am the bread of life. Your ancestors ate the manna in the wilderness, but they died; this is the bread that comes down from heaven so that one may eat it and not die. I am the living bread that came down from heaven; whoever eats this bread will live for ever; and the bread that I will give is my flesh for the life of the world. . . . Whoever eats my flesh and drinks my blood has eternal life, and I will raise him on the last day. (John 6:48-51, 54)

After Mass on Holy Thursday, the Blessed Sacrament is carried with some solemnity to a chapel prepared for reservation; Communion will be distributed the next day. In the older Roman liturgy, the remains of the consecrated bread were placed in a small box and deposited in a drawer in the sacristy, without any special outward signs of honor. At the next Mass, the box was brought to the altar at the moment of the fraction, and its contents were placed in the chalice. At the beginning of that Mass, when the pontiff entered the Church, the box had been presented to him open, and he had venerated the sacred species for a moment.[7] Once devotion to the Blessed Sacrament began to develop, the reserved species also began to receive special honor. In some churches during the eighth century, the ciboria were placed near the reliquaries on the altar; in the eleventh century, tabernacles set in the wall began to appear.

Devotion to the Blessed Sacrament developed gradually; the process was speeded up in the second half of the thirteenth century, once Pope Urban IV extended to the whole Church the feast of Corpus Christi (August 11, 1264). The Holy Thursday repository then became a place for manifesting devotion to the Eucharist on the anniversary of the Last Supper. Once the Holy Thursday liturgy took over some customs that were signs of sadness (no playing of the organ; use of a clapper or rattle instead of bells; etc.), the repository came to be regarded in some places as a symbolic tomb for Christ.

The solemn stripping of the altar seems to have been simply a ritualization of an older utilitarian action, since the altar cloths had always been removed once the Mass was over. An age in quest of (often artificial) symbolisms needed no special prodding to see in the stripping of the altars the stripping of Christ's garments from him in preparation for crucifixion. The altar cloths were left off the altar until Saturday evening, simply because no Mass was celebrated until the Easter Vigil. Here again, however, symbolism came into play. The end result was that Holy Thursday acquired an atmosphere of sadness that the new Holy Week ritual has deliberately removed.

In some monasteries and churches, the altars are washed on Holy Thursday, but it is done without special solemnity. Clerics in surplices first wash the altar with water and wine, then dry it. In the Byzantine Rite, however, there is a solemn washing of the altar; while psalms are sung, the patriarch, prelates, and priests wash the altar with water.

The Three Holy Days of Christ Dead, Buried, and Risen: Good Friday, Holy Saturday, Easter Sunday

28. THE UNITY OF THE THREE HOLY DAYS

In the early centuries the paschal Triduum comprised Good Friday, Holy Saturday, and Easter Sunday.* It was known simply as the Triduum of Christ dead, buried, and risen. The penitential fast of Lent ended on Holy Thursday; on Good Friday there began a festive, intra-paschal fast that ended with Communion during the Easter Vigil.

In Tertullian's time, the paschal fast began on Good Friday and lasted through Holy Saturday until the celebration of the Eucharist during the night between Saturday and Sunday.[†] Friday and Saturday were days of fast for all. At that time people had a very realistic conception of the Eucharist; it was regarded as the most real of all foods, to the point that to receive the Eucharist was to break one's fast. When Tertullian wanted to persuade Christians to celebrate the Eucharist on a fast day, he did not challenge their belief that it would break their fast; he simply argued that to celebrate the Eucharist is more important than to fast.

The fast on Good Friday and Holy Saturday did not mean that there were special celebrations on these days. We remarked earlier that the Church of the first centuries did not think of breaking up the paschal mysteries into stages and celebrating these one by one. The simple structure of the paschal liturgy in the early Church showed, and was meant to show, the real unity of Christ's death and resurrection. Life came from death.

---

* It is clear from his arrangement of this material that Nocent prefers to think of the Triduum this way; however, the postconciliar liturgy starts the Triduum with the Holy Thursday Evening Mass of the Lord's Supper.
† It is unknown how broadly people of this time kept a fast or observed a "Good Friday."

By a normal and inevitable development, the Church gradually came to celebrate the stages of the one mystery; she did not separate the stages, but she did focus her attention on each in turn, while remaining always aware that they formed a unity. In a now classic text, St. Ambrose is a witness to the evolution that had already occurred: "We must observe not only the day of the Passion but the day of the resurrection as well. Thus we have a day of bitterness and a day of joy; on the one, let us fast; on the other, let us seek refreshment." A few lines further on, he presents us with the ancient idea of the paschal Triduum: "the sacred Triduum . . . during which he suffered, rested, and rose, and of which he says, 'Destroy this temple, and in three days I will raise it up.'"[1]

We have already pointed out how the Triduum was organized in the early Church (St. Augustine's "most holy Triduum of the crucified, buried, and risen [Christ]"[2]), and we need not insist further on it. It is clear, however, that this apparent breaking up of the one mystery could lead to the faithful fragmenting the mystery in their own minds and forgetting its basic unity. Yet if we but read the liturgical texts for the three days, we will find the Roman liturgy insisting that the death and resurrection of Christ form a single indivisible mystery.

The Glorious Passion of Christ Our Lord: Good Friday

29. CELEBRATIONS ANCIENT AND MODERN

Celebration of the Word

The liturgy of the day comprises three actions, among which there is no very clear connection. The three are the celebration of the word, the adoration of the cross, and Communion.

The celebration of the word is the basic element, and it is found everywhere in the Good Friday liturgy. It is especially interesting as far as the history of the Roman liturgy is concerned. This is because we still find in it the simple, rather elementary structure that characterized the Liturgy of the Word as described by St. Justin in his *First Apology* (ca. 150). St. Justin tells us that on Sundays "the memoirs of the apostles or the writings of the prophets are read, as far as time allows; then, when the reader is finished, he who presides admonishes and exhorts those present to imitate the splendid things they have heard."[1] The celebration of the word ended with solemn prayers offered by the whole assembly.

The Gospel of St. Luke shows us Christ reading Isaiah (61:1-2) and then explaining what he had read (Luke 4:16-22). The Liturgy of the Word as described by St. Justin was really still the Jewish morning liturgy on the Sabbath. This office consisted of a reading of the Law and the Prophets and of ensuing acclamations. Prayers were then offered by the congregation for all the needs of the community, and a final blessing marked the end of the liturgy. The first Christian liturgies all followed the pattern of the Jewish synagogal liturgy. As late as the time of St. Augustine, we find liturgical meetings in which the word was proclaimed but no Eucharist was celebrated. That was the Roman custom on Wednesdays and Fridays.

The first part of the Good Friday office still reflects this early liturgical pattern and, apart from a few variations, is marked by the ancient simplicity: readings and chants, homily, solemn general intercessions. That is the nucleus of the Liturgy of the Word. As all are aware, the conciliar Constitution on the Sacred Liturgy has restored the more frequent use of Bible services that are not followed by the celebration of the Eucharist.[2]

The precise order followed in this ancient Good Friday Liturgy of the Word has, however, varied in details from period to period and even from place to place. In ancient Roman practice, the service began with the bishop prostrating himself and praying in silence; then there was a first reading followed by a tract, a second reading followed by another tract, the singing of the passion, and the solemn intercessions. These last were the only prayers said during the service.[3]

In some liturgical books, however, when the celebrant had reached the altar, he invited the congregation to pray, and the deacon told the faithful to kneel down. When all had stood up again, the celebrant read the prayer *Deus a quo et Iudas* ("O God, who punished Judas . . ."). There was then a first reading, followed by a tract and the prayer *Deus, qui peccati veteris* ("O God, through the Passion of your Christ . . ."); a second reading, with its tract; the singing of the passion; and the solemn intercessions.[4]

Still another organization of the ceremony was as follows: prostration of the celebrant, who prays silently; a first lesson followed by a tract and the prayer *Deus, a quo et Iudas*; a second reading and tract; the singing of the passion; the solemn intercessions.

Finally, there is the organization we find in the new Holy Week ritual: silent prostration, followed by a prayer; first reading and responsorial psalm; second reading and verse before the gospel; singing of the passion; solemn intercessions. There is no entrance song and no *Gloria*; there is no *Kyrie* because it is replaced by the solemn intercessions.

The "prayer of the faithful" was part of the Roman liturgy down to the time of Pope Gelasius I (492–96). In the Eastern liturgy, it has been preserved down to our time, but in the Roman liturgy, except for its rather archaic use in the Good Friday liturgy, it vanished completely from view. Vestiges of it, such as the prayers of the prone in some countries, would not have reminded anyone but a few specialists of the original prayer of the faithful. But this is not the place to sketch the history of this prayer.

We should point out, however, that since the time (about the fourth century) when the Western and Eastern rites began to be differentiated, the Good Friday prayer of the faithful took on a different form in West and East. In the Western rite, the celebrant announces the intention; everyone prays silently; then the celebrant says a prayer in which the congregation joins with its "Amen." In the East, the deacon proclaims the intentions and the faithful answer each with a *Kyrie eleison* or similar response; only at the end of the litany does the celebrant say a prayer to which the faithful answer "Amen." In Egeria's account of the Jerusalem liturgy, we see the children chanting *Kyrie eleison* in answer to intentions proclaimed by the deacon at the end of Vespers.[5] The *Kyrie* seems to have been introduced into the Roman liturgy at least before 529[6] and to have been sung in response to an intention.

With regard to the *Kyrie*, we still possess an important document that has been attributed to Pope Gelasius. The "prayer which Pope Gelasius determined should be sung throughout the Church" consists of nineteen intentions, each answered with a *Kyrie eleison* or a *Christe eleison*.[7] The ancient prayer of the faithful, in the form of the solemn intercessions, thus took on a new shape and became like the prayer of the faithful as found in the Eastern liturgy. Its greater simplicity and directness undoubtedly helped it replace the older solemn intercessions. It is difficult, however, to determine whether the displacement of the prayer of the faithful occurred at the same time as its form changed (from solemn intercessions to litanic prayer) or whether, on the contrary, there were two stages: introduction of the litanic form and then the shift of the prayer of the faithful to a position before the readings. In any case, by the time the first Roman *Ordines* were composed (around the middle of the seventh century), the offertory rite comes immediately after the gospel and homily, leaving no place for a litanic prayer.[8]

The chanted solemn intercessions of Good Friday are ten in number. We should be aware of the theology implied in putting these solemn intercessions after the proclamation of the word. The faithful are first penetrated by the word that the Lord himself addresses to them; then, as men and women transformed by that word, they join in prayer for the important intentions of the Church.

Adoration of the Cross

Egeria, the fourth-century traveler, is our first witness to this liturgical custom:

A throne is set up for the bishop on Golgotha behind the Cross, which now stands there. The bishop sits on his throne, a table covered with a linen cloth is set before him, and the deacons stand around the table. The gilded silver casket containing the sacred wood of the Cross is brought in and opened. Both the wood of the Cross and the inscription are taken out and placed on the table. As soon as they have been placed on the table, the bishop, remaining seated, grips the ends of the sacred wood with his hands, while the deacons, who are standing about, keep watch over it. There is a reason why it is guarded in this manner. It is the practice here for all the people to come forth one by one, the faithful as well as the catechumens, to bow down before the table, kiss the holy wood, and then move on. It is said that someone (I do not know when) took a bite and stole a piece of the holy Cross. Therefore, it is now guarded by the deacons standing around, lest there be anyone who would dare come and do that again.

All the people pass through one by one; all of them bow down, touching the Cross and the inscription, first with their foreheads, then with their eyes; and, after kissing the Cross, they move on. No one, however, puts out his hand to touch the Cross.[9]

At Rome, where a piece of the wood of the cross was preserved, a ritual of veneration similar to the one described by Egeria was introduced.[10] But, though the seventh-century Mozarabic liturgy has a service of adoration of the cross that it seems to have gotten from Jerusalem,[11] the Roman liturgy did not derive its ritual from Spain. Only in *Ordo* 23 (700–750) do we find a lengthy description (the work of a pilgrim) of the rite of adoration of the cross; the description is quite close to Egeria's,[12] and the ritual undoubtedly did come from Jerusalem. The Eastern influence is evident. For example, the pope himself carries the smoking censer in the procession, something found nowhere else in the Roman liturgy. It has been noted by historians that just at the period when the Good Friday veneration of the cross appears in the Roman liturgy, the See of Peter was occupied by Eastern popes, from John V (685–86) to Zachary (741–52).[13]

The procession starts at the Lateran and moves to Santa Croce de Gerusalemme; the pope, barefooted, carries the censer, while a deacon follows him with the box containing a relic of the cross. The box is placed on the altar and the pope opens it; he then prostrates himself in prayer before the altar, rises, kisses the relic, and goes to his throne. At a signal from him, the bishops, priests, deacons, and subdeacons come up to kiss the cross on the altar; they are followed by the faithful. After the adoration of the cross, a deacon goes into the pulpit and begins the reading from the prophet Hosea. This whole ritual precedes the Liturgy of the Word, and that is exactly the custom of which we learn in Egeria's journal.[14] Neither in *Ordo* 23 nor in Egeria's account is anything said of singing during the adoration; the whole ceremony was probably conducted in profound silence.

From the eighth and ninth centuries on, the procession of the faithful to the altar to adore the cross (a ceremony that took place in the evening) was accompanied by the singing of the antiphon *Ecce lignum crucis* ("Behold the wood of the cross, on which hung the salvation of the world") and Psalm 119, "Blessed are those whose way is blameless, / who walk in the law of the LORD!"[15] Later on, other antiphons were added to the psalmody, for example, *Salva nos, Christe* ("Save us, O Christ") and especially *Crucem tuam adoramus, Domine* ("We adore your cross, O Lord, and we praise and glorify your holy resurrection"). This last is Byzantine in origin[16] and was already known to Amalarius.[17]

According to *Ordo* 31 (850–900), after the pope has communicated, the cross is carried from behind the altar to the front of the altar, while the *Trisagion* is sung, another composition that came to Rome from the Eastern liturgy by way of Gaul.[18] During the adoration of the cross by the lower clergy and the faithful, not only the *Ecce lignum crucis* and Psalm 118 (119) are sung but also the hymn *Pange lingua* ("Sing, my tongue," composed by Venantius Fortunatus, who died in 600), along with the antiphon *Crux fidelis* ("O faithful cross").[19] According to this same *Ordo*, the *Ecce lignum crucis* was sung while the cross was being shown to the faithful.

Nothing is said in these various *Ordines* about unveiling the cross, a ceremony that makes its appearance only in the twelfth century[20] but thenceforth acquires an ever greater importance. With the Roman Pontifical of the twelfth century, the ceremony undergoes a kind of dramatization.[21] Later on, during the adoration of the cross, the *Improperia* ("Reproaches") are joined to the *Trisagion*; the practice can be found as early as the end of the ninth century.[22]

In the new Holy Week rite, two ways of showing the cross are provided. The cross may be brought veiled to the altar, where the celebrant uncovers it in stages, singing at each stage the antiphon, "Behold the wood of the Cross, on which hung the salvation of the world." Or else the celebrant or deacon may carry the cross, unveiled, from the back of the church, stopping to sing the antiphon three times on the way. During the adoration of the cross, the antiphon *Crucem tuam adoramus, Domine,* and the *Improperia* may be sung.

According to the old *Ordo* 31, the faithful kissed the cross immediately before receiving Communion. The adoration of the cross and the reception of Communion were thus brought into close proximity and became in effect a single action.

Reception of Communion

The reception of Communion on Good Friday was not practiced at Rome before the seventh century. In his letter to Decentius, Pope Innocent I (401–17) wrote: "It is clear that during these two days the apostles were filled with grief and even hid themselves out of fear of the Jews. Nor is there any doubt that they fasted during that time; consequently, it is the tradition of the Church that the mysteries not be celebrated on these two days."[23] We saw above that in Tertullian's time reception of the Eucharist was considered to break the fast. The same view prevailed in the time of Innocent I.

In *Ordo* 23 (700–750) we find an interesting rubric to the effect that neither the pope nor the deacons communicate on Good Friday; anyone wishing to communicate may go to some other church of Rome and there receive the Eucharist that had been reserved after the Holy Thursday Mass.[24] Here we have divergent customs existing side by side at Rome. The papal liturgy had no communion rite, while the other churches of the city did have one in which the Eucharist reserved from Holy Thursday was distributed. The introduction of Communion on Good Friday presupposed a mitigation of the intra-paschal fast.

In the present Byzantine liturgy, the liturgy of the presanctified is not celebrated on Good Friday (therefore, no Communion that day), unless the day happens to fall on March 25, the feast of the Annunciation, which is not transferrable. During Lent, Mass is not celebrated in the Byzantine Rite except on Saturdays and Sundays; on the other days of the week, however, a liturgy of the presanctified is celebrated after Vespers. The Romans may have been led to their Good Friday practice of a liturgy of the presanctified by observing the Lenten custom of the Byzantine colony at Rome.

In the Roman liturgy of that period, the people received Communion under both species. The oldest documents expressly mention the reservation of both the consecrated bread and the consecrated wine. Later documents, which seem to reflect Gallican usage, mention only the reservation of the consecrated bread, but, in the same context, they mention that the consecrated bread is silently placed in a chalice of unconsecrated wine. This practice was based on a theological opinion that arose around 800.

It was not an easy matter, of course, to reserve for Friday enough of the precious blood that had been consecrated at the Thursday Mass. Consequently, it had been customary to pour some of the precious blood into a chalice of unconsecrated wine and to use the mixture for the Communion of the faithful on Friday. But around 800 there arose the opinion that by mingling consecrated bread with unconsecrated wine, a consecration of the wine was effected. This was due not to any combining of molecules but simply to contact with the consecrated bread. Amalarius is a witness to the resultant liturgical usage.[25] The Romano-Germanic Pontifical of the tenth century explicitly accepts the belief in consecration by contact: "The unconsecrated wine is sanctified by the consecrated bread."[26]

This, then, was how Communion was celebrated. The bread consecrated the day before was brought to the altar, along with unconsecrated wine. They were incensed; then the celebrant sang the Our Father; the *Pax Domini* was not sung. The host was divided into three parts, one of which was silently placed in the chalice. The Roman Pontifical of the twelfth century still attested to the now longstanding belief: "The unconsecrated wine is sanctified by the mingling with the body of the Lord."[27]

At the beginning of the thirteenth century, however, the theologians, with Peter Cantor (d. 1197) at their head, rejected the theory of consecration by contact. As a result, we find the pope alone receiving Communion at his Mass.[28] From that time on, down to the reform of 1955, only the celebrant communicated at the Good Friday liturgy, but the rite of commingling continued in use. The 1955 reform suppressed the commingling and restored the practice of Communion for all, the first traces of which we saw in the nonpapal Roman liturgy of the seventh century. After Communion there is now a closing prayer, and, by way of dismissal, another that the celebrant says with his hands extended toward the congregation.

30. THE BLOOD OF THE LAMB

The primary concern of the Office of Readings in the Liturgy of the Hours on Good Friday is to situate the passion in its proper messianic context.

The Psalms

Psalm 2 has always been regarded as messianic by both the Jewish and the Christian traditions. It shows enemies rebelling against God: "They arise, the kings of the earth; / princes plot against the LORD and his Anointed" (v. 2). But "He who sits in the heavens laughs; / the LORD derides and mocks them" (v. 4). Then we are told the role of the Messiah: "The LORD said to me, 'You are my Son. / It is I who have begotten you this day. / Ask of me, and I will give you / the nations as your inheritance, / and the ends of the earth as your possession. / With a rod of iron you will rule them; / like a potter's jar you will shatter them'" (vv. 7-9).

The perspective here is already paschal, since the Son, begotten according to the flesh, will shatter his enemies as though they were a potter's dish and will receive the nations as his inheritance.

In Psalm 22 we hear Christ lamenting and praying. A lover of the psalms, he will utter aloud the opening words of this psalm as he hangs on the cross: "My God, my God, why have you forsaken me? / Why are you far from saving me, / so far from my words of anguish? / O my God, I call by day and you do not answer; / I call by night and I find no reprieve" (vv. 2-3).

Verses 7 and 8 of this psalm remind us of the fourth song of the Suffering Servant (Isa 52:13–53:12), and the evangelists took the psalm as a description of the Lord's passion. St. Matthew (27:46), for example, puts verse 2 of the psalm on Christ's lips at the ninth hour when he utters his loud cry, "*Eli, Eli, lema sabachthani?*" In thus verbalizing the Savior's cry, Matthew does not mean that Christ is expressing despair; on the contrary, Matthew has in mind the later part of the psalm in which the psalmist voices his certainty of final victory. At the beginning of the crucifixion scene, Matthew and John allude to (Matthew) or quote (John) verse 19 of Psalm 22, "They divided my garments among them, and for my vesture they cast lots" (John 19:24).

Psalm 38, the third psalm in the Office of Readings, likewise expresses distress. Once again we find the accents of the fourth song of the Suffering Servant (Isa 53:7): "But I, like someone deaf, do not hear; / like someone mute, I do not open my mouth. / I am like one who hears nothing, / in whose mouth is no defense" (Ps 38:14-15). The distress of Christ, weighted down as he is with the sins of the world, finds voice in even more violent words in verses 18-19, "For I am on the point of falling; / and my pain is always with me. / I confess that I am guilty; / and I am grieved because of my sin."

The antiphons are chosen in order to convey the same thoughts and feelings. Thus the antiphon for the first psalm emphasizes the violence used by the enemy: "Earthly kings rise up, in revolt; princes conspire together against the Lord and his Anointed." The second antiphon, taken from Psalm 22 itself, reminds us of Calvary: "They divide my garments among them; they cast lots for my clothing."

Christ the Priest Enters the Sanctuary

The atmosphere in the first reading, from the Letter to the Hebrews, is quite different, as it shows us Christ the High Priest entering once and for all into the Holy of Holies (Heb 9:11-28). The passage gives us a theological vision of the Lamb who is sacrificed. It is not with the blood of goats or calves but with his own blood that Christ enters once and for all into the sanctuary and wins eternal redemption for us (v. 12). He is the mediator of a new covenant (v. 15), but in establishing it he shed his blood only once. Unlike the priests of the Old Testament, he does not have to shed blood over and over but has appeared at the end of the ages to take away sin once and for all (v. 26). Now he has entered heaven in person so that he might appear before God on our behalf (v. 24).

The passage ends with the expression of a great hope of salvation; it is a hope whose reality we already possess in germ: "so Christ was offered up once to take away the sins of many; he will appear a second time not to take away sin but to bring salvation to those who eagerly await him" (v. 28).

The Covenant in the Blood of Christ

The language and imagery of the Letter to the Hebrews should not prevent us from seeing that it is speaking of a true sacrifice and that blood is required by the covenant.

In the eucharistic liturgy, when the celebrant shows the consecrated bread to the faithful he says, "Behold the Lamb of God, behold him who takes away the sins of the world." These words sum up the whole paschal mystery, the life of the Church, and our individual lives. In the Fourth Gospel, John the Baptist already speaks of Christ in the same way: "Behold, the Lamb of God, who takes away the sin of the world" (1:29).

When the Baptist used the title "Lamb of God," he was undoubtedly making his own a current image. But the image was, in fact, a double image. It could refer either to the Passover lamb of the book of Exodus (chap. 12) or to the lamb led to slaughter in the book of Isaiah (chap. 53). In the book of Exodus, the Lord gives instructions to Moses and Aaron: "You will keep it [the lamb] until the fourteenth day of this month, and then, with the whole community of Israel assembled, it will be slaughtered during the evening twilight. They will take some of its blood and apply it to the two doorposts and the lintel of the houses in which they eat it" (Exod 12:6-7). The lamb here is a lamb sacrificed; its blood is shed. Later in the chapter we are told that "when the LORD goes by to strike down the Egyptians, seeing the blood on the lintel and the two doorposts, the LORD will pass over that door, and not let the destroyer come into your houses to strike you down" (v. 23).

Blood thus played a part in Israelite religion as it did in other religions of antiquity. The blood represented the being's life. The book of Deuteronomy, for example, commands: "But make sure that you do not eat of the blood [of the animals slaughtered for food]; for blood is life" (12:23). The life in question depends directly on God: "It is I who make both death and life, I who inflict wounds and heal them" (32:39). The use made of blood in worship thus reflected the outlook of a people that had a sense both of life and of God. They realized that the blood of a being, like the life it supported, belonged to God alone and must be reserved for him in the form of sacrifice (Lev 3:17).

Blood could be used only for expiation (Lev 17:18). It was natural for Israelites to assign blood a redemptive value. It was through the blood of the lamb, after all, that the Hebrews had won freedom from

Egypt. The blood shed in circumcision had already served as blood that sealed a covenant (Exod 4:26), but in Egypt the blood of the lamb also liberated the Hebrews and thus bound them to God in an even firmer covenant, for under this covenant they would become a kingdom of priests and a holy nation (Exod 19:6).

The covenant would later be concluded by means of a communion sacrifice in which blood once again played an essential role:

> Then, having sent young men of the Israelites to offer burnt offerings and sacrifice young bulls as communion offerings to the LORD, Moses took half of the blood and put it in large bowls; the other half he splashed on the altar. Taking the book of the covenant, he read it aloud to the people, who answered, "All that the LORD has said, we will hear and do." Then he took the blood and splashed it on the people, saying, "This is the blood of the covenant which the LORD has made with you according to all these words." (Exod 24:5-8)

The role of the young men is not clear, but the text as a whole conveys valuable information, namely, that part of the blood is poured on the altar, which represents God, and the other part is sprinkled on the people. First, the altar is splashed; then, the conditions of the covenant are announced; finally, the people give their assent, and the rest of the blood is sprinkled on them. There is a point here to which commentators rarely advert. It is that the blood is splashed on the altar before the law is read out. This means that it is primarily the people who commit themselves. Yahweh is not the prisoner of his own covenant; on the contrary, it is he who takes the initiative and offers an unmerited gift. "There are here no reciprocal rights and duties as in human covenants."[1]

Once we realize that blood symbolizes the life over which Yahweh has full rights and which no one but he can dispose of, we can understand that the blood ritual in the covenant signifies a genuine community between God and his people. Yahweh "gives the people a share in what is his by divine right."[2] This is of the utmost importance. We can see that, above and beyond a covenant at the juridical level, this covenant in blood manifests Yahweh's desire to have Israel for a son to whom he will be attached by ties of blood. Then the threat to Pharaoh makes sense: "So you will say to Pharaoh, Thus says the LORD: Israel is my son, my firstborn. I said to you: Let my son go, that he may serve me. Since you refuse to let him go, I will kill your son, your firstborn" (Exod 4:22-23). Later on, the book of Wisdom will say that "at the destruction of the firstborn they [the Egyptians] acknowledged that this people was God's son" (18:13).

The point of the rite of sprinkling thus seems to be to show that the vital bond linking Israel to its God is no less strong than the bond created by flesh-and-blood sonship.[3] The blood of the covenant is not only the blood that ransoms; it is also, and even more, the blood binding God to his people.

Christ the Lamb

The whole Christian tradition has seen in Christ the lamb, the only true Lamb, as the first preface for Easter puts it.

By the very manner in which he relates the events of the passion, St. John tells the world that Christ is the true Lamb. Jesus is put to death on the eve of the feast of Unleavened Bread, as John several times reminds us (18:28; 19:14, 31). In other words, he dies on the day when the Passover lambs are sacrificed in the temple. After his death, as John carefully notes, his legs are not broken, and the evangelist quotes the ritual prescription concerning the paschal lamb: "You shall not break any of its bones" (Exod 12:46; cf. John 19:36).

Writing to the Christians of Corinth, St. Paul urges them to live like unleavened loaves, as it were, "For our paschal lamb, Christ, has been sacrificed" (1 Cor 5:7). In his teaching, the Apostle also emphasized the value of blood in expiation; blood suggests sacrifice as well as ransom and justification.[4]

The First Letter of St. Peter, which is generally regarded as a baptismal catechesis, speaks of Jesus as the Lamb without sin (1:19) whose blood has ransomed humanity (1:18-19). This redemption by the blood of the Lamb means freedom from idols (1:14-18). Since they have been set free by the blood of the Lamb, Christians must be holy in all they do. They are now members of a royal and priestly people and have been called from darkness into the light (2:9).

For St. John too, Christ is the sinless Lamb (1:29 and 8:48; 1 John 3:5), who takes away the sin of the world (1:29). It is especially in the book of Revelation, however, that St. John exalts Christ as the Lamb who has triumphed. Jesus is the Lamb (5:6) who buys humanity back with his blood (5:9). Christians have been ransomed from the world (14:3) and are now a royal and priestly people (5:10). Thanks to the blood of the Lamb, they have overcome Satan (12:1). Now they can sing the canticle of Moses and the canticle of the Lamb (15:3).

In the book of Revelation we are given the basic theology that underlies the paschal mystery, for the Lamb who is slain is also "the lion of the tribe of Judah, the root of David" who "has triumphed, enabling him to open the scroll with its seven seals" (5:5). The Lamb has taken possession of his kingdom and now celebrates his wedding with his Bride, who has beautified herself for this day; she, the Church, joins the Lamb in inviting us to the wedding feast (19:6-9).

In this vision the Lamb is he who "takes away" the sins of the world. But it is also possible to regard the Lamb as the suffering Messiah who "bears" or "carries" the sins of the world. It has often been remarked that at a number of points in the Gospel of St. John words are used that can have two meanings. Thus the Greek verb *airein* can mean either "lift up and take away" or "carry." Given the latter of the two meanings, the word suggests the Servant Song in the book of Isaiah (chap. 53). Under heavy persecution a devout person could liken himself to a lamb led to slaughter (Jer 11:19). Isaiah, in fact, applied the image to the Servant: "Though harshly treated he submitted and did not open his mouth; Like a lamb led to slaughter or a sheep silent before shearers, he did not open his mouth" (53:7).

When the Ethiopian eunuch invited Philip into his carriage, the passage he had been reading and puzzling over was from the fourth Servant Song: "Like a sheep he was led to the slaughter, and as a lamb before its shearer is silent, so he opened not his mouth" (Acts 8:32). With this passage as his starting point, Philip told the eunuch the Good News of Jesus. Faith in this Lamb who was silent was the condition required for receiving the baptism Philip would administer. Philip thus linked up the two aspects of the Lamb that sum up the whole of the Good News: the mute Lamb led to slaughter and the spotless Lamb whose blood is shed for the salvation of the multitude, those whom he draws with him in his victory over the powers of evil.

The Office of Readings in the Liturgy of the Hours has for its second reading a passage from a catechesis of St. John Chrysostom. In it the saint is praising the power of Christ's blood.[5]

"Do you wish to know the power of Christ's blood?" To make his point, Chrysostom has recourse to typology, reminding his readers of the blood that the Israelites smeared on their doorposts. If the angel of death did not dare enter when he saw the blood that was, in fact, only a prefiguration, much more will he be afraid when he sees the real blood of Christ. The preacher then turns to the water and blood that flowed from the side of the crucified Christ. The water symbolizes baptism; the blood is the blood of the eucharistic sacrament. The water comes first, because we are first washed clean in baptism; only then are we sanctified by the Eucharist.

The Jews immolated a lamb; we have come to know the fruit that Christ's sacrifice has produced. For from the pierced side of Christ the Church was born, just as Eve was born from the side of Adam. Chrysostom has St. Paul's teaching in mind when he says, "We spring from his body and blood," alluding to the fruitful side of Christ. Christ made the Church one with himself, and he nourishes us. It is by means of this food that we are both born and fed. As a woman nurtures her child with her blood and her milk, so Christ gives us a new birth through his blood and then feeds us with that same blood.

31. THE SERVANT PIERCED AND VICTORIOUS

The Liturgy of the Word on Good Friday is marked by a notable restraint. The severity, which also shows in the outward decor (the altar is completely bare, without cross, candlesticks, or cloths), could be misleading; it might induce a dramatic sense of sadness and make us forget that the death of Christ is, in fact, a triumph. In reality, bare altars were common in the early Church whenever the altar as such was to play no part. In any case, the prayer that follows the moment of recollection at the beginning of the service expresses in a balanced way the meaning of all that is to follow: "Remember your mercies, O Lord, and with your eternal protection sanctify your servants, for whom Christ your Son, by the shedding of his Blood, established the Paschal Mystery." The alternate prayer conveys the same essential message: "O God, who by the Passion of Christ your Son, our Lord, abolished the death inherited from ancient sin by every succeeding generation, grant that just as, being conformed to him, we have borne by the law of nature the image of the man of earth, so by the sanctification of grace we may bear the image of the Man of heaven."

The two prayers, taking as their point of departure the mission and death of the Son, focus our attention on the mystery of the victorious Passover that is the source of our new life. The whole history of salvation is thus summed up in a few words at the moment when the Church is ready to celebrate the death of her Christ, something she cannot do without at the same time celebrating his triumph and ours.

The Servant Pierced for Our Sins

In the first reading we meet the Suffering Servant. The description Isaiah gives of him cannot but be deeply moving when read on Good Friday (Isa 52:13–53:12). And yet the very first verse of the reading evokes the true spirit that should pervade us on this day: "See, my servant shall prosper, / he shall be raised highly and greatly exalted" (52:13).

The description that follows reveals its full meaning only in the light of that first verse. The Servant's lot is really a passage through

271

suffering and death, a journey through death to exaltation and glory. For this reason, the text became classic from the very first days of the Church as a way of describing the death and victorious resurrection of the Lord.

St. Matthew quotes a verse from it: "He took away our infirmities and bore our diseases" (Matt 8:17; Isa 53:4). In St. Luke, not long before the end, Christ predicts the fulfillment of what the prophets had said: "Behold, we are going up to Jerusalem and everything written by the prophets about the Son of Man will be fulfilled" (Luke 18:31); he is referring here to the prophecies concerning the suffering of the Son of Man. In the Acts of the Apostles, when Philip meets the Ethiopian court official who is returning home from Jerusalem, the latter is reading Isaiah 53:7-8, "Like a lamb he was led to the slaughter, and as a sheep before its shearers is silent, so he opened not his mouth." Philip uses the passage as his starting point in explaining the Gospel of Jesus to the man (Acts 8:26-35).

The First Letter of Peter has a passage (2:22-24) that contains several implicit quotations from the fourth of the Servant Songs: "He committed no sin, and no deceit was found in his mouth" (cf. Isa 53:9); "He himself bore our sins in his body on the cross" (cf. Isa 53:12); "By his wounds you have been healed" (cf. Isa 53:5-6).

The exegetes do not agree on the identity of the servant described by Isaiah. Some believe it to be the prophet himself; others think Israel is meant. It is not easy, however, to apply the description to Israel, for, literary arguments aside, it would be surprising indeed to see Israel declared upright or to liken it to an innocent man being condemned, when everyone knew of its infidelities. It would seem rather that the servant is a prophetic figure.

In any case, when the Church reads this text, we see in it a moving description of the Christ who is laid low and accepts death as an expiatory sacrifice that will bring life to the nations. From our standpoint as Christians, the interpretation given the text by the New Testament is decisive: the Servant is Christ. We admit that by the rules of exegesis the servant may be interpreted as being either an individual or a people. Yet it is impossible for us to hear the poem read on Good Friday and not see in it the image of him whose victorious death the Church is celebrating. There is no need of our commenting on the text here; read it in the Lectionary or in the Bible, and it is perfectly clear.

Psalm 31, which serves as the response to the proclamation of Isaiah's picture of Christ, has a refrain that puts the whole into the context of the cross: "Father, into your hands I commend my spirit" (Luke 23:46). The psalm is especially appropriate, since some of its verses are like an echo of the passage from Isaiah.

> Because of all my foes
> I have become a reproach,
> an object of scorn to my neighbors
> and of fear to my friends.
> Those who see me in the street
> flee from me. (Ps 31:12)

> Let your face shine on your servant. (Ps 31:17)

> He was spurned and avoided by people . . .
> one from whom people hide their faces. (Isa 53:3)

> [H]e shall see his descendants in a long life. (Isa 53:10)

"A Great Priest over the House of God"

In St. John's gospel, Jesus says: "And when I am lifted up from the earth, I will draw everyone to myself" (12:32). Through and because of the sacrifice of the cross, we now have "a great priest over the house of God" (Heb 10:21). To understand this, we must reread the passage from the Letter to the Hebrews in which the author explains the priesthood of Christ; the passage supplies the second reading for Good Friday. The key verses are these:

> Since we have a great high priest who has passed through the heavens, Jesus, the Son of God, let us hold fast to our confession. For we do not have a high priest who is unable to sympathize with our weaknesses, but one who has similarly been tested in every way, yet without sin. So let us confidently approach the throne of grace to receive mercy and to find grace for timely help.
> In the days when Christ was in the flesh, he offered prayers and supplications with loud cries and tears to the one who was able to save him from death, and he was heard because of his reverence. Son though he was, he learned obedience from what he suffered; and when he was made perfect, he became the source of eternal salvation for all who obey him. (Heb 4:14-16; 5:7-9)

Someone—and that Someone is Christ, the all-powerful Intercessor—can now understand our needs and present them to the Father. The Church wants us to relive the passion of Christ on Good Friday. For when the Church, which is God's household, contemplates his suffering and the power of the Christ who overcame suffering so victoriously, she remembers that she has at her head a great Priest. Remembering it, she begins to invoke his aid, or, more accurately, she prays with him for the important intentions of his Body, which she is.

The Glorious Passion

At this point, then, the Church proclaims to her believing members, her catechumens, and the world at large the death of her Lord, as she has done in the past and will continue to do until he comes again. Yet we will not properly understand what she proclaims unless we see it in its context, and for this we must go back even beyond the Last Supper in the Gospel of St. John, whose account of the passion is the one read on this day.

In chapter 12, just before Passover, Jesus announces his death, but also his glorification through and by means of his death: "The hour has come for the Son of Man to be glorified. Amen, amen, I say to you, unless a grain of wheat falls to the ground and dies, it remains just a grain of wheat; but if it dies, it produces much fruit" (12:23-24).

A few moments later, a troubled Christ asks himself whether or not he should pray to the Father to save him from this hour. But he immediately answers his question: " 'But it was for this purpose that I came to this hour. Father, glorify your name.' Then a voice came from heaven, 'I have glorified it, and will glorify it again' " (12:27-28). Then Christ goes a step further in foretelling his glorious death: "Now is the time of judgment on this world; now the ruler of this world will be driven out; and I, when I am *lifted up* from the earth, will draw everyone to myself" (12:31-32).

This cannot be misunderstood. Christ has to pass through suffering and death, but from this death bursts life. Christ *"lifted up"* from the earth will draw everyone to himself. This is the third time in the gospel that John uses the same term "lifted up," while giving it without any doubt a double meaning. In 3:14-16 we read, "And just as

Moses lifted up the serpent in the desert, so must the Son of Man be *lifted up*, so that everyone who believes in him may have eternal life. For God so loved the world, that he gave his only Son."

Earlier, in chapter 8, he says, "When you *lift up* the Son of Man, then you will realize that I AM" (8:28).*

In chapter 12, the word "lift up" reveals its double meaning, as the evangelist explicitly says: "He said this indicating the kind of death he would die" (12:33). The context in which the term is used leaves no doubt as to the two meanings of "lift up": it means the crucifixion, but it also means the glorious ascension that will follow.

The announcement during the Supper of Judas's betrayal links the Supper to the sacrifice of the cross. In other words, the successive moments in which Christ hands himself over as food and is handed over to death belong together. When Judas eats the morsel and goes out into the night, Jesus says, "Now is the Son of Man glorified, and God is glorified in him. [If God is glorified in him,] God will also glorify him in himself, and he will glorify him at once" (13:31-32). Thus, even at the very moment when the betrayal is assured and the passion is imminent, Jesus speaks of his glorification.

In his farewell discourse, Jesus tells his disciples of his departure through death and of his resurrection, but he also tells them that only his disciples will realize his triumph: "In a little while the world will no longer see me, but you will see me, because I live and you will live. On that day you will realize that I am in my Father and you in me, and I in you" (14:19-20). The world will no longer be even thinking about the man who was crucified, but the disciples will see him alive, risen, and glorious. Then, when the disciples are nonetheless saddened, Jesus assures them: "take courage, I have conquered the world" (16:33).

We must also keep in mind the passages in which Jesus speaks of going to his Father and of sending the Spirit who will glorify him and communicate to the disciples the truth that is in Jesus (16:14).

The priestly prayer, in which Jesus offers himself to his Father and intercedes for the disciples, also emphasizes the glorious side of the coming passion: "Father, the hour has come. Give glory to your son, so that your son may glorify you, just as you gave him authority over

---

* Italics in these citations are by Nocent.

all people, so that he may give eternal life to all you gave him. . . . Now glorify me, Father, with you, with the glory that I had with you before the world began" (17:1-2, 5).

In his tenth sermon on the passion, St. Leo the Great comments on this exaltation of Christ. In doing so, he shows how Christ's glorification resulted from his death; more accurately, he shows that there is really no succession of steps here but that Christ's death is already his glorification:

> When, then, Christ Jesus was raised up on the Cross, he brought death to the author of death and broke the power of all the Principalities and Powers ranged against him, by exposing to them his flesh in which he could suffer. He allowed the ancient enemy to assail him insolently; the latter unleashed his rage against a nature that was subject to his attacks, and dared demand tribute from one in whom there was in fact no slightest trace of sin. In consequences, the deadly bond under which we were all sold was rendered void, and the contract that enslaved us now passed into the Redeemer's hands. The nails that pierced the Lord's hands and feet inflicted everlasting wounds on the devil, and the pain which the sacred limbs experienced proved deadly to the hostile powers. Thus Christ won his victory, and in such a way that in and through him all who believed in him likewise triumphed.
>
> When the Lord, glorified by having his crucified body raised aloft, was effecting the reconciliation of the world from his high place of torment and was calling the converted thief to a home in paradise, you, the leaders of the Jews and the teachers of the law, were not touched by the evil you had done, nor softened at seeing the effect of your crime. No, to the sharp nails you added piercing words.[1]

Death and Exaltation

On Palm Sunday the passion is read, with the Synoptics supplying the text in a three-year cycle. On Good Friday, the Gospel of John is read, in accordance with very ancient tradition. We have already had occasion to characterize briefly each of the synoptic accounts of the passion.[2] St. John's account is shorter and less anecdotal. It contains, nonetheless, a vibrant theology, the essential points of which we shall briefly note here.

First of all—and this is true from the very beginning of the account—John emphasizes Jesus' obedience to the Father's will. The theme is, of course, a favorite one with him. In the Garden of Olives, for example, we do not find Jesus praying to be relieved from drinking the cup of suffering; on the contrary, his words indicate that he accepts the cup as a duty and even as a gift that will lead him to his glory: "Shall I not drink the cup that the Father gave me?" (18:11).

Though John usually avoids the anecdotal, he does emphasize many of the details in the scene of Jesus' questioning by Pilate (18:28–19:16). He points out that the kind of death to which Jesus is sentenced is a fulfillment of his own prediction: "in order that the word of Jesus might be fulfilled that he said indicating the kind of death he would die" (18:32). Especially, however, John wants to emphasize the kingship of Christ. Jesus asserts that his coming into this world was motivated by the desire to proclaim the mystery of salvation; that is why his words are so important—because anyone who belongs to the truth hears his voice. But Jesus goes beyond hints of his kingship; he states it openly: "My kingdom does not belong to this world. . . . You say I am a king. For this I was born and for this I came into the world, to testify to the truth" (18:36-37). Here again we have a favorite theme of St. John's. Pilate even hands Jesus over to the Jews with the words, "Behold, your king!" (19:14); it is not clear whether he is speaking ironically or whether he is half convinced.

The kingship of Jesus will be asserted even by the instrument of his death, for the inscription on the cross read: "Jesus the Nazorean, the King of the Jews." The text was written in three languages and proclaimed a fact that has transformed the history of the world. Here, once again, in a new guise, we find the theme of glorification: of the crucifixion that is also a victory, the hour of death that is also the hour of triumph.

The Prayer of the Church

After having listened to the account of Christ's victorious death, the Church now recollects herself for prayer, in accordance with the ancient custom that every Liturgy of the Word should end with a prayer of the faithful. This is a custom that has now been happily restored.

On Good Friday, the general intercessions are of the kind used in the Roman Church down to the time of Pope Gelasius. The order of the intentions has been changed in the liturgical reform, and some intentions have been added. Ten intentions are proclaimed; each proclamation is followed by a moment of silent prayer, and then the celebrant utters a prayer in the name of all.

It will be enough here simply to list the intentions; they instruct us as to the concerns that should be ours as we recall the permanent presence of Christ's passion. We pray for the Holy Church, for the pope, for all orders and degrees of the faithful, for catechumens, for the unity of Christians, for the Jewish people, for those who do not believe in Christ, for those who do not believe in God, for those in public office, and for those in tribulation.

It is good to realize that at the moment when the Church is celebrating the high point in the history of salvation, she does not lose interest in any individual but, on the contrary, seeks to bring into her celebration all things spiritual and human, all the situations people find themselves in, all their anxieties, all their divergent viewpoints.

"Behold the Wood of the Cross"

Communion should have immediately followed on the Liturgy of the Word, but the ceremony of the adoration of the cross was inserted at this point, as an action called for by the proclamation of the passion. The cross is lifted up and shown to the world; here is Christ crucified, and people must choose. The elevation, and the adoration that follows, are also an assertion of the decisive victory Christ has won over the powers of evil that are active in the world. He is "lifted up," and the lifting up means that the human race that had been dispersed has been gathered into unity once again.

The elevation of the cross thus points to the most important act in the history of salvation. The faithful respond by singing "Come, let us adore" and kneeling in a rite that acknowledges a true victory. We have already spoken of the glorious aspect of the Lord's death and of how the Lamb slain on the cross is also the Lamb of St. John's apocalyptic vision of triumph. What more does Christianity have to show to the world? The triumphant cross is the source of all Christian meaning; the sign of the cross, which this world regards as foolishness, is what distinguishes the Christian from unbelievers.

In his second sermon on the passion, St. Leo the Great suggests what our thoughts should be as we gaze upon the cross:

> We, then, beloved, to whom our Lord Jesus Christ crucified is not a stumbling block or folly but the power of God and the wisdom of God; we who are the spiritual seed of Abraham, not begotten of a slave but

reborn into a free family; we who were rescued by God's mighty hand and outstretched arm from oppression and tyranny in Egypt and for whom the true and spotless Lamb, Jesus Christ, was sacrificed—let us embrace this marvelous and saving paschal mystery and be remade in the image of him who became like us in our deformity. Let us rise up to him who turned our lowly dust into his glorious body; and in order that we may merit a share in his resurrection, let us be thoroughly like him in his humility and patience. Great is the name of him whose service we have entered, and great the profession whose discipline we have accepted. Christ's followers may not abandon the royal road.[3]

The Church shows us the cross, and we adore it. It is difficult not to think of John and the words he cites from the prophet Zechariah: "They will look upon him whom they have pierced" (John 19:37; Zech 12:10).

To "look on" means to know and understand the mystery of the cross. The liturgy of the adoration of the cross presupposes that we have this kind of concrete knowledge.

It might be said that the term "adoration" is out of place here, since we do not adore the cross or, for that matter, the death of Christ. We adore his Person and what his Person means to us, symbolizing as it does the love of the Son for the Father and of the Father and the Son for us.[†]

The reproaches that are sung during the veneration of the cross have to do with the exchange of love between God and humanity in Christ. They are a dialogue in which God, through his Christ, tells us of his love and forces us to admit what he has done for us and the world out of love.

The reproaches developed in the course of time. The first part comprises the first three strophes (the third begins: "What more should I have done for you?") and seems to have been composed in the West. The "My people, what have I done to you?" appears for the first time in the seventh-century Spanish liturgical book, the *Liber ordinum*.[4] Scripture has evidently provided the inspiration for these stanzas.

The second part contains nine stanzas (with a refrain repeated after each), likewise inspired by Scripture, but in a much freer fashion. Each stanza contrasts what God has done and what the people have done in return. This second section seems to date from the eleventh century.

---

† The texts and rubrics of Good Friday, however, call on the faithful to adore the wood of the cross, the instrument of salvation, stained with the blood of Christ.

The responses (refrains) throughout are either the *Trisagion* or the words, "My people, what have I done to you? Or how have I grieved you? Answer me!"

The reproaches are an especially moving experience in the Good Friday liturgy. The first three stanzas, to which the *Trisagion* is the response, express the divine initiatives and the hardening of the people whom God wanted for his own. The second part goes into greater detail on God's initiatives on behalf of his people: the liberation from Egypt, the crossing of the Red Sea, the column of cloud, the manna, the water from the rock, the conquest of the kings of Canaan, and the royal house. How stirring a description of God's loving attentions to a people that responded by abandoning and betraying him!

The opening antiphon at the veneration of the cross sums up the real meaning of the ceremony: "We adore your Cross, O Lord, we praise and glorify your holy Resurrection, for behold, because of the wood of a tree joy has come to the whole world."

The Body and Blood of the Lord

Once the veneration of the cross is completed, the reserved Sacrament is brought to the altar. As usual, the celebrant recites the Our Father with the congregation. The words "thy will be done on earth as it is in heaven" take on a special depth of meaning after the reading of the passion, where we saw Christ bowing to the will he had come to do and obeying it with a love that would win him exaltation and a name above every other name.

All the faithful then receive the Body of Christ. It is possible to regret this custom, which was introduced at a recent reform of Holy Week. The reason for the regret is that the practice may distract attention from the climactic point of the sacred Triduum, the reception of the Eucharist during the Easter Vigil. Perhaps we should have followed the practice of the early Church by fasting even from Communion until the Vigil. On the other hand, the reception of Christ's Body, which is the sign of his immolation and glorious passion, is also an especially meaningful act on Good Friday. It is at least understandable that a rite should have been introduced that for a very long time was excluded from the papal liturgy.

The Lord Rests in the Tomb: Holy Saturday

32. CELEBRATIONS ANCIENT AND MODERN

Holy Saturday has a special character. Apart from such Hours as were chiefly monastic in origin (such as Matins), the day used to have no special Office of its own. On this day a fast was observed until into the night, but it was a festive fast, a fast marked by expectation of the Lord's return.

In the early centuries, the only ceremony held at Rome on Holy Saturday morning was the "handing back [recitation]" of the Creed by the catechumens and the final exorcism before the solemn renunciation of Satan.

In the section on Lent, we followed the progress of the catechumens and observed their gradual transformation. On this Saturday, the Church of Rome gave special attention to these catechumens, since that very night they were to become her children.

The old liturgical books have preserved a record for us of how the ceremony was conducted.[1] During Lent the catechumens had undergone three scrutinies, or, at a later period, six; the last scrutiny, a more solemn one, took place on Holy Saturday. Moreover, during Lent the Creed had been presented to the catechumens, along with a short explanation of its articles; now, on Holy Saturday, the catechumens were to recite the Creed, which they had learned by heart. The recital was not their absolute profession of faith. These individuals undoubtedly had an incipient faith, but faith in its fullness would be a gift received through baptism itself. Their profession of faith would, in fact, be part of the sacramental rite, since the officiating priest would ask them three questions: "Do you believe in the Father . . . ," "Do you believe in the Son . . . ," and "Do you believe in the Holy Spirit . . . ," and to each the candidates would answer "I do." They would be immersed in the water of the font three times, once after each response.

The point, therefore, of the Holy Saturday morning ceremony was to gain assurance that the candidates knew the Creed and that they were disposed to profess their faith at the moment of baptism.

Still more impressive was the solemn renunciation of Satan by the catechumens. It was preceded by an imposition of hands by the bishop, the rite of the *Ephphetha*, and an anointing.

After this the catechumens renounced Satan and all his works and "pomps." In the interests of clarity, the word "pomps" has now been replaced by "empty promises."[2] It must be admitted, however, that this and other translations do not really capture the meaning of the original word. A *pompa* was a solemn public procession, and in this context the word called to mind the worship of Gentile divinities, the games at the arenas, and all the extravagant display of a civilization characterized, and undermined, by wealth and conspicuous consumption. In short, catechumens were renouncing the paganism around them.

Sometimes the ceremony became even more expressive, as, for example, in the East, where the catechumens spat in the direction of the West (the place of sunset and darkness), where the powers of evil dwelt. The fathers of the Church enjoyed describing this solemn renunciation in which the catechumens rejected the "world" and pledged their fidelity.

In continuity with the ancient solemn scrutiny, the Church now asks all the baptized (at the renewal of the baptismal promises) to renew their rejection of Satan and the "empty show."

33. HIS BODY REPOSES IN HOPE

The reform of Holy Week has restored to Holy Saturday its authentic meaning and its ancient form. On this day the Church celebrates Christ resting in his tomb, but she also awaits his resurrection, for she knows that his body reposes in hope (cf. Ps 16:9).

The Holy Women Remained Sitting by the Tomb

With the holy women, the Church sits by the tomb and meditates on the Lord as he rests there in peace.

This is the theme of the first antiphon in the Office of Readings: "In peace, I will lie down and sleep," and it strikes the keynote for the whole of the Office: repose in the expectation of a glorious resurrection. The thoughts of the praying Church are concentrated on the event that has just taken place, that is, the suffering and death of Christ, but the Church is also constantly aware that Jesus died certain of ultimate victory. Even as she meditates on the Lord's death and repose, she is, therefore, impatient to proclaim the coming resurrection. In the alternate responsory after the psalms of Lauds, she cannot help breaking out into the words: "For our sake Christ was obedient, accepting even death, death on a cross. Therefore God raised him on high and gave him the name above all other names."

Psalm 4 in the Office of Readings ends with words that tell us of the joy Christ already has, even before the resurrection, for he sees that his mission is completed and he tastes the victory:

> You have put into my heart a greater joy
> than abundance of grain and new wine can provide.
> In peace I will lie down and fall asleep,
> for you alone, O LORD, make me dwell in safety.

Psalm 16 reminds us of the resurrection and of Christ's entry into his inheritance:

> O LORD, it is you who are my portion and cup;
> you yourself who secure my lot.

Pleasant places are marked out for me:
a pleasing heritage indeed is mine! . . .
And so, my heart rejoices, my soul is glad;
even my flesh shall rest in hope.
For you will not abandon my soul to hell,
nor let your holy one see corruption.
You will show me the path of life,
the fullness of joy in your presence,
at your right hand, bliss forever. (Ps 16:5-6, 9-11)

Psalm 24 expresses similar sentiments:

Who shall climb the mountain of the LORD?
Who shall stand in his holy place?
The clean of hands and pure of heart. . . .
Blessings from the LORD shall he receive,
and right reward from the God who saves him. . . .
O gates, lift high your heads;
grow higher, ancient doors.
Let him enter, the king of glory!
Who is this king of glory?
The LORD, the mighty, the valiant;
the LORD, the valiant in war. (Ps 24:3-5, 7-8)

The psalm is describing the victory of the risen Christ, who, after conquering in battle, returns to his Father's house.

The Repose of Christ

The reading from the Letter to the Hebrews bids us strive to enter into Christ's rest (4:1-13). The reading deserves our attention, for the theme of the Lord's rest or repose suggests in turn a whole series of themes of which we, the baptized, should be aware.

The beginning of the passage may mislead us into thinking that the author of the Letter to the Hebrews is indulging in a bit of moralizing. In fact, however, he is simply urging us to learn from what happened to the Hebrews, who received the Good News but did not accept it with faith nor profit by it.

Like the Hebrews, we too are invited to enter into rest. What rest is meant? The Letter reminds us that on the seventh day God rested from his work of creating. In like manner, a sabbath rest awaits those who hear the voice of the Lord and do not harden their hearts against it. "whoever enters into God's rest, rests from his own works as God did from his. Therefore, let us strive to enter into that rest, so that no one may fall after the same example of disobedience" (4:10-11).

The rest of Christ in the tomb thus leads the Church's thoughts to the Creator's rest on the seventh day, to the rest promised the Hebrews but not obtained because they lacked faith and disobeyed, and to the sabbath rest at the end of time for all who believe.

The death and rest of Christ are realities that make claims on us today. Entry into rest supposes obedient faith and a laborious effort to attain life in the Promised Land.

Christ Our Passover: Easter Vigil

34. CELEBRATIONS ANCIENT AND MODERN

A special feast of Easter does not seem to have been celebrated at Rome before the second half of the second century. Elsewhere, if we can trust Eusebius of Caesarea, the celebration of Easter had begun in the early second century.[1] This did not mean, of course, that the early Church did not live by the mystery of the Lord's death and resurrection. Quite the contrary. But every Sunday was a commemoration of the paschal mystery in the form of the eucharistic celebration. Finally, a single Sunday was chosen as a special day for the feast of Christ's resurrection and became the most solemn of Sundays, the Sunday *par excellence*, the Sunday of Sundays.

In acting thus, the Church was, as on other occasions, christianizing a Jewish feast. Since Easter is the feast of the Lord's resurrection and an anticipation of his second coming, St. Jerome writes that our Passover, like the Jewish, is marked by expectation of the Messiah's coming in power: "It was a tradition among the Jews that the Messiah would come during the night, at the hour when the Passover had been celebrated in Egypt. . . . That, I think, is why we have the tradition from the apostles that the congregation is not to be dismissed before midnight during the Easter Vigil, since they await the coming of Christ at that hour."[2]

Jewish Passover and Christian Easter

No one would deny that there are similarities between our Easter Vigil and the Jewish Passover feast. We think, however, that what should be emphasized is not outward likenesses but the theology of expectation that underlies both. The Passover of the Bible is "a religious movement that inspires the entire people of God."[3] A dynamic sense of liberation dominates the Jewish Passover of the Bible, and the idea of "passage" is essential and central to it, as it is to the Christian Pasch. We should be aware, moreover, that in celebrating the Passover the Jews were not simply commemorating a past event. Rather, they were celebrating an event they regarded as a present reality: "To commemorate is not to stand off from what had once taken place; on the contrary, it means eliminating the distance that separates. It means bringing the past to life again."[4]

There are also, however, important differences between the Jewish Passover and the Christian Pasch. The Jewish Passover liturgy is a domestic affair; the Christian paschal liturgy is a community celebration with the Eucharist as its center. Moreover, the Jewish feast was only the starting point for the Christian feast, and the latter represents a goal reached, even if it also looks forward to a definitive fulfillment at the end of time.

In his *Ecclesiastical History*, Eusebius of Caesarea tells us that Christians saw their own Easter as so much like the Jewish Passover feast they had christianized that they wanted to celebrate Easter on the fourteenth day of the month Nisan, that is, on the day when the Jews immolated the Passover lamb. We must qualify Eusebius's statement, however, since it was only the Christians of Asia Minor who insisted on this date. The other Churches, on the contrary, appealed to apostolic tradition and celebrated the feast on a Sunday, which had been the day of the Lord's resurrection. The controversy was quite a lively one, as the reader may know; Pope Victor I (ca. 189–ca. 198) put an end to it by decreeing that the celebration of Easter should take place on the Sunday following the fourteenth day of Nisan.[5]

In any event, the Passover that Christians celebrated had been perfectly described by St. Paul when he wrote, "Therefore, let us celebrate the feast, not with the old yeast, the yeast of malice and wickedness, but with the unleavened bread of sincerity and truth" (1 Cor 5:8).

The Easter Vigil in Earlier Times

Some of the components of the later Vigil are discernible even in Christian antiquity. There was a fast, followed by a nighttime prayer service that concluded with the celebration of the Eucharist. In the third-century Syrian *Didascalia Apostolorom*, these two—the fast and the prayer service culminating in the Eucharist—are the sole observances attested.[6] But one thing is clear: the Vigil service was already a well-established practice.

The *Apostolic Tradition* (ca. 215) of St. Hippolytus of Rome* shows, however, that the administration of baptism had already been linked with the Vigil and was celebrated during the night.[7] Tertullian would write that Easter Sunday was the natural time for baptism.[8] The celebration of baptism during the Vigil became widespread, however, only in the fourth century.

The practice of singing a hymn of blessing at the lighting of the lamp in the home at evening is very ancient. The *Apostolic Tradition* gives a prayer for blessing the lamp at the community meal.[9] Nonetheless, what we now call the *Exsultet* made its appearance only in the fourth century, and in various forms. Moreover, although the blessing of the paschal candle became the practice almost everywhere, even in the churches of Rome (fifth century), it is still missing from the papal liturgy as late as the eleventh century.[10]

For the blessing of the fire, there is no official formulary before the twelfth century. It then appears in the Roman Pontifical of the twelfth century, which describes the procession in which the acclamation "The Light of Christ" is sung.[11] The use of new fire (the old fires had been extinguished on Holy Thursday evening) is attested as a Good Friday usage at Rome in the ninth century.[12]

After this quick glance at the broad development of the liturgy of the Easter Vigil, let us now retrace our steps and look at the various parts of the rite in greater detail.

The Blessing of the New Fire

The blessing of the new fire, as we just indicated, originated in a practical need. And yet the problem is really not that clear, for questions were being raised about the blessing as early as the eighth and ninth centuries.[13] Various traditions have to be considered.

At Rome it was the custom to flood the celebration of the Easter Vigil with light, in order to impress on the participants the idea of Christ as the Light. The lamps were lit even before the Vigil began, and the light only intensified as the rite continued.

From the beginning of the Vigil there were two human-sized candles on the scene. They were to be seen at either side of the altar,

---

* Regarding authorship and dating, see vol. 1, p. 128. Further, the *Apostolic Tradition* never specifies that this was the Easter Vigil.

of the celebrant, and of the baptismal font. Originally these were not blessed. Then, in *Ordo* 16 (680–775) a blessing of the candles appears. According to *Ordo* 23 (700–750), the light for these candles is taken from the light "that was hidden away on Good Friday." In *Ordo* 17 there is a "blessing" of the candle that is lit at the fire hidden on Good Friday. *Ordo* 26 (750–75) provides new details.

According to *Ordo* 26, at the ninth hour on Holy Thursday, fire is struck from flint at the door of the basilica, and from the fire a candle stuck on a reed is lit. A lamp is also lit at the fire and kept until Holy Saturday, when it will be used to light the candle that has just been blessed. This seems to be a strictly Gallican custom. The blessed and lit candle is solemnly carried into the basilica and used to light seven lamps standing before the altar; then the whole church is illumined. At this point the ministers enter for the celebration of Mass. The various lamps are solemnly extinguished again during Matins and Lauds.

From this time on, the usages found in the various *Ordines* intermingle, and the problem becomes complicated. At Mainz in the tenth century, for example, the procession into the church may be done in two ways: in silence or to the accompaniment of the hymn *Inventor rutili luminis, dux bone* ("O good Leader, Creator of the gleaming light").[14] In the thirteenth century, a three-branched candlestick is in use,[15] but this was eliminated in the reform of 1951. The use of a three-branched candlestick may have been taken over from Jerusalem, where the bishop lit three candles, and after him the clergy and finally the entire congregation did the same.[16] But, while the 1951 reform suppressed the three-branched candlestick (the point of which was not very clear), it introduced the practice of lighting the candles of all the faithful; this custom had not hitherto existed in the Roman liturgy, though it did at Jerusalem.

How was the candle blessed? Originally, it seems that the ceremony consisted simply in tracing a sign of the cross on the candle. The minister who was to do the blessing stood at the center of the sanctuary in front of the altar, asked that the others pray for him, and drew the sign of the cross on the candle. Then he received from the subdeacon the light hidden away on Good Friday and lit the candle. Thereupon he said, "The Lord be with you," and a prayer, and continued with the "Lift up your hearts," etc.[17] Several *Exsultet* formulas have come down to us, among them the poem with which we are familiar. In 384, St. Jerome wrote a long letter to Praesidius in which he rather spitefully attacked our *Exsultet* for frivolity.[18†]

The Readings

The readings are an essential part of the Easter Vigil, but the various rites differ in the number, choice, and length of the readings. The Coptic Rite, for example, has a very large number of readings, as does the Byzantine Rite. The Roman Rite has known different systems over the centuries. The history has not yet been fully clarified, and we cannot go into it here. Suffice it to say that the Gregorian Sacramentary has four readings,[19] and the Gelasian has ten,[20] while at Rome there were six lessons, later on twelve. During the period when the popes were Easterners, that is, in the seventh and eighth centuries, there were twelve lessons, sung in both Latin and Greek.[21]

The Blessing of the Baptismal Water

The blessing of the baptismal water seems to have been in use by about the second century. Two important texts of the blessing have come down to us. One was composed by Bishop Serapion of Thmuis (ca. 350). The celebrant asks that the waters be filled with the Spirit; just as the Word went down into the water of the Jordan and sanctified it, so may he now descend into the water of the font and render it spiritual.[22] The other text is by St. Optatus of Milevi (writing ca. 370) and takes the form of a brief acclamation of praise addressed to the water.[23]

Later on, around 400, the *Constitutiones Apostolorum* describes the blessing of the water by the priest. The latter praises and blesses the Lord because he has sent his Son for the world's salvation. Now we have the baptism of regeneration as a symbolic embodiment of the saving cross. May God therefore sanctify the water and make it the medium of his grace and power so that everyone who is baptized in accordance with Christ's command may be crucified with Christ and may die and rise with him to adoption, thus dying to sin and being made alive for holiness.[24]

---

† Jerome gives no indication of the text, and the earliest evidence of "our *Exsultet*" came several centuries later. Jerome was unhappy, but it is not clear why.

The Verona Sacramentary (fifth to sixth century) has a short formula for the blessing of baptismal water:

> We turn to you in prayer, Lord, eternal Creator of all things and all-powerful God, whose Spirit swept over the waters of creation and whose eyes looked from heaven upon the Jordan as John bestowed his baptism of repentance on those who confessed their sins. We pray your holy Majesty to be secretly at work in this water and to thoroughly cleanse the interior of those who will be baptized in it. May they be reborn from their deadly sins and live again according to the new human created in Christ Jesus, with whom you live and reign in the unity of the Holy Spirit throughout the ages.[25]

St. Ambrose speaks of the blessing in his *De sacramentis*. He is addressing the newly baptized and explaining to them the sacrament they have received: "Attend now to this next point. The priest comes and stands by the font; he says a prayer, calling upon the name of the Father and the presence of the Son and the Holy Spirit. He uses heavenly words, for he uses the words of Christ, who told us to baptize 'in the name of the Father and of the Son and of the Holy Spirit.'"[26]

Litanies

Since it took time to get from the church, where the Liturgy of the Word had been celebrated, to the baptistery, where the water was to be blessed, a litany was sung. At Rome a litany served as a processional song. That is why we find a litany at various points in the celebration of the Easter Vigil. In *Ordo* 17 a litany is sung before the blessing of the candle as the clergy and subdeacons enter; another is sung after the blessing of the candle while the priests and deacons, with their lighted candles, are taking their places for the readings.[27] According to another *Ordo*, a litany is also sung during the procession to the font.[28] Finally, a litany is sung that serves as an entrance song for the Mass and ends with the *Gloria in excelsis*.[29] In some places a litany is also sung while the bishop is conferring the sacrament of confirmation after baptism.[30]

The litanies were usually repeated, sometimes as often as seven times. In time, the antiphon *Sicut cervus* ("Like the deer that yearns / for running streams . . ."; Ps 42:2) was introduced for the procession to the font. Then it became customary to divide up a single litany, part being sung before the blessing of the font and the baptisms, part afterward, with the *Kyrie* of the litany serving as the *Kyrie* of the Mass.

Until Vatican II and the most recent reform of Holy Week, the Vigil Mass had preserved some special features in an effort to imitate what was done in early times. For example, there was no *Agnus Dei*, a prayer that had been introduced during the fraction by Pope Sergius I (687–701). There was also no kiss of peace, because at cockcrow, when Easter day began to dawn, a kiss of peace was exchanged, with the greeting, "Peace be with you."[31] The experts in the recent reform judged that the preservation of these peculiarities had no value for the life of the faithful.

35. THE LIGHT OF CHRIST

The New Fire

When the Church introduced the blessing of the new fire, she was simply giving a sacral dimension to a straightforward material necessity. A new source of light was needed for the nighttime Office, since the lamps had been extinguished at the end of the Lucernarium, or evening Office. What this blessing of the new fire shows, as do the blessing of the paschal candle and the consecration of the baptismal water, is the effects of redemption. The world is already taking on a new appearance, as subhuman creatures take their place in the global unity and cease to be enemies. These creatures are servants once again and thus instruments of grace.

The catechumens have long since been awaiting the moment of their enlightenment. Now they see the act of creation being mimed before their eyes. The Lord is asleep in his tomb, but he is also now making his own and acting out the words the prophet Hosea had written: "Death, you shall die in me; hell, you shall be destroyed by me" (13:14).[1] The third antiphon at Vespers on Holy Saturday reminds all that they are to expect Christ's victory over death, for he had said, "Destroy this temple and in three days I will raise it up" (John 2:19).

In short, the now sleeping Lord will soon be the victorious Master of the world. In the canticle for Vespers on Holy Saturday, the Church bids the faithful sing a passage from the Letter to the Philippians that presents both the fact of the resurrection and the title the Lord has to it:

> he emptied himself . . . and found in human appearance, he humbled himself, becoming obedient to death, even death on a cross. Because of this God greatly exalted him and bestowed on him the name that is above every name, that at the name of Jesus every knee should bend, of those in heaven and on earth and under the earth, and every tongue confess that Jesus Christ is Lord, to the glory of God the Father. (Phil 2:7-11)

Christ the Lord is thus given dominion over the whole universe; the Letter to the Philippians expresses it as sovereignty over everything in the heavens, on earth, and under the earth.

In the Letter to the Colossians, Paul again asserts the unqualified lordship of Christ as conqueror of death:

> He is the image of the invisible God, the firstborn of all creation. For in him were created all things in heaven and on earth, the visible and the invisible, whether thrones or dominions or principalities or powers; all things were created through him and for him. He is before all things, and in him all things hold together. (Col 1:15-17)

The Letter to the Ephesians contains a similar assertion:

> [God worked his great might] in Christ, raising him from the dead and seating him at his right hand in the heavens, far above every principality, authority, power, and dominion, and every name that is named not only in this age but also in the one to come. (Eph 1:20-21)

We should note carefully Paul's insistence on Christ's triumph and present dominion over the entirety of creation. The paschal mystery means the renewal of creation as a whole; that is the normal and logical consequence of human redemption. The first human was set in the midst of the world and called upon to bestow names upon creatures; they, in turn, were meant to be his servants. Once humans themselves acquire a new existence as servants of God, the creatures around them are likewise renewed and begin once again to serve, for they were created for the sake of humans, so that they might be stewards of them and make them contribute to the glory of God.

Fire is one such creature that is now humanity's servant, the fire "which was struck from the flint and is destined for our use."[2] The fire becomes at the same time God's servant, and we can therefore ask him: "sanctify this new fire, we pray, and grant that, by these paschal celebrations, we may be so inflamed with heavenly desires, that with minds made pure we may attain festivities of unending splendor."[3] It thus symbolizes a new beginning in our lives.

The New Light

The candle too is a creature renewed and has the sacral function of symbolizing to the world the glory of the risen Christ. That is why the sign of the cross is first traced on the candle, for the cross is what gives all things their meaning. The Roman Canon of the Mass (Eucharistic Prayer I) gives apt expression to this universal significance of Christ's redemptive death when it says, "Through whom you continue to make all these good things, O Lord; you sanctify them, fill them with life, bless them, and bestow them upon us."

As the celebrant traces the sign of the cross and inscribes the Greek letters *alpha* and *omega* along with the numerals of the current year, he says: "Christ yesterday and today; the Beginning and the End; the Alpha; and the Omega. All time belongs to him, and all the ages. To him be glory and power through every age and for ever. Amen." He thus expresses in a few words and actions the entire doctrine of St. Paul on Christ as Lord of the universe. Nothing escapes the influence of Christ's redemptive act; the whole of creation—humanity, things, and time—now belongs to him.

It might be thought that from a pastoral viewpoint the restoration of these rites—some of them ancient, others merely local—was not a very happy idea. Does it not create a kind of dead space in the course of the celebration, inasmuch as the faithful take hardly any part in these ceremonies? People are standing in the dark; they can hardly see what is going on; the words of the celebrant lack unction and are like scattered fragments of a discourse. And yet we have just seen the wealth of teaching this short ceremony contains.

In the recent reform a good deal of freedom was allowed with regard to these ceremonies, since they may be omitted or kept only in part.‡ It was thought proper to retain the practice of inserting the five grains of incense in the candle, although the whole ceremony had its origin in a misreading of the Latin text. The Latin word *incensum*, which in context meant "lighted" and referred to the candle, was mistaken for another word that is spelled the same way but has a different meaning, namely, "incense." It was this misinterpretation that gave rise to the five grains of incense that are inserted in the candle and symbolize the five wounds of Christ: "By his holy and glorious wounds, may Christ the Lord guard us and protect us. Amen." The words admittedly do aptly express the mysterious power of Christ's glorious death, but the symbolism is a bit forced. It could disappear without great loss from a liturgy that is already rich enough and ought not to become excessively freighted with symbolism. Our

‡ This changed with the third edition of the *Missale Romanum*, which now makes obligatory the incision of the candle but leaves optional the insertion of incense grains.

concern, after all, should be that the faithful concentrate on the central aspects of the paschal mystery.

The celebrant ends the preparation of the paschal candle by lighting it from the new fire while saying, "May the light of Christ rising in glory dispel the darkness of our hearts and minds."

The Procession

The ministers now walk in procession behind the lighted candle, which represents Christ, who is the column of fire and light that guides us through the darkness and shows us the way to the Promised Land. The procession begins when the deacon has chanted for a first time, "The Light of Christ," and the congregation answers, "Thanks be to God." The deacon then moves forward and, when he has advanced a bit, chants once again but in a higher tone,§ "The Light of Christ." All again answer, "Thanks be to God," and then light their candles from the paschal candle. The procession advances to the altar, where the deacon sings a third time, "The Light of Christ."

We must attend this ceremony with the simplicity and openness of a child if we are to enter fully into the mind of the Church at this moment of joy. The world knows only too well the darkness that fills the earth with unhappiness and anxiety. Yet at this moment people can tell themselves that their wretchedness has elicited God's pity and that he wants to shed his light everywhere.

The prophets of long ago promised that the light would come: "The people who walked in darkness have seen a great light" (Isa 9:1; cf. 42:7; 49:9). But the light that will shine upon the new Jerusalem (Isa 60:1-2) will be the living God himself, for he shall enlighten his people (Isa 60:19), and his Servant will be a light for the nations (Isa 42:6; 49:6). St. Paul ends his speech to King Agrippa by saying that Moses and the prophets had predicted "that the Messiah must suffer and that, as the first to rise from the dead, he would proclaim light both to our people and to the Gentiles" (Acts 26:23).

Jesus tells his hearers what his own miracles mean; in particular, before healing the man born blind, he says, "While I am in the world, I am the light of the world" (John 9:5). In the Prologue to the Fourth

---

§ A higher tone is traditional, but the rubrics no longer mention it.

Gospel, John has already presented Christ to us as "the true light, which enlightens everyone" (John 1:9).

"It was night," observed St. John (13:30) when Judas left the room after the Last Supper. It was night too when Christ at the moment of his arrest said, "but this is your hour, the time for the power of darkness" (Luke 22:53). Now, during the Easter Vigil, it is again night, but on this night the Church contemplates Christ as the light that dispels all darkness. "God is light," says St. John, and "in him there is no darkness at all" (1 John 1:5).

The catechumens who take part in this celebration of the light have already known from experience that by their natural birth they belonged to the realm of darkness. Now they know as well that God has "called" them "out of darkness into his wonderful light" (1 Pet 2:9). In a few minutes' time, at their baptism, they will experience what St. Paul wrote to the Ephesians: "Christ will give you light" (Eph 5:14). They will cease to be "darkness" and will become "light in the Lord" (Eph 5:8). As a member of the Church, they will be rescued from the power of darkness and be brought into the kingdom of God's Son, where they will share the lot of the saints in the light (Col 1:12-13).

The light also shines on all the faithful present, and they too must choose once again either to accept or to reject it. No celebration, however pastoral, however moving and meaningful, can force people to choose aright, and even in the presence of the risen Christ people will continue to be divided into "children of this world" and "children of light" (Luke 16:8). In order to become a child of the light one must believe, in concrete, practical ways, in him who is the Light; only through conflict does the believer make his way to the heavenly Jerusalem, the city that has no need of sun or moon, because God's glory is its source of light and the Lamb its lamp (Rev 21:23).

The *Exsultet*

The deacon now comes to the celebrant and asks his blessing before singing the Easter Proclamation. Then he incenses the book containing the *Exsultet* and the paschal candle as well. Finally he begins the Easter Proclamation, or the "Praise of the Candle" (*Laus Cerei*), to give it its ancient name.

The word *Exsultet* that begins the song (or, more properly, its prologue) has given the whole piece its name. Another name for it is the "Easter Proclamation" (*Praeconium Paschale*).

In the prologue, the deacon bids all—heaven, earth, the Church, the Christian assembly—to share the joy that comes from Christ's victory over darkness. The prologue, and indeed the body of the song as well, often took the form of an improvised song about the resurrection.

After the prologue the deacon intones the great hymn of thanksgiving for the history of salvation. The Proclamation sums up this history: the redemptive act that ransomed sinful Adam; the great prefigurations of redemption (the Passover lamb, the Red Sea, the pillar of fire). This is the night when people receive salvation and when Christ wins his victory. The deacon then waxes even more lyrical as he praises this night in which God had shown us his tender love by giving his own Son to ransom a slave. He sings of the fault that was a happy fault, the sin that was a necessary sin, because it won for us so glorious a Redeemer.

Next, the deacon speaks of the candle itself, which the entire Church offers to God. May it burn and never be extinguished; may Christ, the Morning Star that never sets, find it always lit.

This very beautiful poem (St. Ambrose of Milan may have written it[4])¶ often stirs the congregation deeply at its beginning, for they are still under the influence of the preceding darkness that had been lit only by the flickering light of the candles. Today, however, it will hardly win adherents through its doctrine. The many images, the tightly packed themes, and a lyricism that does not reflect our modern sensibility make this bravura piece rather difficult for the congregation. After the rapid start in the ceremony of "The Light of Christ," the people may find nothing for them to grasp and become somewhat bored, even though the celebration of the paschal mystery is only beginning.

Regretfully, then (since the *Exsultet* is indeed a masterpiece), we must say that some future reform should shorten the Easter Proclamation and recast it in language more accessible to contemporary people. In this regard, pastors with authority must act courageously to sacrifice a poem that is a theological and artistic success, and to replace it with a composition that may turn out to be even more beautiful if it is a vernacular song with genuine pastoral value.**

¶ The earliest of the current text is several centuries after Ambrose. It is unlikely he is the author.

** The current rubrics, of course, do not allow this. Even the option for inserting congregational acclamations was removed from the third edition of the Missal.

Nothing can be truly beautiful if it is not functional—a principle as valid for liturgy as for architecture. We must live not in the past or the future but in the present, and we must study the solid doctrine given us in the *Exsultet* in order that we may present it in a more suitable manner.

The Today of the Scriptures

In its Constitution on the Sacred Liturgy (no. 7), Vatican II lists the various ways in which Christ is present among his people. He is present not only in the Eucharist (the highest form of his presence) and the other sacraments but also in his word and in the prayer of the Church. The Liturgy of the Word during the Easter Vigil is an especially notable example of this teaching, for the Vigil is constructed as a dialogue (something we would like to find more frequently in the Church).

At this point when the Church is about to baptize the catechumens, she is undoubtedly motivated by a desire to offer them a final instruction.[5] It would be a mistake, however, to concentrate exclusively on the didactic aspect of the Vigil readings. What we should be primarily attentive to is the presence of Christ, who is teaching us himself.[6] That is the point of reading the Scripture lessons near, and by the light of, the paschal candle. The Old Testament is read, but in the light of Christ, and indeed in the light of a Christ who is present today. This bridging of the centuries is especially striking in connection with the third reading, which narrates the first Passover on which the Hebrews were rescued from Egypt and brought safely through the Red Sea.[7]

In this reading the Lord addresses us and tells us what he did for his Chosen People on the first Passover: how he led them out of Egypt and across the Red Sea and how he destroyed Pharaoh's army. The Lord, the Father, speaks to us, and he speaks through his Son, the true paschal Lamb that has been sacrificed. We, for our part, listen to this Lord who speaks to us here and now. We are in the same position as the Hebrews in the book of Exodus (chap. 19), who have crossed the Red Sea and whom the Lord now gathered so that he might speak to them.

On that occasion God spoke from the mountaintop, and the people listened. The atmosphere for their listening was created by songs and prayers; on hearing, they acclaimed God's words and then offered him a sacrifice as a covenant sign. We are that people, and Christ actualizes the narrative for us in our day; he tells us what he did for us and what he is still doing for us. We listen. Then, filled with his words, we stand and sing to the Lord the joy his word has brought us. We sing back to him, in lyrical form, what he has just said to us, as we engage in a dialogue with him that conveys our wonder and thanksgiving: "I will sing to the LORD, for he is gloriously triumphant; / horse and chariot he has cast into the sea" (Exod 15:1).[8]

With his "Let us pray," the celebrant then invites us to pray over this amazing dialogue between the Lord and ourselves. All present reflect in silence on what has been said and on the dialogue in which they have taken part. Then the celebrant brings into the present, in the form of a prayer, the message that has been proclaimed: "O God, whose ancient wonders remain undimmed in splendor even in our day, for what you once bestowed on a single people, freeing them from Pharaoh's persecution by the power of your right hand now you bring about as the salvation of the nations through the waters of rebirth, grant, we pray, that the whole world may become children of Abraham and inherit the dignity of Israel's birthright." (A new, optional prayer similarly brings the message into the present.)

In the light of the paschal candle, and because of Jesus our Messiah, what happened once upon a time in the past is happening again. As the catechumens listen to the reading and the prayer, they can better understand that they are indeed part of the history of salvation. The miracle of the Red Sea will shortly be repeated for them.

We cannot really enter into this liturgy unless we walk the path of typology, for we must not see in the story of the Red Sea simply an illustration of what takes place in baptism. Baptism is not modeled after the crossing of the Red Sea, but neither is the account of the crossing simply an illustrated explanation of the baptismal rite. Instead, baptism is a continuation of the account of the crossing. That is, the passage through the sea takes place this night, and from the historical point of view, the crossing this night is more real than the crossing of long ago; it will be ever more real as we approach closer and closer to the Promised Land.

Unless we thus understand the Scriptures that are proclaimed in the liturgy, they will be for us nothing but a reminder of the past; they will stir a sense of wonder, but we will not grasp the fact that the events narrated are taking place here and now. The other readings and prayers of the Vigil are part of the same process of bringing into the present that is going on in the light of the paschal candle.

The first reading confronts us with the two creations (Gen 1:1–2:2). When the Vigil began, we found ourselves in the presence of Christ, the Lord of the universe. Now this Lord of all things himself tells about the creation of the world—a world that he intended as good but that was ruined by sin. The first human beings found themselves in a splendid world of life where everything was good. Now, in the light of the risen Christ, the world is being created once again.

Jesus is the one Lord, "from whom all things are and for whom we exist" (1 Cor 8:6); he is "the firstborn of all creation" (Col 1:15) and "all things were created through him and for him" (Col 1:16); he upholds "all things by his mighty word" (Heb 1:3). The world he created has been ruined, but Christ's task is to restore it completely; point by point, the new creation wrought by Christ corresponds to the first creation. All things in heaven and on earth are to be brought into unity under Christ (Eph 1:10), for God's plan is to make him the one Head of all.

In the midst of this world that is being renewed stands humanity. Unlike Adam, we are "his [God's] handiwork, created in Christ Jesus for the good works that God has prepared in advance, that we should live in them" (Eph 2:10). Humanity has become a new creation, a new being (Gal 6:15; 2 Cor 5:17), being stripped of the old self with its past deeds and clad in the new self, the new humanity, "which is being renewed in knowledge after the image of its creator" (Col 3:10).

The catechumens know that they are on the way to this marvelous transformation, but they know too that the transformation will not be immediately complete. "We know that all creation is groaning in labor pains even until now; and not only that, but we ourselves, who have the firstfruits of the Spirit, groan within ourselves as we wait for adoption, the redemption of our bodies" (Rom 8:22-23). At the same time, however, we know that the completion will someday come and that John's vision in the book of Revelation is true: the old heavens and earth will pass away, and he who sits on the throne will declare, "Behold, I make all things new" (Rev 21:5).

The prayer after this first reading shows that the new creation is going on here and now: "Almighty ever-living God, who are wonderful in the ordering of all your works, may those you have redeemed understand that there exists nothing more marvelous than the world's creation in the beginning except that, at the end of the ages, Christ our Passover has been sacrificed."

The Only Son, Offered in Sacrifice

The second reading is about the sacrifice of Isaac (Gen 22:1-18), and the choice of it is especially appropriate on this night when the Church is recollecting herself in order to celebrate Easter.

Everyone knows the story. What must be realized is that the sacrifice is an essential "type" in both the Scriptures and the liturgy. In order to appreciate the point of the type, it is not enough to emphasize the faith of Abraham and to draw from it moral conclusions about the need to accept unreservedly all sufferings that God may send us. These reflections are valid enough, but the biblico-liturgical meaning of the text goes beyond them. The Letter to the Hebrews shows us the twofold meaning of the event: "[Abraham] reasoned that God was able to raise even from the dead, and he received Isaac back as a symbol" (11:19). The sacrifice of Isaac, an only son, reminds us of the sacrifice of the Father's only Son, while the rescue of Isaac turns our thoughts to the resurrection of Christ.

The story contains a sentence that is important for interpreting the action of Jesus and indeed all the sacrifices the Church offers along with her Christ: "Take your son Isaac, your only one, whom you love, and go to the land of Moriah. There you shall offer him up as a holocaust on a height that I will point out to you" (Gen 22:2). The point being made in the text is clear: Isaac is a loved possession, "your son," and all the more loved because he is "your only one." The sacrifice being asked is all the more agonizing because Isaac is the only son and because he had been born of a barren mother in order to carry out a mission of great importance in the formation of God's people: Isaac was the son of the promise. Moreover, it was the Lord himself who told Abraham of the son Sarah would bear him: "for it is through Isaac that descendants will bear your name" (Gen 21:12).

When we insisted that the story should not be simply a subject for moralizing, we were not denying that it does invite the catechumens now awaiting baptism to an unconditioned faith in the Lord. On that kind of faith will depend the vital renewal through the sacrament that they are about to receive and that will bring them the sacramental gift of faith. The faith they already have is what has brought them to baptism, yet it is baptism that will instill in them a faith that is the work of the Spirit.

The object they embrace in such faith is the death of Christ as efficacious for redemption and as obedience to God's will, in contrast to the disobedience of Adam. A further object of their faith is the resurrection, which signifies a passage through death to life. All that will be the effect of the covenant. That is why Abraham has always been spoken of as our father in faith.

The reading on the sacrifice of Isaac is, then, essentially paschal in character. On the one hand, it shows an act of unconditional obedience to God's will, even to the extent of offering up an only son and having God accept the offering. On the other hand, the sacrifice leading to death leads also to ultimate life and to the restoration of a people through fulfillment of the promise.

The responsorial psalm (Ps 16) is well chosen. From the very first days of the Church it was interpreted as a prophecy of the resurrection (cf. Acts 2:25-29): "O LORD, it is you who are my portion and cup; / you yourself who secure my lot. . . . [E]ven my flesh shall rest in hope. / For you will not abandon my soul to hell, / nor let your holy one see corruption" (vv. 5, 9-10).

The congregation meditates briefly on the mystery, and the prayer pulls the various threads together: "O God, supreme Father of the faithful, who increase the children of your promise by pouring out the grace of adoption throughout the whole world and who through the Paschal Mystery make your servant Abraham father of all nations, as once you swore, grant, we pray, that your peoples may enter worthily into the grace to which you call them."

The Church: City and Bride

The fourth reading speaks to the faithful and the candidates for baptism of the building of the Church that has come forth from the side of Christ and is now his Bride. There is great depth and richness in the "theology" of the Church that is thus proclaimed during the Easter Vigil and presented in close connection with the mystery of death and resurrection. This Church is the "sacrament" of the encounter with God and a "sacrament" that, by Christ's will, contains within itself all the signs of salvation.

The passage from Isaiah (54:5-14) hymns the merciful love and fidelity of God, while also giving an enthusiastic description of the City that divine love has built and continues to build without ceasing. Here is how the prophet expresses God's tender love: "For a brief moment I abandoned you, / but with great tenderness I will take you back / . . . . [W]ith enduring love I take pity on you" (vv. 7-8). The Lord then recalls the Flood in the days of Noah and his own promise never again to let the waters flood the earth. He has sworn not to be angry at his people, and nothing can change his love for them.

God then promises to build the City: "I will make your battlements of rubies, / your gates of carbuncles, / and all your walls of precious stones. / All your children shall be taught by the LORD / . . . . In justice shall you be established" (vv. 12-14). Isaiah here anticipates the Revelation of St. John in describing the earthly Jerusalem in a celestial fashion. We also find in the passage the theme of the Church as a Bride that St. Paul will enunciate in Ephesians (5:25-28) and the Second Vatican Council will repeat in its Dogmatic Constitution on the Church (no. 7).

The responsorial psalm (Ps 30) emphasizes the mercy of God in raising us up and bringing us back to life when we were doomed to death. He has thus "changed my mourning into dancing" (v. 12). The prayer then shows the present relevance of this vision of the building of the Church: "Almighty every-living God, surpass, for the sake of your name, what you pledged to the Patriarchs by reason of their faith, and through sacred adoption increase the children of your promise, so that what the Saints of old never doubted would come to pass your Church may now see in great part fulfilled."

The Mystery of Water and the Mystery of the Word

Life is the theme of the fifth reading (Isa 55:1-11), and it is approached from two angles. First, life is seen in terms of the food that nourishes it, as God freely offers to all a life-giving water: "All you who are thirsty, / come to the water!" (v. 1). Second, the Lord offers a life that has its source in an everlasting covenant. On this night, then, newly baptized Christians will be given a divine nourishment for their new life, and they will also become sharers in an everlasting covenant.

If this is to happen, the believer must be receptive to God's word. This receptivity usually takes the form of faith pure and simple, since

God's thoughts are not our thoughts. But the faith is justified, since God's word is powerful and accomplishes what he wants: "[S]o shall my word be / that goes forth from my mouth; / my word shall not return to me void, / but shall do my will, / achieving the end for which I sent it" (v. 11).

A strict exegesis would doubtless not justify seeing in this passage any allusion to the sacraments. Christian tradition, however, and the insertion of the reading into this particular liturgical celebration require the presence of such a meaning. Water and word are efficacious sacraments and transform the sinner into a new creature. The prophet urges us to "Seek the LORD while he may be found, / call him while he is near. / Let the scoundrel forsake his way, / and the wicked man his thoughts" (vv. 6-7). God's word converts, and the water he provides nourishes anyone who decides to obey the word. In short, we enter upon a vital relationship to God, and we become aware that our life depends on the water he offers us and on the efficacious word he addresses to us.

The responsory is likewise taken from the book of Isaiah (12:2-6). It sings of our joy and exultation at what the Lord offers us: "God indeed is my savior; I am confident and unafraid. My strength and my courage is the LORD, and he has been my savior" (v. 2).

The prayer reminds us that God proclaimed through the prophets the great deeds he will accomplish this night. It then goes on to say: "only at the prompting of your grace do the faithful progress in any kind of virtue."

Wisdom, the Source of Life; the Efficacious Word

People who are transformed by God are also given a guide and a law so that they can move onward and advance toward the goal. The sixth reading (Bar 3:9-15, 32–4:4) praises the wisdom given those who have received new life through water and the Spirit.

The important thing for us, in the liturgical context, is the Christian and Christological interpretation of Baruch's poem. If we look only at Baruch's words in their immediate historical context, it is evident that wisdom, though personified, is not really a person. In this same wisdom, however, the Church sees Jesus Christ. On this point, there is a solid interpretative tradition.

The sapiential books of the Bible provide a vision of Wisdom that is rich but also quite complex. Wisdom is described as living with

God (Wis 8:3) but also as "a breath of the might of God, and a pure emanation of the glory of the Almighty" (Wis 7:25). St. John completely identifies this Wisdom with Christ, frequently applying to him what the sapiential books say of Wisdom. Here are some examples.

Wisdom is at God's side from the beginning of the world (Prov 8:22-23; Sir 24:9; Wis 6:22); John presents the Word of God in the same way in his Prologue (1:1) and in the priestly prayer of Christ after the Last Supper (17:5). Wisdom is an outpouring of God's glory (Wis 7:25); the Word, for St. John, is a manifestation of the Father's glory (1:14; 8:50; 11:4; 17:5, 22, 24). Wisdom is a reflection of the eternal light (Wis 7:26); Jesus comes forth from God, who is Light (1 John 1:5). Wisdom illumines paths (Wis 9:11); the Word is the Light of the world and of individuals (John 1:4-5; 3:19; 8:12; 9:5; 12:46). Wisdom comes from heaven and seeks to remain among people (Prov 8:31; Sir 24:8; Bar 3:29, 37; Wis 9:10, 16, 17); Jesus, the Son of Man, has come down from heaven (John 1:14; 3:13, 31; 6:38; 16:28). Wisdom has for her mission to make heavenly realities known to people (Wis 9:16-18); Christ reveals to people what he has himself received from his Father (John 3:11-12, 32; 7:16; 8:26, 40; 15:45; 17:18).

Further parallels might be given, but they would perhaps be a bit forced. Can anyone doubt that there is a conscious reference back to the Old Testament texts? Even the Synoptics set up similar deliberate parallels and references. For example, Christ's invitation, "Come to me, all you who labor" (Matt 11:28-30), is an evident echo of the book of Sirach (24:19; 51:23) and of the book of Proverbs (9:3). St. Paul too sees Christ as being "the wisdom of God" (1 Cor 1:24).

All Christians must seek out this Wisdom and follow her teaching, for "She is the book of the precepts of God / . . . . [A]ll who cling to her will live" (Bar 4:1). We must all retrace our steps and advance toward her in her splendor; such is the privilege given to the baptized. The responsorial psalm (Ps 19) bids us sing: "The law of the LORD is perfect; / it revives the soul. / The decrees of the LORD are steadfast; / they give wisdom to the simple" (v. 8).

The prayer asks God for the wisdom that should guide the faithful in all that they do: "O God, . . . graciously grant to those you wash clean in the waters of Baptism the assurance of your unfailing protection."

A New Heart and a New Spirit

The seventh and last of the Old Testament readings for the Vigil is from the book of Ezekiel (36:16-17a, 18-28). It is quite familiar to Christians, yet it never fails to rouse their enthusiasm when they listen to it with faith and with a sense of gratitude for their experience of its truth.

The essential theme of the reading is, on the one hand, the dispersal of a people because of their sins (a dispersal reflected in the divisions within us that our infidelities cause) and, on the other, the benevolence of God who, for his name's sake and in order to glorify his name that has been profaned, wishes to unite us into a single people, just as he sought to gather again the dispersed Israelites. He no longer seeks to unite a single nation but to gather humanity from all nations and lands. He transforms people by pouring out purifying water upon them and giving them a new heart and a new spirit. The Lord puts his own Spirit in them and makes them capable of following his law, observing his commandments, and being faithful to him. They will dwell in the land which he will give them; they will be his people, and he will be their God.

The text needs no further commentary. So clearly does it apply to those who will be baptized during the Vigil and to all Christians whom the same baptism has formed into a single body that further explanations would be an unnecessary distraction.

We ought, however, to advert once again to the way in which the liturgy uses the text. In itself, the passage does not foretell Christian baptism, and yet no one will feel that the Church is misusing or betraying the text in making it a part of her catechesis for baptism. She rightly uses the words to sing of God's initiative in taking pity on people and in saving them by purifying them. It is the Lord who purifies, just as it was the Lord who created. Moreover, we receive the Spirit as a gift when God thus sanctifies us (Rom 5:5).

The paschal movement of the passage from Ezekiel is reflected in St. Paul's words to the Romans: "For Christ, while we were still helpless, yet died at the appointed time for the ungodly. . . . How much more then, since we are now justified by his blood, will we be saved through him from the wrath" (Rom 5:6, 9). We have become new people. Ezekiel's theme is taken up by St. Paul (Eph 4:24); in the Fourth Gospel, Jesus develops it in his conversation with Nicodemus:

"No one can enter the kingdom of God without being born of water and Spirit" (John 3:5).

Two psalms are offered as responses to this splendid reading. Both speak of encountering God—the God who gives life (Ps 42) and the God who purifies and renews (Ps 51). Psalm 42 reminds us of how the catechumens will shortly approach the altar after being baptized. Psalm 51 asks God to create a clean heart for us and to restore to us the joy of being saved.

Three prayers are supplied after this seventh and last reading.[††] The third, which is used if there are to be baptisms, best expresses the yearning of every believer. "Almighty ever-living God, be present by the mysteries of your great love and send forth the spirit of adoption to create the new peoples brought to birth for you in the font of Baptism, so that what is to be carried out in our humble service may be brought to fulfillment by your mighty power."

Alive for God

With the singing of the *Gloria* we pass from the anticipations of the paschal mystery in the Old Testament to its reality in the New.

St. Paul's Letter to the Romans (6:3-11) puts briefly the theology of our baptism. He speaks of our liberation through the sacrament: We are there immersed in death with Christ and laid in the tomb with him, but there too we rise with him to a new life. The old self is nailed to the cross with Christ so that our state of sin might be rendered powerless and we might no longer be enslaved to sin. Now we are dead to sin and alive for God.

Paul shows the conclusions that must be drawn from the fact of our baptism into Christ. Since the baptized person has died with Christ, he is no longer under the domination of sin. The consequences of the first Adam's disobedience are overcome, since the obedience of the second Adam has reconciled us to God and made us members of his people, which is the Church. Our union with Christ is real now and is becoming ever more full and complete, but it will reach its perfect and definitive form only at the end of time. We are therefore

---

†† Three options existed in the 1969 draft of the postconciliar Easter Vigil, but only two options now exist. The prayer to which Nocent refers has been moved to conclude the Litany of the Saints.

saved now, but in principle and according to the degree of our union with God; this means we are saved according to the concrete ways in which we apply the means of salvation that are offered to us.

Christian life, then, is a life of freedom and belongs to those who have now been rescued from enslavement to sin. But the freedom will be lasting only if it is always exercised in ways that respect the new situation given us by our baptism as adopted children of the Father.

The responsorial psalm (Ps 118) sings of the wondrous deeds the Lord has done for us: "The LORD's right hand has done mighty deeds; / his right hand is exalted. / . . . I shall not die, I shall live / and recount the deeds of the LORD" (vv. 15-17).

The Risen Lord

The gospel readings for the Vigil follow a three-year cycle; each deals with the same event, the resurrection of Jesus. To understand them properly, however, we should set them side-by-side and compare them, taking St. Mark's text as our starting point, since Mark seems to be the first witness to the women visiting the tomb.[9] By studying some inconsistencies in the account, the exegetes endeavor to go a step further and get back to Mark's sources; we shall not follow them in this venture, since it would be irrelevant to our purpose here.[10]

It is easy enough to show the similarities between the various narratives in the Synoptics and John. More important, however, is the fact that each of the evangelists approaches the event differently, depending on his own personality and on the task of evangelization that is his. St. Matthew gives a doctrinal synthesis on the resurrection, with the intervention of the angels serving as an introduction to the appearances of the risen Christ to the women (Matt 28:9-10) and to the Eleven (Matt 28:16-20). He is also concerned with apologetics, since "to this day" the Jews have been claiming that the Christians simply stole Christ's body (Matt 28:15).

St. Luke is more interested in the empty tomb; the women discover that it is empty, even before the angels intervene (Luke 24:2-3). Subsequently, some disciples, Peter among them, come to the tomb to check on the women's story (Luke 24:12, 24).

St. John is less interested in details, but he nonetheless, like Matthew, does not exclude apologetic concerns. He makes the point that the discovery of the empty tomb by Mary Magdalene (20:1) makes less probable a transfer of the body (20:2, 6-7, 13, 15). In the main, however, John is true to the central theme of his gospel as a whole, namely, faith, and studies the varied reactions of the disciples in terms of faith. Peter and John, for example, are described as coming to a belief in the resurrection (20:3-10); Mary Magdalene is seen passing from grief at the absence of the body to a joy at the Savior's new presence (20:11-18).

St. Mark's account is the basis for the other narratives. In his gospel the empty tomb manifests God's power, and the visit of the women is the occasion for asserting that Christ has conquered death after his mission had apparently ended in failure.

With these facts as basis and background, the various apparitions of the risen Christ, whom the Apostles at first recognize only with hesitation (since if it is indeed the Lord and if he is present in the body, then his body is also a body transformed!), acquire a central place in the teaching of the early Church. This is clear from the sermons in the Acts of the Apostles and the First Letter to the Corinthians (15:3-8). The fact that Peter and the disciples went and verified the women's story lends special authority to the teaching on the resurrection.[11]

The important thing in the liturgical proclamation of the resurrection during the Easter Vigil is not the historical fact of the empty tomb. The empty tomb, after all, is not the object of our faith, any more than the precise manner of Christ's resurrection is. The important thing is that we should conform our lives to that of the risen Christ, in order that, having died with him, we may also rise with him.

That is the real goal of the faith of those who are preparing for baptism and will shortly receive the sacramental faith that saves. Such too is the real goal of the faith of all Christians; the problem of how the Lord rose from the dead is unimportant.

Three Sacramental Stages

When the baptism of adults is celebrated during the Easter Vigil and by the community that prepared the catechumens for the sacrament, the unity that once marked the three sacraments of Christian initiation (baptism, confirmation, Eucharist) is restored. After the homily and a short litany,‡‡ the water is blessed, the catechumens receive baptism and confirmation, and the community begins the celebration of the Eucharist, the first in which the newly baptized will share.

We want to dwell briefly here on the connections between the three stages of the one total sacrament of initiation. In showing the connections, our starting point must be the history of salvation and the action of the Holy Spirit, who directs the development of that history.

At the first creation, the Spirit of God swept over the waters as God was creating the world in unity (Gen 1:2). It was God's intention that close relations of mutual service should bind subhuman creatures to each other and to humanity, and people to one other and to their divine Lord. Humanity's catastrophic rebellion against God destroyed this unity, and the Old Testament shows us God constantly endeavoring to reestablish it by offering repeated covenants.

Throughout this Old Testament history it is easy to see the Holy Spirit at work in those whose role it was to guide the people of God and reunite them. Thus, it was the Spirit who raised up the Judges for the salvation of Israel (Judg 3:10-11; 14:6; 1 Sam 10:1-6; 11:2-11; Exod 35:31; etc.). The Spirit is bestowed on the prophets so that they may bear witness; important here is the connection between the Spirit and the word (Isa 8:11; Jer 1:9-15; 20:7; Ezek 3:12-14, 24; 8:3; 11:5; Amos 3:8; 7:14; Isa 61:1-8). Through a consecration the Spirit is also given for priestly service. The Spirit makes the Servant a prophet, a king, and a priest who offers God a pleasing sacrifice that he accepts as expiation for sins (Isa 53). Joined to the priestly service here is the mission of the prophet and the witness.

Yet all these missions were unsuccessful. At the end of the ages, therefore, the Lord sends his own Son. Here again we find the Spirit at work in bringing about the birth of the eternal Word in the flesh. The birth of the Word made flesh from the Virgin's womb is due to the action of the Spirit, and once again God's intervention—in this case, his coming in person—is aimed at the restoration of unity. From the moment of his conception, moreover, the Word incarnate is Messiah, Prophet, Priest, and King.

---

‡‡ The 1969 draft of the postconciliar Vigil, which apparently Nocent was using, had abbreviated the Litany of the Saints. It is no longer "a short litany."

We can link our baptism directly to the incarnation. By the power of the Spirit, the Word came among us and took a human nature to himself. By the power of the same Spirit, who acts now through the instrumentality of the baptismal water, we become new creatures and adopted children; we are "divinized." Baptism gives us a specifically "Christ-ian" existence, which is that of an adopted son or daughter of the Father.

In the life even of Jesus himself, the Spirit intervened in a special way at his baptism in the Jordan and at his transfiguration. By his baptism Jesus was officially assigned to carry out his roles as Messiah, Prophet, Priest, and King. These functions already belonged to him ever since his birth as a man, but now he was publicly, officially deputed to carry them out so as to create a new people. In this context, the words of the Father point to the mission of this Son who was so pleasing to him. If the Father is pleased with the Son, it is because the Son does his will. Tradition has therefore justifiably enriched the word "Son" with the further meaning of "Servant," that is, the one who proclaims God and offers sacrifice by offering his own life for the redemption of his people.

At his baptism, then, Jesus is consecrated for the sacrifice he will offer his Father as a Priest. The baptism also signals the beginning of Jesus' preaching, and the transfiguration is the point at which he begins to predict his own death and resurrection. To the intervention of the Spirit in the life of the incarnate Word in order officially to bestow upon him his mission we can connect the intervention in our lives of the Spirit of Pentecost. Confirmation, which gives us Christian "perfection" and thus complements the "Christ-ian" existence given us at baptism, is the sacrament officially assigning us our Christian mission. It deputes us to be witnesses and to offer sacrifice.

Christ carried out his own priestly mission first and foremost through the paschal mystery of his death, resurrection, and ascension and his sending of the Spirit. We too fulfill our priestly task when we offer sacrifice in union with the ordained priest who has been consecrated by the Spirit so that he may make the sacrifice of Christ present for us.

These various considerations drawn from the history of salvation and the action of the Spirit make clear the close union that exists between the three sacraments of initiation. The first two of these sacraments give us a mode of existence that theologians call a "character" and that is definitive. Through baptism, we are destined for a Christian life under the sway of the Spirit, and we become adopted sons and daughters of God. Confirmation puts an official seal upon our existence and role as Christians. The third sacrament of initiation, the Eucharist, has for its purpose to revive and renew in us the character we received in baptism and confirmation. In celebrating the Eucharist, we give witness and proclaim to the world the death and resurrection of Christ until he comes again.

Wellspring of Life

Once the Liturgy of the Word is completed, the liturgy of baptism begins. The cantors start the ceremony by singing the litany that will lead up to the blessing of the baptismal water. The water is blessed in the baptistery if the place is so situated that the faithful may easily take part in the ceremony; otherwise the water to be blessed is placed in a vessel in the sanctuary.

The prayer now used for the blessing of the baptismal water is no longer the one found in the old liturgical books for the Easter Vigil. Yet, even though it is much shortened, it has preserved the important passages that link the blessing with the history of salvation. We still find in it the "types" of baptism, that is, the past events that are not simply illustrations but find a genuine fulfillment in the Church. The prayer mentions in turn the Spirit who breathed over the waters at the beginning, the waters of the Flood (signifying death to sin and the rebirth of the just one), the crossing of the Red Sea, the waters of the Jordan, and the water that flowed from the wound in Christ's side. Then Christ's command to go and baptize all nations is recalled, and the blessing proper ends with a prayer: "May the power of the Holy Spirit, O Lord, we pray, come down through your Son into the fullness of this font, so that all who have been buried with Christ by Baptism into death may rise again to life with him."

In his *De sacramentis*, St. Ambrose comments on the various scriptural "types" of baptism. With regard to the Flood, he says:

> We began to explain yesterday that the Flood is a prefiguration of baptism. What is the Flood, after all, but the means by which the just one dies to sin and is preserved in order to propagate justice? The Lord saw that the sins of humanity were multiplying; he therefore rescued only the just one and his posterity when he bade the waters rise above even

the mountaintops. Thus all fleshly corruption was itself destroyed in the Flood, and only the stock and example of the just one remained. Is not the Flood, then, the same as baptism, in which all sins are washed away and only the spirit and grace of the just one revive?[12]

Tertullian writes in his treatise on baptism:

> After the waters of the Flood had cleansed away the ancient stain, that is, after what I might call the baptism of the world, the dove was sent forth from the ark and returned with an olive branch as a sign that heaven's wrath had ceased. This olive branch was a sign of peace extended even to the Gentiles. By a similar ordinance, but one that is spiritually effective, the Dove which is the Holy Spirit is sent upon the earth, that is, upon our flesh as it emerges from the bath with its old sins wiped away. The Dove comes bringing the peace of God, a messenger from heaven, where the Church, prefigured by the ark, has her dwelling.[13]

An inscription in the Lateran baptistery from the time of Sixtus III gives poetic expression to the maternal aspect of the font:

> Here a race divine is born for heaven,
> begotten by the fruitful Spirit in this font. . . .
> Nothing separates those reborn and made one
> by the one font, the one Spirit, the one faith.
> Mother Church gives birth in these waters
> to the virginal fruit she conceived by the Spirit.[14]

St. Justin, in his *First Apology*, had already seen in the baptismal font an image of the Church's maternal womb.[15] St. Leo the Great takes up the theme in one of his sermons: "For every one who is reborn, the water of baptism is like the Virgin's womb, since the same Holy Spirit who filled the Virgin fills the font."[16]

These various types of baptism and the font (Flood, womb, etc.) became part of the early Church's teaching on baptism. St. Ambrose comments on most of them in his catechetical writings. He speaks as follows, for example, of the bitter waters of Marah:

> Moses had entered the desert, and the thirsting people had reached the spring of Marah and wanted to drink. But no sooner did they draw the water than they tasted its bitterness and could not drink it. Then Moses threw a piece of wood into the spring, and the bitter waters turned sweet.

What does this tell us but that every creature subject to corruption is a bitter water to humanity? It may be sweet for a moment, it may be pleasurable for a moment, but it is bitter, since it cannot take away sin. Drink it and you will go on thirsting. . . . But when it receives the Cross of Christ, the heavenly sacrament, it becomes sweet and pleasant—rightly "sweet" because it takes guilt from us.[17]

Born again of Water and the Spirit

The decisive moment is now at hand for which the Church has long been preparing the catechumens by means of frequent exorcisms. The priest asks them whether they believe; then he proceeds to baptize them.

At an earlier time, these two actions, now separate, formed a single whole. The candidates put off their garments and went down into the pool of water that was the baptismal font. As they stood there, the priest asked them: "Do you believe in God, the Father almighty, Creator of heaven and earth?" The candidate, moved by the grace of the Holy Spirit, answered, "I believe." The priest then submerged the candidate's head under the water of the pool or else collected a little water from the pipes feeding the pool and poured it over the candidate's head as he stood in the pool.[§§] The priest then questioned the person again: "Do you believe in Jesus Christ, his only Son, our Lord, who was born and suffered?" The answer came again: "I believe," and the priest performed the second immersion or infusion. Finally, "Do you believe in the Holy Spirit, the holy Catholic Church, the communion of saints, the forgiveness of sins, the resurrection of the dead, and everlasting life?" The third profession of faith was followed by the third immersion or infusion. Such was the early form baptism took; it consisted of the triple question-and-answer and the triple immersion.

That type of baptism imaged forth in a more perfect way the reality of which St. Paul speaks: "We were indeed buried with him through baptism into death, so that, just as Christ was raised from the dead by the glory of the Father, we too might live in newness of life" (Rom 6:4). The baptized also showed outwardly their active receptivity

---

§§ Nocent gives no citation here. It is hard to deduce such methods of baptism from early Church literature.

toward the baptismal grace given to them by answering, "I believe." Later on, however, toward the seventh century, when it was primarily infants who were being baptized and who could not answer for themselves, the questions came to be directed to the godparents. For the act of baptism itself, the minister declared: "I baptize you in the name of the Father and of the Son and of the Holy Spirit."

The priest now goes on to anoint the newly baptized persons with holy chrism, signifying that they now share in the Messiah's role of Prophet, Priest, and King. They are then given a white garment, which they are urged to wear unstained until the day of judgment. The garment is a sign of the resurrection; the candidates have gone down into death with Christ then risen to life again with him, thereby becoming new creatures. Finally, the newly baptized are given a lighted candle and bidden to walk as children of light and to keep the candle lit until the Lord comes for the everlasting marriage feast; at that moment faithful Christians will go out with the saints and the elect to meet him.

St. Ambrose reminds the newly baptized Christians of the questions they were asked and the answers they gave:

> They asked you, "Do you believe in God, the Father almighty?" You answered, "I believe," and you were immersed, that is, buried. Again they asked you, "Do you believe in our Lord Jesus Christ and in his Cross?" You said, "I believe," and were immersed again. You were thus buried with Christ; but anyone buried with Christ also rises with Christ. A third time they asked, "Do you believe in the Holy Spirit?" You said, "I believe," and you were immersed a third time so that the triple profession of faith might free you from the many sins of the past.[18]

The saint explains another aspect of the immersion and the emergence from the font:

> Listen carefully, for in order to break the bonds of Satan even in this world, a way was found for one to die while still alive and to rise again. What do we mean by "still alive"? We mean living a bodily life when coming to the font and being immersed in it. Water comes from the earth, does it not? In baptism, therefore, one satisfies the sentence passed by God, but without being swallowed up in bodily death. By being immersed, you suffer the sentence, "Dust you are, and to dust you will return." Once that sentence has been executed, there is room for the heavenly remedy and blessing. Water comes from the earth, but

the nature of our bodily life did not permit us to be covered with earth and to rise again from the earth. Therefore we are cleansed not by earth but by water, and the font is a kind of tomb.[19]

The fathers generally like to think of the baptismal font as both a tomb and a life-giving mother.

St. Ambrose focuses his attention above all on the rite of immersion. He has already described it; now, in his commentary on it, he takes as his point of departure the well-known sentence of St. Paul in his Letter to the Romans (6:3):

> The Apostle therefore cries out, as we have just heard in the reading, that whoever is baptized is baptized into the death of Jesus. What does he mean by "into the death of Jesus"? His point is that just as Christ died, so you must taste death, and that just as Christ died to sin and lives for God, so you have died, through the act of baptism, to the attraction that sin used to have for you, and you have risen through the grace of Christ. The "death," then, is indeed a death, but it is a symbolic death, not a bodily death. When you were immersed, you received the likeness of his death and burial and the sacrament of his Cross, for Christ hung on the Cross and his body was fixed to it with the nails. You were thus crucified with him and are now attached to Christ, attached by the nails of our Lord Jesus Christ lest the devil be able to detach you from him. Let these nails of Christ keep you his, though human weakness draws you away.[20]

In his *De mysteriis*, St. Ambrose points out the meaning of the white garment that is given to the newly baptized Christian:

> You then received white garments as a sign that you have put off the wrappings of sin and put on the pure veils of innocence. . . . For Christ's garments became as white as snow when, in the Gospel, he showed the glory of his resurrection. . . . After donning these white garments through the bath of rebirth, the Church says in the Canticle, "I am very dark, but comely, O daughters of Jerusalem." She is very dark through the weakness of the human condition, comely through grace; very dark because made up of sinners, comely through the sacrament of faith.[21]

The saint continues his commentary on the Canticle of Canticles: The Lord sees his Church as beautiful because she has been redeemed by his blood; he engages in dialogue with her, with the text of the Canticle supplying his words to her.

Many other fathers of the Church likewise commented on the baptismal rites. It is impossible for us to give further examples here, but what St. Ambrose says gives us a good idea of what the fathers in general taught.

In the ancient baptismal rite, the baptized were clad in or received an alb (after the postbaptismal anointing) and then advanced toward the bishop. The latter laid his hands on them, anointed their heads, and gave them the kiss of peace. Carrying their candles, the newly baptized then moved on to the altar, where for the first time they would share in the celebration of the Eucharist. The Eucharist was for them, as for the rest of the faithful, the high point of the Easter Vigil. They would now eat the Body and drink the Blood of the dead and risen Christ and thus receive the pledge of everlasting life.

As the procession moved toward the altar, the newly baptized sang Psalm 23 (22), "The LORD is my shepherd." Patristic commentaries on this psalm are numerous and often quite interesting; we must, however, read the psalm in its entirety if we are to understand the patristic interpretation of it.

> The LORD is my shepherd;
> there is nothing I shall want.
> Fresh and green are the pastures
> where he gives me repose.
> Near restful waters he leads me;
> he revives my soul.
> He guides me along the right path,
> for the sake of his name.
> Though I should walk in the valley of the shadow of death,
> no evil would I fear, for you are with me.
> Your crook and your staff will give me comfort.
> You have prepared a table before me
> in the sight of my foes.
> My head you have anointed with oil;
> my cup is overflowing.
> Surely goodness and mercy shall follow me
> all the days of my life.
> In the LORD's own house shall I dwell
> for length of days unending.

Let us turn once again to St. Ambrose for commentary:

Learn again what sacrament you received. Listen to what holy David says, for he too foresaw this mystery and rejoiced at it. He said that he lacked nothing. Why? Because one who receives Christ's Body will not hunger for ever. How often have you not heard the twenty-second [twenty-third] psalm, but not understood it? See how it applies to the heavenly sacraments![22]

Elsewhere the saint tells us just at what point Psalm 23 was sung: "He has sloughed off the ancient error and renewed his youth like the eagle; now he hastens to this heavenly banquet. He comes in and sees the sacred altar made ready, and he cries out: 'You prepare a table before me!'"[23]

The fathers interpret the "table" of Psalm 23 as referring to the Eucharist that the newly baptized Christians are about to receive for the first time. But the preceding verses too have their Christian significance. For example, they see the words "near restful waters he leads me" as indicating baptism. St. Cyril of Alexandria writes, "This grassy place [= the 'green pastures'] is the paradise whence we fell; Christ brings us back to it and settles us therein through the waters that give rest, that is, through baptism."[24]

The anointing with oil was understood as referring to confirmation. St. Cyril of Jerusalem thus interprets it in the fourth of his *Mystagogical Catecheses*: "He has anointed your forehead with oil, in the form of the seal you have received from God; this was that the seal might be impressed upon you and you might be consecrated to God."[25] The psalm also mentions an overflowing cup; the same commentator compares it to the cup of the Eucharist: "'Your cup intoxicates me like the best wine.' Here is mention of the cup that Jesus took in his hands and over which he gave thanks and said, 'This is my blood, which is shed for many for the forgiveness of sins.'"[26]

The new rite of initiation provides that adults be baptized and right away confirmed and that any children then be baptized.¶¶ After this, the rest of the faithful renew their baptismal promises.

The celebration of the Eucharist then begins. Here is how the preface sings of the mystery:

¶¶ The third edition of the Roman Missal sets forth a different sequence. All the baptisms of adults and children take place together. Then the children are given the postbaptismal anointing with chrism, and adults are confirmed after that.

It is truly right and just, our duty and our salvation,
at all times to acclaim you, O Lord,
but (on this night / on this day / in this time) above all
to laud you yet more gloriously,
when Christ our Passover has been sacrificed.

For he is the true Lamb
who has taken away the sins of the world;
by dying he has destroyed our death,
and by rising, restored our life.

Therefore, overcome with paschal joy,
every land, every people exults in your praise
and even the heavenly Powers, with the angelic hosts,
sing together the unending hymn of your glory,
as they acclaim.

The whole service ends*** with a prayer that all may be united in love: "Pour out on us, O Lord, the Spirit of your love, and in your kindness make those you have nourished by this paschal Sacrament one in mind and heart."

The "Perfect Christian"

The catechumens have now completed their initiation; they are "complete," "finished," "perfect" Christians. Now that we have seen the stages in this initiation, we want to go back to the second and third stages so that we may gain an understanding of what a lay Christian life in the Church means.

Here we run into a problem: What is the meaning of confirmation? The question is a complicated one and has been the subject of much discussion. This, however, is not the place for reviewing the controversies; we are not interested here in scholarship but only in helping Christians understand better what they are and to comprehend what the former catechumens have now become.

In the discussion of and preaching on confirmation, it is usually said that the sacrament makes the baptized persons witnesses; they are now a witness to, and a soldier of, Christ. This approach seems rather narrow. We may also ask whether the interpretation of confir-

***This is the prayer after Communion. The solemn blessing and dismissal follow.

mation as the sacrament of witnessing is not due to a particular situation. I am referring to the fact that in most Western countries confirmation is the last of the sacraments of initiation to be given, being administered often quite a few years after the Eucharist has been received for the first time. In these circumstances, emphasis has been placed on the idea that the sacrament gives the strength and courage for bearing witness and that it "completes" the formation of a Christian.

We may ask whether such a theology of confirmation is not the result of circumstances, instead of being the source of the liturgical practice found in many parts of the Church. This is not to deny that the theology has a certain validity. The Church certainly has the right to preach a theology of the sacraments that has a real basis in the sacraments. She may also emphasize at a given moment one aspect of a complete theology rather than another. Moreover, in her liturgical practice she can act in a way that corresponds to the theology being preached.

The Church of today could, for example, determine that the central focus in the theology of confirmation should be on witnessing and could therefore prescribe that the sacrament is to be conferred when the recipient reaches adulthood and after admission to the Eucharist. Christ himself gave no precise instructions on this matter, and the Church, his Body, has the right to take the initiative and issue such instructions.

As a matter of fact, however, the present practice of the Church is not such that we can deduce a specific theology from it. Usage differs widely. In the Eastern Church the three sacraments of baptism, confirmation, and Eucharist are always given together, even to an infant. Elsewhere, confirmation is given immediately after baptism or conjointly with First Communion or several years after First Communion. What conclusion can we draw from such a varied practice—conclusions not about pastoral practice but about what a Christian is?

If we are to understand the action of the Spirit in this sacrament, it would be better to begin, not with the effects the Spirit produces in people, but with the Spirit's role in the history of salvation, that is, in God's plan for the world. To start with the effects of the Spirit's action in people is to get ourselves into difficulty right from the beginning. For if the Spirit has already acted in baptism, how are we to conceive of him acting in confirmation? Conversely, if the Spirit does act in confirmation, how are we to conceive of him having already acted in baptism? If we concentrate on effects, we will be led to think that there is really only one sacrament involved in baptism and confirmation and that confirmation is simply an aspect of baptism. But then we would be denying the formal teaching of the Church, which distinguishes them as two sacraments. (The fact that baptism, confirmation, and Eucharist are three distinct sacraments does not prevent us from legitimately considering Christian initiation to be a single whole with three stages.)

It will be profitable, then, to approach the problem, not by inquiring into the effects of the Spirit's action in people, but by distinguishing his various activities in God's plan for the world. Such an approach brings us back to what we said earlier about the unity of the three sacraments of initiation.[27]

We see, to begin with, that the Spirit is at work in the creation of the world; according to the opening verses of Genesis, he seems to act as the mighty "Breath" that he is by his very being. Once the world has been created, the Spirit's habitual role is to bring into existence, raise up, transform, and, above all, to unify. Unity is the goal that controls the whole work of creation: the union of a person with God, union within a person, the union of people with one another, the union of people with subhuman creatures, and the union of subhuman creatures with one another in the service of people and for the glory of God.

Sin rends, separates, dislocates. Once sin has come on the scene, God's plan becomes that of bringing humanity back to union and of restoring unity to the world. Can we discern how the Lord God goes about implementing his plan for rebuilding? In the Old Testament we see the Spirit of God acting to raise up people for needed tasks; we cannot say that the Old Testament presents the Spirit as a distinct Person in God, but we certainly can see the Spirit of God acting in the prophets, for example. In order to reach people at their own level, that of an incarnated spirit, God sent envoys, representatives, so that in touching and hearing them and in seeing the signs they offered, people could come in contact with God himself. (Recall how important the theology of "mission" is in the Old Testament.)

God's preliminary work needed implementation, and therefore, because he always loved the world, he sent his only Son. Now, in touching Jesus, people could truly be in contact with the Father. But as God's plan enters this new stage, there is also a major action of the Spirit, for it is by the power of the Spirit that Jesus is conceived in the Virgin's womb. It is through the action of the Spirit that the Word becomes flesh in the fullest and most concrete sense. From his conception, Jesus is Messiah, Prophet, Priest, and King and is thus qualified for the role he must play in the plan of salvation.

Before he begins to exercise that role, Christ is officially declared before the world to be Messiah, Prophet, Priest, and King; this happens at his baptism and involves the intervention of the Spirit. A voice from heaven describes Jesus as the one on whom the Father's favor rests; the dove descending is the symbol of the Spirit. Later on, at the transfiguration, in an account that has a function similar to that of the baptism, we see the Spirit manifesting himself once again, and we hear the voice declaring, "This is my beloved Son, with whom I am well pleased; listen to him."

If we ask where the essential fulfillment of Christ's mission as Messiah, Prophet, Priest, and King is to be found, we must say that it is to be found in the paschal mystery. He fulfills his role most perfectly and completely in this mystery, which includes his priestly action on Calvary, his resurrection and ascension, and his sending of the Spirit, who will unify the Church.

We can now see which were the major actions of the Spirit in carrying out the plan of salvation in Christ. He acted at the moment when the world was created in unity, in the conception of Christ, in Christ's official deputation to his role as Savior, and in the restoration of unity at Pentecost.

Against this background we may now inquire into the activities of the Spirit within the Christian. The fathers of the Church, like St. Paul, explicitly state that the Christian has become so like Christ in his death and resurrection that if we look at Christ, we can understand what takes place likewise in the Christian. It is legitimate, in other words, to parallel what happened in the case of Christ and what happens now in the Christian. If such-and-such were the activities of the Spirit in the plan of salvation and especially in the person of Jesus, then his activities in the Christian will be similar.

Consequently, just as the Word became a human being through the action of the Spirit, so the Christian becomes a Christian through the Spirit's action in the font. The early Church thought of the font as being both tomb and mother: in the font we are immersed in death with Christ so that we may rise with him; from it we receive a new life in a second birth through water and the Spirit. When Christians are thus reborn, they receive powers and qualifications that are essential for being what they should be. The postbaptismal anointing makes it quite clear that each Christian is now prophet, priest, and king.

At a second stage, we can draw a parallel between what took place for Christ at the Jordan and in his transfiguration and what takes place for Christians at confirmation, which is the Spirit's second action in them. Like Christ, the Christian is now officially deputed to the role of prophet, priest, and king.

What do these roles mean for Christians? When do they carry them out most intensely? For an answer, we must keep looking at the parallel between Christ and the Christian. Christ most perfectly carried out his role as Messiah, Prophet, Priest, and King in the paschal mystery (passion, resurrection, ascension, sending of the Spirit). When, then, does the Christian actively exercise the role the Spirit gave in confirmation? One does it first and foremost in the celebration of the Eucharist, which makes present the paschal mystery, especially the death on the cross.

In confirmation, then, the Spirit officially deputes the Christian to the sharing with Christ of his paschal mystery; the Christian does this, above all, by celebrating the mystery through an active participation in the Eucharist. Here we have theological justification for the practice of always administering confirmation before the Christian is admitted to the celebration of the Eucharist, since it is to participation in the Eucharist that confirmation officially deputes a person.

There is no text from Christian antiquity that proves a necessity of administering confirmation before the person can participate in the Eucharist. We think, however, that a passage from the *Apostolic Tradition* speaks of a prescription that is not simply juridical: after describing baptism and confirmation, it says, "Then let them join the whole people in prayer; they are not to pray together with the faithful until they have received all that."[28] In the context, the *Apostolic Tradition* seems to be referring to the prayer of the faithful at the beginning of the eucharistic liturgy. This would mean that in its eyes confirmation makes Christians "perfect" or "complete," that is, enables them to take part in the celebration of the Eucharist, the greatest prayer the Church has.

It is in this Eucharist that the Christian is now called upon to give witness. And indeed by celebrating the Eucharist with the Church, the Christian gives the most powerful of all testimonies, since it is not only a human testimony but one with sacramental efficacy. For, "as often as you eat this bread and drink the cup, you proclaim the death of the Lord until he comes" (1 Cor 11:26). In thus bearing witness through active participation in the Eucharist, the Christian performs a priestly act.

No confusion is really possible between this priesthood and that of the ordained priest. The priesthood of the believer is a genuine priesthood, not simply a "priesthood" by some extension of the term. The priesthood of the ordained priest, however, is ministerial; through his action the reality of the paschal mystery is made present in the real presence of the Eucharist. The priesthood of the believer, on the other hand, consists in one's power and right to take a fully active part in the sacrifice of Christ that the action of the ministerial priest has rendered present.

To be a "perfect" or "complete" Christian, then, means primarily to fulfill the priestly role and, by so doing, to bear witness. For the fulfillment of that role, the Christian is made part of the Church that the Spirit of Pentecost has gathered into unity; the same Spirit structures the Body of Christ and gives it its apostolic mission.

This, then, is the height now reached by the catechumens whom the Church began preparing for baptism at the beginning of Lent. They are now part of the Church and have the mission of living the paschal mystery and spreading its influence.

Climax of the Vigil: The Eucharist, Pasch of the Church

We must be on guard lest, after giving so much attention to the blessing of the fire, the singing of the *Exsultet*, the blessing of the water, the celebration of baptism and confirmation, we end up celebrating the Eucharist as though it were an ordinary, everyday Eucharist. As a matter of fact, however, the Eucharist is the climax of the Vigil service. It is to it that baptism and confirmation are leading, and this Eucharist is, moreover, the most solemn of the year, more solemn even than that of Holy Thursday evening.

The Eucharist is in a true sense the Pasch, or Passover, of the Church.[29] It is constantly effecting the Church's passage to definitive life, constantly actualizing the paschal mystery and purifying people. The forgiveness of sins in baptism depends on the Eucharist; the early Church felt that we must be purified before participating in the Eucharist, but at the same time, it thought of the Eucharist as cleansing from sin those who were truly repentant. The Church is thus constantly being built in solid foundations by the repetition of the Paschal Supper; it is constantly being brought into the presence of the one sacrifice of the cross and constantly offering it, with the Son, to the Father.

The Eucharist is also very closely connected with the Lord's resurrection. For if Christ is not risen, the Eucharist is emptied of content and meaning. The Eucharist presupposes the resurrection and gives people a share in it: the same Jesus said, "I am the resurrection and the life" (John 11:25) and "I am the bread of life" (John 6:48). Without the resurrection, the Eucharist would be a simple fraternal meal; it would not communicate divine life and be creative.

There is a further side of the Eucharist that we should bear in mind: the eucharistic Christ, because he is the risen Christ, truly rules the world. He has overcome our death by his resurrection and is now slowly transforming the world through the Eucharist, which is rendering the world incorruptible.[30]

Especially, then, on this night of Christ's resurrection, the celebration of the Eucharist is the climax of the Church's activity and thus the key to the whole celebration of the Easter Vigil.

Easter Time

Structure and Themes of Easter Sunday and Easter Time

The Distribution of Readings

The following tables will list the readings from Scripture for Easter Time, both at Mass and in the Liturgy of the Hours.

Beginning in the second week of Easter, the principle of continuous reading is applied at Mass, both for the first reading (continuous reading of Acts) and for the gospel (continuous reading of St. John). As a result, we may not look for close parallels between the two readings at each Mass; the two collections of readings, however, do provide an important doctrinal synthesis.

In the Office of Readings, the First Letter of St. Peter is read during the octave. The next four weeks are given over to a semicontinuous reading of the book of Revelation, and the final two weeks to a reading of the letters of St. John.

In the following table, the number given before each reading will be used later to refer to it.

Readings for the Easter Season							
Sundays and Feasts							
Sundays		Acts of the Apostles		The Apostle		The Gospel	
I. Christ is risen	1	We ate and drank with him after he had risen; Acts 10:24a, 27-43	2	Look for the things that are above, where Christ is risen; Col 3:1-4	3	*Morning*: Jesus risen from the dead; John 20:1-9 *Evening*: They knew him in the breaking of bread; Luke 24:13-35	
			or 2	Be a new leaven; 1 Cor 5:6b-8	*or* 4	Gospel of the Easter Vigil	
II. The community of believers grew; doubting Thomas	5	A. The community of believers; Acts 2:42-47	8	A. Rebirth through the risen Jesus; 1 Peter 1:3-9	11	A. Jesus appears on Sunday evening; John 20:19-31	

	6	B. One heart and one mind; Acts 4:32-35	9	B. The Sons of God overcome the world; 1 John 5:1-6	12	B. same
	7	C. Growth of the community; Acts 5:12-16	10	C. Christ who was dead lives forever; Rev 1:9-11a, 12-13, 17-19	13	C. same
III. The risen Christ appears to his followers	14	A. Sermon of Peter on the risen Christ; Acts 2:14, 22-28	17	A. Redeemed by the blood of the Lamb; 1 Pet 1:17-21	20	A. They knew him in the breaking of bread; Luke 24:13-35
	15	B. Sermon of Peter: Christ died and rose; Acts 3:13-15, 17-19	18	B. Christ, the victim; 1 John 2:1-5a	21	B. Christ appears and eats with the disciples; Luke 24:35-48
	16	C. Sermon of Peter: the apostles are witnesses; Acts 5:27b-32, 40b-41	19	C. The Lamb receives power and riches; Rev 5:11-14	22	C. Peter, fisherman and shepherd; John 21:1-19
IV. The Good Shepherd	23	A. Sermon of Peter: Jesus is Lord and Christ; Acts 2:14a, 36-41	26	A. We are healed and have come back to our Shepherd; 1 Pet 2:20b-25	29	A. Christ the Sheepgate; John 10:1-10
	24	B. Sermon of Peter: No salvation but in Christ; Acts 4:8-12	27	B. We have become children of God; 1 John 3:1-2	30	B. The true shepherd gives his life for his flock; John 10:11-18
	25	C. Sermon of Paul and Barnabas: Salvation to the ends of the earth; Acts 13:14, 43-52	28	C. The Lamb leads to the living waters; Rev 7:9, 14b-17	31	C. Christ gives eternal life to his flock; John 10:27-30
V. Ministries	32	a. Seven men chosen who are filled with the Spirit; Acts 6:1-7	35	A. The royal priesthood; 1 Pet 2:4-9	38	A. Christ the Way, the Truth, and the Life; John 14:1-12
	33	B. Paul is presented to the community by Barnabas; Acts 9:26-31	36	B. Believe, and love one another; 1 John 3:18-24	39	B. Dwell in Christ so that you may bear fruit; John 15:1-8

	34	C. Preaching of Paul and Barnabas; choice of elders; Acts 14:21-27	37	C. The New Jerusalem; Rev 21:1-5a	40	C. The new commandment of love; John 13:31-33a, 34-35
VI. Expansion of the Community	41	A. Imposition of hands and gift of the Spirit; Acts 8:5-8, 14-17	44	A. Christ dead and risen is our hope; 1 Pet 3:15-18	47	A. Promise of the Spirit; John 14:15-21
	42	B. The Spirit is given even to pagans; Acts 10:25-26, 34-35, 44-48	45	B. God loved us and sent his Son; 1 John 4:7-10	48	B. The proof of love: to give one's life for one's friends; John 15:9-17
	43	C. Leaders chosen for the community; Acts 15:1-2, 22-29	46	C. The holy city descending from heaven; Rev 21:10-14, 22-23	49	C. The Spirit will teach us everything; John 14:23-29
Ascension	50	A. Account of the Ascension; Acts 1:1-11	51	A. Christ seated at the Father's right hand; Eph 1:17-23	52	A. All power is given to Christ; Matt 28:16-20
		B. same		B. same	53	B. Christ exalted to the Father's side; Mark 16:15-20
		C. same		C. same	54	C. Christ was taken up to heaven; Luke 24:46-53
VII. Witnesses to the Son, glory of Christ; the prayer of Jesus	55	A. Prayer of the community; Acts 1:12-14	58	A. Insulted for the name of Christ; 1 Pet 4:13-16	61	A. Father, glorify your Son of Christ; John 17:1-11a
	56	B. Choice of Matthias as a witness to the resurrection; Acts 1:15-17, 20a, 20c-26	59	B. We have seen, and we await the sending of the Son as savior; 1 John 4:11-16	62	B. May they be consecrated by the truth; John 17:11b-19
	57	C. Stephen's vision and martyrdom; Acts 7:55–8:1a	60	C. I am the Alpha and the Omega; Rev 22:12-14, 16-17, 20	63	C. May they be one in us; John 17:20-26

Pentecost Vigil	64	Babel and the scattering of humankind; Gen 11:19						
	65	The Lord on Sinai; Exod 19:3-8a, 16-20b						
	66	The dry bones; Ezek 37:1-14						
	67	I will pour out my spirit on my servants and handmaids; Joel 2:28-32	68	The Spirit prays for you; Rom 8:22-27	69	The Spirit is given, a flood of living water; John 7:37-39		
Sunday	70	They were filled with the Spirit; Acts 2:1-11	71	Baptized in the one Spirit into a single body; 1 Cor 12:3b-7, 12-13	72	I send you; receive the Spirit; John 20:19-23		

Readings during the Octave of Easter				
		Witnesses to the Resurrection		*Faith and Conversion through Proclamation of the Resurrection*
Monday	73	Witnesses to the resurrection; Acts 2:14, 22-32	74	The risen Christ meets the women who are to tell his brothers of his resurrection; Matt 28:8-15
Tuesday	75	Be converted, believe, and be baptized; Acts 2:36-41	76	Appearance to Magdalene: "I have seen the Lord"; John 20:11-18
Wednesday	77	Peter cures a paralytic; Acts 3:1-10	78	The disciples at Emmaus; Luke 24:13-35
Thursday	79	Sermon of Peter: Jesus died but rose again; Acts 3:11-26	80	The prophecies have been fulfilled: Christ rose on the third day; Luke 24:35-48
Friday	81	Salvation is to be found only in Jesus; Acts 4:1-12	82	Appearance at the Sea of Tiberias: Jesus gives the disciples bread and fish; John 21:1-14
Saturday	83	We cannot be silent about what we have seen; Acts 4:13-21	84	Go and proclaim the good news to all humankind; Mark 16:9-15

Readings for Weekdays during the Easter Season							
		Continuous Reading of Acts			*Continuous Reading of John*		
Second Week	Monday	85	4:23-31	Prayer for the Spirit and courage to preach	86	3:1-8	Rebirth from water and Spirit for the kingdom
	Tuesday	87	4:32-37	The faithful were of one heart and one mind	88	3:7-15	Christ comes from God, reveals the Father, and returns
	Wednesday	89	5:17-26	The apostles escape from prison and preach in the temple	90	3:16-21	God sent his Son to save the world
	Thursday	91	5:27-33	We testify to the resurrection	92	3:31-36	The Father has put everything in the Son's hands
	Friday	93	5:34-42	The apostles are beaten for the name of Jesus	94	6:1-15	Multiplication of bread; Jesus eats with his disciples
	Saturday	95	6:1-7	Appointment of seven men who are filled with the Spirit	96	6:16-21	Jesus walks on the water
Third Week	Monday	97	6:8-15	Stephen speaks with wisdom and the power of the Spirit	98	6:22-29	Seek the food that does not perish
	Tuesday	99	7:51-59	Martyrdom of Stephen	100	6:30-35	My Father gives you the true bread from heaven
	Wednesday	101	8:1-8	The good news is preached everywhere	102	6:35-40	Whoever sees the Son will live forever
	Thursday	103	8:26-40	Philip baptizes an Ethiopian	104	6:44-51	I am the living bread come down from heaven

	Friday	105	9:1-20	Paul, God's instrument for the Gentiles	106	6:52-59	My flesh is real food and my blood real drink
	Saturday	107	9:31-42	The Church progresses and is consoled by the Spirit	108	6:60-69	To whom shall we go? You have the words of eternal life
Fourth Week	Monday	109	11:1-18	Even the pagans are converted	110	10:1-10	I am the gate for the sheep
	Tuesday	111	11:19-26	The good news is preached to the Greeks	112	10:22-30	The Father and I are one
	Wednesday	113	12:24–13:5a	The Spirit chooses Saul and Barnabas	114	12:44-50	I have come into the world to be its light
	Thursday	115	13:13-25	Jesus of the race of David has been raised up	116	13:16-20	Receive the one I send, and you receive me
	Friday	117	13:26-33	Sermon of Paul: God has raised up Jesus	118	14:1-6	I am the Way, the Truth, and the Life
	Saturday	119	13:44-52	We now turn to the Gentiles	120	14:7-14	He who sees me sees the Father
Fifth Week	Monday	121	14:5-18	Sermon of Paul and Barnabas: Turn from idols to the living God	122	14:21-26	The Spirit will teach you everything
	Tuesday	123	14:19-28	Address of Paul and Barnabas to the community, telling what God had done for them	124	14:27-31a	I give you my peace
	Wednesday	125	15:1-6	The problem of whether to circumcise the Gentiles	126	15:1-8	If you remain in me and I in you, you will bear much fruit

	Thursday	127	15:7-21	Counsels of Peter and James: Do not burden the converted pagans	128	15:9-11	Love me and you will have joy
	Friday	129	15:22-23	No unnecessary burdens	130	15:12-17	Love one another
	Saturday	131	16:1-10	The Spirit sends forth Paul and Luke	132	15:18-21	I have chosen you; you no longer belong to the world
Sixth Week	Monday	133	16:11-15	Conversion and baptism of Lydia and her household	134	15:26–16:4a	The Spirit of truth will bear witness to me
	Tuesday	135	16:22-34	Paul and Silas in prison: Believe and be saved	136	16:5-11	If I do not go, the Spirit cannot come
	Wednesday	137	17:15, 22–18:1	I proclaim him whom you worship without knowing him	138	16:12-15	The Spirit of truth will lead you to the entire truth
	Thursday	139	18:1-8	Each Sabbath Paul spoke in the synagogue	140	16:16-20	Jesus announces his departure and new presence
	Friday	141	18:9-18	Paul's vision: Speak fearlessly to the Corinthians	142	16:20-23a	A joy no one can take away
	Saturday	143	18:23-28	Teaching of Apollos about Christ	144	16:23b-28	My Father loves you because you love me and believe in me
Seventh Week	Monday	145	19:1-8	Paul baptizes and lays hands on the baptized to confer the Spirit	146	16:29-33	Courage! I have overcome the world
	Tuesday	147	20:17-27	Paul wants to carry out his mission fully	148	17:1-11a	Father, give glory to your Son

	Wednesday	149	20:28-38	God has power to build and to give an inheritance	150	17:11b-19	May they be one
	Thursday	151	22:30; 23:6-11	Paul bears witness and is ordered to Rome	152	17:20-26	May their unity be complete
	Friday	153	25:13-21	Jesus died, but Paul claims he is alive	154	21:15-19	Shepherd my flock
	Saturday	155	28:16-20, 30-31	Paul proclaims God's rule at Rome	156	21:20-25	John has written all this, and it is true

Sunday Readings in the Liturgy of the Hours

First Sunday	157	The Israelites pass dryshod through the Red Sea; Exod 14:15–15:1a	Fifth Sunday	161	The wedding day of the Lamb; Rev 18:21–19:10
Second Sunday	158	A new life; Col 3:1-17	Sixth Sunday	162	The word of life; God is Light; 1 John 1:1-10
Third Sunday	159	The Lamb breaks the seals of the book; Rev 6:1-17	Ascension	163	He ascended on high with a host of captives; Eph 4:1-24
Fourth Sunday	160	The sign of the woman; Rev 12:1-17	Seventh Sunday	164	The commandment of faith and love; 1 John 3:18-24
			Pentecost	165	Those led by the Spirit are the children of God; Rom 8:5-27

Weekday Readings in the Liturgy of the Hours

First Week	Monday	166	1 Pet 1:1-21	Thanksgiving
	Tuesday	167	1 Pet 1:22–2:10	The way of God's children
	Wednesday	168	1 Pet 2:11-25	Christians are aliens in the world
	Thursday	169	1 Pet 3:1-17	The imitation of Christ
	Friday	170	1 Pet 3:18–4:11	Waiting for the Lord's coming
	Saturday	171	1 Pet 4:12–5:14	Exhortation to the faithful and the elders

Second Week	Monday	172	Rev 1:1-20	Vision of the Son of Man
	Tuesday	173	Rev 2:1-11	To the churches of Ephesus and Smyrna
	Wednesday	174	Rev 2:12-29	To the churches of Pergamum and Thyatira
	Thursday	175	Rev 3:1-22	To the churches of Sardis, Philadelphia, and Laodicea
	Friday	176	Rev 4:1-11	Vision of God
	Saturday	177	Rev 5:1-14	Vision of the Lamb
Third Week	Monday	178	Rev 7:1-17	A great throng with the seal of God
	Tuesday	179	Rev 8:1-13	Seven angels chastise the world
	Wednesday	180	Rev 9:1-12	The plague of locusts
	Thursday	181	Rev 9:13-21	The plague of war
	Friday	182	Rev 10:1-11	The seer is confirmed in his role
	Saturday	183	Rev 11:1-19	The two witnesses
Fourth Week	Monday	184	Rev 13:1-18	The two beasts
	Tuesday	185	Rev 14:1-13	The conquering Lamb
	Wednesday	186	Rev 14:14–15:4	The harvest of the last days
	Thursday	187	Rev 15:5–16:21	The seven bowls of God's anger
	Friday	188	Rev 17:1-18	Babylon, the great harlot
	Saturday	189	Rev 18:1-20	The fall of Babylon
Fifth Week	Monday	190	Rev 19:11-21	Victory of God's Word
	Tuesday	191	Rev 20:1-15	Final struggle with the dragon
	Wednesday	192	Rev 21:1-8	The new Jerusalem
	Thursday	193	Rev 21:9-27; 22:1-9	Vision of the heavenly Jerusalem
	Friday	194	Rev 22:1-9	The river of life
	Saturday	195	Rev 22:10-21	Our hope is sure
Sixth Week	Monday	196	1 John 2:1-11	The new commandment
	Tuesday	197	1 John 2:12-17	Doing God's will
	Wednesday	198	1 John 2:18-29	The antichrist
	*Thursday	199	1 John 3:1-10	We are children of God
	Friday	200	1 John 3:11-17	Love for the brothers
	Saturday	201	1 John 3:18-24	The commandment of faith and love

Seventh Week	Monday	202	1 John 4:1-10	God first loved us
	Tuesday	203	1 John 4:11-21	God is love
	Wednesday	204	1 John 5:1-12	Our faith conquers the world
	Thursday	205	1 John 5:13-21	Prayer for sinners
	Friday	206	2 John	Be faithful
	Saturday	207	3 John	Let us walk in truth

* If Ascension is celebrated on this day and not on Sunday, today's reading is shifted to Friday, Friday's to Saturday, and Saturday's to the Seventh Sunday.

Easter Sunday

36. THIS DAY THAT THE LORD HAS MADE

"This Is the Day the Lord Has Made"

The day has dawned at last, the day of days; indeed, the feast we celebrate we call simply "the Day of the Lord." At this moment we experience a reality that is both past and present: "The Pasch is indeed 'the Passover of the Lord': Has the Spirit ever made any truth more clear than this: that Easter is not a figure or a story or a distant image, but the real Passover of the Lord?"[1]

As the celebrant enters the church to celebrate the Mass of Easter Day, he may remind all of both baptism and the blood of the covenant by sprinkling those present with holy water. Meanwhile, all may sing, "I saw water flowing from the Temple, from its right-hand side, alleluia: and all to whom this water came were saved and shall say: alleluia, alleluia."

The great news is proclaimed once again in the entrance song, but this time it is Christ himself who proclaims it through the mouths of his faithful: "I have risen, and I am with you still, alleluia. You have laid your hand upon me, alleluia. Too wonderful for me, this knowledge, alleluia, alleluia." The hand the Father placed on the Son he now places on the Church and on each of us.

"We Ate and Drank with Him"

The first reading in today's Mass is from Peter's sermon in the house of Cornelius the centurion. These two men were deeply moved when they met for the first time. Cornelius had had a vision in which he was told to send for Peter. Peter came, learned of what had happened, and responded with the catechesis that forms today's reading [1].

The passage raises historical and literary problems that we shall not go into. In any event, it is generally accepted that the account is historical as far as its substance goes. It can readily be admitted that,

339

under the inspiration of the Holy Spirit, Luke has made contributions of his own in respect to both the literary form and the exposition of the problems caused by the law-gospel conflict in the life of the young Church.[2]

It is chiefly because of verses 40-43 that the Church today bids us read this discourse that Cornelius's conversion elicits from the deeply moved Apostle. Cornelius's vision and conversion mark a major turning point for Peter and the entire Church, for the Spirit seems to be clearly pointing out the direction the Church should take. The Spirit has now revealed that "in every nation whoever fears him and acts uprightly is acceptable to him" (Acts 10:35). Yet the revelation that the Church's mission is universal turns Peter's world upside down. Others had already learned this truth, either from personal experience, as Paul did in his own sudden conversion, or from the experience of converting others, as Philip did in baptizing the Ethiopian official. Peter, on the other hand, while never denying it (after all, he stated the truth on Pentecost! [Acts 2:14]), had not come to a personal realization that the Spirit was demanding the mission to the Gentiles. The chief of the apostles will not forget his experience, as he makes clear in his explanation to the church at Jerusalem (Acts 11:1-8) and in his words to the Council of Jerusalem (Acts 15:7-9).

The few verses read today sum up both the Church's mission and the essential object of saving faith: God raised Jesus up on the third day and had him appear to the witness chosen beforehand by God. One requirement for being an apostle was to have been a witness of the resurrection. That is why Peter adds, "us . . . who ate and drank with him after he rose from the dead" (Acts 10:41). The mission of the apostles and of the entire Church is to bear witness to this resurrection and to proclaim it as the object of a faith that saves because it brings the forgiveness of sins (v. 43).

The three essential points of this message are meaningful for each of us and should stimulate our reflection: the universalism of the Church; the witness to the resurrection of Christ; our faith in the risen Christ. The preaching of the Church, and the witness each of us must give, can be summed up, at every point in time until Christ comes again, in the paschal message that Christ is risen from the dead and is now living.

The responsorial psalm (Ps 118) proclaims our new condition, now that the mystery of the resurrection has been fulfilled in us: " 'his right hand is exalted. / The Lord's right hand has done mighty deeds.' / I shall not die, I shall live / and recount the deeds of the Lord" (Ps 118:16-17).

If You Have Been Raised with Christ

The second reading rouses us from a contemplation that might possibly be that of the mere spectator and thus leave us personally uncommitted. For baptized Christians, the resurrection of Christ is not merely a historical event; it affects them personally, and its reality and the demands it makes are felt each day: "If then you were raised with Christ . . ." (Col 3:1) [2].

St. Paul tells us that these demands are laid upon us by our baptism. In his Letter to the Romans, and with the ritual of baptism as his point of reference, the Apostle teaches that we have been buried with Christ in death; consequently, we must also live a new life with him (Rom 6:4-5). The way Paul speaks might make us think that our risen life is entirely in the future. The Letter to the Colossians, however, makes it clear that we live here and now with the risen Jesus and that our lives must be the lives of those who are risen with Christ.

The concrete conclusion that follows from this premise is perfectly clear and forms the basis of Christian morality: "Think of what is above, not of what is on earth" (Col 3:2). Christians must live according to what they really are; this means that their life is lived under the sign of hope. Only in faith do they understand that their personal renewal is something already real. While on earth, they pass through a time of testing, and only as in a mirror, indistinctly, do they come in contact with the mysteries of salvation (1 Cor 13:12; 2 Cor 5:6-7). Nonetheless, they do possess the pledge that is the Spirit (2 Cor 1:22; 5:5; Rom 2:23; Eph 1:13-14). We must strengthen within us the new life we received in baptism. That life is truly ours, but we must live it in paradoxical condition: we must be in the world without belonging to it (Col 2:20; 1 Cor 7:31); we must suffer even though we are already risen (2 Cor 4:10-11). In this way, we Christians make up what is lacking in the sufferings of Christ, even as we live by his resurrection and wait to "appear with him in glory" (Col 3:4).

Here is a doctrine that is both optimistic and demanding. The collect of the Mass translates it into fervent prayer: "O God, who on this day, through your Only Begotten Son, have conquered death and unlocked for us the path to eternity, grant, we pray, that we who keep the solemnity of the Lord's Resurrection may, through the renewal brought by your Spirit, rise up in the light of life."

A New Dough

The Easter Sunday liturgy provides an alternative second reading, taken from the First Letter to the Corinthians (5:6-8). This reading makes the point that the feast of Easter is not a celebration limited to externals but that, on the contrary, there is only one way of properly celebrating it: to put away all corruption and wickedness. These are the "old yeast" and we must get rid of them so that we may celebrate with the unleavened bread of sincerity and truth. We ourselves must be like Passover bread that is unleavened. We must be a new dough.

St. Paul likes to relate Christ's Pasch and ours to the Pasch of the Church as she first celebrated it in the context of the Jewish Passover. The first ritual step taken for the latter celebration was to rid the house of any old yeast. Paul also, and more importantly, compares the sacrifice of Christ to the sacrifice of the Passover lamb. As the Passover sacrifice commemorated the liberation and Exodus from Egypt, so the blood of Christ the Lamb sealed the new and eternal covenant.

The Easter Sequence sums up in poetic style the meaning of the feast. In this poem the Church sings: "Christ indeed from death is risen, our new life obtaining. Have mercy, victor King, ever reigning!"

"They Did Not Yet Understand . . . That He Had to Rise from the Dead"

The gospel passage proposed for reading at a morning Mass on Easter Sunday[3] might well stir our enthusiasm by its literary character and by the apologetic emphasis it contains. By "apologetic emphasis" I mean the importance John attributes to the witness of Mary and of the two disciples, namely, Peter, the chief of the apostles, and John, who, though not the chief, runs ahead of Peter to the tomb [3].

The account is undoubtedly important for its details, especially since John, while agreeing with the Synoptics on a number of points, also has his own way of describing the events. Nonetheless, it seems to me, especially since the Church has already greatly emphasized the event itself of the resurrection during the Easter Vigil service, that we should pay special attention to the final sentence of the passage: "For they did not yet understand the Scripture that he had to rise from the dead" (John 20:9).

Here was a blindness that the disciple whom Jesus loved made no attempt to hide. That should encourage us to renew our own faith. Here were people who had lived with Jesus and had listened time after time to his teaching and his references to his death and resurrection. Yet they did not even now understand him or the Scriptures with all those prophecies of the resurrection that we heard read during the Vigil. As a matter of fact, the two disciples in today's gospel believe only when they see: Peter, who enters the tomb, sees and believes; John, who arrives first, looks in without entering (that privilege is for Peter) and likewise sees and believes.

The account, which poses numerous problems for the exegete, contains three important points: the empty tomb, the haste of the disciples, and their faith.

The discovery takes place "on the first day of the week." Here we have the reason for the celebration of Sunday. The Jews celebrated Saturday, because that was the day on which the Lord rested after his six days' work of creation. But the Lord rose "early in the morning" on the first day of the new week, and that is the day Christians would henceforth celebrate. It would be for them, however, not only the first day of the week but also the eighth day, a day that in a sense falls outside the system of the week. For it is not only the day on which God began the work of the first creation but also the day of the new creation and the resurrection from the dead.

Christians did not think of this day in terms of apologetics, that is, as a proof that the mission of Jesus had been successful. They thought of it as first and foremost the day when the whole of creation is renewed.

The rock has been taken from the door of the tomb. Mary Magdalene, seeing this, runs to tell the disciples. John makes it a point to tell us who the two disciples are that hasten to check on Mary's report: they are Peter, the leader of the new Church, and "the other disciple whom Jesus loved." The latter, so eager in love for Christ, reaches the tomb first but holds back and lets Peter enter the tomb, for Peter's testimony will carry greater weight with the community as a whole. The other disciple does, however, see immediately that the tomb is empty, even if everything in it is neatly disposed (as Peter could attest). That other disciple then entered the tomb and "saw and believed." We are reminded of the story of Thomas, which will be read on the Second Sunday of Easter: "Have you come to believe because you have seen me? Blessed are those who have not seen and have believed" (John 20:29).

The Church and every Christian now have at their disposal two testimonies: that of the ancient Scriptures, as read now in and by the Church, under the guidance of the Spirit of Pentecost, and that of the two disciples and Mary Magdalene.

"He Was Made Known to Them in the Breaking of the Bread"

At an afternoon Mass on Easter Sunday, the familiar gospel of the disciples at Emmaus is read [4]. In it we find exemplified the same kind of failure to understand the Scriptures. Here Jesus himself makes this point as he walks along with the two disciples on the evening of Resurrection Sunday: " 'Oh, how foolish you are! How slow of heart to believe all that the prophets spoke! Was it not necessary that the Christ should suffer these things and enter into his glory?' Then beginning with Moses and all the prophets, he interpreted to them what referred to him in all the Scriptures" (Luke 24:25-27). Christ gives the kind of catechesis that the fathers of the Church will later adopt; they will search out the types or prefigurations and then study the fulfillment of them: type, prefiguration, preparation—antitype, realization, fulfillment.

We have on several occasions emphasized the fact that the Church's traditional liturgical reading of the Scriptures, while not neglecting exegesis, brings to light special values in the gospel passages she proclaims. Thus, a strict application of the principles of exegesis will not allow us to assert that the meal Jesus took with the disciples at Emmaus was a eucharistic meal; and yet it is impossible not to see in the words Luke uses a reference to the Eucharist: "he took bread, said the blessing, broke it, and gave it to them" (Luke 24:30). Surely Luke had the Eucharist in mind both here and in Acts 2:42. He may not say in so many words that the meal at Emmaus is a repetition of the Supper, but he surely is thinking about it; nor can the Church think otherwise.

In other words, the simple fact that the disciples recognized Jesus in the breaking of bread does not prove that the meal was a eucharistic celebration, since it could have been simply the case that the

Lord's manner of performing the actions made him immediately recognizable. Yet neither Luke nor the Church as she proclaims this text can help but recall the Last Supper. Moreover, while the disciples recognized Jesus in the breaking of bread, what inflames their hearts is above all the Lord's explanations of the Scriptures: "Were not our hearts burning within us while he spoke to us on the way and opened the Scriptures to us?" (Luke 24:32) It was doubtless that experience that made them urge Jesus: "Stay with us, for it is nearly evening and the day is almost over" (Luke 24:29). And yet, in telling their story to the apostles, they refer only to the breaking of bread and do not mention the explanation of the Scriptures. "Then the two recounted what had taken place on the way and how he was made known to them in the breaking of the bread" (v. 35).

From that time forward it is in the breaking of bread that the Church has manifested her faith in the resurrection of Jesus. The Eucharist is the distinctive sign by which a Catholic professes faith in the paschal mystery and celebrates that mystery in the joyous Eucharist, which is inseparable from Easter.

Living the Paschal Mystery

The Church does not limit her celebration of her Lord's resurrection to Easter Sunday but continues it until the day when the Lord sends his Spirit. The reason for this unbroken celebration is that Pentecost marks the full impact of salvation on the world and the outpouring of God's life.[4]

This does not mean, however, that Christians need not themselves face death. On the contrary, the vision of glory never comes save after the passage through death. The "rediscovery" of the paschal mystery undoubtedly has made us aware that the term "redemption" tended to be too juridical, to the point at times of making Christians forget that the resurrection too was a mystery of salvation and not simply a kind of appendix or a proof that Christ's mission had been successful. It is also true, however, that the paschal mystery directs our attention back to the beginning of God's creation and to the catastrophe that had left its mark on the world. The paschal mystery includes the incarnation and all the deeds of Christ. Consequently, though it ends in glory, it also requires the passage through death. In fact, we must even maintain that life springs from death.

These remarks enable us to pinpoint the true nature of Christian asceticism. Of Christians, as of Christ himself, it must be said not simply that their glory comes after death but that their self-renunciation and death are already part of their paschal victory.

The Paschal Mystery and the Fathers

Our purpose here is not to provide an anthology of patristic texts on the paschal mystery; that would require more pages than we have at our disposal. We wish only to bring to the reader's attention some thoughts of the great writers whose voices still echo in the Church.

An author whose poetic freshness and profound yet simple theology still have power to move us deeply is Melito of Sardis.[5] His poem *On the Pasch* displays, as early as 160–70 (the most probable period of composition), a procedure that will be typical of the later patristic catecheses, namely, the use of typology. The poet gives a typological interpretation of Exodus 12:3-28, namely, just as Israel was protected by the blood of the lamb, so the new people of God will be preserved by the blood of the sacrifice on the cross. The person, nature, and work of Christ are presented in the framework of the economy of salvation, that is, of the developing plan God has for humanity's redemption. The passion of Christ is foretold by types. Finally, he wins the victory in his resurrection.

Here is how the poem begins:

> The Scripture account of the Hebrew Exodus has been read, and the words of the mystery have been explained: how the lamb is sacrificed and the people saved. Therefore, beloved, observe and understand! The paschal mystery is new and old, eternal and temporal, corruptible and incorruptible, mortal and immortal. It is old according to the Law, new according to the Logos; temporal in its prefiguration, eternal in the grace it bestows; corruptible in the immolation of the sheep, incorruptible in the life of the Lord; mortal through burial in the earth, immortal through the resurrection from the dead. The Law is old, but the Logos new; the figure is temporal, grace eternal; the sheep is corruptible, the Lord incorruptible; he is sacrificed as a lamb, raised up as God. For, "like a sheep he was led forth to be slaughtered," but he was not a sheep; he was led forth like a silent lamb, but he was not a lamb. The figure is gone and outstripped, the truth has been found [fulfilled]. For instead of a lamb it is God who has come; instead of a sheep, a human being, and in the human the Christ who contains all things. Thus the

sacrifice of the sheep and the Passover rite and the letter of the Law have given way to Christ Jesus.[6]

Further on, Melito explains that what is prefigured in the Old Testament is fulfilled in the New: "The people [Israel], therefore, were like the outline of a plan, and the Law was like the letter of a parable; the Gospel, however, is the explanation and fulfillment of the Law, and the Church is the place where it is carried out."[7]

It is when Melito defines the Pasch on the basis of a false etymology, however, that he best expresses the meaning of the mystery and opens the door for an interpretation that will always remain valid, even when its erroneous etymological basis is removed. Melito writes: "What, then, is the 'Pasch'? The name is derived from what happened, for the verb *paschein* [to suffer; also, to celebrate the Passion = Pasch = passage] is derived from *pathein* [to have suffered]."[8]

Here is a valid theology despite its being based on a false etymology. The Pasch *is* a passage through suffering to victory; *paschein*, "to suffer," is indeed connected, in its content, with *pascha*, "passage." As a result, the word *passio* will connote triumph through suffering, rather than simply suffering itself. This is true of the *Passio*, or gospel of Christ's passion, that is proclaimed on Good Friday: it is first and foremost an account of Christ's victory through suffering. So too, the *passio* of a martyr, despite its legendary details, means chiefly an account of how the martyr triumphed through sufferings.

This, at any rate, is how we must understand the "Pasch" of the Lord as well as our own and the Church's "pasch." It was worth our while to recall the false etymology that served as a point of departure, for it helps us understand the way in which the fathers approached the paschal mystery.[9]

Some Patristic Texts: St. John Chrysostom and St. Ambrose

In one of his Easter catecheses, St. John Chrysostom reminds his hearers of the power still present in the blood that Christ shed for us:

> Do you wish to know the power of this blood? Go back to what prefigured it, to the ancient accounts of what happened in Egypt. God was about to inflict the tenth plague on the Egyptians, slaying their firstborn because they were holding his firstborn people captive. But how could he avoid harming the Jews along with the Egyptians, since

all alike dwelt in the same place? See now the power of the prefiguration so that you may understand the power of the reality that fulfilled
it. The blow inflicted by God was about to descend from heaven, and
the destroying angel was about to make the round of the homes.

What did Moses do? He told the Jews: "Sacrifice an unblemished
lamb and smear your doorposts with the blood."

What do you respond to Moses? "Can the blood of a mindless beast
save those who are endowed with reason?" "Yes," he says, "not because
it is blood but because it is a figure of the Savior's blood. Just as an
emperor's statue, though it lacks all sense, safeguards those endowed
with reason and sense when they seek refuge at it, not because it is a
piece of bronze but because it is an image of the emperor, so this lifeless
and unfeeling blood saved living human beings, not because it was
blood, but because it prefigured the blood of the Lord."

Here is another way to appreciate the power of this blood. Observe
where it began to flow and what its source was. It flowed down from
the Cross and from the Lord's side. While the dead Jesus still hung on
the Cross (the Gospel tells us), a soldier approached and opened his
side with a spear, and water and blood flowed out. The water symbol-
ized baptism, and the blood the mysteries. . . .

Blood and water flowed from his side. Beloved, do not pass this
mystery by unheeding, for I have yet another mystical interpretation
to offer you. I said that the water and blood were the symbols respec-
tively of baptism and the mysteries. Now it is from these two sacraments that the Church is reborn, in the bath of rebirth and renewal in
the Holy Spirit, through baptism and the mysteries. The symbols of
baptism and the mysteries, however, came from Christ's side. Therefore
it is from his side that he formed the Church, just as he formed Eve
from the side of Adam. . . .

Have you seen how Christ made his Bride one with himself? Have
you observed the food with which he nourishes her? Well, it is the same
food that has formed and nourished us.[10]

Note the procedure, which is a favorite with the fathers. It consists
in going back to the types and figures in the Old Testament and making these the basis for instructing Christians on the sacraments and
situating the sacraments in the history of salvation. Such a catechesis
highlights the connection between the sacraments of Christian initiation and the Pasch.

In his explanation of the Creed, St. Ambrose approaches the resurrection from a special point of view, seeing in it a sign of Christ's
divinity, which the incarnation had in no way diminished:

"On the third day he arose from the dead." There you are told of his resurrection. "He ascended into heaven, and sits at the right hand of the Father." You see that the flesh could in no way detract from the divinity, but that on the contrary the incarnation brought Christ a great triumph. Why, after rising from the dead, does he take his seat at the Father's right hand? Because he has thus brought back to the Father the fruit of his "good pleasure." There are two facts of which you are sure: he rose from the dead, and he sits at the Father's right hand. The conclusion is that the flesh could not diminish the glory of the divinity.[11]

In emphasizing this unwonted aspect of the resurrection and ascension, the Doctor of the Church should not be regarded as developing an apologetic argument. His aim is rather to call our attention not only to the glorification of Christ but to ours as well, for once sins have been forgiven, the flesh is not of itself an obstacle to the glorious transfiguration.

St. Leo the Great

St. Leo is what we might call the classical catechist of the great mysteries of the Lord, such as the incarnation, passion, and resurrection. In discussing each of the mysteries, he likes to emphasize three points: the actualization of the mystery that the Church celebrates in her liturgy as a present and not a purely past reality; the integration of the mystery being celebrated into the overall history of salvation; the consideration of the mystery as being not simply an event but an example as well. Christ's actions have a present reality and, as such, are fully efficacious, but at the same time they are an example for us.

St. Leo begins a sermon on the passion by saying:

Beloved, the Lord's glorious passion, concerning which we promised we would speak today, is most to be admired for the mystery of humility it embodies. It redeemed us all, and it instructs us, so that after having paid our ransom it also helps us to holiness. . . .

Beyond a doubt, beloved, the Son of God so closely united human nature to himself that Christ is one and the same not only in that individual who is the firstborn of all creatures but in all his saints as well. As the Head cannot be separated from the members, neither can the members be separated from the Head. For although it is true not of this life but of eternal life that God is all in all, yet even now he inhabits, and cannot be separated from, his temple which is the Church, as he promised when he said: "Lo, I am with you always, to the close of the age." The Apostle concurs when he writes: "He is the head of the body, the Church; he is the beginning, the firstborn from the dead, that in everything he might be preeminent. For in him all the fullness of God was pleased to dwell, and through him to reconcile to himself all things."[12]

From the very beginning of this sermon, St. Leo makes it clear what a mystery of Christ is for us: a fact, and indeed a sanctifying fact, but an example as well. Taking as his starting point the incarnation and the bonds uniting Christ and his Church, the saint draws concrete conclusions for us. He continues: "Thus our Savior, the Son of God, gave all who believe in him an efficacious sign and an example; through rebirth they lay hold of the former, through imitation they follow the latter."[13]

We have already seen how the fathers like to refer back to scriptural types. St. Leo does not neglect this method:

> Everything that was formerly done in obedience to the law—the circumcision of the flesh, the varied sacrifices, the observance of the Sabbath—was a testimony to Christ and a prophecy of his grace. He is the end of the law, not in the sense that he empties the law of further meaning, but in the sense that he fulfills it. Though he is the author of the old as well as the new, he changed the mysteries hidden in the figurative promises by bringing to pass what was promised; he put an end to prophecy, because he who was prophesied had now come.[14]

St. Leo goes on then to present salvation as a present reality in the liturgy, so much so that we are in contact with the mystery we celebrate. The passage is extremely important for a theology of the liturgy.

> All that the Son of God did and taught for the reconciliation of the world is not simply known to us through the historical record of the past; we also experience it through the power of his present works. . . . It is not only the courageous, glorious martyrs who share in his suffering; all the faithful who are reborn also share it, and do so in the very act of their rebirth. For when people renounce Satan and believe in God, when they pass from corruption to a new life, when they lay aside the image of the earthly human and take on the form of the heavenly human, they go through a kind of death and resurrection. One who is received by Christ and receives Christ is not the same after baptism as before; the body of the reborn Christian becomes the flesh of the crucified Christ.[15]

Commenting on St. Paul's words in his First Letter to the Corinthians, "Christ has been raised from the dead, the firstfruits of those who have fallen asleep" (15:20), St. Leo writes, "He who was the first human being to rise from the dead was part of the totality that followed; moreover, we piously believe that what first took place in the Head will take place in the members as well, since 'as in Adam all die, so also in Christ shall all be made alive.' "[16]

In the saint's two sermons on the resurrection, we find passages that speak to some of our contemporary preoccupations. He speaks, for example, of the state of Christ's risen body:

> He would also show them the wounds in his side, the holes left by the nails, and all the marks of his recent passion—all this in order to show that the divine and human natures remain distinct in him, and in order that we might be sure the Word is not identical with the flesh he assumed, but might confess that the Son of God is both Word and flesh.
>
> Paul, the Apostle of the Gentiles, does not disagree with this belief, beloved, when he says: "Although we used to know Christ according to the flesh, now we no longer know him thus." For the resurrection of the Lord signals, not the end of the flesh, but a transformation of it, nor does the increased power mean that the substance is consumed. The nature remains; only its state changes. The body that could once be crucified is now impassible; the body that could once be slain is now immortal; the body that could once be wounded is now incorruptible. Rightly, then, does Paul say we no longer know Christ's flesh in the state in which it used to be known, for now everything weak and passible has been eliminated, so that while remaining what it was in its essence, it is no longer what it was as far as its glorified state is concerned.[17]

The second sermon on the resurrection is especially rich; it follows a method with which we are by now familiar: "The cross of Christ by which humanity was saved is both a sacred sign and an example: a sacred sign through which the power of God works, and an example to stimulate devotion. Once people have been freed from the yoke of slavery, they are given this further blessing, that they can then imitate the work of redemption."[18]

To the feast we call the Pasch the Hebrews gave the name *Phase*, or "passage," as the evangelist shows when he writes: "Before the feast of Passover, Jesus knew that his hour had come to pass from this world to the Father" (John 13:1). But in which of his two natures did he make this passage? In ours, of course, since the Father was in

the Son and the Son in the Father beyond any possibility of separation. Nonetheless, since the Word and his human nature are but a
single person, the nature he assumed is not separated from him who
assumed it. Consequently, the honor given to him who is exalted
means an increase of glory for him who does the exalting. St. Paul
says as much: "Because of this, God greatly exalted him and bestowed
on him the name that is above every name" (Phil 2:9).

Paul is here referring to the exaltation of Jesus in the human nature
that had been assumed by the Word; just as the divinity is inseparable
from Jesus in his sufferings, so it is coeternal with him in his divine
glory.

The Lord wanted his faithful followers to share in the passage to
glory that would shortly be his. He prepared them for it when, with
his passion imminent, he prayed to his Father not only for his apostles
and disciples but for the entire Church: "I pray not only for them,
but also for those who will believe in me through their word, so that
they may all be one, as you, Father, are in me and I in you, that they
also may be [one] in us" (John 17:20-21). "Therefore, too, as the
Apostle says, 'we await a Savior, the Lord Jesus Christ, who will
change our lowly body to be like his glorious body,' he who lives and
reigns with the Father and the Holy Spirit for ever and ever. Amen."[19]

This quite simple theology of the paschal mystery emphasizes our
close and very concrete participation in the mystery that we are already
living out in our lives. It was the great merit of the fathers that they
gave such vibrant expression to it. No one has ever been able to improve on it without complicating it and without making abstract and
conceptual something meant to be lived out in concrete experience.

Second Sunday of Easter

37. BELIEVING WITHOUT SEEING

The Faith of Thomas

On the Second Sunday of Easter the same gospel pericope is read in all three years of the cycle. The passage relates the appearance of Christ to his disciples and the faith of Thomas, who had been absent on the occasion of Christ's first appearance to them. Thomas had withheld his assent and was waiting to verify in a personal, concrete way the Lord's resurrection. We all know of the deeply moving encounter between Christ and his doubting disciple and of the gentle but firm way in which the Lord brought Thomas to faith, even while proclaiming a demanding ideal of unconditional faith: "Blessed are those who have not seen and have believed" (John 20:29).

It is important that the liturgy, before embarking on a presentation of the Church's paschal life, should emphasize the nature of Christian faith. This passage from John's gospel [11] was perfect for the purpose.

As the reader may know, chapter 20 of St. John's gospel is regarded as the last of his writings. It is one of the best constructed chapters in the whole gospel, and its content is extremely important for the life of the Church as a whole and for the life of each member. Why so? Because, although the apostles were in a position to have concrete experience of the risen Christ, that kind of experience must in the future be replaced by a purely spiritual faith. In the future, to be converted would mean to believe in the word, the kerygma or authoritative proclamation of the Church, without there being any possibility of controlling through external evidence the truth the Church proclaims.

This new situation means a new difficulty for the Christian of later times as compared with the apostles; at the same time, however, it marks a certain superiority of the later Christian over the first disciples. For when Thomas wanted to control belief by facts and when the Lord was forced to tell him, "Blessed are those who have not seen and have believed," he was uttering a reproach that also applied to the other disciples, including John, of whom we are told that "he saw and believed" (John 20:8). Neither Peter nor John believed what Mary Magdalene told them; instead they ran to the tomb to see for themselves. Mary herself, no less than Thomas, had a quasi-material experience of the resurrection (John 20:17; 20:25, 27).

The starting point, then, was a faith that went beyond any physical control of evidence for the resurrection but was nonetheless still dependent on an experience of the visible and tangible. The goal was a much broader and deeper kind of faith that must characterize the Church as a whole and each individual member. For the Church, in days to come, would have to proclaim the resurrection and, with the help of the Spirit, rouse faith in the risen Jesus. Let us look now at the profound meaning this gospel pericope has in its liturgical proclamation. (In so doing, we shall leave aside the critical exegetical problems with regard to verses 30-31, which, according to some, mark the end of the Fourth Gospel, and the problem of the possible revision of verse 21 by a contemporary of John, possibly one of his disciples.)

The appearance of Christ occurs at a new gathering of his disciples. John dates the event precisely: "a week later" (v. 26). On that day "his disciples were again inside"; the word "again" would seem to indicate that the disciples did not gather daily. Christ appears in their midst with a body that is his own yet transformed, for he comes through "doors [that] were locked." This glorified body still bears the marks of the passion, so much so that Thomas is forced to cry out, "My Lord and my God!" Here is a clear assertion about the person of Jesus, and the first to be put in such concrete words in the New Testament writings. We must bear in mind that faith is the theme of John's gospel. The miracles of Jesus and the concomitant intensification of Jewish disbelief form the very framework of this gospel. Here, on Thomas's lips, we have the climactic affirmation that will henceforth be used by the Church and the individual Christian when in the presence of Christ the Lord: "My Lord and my God!"

Let us turn now to verse 29. It contains two statements that need to be carefully distinguished. The first applies to Thomas and, as we noted earlier, to the other disciples as well: they believed because they had seen. The second statement, however, is addressed to the entire Church: "Blessed are those who have not seen and have believed." The first part of this verse, then, is addressed to the apostles, the second part to the Church and to us. And yet the first part of verse 29 is important for us too. Our faith, after all, is not faith in a doctrine but faith in a historical person, in the Jesus who died and rose. The reality of the historical person and his glorification is assured us by the apostles, whose essential role was to be witnesses to others.

The end of the pericope (vv. 30-31) makes clear the purpose of John in writing his gospel. He has carefully chosen the "signs" or miracles of Jesus that he found the most suitable for rousing faith. His gospel is in the service of the Church's faith and mission, which is to bring others to faith in Jesus. The recently founded Christian community will perdure and grow only if its faith is strong and persevering. In the Fourth Gospel, faith is either stimulated by the "sign" or miracle, or it is the direct result of the "sign."

The same law holds in the sacramental life of the Church. If a person is to enter into that life, he or she must already have the gift of faith to some degree. And yet, at the same time, faith is a gift received in and through the sacrament itself. If we are to be transformed and to live in Christ, we need faith, which is the condition for the sacramental life and the access to the "signs." Yet it is these very "signs" that bestow faith on us and ensure its growth and strength.

The Life of the First Community

The faith we have been discussing is a faith that does not depend on seeing; it does, however, depend on the full experience of the sacramental signs and, even more basically, of the ecclesial community, which is itself a sign of the death and resurrection of Christ. That is the kind of faith that characterizes the first Christian community, as it must characterize every community that claims Christ for its Lord.

The first reading in each year of the three-year cycle presents this first Christian community to us. Year A shows us the group in its life of faith [5]. The activity of this united community for which Christ prayed in chapter 17 of the Fourth Gospel has four components that are especially singled out: fidelity in listening to the instruction of the apostles, a life of familial communion, the breaking of bread, and common prayer. These four characteristic activities are briefly stated in the first reading.

The first community was the fruit produced by the Spirit of the risen Christ; it was also constantly being sustained and built up by the hearing of the words of the apostles, who had been witnesses to the resurrection. Note how the passage begins by emphasizing the patience and continuity that characterize each of the four activities: the first Christians "devoted themselves to" (literally: they persisted or persevered in) the four activities that their life as a group comprised.

The faithful listened, then, to the teachings and instructions of the apostles. From now on, it was through the apostles that the Lord would speak; they are the ones the Lord has "sent," and it is their task to present the faith to others, since they have been witnesses of all that occurred from the beginning to the day when the Spirit was sent (Acts 1:8, 21; Luke 24:48). The teaching and instruction the apostles gave has come to us in those marvelous documents whose truth is guaranteed by their divine inspiration: the four gospels and the letters of the apostles, the latter being, as it were, a more concrete commentary on the gospels, with emphasis on particular points of which the faithful needed to be reminded. Other readings from the Acts of the Apostles will give us an idea of how the apostles went about their task of instructing; especially to be noted are the sermons of Peter and Paul.

This picture of the first Christians perseveringly listening to the instruction of the apostles will always be relevant to the Church. Heresy and schism result precisely from a failure to listen perseveringly and from a refusal to accept the teaching of the Lord's envoys. Surely this example of the first community is especially necessary today.

The faithful also lived in close communion with one another. Familial communion, however, does not mean having a shared mystical vision of reality or repeating platitudes that never flow over into action. On the contrary, the *koinonia*—a word that people today are constantly using in and out of season, but that Luke uses only in this passage—quite clearly means, in its context here, the sharing of all possessions, as is made clear in Acts 2:44-45, "All who believed were together and had all things in common; they would sell their property and possessions and divide them among all according to each one's need."

The *koinonia*, or communion, is thus very realistic and affects people at the material level. And yet, if the communion were limited to this, it would not suffice to make the community "Christian," for we can find the sharing of possessions practiced apart from any reference to Christianity. "Communion" here looks beyond material sharing to an attitude inspired by a living faith and manifested in prayer and especially in the celebration of the Eucharist in the homes of the community.

The faithful devoted themselves, we are told, "to the breaking of the bread." The words and their specific meaning are much discussed. We may admit, however, with a good number of exegetes, that the words refer to the Eucharist and not simply to the ritual that marked the beginning of an ordinary meal. At the same time, we should not focus on this verse with the intention of giving a historical or theological proof that a eucharistic celebration was indeed meant. It is better to say simply that Christian tradition has seen in the words a reference to the Eucharist. As for its being celebrated in homes, that is something that is frequently mentioned (1 Cor 16:19; Rom 16:5; Col 4:15; Phlm 2).

The faithful also devoted themselves to prayer in the temple. This explains why the patterns of Christian prayer will be those of Jewish prayer before it. What we now call the "Liturgy of the Word" at Mass took over the outline of the Jewish liturgy and especially of prayer in the synagogue. When St. Justin Martyr describes the Christian celebration on Sundays, his account of the Liturgy of the Word might well be an account of the Jewish synagogal liturgy.[1]

The final point made in today's first reading is that the community grew because the Lord drew into it those whom he was calling to salvation.

Such was the character of the first Christian community. The first reading in Years B and C will fill out the picture a bit more.

Psalm 118, chosen as the responsorial psalm for this reading, sings of the stone that was rejected by the builders but nonetheless became the cornerstone.

One Heart and One Mind

The first reading in Year B once again characterizes the community, but this time by means of a trait that was among the most eye-catching of all: the unity that allows St. Luke to speak of the community as possessing "one heart and mind" [6]. The sharing of possessions, however, is also mentioned once again, while a new characteristic makes its appearance: the witness given by the apostles.

If, then, the early community as a whole, because of its unity and its sharing of possessions, played a prominent part in the life of the

Church, we should not let that make us forget the role of the apostles. The latter have a place apart in the Acts of the Apostles, and their most characteristic function is to give witness. They continue to be teachers, as we have already seen, and the community listens devotedly to them, but they also carry out this ministry of witnessing on the broader scene to the world at large. They do this in two ways: through preaching (preaching that is frequently bold and courageous, leading to beatings and imprisonment) and, in imitation of Christ, through miracles, as Acts specifically mentions (2:43; 5:12). The purpose of these miracles is to rouse faith in the presence of the risen Christ. In Acts, Peter is the one who most frequently gives witness by his sermons and miracles (3:1-10; 9:32-35, 36-42). The envoys of Christ are thus able to see in their own persons the fulfillment of Christ's promises (Luke 9:1; 10:9).

A Growing Community

The first reading in Year C emphasizes the growth of the community [7]. What Acts is here reporting is a kind of miracle of faith, and the miracle is due to the Spirit who guides the Church in its mission and expansion. The expansion, in other words, is not the result of propaganda that is intended, as in politics, to augment the number of sympathizers and adherents. The truth is that "every day the Lord added to their number those who were being saved" (Acts 2:47). The source of the Church's fruitfulness in her mission is Jesus and the Spirit whom he has sent (Acts 2:41, 47; 4:4; 5:14; 6:7; 11:21; 21:20). In today's reading, St. Luke observes that more and more men and women were "added to" believers in the Lord through faith. He is showing how powerful was the gift of the Spirit who led people to faith in the resurrection of Christ and in his various mysteries.

Faith in the Risen Christ

The second reading in each of the three years focuses on an aspect of the theology of the resurrection.

The Risen Jesus and Our Rebirth

The second reading in Year A reminds us that we owe the grace of our rebirth to the resurrection of Jesus [8]. The "blessing" or thanksgiving with which the letter begins (after the greeting) and its reference to rebirth have suggested to exegetes that the letter here incorporates a baptismal liturgy. That is quite possible. At any rate, there can be no doubt that the author is referring to rebirth through baptism. It is another matter, of course, to see in the passage a liturgical composition used in baptism, namely, a hymn composed for the baptismal liturgy of that time.[2]

The structure and style of the first verses are not original but reflect Jewish prayer patterns in which the person praying blesses or praises the Lord and marvels at what he has done and continues to do for his people. The formula is one that we find even in our oldest eucharistic prayers.[3] In the passage from the First Letter of Peter, the Jewish prayer form is immediately filled with a Christian content: he who is "blessed" or praised is the Father of our Lord Jesus Christ who has given us rebirth and a living hope by raising Jesus from the dead. The words "new birth" do not of themselves necessarily refer to baptism, but we must bear in mind the liturgical context of the reading on the Second Sunday of Easter, a time when we are still in the atmosphere created by the Easter Vigil, in which rebirth is so closely linked to the death and resurrection of Christ.

The most important point in the reading, however, and the point that should give strength and vitality to the Christian community, is the fact of the resurrection, for that is the basis of the hope shared by all the children of God. Hope here does not mean expectation pure and simple, for we already possess, in a way, the reality for which we hope. The passage makes this reality—that is, the object of our hope—quite clear: it is the inheritance being kept for us in heaven.

Because we are advancing toward the goal, present trials cannot deaden our sense of joy; no crisis, however serious, can lessen the interior joy of the community and of individual Christians who know by faith the treasure that is already theirs. The faith, however, must be of a high order; it must have a quality that is tested by the trials they must yet endure for a while. The joy that springs from faith—the faith that believes without seeing, faith in the person of Christ who died but has risen and is now living in the Church—should transform individual Christians and their entire life, for, as the end of the pericope says, "you attain the goal of your faith, the salvation of your souls."

If we look back now over the whole Liturgy of the Word for the Second Sunday of Easter in Year A, we do not find the kind of thematic unity that forces itself on our attention. Yet, without straining for points of contact, we can say that the liturgy possesses a real unity. Christ appears to Thomas and tells him what he, Christ, understands by faith. This faith, which is of a spiritual kind, being faith in the word of God, gives rise in the Christian community to deep-rooted attitudes of prayer, sharing of material goods, and perseverance in breaking bread together; these attitudes in turn astonish outsiders and bring new members into the community. The community is constantly "blessing" the God who, through faith in the resurrection of his Son, sustains it in the joy of possessing, in sure hope, the inheritance of salvation.

Such is the vitally important and always relevant lesson the Lord himself teaches his disciples who listen to him in the liturgical proclamation that actualizes his word.

Child of God and Conqueror of the World

The second reading for this Sunday in Year B emphasizes the efficacy of faith; it tells us that the believer is a child of God and overcomes the world [9]. The community that sought to live as having "one heart and mind" [6] needed this encouraging vision at the moment when it had to move out into a hostile world. Earlier in this same letter John had written: "everyone who loves is begotten by God" (1 John 4:7). Now he shifts his attention to faith in the person of Christ: "Everyone who believes that Jesus is the Christ is begotten by God" (1 John 5:1).

This personal faith was all the more necessary at a time when the new community was hardly fully distinct as yet from Judaism; it must inevitably think of Jesus as Messiah and believe him to be the expected Messiah. This is also a frequent topic of preaching in the early Church (Acts 5:42; 9:22; 17:3; 18:28; John 9:22). Faith, then, insofar as it meant adherence to the person of Jesus, could not but be the belief that he was both Messiah and Son of God.

Overcoming the world presupposes such a faith in the Son of God. St. John is certainly concerned to make it clear just what "faith" involves, since there was, and always will be, the danger of self-deception, inasmuch as people may "believe" and yet in no way alter the way they live. St. John, therefore, knowing his Church from experience, wants to make plain the realistic conditions that faith requires. Concretely, a person who believes will obey the commandments; that is what enables the faith of Christians to overcome the world and makes faith a conquering power.

Christ had said, in order to hearten his disciples, "take courage, I have conquered the world" (John 16:33). If we believe in the person of Christ Jesus, we shall share in this victory of his, which is such a favorite theme of John's. In other words, the person (after Christ) who overcomes the world is the one who believes that Jesus is the Son of God and who—we must add with St. John—lives in accordance with this faith of his.

Such a faith would not be possible in a world so opposed to it unless the Spirit himself bore witness. Amid the storm, when the entire world is rejecting Christ, Christians will have the help of the Spirit whom Christ promised them for their witnessing (John 15:26) and will continue to believe unwaveringly in Jesus. It is the Spirit who will make their faith unwavering, and he will make known to us the full revelation that is present in the person of Jesus (John 14:6).

If we look back over the Liturgy of the Word for the Second Sunday of Easter in Year B, we find that it embodies a rich conception, namely, that Christ by his resurrection has created a community that is one in heart and mind, a community convinced that it will overcome the world because it believes in the person of Christ, a community enlightened by the Holy Spirit who manifests divine revelation in its fullness.

Christ Died but Now Lives Forever

In continuity with ancient tradition, especially in the Spanish Church, the Church chooses a pericope from the book of Revelation for the second reading in Year C [10]. The passage is a thrilling proclamation of the reality of the Lord's resurrection. The Jesus of whom the passage speaks is the Son of Man, the Head of the Church, and the Master of the entire history of salvation.

The letter to the seven churches of Asia is addressed to a suffering Christian community that is being persecuted but at the same time is persevering with Jesus like the royal nation of priests that it is. The only reason, moreover, why the Church and the Apostle are experiencing this difficult time is their faith in the risen Jesus and their preaching of the word.

It is on a Sunday, the Lord's Day, that John has his first vision (v. 10). This simple fact has a deeper significance, since Sunday is the day when the Church is most deeply aware of the resurrection of Christ. That is also the day on which he writes, and his correspondents are the churches of Asia Minor.

His vision, though written in the style of the time, is easy to interpret. The seven golden lampstands are evidently the seven churches to which John is to write. The central figure, however, is the Son of Man; this is important, because the vision is meant to tell the seven churches the precise object of their faith.

The expression "Son of Man" occurs first in the book of Daniel (chap. 7). It becomes complex and acquires various meanings in the course of time, but the important thing for us is that Jesus himself uses the expression with the reference to himself (Matt 17:9 and Mark 9:9-13; Matt 17:22; Mark 9:30-32; and Luke 9:44-45; Matt 20:18; Mark 10:32-34; and Luke 18:31-33; Mark 8:31; Matt 16:13-20; and Luke 9:18-21). The title comes from Jewish apocalyptic writing, but Jesus enriches it by applying it to the one who came as "Servant" to save others by sacrificing his own life and to be glorified. In addition, the title has an eschatological aspect as it is used by Christ: The Son of Man will come at the end of time in order to judge. According to the Synoptics, Jesus presents himself to the Sanhedrin as Son of Man (Matt 26:57-66; 27:2; Mark 14:53-64; 15:1; Luke 22:66-69). John has his own way of putting it: "[The Father] gave him power to exercise judgment, because he is the Son of Man" (John 5:27). The title became important to the faith of the early Christians, and St. Stephen will say when he is about to die: "Behold, I see the heavens opened, and the Son of Man standing at the right hand of God" (Acts 7:56).

The book of Revelation enters into even greater detail on the person of the Son of Man. The latter himself tells John who he is: "I am the first and the last"—that is, God—"the one who lives," an expression that conjures up the paschal mystery in which the dead Christ rises to everlasting life and henceforth holds "the keys to death and the netherworld."

John's vision in the book of Revelation thus shows us the Son of Man as possessed of the new status that is his by reason of the resurrection. In Christian eyes, the Son of Man is first and foremost the risen Christ who sits at the Father's right hand and will come to judge the living and the dead.

The three readings in Year C thus show us the risen Christ as the object of the community's faith and the focus of its life; he draws people to the Church so that he may bestow salvation on them.

The collect for this second Sunday emphasizes the role of faith and asks God's help in living that faith: "God of everlasting mercy, who in the very recurrence of the paschal feast kindle the faith of the people you have made your own, increase, we pray, the grace you have bestowed, that all may grasp and rightly understand in what font they have been washed, by whose Spirit they have been reborn, by whose Blood they have been redeemed."

The first option for the entrance antiphon exhorts the Christian community to be eager for God's word, which will make it grow toward salvation: "Like newborn infants, you must long for the pure, spiritual milk, that in him you may grow to salvation, alleluia."

Third Sunday of Easter

38. THE RISEN CHRIST APPEARS TO HIS DISCIPLES

[A] "He Was Made Known to Them in the Breaking of the Bread"

We have already read and commented on the story of the two disciples at Emmaus, since it was read at the afternoon Mass on Easter Sunday.

The first reading is from St. Peter's sermon on Pentecost [14]. In it Peter proclaims the resurrection of Christ and does it firmly and even harshly: "This man, delivered up by the set plan and foreknowledge of God, you killed, using lawless men to crucify him. But God raised him up, releasing him from the throes of death, because it was impossible for him to be held by it" (Acts 2:23-24).

Peter's words are addressed to people who know the facts, and he reminds them that God has sent Jesus to them "with mighty deeds, wonders, and signs . . . as you yourselves know" (v. 22). Despite the signs, they put him to death; others did the evil deed, but the Jews were no less guilty. Now this Jesus has risen from the dead! Peter here quotes Psalm 16, which also serves as the responsorial psalm after the reading: "For you will not abandon my soul to hell, / nor let your holy one see corruption" (v. 10).

Redeemed by the Blood of the Lamb

The second reading continues to develop this life-giving theology of Christ's death and resurrection [17]. The First Letter of Peter reminds us that we have been redeemed by the blood of the Lamb, and the Christian community must bear its true state in mind: "realizing that you were ransomed from your futile conduct, handed on by your ancestors . . . with the precious blood of Christ as of a spotless unblemished lamb" (1 Pet 1:18-19).

Peter is here giving a Christian content to Isaiah's Servant Songs (Isa 42:1-4; 49:1-6; 50:4-9; 52:13–53:12). We must be on guard, however, against thinking that our redemption was effected solely by the blood of the Lamb, thus separating our liberation from the guilt of sin from the gift of new life that comes through the resurrection. That kind of one-sided theology misses the full content of the paschal mystery; there have been writers accustomed to speak simply of "redemption." There was nothing wrong with the term itself; the mistake was to stop short at the death of Christ and to link our redemption exclusively with this death, the resurrection of Christ being simply a proof of Christ's divinity and of the success of his mission. Many manuals of theology and a large number of spiritual books followed this line. It was even thought at times that the Quartodecimans (who celebrated the Pasch on the fourteenth day of Nisan, date of the Jewish Passover) were celebrating chiefly the death of Christ, while the rest of the Church, which celebrated the Pasch on the Sunday after the fourteenth day of Nisan, was thinking primarily of the resurrection. This interpretation, based on imagination rather than on texts and facts, has now been shown to be false.[1]

We need not force the texts in order to show the liturgical unity of this third Sunday in Year A. The gospel pericope, in the context of the liturgical celebration, acquires a properly eucharistic reference: the two disciples at Emmaus had come to know him "in the breaking of the bread." The Jesus who broke bread for his disciples at Emmaus is the Nazarene whose death and resurrection Peter proclaims on Pentecost. He is the spotless Lamb who shed his blood and has risen from the dead to liberate us. It is this one Christ who is the object of our faith and of the faith of the Church.

[B] The Resurrection on the Third Day as Foretold by the Prophets

The gospel for the third Sunday in Year B likewise tells the community about an appearance of the risen Jesus [21]. The new appearance takes place while the two disciples who have returned from Emmaus are still telling their fellows what had happened to them.

The ending of this pericope is very important, for it provides us with insight into the method followed in catechetics by the early Church: the method of starting with Scripture. Here the risen Christ opens the minds of his disciples to the understanding of the Scriptures and shows how the prophets had foretold the sufferings of the Messiah, his resurrection from the dead on the third day, and the fact that "repentance, for the forgiveness of sins, would be preached in his name to all the nations, beginning from Jerusalem" (Luke 24:47). The apostles are to be his witnesses.

Here we have a catechesis but also a mission or program that the risen Christ assigns to his new community. But the catechesis comes after he has first given them a physical demonstration of his resurrection by showing them his wounds and eating a piece of broiled fish that they offer him. Christ wants to make sure that the disciples realize that he is the same Jesus who had lived with them before, that he is now alive again, still in the body, even if a transformed body. He is present with them again as a sign that all the prophecies are now fulfilled.

We must remember, however, that while Jesus thus gives signs showing that he has truly risen, these signs are not enough by themselves. They have to be understood, and this requires faith, since a true recognition of the risen Christ does not stop short at his human nature but penetrates beyond it.

Luke is very much concerned with the theme of the fulfillment of the Scriptures; he is the only one of the evangelists to emphasize it to such an extent. St. John says that the Scriptures could not be understood until Christ had risen from the dead, entered his glory, and sent his Spirit (John 2:22; 12:16; 13:8; 14:26). Luke tells us how the Scriptures, in fact, came to be understood, but he does not wait for the sending of Jesus' Spirit; instead, he describes the enlightenment as taking place when Christ appears to his disciples after the resurrection. Are John and Luke to be reconciled? Yes. The disciples begin to understand the Scriptures from Easter on; at the same time, however, there are moments when their understanding is radically increased, and the coming of the Spirit is a moment that advances this considerably.

The apostles are witnesses to the resurrection and to the fulfillment of the Scriptures. They must now proclaim to the Gentiles what they have seen and what they know. That is the starting point for the expansion of the Church.

Peter and His Message

Peter is fully aware of his mission to be a witness and to preach conversion, as his discourse in chapter 3 of the Acts of the Apostles shows [15]. He addresses the people and proclaims the Lord's resurrection, reminding them once again that it was the Jewish people who put the Messiah to death, though he was the Author of life. Peter himself is a witness to the resurrection. He reminds his hearers that in the recent events the Scriptures have been fulfilled. The people must therefore be converted and return to God so that their sins may be forgiven.

Such is the theme of the first reading, and it is closely related to the gospel of the day, since conversion is precisely what Christ bids his apostles preach as witnesses to the resurrection, which is the central object of faith.

The responsorial psalm (Ps 4) prays the Lord to make himself known: "Lift up the light of your face on us, O LORD. / You have put into my heart a greater joy" (vv. 7-8).

Christ, the Victim for Our Sins

Faith in Christ brings forgiveness of our sins, but the daily struggle remains. St. John was very conscious of it and speaks of it in the second reading [18]. He seems to have been afraid of any abstract mysticism. The resurrection of Christ is not simply an external fact that should induce wonder; it must lead to conversion, and conversion supposes an effort to observe the commandments and avoid sin. Only if we meet this condition can we be sure that we really "know" Christ, the Victim who was sacrificed for our sins.

The love of God reaches its perfection in the person who faithfully keeps God's word. The believer, then, faces moral demands that he must take very seriously. Yet John is also aware how weak people are, and he assures his readers: "if anyone does sin, we have an Advocate with the Father, Jesus Christ the righteous one" (1 John 2:1).

This statement requires at least a brief explanation. How does John understand Christ's role as "Advocate"? We shall have occasion later on to focus our attention again on the meaning of the term *parakletos*, "Paraclete," which means in general "someone called to another's side," a defender whose function is to help and encourage. In our present passage Jesus himself acts as Advocate before the Father. He is a Mediator, and the language here refers us to the priestly activity of Christ as presented to us in the Letter to the Hebrews (7:25; 9:24).

It is as Victim for our sins that Christ stands as our Advocate before the Father. But he cannot exercise this role in our favor unless we know him. The Christian must therefore "experience God," as we like to say nowadays. This experience, however, is not some abstractly mystical experience but takes the form of observing the commandments. It is easy to determine whether or not we "know" Christ. Simply ask: Do I observe his commandments? For knowing Christ, like knowing God, is not, in John's view, a narrowly intellectual, conceptual activity; knowledge in this instance means a concrete, interpersonal relationship with Christ, and the moral quality of our life provides a criterion for determining how real the relationship is.

"[W]hoever keeps his word, the love of God is truly perfected in him" (1 John 2:5). We might think that "love of God" here means our love for him, that is, the love in which we take a certain initiative by giving ourselves to him because we obey his commandments and thus truly "know" him. But the text is susceptible of another interpretation: in those who observe the commandments and thus know Christ, divine love is able to enter in without hindrance; it can fill them completely and free them by making them fully adoptive children of God.

[C] Peter, Fisherman and Shepherd

The gospel for the third Sunday in Year C tells us of the appearance of the risen Christ to his apostles as they were fishing in the Sea of Tiberias [22]. There is a miraculous catch; Christ gives his disciples bread and fish to eat; Peter avows his love and is appointed shepherd of the Church. The passage has a grandeur about it, and it is so important for the life of the Church of every age that it calls for some words of commentary.

To begin with, the writer of the passage seems to have freighted it with symbolism, and we must find the key that will unlock for us the meaning of the words and the events. Critical exegetical scholarship regards chapter 21 as a later addition to the gospel, whether by John himself or by one of his collaborators. The gospel could nicely have ended with chapter 20, although every known manuscript of the gospel contains chapter 21; evidently this chapter was always known as part of the Fourth Gospel. On the other hand, the exegetes also think that chapter 21 was written long after Peter suffered martyrdom (about thirty years later). These various points must be kept in mind as we listen to the gospel being read.

This particular passage seems to have been chosen for this Sunday's liturgy in order to call attention to Peter as the witness who converts others and as the shepherd of the Church. The first reading [16] likewise presents Peter as the witness who is willing to be a martyr: he preaches the death and resurrection of Christ and is beaten for his preaching.

In the gospel pericope, Peter says that he is going fishing; Thomas, Nathanael, the sons of Zebedee, and two other disciples decide to go with him. We may legitimately discern a deliberate message being conveyed through the simple statement of fact: Peter is a fisher and will be a fisher of people, but he is accompanied by other apostles and disciples who share his role. Apart from the command and power of Christ, however, the fishing is fruitless; St. John emphasizes the point, telling us that "that night they caught nothing" (John 21:3). Then, at dawn, Christ stands there on the shore, and when he gives the order to cast the net, it is soon so filled with fish that it is in danger of breaking.

It is at this moment that John, the disciple whom Jesus loved, recognizes the risen Christ. We should note, here as elsewhere, the difficulty that the disciples had in immediately recognizing the risen Christ and the concern of John to emphasize that the Christ was real.

The catch is clearly miraculous, and it is the stimulus that causes the disciples to recognize Jesus at last, even though all along he has been only about a hundred yards away. There are 153 fish in the net, but despite this the net has not broken, as John points out. The number, which is clearly arbitrary, must have had a symbolic meaning that escapes us. Just what the meaning was is not important (since no hint of it is given), but it shows that the author had a specific intention in writing the story and that we must in general be attentive to the symbols he uses.

The apostles and other disciples now eat with Jesus, but it is Jesus who gives them the bread and fish—purely an inescapable reminder of the multiplication of the loaves and fishes (John 6:1-21). There is no multiplication in the present case, but there seems to be the same eucharistic significance: Jesus gives the bread that is the bread of life, and he gives the fish that is himself. (We may recall that the Greek word for "fish," *ichthus*, was also an acronym used by the early Christians and stood for "Jesus Christ, Son of God, Savior" [*Iesous Christos theou uios soter*].) In addition, just as the story of the multiplication of the loaves and fishes had an eschatological reference, that is, reminded the hearers of the banquet of the kingdom at the end of time (this is why the passage is read during Advent), so this meal of Christ with his disciples has the same eschatological reference. We need not press the symbolism too far and try to find in the details of the account a whole set of eschatological symbols. The fact that the risen Christ, victorious over death, is eating with his disciples, and the presence of the fish, which symbolizes the saved, are sufficiently eloquent; no further details are needed.

Now we come to the main point of the account, at least from the viewpoint of the Church as it celebrates this Liturgy of the Word, namely, Peter's protestation of love and his investiture as shepherd of the flock. Here, perhaps, we should recall that at the beginning of the story Peter had stripped as he worked in the boat. Should not this fact be noted? John points it out and remarks that Peter threw on some clothes before jumping into the water and going ashore. His nakedness reminds us, does it not, of his human condition, nudity being the sign both of sin and of wretchedness generally?

We may ask why Christ, in his desire to know Peter's love from his own mouth, should ask the question three times. Perhaps the triple repetition simply reflects Christ's concern. May we also see in it Christ's intention of eliciting a triple profession of love that will counterbalance Peter's triple denial? But the repetition seems due rather to the solemnity of the moment and to a form of investiture often used in order to emphasize importance; it is the kind of thing people used to do in sealing unwritten contracts.

In any case, the important thing for us is the investiture of Peter as leader of the flock. It is because of his great role as shepherd that his Lord requires of him a special love beyond that which others have. Peter will have to bear witness to the point of martyrdom and will have to strengthen his companions in the faith. The account implies that the task entrusted to Peter is entrusted to his successors as well. They too will have to have a love for the Lord greater than that of others.

The Lord then tells Peter that his role of witness will lead him to a violent death for the glory of God.

Peter, the Witness

The first reading [16] shows Peter exercising the function he had received of being a witness to the resurrection. He answers the high priest's accusation of disobedience by saying that the apostles must obey God rather than people. He then goes on to tell the Jews that though they had put Jesus to death, God raised him up and made him the Savior who brings Israel repentance and the forgiveness of sins. He then asserts, as he had on previous occasions, "We are witnesses of these things." The apostles are whipped but nonetheless they depart "rejoicing that they had been found worthy to suffer dishonor for the sake of the name."

The Lamb Slain and Glorified

The second reading proclaims John's fervent vision of the risen Christ's glorification as the Lamb triumphant whom the whole world blesses and praises in a majestic doxology [19]. This Christ, slain but now victorious, is the one who has appeared to the apostles and given them the commission to preach his paschal mystery; he is the one who appeared to Peter and made him shepherd of all who will enter the community.

Fourth Sunday of Easter

39. THE GOOD SHEPHERD

The theme of the Good Shepherd appears in the gospel throughout the three-year cycle, since the three pericopes are taken from chapter 10 of St. John. At first sight, it seemed better to give here, under the fourth Sunday, a complete picture of Christ the Good Shepherd as it is presented in the three passages. But a further factor had to be taken into account, namely, that in each year of the complete cycle the other readings provide a specifying framework for the gospel pericope. We prefer, therefore, to limit ourselves in each instance to the complex of readings as offered in the liturgy for each year of the cycle.

[A] Christ, the Gate of the Sheep

"I am the gate": this statement, which comes after a careful explanatory preparation, is the central theme of the gospel for the fourth Sunday in Year A [29]. How is the statement to be understood? A door opens and closes—and such is the activity Jesus exercises. He speaks of "All who came before me" as "thieves and robbers," for he alone is the Gate; anyone, therefore, who attempts to enter by any other gate can be only a thief and a robber.

When others came, before Jesus, and called to the sheep, the sheep did not heed and follow them, for in their call the sheep did not recognize the voice of the true Shepherd. Jesus thus condemns his enemies and all who seek to teach without having been sent by the Father. All such come forward on their own authority, and whatever they do is for their own profit; they seek their own glory (cf. John 7:18), and their deeds are destructive. But if anyone enters through the only true Gate, which is Jesus, he finds salvation and life. Entering through Jesus is thus a necessity for anyone who wants to be saved; if he enters through Jesus, he enters the fold of which Jesus alone is the Shepherd.

The Glorified Christ

In his sermon on Pentecost, Peter exhorts his hearers precisely to enter into the fold through the only true Gate: Christ, who is risen from the dead and lives forevermore [23]. The theme of Peter's preaching never varies: it is always Christ, whom the Jews crucified and whom God raised up. The Jews must therefore be converted and accept baptism in the name of Jesus if they are to receive the gift of the Spirit. They must pass through the true Gate into the fold, where they will find green pastures. That means, however, that they must turn away from the thieves and marauders, "this corrupt generation," and listen to the voice of the true shepherd.

The responsorial psalm (Ps 23) expresses this faith in the true Shepherd; it also sketches out the journey of the baptized person through the sacramental mysteries. It is the classic psalm to be sung at Christian initiation, and the Church has restored it to its rightful place.

We Are Healed and Have Come back to the Shepherd

We must therefore be converted, that is, stop wandering hither and yon and return to the Shepherd who is "the guardian of your souls" [26]. To this we are exhorted in the second reading. Returning to the Shepherd, however, also means imitating him in our everyday lives. If we suffer, we should praise God for it; suffering, after all, is what we have been called to, since Christ first suffered for us and left us an example so that we might follow after him. We must die to our sins and live holy lives. Such a course is really possible for us, since our Shepherd carried our sins in his own body on the wood of the cross.

The unity of the three readings is clear by reason of the very broad but meaningful link between them. Anyone who wants to hear and understand and who believes that Christ, really present, is addressing his kindly but demanding message to us today cannot continue to live as he did before. The celebration of the liturgy requires that we examine our conscience and be converted to a truly Christian life within Christ's fold.

[B] "The Good Shepherd Lays down His Life for the Sheep"

On the fourth Sunday in Year B, Christ shows himself to us as the Good Shepherd who gives his life for his sheep [30]. In fact, giving his life is the sign by which we recognize him as a genuine shepherd. But among all the shepherds, Christ alone can give his life in a way that is completely effective, for his sacrifice is unique, being the self-giving of the Son to the Father in obedience to the Father's will. Christ is the only shepherd capable of giving his life in such an efficacious manner.

Because of his total dedication, the Good Shepherd knows his sheep and they know him. The "knowledge" here consists in the active, personal relationship described in the first part of the chapter: the Shepherd calls his sheep by name (John 10:3); he takes jealous care of them (10:8, 12); above all, he gives them life by sacrificing his own (10:10). The sheep in turn know their Shepherd, recognize his voice, and follow him (10:4). We must also note, however, the parallel Jesus uses: he knows his sheep and his sheep know him "as the Father knows me and I know the Father" (10:15). This parallel shows the knowledge to be interpersonal, involving the closest possible kind of union, namely, a union of the kind that exists between Father and Son.

In applying the title of Shepherd to himself, Jesus takes over a favorite theme of the Old Testament. A person can enter into a relation with the Lord and know him only if the Lord himself offers it. It is the Lord who chooses and calls people to the office of shepherd (Isa 16:7; Jer 1:5). The result is a close relation between shepherd and sheep, comparable to the relation between the Lord and the one who reverences him.

St. John then goes on to speak of one of his central concerns: the Church, its formation and its future. Church means unity, and the unity comes from Christ: "there will be one flock, one shepherd" (John 10:16). The flock is formed by Christ himself, for it is he who calls the disciple (John 19:35; 20:29; 1 John 1:1-4). It is he who gives his life for the unity of the flock. To that end he has power from the Father.

No Salvation but in Christ

The words we just quoted—"there shall be one flock, one shepherd"—have caused questioning and remorse among believers down to our own day. For over against those words there is "the scandal of the separation of Churches," and the faithful of today feel it more than ever before. The quest for union between the Churches is the response people of goodwill make to the words of Christ with their implicit command; these people hope that the Lord's words are a prophecy that describes the situation at the end: one flock at last.

The first reading emphasizes the need for such oneness: "There is no salvation through anyone else" [24]. The problem is that each Church believes in good faith that it is indeed with and in Christ! A single flock is possible only under a single Shepherd. The challenge, however, is to accept not only Christ, the one Shepherd, but also the human being who represents the one Shepherd. The drama of the incident reported in the first reading is concentrated precisely in that point: Peter is asked by what power or in whose name he has cured a cripple; he answers that he performed the cure, which was a sign, in the name of the risen Jesus, who is the Cornerstone; apart from this Jesus there is no salvation, for the Lord had made his Christ the foundation of his entire work.

The responsorial psalm (Ps 118) makes the same point about Christ as the foundation: "The stone that the builders rejected / has become the cornerstone. / By the LORD has this been done, / a marvel in our eyes" (vv. 22-23).

"We Are God's Children Now"

Christ is the Shepherd of those who know God and have become his children. This relationship—being a child of God—is what God's love for us has given us. It is also what distinguishes us from, and opposes us to, the world: we are now the children of God, but "the world . . . did not know him" [27]. The theme of the second reading is thus a tragic one. We are now the children of God, and that is all that separates us from the world—but what a radical separation!

At the same time, however, we are ignorant of what we shall one day be, or at least that future state is not clear to us. We are certain, however, of one thing: when the Son of God appears, we shall be like him, for we shall see him as he is. Evidently there is an immense distance between what we now are and that future condition of which we are still ignorant and that others cannot see in us.

This First Letter of John really brings out the great problem that Christianity and the individual Christian face. We know what we really are, and we must live lives befitting men and women who are God's adopted children. But the world does not see or understand what we know to be true. In fact, we ourselves, though knowing that we are now God's children, do not know in any clear way what we shall one day be; that will become clear to us only when Christ returns. In the interim, we must live our lives both apart from the world and in the world, since we have already been bidden to live for the things above.

The entrance antiphon, aware of what we already truly are, proclaims to the world: "The merciful love of the Lord fills the earth; by the word of the Lord the heavens were made, alleluia." The collect expresses an awareness both of what we have become and of the difficulty of our present state: "Almighty ever-living God, lead us to a share in the joys of heaven, so that the humble flock may reach where the brave Shepherd has gone before."

[C] The Shepherd Gives Eternal Life to His Sheep

The very short gospel for the fourth Sunday in Year C is rich in the revelation it contains [31]. The key statement in it is: "I give them [my sheep] eternal life, and they shall never perish" (v. 28). The other theme has already been heard in Christ's portrayal of the Good Shepherd, namely, the interpersonal knowledge that is based, as far as humanity is concerned, on docility in hearing the word and on obedience in following after Jesus in everyday life.

The most important point made there, then, is that eternal life is the Good Shepherd's gift. Jesus is Life: he gives his own life for his flock (10:15) and wants them to have life in abundance (10:10). Now we are told that those who accept the relationship of interpersonal "knowledge" will never perish. This is a new way of promising the eternal life with which the Fourth Gospel is so concerned. Jesus continues the image of the shepherd who possesses and defends his sheep by saying that no one can snatch them from the hand of the Father to whom he entrusts them, because he and the Father are one.

Baptized Christians feel a new strength flow into them from these words of Christ; they are also compelled to reflect on the responsibility that such a gift demands. The protection to which Christ refers is, after all, not a purely mechanical thing, an activity in which our receptivity plays no part. No, acceptance is a positive act, for it means heeding and following; it means being disposed for a difficult life of conflict, but one in which we are sure that victory is possible.

Salvation to the Ends of the Earth

This eternal life is the subject of the apostolic preaching; we hear Paul and Barnabas preaching it in today's first reading [25]. They had preached it first to the Jews but were attacked for their pains. Now they turn to the Gentiles. They cannot remain silent, "For so the Lord has commanded us, *I have made you a light to the Gentiles, that you may be an instrument of salvation to the ends of the earth*" (Acts 13:47). The preaching is effective, and Luke tells us why, in a sentence not easy to interpret: "All who were destined for eternal life came to believe" (v. 48).

The Chosen People of God would not believe in his Son, who died and rose for their salvation. Therefore, the preachers of the Good News turn to the Gentiles, whom the Lord has already disposed. They turn to the Gentiles because salvation is meant to be universal, even if the Chosen People rightly had first place in the implementation of God's saving will. God must dispose people's hearts, for the Shepherd can give eternal life only to those who are willing to hear and accept him and follow him into the one fold.

The responsorial psalm (Ps 100) picks up the theme of the first reading: "Know that he, the LORD, is God. / He made us; we belong to him. / We are his people, the sheep of his flock" (v. 3).

The Lamb and Shepherd

The second reading, from John's apocalyptic vision, speaks of the fulfillment of what we heard about in the first reading [28]. The Apostle sees a huge crowd from every nation and race, people and tongue. They are standing before the throne and the Lamb, clad in white and carrying palm branches. One of the elders explains who these people are and whence they come: "These are the ones who have survived the time of great distress; they have washed their robes and made them white in the blood of the Lamb. . . . They will not hunger or thirst any more / . . . . For the Lamb who is in the center of the throne / will shepherd them / and lead them to springs of life-giving water, / and God will wipe away every tear from their eyes" (vv. 14-17).

There is no need to dwell on the universality represented by the huge crowd. They give glory to God, and their whole attitude is one of contemplation and liturgical thanksgiving, for they are a people who have won a victory. They wear the white garments that symbolize the purification received in baptism. The idea of purifying garments in blood is doubtless strange, but the point is clear; the theology of purification and renewal has simply twisted the image for its own purposes. The blood is that which renews people and prepares them for the glorious resurrection with Christ; the white garments are thus a sign of victory and resurrection.

The crowd is a single unit directed by the staff of the Lamb, who is thus represented here as a Shepherd. The passage draws on two classic texts from the earlier Scriptures: Psalm 23, in which the Lord is depicted as Israel's Shepherd, and the book of Isaiah, chapter 49 (second Servant Song), on which verses 16-17 of the passage are based (cf. Isa 49:10).

John's vision is a vision of the victory of the one flock, which at last is united under a single leader: the Shepherd-Lamb who gave his life for his sheep.

Fifth Sunday of Easter

40. MINISTRIES IN THE NEW COMMUNITY

The continuous reading of the Acts of the Apostles and of St. John's gospel has the drawback that it is not always easy to link the various themes contained in the Liturgy of the Word. Nonetheless, we may note certain emphases that do give the Fifth Sunday of Easter a character of its own. One such emphasis is on the organization of the new Christian community now that its Lord had risen and withdrawn his visible presence from his disciples. There was need of ensuring that the services provided in the Church would be continuous, since ministries are indispensable not only for external organization but also for transmitting the word and the sacramental signs that the Lord had left to his followers.

While the reading of the Acts of the Apostles shows us the early Church's concern for the establishment of the needed ministries, the gospel puts the emphasis rather on the deeper spiritual formation of this community that was called to follow Christ, the Way, the Truth, and the Life [38], to remain in Christ so that it might bear fruit [39], and to live in mutual love [40].

[A] Christ, the Way, the Truth, and the Life

The young Church had to be made deeply aware that no one can come to the Father except through Christ; that is a major theme in this Sunday's gospel [38]. When Philip asks, "show us the Father," and thereby reveals the apostles' continued failure to understand, Jesus takes the opportunity to emphasize once again his oneness with the Father: "I am in the Father and the Father is in me" (v. 10). Faith in this truth is an absolute necessity; the energy for accomplishing great things comes from belief in the person of Christ. All the activity of the Church would be fruitless if she did not believe unconditionally in the true reality of Christ and in his oneness with the Father.

The whole point of Christ's earthly works (according to the Fourth Gospel) was to give proof of the unity that exists between the Father and himself.

Now Jesus foretells his departure from the earthly scene. At the moment when he is about to leave his disciples behind, he is concerned with the depth and clarity of their faith, since authentic faith is the basic reality that will direct the life of the young Church. Christ is truly the means of humanity's encounter with God, and the Church must continue this role of Christ, showing people the way to the Father. The Church is, of course, not identical with Christ, but Christ wills that the Church be, like him, the sign of the Father. In her lowly state (in this she is, once again, like Christ) and always under the guidance of the Spirit, she too must be the Way, the Truth, and the Life.

In this passage from St. John, we find once again the word "know": "know" the Father, "know" Christ. The pericope clearly, if implicitly, shows the difference between the idea of "knowledge" as Hebrew speakers understood it and the idea of knowledge found in the Greek philosophers. To the Greek mind, knowing means abstracting, or else it means contemplating from without an object that is definitively what it is, so that we can form a concept of it. In this view of reality, God is outside of and apart from us; we contemplate him in himself as someone we try to reach by gradually elaborating a concept of him. "Truth" is attained when we grasp the essential characteristics of this God whom we contemplate and who remains always external to us.

For the Hebrew mind, knowing means experiencing the object of knowledge and entering into close relations with it. The Greek thinks of contemplating a God who remains changeless and apart from us; the Hebrew seeks to gain concrete experience of God in his relations with humanity, to know God through his works. John's gospel must be read against its cultural background. This means a context that is basically Hebrew but into which certain Greek elements have made their way; in other words, if we want to understand the terminology of the Fourth Gospel, we must not distinguish too simplistically and undiscerningly between Greek "knowing" and Hebrew "knowing." Nonetheless, Christ himself makes it quite clear what he means by "knowing." He means a concrete experience that is gained by seeing the works he himself does. Seeing them, the observer gains a concrete grasp of Christ's person. Once Christ has returned to the Father, our experiential knowledge of the Father will be gained by means of the signs Christ has left.

The Spirit and the Laying on of Hands

The Church's chief concern, then, is to continue to give the "signs" of Christ in order to make God visible and to enable people to experience him: to "see our God made visible," as the first preface for Christmas puts it. To this end, she must have at her disposal human beings who will devote themselves to the ministry of the word and to the humbler services that sustain even the material life of the faithful. In fact, it is the Spirit who chooses the individuals and gives them a special charism for the accomplishment of their task. Thus, in the first reading for today, seven spiritual men are chosen; the apostles then pray over them and impose hands on them [32]. Luke notes that the number of the disciples "increased greatly" and explicitly notes that among the converts were many Jewish priests.

A Chosen Race, a Royal Priesthood

Apart from these individuals with their special roles, the whole Church is a sign giving people access to the Father. As the Church grows, each Christian is a living stone in the building; that is, each is called to be such a stone, but if one is, in fact, to be such, one must have a vital faith in the person of the risen Jesus.

The second reading in today's liturgy, a passage from the First Letter of Peter [35], has at times been used as the foundation for a somewhat subjective theology that does not properly harmonize with the theology of the ordained ministry (itself admittedly not easy to establish on a scriptural basis). The "priesthood" of which Peter speaks here has either been unduly limited or unduly extended. Some have interpreted the "priesthood" of the faithful as a simple analogy; that is, baptism and confirmation confer a priesthood that is merely analogous. At the other extreme, the text has been turned into a kind of priestly manifesto, a charter for an undifferentiated priesthood of all the faithful without distinction: every baptized person is in the fullest sense a priest; there can be no hierarchy within the Christian priesthood. The second interpretation was put forward by the Reformers at the time of the Council of Trent: "Every Christian a priest!"

The true meaning of the passage from the First Letter of Peter has been explained by the Second Vatican Council in its Dogmatic Constitution on the Church. Here is what the Council says:

> Christ the Lord, high priest taken from among men (cf. Heb. 5:1-5), made the new people "a kingdom of priests to God, his Father" (Apoc. 1:6; cf. 5:9-10). The baptized, by regeneration and the anointing of the Holy Spirit, are consecrated to be a spiritual house and a holy priesthood, that through all the works of Christian men they may offer spiritual sacrifices and proclaim the perfection of him who has called them out of darkness into his marvellous light (cf. 1 Pet 2:4-10).

If we were to stop here, we might interpret the Council as saying that the faithful are only analogously priests and make their offering in an exclusively spiritual way. But the text continues a few lines later:

> Though they differ essentially and not only in degree, the common priesthood of the faithful and the ministerial or hierarchical priesthood are none the less ordered one to another; each in its own proper way shares in the one priesthood of Christ.[1]

There is thus, in fact, only one priesthood, that of Christ; there are two essentially differing kinds of participation in it: the priesthood common to all the baptized and the priesthood of ordained ministers. The Constitution does not, however, give us full clarity on the real priesthood of the faithful. It speaks of the spiritual sacrifices the faithful are to offer, but when there is question of the Eucharist, the Council speaks only of the ministerial priesthood. Are we then to understand the "offering of sacrifice" in two different ways: a spiritual and purely interior offering, which is the task of the common priesthood, and a ritual, visible, external offering of the true sacrifice, which is the task of the ministerial or ordained priesthood? From such a distinction it would follow that the only true sacrifice is ritual and external and thus offered solely by the hierarchical priesthood.

If such a distinction were proper, it would have serious consequences for the participation of the faithful in the liturgy. The center and high point of the whole liturgy is, after all, the eucharistic sacrifice. If the sacrifice were offered visibly only by the ministerial priest, while the faithful with their common priesthood could offer only in a spiritual way, the priesthood of the faithful would indeed be merely analogous and reducible to a nominal attribution to the faithful at large of prerogatives that were really proper to the ordained priest alone. But then how could we speak of the liturgy being offered by the Church as a whole, except in an analogous and metaphorical way? In any true and proper sense, the liturgy would really be the action only of the ordained priesthood.

Now, as a matter of fact, nowhere in the Christian tradition do we find such a distinction between a visible, external, ritual sacrifice and a spiritual sacrifice. On the contrary, in the teaching both of the prophets and of Christ we find that there is only one sacrifice: the spiritual sacrifice that consists in doing the Father's will (Jer 7:22; Amos 5:21-25; Matt 9:13; 12:7; Mark 12:33-34; John 4:23-24 and especially 2:14-17; Matt 26:61; Mark 14:58). Thus, the death of Christ is a spiritual sacrifice, the only kind that the Father can accept.

Christians too offer a spiritual sacrifice. The celebration of the Eucharist, being sacramental, is external and ritual, but the sacrifice of Christ that is actualized under the sacramental exterior is itself a spiritual, not an external, sacrifice. The spiritual sacrifice of Christ is rendered present, and the faithful are thus enabled to unite themselves fully with it; they unite themselves to the submission of Christ in doing the Father's will. The obedience and self-giving of the faithful—that is, their spiritual sacrifice—becomes, in fact, the matter for Christ's own sacrificial offering to the Father, inasmuch as he, the Head of the Church, joins their offering to his own; he unites his whole Church with him in offering his spiritual sacrifice of obedience to the Father's will.

While, then, we must not exaggerate what Peter says in his first letter and turn the faithful into the same kind of priests as the ordained ministers, neither must we set up an opposition between the sacrifice offered by the ordained priest—an external, visible, ritual sacrifice, which alone would truly be sacrifice—and the sacrifice offered by the priestly faithful, which would consist simply in making an interior, spiritual offering.

We should recall here what was said earlier in this volume about the three sacraments of Christian initiation. God's plan of salvation is to restore the world to unity both within itself and with God so that he may thereby be glorified. Such a goal necessarily requires that people should do the Father's will. The Word incarnate can effect the restoration by offering his life as a sign of the complete dedication of his own will to the Father's. It is because he thus responds to the

Father that he is the beloved Son the Father's voice proclaims him to be at his baptism and again at his transfiguration.

Through our baptism, the Spirit has made us adopted children of God; in our confirmation we have been officially deputed to share in the work of Christ. Doing his work requires that his sacrifice (the spiritual sacrifice signified by the shedding of his blood and his death) be actualized for us. The ministerial priest renders this service to the baptized and confirmed, having received from the Spirit the power to render the sacrifice of Calvary present. The ordained priest offers the sacrifice along with Christ, Head of the Church, whose priesthood as Head the ordained minister shares. The baptized and confirmed likewise offer the sacrifice thus rendered present, exercising the priesthood that is theirs as members of the Church. Christ makes his own the goodwill, the effort to live a better life, the sufferings of each of us, and makes them part of the spiritual sacrifice of praise, whose sign is the sacrifice of the cross as made present in an unbloody manner.

On this fifth Sunday (Year A), then, we must learn to think of the Church as not being made up solely of the ministers who are ordained to provide the Church with a structure. We are urged, on the contrary, to look to our own priesthood, which is admittedly of its own kind yet which also complements that of the ordained priest. Ordained priests and the rest of the baptized, even if their priesthood be essentially different in degree, must alike offer the one true spiritual sacrifice.

[B] Remain in Christ so That You May Bear Fruit

In the gospel for the fifth Sunday in Year B, St. John uses a symbolism already familiar from the Old Testament [39]; in fact, it had been used in Hellenistic literature as well, the language being taken from agriculture. Yet, from the beginning, we sense that we must not get lost in symbolic details and that John is seeking to express in material terms the spiritual doctrine that Christ wants to teach. The aim is to bring out the unity and fraternal spirit proper to the Church. We must not, therefore, overemphasize the material details; the symbolism is evidently only a docile instrument, so much so that at points it is, as it were, overwhelmed by the higher doctrinal meaning John wishes to communicate.

The symbolism is that of the vineyard, but a grower who does not know what John is trying to express through it, and does not realize how the symbolism has been built up in the course of the centuries, would find it all very confusing.

The Old Testament applies the symbolism of the vine and vineyard to Israel, which is God's vineyard, but an unfaithful one. God's people, Israel, is his vineyard, yet Israel has attributed her fruitfulness to other gods rather than to the true God who is her Spouse (Hos 10:1; 3:1). The theme of the vine or vineyard is used in this context to highlight both the covenant and Israel's fruitfulness. Isaiah will make extensive use of the image. He describes the anger of God, who loves his vineyard yet receives from it nothing but wild grapes; he will therefore lay it waste (Isa 5:1-7). The situation changes, however, and love triumphs. Israel is a vine that the Lord transplanted from Egypt, where it had been held prisoner, and set in the soil of its own land.

Jeremiah likewise deplores the sad state of the chosen vine (2:21; 8:13), which in the end will be destroyed (5:10; 12:10). Ezekiel too describes the infidelity of the vine (19:10-14; 17:5-19).

The gospel pericope reminds the hearers of the need to bear good fruit and of the vinegrower's anxious concern for his vine. But this is not the main point of the passage. The central interest is in being united with the Lord and in glorifying him by bearing the fruit he wants. The main theme, therefore, is the close union between the Lord and his disciples. The Lord is the true Vine, of which the Father takes such care, and the branches grafted onto it must be careful to remain united to him.

Christ is evidently speaking of his Church and voicing his concern for the future of his Body. His desire is that each of us should remain united to him, for we will bear fruit only if we are one with the Church and thus with him. In this context, we cannot but recall the splendid passage from the *Didache* that speaks as follows in a eucharistic prayer over the cup: "We thank you, our Father, for the holy vine of David, your servant, which you revealed to us through Jesus, your Servant."[2] The *Didache*, however, seems to be thinking simply of the Church that is revealed by Jesus. St. John, on the other hand, applies the symbol of the vine directly to Christ who unites the members of the Church to himself and to one another.

There is, then, an exchange of love between Christ and each member of the Church, and between each member of the Church and the other members who are united to Christ. This love and this union are the conditions required if the branches are to bear fruit and thus give glory to God. We remain in God through faith and through mutual love.

The second reading for this Sunday is a passage from St. John's first letter [36] and serves as a kind of commentary on the gospel passage. We will bear fruit, we are told, only if we believe in Jesus and if we love one another as he has commanded us. Through fidelity to the commandments, we remain in God and he remains in us; the gift of his Spirit is his sign to us that he indeed remains in us. We must take careful note of how very concrete John's instruction is, for its down-to-earth character will prevent us from indulging in a purely literary kind of theology of God's indwelling in us and our indwelling in God. John forces us to be very concrete and to measure our union with God by our observance of the commandments, especially the commandment of mutual love, practiced in an atmosphere of authentic faith in Christ.

The Gradual Expansion of the Church

The first reading for the fifth Sunday in Year B describes how Barnabas vouched for Paul to the community at Jerusalem [33]. The reading may seem rather remote from the other two readings of this liturgy, and yet a closer look will show that we are still speaking of the progressive building up of the Church in the years after the resurrection of Christ. Paul had seen the risen Christ and qualifies as an apostle and leader. The Church is gradually expanding as the Spirit brings in new members. The vine is becoming larger as new branches are grafted on through faith in the risen Christ, who is the primary object of the preaching of Paul and the other apostles.

[C] "Love One Another"

The eucharistic meal is finished, and Judas has left the Supper room [40]; the passion of Christ has already begun. Jesus links his own glorification and that of his Father to the death that he foretells in veiled terms. His words are those of the Christ who has freely offered his life for the sake of doing the Father's will. His death is, however, also a sign of his love for his disciples (cf. 13:1), who must have the same kind of love for one another. "I give you a new commandment: love one another. As I have loved you, so you also should love one another. This is how all will know that you are my disciples, if you have love for one another" (13:34-35).

As we listen to these words, we must not fail to link them with the Supper that Christ has been celebrating. Neither the words nor the Supper belong simply to the past. Christ speaks the words here and now as we listen to them; Christ is here and now celebrating the Supper he instituted the night before he died, thereby bringing his glorious passion into the present and making it the source of our union with him and with each other. The sign by which people will recognize us is the sign of charity that is grounded in the Eucharist, that is, in the ongoing actualization of the paschal mystery that restores the world to unity.

A New City

The new commandment and the new being that is the Christian are creating a new world and a new city. That is the theme of the second reading [37], which is closely connected with the gospel pericope. John's vision is of the new city, the new Jerusalem (the Church), the new earth, whereon God dwells with people. Everything is renewed: "Behold, I make all things new" (Rev 21:5).

We must not, of course, confuse the earthly Church with the kingdom in its final state. While the Church of the present time is indeed the place where God dwells with people, it also contains those who are dead; its people still weep and utter cries of sorrow. On the other hand, the Church is moving toward that ultimate Jerusalem, and we are bidden to go with her, trusting that the mysteries of Christ will be successful in what they seek to accomplish.

The new commandment of love gives rise to the new city that is set over against the world, in whose eyes we Christians are such strange beings; the unbeliever cannot understand our attitudes or the choices we make. Our task, therefore, is to help the Church, whose members we are, to become ever more fully and perfectly the Spouse of Christ, a Bride adorned for her Bridegroom. Love exercised in concrete, practical ways is what will enable the Church to be what she should be.

Negative criticism, on the other hand, is destructive and never constructive. It is easy, after all, to find fault with failures and deficiencies but much less simple to provide the positive help that remedies a defect and gives others the courage to move forward. Such an attitude does not require that our love be a bland, insipid thing or that we cultivate a complacent, childish admiration for everything the Church says and does. We're quite accustomed nowadays to thinking of the Church as sinful on her human side. Perhaps we're even overly accustomed to it, so that our faith has become less lively. We're preoccupied with counting all the wrinkles, and we forget the spiritual beauty of this Bride that is preparing to meet her Spouse. Is our derisive laughter really a source of fruitfulness for the Church?

Men and women show a special kind of bigness and a special kind of balance when they know how to point out the defects of the institution in a sure but tactful way, while preserving at the same time the unqualified respect owed to the Church that God has established and from which we receive the divine life that is in us. Our criticism, no matter how severe it must sometimes be, should never encourage others to abandon the Church or even to be less than enthusiastic about her. Criticism will not have such effects if it truly proceeds from faith and from love of our brothers and sisters.

The Church Grows; Elders Are Needed

The first reading for the fifth Sunday in Year C is not closely connected with the other two readings, yet it can be linked to them without forcing the texts [34]. The new Jerusalem that is the Church was growing slowly. If it was to grow, the disciples had to persevere in the faith and had to survive many trials on their way to the kingdom. For this they needed help such as the apostles provided. Meanwhile, however, the number of believers who had made the decision to live the commandment of love as members of the new people of God was increasing rapidly; in particular, the Gentile nations were accepting the Good News, and the door of faith was being thrown open to them. Paul and Barnabas therefore installed elders in each community.

What a transformation had taken place since the resurrection of Jesus! Unity should be attained through mutual love and on building together the new Jerusalem into which even Gentiles were called.

Sixth Sunday of Easter

41. THE SPIRIT AND THE CHURCH

[A] Promise of the Spirit

Christ speaks to his disciples; he also speaks to us who celebrate his Eucharist. Addressing thus his entire Church, he announces in his farewell discourse that he will send the Paraclete and that he will himself return at the end of time [47]; that is the message the Church passes on to us today.

In his farewell discourse, Christ tells us his final wish for us: that we should be faithful to his commandments, since this obedience is the proof of our love for him. St. John is careful to pass these words on to the young Church experiencing so many difficulties and enduring so much conflict. Another theme of the discourse is that of mutual immanence: the Father in me and I in the Father; I in you and you in me. It is a favorite theme of St. John's, for it sheds a great deal of light on the deeper meaning of the Church's life and the life of her individual members. Closely connected both with the observance of the commandments and with the mutual love of Christ and others is the theme of the sending of the Spirit. The Spirit will sustain the Church; at the same time, we have the impression that the gift of the Spirit is conditioned by that observance of the commandments that is the sign of love.

The Spirit who will be sent will be "another Advocate," the Spirit of truth, and he will be with us always. What will his role be? It will be to make ever more fully known the mysteries of Christ, that is, the meaning of his life and words and actions. But at the same time the Spirit of truth will give Christians the strength to live in a world that does not understand them or see what they see. For, as Jesus points out emphatically, only those who believe and lovingly obey the commandments can receive, see, and know this Spirit. The Spirit is with and in such people and not in unbelievers.

"Another Advocate" may seem a rather odd expression, but the meaning is easily grasped. Throughout his earthly life Jesus had been at his disciples' side; now the Spirit will take Jesus' place and continue his work, and the disciples will not be left orphans. As far as the world is concerned, Christ will have disappeared, but the disciples will see him and see him as a living person. This last statement refers to Jesus' return at his resurrection but also to his return at the end of time. Nonetheless, this knowing and seeing of Jesus does not imply merely a vision of his physical presence but rather a true understanding of what he is. The disciples will know that he is in the Father and that his disciples are in him and he in them.

Observe how solemnly Christ introduces these words about the mutual presence and immanence of himself and his disciples: "On that day you will realize . . ." (v. 20). "That day" is the day of his glorious resurrection. Yet Christ also has in mind here the Church, with which he will continue to be present until the great Day of definitive encounter. Throughout that whole time he will manifest himself, but only to those who love him, that is, those who accept his word and are faithful to it.

The Laying on of Hands and the Gift of the Spirit

The first reading for the sixth Sunday in Year A tells how the apostles Peter and John laid hands on the Samaritan converts so that they might receive the gift of the Spirit [41]. The reading is evidently related to the gospel pericope, for the Spirit thus communicated is the Spirit of truth who remains with us and guides us.

Some Samaritans have been converted by the preaching of Philip; Peter and John are then sent into Samaria to continue Philip's work. This they do by imposing hands so that the recently baptized may receive the Holy Spirit. The statement can be misinterpreted to mean that baptism had not conferred the Spirit (as though he had not effected the rebirth through baptism by water for the forgiveness of sins) and that the laying on of hands was required if the Spirit were to be bestowed. No, the point is evidently that some special gift of the Spirit is bestowed through the laying on of hands, even though the Acts of the Apostles does not tell us in what this special gift consists. Later on, at Ephesus, Paul will confer baptism on those who had received only the baptism of John, and then he will lay hands on them for the gift of the Spirit (Acts 19:1-7).

In today's reading the gift of the Spirit takes the form of the gift of tongues and the gift of prophecy. In other words, the gift of the Spirit represents a completion that takes outward form in a kind of witnessing. In any event, we can discern here the link between baptism and that gift of the Spirit that will later on be called "confirmation."

The Risen Christ Is Our Hope

The second reading, from the First Letter of Peter, refers to the difficult situation of Christians amid a world that does not understand them [44]. The letter aims at encouraging the persecuted Christians to bear witness to their hope. They must be ready to suffer for having done only what is good and right. Peter then points to the example of Christ, who, though innocent, died for the guilty and their sins.

The reason why this passage was chosen for today's liturgy seems to be the implied action of that Spirit of whom we hear in the first reading and in the gospel. He it is who raised Christ from the dead and gave him the victory over the powers of evil. This same Spirit is our hope, since he gives us rebirth and a participation in the life of God and Christ. In the flesh Christ was put to death, thus sharing the common lot of humanity, but the Spirit has given him a new kind of life. That is the basis for our hope that we too will be transformed and glorified. For people with such a hope, difficulty and persecution hold no terrors, for they are the way by which we attain a share in Christ's victory.

[B] Giving One's Life for One's Friends

The theme of the sixth Sunday in Year B is love. The salient phrases in the gospel pericope make this clear: abide in Christ's love; love one another; give one's life for one's friends [48]. In fact, the whole process of salvation is shown to be at bottom a matter of love: "As the Father loves me, so I also love you. . . . love one another as I love you" (vv. 9, 12).

Everything in this passage has to do with love. Love has been given to us: "As the Father loves me, so I also love you" (v. 9). We must therefore be faithful to love: "Remain in my love" (v. 9). We know from elsewhere in what this love given to us consists: "In this is love: not that we have loved God, but that he loved us and sent his Son as expiation for our sins" (1 John 4:10; from the second reading). Christ's great desire is that his disciples and we with them should live on, or abide, in his love. He also tells us in what this abiding concretely consists: "If you keep my commandments, you will remain in my love, just as I have kept my Father's commandments" (John 15:10). (John, we should note, never indulges in what might be called an abstract metaphysics of love; he always gives love a concrete, realistic meaning.)

In speaking of our union with him, Jesus uses the same terms that he uses to describe his own union with the Father. While our union with him is only analogous to his union with the Father, the identity of the language indicates how very close our relation to God can become. The very love that unites the two divine Persons, Father and Son, is communicated to people. Christ tells us what the quality of this love is: "No one has greater love than this, to lay down one's life for one's friends" (v. 13). Jesus then identifies his own friends: they are his disciples, and the laying down of his life for them is a clear reference to his passion. We must observe, however, that a "friend" cannot lay down his or her life for us unless we have been obeying that person's commandments, since otherwise there would have been no friendship.

It is characteristic of friends that they hide nothing from one another but share everything. That is what Jesus does, as he tells us here: "I have called you friends, because I have told you everything I have heard from my Father."

The friendship in question here is, concretely, not a friendship between mere human beings but between God and the sinner. Inevitably, then, the initiative in the invitation to friendship must come from God (v. 16). Jesus had already made this point earlier: "No one can come to me unless the Father who sent me draws him" (John 6:44). At the same time, however, this friendship to which God invites us is impossible unless we also love one another (v. 17).

Because of God's love for us and our response to his invitation to friendship, we must "go and bear fruit" (v. 16). How are these words to be understood? According to the translation just given, "going" and "bearing fruit" are distinct ideas, and we must attend to each of them. The first indicates a mission; the second points to the result of the mission and the love. Other translators prefer to turn the two expressions into one: "go to bear fruit." In any case, love is presented as taking concrete form in the observance of the commandments that is indispensable if we are to bear fruit. Note that the controlling image is still that of the vine, whose branches bear fruit as long as they remain connected with the vine.

A further consequence of the love that unites us to the Father and Son in the Spirit is that we can ask anything of the Father in Christ's name, and it will be given to us.

The passage ends with a repetition of the key idea: "This I command you: love one another" (v. 17).

God Loved Us and Sent His Son

The second reading [45] also deals with John's favorite theme: mutual love. We must love one another, he says, because all love is from God. "[L]ove is of God; everyone who loves is begotten by God and knows God" (v. 7): here we have some of John's characteristic expressions: love, knowledge, adoption. We also find John telling us that God's love never remains at the abstract level but manifests itself in concrete ways, most especially in the sending of the Son so that he may give us life (v. 9). There we have the real sign of love: God "sent his Son as expiation for our sins" (v. 10).

The proposition that "God is love" (v. 8) had to take concrete form, since love does not exist if it does not manifest itself. But God did manifest his love by sending Jesus. The incarnation of the Word is the supreme sign of God's love for us. Was this an isolated gesture of love? No, for the sending of the Son is bound up with the whole history of salvation. In sending him, then, God did not make an isolated, passing gesture, however grand and glorious; rather, the whole history of salvation is there to prepare for and complete the mission of the Son.

It is important to emphasize the free and unmerited character of God's love for us. He loved first and took the initiative; he chose us, not we him. It is understandable, then, that the Greek text of the New Testament should use the word *agapē* to express this divine love and should reject the terms *eros* (love based on desire that seeks fulfillment; love associated with passion) and *philia* (mutual friendship of equals). The term *agapē* brings out the divine goodwill and initiative.

John's main concern for the young Church is that charity should rule the life of its members, thus reflecting the love of God that caused him to send his Son. If the expansion of the Church is effected through the revelation to people of God's love for them, then the revelation itself is effected chiefly through the sign of the familial love that unites Christians with one another. It is our task to communicate to others the love of God that made him send his Son, just as it is our task to communicate to them the "knowledge" of God. We can carry out our task, however, only as members of a community that will be a sign of God's *agapē*—in other words, a community whose life is marked by the bonds love fashions.

The Spirit Is Given without Partiality

The love thus manifested by the sending of the Son and the giving of the Spirit reaches out to all people; the Father loves all and intends all to be saved [42]. In the first reading, Peter is forced to acknowledge that the Spirit does indeed breathe wherever he wishes (cf. John 3:8). This is an important moment in the history of the Church, for without this acknowledgment the Church would have been the captive of one nation and one race, but instead the Spirit manifests even to Gentiles. As long as one fears God and acts uprightly, one can become a believer and receive the gift of the Spirit.

The responsorial psalm (Ps 98) for the sixth Sunday in Year B is an enthusiastic response to God's desire for the salvation of all. "The Lord has revealed to the nations his saving power," says the response, while in verses 2-3 we sing: "The LORD has made known his salvation, / has shown his deliverance to the nations. / . . . All the ends of the earth have seen / the salvation of our God."

[C] The Holy Spirit Will Teach Us Everything

In the gospel passage for the sixth Sunday in Year C, Jesus is preparing his disciples for his departure and return to his Father [49]. Chapter 14 of the Fourth Gospel is, of course, a farewell address. Toward the end of it Jesus promises that God will come to those who believe and that he will send the Spirit to teach them everything. We find once again the familiar theme of "remaining" or "dwelling": "we will come to him and make our dwelling with him" (v. 23).

The Father and the Son come to those who believe with a faith that has its origin in the Spirit. This trinitarian coming is a new revelation for the disciples. The condition for the coming of the Trinity, however, is that the disciple must love and be faithful to Jesus' word.

The departure of Jesus is necessary if the Spirit is to come and carry out his mission of instructing the disciples and making Christ's words alive for them. What Jesus is here doing is to explain the necessity of the mystery of the ascension: If he does not go, the Spirit cannot be sent; and this sending is necessary for the completion of Jesus' work and for bringing the disciples to an understanding of all that Jesus had taught them.

The disciples realize that Jesus is going to leave them, and the news devastates them. Jesus reassures them: he is leaving, but he will return. Yet, even his return will leave the young Church subject to trial and needing to live by faith; people must believe in Jesus without seeing him. The disciples should not be fearful at this thought, for Christ gives them a peace that is of God himself. They will have the joy of knowing that Christ is glorified and seated at the Father's right hand, the joy of fully grasping the teaching of Jesus, the joy that comes from the indwelling of the Trinity. Such peace and joy are unintelligible to the world, for the joy is a joy amid suffering, the peace a peace amid conflict. Yet they belong to those who believe in the victory of Christ, for this victory is the firm foundation of hope.

The Holy City Coming down from Heaven

The departure of Jesus and the sending of the Spirit announce the building of a new city, a new kingdom, the Church of the saved. Such is the meaning of the second reading [46]. But the city is not the present Church; neither is it the future Church, as though the vision were talking about the present Church in its perfect state. The vision is of a new creation: the heavenly city. The present Church is, however, a sign of the heavenly city and constantly refers its present life to that future reality.

The new city gleams with the splendor of God. The details of its description are of little interest to us here, though we should note the reference to the twelve tribes of Israel and to the wall built on twelve foundations, which are the twelve apostles. The city has no temple. What is the significance of this statement? Is it a condemnation of all liturgical worship? Is it an echo of prophetic warnings against the dangers of external worship (cf. Jer 7:4)? Not at all! There is no opposition between liturgy, external worship, and true adoration; there is only complementarity, provided the gesture and the words reflect genuine interior adoration. The point of the statement that the city has no temple is simply that there is no need for a material building, because God himself is the temple of the new city. Neither is there any longer need of sun and moon, since the Lord is the city's light. He is all in all.

We may ask whether such a vision is not discouraging to the Church and does not take the heart out of those who want to work in the present Church. The question implies a misconception. It is, after all, the present Church herself that prepares us for her future elimination and replacement by the new city, just as every celebration of the liturgy takes us a step closer to the elimination of every temple and every liturgy. Why? Because on earth we toil in darkness and see reality only in a mirror and through signs, whereas in the new city we shall see without the mediation of mirrors and shall see God himself face-to-face.[1]

Choice of Leaders for the Community

In the first reading we are at a decisive moment for the new Church: it must decide on the attitude it will take toward the people among whom it first came into existence [43]. Radical decisions have to be made, yet a certain flexibility must also be preserved. The scene is the famous Council of Jerusalem, the first example of a Church council. Leaders are chosen from the Jerusalem community, and they set out for Antioch with Paul and Barnabas to announce the decisions reached by the Council.

Two points are noteworthy. The first is that the leading men chosen by the Council and sent out from Jerusalem are the ones with authority; any others claiming the right to lay down the law have no mandate to do so, and no one should pay any attention to them. The second point is that the conciliar decision has been made with the help of the Holy Spirit. It is this second point that establishes a connection between this reading and the gospel of the day. The Spirit whom Jesus has sent teaches everything and bestows perspicacity of judgment on those who exercise authority in the Church. Circumcision will not be required of Gentile converts. The only prohibitions are not to eat meat sacrificed to idols, or blood, or the meat of strangled animals, and to abstain from illicit sexual unions.

At first sight this reading seems to have little connection with the overall theme of this Sunday in all three years. But it does, in fact, have a connection, for it is dealing with the formation and growth of the Church. It provides us with a typical example of the difficulties that the establishment of the Church entailed and of how the Spirit of Christ helped the disciples reach a sound decision in a matter that was agitating a local church.

42. THE ASCENSION OF THE LORD

In the liturgy for the feast of the ascension, the first two readings are the same in all three years of the cycle;* for the gospel, however, a different pericope has been chosen in each of the three years. Of the three gospel passages, however, only those from Mark [53] and Luke [54] narrate the ascension. Luke tells the story again in the Acts of the Apostles, in a passage used for the first reading of the feast [50], while the second reading, from the Letter to the Ephesians, gives a theology of the mystery [51]. The three gospels locate the ascension (explicitly or implicitly) after a discourse in which Jesus sends his apostles forth into the world to proclaim his resurrection, to teach, and to baptize. The Acts of the Apostles locates the ascension in the same context.

Since the liturgies for the three-year cycle overlap, we shall treat them as one and discuss all the readings together.

"He Was Lifted up, and a Cloud Took Him from Their Sight"

The first reading, from the Acts of the Apostles [50], puts the mystery of the ascension into its historical context. Luke intends that what he writes here should be read in continuity with what he had already written in his first book, that is, the gospel. Both here and in the gospel, chapter 24 [54], Jesus leaves his disciples only after giving them explicit instructions. Matthew and Mark too relate the final instructions that Jesus gives his disciples before leaving them and ascending to heaven.

We should note the way in which Luke, in the Acts of the Apostles, speaks of Christ giving these final instructions: he gives them in the Holy Spirit. The evangelist here points out that the Spirit who will be guiding the apostles in their missionary work is already present

* After Nocent wrote this, optional second readings were added to Years B and C. Hence, he has no commentary on them.

and active in the final words Christ speaks before his departure. Nor does Luke fail to give a reason why Christ gives his instructions to a limited group. This is the group to whom he has shown himself alive after his passion, appearing to them during a period of forty days and giving them proofs of the resurrection; this was also the group to which he had been speaking about the kingdom of God.

In Luke's account here, Jesus insists that the apostles must stay in Jerusalem and wait for the fulfillment of the Father's promise. Luke is also the one who, both in his gospel and in the Acts of the Apostles, emphasizes the place that Jerusalem has in the events of the mystery of salvation. It is at Jerusalem that Jesus is presented in the temple and recognized as the Messiah by Simeon and Anna (2:22-38). It is at Jerusalem that Jesus, still a child, will teach the teachers of the law (2:41-50). The ascent to Jerusalem later on is therefore significant: the public life of Jesus had begun at Jerusalem, and so it must end there.

It is at Jerusalem too that the apostles will receive their baptism in the Holy Spirit, which will give them the strength and courage they need if they are to be witnesses in Jerusalem, throughout Judea and Samaria, and to the ends of the earth. In their last conversation with Jesus just before his ascension, the apostles ask whether the fulfillment of the Father's promise means that Israel is about to be restored. Jesus answers with firmness and restraint. The answer implicitly distinguishes between the imminent coming of the Spirit, who will give the strength the apostles need for bearing witness, and the definitive establishment of the kingdom. Before the latter can occur, the Gospel must be carried beyond the boundaries of Israel; the kingdom will come at a time the Father has determined.

After reporting Jesus' instructions, Luke narrates the ascension itself. He writes as a historian of events, in a sober way. The "cloud" is the cloud found in various theophanies in both the Old and the New Testaments, but Luke strikes no note of triumph in his description. Jesus simply vanishes into the cloud, and the angels tell the disciples that he will someday return.

Despite what Luke says, we may well find the account perplexing, for Luke provides no theological interpretation. He prepares us for Jesus' departure, and we know that if Christ does not ascend to heaven and take his place at the Father's side, the Spirit cannot come. But if we had only Luke's account, we would be unable to elaborate a theology of the ascension.

Though there is no triumphal ring to Luke's story, the liturgy strikes this note in the responsorial psalm (Ps 47): "God goes up with shouts of joy. / The LORD goes up with trumpet blast. / . . . God is king of all the earth. / Sing praise with all your skill. / God reigns over the nations. / God sits upon his holy throne" (vv. 6, 8-9).

[A] Christ Is Seated at the Right Hand of the Father

The second reading gives a more doctrinal vision of the ascension [51], showing us Christ as the sign of God's strength and wisdom. The passage is one of enthusiastic praise for the victorious Christ. He is the Christ of glory, whom God raised from the dead, set at his own right side, and made Master of all things. Above all, God has made him Head of the Church, which is his Body and fullness.

The passage is thus another summary of Paul's theology (see also, for example, Col 2:10; Eph 1:15-16; 3:6; 4:4, 12, 16; 5:23, 29). The Church is here called the "fullness" of Christ, his *plērōma*. Paul uses the same term elsewhere in Ephesians when speaking of the perfect human (3:19; 4:13). Christ does not, of course, require any perfection from outside himself. The Church is his "fullness" because in her the saving action of God is seen in a maximum degree. The Church is the privileged locus of the action of God and Christ.

The victory and glory of Christ, now Master of all things, is a source of hope for us, because what belongs to Christ belongs also to his followers. We can see in the heavenly Christ the inheritance that shall someday be ours.

"All Power in Heaven and on Earth Has Been Given to Me"

The passage from St. Matthew's gospel [52] gives us Christ's last words before his departure. He speaks of his glory and power: "All power in heaven and on earth has been given to me." The moment is a solemn one, and when the disciples see Jesus, they fall down in homage; his presence is already so filled with majesty that it forces people to their knees in adoration.

Until now, some had had their doubts. That is why Jesus presents himself to them as "Lord" and possessor of supreme authority; he is Lord of both heaven and earth. He also gives the disciples their mission, which is universal in scope: they are to make disciples of all nations and baptize them in the name of the Father and the Son and the Holy Spirit; they are also to teach people to observe Christ's commandments. In short, they are to transmit a complete program of Christian life, once they have proclaimed the basic message of faith in the Christ who has been raised from the dead and now lives forever. The account ends with a promise of Christ's efficacious presence to his Church: "And behold, I am with you always, until the end of the age."

[B] "The Lord Jesus, after he Spoke to Them, Was Taken up into Heaven"

In the reading from Mark's gospel (Year B), Christ's final words have to do with faith, baptism, and the signs that will accompany those who believe [53]. He bids his disciples go and proclaim the Good News to all creation. The words reflect the evangelist's experience as viewed in the light of the Spirit. It is hardly probable, after all, that Christ gave so concrete an order. If he had, how could we explain either the hesitations of the apostles in the early years or their insistence that the Gospel must be preached even to the Gentiles?

The apostles are to preach the Good News. The result of their *kerygma* (an authoritative proclamation not based on arguments) will be the faith that saves, or, if people reject the proclamation, their condemnation. Faith in turn leads to baptism, or, rather, it is professed in the reception of baptism. Note that the condemnation is pronounced against those who *refuse* to believe. There is thus a middle ground left open in Christ's statement; we may not simply condemn all who do not believe but must examine their basic attitudes and motivations.

Those who believe will have power to perform "signs." This is especially true of the apostles, who must use the signs to back up their preaching. In the Fourth Gospel (14:12), Christ again says that "whoever believes in me will do the works that I do and will do greater ones than these." And we know from the Acts of the Apostles the wonders that the apostles did perform in order to confirm the truth they preached and to arouse or intensify faith.

After relating Christ's final words, Mark mentions the ascension itself. We should note especially his addition of the fact that Jesus now took his seat at God's right side. What Mark is emphasizing here is the glorification of Jesus' humanity.

As Mark tells it, the apostles let no time elapse between Christ's commission to them and their departure for their missionary work: they go forth and preach the Good News everywhere. The evangelist notes that the Lord continued to work with them, thus fulfilling his promise as recorded by Matthew: "Go . . . I am with you always, until the end of the age" (28:19-20).

[C] "He Was Carried up into Heaven"

Luke's account of the ascension in the gospel [54] must be compared with his account in Acts; the latter was written at a later date, and in it Luke refers back to his gospel.

The pericope contains an important statement by Christ: "Thus it is written that the Christ would suffer and rise from the dead on the third day and that repentance, for the forgiveness of sins, would be preached in his name to all the nations, beginning from Jerusalem" (24:46-47). There are several essential points made here which together form a doctrinal synthesis that can be described as the paschal mystery of death and resurrection. Those who had been witnesses of the events are to go forth to proclaim them and thus bring people to conversion; they are to make their proclamation to all the nations, but they are to start at Jerusalem. Christ will even tell them to stay in Jerusalem until the promised Spirit comes (cf. Acts 1:1-11).

In Luke's gospel account of Jesus' final words, the Lord teaches his disciples the meaning of the Scriptures, as he had done for the disciples at Emmaus when he told them: "Was it not necessary that the Messiah should suffer these things and enter into his glory?" (24:26). Jesus then promises to send the Spirit. Finally, he blesses the disciples and ascends into heaven. Here again, there is no air of triumph about the story; the facts are related very simply. Nonetheless (but expressing the evangelist's own reaction at a later time?), the apostles fall to the ground in worship of Jesus; they understand now that he is glorified, and they return to Jerusalem rejoicing.

"It Is Better for You That I Go"

Has the Christian of today any reason to be really interested in the ascension that took place so many centuries ago? After all, our concern now is to live the life of the Church under the guidance of the

Spirit. How can the ascension be anything to us but a past historical event, albeit an important one, in the life of the Savior?

Let us ask St. Leo the Great what he thinks about the ascension. In the first of his two sermons on the mystery, the saint makes the point that the ascension of Christ means that his human nature is now enthroned at the Father's side. He then turns his thoughts to us, the disciples Christ has left behind:

> The ascension of Christ thus means our own elevation as well; where the glorious Head has gone before, the Body is called to follow in hope. Let us therefore exult, beloved, as is fitting, and let us rejoice in devout thanksgiving. For on this day not only have we been confirmed in our possession of paradise, but we have even entered heaven in the person of Christ; through his ineffable grace we have regained far more than we had lost through the devil's hatred.[1]

In this sermon, then, the saint sees in Christ's ascension and heavenly glorification the pledge of what we too shall someday be and a vision of what we already are. In St. Leo's view, the feast of the ascension is not simply the celebration of a historical event; it is also a celebration of what we ourselves now are.

In the second sermon, the saint returns to this same theme, which, as he sees it, is the real object of the feast: "At Easter the Lord's resurrection was the source of our joy; today his ascension into heaven is our reason for rejoicing, for today we recall and duly venerate the day on which our lowly nature was elevated, in Christ, far above the heavenly host."[2]

But St. Leo goes further in responding to our modern questions about the practical meaning of the feast of the ascension. In the same second sermon he writes:

> Forty days after his resurrection, our Lord Jesus Christ was raised up to heaven before his disciples' eyes, thus ending his bodily presence among them. He would remain at the Father's right side until the time divinely appointed for multiplying the children of the Church had passed. Then he would come, in the very body in which he had ascended, to judge the living and the dead. Thus what formerly had been visible in our Redeemer now took the form of sacred rites; and in order that faith might be purer and stronger, bodily vision was replaced by teaching whose authority the divinely enlightened hearts of the faithful might accept and follow.[3]

St. Leo makes an important point in this passage, namely, that on the visible scene the Redeemer is replaced by sacred rites; it is through these sacramental signs that we now encounter the Christ who has ascended to the Father's side.

St. Leo's theological approach here has inspired most modern study and presentation of the sacramental life. Its starting point is Christ's assurance to his disciples. "It is better for you that I go" (John 16:7). But Christ had previously said: "Whoever has seen me has seen the Father" (John 14:9). How, then, can he say, "It is better for you that I go," when his going deprives us of real contact with the Father? Christ's second statement would indeed be meaningless unless his departure led to a contact of all believers both with him and with his Father. That is precisely what has happened: Christ's departure paved the way for the activity of the Spirit in the sacraments, which are the symbolic extensions of Christ's glorified body throughout the world. Unless Christ were both glorified and departed from us, the sacraments would be impossible. Any contact with a Christ still present in bodily form on earth would be limited by the conditions of space and time. Now, however, Christ is present to us in every place and at all times through signs that draw their efficacy from his Spirit.

The incarnation of the eternal Word made it possible for the world to encounter God and thus changed the course of history. The ascension of the glorified Christ and the subsequent sending of the Spirit allow all believers to touch Christ, to see and know God, and to live his life, by providing a mode of contact with the Lord. Each sacrament is a sign of his presence; this is especially true of the Eucharist, which is specifically the sign of the presence of his now glorified body. Reflection on each of the sacraments (including the word that is part of the rite, and against the background of the sign-nature of the Church herself) will enable us to see how truly Christ spoke in saying that his departure was to our advantage. It will also enable us to understand better the deeper significance of the ascension in the history of our salvation.[4]

The Prayers for the Feast of the Ascension

The reformed liturgy provides two prefaces for the feast of the ascension. The second of them, used already in the Roman Missal of 1570, links resurrection and ascension, the purpose of the latter being to make us sharers in the divinity of Christ: "For after his Resurrection he plainly appeared to all his disciples and was taken up to heaven in their sight, that he might make us sharers in his divinity."

The first preface expands on the same point: "For the Lord Jesus, the King of glory, conqueror of sin and death, ascended (today) to the highest heavens, as the Angels gazed in wonder. Mediator between God and man, judge of the world and Lord of hosts, he ascended, not to distance himself from our lowly state but that we, his members, might be confident of following where he, our Head and Founder, has gone before."

The other prayers of the Mass[†] concentrate chiefly on our passage to heaven as prefigured in the Lord's ascension. "Gladden us with holy joys, almighty God, and make us rejoice with devout thanksgiving, for the Ascension of Christ your Son is our exaltation, and, where the Head has gone before in glory, the Body is called to follow in hope." Or again: "Almighty ever-living God, who allow those on earth to celebrate divine mysteries, grant, we pray, that Christian hope may draw us onward to where our nature is united with you."

A preface in the Verona Sacramentary (a preface that resembles the first, and newer, of the current prefaces) sums up the reason for our joy on this feast:

> Rightly do we exult and rejoice on today's feast. The ascension into heaven of the human Jesus Christ, Mediator between God and humanity, is not an abandonment of us to our lowly state, for he exists now in the glory that he always had with you and in the nature he took from us and made his own. He deigned to become a human, in order that he might make us sharers in his divinity.[5]

---

† After Nocent wrote this, a Vigil Mass was added to the missal. This commentary pertains to the prayers at the Mass during the Day.

Seventh Sunday of Easter

43. JESUS PRAYS FOR HIS DISCIPLES

[A] "Father, . . . Give Glory to Your Son"

The focus of the gospel reading is on the glory of the Christ [61]. Jesus had earlier spoken of this glory when he said, "The Son of Man will come with his angels in his Father's glory" (Matt 16:27), and Mark reports Christ's words to the effect that if anyone is ashamed of Jesus, Jesus will in turn be ashamed of him when he comes in his Father's glory (Mark 8:38; cf. Luke 9:26).

In the Fourth Gospel, Jesus speaks more pointedly of this glory that will be his: "The hour has come for the Son of Man to be glorified" (12:23). It is a glory he does not seek for himself, but there is an Other who seeks it for him (8:50). John ends his account of the miracle at Cana by saying, "this . . . revealed his glory, and his disciples began to believe in him" (2:11). Finally, in the priestly prayer, Jesus asks that those whom the Father has given him may contemplate his glory (17:24). There is thus a connection between glory and faith by which the glory of Jesus is contemplated.

There can be no doubt that Christ's hearers understood this "glory" to be connected to his person. The word "glory" to us is chiefly a synonym for "reputation" or "renown"; the Semite, however, took it rather to mean "a value that elicits respect." That is why the "glory" of Yahweh can be identified with God himself and his omnipotence. His glory is manifested in his interventions, as, for example, the well-known miracle at the Red Sea (Exod 14:18) or his various appearances (e.g., Exod 16:10). God's "glory" is his self-manifestation; thus, Moses asks the Lord to show him his glory (Exod 33:18). This presence of the Lord in all his splendor is later on somewhat materialized, so to speak; thus, the glory of Yahweh is said to fill the temple (1 Kgs 8:10).

In the New Testament, "glory" is connected with the person of Jesus and is consequently manifested by various actions of his earthly life, as we noted in connection with the miracle of Cana. Especially, however, do we see Jesus' glory at his baptism and his transfiguration (Luke 9:32, 35; 2 Pet 1:17). Even the passion will reveal his glory, and Paul will speak of "crucifying the Lord of glory" (1 Cor 2:8).

John, above all, is the one who directly connects "glory" with the person of Jesus. This glory is manifested by the unity between Father and Son (10:30), by Jesus' works (11:40), and in a very special way by the paschal mystery of his death and resurrection. The glory belonged to him since before the creation of the world (17:24), but his death, resurrection, and ascension make it manifest to all.

Jesus has now been taken up into glory (1 Tim 3:16), for God has glorified his Servant (Acts 3:13). He has raised him up and given him glory (1 Pet 1:21).

We are now in a position to understand better the pericope read in this day's liturgy (Year A). The prayer remains, however, a complicated composition. In the part read today, Christ is saying that he has glorified his Father by carrying out the task entrusted to him; now he in return must be glorified by the Father. Any glory given him, however, means the glorification of the Father as well, since there is no separation between the two glories. The glory that the Son gives the Father consists in the accomplishment of his mission; he has made the Father known to people who have come to realize that he came from the Father and have accepted the word that had been communicated to the Son and that he in turn has communicated to them. They have believed, and they know; consequently, they have eternal life, for eternal life consists in knowing the only true God.

The climactic statement in this reading is that Jesus is glorified in his disciples. He can say this because they make clear the successful accomplishment of his mission: he has united them to himself and transformed them into his likeness; they now belong to the Father, just as they do to the Son. The Son's glory is the Father's glory, and the Father's glory is the Son's glory, and the Son's glory is ours as well.

The Spirit of Glory Rests upon Us

The second reading connects the glory of Christ with the way in which the Christian should live [58]. God's Spirit, the Spirit of glory, rests upon us, and therefore nothing, not even persecution or insult, can take our joy away. In fact, condemnation for being a Christian is an occasion for giving glory to God. During our trials and until the time when Christ's glory will be manifested on the last day, we must share that glory and live joyously. The interim is simply a delay and should therefore be a joyful time.

Persevering in Prayer

The apostles and other disciples were steadfast in prayer; with them were some women, among them Mary, the Mother of Jesus. They were all gathered on the upper floor of a house; there the little community, Mary included, contemplated the glory of the risen and ascended Christ while they waited for the promised Holy Spirit [55].

[B] Consecrated in Truth

In this section of Christ's fervent prayer, there are three principal themes: life in the truth, life in unity, life in the world but not of the world [62].

God's word is truth, and Jesus has communicated it to his disciples; now these disciples must be consecrated in and by the truth. What does "truth" mean for St. John? It means eternal reality as revealed to people—"either the reality itself or the revelation of it."[1] The final words of today's pericope—"consecrated in truth"—thus reveal their full weight of meaning: when Jesus asks the Father to consecrate his disciples in truth, he is asking that they "be sanctified upon the plane of absolute reality."[2]

The disciples are thus meant to attain to the holiness of God himself, since Jesus is putting them into the very sphere of God. They are God's adopted children, chosen as such by the Father and given to him by the Son. Consecration in truth and participation in the holiness of the Father will in turn bestow on them the plenitude of joy—that joy which Christ himself experiences now as he looks back at what has been successfully accomplished.

The disciples must, however, remain united and one, just as the Father and the Son are one. We have met with this theme already; it is a favorite of John's and will be developed further in the next part of the chapter (vv. 21-24). The one reality that the body of disciples should become is identically the one reality that is the Father and the Son. If they remain in this unity, the disciples will be able to remain also in the truth, that is, in the eternal absolute reality.

Such an existence does not remove the disciples from the world, but it does set up an opposition between them and the world. The world cannot understand them, and it will end up by hating them because they are such a stumbling block for it. What is said of the disciples here applies to all Christians: they are in the world, for the sake of the world's life, but they are not of the world. This tension is part of every baptized Christian's life. The opposition is one that can neither be glossed over or watered down, under penalty of not remaining in either truth or unity.

We Have Seen God's Love

The second reading consists of reflections by St. John (first letter) that run parallel to chapter 17 of the gospel [59]. The themes of unity and of God's indwelling in us are taken up. While no one has ever seen God, the apostles have been witnesses of the Son in his mission as Savior of the world. We do not see God, but we do see his love at work. He is Love, and anyone who abides in love abides in God. "Remain in love" is the same as "remain in the truth" and "be consecrated in truth." If we have faith, we can discern the love of God at work in our midst. We can also recognize it in ourselves, for in us it achieves its perfect operation, consecrating us in truth.

Here is the source of Christians' dignity and joy but also of their responsibility to the world. Christians are people who by faith see how the sacramental signs actualize the history of salvation. Their way of life has been established by the Spirit for the period that runs from the ascension to the end of time. Our need now is to abide in love so that we may abide in God and God in us. Such is our privileged situation; we know what consequences flow from it. It is the foundation of the Christian outlook and the Christian moral stance. Morality is a word that has often been debased, but we can see how it far transcends juridicism and codes of precepts. Morality points to and helps preserve our union with God and others.

A Witness to the Resurrection

The loving faith of which we have been speaking rests ultimately on witness given to the resurrection; the community whose life is one of loving fidelity to truth is founded on the testimony of those who saw the risen Christ. The group of apostles, reduced to eleven by the betrayal and death of Judas, felt it necessary to restore its full complement of twelve and therefore chose Matthias to join their ranks. Along with the others, he was to be a witness to the resurrection and thus a witness to the Father's love that had been revealed in the mission of the Son.

The Church has continued through the centuries to be a community of faith and love, and the successors of the apostles, with the Spirit's aid, have continued to help the people of God, the Church, to abide in truth and love. That is the bishop's chief function. The successors of the apostles are thus the foundation of the community that continues to live in the world without being of the world but, on the contrary, being hated by the world. That is the Christian ideal; the gift of the Spirit enables Christians to attain the ideal amid conflict and despite their own weakness.

[C] Perfect Unity, Sign of the Son's Mission

In the last part of John 17, Christ's priestly prayer broadens in scope, as he prays not only for those who already belong to the little community but for all who will enter it in the future [63]. His thoughts focus here on unity. The unity he has before him is the unity that marks the life of Father and Son and makes of them a single Being. The members of the little community have received from Jesus a share in the glory that the Father had given to him. They have been given that share so that they too might be one as Father and Son are one.

It follows from this that the life of the community is chiefly devoted to showing forth the love that is manifested by unity. If the members are successful in this, they will be signs amid the world: "This is how all will know that you are my disciples, if you have love for one another" (John 13:35). In this context, Jesus once again emphasizes the opposition between the world and the disciples. The world has not known the Father; it has refused his love, rejected the One he sent. The disciples, on the other hand, have accepted both the love and the One he sent; that is why they can be children of God (1:12).

This final section of the priestly prayer may be said to sum up John's thoughts on the fulfillment of God's plan of salvation; the key words in the synthesis are love, unity, indwelling. The disciples in Jesus, and Jesus in the disciples; the disciples with Jesus in the Father; the disciples united with one another; the world being restored to the unity God intended for it when he first created it. The prayer is a hymn to the glory of God and Christ.

The Son of Man at the Father's Right Hand

This hymn of glory is addressed to the Son who has risen from the dead and ascended into heaven. It also shows us what the object of Christians' contemplation should be; they are to "see my glory" (17:24). In the vision given to him as he undergoes martyrdom, Stephen achieves this contemplation [57]. He is hated by the same world that rejected the Son and Savior; now, like Christ, he gives his life, and therefore the vision of Christ in glory, seated at the Father's side, is given to him at the moment of death. He is the first of many believers to sacrifice themselves for the glory of the Father and the Son.

The Alpha and the Omega

The second reading [60] is a contemplation of the Lord who is Alpha and Omega, the first and the last, the beginning and the end; at the same time, it is a proclamation of the Lord's coming. The Christian community is encouraged to await that coming, not in a passive way, but with the cry, "Come, Lord Jesus!"

Those who have washed their robes so that they may have access to the tree of life and may be able to enter the city gate, that is, those who have believed, been converted, and been washed of their sins in baptism, are called. They hear the Spirit and the Bride saying, "Come." Therefore, "Let the one who thirsts come forward, and the one who wants it receive the gift of life-giving water" (22:17). The image taken from the prophet Isaiah (55:1) and now used during the Advent season had acquired a sacramental meaning for the young Christian community.

The choice of such a reading at this point in the liturgy suggests a twofold attitude that we should cultivate: expectation of the Spirit to whom the Church of today addresses its appeal, "Come, Holy Spirit!" and expectation of Christ's return on the last day. For if the Spirit comes, he does so in order to lead the Church toward its completion on the final day when it encounters the Lord; the Spirit is pledge of his coming and proclaims it to the Church. The Pentecostal event we are now about to celebrate has thus a double weight of meaning: it means strength and light for the pilgrim Church; it leads us to await Christ in company with the Spirit, our Advocate and Guide as we move toward the day of Christ's return.

Pentecost Sunday

44. THE MISSION OF THE HOLY SPIRIT

Vigil Mass

We have come to the end of the fifty-day Easter Time. The day that terminates the season is not a feast of the Holy Spirit but proclaims that God has sent him and that the Church has received him as a gift. The gospel for the Vigil Mass emphasizes this point, since Jesus' allusion to the Spirit is spoken on "the last and greatest day of the feast" [69]. It was on the last day too of the fifty-day period after Easter that the gift of the Spirit was bestowed on the apostles and that they departed to give witness to the life, death, and resurrection of Jesus. Because Pentecost was so closely related to Easter (the whole fifty-day period after Easter was a single long feast), the Church adopted the practice of conferring the sacraments of Christian initiation on Pentecost on those who had not been able to receive them during the Easter Vigil. In the reformed liturgy, therefore, the "Vigil" of Pentecost has been given back its true structure as a vigil celebration.

There are four Old Testament texts [64–67], a single second reading [68], and a gospel pericope; the readings are the same in all three years of the cycle.

Babel and the Scattering of Humankind

The unity in which the world was created was not welcomed by Adam or those who came after him. The story of Babel and the scattering of humankind brings home the breaking of unity by sin [64].

The reading is well chosen, since the Spirit is he who brings back into unity what had been scattered, just as he had been present and active when the world was created in its original unity. It is quite fitting, therefore, that at the moment when the Church is about to celebrate the sending of the Spirit, she should recall the disunity and dispersion represented by the tower of Babel.

411

The descendants of Noah did not turn out any better than the human beings the Lord had earlier decided to destroy in a violent way through the Flood (Gen 6:5). In this story of the scattering of humankind at Babylon (Babel = Babylon), some scholars see a conflation of two stories, one relating to the city of Babylon, the other to the tower that was to reach the heavens. Possibly, but the exegetes generally do not see the text, in its present form, as requiring a dissection that would produce two stories; as it stands, the story is now one, even if it was shaped out of what had earlier been two stories.

The story of the destruction of Babylon and its tower comprises verses 2-5, 6b-7a, 8-9a. The emphasis here is on dispersion. The city was named Babel (*Babilu*), because its inhabitants had been ejected from it (*ibbabilu* = *cast out*, according to one etymology) and scattered throughout the world. Note the details: "They used bricks for stone, and bitumen for mortar" (v. 3); the writer is a Palestinian, and in Palestine stone and mortar were used for building. In any case, the people were forced to stop building and were scattered abroad.

The problem of languages was less important, and the populations in question perhaps did not regard it as so great a misfortune. In fact, the Egyptians sometimes thought of the multiplicity of languages as wealth from the gods.

Luke, in Acts, implicitly regards the tower of Babel as being at the source of the most profound division between humans. The Spirit comes to repair the damage, and the sign he gives on Pentecost is that listeners hear in their own language the message preached by the apostles (Acts 2:4, 8).

This first reading has been chosen, then, because the Church wishes to remind us of creation's original unity, of the division caused by sin, and of the restoration of unity by the Holy Spirit.

The Lord Speaks to Moses on Sinai

The choice of this next reading [65] is, to some extent, due to its framework or scenario. The Lord comes down in the midst of fire, and the mountain is covered with a cloud of smoke. Fire, smoke, and flames, along with thunder and lightning, are the Old Testament signs of the Lord's presence. The signs point to, while hiding, the majesty and holiness of God; they are signs that both attract and repel, for humanity wants to see God, yet to see God is to die.

Passages that speak of fire as a sign are numerous in the Old Testament (for example, Exod 3:2; 13:21; 40:38; Deut 1:33; 4:11-12, 33; 5:22; 9:15; Neh 9:12; Isa 4:5; 10:17; 31:9; 66:15, to list but a few). On Mount Horeb, Moses sees a bush that is on fire yet is not consumed (Exod 3:2); it is a sign of God's presence and is similar to the sign in today's reading. A dialogue ensues here between God and Moses. The Lord had earlier (vv. 3-6) assured Moses that if Israel proved faithful to the covenant, it would become a kingdom of priests and a holy nation. St. Peter, in his first letter (2:9), would apply these words to the baptized.

It is easy to understand why this text was chosen for the Vigil of Pentecost and easy to transpose it to the Christian sphere. In fact, it is when the text is read during the Vigil Mass that we perceive its full resonances. The Spirit of Pentecost comes in the sign of tongues of fire; he consecrates a new people and reasserts his covenant with the new kingdom of priests and holy nation that is the newborn Church.

The Spirit and Life

The third reading links the Spirit with life [66]. It records Ezekiel's vision of the dry bones that come to life and the Lord's interpretation of the vision.

The prophet is walking through a desolate place that is strewn with dried-up bones. The Spirit has brought him to this place, and now the Lord asks him how these bones may be brought back to life. The prophet's answer is inspired by faith: "Lord GOD, you alone know that" (v. 3). Because of his great faith, the prophet is bidden to pronounce an oracle in words that the Lord himself gives him. He is bidden to command the bones to become alive once more; he does so and describes what happened.

The Lord next orders Ezekiel to invoke the Spirit and to "prophesy" (a word that means not only to predict something but to bring it to pass by predicting it). He prophesied as commanded: "From the four winds come, O spirit, and breathe into these slain that they may come to life" (v. 9). The result: "they came alive and stood upright" (v. 10). The Lord explains the vision: The dry bones represent the people of Israel, who are now without hope. It is they whom the prophet is really addressing; he is to say to them in the Lord's name, "my people! I will put my spirit in you that you may live, and I will settle you upon your land; thus you shall know that I am the LORD. I have promised" (vv. 13-14).

The proclamation concerns Israel's survival and its liberation as a renewed people. In the resurrection that is depicted (supposedly situated, in the vision, in the Valley of Jehoshaphat) the Church has seen the resurrection of the dead. Both Tertullian[1] and Jerome[2] refer to the passage in the context of this doctrine. We can go a step further, however, and see in the story the Holy Spirit, who gives life and creates a new people; the dry bones that are brought to life are the Church, which is brought to life on Pentecost by the Spirit of God.

"I Will Pour out My Spirit"

In his sermon on Pentecost morning, Peter quotes a long passage from the prophet Joel (Acts 2:17-21; Joel 3:1-5). This passage constitutes the fourth of the Old Testament readings during the Vigil [67].

The text is an intricate one; the prophet is speaking of the last day and also reporting some of the catastrophes that will mark it. We are familiar with this approach, since Jesus himself uses it (Matt 24:6-9; 27:45-54; Mark 13:7; Rev 6:11-13). In the Old Testament, Amos (8:9), Isaiah (13:10), and Ezekiel (32:7) all make similar predictions of catastrophes when speaking of the Day of the Lord. The scene, then, in which we are placed is the last day, the day of judgment, when the only ones to be saved will be the just who call upon the name of the Lord; at that point the people of God will enter into its peace.

The passage from Joel also tells, however, of an outpouring of the Spirit on all humankind, a gift of the Spirit to the whole people without exception. Comings of the Spirit are frequent in the Old Testament; let us briefly review some of them. At times, the Spirit is given for the salvation of the people; a typical case is the coming of the Lord's Spirit upon the judges for the exercise of their office (Judg 3:10-11; 14:6; Isa 10:1-16; 11:2-11; Exod 35:31). At other times the Spirit is given so that people may bear witness in the form of an oracle that brings about what it predicts; we can see here the connection between the Spirit and the efficacious word (Isa 8:11; Jer 1:9-15; 20:7; Exod 3:12, 14; Amos 3:8; 7:14; and especially Isa 61:1-8, where the Servant prefigures Jesus, the Servant of the New Testament). Finally, the Spirit is also given in order to consecrate someone for a priestly service (Isa 42:1); in Isaiah 53:11 we are told that the Servant's sufferings will justify many. Jesus will later fill the role of the Servant who gives his life for the ransom of the many.

In the reading from Joel, the Spirit is given to all people, and the liturgy sees in this statement a typological prediction of Pentecost. Certain characteristics attach to this coming of the Spirit. It is universal: "I will pour out my spirit upon all flesh." It leads to prodigies, such as the gift of tongues (Acts 2:3). The Spirit also (a point placed in special relief in this passage from Joel) proclaims judgment and the end of the world. That is one aspect of the gift of the Spirit whose overall purpose is to rebuild and bring to completion.

The responsorial psalm (Ps 104) complements the readings, since it is concerned with praising God for the activity of his Spirit. The response situates the activity in a specifically Christian context: "Lord, send out your Spirit, and renew the face of the earth." The whole psalm is thereby turned into a glorification of the life-giving Holy Spirit.

The Spirit Prays for Us

We turn now to the New Testament, where St. Paul gives us a "theology" of the Holy Spirit [68]. Paul is concerned in this part of the Letter to the Romans with the reality of the Christian's condition while on earth. He speaks very concretely and makes no effort to play down the difficulties the Christian faces. At the same time, Paul is not a pessimist but, on the contrary, full of hope. The world has been rent asunder and needs to be wholly refashioned; creation in its entirety suffers and groans. So do we. But we have already received the Spirit; how, then, is our deep interior division to be explained?

St. Paul's answer is that we have indeed received the Spirit, but the deliverance of our bodies is something we still await. We have been saved, but only in hope; what we hope for is itself unseen, and we must await it with perseverance. At the same time, we are creatures who lack a great deal. In fact, of ourselves we are not even capable of crying out to the Father. Here is where the Spirit intervenes in his role of Advocate.

The Christian's condition, then, does differ from that of others, because a Christian has received the Spirit yet remains weak. Even after the work of redemption has been accomplished, we experience a constant desolating weakness that is inherent in our nature (Rom

6:19). That will continue to be our situation until the moment when we are glorified with Christ (Rom 8:11).

Meanwhile, the Spirit intercedes for us. We cannot pray? The Spirit prays in our stead! This prayer of the Spirit in believers is part of the carrying out of God's plan of salvation: the Spirit "intercedes for the holy ones according to God's will" (Rom 8:27). The Spirit's prayer can be summed up in a "Thy will be done"—a sentiment that the Spirit accepts and proclaims in us and with us. The Spirit, therefore, helps us to pray in order that God's plan may be carried out and in order that we may be able to collaborate in the salvation that is the Lord's gift.

"Rivers of Living Water Will Flow from Within"

The gospel situates us on the solemn day that marks the ending of the feast of Booths [69]. The book of Leviticus tells us how this feast was celebrated (23:33-43). We know that the celebration lasted for a week, that it was a time of rest, like a lengthy Sabbath, and that it involved gathering for worship. The people built huts of branches as a reminder of the years their ancestors had spent in the wilderness. There was also a procession in which the marchers carried palms and fruits. At a later period, the practice of offering a libation each morning was introduced, while in the evenings the temple was illuminated.[3]

The illumination of the temple and the morning libation are important for the understanding of the gospel text in which Jesus speaks of rivers of living water and of himself as the Light of the world. The mention of water occurs in the short passage read at Mass during the Pentecost Vigil.

When we read this passage, we are reminded, of course, of Jesus' conversation with the Samaritan woman (John 4:11-14). Elsewhere in the Fourth Gospel, Jesus says, "whoever comes to me will never hunger, and whoever believes in me will never thirst" (6:35). Now, in today's pericope, he says, "Let anyone who thirsts come to me and drink. As Scripture says: *Rivers of living water will flow from within*" (7:37-38), words that also remind us of the book of Isaiah (55:1, 3).

The evangelist here refers to and quotes Scripture, but a search of the Old Testament has not discovered such a text. Perhaps the words are intended as a reference to Ezekiel (47:1-12), who speaks of the water that flows from the temple and, in its passage to the Dead Sea, becomes a stream on whose banks trees grow. Perhaps they refer rather to the rock from which water flowed in the desert (Pss 78:16; 105:41).[4] Both hypotheses can be defended; in fact, both can be accepted simultaneously, since they are not opposed to each other but can be harmonized. Christ, after all, is regarded in the New Testament as the spiritual Rock (1 Cor 10:4), and he is also the Temple of the last times (John 2:20-22).

John himself comments briefly on Jesus' words, telling us that the rivers of living water symbolize the Holy Spirit who will be given to those who believe in Jesus. Water as a symbol of the Spirit is, of course, not John's invention; it is already to be found in the Jewish tradition. In the book of Isaiah, for example, we read: "I will pour out water upon the thirsty ground, / streams upon the dry land; / I will pour out my spirit upon your offspring, / my blessing upon your descendants" (44:3).

In John's view, however, the water is a symbol not simply of power or strength but of a person, namely, the Spirit whom the Father sends: "There was, of course, no Spirit yet, because Jesus had not yet been glorified." The death, resurrection, and ascension of Jesus will introduce a new stage in the history of salvation, for they will lead to the sending of the Spirit who slakes the thirst of believers.

Mass during the Day

"Receive the Holy Spirit. I Send You"

The gospel read during the Mass on Pentecost day tells us of Jesus' appearance to his apostles in Jerusalem on Easter evening [72]. He is suddenly there, even though the doors were locked, as the evangelist notes; he shows his hands and side to his disciples. Should we not connect this action with the greeting Jesus gives his disciples, "Peace be with you"? This is not an ordinary greeting. In John's view, it is connected with the wounds, because peace flows from the passion and resurrection. (The idea of Christ's display of his wounds as a way of assuring the disciples of his identity is Lukan [see 24:39] rather than Johannine.)

Now Christ "sends" his disciples. In doing so, he uses the kind of formula we find frequently in the Fourth Gospel: "As the Father has sent me, so I send you" (v. 21; see the many other formulas that establish a parallel between the activity of the Father in relation to the Son and the activity of the Son in relation to his disciples: for example, 6:57; 10:15; 15:9; 17:18). For John, however, such formulas express more than a simple parallelism; they do more than affirm the divinity of Christ on the grounds that he acts as the Father acts. They are also a theological statement that believers share in the very life that is common to Father and Son.

The formula here ends rather abruptly: "I send you." He is not sending them to a place but giving them a mission that they must carry out. What is the mission? It is that of forgiving sins, as Christ immediately makes clear. Since, however, Christ draws a parallel between his action in sending the disciples and the Father's action in sending him, he is also telling the disciples that they are to continue the work that Jesus himself has been doing for the reconstruction of the world. They too are to do the Father's work. As Jesus reveals the Father and makes him known, so the disciples are to reveal Jesus and make him known.

The passage confronts us with a problem: How is the giving of the Spirit here to be related to Pentecost?

"They Were All Filled with the Holy Spirit"

St. Luke tells us in today's first reading of how the Spirit came upon the disciples as they were gathered in the upper room [70]. In describing this coming of the Spirit of the Lord, he uses the classical language of the Old Testament. We saw earlier in this chapter how descriptive traits keep recurring throughout the Old Testament: the rush of wind, the fire that divides into tongues and rests on each individual. As a result of this descent of the Spirit, the disciples proclaim the marvelous deeds of God, and listeners hear them in their own language.

Luke thus puts the coming of the Spirit on Pentecost. John, however, speaks of the Spirit being given on Easter evening. Is there a contradiction here between Acts and John? Has John conflated Pentecost and Easter? According to some exegetes, John is not conflating the two events, but neither is he distinguishing them; he is interested, rather, in giving expression to the paschal mystery as a unitary whole.[5]

We should note that Luke too has an anticipation of Pentecost inasmuch as he speaks of the apostles having been chosen by Christ "through the holy Spirit" (Acts 1:2). It seems more accurate, therefore, to say that these various actions and gifts of the Spirit (including John 20:22) were all a preparation for the definitive coming of the Spirit. When we say that the Church was born on Pentecost, we are undoubtedly simplifying somewhat. After all, the Church was also born from the side of Christ on Calvary, while the various appearances of Christ after his resurrection were so many stages in the formation of the Church. The Church was born on Calvary and born of his resurrection, no less than she was born of the Spirit on Pentecost. The whole first chapter of the Acts of the Apostles is concerned with this gradual formation that was going on even before the Spirit was poured out on Pentecost.

We may say that St. Luke lays greater emphasis on the historical facts, while John is more concerned with the close connection between Calvary, the resurrection, the appearances, and the gift of the Spirit on Pentecost. As for ourselves, it is important to be aware of how the liturgy understands the gospel text that it links to the account of Pentecost and to the second reading, in which St. Paul reminds us that we were baptized in one Spirit in order to form one Body.

Baptized in the One Spirit to Form a Single Body

Here, as on other occasions, the liturgy transcends, without ignoring, exegetical difficulties and presents the Scripture texts in its own way so as to bring them to life for us.

In the second reading St. Paul tells us of his experience of the Spirit in the Church [71]. He describes the experience by referring to the Spirit's various manifestations, but he also insists on the unity of the Spirit who thus manifests himself in a variety of ways. He seems to connect the diversification of the manifestations with the diverse functions that are needed for the Church's life, but despite the diversity, all the activities have their origin in one and the same Spirit.

We receive various gifts that manifest the Spirit, and we receive them for the good of the community as a whole. When, in this First Letter to the Corinthians, Paul explains the diversity of gifts and offices in the Church, he shows how it is the very richness of the Church's unity that leads to a diversity of spiritual gifts. There is, then, a plurality of gifts, but they exist for the sake of the unity and perfection of a Body that is one. That is why Paul can use the image of the human body to describe the diversity that the unity of the Church entails. There is but one Spirit and there is but one Body of Christ. We have all drunk of the same Spirit and we all form a single Body through our baptism.

In the gospel pericope for today, John shows us Christ in the act of conferring a special charism on the apostles: the charism of the forgiveness of sins and of going forth to preach. In Acts, St. Luke speaks of the coming of the Spirit, a coming that relates to the Church insofar as she addresses herself to the entire world and actually reaches all nations by speaking their various tongues; here the divided world is reunited, and a sign is given that offsets the sign of Babel, now reduced to a simple memory.

From this time forth, Christians can always be mindful of the outpouring of the Spirit on the apostles. They need only recall their own baptism, and they will understand what the Spirit wants of those who are their fellow Christians, according to the gift each one has for the good of the whole Body. They must also learn what special gift they themselves have that can be put at the service of all. The gift of Pentecost is not meant to be a stimulus to triumphalism. On the contrary, it is the stimulus for the Church to realize that she must communicate the gifts of the Spirit to each of her members and that she must preserve these gifts and encourage their use for the good of all.

The collect of this Mass expresses succinctly the mystery of Pentecost as a gift to the Church for the sake of the world. The Church, which has the Spirit for her guide, is above all a catholic, or all-embracing, Church: "O God, who by the mystery of today's great feast sanctify your whole Church in every people and nation, pour out, we pray, the gifts of the Holy Spirit across the face of the earth and, with the divine grace that was at work when the Gospel was first proclaimed, fill now once more the hearts of believers."

The preface emphasizes the connection between Pentecost and the paschal mystery: "For, bringing your Paschal Mystery to completion, you bestowed the Holy Spirit today on those you made your adopted children by uniting them to your Only Begotten Son." Then, picking up the theme of the second reading, it adds: "Therefore, overcome with paschal joy, every land, every people exults in your praise."

The prayer after Communion reminds us that the Spirit is permanently at work in the Church, especially through the sacraments: "O God, who bestow heavenly gifts upon your Church, safeguard, we pray, the grace you have given, that the gift of the Holy Spirit poured out upon her may retain all its force and that this spiritual food may gain her abundance of eternal redemption."

The Paschal Mystery

Now that we have made our way through the major seasons of the Christian year—Advent, Nativity and Epiphany, Lent, and Easter Time—we are in a position to appreciate better the unity of the paschal mystery. We can see that everything in the Church's life has this mystery for its center, leads into it, and depends on it. The celebration of the incarnation would simply be the recalling of a historical event if we did not know that the incarnation is the necessary starting point for Christ's carrying out of the Father's will that he offer a sacrifice on humanity's behalf for the sake of the covenant. We are also better able to grasp the mystery as a whole, comprising as it does the death, resurrection, and ascension of Christ and the sending of the Spirit. That is the total mystery that the Church lives out in each of her members, and the only real purpose of the liturgy is to assure the actualization of it.

In his first sermon on Pentecost, St. Leo the Great speaks as follows:

> This day contains within itself the great mysteries of the old and new economies, showing clearly that the law had foretold grace and that grace brought the fulfillment of the law. It was on the fiftieth day after the sacrifice of the lamb that the law was given on Mount Sinai to the Hebrews who had been liberated from Egypt. So too, once Christ had suffered and the true Lamb of God had been slain, it was on the fiftieth day after his resurrection that the Holy Spirit came upon the apostles and the multitude of believers. The alert Christian will readily see that the initial events of the Old Testament served the gospel in its beginnings and that the second covenant had its origin in the same Spirit who had instituted the first.[6]

There is an interesting passage in the saint's second sermon on Pentecost in which he insists that the gift given on Pentecost is not an absolute beginning but rather a new outpouring of grace:

> Let us not doubt that when on Pentecost the Holy Spirit filled the Lord's disciples, he was not giving his gift for the first time but was rather extending a gift already given. The patriarchs, the prophets, the priests,

and all the saints of earlier times were nourished by the same sanctifying spirit. No sacrament was ever instituted, no mystery ever celebrated, that did not involve his grace. The power of his gifts had ever
been the same, though the gifts had not previously been given in so
great a measure.[7]

The Spirit Today

The sequence for Pentecost, though grandiose and perhaps even
somewhat outmoded in style, sings compellingly of the Church's joy
and of all that the world owes to the Holy Spirit. The Spirit's activity
has not ceased. Pentecost was doubtless a climactic moment in which
the Spirit showed how generous his gifts are, but, as St. Leo has just
told us, the Spirit had acted in the world before Pentecost and he has
not ceased to act since then. The constitutions and decrees of the
Second Vatican Council are filled with references to the Holy Spirit;
in fact, a study of the theology of the Holy Spirit as found in these
documents would be most worthwhile.

We have the impression that the Catholics of our day restrict the
activity of the Spirit to the elaboration of dogma and to the making of
decisions with regard to the present circumstances of the Church's life.
They too readily forget the constant activity of the Spirit in the sacraments. Every Christian lives under the influence of the Spirit given in
baptism and confirmation. It is the Spirit who strengthens our faith and
unity each time we receive the Eucharist. The epiclesis that has been
made a part of the new eucharistic prayers should remind us that the
Spirit acts in the Eucharist not only to transform the bread and wine
but also to intensify our faith and deepen our unity within the Church.

The Spirit also acts in priestly ordination to give the person called
the power to actualize the mysteries of Christ. He is present in the
sacrament of marriage to give the partners the strength and courage
they need for fidelity to their mutual union in imitation of the union
of Christ and his Church. At every moment, in fact, we are permeated
by the Spirit. There is no prayer meeting and no Liturgy of the Word
in which the Spirit is not actively enabling us to pray and converse
with the Lord present among us by the power of the same Spirit, for
it is the Spirit who brings the Scripture text to life. It is the Spirit who
enables us to say, "Father!"

45. THE WEEKDAY READINGS OF EASTER TIME

The readings for the weekdays of Easter Time are chosen according to a principle that allows little scope for a coherent commentary. As on the Sundays of Ordinary Time, one gospel is read continuously. On these Sundays, however, the other reading suggests the viewpoint from which the Church reads each of the successive gospel pericopes. But on the weekdays of Easter Time the first reading cannot serve this purpose, since, along with the continuous reading of St. John's gospel, there is also a continuous reading of the Acts of the Apostles. The two series of readings advance side by side but without any intrinsic relation to each other.

This practice is the renewal of an ancient tradition that has been followed in almost all the other liturgies. The reading of the Acts of the Apostles is quite suited to this period of the Church year, since it brings us into vivid contact with the Church of the risen Christ, who has now sent his Spirit upon it. Similarly, there is great profit to be drawn from the reading of the Fourth Gospel during this season. We must not, however, try to correlate the two readings; there is no specific connection between them. The spiritual fruit that we are offered consists of a global vision, and on this there is no point in trying to offer a commentary, since such a commentary would amount to commentaries on the Fourth Gospel and on the Acts of the Apostles.

Even if we were to attempt a commentary on these two books of the New Testament, it would contribute nothing as far as an understanding of the liturgical celebration goes, since the Fourth Gospel and the Acts of the Apostles are not related to each other on each successive day in accordance with some pattern that the liturgy intends to impose. All we can do here, then, is to refer the reader to good commentaries on the two books and to urge the reading of the texts in the light of Easter and the paschal mystery.

Octave of Easter

As we read the texts for the octave, we can at least note that while the Acts of the Apostles is read continuously, the texts from the gospels are each chosen, not by reference to Acts, but by reference to the resurrection celebrated a few days before. To this extent the octave does form a whole and can be presented as such.

The gospel pericopes [74–84] all relate various appearances of the risen Christ to such witnesses as the holy women, the disciples at Emmaus, and the disciples on the shore of the Sea of Tiberias. The fact of being chosen as a witness always requires of the one chosen the giving of testimony to others, since the resurrection is Good News that must be proclaimed to the world. The resurrection also looks to the past, inasmuch as it is the fulfillment of the prophecies relating to the history of salvation.

The readings from the Acts of the Apostles [73–83] emphasize the apostles' role as witnesses of the resurrection. They cannot remain silent about what they have seen [83] but must preach Christ dead and risen [79], in whom alone salvation is to be found [81]. It is in the name of this Jesus that Peter heals a paralytic [77]. Let everyone therefore be converted, begin to believe, and be baptized [75].

Second Week

We may, in a similar way, attempt to pull together the teaching of each of the other weeks, as presented in the continuous reading of the Fourth Gospel and the Acts of the Apostles. We need not, however, expect any great unity of thought that would bind the two series of readings together, since the Church has not chosen the texts in view of a theme.

The gospel pericopes of this week continue to show Christ to us: he comes from God and enables us to know God [88]; God sent him so that he might save the world [90], for the Father has now put everything into his hands [92]. It is the risen Christ who continues to secure the salvation of the world, and that is why he shows his disciples how real his resurrection was and how real his risen body now is [94]; that is why he walks on the water [96]. If we too want to enter upon the way of salvation and reach the kingdom, we must be reborn of water and the Spirit [86].

The Acts of the Apostles shows us the new life of the young community. We see the community praying for the power the Spirit gives so that Christians may proclaim the Good News [85]. Deep love binds the community together; the faithful have but one mind and one heart [87]. The apostles, for their part, cannot but testify to what they have witnessed [91]; they may have to suffer imprisonment, but that will not prevent them from continuing their teaching [89]. The choice of seven men for stewardship functions ensures the proper organization of the Church's life [95].

Third Week

Each Christian's life comes from the risen Christ, but that life must then be focused on eternal life and the demands the Lord makes of us—such is the teaching of the gospel pericopes during this week. We must look for the food that does not perish [98]; it comes from God our Father [100]. Christ's flesh is truly food [106], for he is the living Bread that has come down from heaven [104]. Anyone who sees the Son has eternal life [102]. Christ is thus the center of our lives; to whom else shall we go [108]?

The Acts of the Apostles shows us the ongoing witnessing activity of the disciples: they proclaim the Good News everywhere [101]. Philip baptizes an Ethiopian [103] while Paul proves to be an instrument God has chosen for the conversion of the Gentiles [105]. The Church is thus continually growing under the guidance of the Spirit [107]. The obligation to preach the Good News may even bring a person to martyrdom: the wisdom and the Spirit of God fill Stephen [97], and he gives his life in testimony to the message entrusted to him [99].

Fourth Week

The gospel pericopes emphasize the fact that the person of Jesus is our sole way to salvation. He and the Father are one [112], so that whoever sees him sees the Father [120]. He is the Gate [110], the Light that has come into the world [114], the Way, the Truth, and the Life [118]. Those whom he sends represent him [116].

The readings from Acts show us Jesus, who is of the race of David [115], as risen from the dead [117]. This proclamation of the person of Jesus leads to conversions among the Gentiles [109–19], even among the Greeks [111]. The Church faces a continuing need to organize itself for its missionary task, and Barnabas and Paul are chosen under the inspiration of the Spirit [113].

Fifth Week

During this week the gospel pericopes emphasize the special situation of Christians: they are called upon to remain in Christ so that they may bear fruit [126] and find joy [128], for Christ is the giver of true peace [124]. To remain in Christ means loving one another [130]. The disciples, to whom the Spirit now teaches everything [124], are so permeated by the life of Christ that, like the original disciples whom Jesus chose, they no longer belong to this world [132].

The readings from the Acts of the Apostles continue the story of the new Church's life. She is ever faithful to her mission of preaching that people must abandon idols [121], while the community also keeps constantly before it the memory of what God has done for it [123]. The problem of the conversion of the Gentiles is resolved, as is the problem of circumcision [125]. Missioners are not to lay excessive burdens on the Gentiles who are converted [127]; in fact, nothing extra that is unnecessary is to be required of them [129]. The Church continues to grow; Paul and Luke set off on a missionary journey [131].

Sixth Week

In the gospel, Jesus announces his departure [140], which is necessary if the Spirit is to come [136]. The Spirit will bear witness to Jesus [134] and will guide the disciples to the truth in its entirety [138]. The disciples have now found their true way: The Father loves them because they have loved Jesus and have believed in him [144]; no one will be able to take their joy from them [142].

The community's life is focused chiefly on the mission of witnessing. Thus Paul and Silas, while in prison, preach conversion [135] and continue to proclaim Jesus [137]; each Sabbath Paul addresses the congregation in the synagogue [139]; the Lord also sends him to the Corinthians [141]. The witness of the apostles is so convincing that it leads others likewise to bear witness, for example, Apollos the Jew, who preaches to his fellow Jews about Christ [143]. New members are constantly entering the community, for example, Lydia and her household [133].

Seventh Week

Jesus reaches the end of his time on earth and prepares to sacrifice his life. His priestly prayer is broad in scope: May the Father glorify him, now that his mission is accomplished, so that his disciples may be glorified in him [148]. His disciples must seek unity above and before all else [152] and be one as Jesus and his Father are one [150]. They must not be fearful or downcast, for Christ has conquered the world; this should fill them with courage [146]. To secure this unity and renew this courage, the disciples need a leader who will represent Jesus in this world and be the shepherd of his sheep [154]. John ends his gospel by asserting his own apostleship: he is one who has seen the risen Jesus, and he bears witness to him [156].

The Acts of the Apostles continues the story of the community's missionary activities: Paul baptizes and bestows the Spirit at Ephesus [145], where he also preaches a sermon in which he asserts that God has the power to build up the community and give its members a share in his heritage [149]. Paul continues to bear witness to Christ and is ordered to go to Rome [151]. He never stops preaching the resurrection of Christ as the center of Christian faith [153], for his great desire is to carry out fully the ministry Christ gave him [147]. He will die at Rome after proclaiming the kingdom of God [155].

The two books that are thus continuously read during the weeks of Easter Time have the power to enable us to grasp vividly what the Lord did and is still continuing to do. When we read the Acts of the Apostles, we are reading our family history, but not simply as though it concerned only past events. The Gospel of John, with its many deeply moving passages, brings home to us the reality of what we are, for Jesus' words, addressed long ago to his first disciples, are addressed now to us.

46. MISSAL PRAYERS DURING EASTER TIME

It will be worth our while to take a look, even a hurried and superficial one, at the various prayers said in the Masses of Easter Time. Our purpose is to discern the chief points of theology that the Church is emphasizing during the season.

The Liturgical Mystery

The paschal mystery is not simply a memory but a present, transforming reality. Each year, therefore, we must ask the Lord for the power to live Easter Time as we should:

> As we recall year by year the mysteries by which, through the restoration of its original dignity, human nature has received the hope of rising again, we earnestly beseech your mercy, Lord, that what we celebrate in faith we may possess in unending love.[1]

The Pasch is a present reality and not a mere memory. It is a continuation of redemption, and God must help us if we are to keep it present, not only at the moment when it is celebrated, but throughout our Christian lives, which are meant to be paschal lives:

> Grant, we pray, almighty God, that we, who have celebrated the paschal festivities, may by your gift hold fast to them in the way that we live our lives.[2]

The mystery thus present has transforming power and continues to work its effects in us:

> Grant, almighty God, that we may celebrate with heartfelt devotion these days of joy, which we keep in honor of the risen Lord, and that what we relive in remembrance we may always hold to in what we do.[3]

> Grant, we pray, O Lord, that we may always find delight in these paschal mysteries, so that the renewal constantly at work within us may be the cause of our unending joy.[4]

The transformation we undergo is entirely the work of the Spirit; he it is who disposes us to do the Father's will:

> May your Spirit, O Lord, we pray, imbue us powerfully with spiritual gifts, that he may give us a mind pleasing to you and graciously conform us to your will.[5]

It is also the power of the Spirit that enables us to discern just what God's will for us is:

> May the power of the Holy Spirit come to us, we pray, O Lord, that we may keep your will faithfully in mind and express it in a devout way of life.[6]

We have now passed from our former world and live among the signs of the new age:

> Hear in your compassion our prayers, O Lord, that, as we have been brought from things of the past to new mysteries, so with former ways left behind, we may be made new in holiness of mind.[7]

Faith and baptism are the source of our rebirth and renewal:

> Accept, O Lord, we pray, the oblations of your people (and of those you have brought to new birth), that, renewed by confession of your name and by Baptism, they may attain unending happiness.[8]

Baptism purifies us, and the celebration of the paschal mystery reinvigorates our faith:

> God of everlasting mercy, who in the very recurrence of the paschal feast kindle the faith of the people you have made your own, increase, we pray, the grace you have bestowed, that all may grasp and rightly understand in what font they have been washed, by whose Spirit they have been reborn, by whose Blood they have been redeemed.[9]

The prayers of Easter Time call attention to the action in us of the paschal liturgy:

> Look upon your Church, O God, with unfailing love and favor, so that, renewed by the paschal mysteries, she may come to the glory of the resurrection.[10]

Those who have been initiated into the Christian mysteries are now capable of leading a transfigured life:

> Graciously be present to your people, we pray, O Lord, and lead those you have imbued with heavenly mysteries to pass from former ways to newness of life.[11]

The ultimate reason for this possibility is that we are nourished by the Easter sacraments; they are the foundation of our abiding transformation in Christ:

> Pour out on us, O Lord, the Spirit of your love, and in your kindness make those you have nourished by this paschal Sacrament one in mind and heart.[12]

It is, therefore, not only at the moment of the celebration that we are touched by God's renewing grace; the effects of the Easter mystery are constantly being produced in us:

> O God, who for the salvation of the world brought about the paschal sacrifice, be favorable to the supplications of your people, so that Christ our High Priest, interceding on our behalf, may by his likeness to ourselves bring us reconciliation, and by his equality with you, free us from our sins.[13]

Some of the postcommunion prayers take up this last theme but connect it specifically with the Eucharist:

> Almighty ever-living God, who restore us to eternal life in the Resurrection of Christ, increase in us, we pray, the fruits of this paschal Sacrament and pour into our hearts the strength of this saving food.[14]

Some prayers go even further in linking Easter and the sacraments by seeing the latter as the means of our redemption and our participation in the divine nature:

> Hear, O Lord, our prayers, that this most holy exchange, by which you have redeemed us, may bring your help in this present life and ensure for us eternal gladness.[15]

> O God, who by the wonderful exchange effected in this sacrifice have made us partakers of the one supreme Godhead, grant, we pray, that, as we have come to know your truth, we may make it ours by a worthy way of life.[16]

All this is not independent of us and our inner attitudes. On the contrary, our minds and hearts must be fully involved in the celebration and must truly participate in the paschal mystery:

> Grant us, Lord, we pray, that, being rightly conformed to the paschal mysteries, what we celebrate in joy may protect and save us with perpetual power.[17]

Victory over Sin and Death

The prayers at times present the "negative" side of the paschal mystery, that is, the abandonment or elimination of a past situation so as to make possible the creation of a new being. The negative aspect (destruction of sin and death) and the positive aspect (rebirth, new life, glory) are not always brought together in the prayer. We shall therefore illustrate each aspect separately.

We are liberated from our errors and sins, from death and a corrupt world:

> Almighty ever-living God, let us feel your compassion more readily during these days when, by your gift, we have known it more fully, so that those you have freed from the darkness of error may cling more firmly to the teachings of your truth.[18]

> His death is our ransom from death.[19]

Because Christ has conquered, we are freed and share in his conquest:

> For the Lord Jesus, the King of glory, conqueror of sin and death, ascended (today) to the highest heavens . . . not to distance himself from our lowly state but that we, his members, might be confident of following where He, our Head and Founder, has gone before.[20]

He has destroyed the old order;[21] by being sacrificed he has conquered death,[22] that is, by dying, he has destroyed death itself.[23] Easter is for us, as it was for the Israelites, a night of liberation.[24]

A New Being

Far more attention is given in the prayers to the positive side of the paschal mystery. We are a new creation; we are beings made new by the Lord's paschal mystery. Some prayers simply state the fact without giving the reasons for the renewal and without specifying its nature. They simply emphasize that we are now new people. Moreover, the renewal affects not humanity alone but the whole of creation:

> We pray, O Lord, that the reverent reception of the Sacrament of your Son may cleanse us from our old ways and transform us into a new creation.[25]

The paschal mystery is the source of our rebirth to a new life, and the Holy Spirit is the one who effects the transformation.[26] In a literal sense, we are made new creatures along with the rest of the created order.[27] Our being is wholly renewed.[28]

We experience a new birth[29] and become new people.[30]

Adoption

The goal of the whole history of salvation is to make us God's adopted sons and daughters. That is the viewpoint of the prayers during Easter Time; they contain many references to this adoption.

Sometimes the adoption is linked to faith, freedom, and eternal life:

> O God, by whom we are redeemed and receive adoption, look graciously upon your beloved sons and daughters, that those who believe in Christ may receive true freedom and an everlasting inheritance.[31]

Other prayers remind us that humankind had at one time possessed the rank and dignity of God's children but had lost it; God's action, then, was really one of restoration:

> May your people exult for ever, O God, in renewed youthfulness of spirit, so that, rejoicing now in the restored glory of our adoption, we may look forward in confident hope to the rejoicing of the day of resurrection.[32]

Sometimes our adoption is seen as a grace contributing to the growth of the Church:

> Almighty, ever-living God, . . . through sacred adoption increase the children of your promise.[33]

Another prayer of the Easter Vigil touches on the same theme:

> increase the children of your promise.[34]

Adoption is given bolder expression in the alternate prayer for the beginning of the Good Friday service. Here the Church asks that we become like God's own Son:

> O God, who by the Passion of Christ your Son, our Lord, abolished the death inherited from ancient sin by every succeeding generation, grant that just as, being conformed to him, we have borne by the law of nature the image of the man of earth, so by the sanctification of grace we may bear the image of the Man of heaven.[35]

Adoption is a gift already bestowed on us. If, however, we are to live as God's children should, then our own inner attitudes must progressively deepen and become more perfect:

> bring, we pray, to perfection in our hearts the spirit of adoption as your sons and daughters.[36]

The adoption means a sharing in the divine nature. The prayers that speak of it link this sharing with our sharing in the Eucharist:

> O God, who by the wonderful exchange effected in this sacrifice have made us partakers of the one supreme Godhead, grant, we pray, that, as we have come to know your truth, we may make it ours by a worthy way of life.[37]

In this context, the ascension of Christ into heaven has special meaning for Christians, being a sign that they are already, in a measure, divinized:

> For after his Resurrection he plainly appeared to all his disciples and was taken up to heaven in their sight, that he might make us sharers in his divinity.[38]

Through adoption, our human nature is not only restored to its pristine condition; it is even exalted beyond that:

> O God, who restore human nature to yet greater dignity than at its beginnings, look upon the amazing mystery of your loving kindness.[39]

One prayer looks even beyond humanity to the world at large when it speaks of the effects of redemption:

> O God, who in the abasement of your Son have raised up a fallen world, fill your faithful with holy joy.[40]

The paschal mystery, then, has truly wrought a change in us. It has sanctified us:

> Remember your mercies, O Lord, and with your eternal protection sanctify your servants, for whom Christ your Son, by the shedding of his Blood, established the Paschal Mystery.[41]

It has also made us so like to Christ that we have already been clothed in his immortality:

> O God, . . . look with favor on those you have chosen and clothe with blessed immortality those reborn through the Sacrament of Baptism.[42]

The Baptized People

All these graces are not only given to us as individuals but meant to form a people. The kingdom is open to those reborn of water and the Spirit:

> O God, who open wide the gates of the heavenly Kingdom to those reborn of water and the Holy Spirit, pour out on your servants an increase of the grace you have bestowed.[43]

The reference here is to the whole baptized people, who are renewed by the joy of the resurrection;[44] the whole Church is the subject of God's sanctifying action.[45] Christ, the Head, is now glorified, and the Church, his Body, shares his glory and is advancing toward the completion of that glorification:

> Accept, O Lord, the prayers of your faithful with the sacrificial offerings, that through these acts of devotedness we may pass over to the glory of heaven.[46]

In her celebration of the paschal mystery, the Church prays that God's people in its entirety may enter the glory of heaven:

Almighty ever-living God, lead us to a share in the joys of heaven, so that the humble flock may reach where the brave Shepherd has gone before.[47]

Created Anew for Resurrection and Eternal Life

We have been created anew, and the change that has been worked in us, making us adoptive children and sharers in the divine life, is leading us to our own resurrection and to eternal life:

Almighty ever-living God, who restore us to eternal life in the Resurrection of Christ . . .[48]

Christ's resurrection has thus become ours; for us individually, however, the resurrection is still an object of hope:

. . . rejoicing now in the restored glory of our adoption, we may look forward in confident hope to the rejoicing of the day of resurrection.[49]

The resurrection certainly lies ahead as an objective we can attain, but our weakness is also a fact, and the resurrection is a grace:

grant us, your servants, to attain the grace of the resurrection.[50]

Our Victory

The resurrection, in which we became sharers through baptism when we passed from death to life,[51] is for us, as it was for Christ, a victory:

For the Lord Jesus, the King of glory, conqueror of sin and death, ascended (today) to the highest heavens.[52]

Or again:

he is the sacrificial Victim who dies no more, the Lamb, once slain, who lives for ever.[53]

We share this victory with Christ:

the Ascension of Christ your Son is our exaltation.[54]

It is a victory that should shine out in our lives and be visible to those around us because of our outlook and conduct:

> Enable us, we pray, almighty God, to proclaim the power of the risen Lord.[55]

The reason is that Christ's victory, which is the condition of ours, is a victory that opens the door to eternal life for us:

> O God, who on this day, through your Only Begotten Son, have conquered death and unlocked for us the path to eternity . . .[56]

47. THE EASTER VIGIL IN OTHER LITURGIES

There is no point in printing a table of the readings found in the older Latin liturgies for the paschal Triduum and for Easter Time. Such a table would show us little that is different in any significant way.

The Würzburg Lectionary[1] provides readings for nine Sundays after the octave Sunday of Easter; not all of these could have been used, since at no period was there ever so long an Easter Time. The readings continue the reading from the letters of Peter and the Gospel of John. The Murbach Lectionary[2] has almost exactly the same list of readings as are to be found in the epistolary and evangeliary of Würzburg. The Missal of 1570 in turn adopted almost without exception the readings proposed by the Murbach Lectionary.

On the Milanese and Gallican liturgies, it is quite difficult to express an opinion, since the readings are presented in various ways by a number of lectionaries and sacramentaries; on some days no readings are indicated. The same is true of the Spanish liturgy.

This is not the place for suggesting explanations of such phenomena as the one just mentioned; it is far better to point out what may be still useful and manifests some real originality. For this reason, we have decided to limit ourselves to a list of the readings used in the Roman liturgy of the Easter Vigil until the first of the recent reforms (1955); a list of the readings for the Vigil in the Byzantine liturgy; and, finally, a list of the Vigil readings in the Coptic liturgy.

The current reform has considerably enriched the lectionary for Easter Time. There is nothing to be gained by printing the far less substantial lists of readings from the Würzburg Lectionary and Evangeliary, especially since it is difficult to see what principle was at work. Why, for example, should the so-called Catholic letters be read during Easter Time? It looks as if their introduction into this season was due to an early reform of the lectionary; the reformers realized that certain books of Scripture were not being read and decided to get them in on the Sundays of Easter Time. This would also explain why readings are provided for nine Sundays after Low Sunday in the Würzburg Lectionary.[3]

The Vigil Readings in the Roman Liturgy of 1570

1. Genesis 1:1-31; 2:1-2 Creation.
2. Genesis 5:32–8:21 The Flood.
3. Genesis 22:1-19 The sacrifice of Isaac.
4. Exodus 14:24-31; 15:1 Crossing of the Red Sea.
5. Isaiah 54:17; 55:1-11 Come and draw water.
6. Baruch 3:9-38 Praise of wisdom.
7. Ezekiel 37:1-14 The dry bones come alive.
8. Isaiah 4:1-6 The remnant of Israel; the vine.
9. Exodus 12:1-11 The Passover lamb.
10. Jonah 3:1-10 Jonah at Nineveh.
11. Deuteronomy 31:22-30 Last words of Moses.
12. Daniel 3:1-24 The youths in the fiery furnace.

Byzantine Liturgy[4]

1. Genesis 1 Creation.
2. Isaiah 60:1-16 The glory of the new Jerusalem.
3. Exodus 12:1-11 The Passover lamb.
4. Jonah 1–4 Story of Jonah.
5. Joshua 5:10-16 Circumcision of the Hebrews.
6. Exodus 13:20–15:19 The pillar of cloud; the covenant.
7. Wisdom 3:8-15 Remnant of Israel.
8. 1 Kings 17:8-24 Raising of widow's son to life.
9. Isaiah 61:10–62:5 Resurrection of Jerusalem.
10. Genesis 22:1-18 Sacrifice of Isaac.
11. Isaiah 61:1-10 Mission of the redeemer.
12. 2 Kings 4:8-27 Elisha revives a child.
13. Isaiah 63:11–64:5 Divine vengeance.
14. Jeremiah 31 Restoration of Israel.
15. Daniel 3:1-56 The youths in the fiery furnace.

Coptic Liturgy[5]

1. Gospel of John (entire).
2. Deuteronomy 32:39-43 Canticle of Moses.
3. Isaiah 60:1-7 Glory of the new Jerusalem.
4. Isaiah 42:5-17 Song of the Suffering Servant.
5. Isaiah 49:13-23 Renewal of Jerusalem.
6. Jeremiah 31:23-38 Restoration of Jerusalem.
7. Habakkuk 3 The prophet's prayer.
8. Zachariah 2:10-13 Liberation of Zion.
9. Isaiah 49:6-11 The Servant, light to the nations.
10. Wisdom 5:1-17 Remorse of the wicked who did not recognize the just man.
11. Psalm 7:7-9 The persecuted just man.
12. Psalm 11:6 The Lord saves the poor man.
13. Psalm 23:7-10 Triumphal entrance song of the Lord.
14. Psalm 46:6-9 The Lord, King of Israel and the world.
15. Psalm 75:9-10 Hymn to the awesome and conquering Lord.
16. Psalm 67:19-34 The glorious epic of Israel.
17. Psalm 77:65-66 History of the Chosen People.
18. Psalm 81:1-8 The Lord's judgment against wicked judges.
19. Psalm 95:1-2, 10 The glory of the Lord.

Solemnities and Feasts of the Lord

48. SOLEMNITY OF
THE MOST BLESSED TRINITY

Two Approaches to the Trinity

It may seem strange that a special feast of the Blessed Trinity should ever have been established, since such a feast may seem to be a celebration of an abstraction. Latin theology approaches the Trinity in a highly metaphysical way by analyzing the concepts of person and nature and speaking of the Trinity as consisting of three distinct Persons, each with its complete personality but with all three possessing a single divine nature. Try as we will, that is bound to remain rather abstract!

The liturgy, on the other hand, both Latin and Eastern, constantly shows us the three divine Persons engaged in the work of saving and rebuilding the world. Greek theology likewise takes a more vital approach to the Trinity. It speaks of the Father so loving the world that to save it he sends his Son, who gives his life for us, rises from the dead, ascends to heaven, and sends his Spirit. The Spirit forms the image of the Son in us, so that as the Father looks at us, he sees in us his own Son. This "economic" approach to the Trinity, as it is called, gives us a more concrete grasp of the Trinity and enables us to situate ourselves in relation to the divine Persons, for we are better able to understand how our baptism and our entire Christian activity is connected with the Trinity.[1] In this approach, the Trinity is no abstraction.

The liturgy thus takes the same approach as Greek theology: it shows us the activity of the divine Persons. The liturgy of the sacraments and the various prayers of the liturgy have from the very beginning emphasized either the action of the Trinity or our response of praise. Think, for example, of the various doxologies (the "Glory be to the Father . . . ," etc.) and ancient hymns such as the *Gloria* and the *Te Deum*.

Establishment of the Feast

By the ninth century there were churches dedicated to the Trinity, for example, in the monastery of St. Benedict of Aniane.[2] There was a votive Office composed by Stephen, bishop of Liege (d. 920).[3] At that period, however, there was no feast of the Trinity. Yet we do find a feast being celebrated in 1030 on the first Sunday after Pentecost, and it quickly became popular and widespread. We are informed of the event because it roused opposition, including that, later on, of Pope Alexander III (d. 1181). Nonetheless, the feast continued to be celebrated and became increasingly popular, to the point where Pope John XXII approved it in 1334 as a feast of the universal Church, to be celebrated on the first Sunday after Pentecost.

It is not easy to determine the reasons for placing the feast on the Sunday after Pentecost. It may be that once Pentecost had climaxed Easter Time by celebrating the sending of the Spirit, and thus the cycle of activities of the three Persons, there was a desire to sum up their work, as it were, in a single celebration. Not all the churches celebrated the feast, however, on the Sunday after Pentecost; in fact, some celebrated it on the last Sunday after Pentecost.

It must be acknowledged that a celebration of this type could become popular only at a time when the liturgical life and the proper understanding of the Bible were on the wane. Close contact with the Scriptures as proclaimed in the Church and with a liturgy that expressed at every moment the activity of the three divine Persons would not have roused a desire for such a feast. On the other hand, the theological mentality of the age when the feast became universal could only have been pleased by it. The feast has at least this advantage, that it draws our attention to the fact that the Trinity is active in every liturgical celebration throughout the entire Church year.

Readings

[A] Believe in the Love of God (John 3:16-18)

The gospel for this Sunday does not deal in abstractions but confronts us in a very concrete way with the activity of the Trinity. More accurately, it speaks of the Father and the Son, but it does so in the same manner that Greek theology was later to adopt: "God so loved the world that he gave his only Son" (John 3:16).

This passage has already been used on the Fourth Sunday of Lent (Year B), but the perspective there was different. This twofold use of the same passage should remind us of a point we have emphasized several times before, namely, that the texts of the liturgy take on a coloration from their liturgical context. On the Fourth Sunday of Lent, attention was focused on what Jesus had to say to Nicodemus about rebirth, since at that time the catechumens were being prepared for baptism, and the Christian community as a whole was preparing for Easter and the commemoration of its baptism in water and the Spirit. Here, on Trinity Sunday, the emphasis is on our contact with the divine Persons who effect our salvation.

The work of salvation that the Son accomplishes (and of which the Scriptures tell us) is also a sign of the Father's love for us. We can glimpse something of the character of this fatherly love, for when Jesus tells us that the Father has sent his "only" Son, we cannot help thinking of Abraham and his unconditional surrender of his son Isaac. That is the kind of love the Father shows us in sending his only Son—not to condemn the world but to save it.

If the encounter with the divine Persons is to be authentic, we must have faith. Not to believe in the name of the only Son of God is already to be condemned; to believe in the Son and therefore in the Father's love for us is to possess eternal life.

The Trinity, then, is Love. It is entirely at the service of the world, which it intends to re-create and thereby save.

A God Merciful and Gracious (Exod 34:4b-6, 8-9)

When God reveals himself to Moses, he presents himself as a merciful and gracious God: "The LORD, the LORD, a merciful and gracious God, slow to anger and rich in kindness and fidelity" (Exod 34:6). The inspired writers were awestruck by the graciousness of God and by the fact that God should reveal himself in this way and speak thus of himself: "The LORD, your God, carried you, as one carries his own child" (Deut 1:31); "I trust in the mercy of God, / forever and ever" (Ps 52:10); "Now [my loving] God will proceed before me" (Ps 59:11); "for you, O God, are my stronghold, / the God who shows me merciful love" (Ps 59:18); "Let your compassion hasten to meet us" (Ps 79:8); "The loving deeds of the LORD I will recall, the glorious acts of the LORD, Because of all the LORD has done for us, the immense goodness to the house of Israel, Which he has granted according to his mercy and his many loving deeds" (Isa 63:7). There are many other passages that exalt the tender, gracious love of God.

It would be impossible to list all the passages in which the Old Testament praises the mercy of God. Here are a few of the themes. Mercy is identical with God: he is the God of mercy (Deut 4:31; Ps 86:15; Wis 9:1); he always acts mercifully (Exod 20:6; Deut 5:10), and his mercy is immense and without limit (Pss 51:3; 115:5; 117:2; Dan 3:42); it is even eternal (1 Chr 16:34, 41; 2 Chr 5:13; 7:13; 20:21; Pss 100:5; 103:17; 107:1; 118:1, 29).

This is the God who appeared to Moses and whom Moses asked to remain in our midst (Exod 34:9). The encounter with the God who loves gave Moses confidence, so that he can ask with hope and without fear: "If I find favor with you, O LORD, do come along in our company. This is indeed a stiff-necked people; yet pardon our wickedness and sins, and receive us as your own" (Exod 34:9).

The God of Peace and Love Will Be with You (2 Cor 13:11-13)

The end of the second reading confronts us with the full mystery of the Trinity but does so in the atmosphere of love that is already characteristic of God in the Old Testament when he decides to make himself known. This same ending provides one of the greetings the celebrant may use at the beginning of the eucharistic celebration: "The grace of the Lord Jesus Christ and the love of God and the fellowship of the Holy Spirit be with all of you" (2 Cor 13:13).

St. Paul usually ends his letters with the formula: "The grace of our Lord Jesus be with you" (Rom 16:20; 1 Cor 16:23; 1 Thess 5:28; etc.). This may explain why he begins his letters with greetings from one who comes in the name of Jesus Christ. In any event, the "grace" of Christ is evidently the redemption he won for us. Christ's act of ransoming us and our resultant salvation have God the Father for their ultimate source; it is he who out of love sent us the only Son, in whom we find salvation (Rom 5:1-11; 8:28, 39). Finally, the Spirit gives himself to us through the faith we receive in baptism; he transforms us into new creatures as adopted children of God and members of Christ's Body, the Church; he makes us his temples.

It is God's love, then, that bestows salvation on us by handing over his Son to death for us and raising him to glorious life again. The Father also sends us the Spirit, who unceasingly gives us the salvation that Christ acquired for us once and for all and that we progressively make our own by means of the Church's sacraments.

It would be difficult to find a better expression of what the Trinity is than the ending of Second Corinthians. We are also told there that by living in permanent union with the divine Persons, the Christian is to seek perfection and to live in peaceful unity (2 Cor 13:11).

In the Liturgy of the Hours, at the Office of Readings, St. Athanasius describes the splendors of the trinitarian life in a letter to Serapion, bishop of Thmuis in Egypt. Here are two sections from the reading:

> [T]he Father makes all things through the Word and in the Holy Spirit, and in this way the unity of the holy Trinity is preserved. Accordingly, in the Church, one God is preached, one God who is *above all things and through all things and in all things*. God is *above all things* as Father, for he is principle and source; he is *through all things* through the Word; and he is *in all things* in the Holy Spirit. . . . Even the gifts that the Spirit dispenses to individuals are given by the Father through the Word. . . . Similarly, when the Spirit dwells in us, the Word who bestows the Spirit is in us too, and the Father is present in the Word.[4]

Commenting on the final verse of Second Corinthians, the saint writes:

> [T]he grace and gift of the Trinity are given by the Father through the Son in the Holy Spirit. Just as grace is given from the Father through the Son, so there could be no communication of the gift to us except in the Holy Spirit. But when we share in the Spirit, we possess the love of the Father, the grace of the Son and the fellowship of the Spirit himself.[5]

[B] Baptized in the Father and the Son and the Holy Spirit (Matt 28:16-20)

What we might call the "proccupation" of the Trinity is that the nations of the world should become "disciples." This means the nations must heed the Trinity, observe the commandments, and, because of this observance, be sure that the Lord is with them to the end of time.

All authority in heaven and earth has been given to Jesus, the Son. Now that he has risen and acquired the title *Kyrios*, that is, Lord of heaven and earth, Jesus has the authority to send his disciples on a mission that is of radical importance for the Church and for the world as a whole. The apostles are to "make disciples."

According to Mark (13:10; 14:9; 16:15) and Luke (24:47), the apostles are to "preach" the Good News. Here the language is stronger: not only are they to present the message objectively, but they are also to forge a bond between the message and those who accept it so that the message will work a profound change in them. Christians, after all, are not simply people who listen to teaching, study it, and contemplate it as something outside themselves. Christians absorb the message into their lives and become disciples. This, however, supposes faith, a gift bestowed by the Spirit in baptism.

Are the words "baptizing them in the name of the Father, and of the Son, and of the Holy Spirit" a reflection of the baptismal formula? I personally do not think so, despite the commentaries that argue that they are. I do not think we can say that in the apostolic period baptism was administered with a trinitarian formula, in the sense that the formula with which we are familiar was already in use: "N., I baptize you in the name of the Father, and of the Son, and of the Holy Spirit." If we study the ancient liturgical books, we will soon be convinced that this formula did not appear in the Roman liturgy before the end of the seventh or the beginning of the eighth century. It is true, however, that in the earlier period baptism involved a triple immersion, each immersion being accompanied by a question put to the candidates about their faith in each of the three divine Persons successively and by each one's response: "I do believe." Properly trinitarian formulas did, of course, exist from a very early time, and we find a number of them in Paul; there is no evidence, however, that they were used in the conferring of baptism.

We may think that the words "baptizing them in the name, etc." mean bringing them into union with the Father, the Son, and the Holy Spirit. When all is said and done, to be a disciple and a Christian is to live in union with the divine Persons. Baptism establishes a close bond between each of us and the Trinity. We have been baptized into a relationship with them; this was always true, even when the formula "in the name of the Father, and of the Son, and of the Holy Spirit" was not used, as, in fact, it was not until the eighth century in the Latin Church. The very meaning of the sacrament is, in part, that it makes people share the life of the Trinity.

A God Who Took a Nation for Himself from the Midst of Another Nation (Deut 4:32-34, 39-40)

Concrete deeds manifest love. That principle holds for the Lord and all he did for his people. His preoccupation was to unite that people to himself. Thus, the order given to the apostles to make disciples means that Christ wants to unite the nations to himself and thereby make them sharers in God's trinitarian life.

The passage from the book of Deuteronomy focuses attention on this desire of God to encounter a people and make it his own. "Did a people ever hear the voice of God speaking from the midst of fire, as you did, and live? Or did any god venture to go and take a nation for himself from the midst of another nation, . . . with strong hand and outstretched arm?" Because of God's actions, history itself becomes an ongoing revelation of the Divinity.

The concrete conclusion to be drawn from this revelation of God through his actions is that we must obey the commandments. Today's passages from the gospel and from the Old Testament thus reach the same conclusion. Because the triune God has revealed himself and because we are now really incorporated into the mystery, an attitude becomes obligatory and indeed increasingly urgent: we must heed God's commands and follow in his paths.

The Spirit Makes Us Children (Rom 8:14-17)

The theme of union with God is also developed in the second reading. We are children of God and heirs of God along with Christ. God's promise to us is the promise of an inheritance (cf. Eph 3:6; 2 Tim 1:1; Titus 1:2). The Spirit who makes us children of God also leads us to our promised inheritance.

What is it that is promised us? In what does the inheritance consist? St. Paul speaks frequently on this subject. For him, the heritage that God intends for his children is his own kingdom and glory (1 Thess 2:12). If we study the vocabulary of Paul a little more closely, we will find him saying the same thing in various ways: the heritage is the kingdom (1 Cor 6:9-10; Gal 5:21; Eph 5:5), or it is glory (Rom 5:2; 8:18; Eph 1:18); it is also eternal life (Rom 6:22-23; Gal 6:8; Titus 1:2) or glory and eternal life (Rom 2:7). And this heritage is ours because we are God's children.

We must therefore allow ourselves to be "led" by the Spirit who is constantly active within us. He wishes to lead us, and we must let ourselves be led. That is what Paul means by saying that we should not "grieve the holy Spirit" (Eph 4:30).

All this amounts to saying that the Spirit radically transforms us, making us children of God and heirs to the promise with Christ. The

Spirit makes the Christian so like Christ that the Father finds in the Christian the very image of the Son whom, out of love for us, he sent to save us.

Paul's language renders almost sensible to us the Trinity to which we are bound through baptism. Once again, all this supposes faith, but faith itself is something the Spirit constantly strengthens in us. If the beginning of faith leads us finally to the Trinity, it is the Trinity that bestows on us, through the sacraments, the faith that leads us to it. Thus we are the constant object of the Trinity's action in our lives.

[C] The Spirit Will Guide Us to All Truth (John 16:12-15)

The gospel passage is part of the discourse after the Last Supper and contains words spoken by Jesus shortly before his earthly links with the apostles would be at an end.

The statement at the beginning of the passage is important: Jesus tells us he cannot teach us everything he would like to. The reason is not any indisposition on his part to do so or any failure to have used his time well while he was with the disciples; the reason is that his hearers were not yet capable of entering into the necessary dialogue with him.

To understand this, we must realize that Christ's teaching is not primarily a matter of doctrine; his teaching is indistinguishable from his person, and it is his person we must receive and accept. As John says in his Prologue, the message of Jesus takes the form of a gift of himself (John 1:4, 10), so that we must enter into dialogue with him rather than simply discuss a doctrine. Despite the time he had spent with his disciples, they had not, however, advanced far enough in this dialogue to be able to understand everything.

John had frequently been struck with the disciples' inability to enter into a true dialogue with Christ and to understand his mystery. Recall, for example, Thomas's question when Jesus says he is going away in order to prepare a place for them: "Master, we do not know where you are going; how can we know the way?" (John 14:5). In reply, Jesus asserts that they can indeed know him and that they now do know him: "If you know me, you will also know my Father. From now on you do know him and have seen him" (14:7). At this point, it is Philip who shows his lack of understanding: "Master, show us the Father, and that will be enough for us." Jesus replies, "Have I been with you for so long a time, and still you do not know me,

Philip? Whoever has seen me has seen the Father. How can you say, 'Show us the Father'? Do you not believe that I am in the Father and the Father is in me?" (14:8-10).

In the same chapter, Judas asks, "Master, [then] what happened that you will yourself to us and not to the world?" Jesus answers, "Whoever loves me will keep my word, and my Father will love him, and we will come to him and make our dwelling with him" (14:22-23). Still later, immediately after today's passage, we see the disciples wondering what Jesus could mean by his words about going to the Father (John 16:16-17).

It is evident, then, that the Spirit will have to continue Christ's work and help the disciples understand the truth. Jesus seems here to be thinking of the Spirit's work in guiding the entire Church of the future; the Spirit will have to help the Church understand all that happens and give it meaning.

The passage thus shows us the relations between Father, Son, and Spirit. Jesus is sent by the Father; the Spirit too is sent by the Father to continue the Son's work in the Church. It is because of Jesus' prayer that the Father sends the Spirit (14:16). But Jesus himself also sends the Spirit from the Father (15:26).

Our whole lives as Christians in the Church are guided by the Spirit toward the full grasp of the truth. The Church's entire life is trinitarian, for it is a sign of the Father's love that gives us the Son through whom we touch the Father, and does so in the Spirit, who is constantly leading us more fully to the truth in its whole extent.

The Work of God Is Revealed as God's by Its Wisdom (Prov 8:22-31)

We may be struck by the poetic beauty of this passage from the book of Proverbs and be tempted, at a first reading, to see in it a hymn to the Person of the Son or the Person of the Spirit. And as a matter of fact, the New Testament identifies Christ as Wisdom that has become incarnate (Col 1:15, 18; Rev 3:14); the fathers also often identify Christ with Wisdom, or if they do not, they identify the Spirit and Wisdom. And yet the passage does not allow the exegete to say that wisdom is here a person; it is rather a personification, used in order to exalt God's work, which in its entirety is a manifestation of divine wisdom. We should not therefore exaggerate the importance of the text as though it contained a theology of Christ himself or of the Spirit.

In the passage, Wisdom steps forward and describes herself. She was created by God, and this before anything else was created; she exists, therefore, before the world was made.

How is the passage to be understood in its liturgical context, that is, as part of the celebration of the Blessed Trinity? We shall not undertake a detailed interpretation of the verses, but this much can be said: we should see expressed in the passage the Church's intention of showing how God had from the beginning prepared the mystery of love that he would later reveal in his Son through the Spirit. The passage in its context is thus an invitation to marvel at the entire great work of God that ultimately leads us to share in the life of the Trinity.

That, certainly, is how the responsorial psalm interprets the passage, for it bids us say, as a refrain, "O LORD, our Lord, how majestic / is your name through all the earth!" (Ps 8:2).

Sharing the Glory of God (Rom 5:1-5)

"Hope of the glory of God" (Rom 5:2) is a hope that is already being fulfilled.

A very ancient prayer of exorcism that is still used in the baptismal ritual tells us that we already possess the *rudimenta gloriae*, that is, the beginnings of our future glory.[6] We already live with the Trinity in the "love of God [that] has been poured out into our hearts through the Holy Spirit that has been given to us" (5:5). We are already justified by faith (5:1) and "have gained access by faith to this grace in which we stand" (5:2). In other words, we are experiencing God's love for us.

This does not mean that all problems are solved; no, we are still in the stage of struggle and testing. But because we have faith and the assurance that we are united to the triune God, the trials and struggles take on a meaning they can have only for someone who has received the Spirit: "we even boast of our afflictions, knowing that affliction produces endurance, and endurance, proven character, and proven character, hope" (5:3-4).

Life in the Spirit thus brings us peace with God through Christ in the Spirit, who pours out the love of God in our hearts.

49. SOLEMNITY OF THE MOST HOLY BODY AND BLOOD OF CHRIST (CORPUS CHRISTI)

Devotion to the Reserved Sacrament

The twelfth century saw the rise of a desire for a more intense devotion to the Eucharist, but in a specialized form. Although it was not forgotten that the Eucharist is a sacrifice, the devotional impulse was focused especially on the real presence and on the need of paying Christ thus present the tribute of adoration and splendid surroundings. This new devotion to the Blessed Sacrament came into existence particularly in Belgium.

Hitherto the reserved sacrament had, of course, been treated with great respect, but the Latin Church did not develop a special devotion to it, any more than had the Eastern Churches. The reasons for the growth of the new devotion were complex. It may have initially been a byproduct of canon law; apologetic needs and theological developments then played a part. The end result, however, was a mysticism that eventually gave birth to religious congregations dedicated to the devotion and adoration of the Blessed Sacrament.

Motives

The penitential discipline continued to be quite severe, and many Catholics could not readily approach the eucharistic table and communicate. At this same time there developed a widespread desire to look upon the Host; so intense was this wish that in some places the faithful would go from church to church, arriving at each just in time for the elevation of the Host at the consecration. For some classes of sinners, the only way they could participate in the eucharistic celebration was to gaze at the Host.

At this period the Church was also busy defending the faithful against doubts about the reality of Christ's eucharistic presence. These were the years when a number of miracles took place in which blood was seen to flow from the Host; we meet these phenomena in Belgium,

Italy, and elsewhere. Meanwhile, in the theological schools, there had been a shift of emphasis in the treatment of the Eucharist. The Mass was always regarded as a sacrifice, but the aspect of sacrificial meal receded very much into the background, and attention was focused rather on the idea of God's majestic descent to the altar at the consecration. As a result, celebration of the Mass came to be characterized by profound reverence; increasingly monumental and majestic altars were built; the ritual became ever more solemn.

Development of the Feast

Juliana of Retinnes (1192–1258), a nun in the Augustinian convent of Mont Cornillion near Liège (Belgium) and later prioress, revealed a series of visions that had been granted her, the first of them occurring in 1208. She saw a lunar disk surrounded by rays of dazzling white light; on one side of the disk, however, there was a dark spot that spoiled the beauty of the whole. The Lord explained to her that the dark spot meant that the Church still lacked a solemn feast in honor of the Blessed Sacrament.

Such a feast was introduced at Liège in 1246 and celebrated on the Thursday within the octave of Trinity Sunday. James Pantaléon, archdeacon of Liège and a confidant of Juliana, later became Pope Urban IV (1261–64) and extended the feast to the universal Church. While living as pope at Orvieto, he was overwhelmed at the news of a eucharistic miracle in nearby Bolsena: a priest tormented by doubts about the real presence saw a host change before his eyes into a bit of bloody flesh that left stains on the corporal.

The procession in honor of the Blessed Sacrament was not prescribed in the papal bull promulgating the feast, but the practice arose spontaneously and quickly spread.

Readings

[A] His Flesh Is True Food and His Blood Is True Drink (John 6:51-58)

The pericope is from the end of the discourse on the bread of life. Using different language, John often refers throughout the discourse to what we know elsewhere as the account of institution (Matt 26:26-29; Mark 14:22-25; Luke 22:15-20; 1 Cor 11:23-25). The whole of chapter

6, after the story of the multiplication of the loaves, is really a discourse on the Eucharist. The exegetes raise problems concerning the discourse, however, and some have even denied that it alludes to the Eucharist at all. We shall not enter into these discussions; what is of interest to us is the spiritual value of the passage on this feast when the Church reads it as the word of the Lord who, in the final analysis, is therein proclaiming himself.

It has been maintained that the verses in today's pericope were a later addition, because they show a certain lack of coherence. In any case, the whole discourse bears the marks of being the result of reflection by St. John long after the actual events. This is not to challenge the authenticity of the discourse; it is simply to indicate that the Savior's original words have been meditated on and recast for catechetical purposes.

Despite a superficial lack of unity, chapter 6 is, in fact, an excellent example of how John went about writing his gospel. The procedure here can be paralleled elsewhere: Christ presents a truth in such a way that it can be interpreted in at least two different senses; the reactions of the hearers then lead him to correct misunderstandings and to explain more fully the truth he wants to teach. Other passages in which he follows the same pattern are the conversations with Nicodemus (chap. 3) and with the Samaritan woman (chap. 4).

In the discourse of chapter 6, the starting point is the exhortation: "Do not work for the food that perishes but for the food that endures for eternal life" (6:27). The language is such as to permit the hearers to mistake the true meaning, so that Christ then has the opportunity to specify his thought and lead the hearers more deeply into the mystery. The explanations finally become so clear that they provoke among the disciples a crisis that Jesus has been expecting. Their faith is tested, and some of them leave him.

Jesus' explanation proceeds by contrasting the manna in the desert with the bread of life, which is the true bread for humanity. Before identifying himself as the true Bread of life, the true Manna, Jesus must first show who he is. He does so by presenting himself as the Son of Man who is to come on the clouds of heaven; to the great scandal of the Jews, he speaks of himself as coming from heaven and as of divine origin (6:32-33). He can then go on to assert that he is the true Manna or Bread from heaven and to compare it with the manna that Moses obtained from God: those who ate the manna in the desert are now dead, whereas the food Jesus offers gives unending life (6:30-35). Jesus is himself the Bread of life, and his hearers must seek this bread that does not become corrupted. He is the eucharistic Bread; those who eat his body and drink his blood will abide in him and he in them (6:56). Jesus is here asserting the union that exists between himself and his disciples; in chapter 15 he will use the same language to teach the same truth.

He Fed You with Manna (*Deut 8:2-3, 14b-16a*)

We know how fond the Jews were of remembering the past in their prayers. It was natural that they should do so, for the experience of the deliverance from Egypt had left a permanent mark on Jewish life. We also know that for the Hebrew mind, "remembering" meant not simply recalling but actualizing the past, that is, making it present and operative. To recall the past was to make it present and thereby give the present the power it needed to face the future. Past events were therefore recalled with love; the great crises of the journey in the desert were a source of glory for Israel's God, and Israel shared the glory. The forty long years of wandering in the wilderness taught the people lessons they would never forget. It was a time when God could test his people's hearts and learn whether or not they would obey his commandments.

The time of testing did not end when the desert journey was over. It was an ongoing thing, and the people of later generations had to make their own the experiences their ancestors had undergone at a time when they were cast down and yet were also sure of God's presence and his gift of life.

In the passage read in today's Mass, the manna is the focus of attention. The passage makes the point that the later generations had to learn, like their ancestors before them, that their lives depended not on material bread alone but on every word that came from the mouth of God. What did this statement mean? It meant that God gives life through his word, as he did first at creation. The word of God was given, for example, through the prophets, and the Hebrews looked upon it as truly a form of food. The manna was food also, a material food, but it was also a sensible sign, a kind of materialization, of God's life-giving and nourishing word. At a later point in the book of Deuteronomy (30:15, 20, etc.), we are told again that God gives his people life through his word. He is the God who saves, and it is as Savior that he was the object of the people's remembrance and praise.

All this holds true for us, the new people of God. The gospel tells us that Christ, the Word of God, is the true Bread of life. He is also the Bread of the covenant but now of a new and everlasting covenant, the covenant that achieves its purpose.

The responsorial psalm, Psalm 147, sings of the Lord who "reveals his word to Jacob; / to Israel, his decrees and judgments" (v. 19). Proudly and jealously it adds: "He has not dealt thus with other nations; / he has not taught them his judgments. / Alleluia!" (v. 20).

The Bread That Makes Us One: One Bread, One Body (1 Cor 10:16-17)

While the manna helped the people's physical life, the word of God sustained and united and refreshed them. These last words describe the role of the Eucharist.

Jewish rites were no longer practiced by those who had converted to Christianity, but the apostles were fully cognizant of the Jewish context in which the Lord had instituted the Eucharist. The language that the apostles use reflects that context and background, as do the accounts of institution. Speaking a blessing and breaking bread—that is what happened at the Passover meal, and that is what Christ likewise did. For the Jews, the Passover meal was a commemorative meal that actualized the "passage" of the people from slavery to freedom. Christ took the rite and made it his own, but the bread broken was now the true Bread, his body, and the cup of the covenant was the cup of his blood. The Bread broken, the one Bread that is shared by many, is the sign that effects community: one Bread, one Body.

The eucharistic meal is a sacrificial meal that unites the faithful to Christ their Head. As the theologians put it, the Eucharist builds the Church. We are "one thing" (cf. John 17:21): the Lord and we, each of us with all the others.

The well-known sequence for Corpus Christi is really not poetic in character but rather takes a metaphysical approach to the Eucharist. In its own way, however, it expresses all aspects of the mystery by which the Church has lived through the centuries and by which we continue to live today: God's word and God's bread.

[B] This Is My Body, This Is My Blood of the Covenant (Mark 14:12-16, 22-26)

This is a text we already met when we were meditating on the readings for Holy Thursday. As we shall see, however, the accompanying Old Testament reading here puts the New Testament text in a special light, emphasizing the "new covenant" aspect of it. This is to say that the passage from Mark was chosen for Corpus Christi, not so much to glorify the real presence (though this presence is certainly presupposed) as to underline the fact that the Eucharist is the sacrifice of the new covenant. It is for this reason that the gospel passage includes so much detail about the preparation for the Passover and about the room where the meal will be eaten.

The "blood of the covenant" is thus the main reason why the pericope is used on this day. In the New Testament, blood acquires great importance because of Christ's death. References to the blood of Christ occur quite often (1 Cor 10:16; 11:27; Eph 2:13; Heb 9:14; 10:9; 1 John 1:7; 1 Pet 1:2; Rev 7:14; 12:11). These references, with their explicit or implicit allusion to the sacrifice of the cross, are a way of emphasizing the saving power of Christ's death, by which the new covenant was concluded. As the old covenant of Sinai was sealed by blood (Exod 24:8), so the new covenant is sealed in an incomparably more perfect way by the blood of Christ (Heb 9:18). The effect of the new covenant is the forgiveness of sins, as foretold by the prophets (Jer 31:31-34).

We may ask whether, in the thinking of Jesus, this covenant blood, like the covenant blood of Sinai, is connected with the book of Isaiah (42:6; 49:8) and the Servant of Yahweh, who gives his life for his people. In any case, the new covenant represents a new stage in the history of salvation. Henceforth, the relations between God and humanity will concern the effective fulfillment of the divine plan of salvation. It was God who took the initiative in the earlier covenants; it is he who has now brought into being the new, definitive, everlasting covenant.

The new covenant is an anticipation of the end of time. The reference to drinking the wine new in the kingdom shows that the messianic age has begun and that participation in the Eucharist is already a participation in the eschatological banquet.

The Blood of the Covenant Which the Lord Has Made with Us
(Exod 24:3-8)

The choice of this passage from the book of Exodus as a first read-ing justifies us, as we have already pointed out, in concentrating, in the gospel reading, on the new covenant that is renewed and actual-ized in the eucharistic celebration.

The text from the book of Exodus does not, however, simply detail the rites in which the covenant is concluded by means of the blood of animals. The passage also emphasizes the concrete commitment on the part of the people that the conclusion of this divinely initiated covenant supposes. The outward rite and its bloodshed will not save; the people must live by the words the Lord has spoken.

What is God's will as expressed in his words here? It is clear that he wants to bring humanity together into a people that will worship him and be devoted to his service; he, for his part, will keep the promises he has made. On Sinai, then, God links himself to a people. We may think that the juridical manner in which the covenant is concluded renders it too exclusive and that salvation is too much connected with the existence of a nation and with its temporal prosperity. We may also ask whether salvation is not turned too much into a reward for obedi-ence, so that its character as a free gift is diminished.

Whatever be the validity of these objections, the new covenant eliminates all such ambiguities. It is addressed to all the peoples of the earth, and it involves first and foremost a changing of one's heart through the power of Christ's blood and the sending of the Spirit. Participation in the Eucharist draws the Christian ever more fully into the covenant and ensures its concrete fulfillment both individu-ally and in the world at large.

The responsorial psalm, Psalm 116, is a thanksgiving for the cove-nant and an expression of the desire to offer sacrifice while invoking the Lord's name: "The cup of salvation I will raise; / I will call on the name of the LORD" (v. 13).

Christ, Mediator of a New Covenant (Heb 9:11-15)

The Letter to the Hebrews looks at the new covenant from a cultic and priestly point of view. In the opening lines of the pericope, Christ is seen as the High Priest of the new covenant, and the temple that is his own body is said to be more perfect than the temple of the former covenant, because Christ's temple was not of human construction and therefore does not belong to this world.

The passage continues the comparison of the two covenants by giving a theological description of Christ's priestly activity. The blood of the covenant is no longer that of an animal but the blood of Christ himself. There is no longer a mere sprinkling with blood that purifies people only outwardly so that they can legally engage in worship; in the new covenant, the blood of Christ, who has offered himself as a spotless victim, purifies people's very consciences.

The passage thus provides several profound ideas: Christ as the High Priest who enters once and for all into the sanctuary and there offers his own blood; the sacrifice of Christ, who offers himself to God as a holy victim; the blood of Christ that purifies people's consciences; the new covenant.

To begin with, Christ is the High Priest of the good things to come, for he is Mediator between God and humanity (Heb 5:1). He gives humans the objective possibility of entering into a covenant with God and of receiving superior blessings and the good things to come. "To come," because while on God's part the offering of a covenant is complete and unreserved, our acceptance of it is still imperfect. In the covenant, God made his plan of salvation fully available, but we must respond to it with a completeness as yet unrealized. Nonetheless, Christ, prefigured by the Jewish priesthood, has now supplanted that priesthood, because the covenant promises are totally fulfilled in his person.

Christ needed to enter the sanctuary only once (Heb 9:12). He did so by passing from this world to his Father. Consequently, his entry into the heavenly sanctuary was not merely symbolic, as it was in Old Testament ritual, but fully real. Moreover, he made his offering in the temple of his own body, which, though belonging to humanity and being a truly human body, is no longer part of the present creation.

The victim that Christ offers is himself. Here the Letter to the Hebrews shows how the theology of Christ's sacrifice differs from the theology of Old Testament sacrifice. In the latter, the important thing was the sprinkling of blood; in the former, death and bloodshed are symbols of the inner attitude of Christ. What redeems us is not, strictly speaking, the shedding of his blood and his death but what these signify, namely, his perfect self-giving to the Father by doing the Father's will. This inner attitude of Christ was and continues to be a permanent reality; consequently, he offers once and for all, yet his intercession is ongoing.

The blood of Christ, that is, the interior offering of himself that is signified by the shedding of his blood, purifies our consciences. This is to say that Christ's self-giving has a purifying power that produces its effect in us whenever we have recourse to it. Christ did not offer a victim distinct from himself; he offered his very self. Consequently, once our consciences are purified, we can offer worship to the Father in union with Christ the Priest.

The covenant is now objectively, fully, definitively in existence. The task set before us is to enter as perfectly as we can upon the way opened to us by this covenant.

In the Office of Readings, a reading from St. Thomas Aquinas explicates the thought of the Letter to the Hebrews. Here are a few lines from this reading:

> Since it was the will of God's only-begotten Son that men should share in his divinity, he assumed our nature in order that by becoming man he might make men gods. Moreover, when he took our flesh he dedicated the whole of its substance to our salvation. He offered his body to God the Father on the altar of the cross as a sacrifice for our reconciliation. He shed his blood for our ransom and purification, so that we might be redeemed from our wretched state of bondage and cleaned from all sin.[1]

[C] Jesus Took the Loaves, Said the Blessing over Them, Broke Them, and Gave Them to His Disciples (Luke 9:11b-17)

The mystery of the bread is the central focus of the gospel pericope in Year C. The first reading recalls the prefigurative sacrifice of Melchizedek, which consists of an offering of bread and wine (Gen 14:18-20). The second reading records the actions and words of Jesus at the institution of the Eucharist (1 Cor 11:23-26). In proper sequence, then, we move from Melchizedek's sacrifice, through the multiplication of the loaves as told by Luke, to the eucharistic meal as described by Paul.

There is no denying that the gospel pericope reflects a concern of the early Church: to show how its sacramental life was continuous with the actions of Jesus during his earthly life. To put it another way, we have here a typical example of a catechesis that uses an action of the earthly Jesus in order to teach the meaning of the sacrament. The Fourth Gospel, which is the most catechetically oriented of the four gospels, makes frequent use of the method, and the fathers would later adopt it in their turn.

The earliest teaching method used by the Church, then, was to bring the sacraments and their meaning alive by seeing them in the light of the Old Testament types and of events in the life of Christ. The pericope from Luke applies the method even in the style chosen for the account. A historical context is given: the wilderness and the hunger of the people who followed Jesus there in order to hear him. From a literary point of view, however, it is as though we were already at the Last Supper, for the language used at the multiplication is the language to be used later in describing the institution of the Eucharist. Evidently the intention is to present the multiplication of the loaves as a "type," prefiguration, anticipation, and implicit announcement of the Eucharist. For this reason nothing is said of the wonder that the crowd felt at the event. The whole is presented rather as an introduction to an infinite mystery: the mystery of the Eucharist, which fulfills human need and desire abundantly.

At the same time, however, we should not forget that every meal in the Bible functions as an anticipation of the messianic banquet. This is why the ancient liturgies, and ours today, make use of the account of the multiplication of the loaves during Advent.

Melchizedek Brought out Bread and Wine (Gen 14:18-20)

As is well known, the Roman Canon mentions the sacrifice of Melchizedek, along with those of Abel and Abraham, as prefigurations of the Christian sacrifice. In a similar manner, today's liturgy links Melchizedek's sacrifice with that of the Eucharist (second reading).

The fact that Melchizedek's ancestry was unknown ("without father, mother or ancestry" Heb. 7:3) and that he was a priest gave him considerable prestige in the Old Testament and the New as well. So special was his priesthood that people could speak of a priesthood "according to the order of Melchizedek" (a phrase from Heb 5:6, which cites Ps 110:4). Melchizedek was not a priest like other priests;

his priesthood was not governed by the Law but was in the prophetic line. For that reason he is a type or figure of Christ; Psalm 110 foresees the Messiah as being a priest not in the line of Aaron but in the line of Melchizedek.

While the priesthood of Melchizedek is extremely important, since it prefigures that of the Messiah, in the present context the passage from the book of Genesis is chosen for the offering of bread and wine, which is seen in the liturgy as a prefiguration of the eucharistic offering. The passage also gives an example of the Hebrew "blessing" that will leave its imprint on the eucharistic prayers of the Church.

The liturgy showed an early awareness of the significance of Melchizedek's sacrifice for the sacrifice of the Mass. That is why the Roman Canon mentions him. The reader will readily recall the passage: "Be pleased to look upon these offerings with a serene and kindly countenance, and to accept them, as once you were pleased to accept the gifts of your servant Abel the just, the sacrifice of Abraham, our father in faith, and the offering of your high priest Melchizedek, a holy sacrifice, a spotless victim." In this prayer we pass from prefigurations to fulfillment.

The responsorial psalm, Psalm 110, sings of the supreme kingship of Christ, who is Messiah and Priest par excellence. As we know, there is only one priesthood, that of Christ, and there are two fully real but essentially different participations in it: priesthood through ordination and priesthood through baptism. Both of these priesthoods, like that of Christ himself, are prefigured by the sacrifice of Melchizedek.

Bread and Wine Proclaim the Lord's Death (1 Cor 11:23-26)

This passage from St. Paul parallels the accounts of institution that we find in the Synoptic Gospels. St. Paul's points of reference are the Jewish Passover and its meal, which signified covenant and liberation. The death and resurrection of the Lord are seen by Paul as the foundation of the definitive covenant, and this covenant is actualized in the eucharistic celebration.

This passage has been chosen for the feast, not so much because it enunciates the theme of covenant as because the covenant is concluded under the signs of bread and wine. This is what puts the Supper in continuity with the sacrifice of Melchizedek.

The celebration as a whole, then, calls to mind the sacrifice of Melchizedek, who brought out bread and wine and gave a blessing to Abraham; that is the theme of the first reading (we should not overlook the presence of Abraham, father of all who believe and father of the covenant as well). In the third reading, Christ gives bread to eat, a sign both of the Eucharist and of the messianic banquet. He is the eternal High Priest, and the Eucharist perpetuates the exercise of his priesthood under the signs of bread and wine. The second reading explicitly describes the Eucharist.

50. SOLEMNITY OF THE MOST SACRED HEART OF JESUS

The Earlier Approach to Christ

It is not true, of course, that no one in the course of Church history ever focused attention on the love of Christ's Heart for us until the last few centuries. On the contrary, we need but read St. Paul's Letter to the Romans (8:28, 39) and especially the Gospel of St. John to see how close to the Christian mind was the image of Christ's loving Heart.

Down to the Scholastic period, however, the Christian mentality was very biblical. This means that Christians attended more to the global mystery of salvation than to the precise details by which the mystery was implemented in time. In the earlier ages of the Church, worship was addressed to the person and not to particular attitudes or actions of his. Consequently, the love of God and the love of Christ, though always present in Christian thinking, were not expressed in a specialized way and in a special feast. The death of Christ and, more generally, the whole mystery of Christ were a constant and sufficient reminder of the Lord's love for us. No one would have dreamed of celebrating a special feast in honor of his love, still less a feast that concentrated on the Heart of God.

A Shift in Theological Outlook

The development of theology and its methodology, together with the growing desire of the theologians to enter into details and to systematize, led to the contemplation (first private, then publicized) of the Lord's love as seen in the popular image of the heart, the seat of love.

The Franciscans, and especially St. Bonaventure with his fervent style, contributed greatly to spreading this special devotion to the Heart of Christ. The pierced Heart became the object of intense contemplation. At almost the same time, various holy nuns in Germany and Italy, in their intimate colloquies with the Lord, were struck by the love manifested in the Heart of Jesus. In Italy there were St. Margaret of Cortona (1247–97) and Blessed Angela of Foligno (1248–1309), the latter of whom wrote an account of her visions. In Germany, St. Mechtild of Magdeburg (1210–80) and St. Gertrude of Helfta (1256–1302) spread the devotion by their visions and revelations, though the devotion was already known in Flanders and practiced there by two nuns, Blessed Mary of Oignies (1177–1213) and St. Luitgard of Tongern (1182–1246). Nevertheless, the devotion, which initially spread rather rapidly, eventually declined somewhat.

The Sixteenth Century On

From the sixteenth century on, the devotion gained ground again. In France, St. John Eudes (1601–80) based his devotion to the Sacred Heart on the theology of St. John and gained permission for his congregation to celebrate the feast of the Sacred Heart on August 30, using a Mass and Office that he himself had composed. The experiment was initially limited to the Diocese of Rennes but was soon adopted in other dioceses. It is worth noting that St. John Eudes won recognition of the devotion in his diocese in 1670.

The appearances of the Lord to St. Margaret Mary Alacoque (1647–90) at Paray-le-Monial occurred some years after the devotion proposed by St. John Eudes had been allowed. These visions roused such enthusiasm that fervent petitions were submitted to Rome to make the celebration of the feast universal. It was only in 1856, however, that Pius IX took this step, assigning the feast to the Friday after the octave of Corpus Christi. Later on, additions were made to the celebration: the consecration of the human race to the Sacred Heart and then, under Pius XI, the act of reparation to the Sacred Heart.

Readings

[A] The Meek and Humble Heart (Matt 11:25-30)

The passage from the Gospel of Matthew has been chosen because of the qualities Jesus there ascribes to his own Heart: "I am meek and humble of heart" (v. 29). The meaning of the words is not so obvious, and to grasp it we must read them in their context. Jesus is urging his hearers to become his disciples, and he tells them that any demands he makes can be met. His attitude is thus in contrast to that of the scribes and Pharisees, whom he accuses elsewhere because "they tie up heavy burdens [hard to carry] and lay them on people's shoulders" (Matt 23:4). Jesus addresses himself precisely to those who "labor and are burdened" (Matt 11:28); that is, he is solicitous about those who are crushed by the heavy burden of Jewish observances. The yoke Jesus lays on his disciples is easy to carry, and the burden is light. He himself is meek and humble of heart and will not crush those who entrust themselves to him as their master.

All of this does not mean that the life to which he summons his disciples is not a demanding one. They must after all carry a yoke, the very same one Christ carries, but the yoke, though it remains a yoke, is easy to carry because it is not a yoke made up of outward observances but a yoke consisting of the service of others out of love.

We must not draw hasty conclusions from this passage, as though Christ did not take seriously the life of the community he founded or as though he were tricking his disciples into an undertaking by describing it as easy when, in fact, it is difficult. There are demands that can be crushing because they are demands for meticulous, legalistic observances that do not foster love and concern for others. Such are not the demands Jesus makes. He is meek and humble of heart; he does not break the bruised reed or quench the still smoldering wick (Matt 12:19-20). The God he brings to humanity is a God who desires mercy, not sacrifice (Matt 9:13; 12:7). Jesus offers those who wish to be his disciples the opportunity to follow him along the way of love. If they accept, they will find rest.

Redeemed from the House of Bondage (Deut 7:6-11)

In his love, God has gathered an insignificant people whom he himself has chosen and freed from the yoke of slavery. We are therefore invited to contemplate God's love for his people, a love shown in the fact that he freely chose them. This love that redeems is, however, also a love that demands fidelity. God liberates, but he also requires that people keep his covenant and obey his commandments.

God himself is a faithful God and gives himself to his people to the point of freeing them from captivity and creating them anew. He is not now proposing to enslave them all over again! The observance of his commandments is meant not as a crushing burden but as a way of continuing to draw down God's fidelity. If one commits oneself to God, God pledges himself in return. The issue here is not a juridical contract but the mutual self-giving in fidelity that is the very heart of love.

The responsorial psalm, Psalm 103, captures perfectly the meaning of the first reading and also prepares the community for the gospel: "The LORD is compassionate and gracious, / slow to anger and rich in mercy. / . . . He does not treat us according to our sins, / nor repay us according to our faults" (vv. 8, 10).

Unity in Love (1 John 4:7-16)

The statement made early on in this reading, "God is love," is not a kind of theological declaration. St. John is concerned not with concepts but with history, with the experience that the world, and especially the Jewish people, has had of God's concern to preserve, deliver, and lead onward.

In John's case, it is evidently the Christian experience of God's incarnation that enables him to say, not as a theological abstraction, but as a historical fact, that "God is love."

The number of passages in the Old Testament that speak of God's love for his people is quite impressive. At least thirty times the Old Testament books tell in one way or another of this faithful love on God's part. The prophet Hosea boldly uses the image of husband and wife to describe the relation of love that God desires should exist between himself and his people; because that love truly exists in him, he pardons his people's infidelity over and over (Hos 2:18-25). This theme will be picked up by other books and by various prophets (e.g., Jer 2:2).

St. John is heir to this tradition, but he goes further. He bases his assertion that God is love on the fact that the Father has sent his only Son into the world so that we might have life through him. To convince us of God's love, he gives us not a definition but the sign by which we can discern that love. The sign is this: "In this is love: not that we have loved God, but that he loved us and sent his Son as expiation for our sins" (1 John 4:10).

The love of God for us and the love of his Son for the world entail consequences for us—and not simply moral consequences imposed on us from outside. Rather, since God has so loved us and since we are his children, we must love one another. Here again John seeks to be very concrete. After all, no one has ever seen God. But if we love one another, God dwells in us and his love is perfected in us. By faith we know God's love to be present among us. He is love; therefore, those who abide in love abide in God and God in them.

This feast of God's love for us will normally influence our behavior toward others, and this behavior will be a sign to the world that God has loved us and continues to love us.

[B] They Will Look upon Him Whom They Have Pierced, and They Shall Believe (John 19:31-37)

Exegetes have seen in chapter 19 of the Fourth Gospel and especially in verses 34-35, on the blood and water that flow from the lance-pierced side of Jesus, an allusion to chapters 6 and 7 of the same gospel. In chapter 6 Jesus spoke of the gift of his own flesh and blood that he would give to his disciples; verses 51-58 gave a hint as to the form the gift would take. Now, in chapter 19, seeing the blood flow from the side of the dead Christ, we realize that the food spoken of in chapter 6 is closely connected with the death of Christ and with the sacrifice of himself that he offered by doing the Father's will.

Verse 38 of chapter 7—"Rivers of living water will flow from within"—likewise yields its full meaning now. We cannot but observe that in the account of the passion every detail is a sign. In fact, every event of Christ's life has its permanent consequences.

We must keep our attention focused not so much on the event as on the abiding reality that it signifies. In this case, however, the event is one that is a turning point of universal history. In fact, we must say that the cross is not only a sign; it is itself also the thing signified. Water flows from the body of Jesus; the water is the life he gives to those who believe in him (John 7:38-39). Whoever drinks this water will never thirst again (John 4:14). The blood of Jesus is true drink (John 6:55).

In short, it makes little difference whether the fact related by John is historical or simply a symbolic way of relating Jesus to the prophecies. At the same time, however, John does appeal to what he has seen with his own eyes, that is, to historical facts. It would be imprudent to refuse him credence.

We are here confronted with a sign of Christ's love and of the love of the Father who accepts the sacrifice Christ offers in our name. The sign refers to the grace that is bestowed through water and the Spirit and that truly quenches our thirst. The Father wants to rebuild the world; the Son offers himself for the work and communicates to us the life that flows from his death and resurrection as from a well-spring. In Jesus who sacrificed himself for us we find both love and reconciliation. This is the point made in the second of the Alleluia verses before the gospel.

Believe in the Love That Forgives (Hos 11:1, 3-4, 8c-9)

God does not come to destroy. He may in the past have been "forced" to punish Israel, but now he repents of that. What he did, he did for the sake of his people: he saved them from Egypt, called them his children, taught them to walk in his ways. But he will not execute his anger, for he is the Holy One who does not come to destroy. As the gospel account tells us, the blood and water that flow from the side of the crucified Christ are signs that God is a loving and forgiving God.

The responsorial psalm, taken from the book of Isaiah, reminds us of the water flowing from Christ's side: "You will draw water joyfully from the springs of salvation" (Isa 12:3). It also reminds us of Christ's words: "Let anyone who thirsts come to me and drink" (John 7:37).

You Will Know the Love of Christ (Eph 3:8-12, 14-19)

Unless we are rooted and grounded in love, we cannot comprehend the breadth and length and height and depth of Christ's love, which surpasses knowledge. This is Paul's enthusiastic outburst in the Letter to the Ephesians. As a matter of fact, any contact with the cross of Christ, and the quenching of our thirst by drinking his blood, after having been washed by the water from his side and having become one body in the Church—that too is too much for our imaginations to grasp.

God's plan, hidden through the ages within his bosom, has now been revealed through his Son, and all of us are commissioned to proclaim it and help it transform other lives. We must make all people see that we approach God with confidence, because we trust in the pierced Christ, to whom we raise our eyes and who is the wellspring and fountainhead of our life.

The religion we are to proclaim is not primarily an institution. Its characteristic trait is that it is a religion of love in which God and humanity are intimately united and in which the chief preoccupation is that the community should be a sign of love at work. That is how we achieve our fulfillment and can enter into the fullness of God himself.

[C] We Have Been Sought and Found (Luke 15:3-7)

God's love for humanity finds expression here in a parable that is well known to us yet never fails to move us deeply: the parable of the lost sheep, which the shepherd anxiously searches out and carries home on his shoulder and for which he then celebrates a joyful feast: "I have found my lost sheep" (v. 6). How could the Lord's attentive love for us be better expressed?

The parable reminds us of other passages, especially in St. John, where Jesus speaks of himself as a shepherd: "This is the will of the one who sent me, that I should not lose anything of what he gave me" (John 6:39); "My sheep hear my voice; I know them, and they follow me. I give them eternal life, and they shall never perish. No one can take them out of my hand" (John 10:27-28); "I will lay down my life for the sheep" (John 10:15). We know how the Synoptic Gospels describe the shepherd's role: he gathers his sheep together (Matt 15:24); he gives his life for them and then returns to life again for them (Matt 26:31; Mark 14:27). To this St. John adds the intimacy created by the reciprocal knowledge of the Good Shepherd and his sheep: "I know mine and mine know me" (John 10:14). The image of the shepherd becomes an authentic revelation of love.

God Will Feed His Flock (Ezek 34:11-16)

The New Testament revelation of God as the loving Shepherd fulfills the promise God made through Ezekiel: "I myself will look after and tend my sheep" (34:11). The image of the shepherd is much used in the Old Testament, where it is applied to earthly kings and to God himself, who is called the "shepherd of Israel" (Ps 80:2). The image is especially popular in the psalms. Psalm 23, for example, reflects the experience of God's people, whom he had led as a shepherd leads his flock and to whom he had given peace and joy. In the present passage, Ezekiel adopts a wholly unpolitical perspective; the God whom he sees as a shepherd will lead all the nations of the earth to good pasture. "The lost I will seek out, the strayed I will bring back, the injured I will bind up, the sick I will heal, but the sleek and the strong I will destroy, shepherding them rightly" (Ezek 34:16).

The gospel parable and Ezekiel's prophecy give a true and permanently valid picture of God. In fact, it is God himself who presents himself to us under this image.

The Proof That He Is a Shepherd and Loves Us (Rom 5:5-11)

Both the prophecy of Ezekiel and the parable of Luke might well be simply literary dressing. In his Letter to the Romans, St. Paul shows us that the image points to a reality. "God proves his love for us in that while we were still sinners Christ died for us" (Rom 5:8). Christ's death reconciled us to God when we were still in sin; now that we have been reconciled by his blood, we shall surely be saved by him in his risen life. We are sure because, as Paul says at the beginning of the pericope, "The love of God has been poured out into our hearts through the Holy Spirit that has been given to us" (v. 5).

Today's celebration does not specify the response we are to make to God's love. Each of us must respond as God wishes us to do in our daily lives.

In a passage read in the Office of Readings, St. Bonaventure writes: "From you flows *the river which gladdens the city of God* and makes us cry out with joy and thanksgiving in hymns of praise to you, for we know by our own experience that *with you is the source of life, and in your light we see light.*"[1]

51. DECEMBER 8: THE IMMACULATE CONCEPTION OF THE BLESSED VIRGIN MARY

At the beginning of the eighth century we find in the East a feast celebrating St. Anne's conception of Mary. In the ninth century the feast appeared at Naples and, a century later, began to spread from there. It was still an optional feast, and the emphasis was on the special favor God gave to Anne of conceiving after so many years of barrenness; the celebration had no further dogmatic dimension. In about the eleventh century the feast became widespread in the West.

In the course of time, the celebration began to take on a greater solemnity and, above all, a new doctrinal meaning. Through a great deal of discussion in the theological schools, clarification was gradually achieved on the special privilege the Blessed Virgin had received of being preserved free from original sin. It was only in 1854, however, that Pope Pius IX proclaimed the dogma of the immaculate conception.

Readings

The Holy Spirit Will Come upon You (Luke 1:26-38)
See "Fourth Week of Advent," vol. 1, pp. 127–35.

Enmity between You and the Woman (Gen 3:9-15, 20)
See the "Tenth Sunday: Evil Overcome," Year B, vol. 3, pp. 211–14.

Chosen before the Foundation of the World (Eph 1:3-6, 11-12)
See "Mary, Mother of God (January 1)," vol. 1, pp. 201–10.

The prayers and the preface bring out the essential content of the dogma: the fact that the Virgin was preserved from original sin by prevenient grace and thus prepared to be a worthy mother for God's

Son. The preface also sees the Immaculate Virgin as prefiguring the Church, Christ's beautiful Bride, who is without spot or wrinkle. We have recourse to Mary's intercession because she was chosen in a unique way from among all women and because she intervenes on behalf of God's people, for whom she is a figure of ideal holiness.

52. FEBRUARY 2:
THE PRESENTATION OF THE LORD

In order to obey the Mosaic law, Mary took the child Jesus to the temple forty days after his birth and presented herself for her legal purification. This required an offering; in her case it was the offering of the poor: a pair of turtledoves or of young pigeons. The elderly Simeon and Anna the prophetess received from God the great favor of meeting the child and recognizing in him the awaited Messiah.

In the East, the meeting of Jesus and Simeon was commemorated in a feast known as *Hypopante* ("Meeting"). It is first attested for the fourteenth of February at Jerusalem toward the end of the fourth century. A procession was part of the celebration, and the day was spent in meditation on the words of Simeon, "a light for revelation to the Gentiles." It was probably around the middle of the fifth century that lamps were carried in the procession, with the intention of thus representing Christ as the Light that enlightens the nations.

Under Pope Sergius I, a Syrian pope (687–701), the feast came to be celebrated at Rome, but on February 2, which was the fortieth day after the birth of Jesus. The celebration included a procession from the church of St. Hadrian to the basilica of St. Mary Major and an Office containing elements of Eastern provenance. Only belatedly, beginning in the ninth century, did the feast spread from Rome throughout the West; for the most part it had something of a penitential character, especially at Rome.

The older liturgical books titled the feast the Purification of the Blessed Virgin. Happily, this law-centered approach to the feast has been abandoned, and the feast now celebrates a new manifestation of Jesus as Messiah. In the new Missal the feast is known as the Presentation of the Lord.

Readings

"My Eyes Have Seen Your Salvation" (Luke 2:22-40)

The Canticle of Simeon, which has become one of the classic hymns of the Church and is recited at Compline in the Roman Office, proclaims the Messiah whom the old man recognizes in the child he holds in his arms. Anna the prophetess also recognizes in the child the one who is to liberate Jerusalem. The presentation is thus a second feast of Epiphany. We, for our part, are being urged to recognize in the Church, in other human beings, and in events the salvation that is being offered to us. Above all, each sacrament is a manifestation of the Lord: we meet him in the sacrament, and he prepares us for the definitive meeting at the end.

The Lord Comes to His Temple (Mal 3:1-4)

The reason why this passage is read today is not chiefly the mention of the temple but rather the fact that it concerns the coming and manifestation of the Lord. Malachi is describing a solemn epiphany and is also foretelling the role of John the Baptist: "I am sending my messenger / to prepare the way before me." The Lord's coming is awesome: "who will endure the day of his coming?" The images used to describe his power and action are strong ones, for his role is primarily to purify so that a sacrifice pleasing to the Lord may be offered.

The responsorial psalm (Ps 24) was written for a glorious entry into Jerusalem, and it foretells the manifestation of the Savior: "Who is this king of glory? / He, the LORD of hosts, / he is the king of glory."

A High Priest Who Is Like His Brothers (Heb 2:14-18)

God chose a unique way of saving the world: he sent his Son and bade him share the human condition; then, through the Son's death, he reduced to impotence the one who had the power to inflict death. The passage goes on, in a Pauline style and a Pauline theological vein, to explain God's plan as it was implemented in the *kenosis*, or self-emptying, of his Son. The result is that we have a High Priest who has been able to offer the perfect sacrifice and take away the sins of the world.

Today, this savior is presented in the temple. The High Priest enters for the first time into the place of sacrifice, but his own sacrifice will be offered on the cross and will be more efficacious than all the sacrifices hitherto offered.

53. MARCH 19:
ST. JOSEPH, HUSBAND OF
THE BLESSED VIRGIN MARY

This feast was introduced into the calendar at a relatively late date. The proclamation of the gospel had often reminded Christians of this saint and offered him to them for their veneration. The Eastern rites made frequent mention of him in their chants. In the West, there is evidence of a popular devotion as early as the seventh century, but there was no organized veneration until about the twelfth century. The reader will recall that Pope John XXIII introduced the name of Joseph into the Roman Canon.

Readings

Joseph Did as the Angel Had Commanded Him (Matt 1:16, 18-21, 24)

The first part of the passage consists of the mention made of Joseph in the genealogy of Jesus. The text then passes immediately to the miraculous conception of Jesus and to the quandary in which Joseph was placed by Mary's condition. The angel explains the mystery to him in a dream. Joseph is thus the first after Mary to receive word from God of the coming and proximate birth of the Messiah, a child who will be named Jesus, that is, "The Lord saves." The gospel shows that Joseph does not hesitate, once the angel has informed him of the true state of affairs. With a restraint we may find surprising, the evangelist says simply, "When Joseph awoke, he did as the angel of the Lord had commanded him."

Your Father and I Have Been Looking for You Anxiously (Luke 2:41-51; Alternate Gospel)

See vol. 1, p. 209.

Joseph, Descendant of David; Jesus, Son of David (2 Sam 7:4-5a, 12-14a, 16)

See vol. 1, p. 127.

The Faith of Abraham, Father of Believers (Rom 4:13, 16-18, 22)

See vol. 3, pp. 96–97.

In celebrating this feast, the Church wants to exalt the servant who is faithful in doing God's will. Abraham is the great Old Testament type of such obedience, and Jesus is its perfect fulfillment. The new and eternal covenant was made possible, in part, because Joseph too obeyed so fully and devoutly, just as the old covenant was made possible by Abraham's obedience.

The collect of the Mass underscores Joseph's role: to his care God entrusted the beginnings of the mystery of salvation. The prayer over the offerings reminds us of Joseph's complete dedication to the service of God's Son, who had been born of Mary. The preface of St. Joseph likewise praises Joseph as the wise and faithful servant whom God had put in charge of the Holy Family and who watched like a father over God's Son.

54. MARCH 25:
THE ANNUNCIATION OF THE LORD

Mention of this feast occurs first in an evangeliary of the seventh century. An inscription found in the ruins of an ancient basilica at Nazareth may contain the words *Ave Maria*, but this does not allow us to assert that as early as the fourth century there was a church dedicated to the Annunciation or a feast celebrating this mystery. Only in the seventh century do we find sure evidence in East and West of a feast of the Annunciation.

He Will Be Called Son of the Most High (Luke 1:26-38)

See vol. 1, pp. 129–30.

Behold, a Virgin Shall Conceive (Isa 7:10-14)

See vol. 1, p. 132.

I Have Come to Do Your Will, O God (Heb 10:4-10)

See vol. 1, pp. 191–93.

The preface for this feast as well as the presidential prayers speak of the annunciation as the fulfillment of God's promise (the preface) and emphasize the two natures of Christ.

The feast is, in fact, a repetition of what has already been celebrated during Advent. It is understandable, however, that the expansion of the Christmas cycle should have led to a desire for a special celebration of this moment in the coming of the Word.

55. JUNE 29: SS. PETER AND PAUL, APOSTLES

The two pillars of the Church, each of whom has his own basilica at Rome, have always been celebrated together by the Church of Rome. The Philocalian Calendar and the Hieronymian Martyrology (June 29) show that a feast was being celebrated at Rome as early as the middle of the fourth century. These two documents announce the feast and tell us that it was celebrated successively at St. Peter's on the Via Aurelia (a liturgy in honor of St. Peter), at the catacombs on the Via Appia (a liturgy in honor of both apostles), and at St. Paul's on the Via Ostiensis (a liturgy in honor of St. Paul). A fifth-century hymn confirms the fact of this triple liturgical celebration on the one day.

We cannot go into the archeological and historical studies that have been done on the history of the feast and on the place where the two Apostles were martyred and buried. The reader will have ready access to material on these questions.

Readings

You Are Peter, and upon This Rock I Will Build My Church (Matt 16:13-19)

See vol. 3, pp. 129–32.

The Lord Rescued Me from the Hand of Herod (Acts 12:1-11)

Receive the Reward of a Winner (2 Tim 4:6-8, 17-18)

See vol. 3, p. 385.

56. AUGUST 15:
THE ASSUMPTION OF
THE BLESSED VIRGIN MARY

The Greeks gave the name *Koimesis* (falling asleep) to this feast that celebrated not only the Blessed Virgin's Assumption but also her death. Some of the Latin names for it were *Dormitio* (falling asleep), *Depositio* (burial), *Natale* (birthday), *Transitus* (passage). As a matter of fact, however, we know nothing of how the Virgin's earthly life ended.

In the middle of the fifth century, the feast appears in the liturgical books. The liturgy of Rome had a feast of the Virgin on January 1, which has been restored in the new calendar; there was no other feast of Mary in the Roman calendar until the seventh century. But we must realize that the official establishment of a feast usually follows upon the existence of a long-established devotion; in the case of the assumption, such a devotion can be traced back very far. The dogmatic definition of the assumption in 1950 thus simply confirmed the faith of the entire Christian people. It can be said that the liturgical feast of the assumption was first celebrated at Jerusalem toward the middle of the fifth century; in the seventh century it spread throughout the whole Latin world as an official feast.

Readings

The Lord Has Lifted up the Lowly (Luke 1:39-56)

A Woman Clothed with the Sun, with the Moon under Her Feet (Rev 11:19a; 12:1-6a, 10ab)

In Christ Shall All Be Brought to Life (1 Cor 15:20-27)
See vol. 3, pp. 174–75.

The presidential prayers of the Mass give clear expression to the faith of the Church and the spirituality of the feast. The assertion that God assumed the Blessed Virgin body and soul into heaven is forcefully made in the collect, in the prayer over the offerings, and in the preface.

The preface says that God preserved from the corruption of the tomb the body that had carried his Son and brought the Author of life into our world. The preface also speaks of the Blessed Virgin as the perfect image of the Church as it will be in eternity.

The Church places herself under the protection of God's Mother, who is now in heaven, for Mary is a sign of the hope of God's pilgrim people (preface). We lift our hearts to the things that are above (collect); she intensifies our longing for the resurrection and our own entry into heavenly glory (collect; prayer after Communion).

57. NOVEMBER 1: ALL SAINTS

It was in the East that Christians first had the idea of celebrating all the martyrs together on one day; we find such a feast celebrated at the end of the fourth century on the first Sunday after Pentecost. A similar feast was celebrated on May 13 at Edessa and another in eastern Syria at the beginning of the fifth century, during the Easter octave. A lectionary of the sixth to seventh centuries indicates such a celebration in the West on the first Sunday after Pentecost. Finally, in 835, Pope Gregory IV decreed a feast of all the saints for November 1, in the territory of Louis the Pious.

Readings

The Reward of the Righteous (Matt 5:1-12)

A Great Multitude, from Every Nation, Race, People, and Tongue (Rev 7:2-4, 9-12)

We Shall See God as He Is (1 John 3:1-3)

The feast focuses on the intercession of the saints in heaven for us who are still on earth; the collect and the prayer over the offerings allude to this intercession. In general, the celebration has a strongly eschatological tone. The preface describes the saints as singing eternally the praises of the Father. Yet even this eschatological vision should be a source of encouragement for the entire Church as she walks by faith, helped by the example of the saints (see the preface). The prayer after Communion, which has its usually eschatological orientation, asks that we may pass from the table at which we are still pilgrims, to the heavenly banquet.

Notes

1. The Anthropology of Lent

1. C. Charlier, editorial in *Bible et vie chrétienne*, no. 4 (December–February 1953–54): 3–4.

2. C. Duquoc, "Acte chéateur et humanitéde Dieu," *Lumière et vie* 49 (June–August 1960): 88.

3. Pseudo–Chrysostom, *In Pascha sermons* 2 (*PG* 59:725), quoted by H. de Lubac, *Catholicism*, trans. L. C. Sheppard (New York: 1950), 4. The first chapter of de Lubac's book offers numerous citations from the fathers that make the same point.

4. See A.-M. Dubarle, *The Biblical Doctrine of Original Sin*, trans. A. M. Stewart (New York, 1965).

5. J. Guillet, *Themes of the Bible*, trans. A. J. LaMothe Jr. (Notre Dame, 1960), 99.

6. *Odes of Solomon*, chap. 12; French translation in J. Labourt, "Les Odes de Solomon," *Revue biblique* 7 (1910): 493.

7. See J. Jeremias, "Adam," *TDNT* 1:141–43.

2. The Experience of Lent in the Fathers

1. *Quaestiones ex utroque [Testamento] mixtim* 70: *De ieiunio* (*PL* 35:2364).

2. *Sermo* 206, 2–3 (*PL* 38:1041–42).

3. *Sermo* 207, 3 (*PL* 38:1044).

4. Ibid.

5. *Sermo* 39, 6 (*SC* 49bis:77; *CCL* 138A:220).

6. *Sermo* 40, 5 (*SC* 49bis:91; *CCL* 138A:231).

7. *Sermo* 41, 3 (*SC* 49bis:99; *CCL* 138A:237).

8. *Sermo* 43, 4 (*SC* 49bis:127; *CCL* 138A:256).

9. *Sermo* 47, 3 (*SC* 49bis:169: *CCL* 138A:277).

10. *Sermo* 48, 4 (*SC* 49bis:179; *CCL* 138A:283).

11. *Sermo* 49, 5 (*SC* 49bis:191; *CCL* 138A:290).

12. *Sermo* 50, 3 (*SC* 49bis:201; *CCL* 138A:294).

13. *Sermo* 211, 1 (*PL* 38:1054).

14. *Sermo* 211, 2 (*PL* 38:1055).

15. *Sermo* 208, 2 (*PL* 38:1045).

16. *Sermo* 205, 3 (*PL* 38:1040).

17. *Sermo* 39, 6 (*SC* 49bis:77; *CCL* 138A:221).

18. *Sermo* 41, 3 (*SC* 49bis:97; *CCL* 138A:23S).

19. *Sermo* 43, 4 (*SC* 49bis:127; *CCL* 138A:2s6).

20. *Sermo* 48, 5 (*SC* 49bis:179; *CCL* 138A:283).

21. *Sermo* 49, 6 (*SC* 49bis:193; *CCL* 138A:290).

22. *Sermo* 40, 4 (*SC* 49bis:87; *CCL* 138A:228).

23. *Sermo* 42, 2 (*SC* 49bis:103; *CCL* 138A:240).

24. Ibid.

25. *Adversus ebriosos et de resurrectione sermo* (*PG* 50:433).

26. *Sermo* 44, 2 (*SC* 49bis:133; *CCL* 138A:259).

27. *Sermo* 43, 3 (*SC* 49bis:123; *CCL* 138A:254).

28. *Sermo* 50, 3 (*SC* 49bis:199; *CCL* 138A:294).

29. *In Genesim homiliae* 1, 4 (*PG* 53:25).

30. *Quaestiones ex utroque [Testamento] mixtim* 70: *De ieiunio* (*PL* 35:2364).

31. *Sermo* 207, 2 (*PL* 38:1043).

32. *Sermo* 47, 1 (*SC* 49bis:161; *CCL* 138A:279).

33. *Sermo* 41, 2 (*SC* 49bis:95; *CCL* 138A:234).

34. *Sermo* 210, 10–11 (*PL* 38:1052–53).

35. St. Leo the Great, *Sermo* 49, 3 (*SC* 49bis:187; *CCL* 138A:287).

36. St. Leo the Great, *Sermo* 48, 1 (*SC* 49bis:173; *CCL* 138A:280).

37. *The Rule of St. Benedict*, ed. Timothy Fry, et al. (Collegeville, MN: Liturgical Press, 1980).

38. "Tamen quia paucorum est ista virtus." Cf. St. Leo, *Sermo* 42: "Sed quia haec fortitudo paucorum est" (*SC* 49bis:102; *CCL* 138A:238).

39. "Omnes pariter et neglegentias aliorum temporum his sanctis diebus diluere." Cf. St. Leo, *Sermo* 39: "Omnes praeteritae desidiae castigantur, omnes neglegentiae diluuntur" (*SC* 49bis:68; *CCL* 138A:214).

40. "Ergo his diebus augeamus nobis aliquid solito penso servitutis." Cf. St. Leo, *Sermo* 40: "Omnem observantiam nostram ratio istorum dierum po scat augeri," and again: "Ad mensuram consuetudinis nostrae necessariis aliquid addamus augmentis" (*SC* 49bis:78; *CCL* 138A:223).

41. L. C. Mohlberg, ed., *Liber sacramentorum romanae aeclesiae ordinis anni circuli* (*Sacramentarium Gelasianum*) Rerum ecclesiasticarum documenta, Series maior: Fontes 4 (Rome, 1960), no. 53. (Henceforth: Gel. with number of text, e.g., Gel. 53).

3. The Church, Place of Divinization

1. See Tertullian, *De praescriptione haereticorum* 1, 3 (*CCL* 1:187).

2. See *La Tradition Apostolique de saint Hippolyte: Essai de reconstitution*, ed. B. Botte, Liturgiewissenschaftliche Quellen und Forschungen 39 (Munster, 1963), chaps. 15–20, pp. 33–59.

3. G. Hudon, *La perfection chrétienne d'après les sermons de saint Leon*, Lex orandi 26 (Paris, 1959), 253. Vatican II's Dogmatic Constitution on the Church speaks of the Church as a "sacrament."

Lent used to begin, for the entire Church, on the First Sunday of Lent. This is why on the Wednesday of Quinquagesima (Ash Wednesday), when the fast of public penitents began, the prayer over the offerings in the Gelasian Sacramentary asks that God prepare the faithful "to celebrate the imminent beginning of the holy sacrament [sc., of Lent]" ("venerabilis sacramenti venturum celebramus exordium": Gel. 91).

4. Gel. 91.

5. Gel. 104.

6. Gel. 235.

7. Saturday of third week, collect; cf. Gel. 99.

8. Thursday of second week, prayer over the offerings.

9. Friday of first week, collect.

10. Ash Wednesday, collect.

11. Gel. 138: "Da nobis observantiam, domine, legitimam devotione perfectam."

12. Gel. 245: "Prosequere, quaesumus, omnipotens deus, ieiuniorum sacra mysteria."

13. "Annua nobis est, dilectissimi, ieiuniorum celebranda festivitas," in L. C. Mohlberg, ed., *Sacramentarium Veronense*, Rerum ecclesiasticarum documenta, Series maior: Fontes 1 (Rome, 1960), no. 860. (Henceforth: Ver. with number of text, e.g., Ver. 860).

14. Ver. 209.

15. This gospel pericope is read on the First Sunday of Lent, the day that originally signaled the beginning of the Lenten season.

16. This prayer is from the Verona Sacramentary (no. 207), where it served as the collect for Ember Wednesday after Pentecost.

17. Ver. 894.

18. Ver. 927: "Ad hostes nostros, domine, superandos praesta quaesumus ut auxilium tuum ieiuniis tibi placitis et bonis operibus impetremus."

19. Ver. 864, prayer over the offerings on Ember Saturday in September: ". . . sed cum in ipsis nostris observationibus a noxiis et illicitis non vacamus, non hoc te ieiunium delegisse prophetica voce testaris quoniam non solum prodesse non poterit castigatio corporalis si spiritus noster nefandis cogitationibus implicetur sed hoc constat esse deterius si etiam terrena conditione mitigata mens ab iniquitatibus non quiescit."

20. H. Küng, *The Council, Reform, and Reunion*, trans. C. Hastings (New York, 1961), 31–32, alt.

21. The Latin text is from Gel. 104.

22. Ver. 1313: "Quoniam . . . per observantiae competentis obsequium de perceptis grati numeribus de percipiendis efficimur gratiores."

23. Ver. 229: "post illos enim laetitiae dies quos in honorem Domini a mortuis resurgentis et in coelos ascendentis exigimus postque perceptum Sancti Spiritus donum necessarie nobis haec ieiunia sancta provisa sunt ut pura conversatione viventibus quae divinitus ecclesiae sunt collata permaneant."

24. Monday of first week, collect; cf. Gel. 1170.

25. Fifth Sunday, prayer over the offerings; cf. Gel. 255.

26. Gel. 210: "Deus, qui nos formam humilitatis ieiunando et orando Unigeniti tui Domini nostri imitatione docuisti."

27. Gel. 178.

28. See Ash Wednesday, collect; cf. Gel. 654.

29. Monday of second week, collect. ("Deus, qui ob animarum medelam castigare precepisti . . ."); cf. Gel. 173.

30. Monday of fifth week, prayer over the offerings.

31. See the Friday of fifth week, collect.

32. See the Thursday of fifth week, prayer over the offerings.

33. See the first prayer for the blessing of the ashes: "as they [all who receive these ashes] follow the Lenten observances, they may be worthy to come with minds made pure to celebrate the Paschal Mystery of your Son." ("ut, quadragesimalem observantiam prosequentes, ad Filii tui paschale mysterium celebrandum purificatis mentibus pervenire mereantur").

34. Monday of fifth week, collect.

35. Friday of first week, prayer after Communion. ("a vetustate purgatos, in mysterii salutaris faciat transire consortium").

36. See Monday of fourth week, prayer over the offerings.

37. Wednesday of fourth week, prayer over the offerings; cf. Gel. 377.

38. Cf. Gel. 257.

39. Tuesday of fourth week, prayer after communion, which is derived from Gel. 488 or 1225.

40. Gel. 1204.

41. Gel. 251.

42. Wednesday of second week, prayer after Communion.

43. Saturday of second week, collect. Gel. 129.

5. Lent Then and Now

1. An *ordo* is a document showing in detail the rubrics to be followed in a celebration; as such, it is an essential complement to the Sacramentary, which normally contains only the prayers the celebrant needs to say. *Ordo XI* dates from the second half of the seventh century and evidently is closely related to the Gelasian Sacramentary. It has been edited by M. Andrieu in his *Les Ordines Romani du Haut Moyen Age* 2, Spicilegium Sacrum Lovaniense 23 (Louvain, 1948), 380–447. See A. Chavasse, "La discipline romaine des scrutins," *Recherches de science religieuse* 48 (1960): 225–40.

6. First and Second Sundays of Lent (Year A): Our Victory and Transformation in Christ

1. In Luke 10:17-20 we are told of the disciples' amazement at seeing the demons subject to them in the name of Christ.

2. "You belong to your father the devil" (John 8:44).

3. *Enarrationes in Psalmos* 60, 3 (*CCL* 39:766). In *The Liturgy of the Hours*, vol. 2: *Lenten Season, Easter Season* (New York: Christian Book Publishing, Co., 1976), 88.

4. J. Mouroux, *The Meaning of Man*, trans. A. H. G. Downes (New York, 1948), 141.

5. *Breviarium in Psalmos* (*PL* 26:1163).

6. *De mysteriis* 7, 34 (*SC* 25bis:174).

7. *Sermo de Transfiguratione* 3 (*SC* 74:17–18; *CCL* 138A:299), in *The Liturgy of the Hours*, vol. 2, 149.

8. Gel. 286.

9. For the ritual, see *Rite of Christian Initiation of Adults* (Collegeville, MN: Liturgical Press, 1988).

10. Ibid., no. 53.

11. Ibid., no. 55.

12. Ibid., no. 57. Cf. Gel. 286. [The Latin text in the *Ordo initiationis christianae adultorum* has "gloriae tuae rudimenta," which is here translated as "grace which has begun." ' Mohlberg's critical edition has "magnitudinis gloriae rudimenta" (i.e., without "tuae"), which Nocent interprets above (see text corresponding to footnote 97) as meaning "the beginning of his (the catechumen's) future great glory."—Trans.]

13. Ibid.

14. Ibid., no. 66; cf. Gel. 285.

15. Ibid.

16. Ibid., no. 135; cf. Gel. 287.

17. Ibid.

18. *Adversus eos qui differunt baptismum oratio* (*PC* 46:417), trans. in J. Daniélou, *The Bible and the Liturgy* (Notre Dame, 1956), 22.

19. *Egeria: Diary of a Pilgrimage*, trans. G. E. Gingras, Ancient Christian Writers 38 (New York, 1970), 123.

7. Third Sunday of Lent (Year A): The Thirst for the Water of Life

1. *Homilia in dictum Pauli: Nolo vos ignorare* 4 (*PC* 51:248–49).
2. *De sacramentis* 5, 3 (*SC* 25bis:120–22); cf. *De mysteriis* 8, 48 (*SC* 25bis:183).
3. *Tractatus in Evangelium Ioannis* 26, 12 (*CCL* 36:265).
4. *Epist.* 63, 8 (*CSEL* 3:706–7), in J. Daniélou, *From Shadows to Reality: Studies in the Biblical Typology of the Fathers*, trans. W. Hibberd (Westminster, MD, 1960), 195.
5. *Tractatus in Evangelium Ioannis* 15, 6 (*CCL* 36:152).
6. Ibid., 26, 12 (*CCL* 36:265).
7. See M.-E. Boismard, "Water," in X. Léon-Dufour, ed., *Dictionary of Biblical Theology*, trans. under the direction of P. J. Cahill (New York, 1967), 567.
8. *Roman Missal*, Ritual Mass for the Conferral of the Sacraments of Christian Initiation, For the Celebration of the Scrutinies; the prayer is taken directly from the Gelasian Sacramentary (no. 193).
9. Gel. 291. Text and translation in *Collectio Rituum*, ed. W. J. Schmitz (Milwaukee, 1964), 85.
10. Gel. 292; translated in Schmitz, *op. cit.*, 87.
11. Gel. 293; translated in Schmitz, *op. cit.*, 103–5.
12. Gel. 298; translated in Schmitz, *op. cit.*, 119–21.
13. *Rite of Christian Initiation of Adults*, no. 154.
14. The Latin original of these prayers is taken over from Gel. 194–98; see *Ordo initiationis christianae adultorum*, no. 377. The English version in the *Rite of Christian Initiation of Adults* is an adaptation of the Latin prayers. Revised translations appear in the third edition of the *Roman Missal*.
The Gelasian Sacramentary adds an *Oratio super populum* (no. 199): "Lord, your holy family humbly awaits the gift of your mercy. Grant that they may receive from your generous hand what at your bidding they desire."
15. At this point, in the Gelasian Sacramentary (no. 197), though not in the *Ordo* or the *Rite*, it is explicitly stated that the names of the candidates are to be read out. The prayer then continues: "Lord, we ask you to bestow the gift of your Spirit on those who are to be made new in the baptismal font, and thus to prepare them for the full effect of your sacraments."

8. Fourth Sunday of Lent (Year A): The Light of Truth

1. *De sacramentis* 3, 12–15 (*SC* 25bis:98–100).
2. *Tractatus in Evangelium Ioannis* 44, 2 (*CCL* 36:382).
3. Ibid., 34, 9 (*CCL* 36:315–16), in *The Liturgy of the Hours*, vol. 2: *Lenten Season, Easter Season* (New York: Catholic Book Publishing Co., 1976), 276.
4. Gel. 294; translated in Schmitz, *Collectio Rituum* (1964), 93–95, with the same second exorcism for women, 11–13.
5. Gel. 295.
6. *Rite of Christian Initiation of Adults*, no. 168.

9. Fifth Sunday of Lent (Year A): Arise and Live

1. *Tractatus in Evangelium Ioannis* 49, 12 (*CCL* 36:426).
2. A. Rose, "Les grands évangiles baptismaux du careme romain," *Questions liturgiques et paroissiales* 43 (1962): 15.

3. Quoted in ibid., 16.
4. *Tractatus in Evangelium Ioannis* 49, 5–6 (*CCL* 36:422).
5. *Commentaria in Ezechielem* 37, 14 (*CCL* 75:515).
6. *Rite of Christian Initiation of Adults*, no. 175.
7. Gel. 310.
8. Gel. 315–18.
9. Gel. 319–28.
10. *Rite of Christian Initiation of Adults*, no. 161. The prayer is based on Gel. 298.
11. See A. Chavasse, "La discipline romaine des scrutins," *Recherches de science religieuse* 48 (1960): 237–38.
12. *Rite of Christian Initiation of Adults*, no. 182.
13. Gel. 299–309.

10. First Sunday of Lent (Year B): The Flood and the Covenant

1. On the Flood, see J. Daniélou, *The Bible and the Liturgy*, chap. 4: "The Types of Baptism: Creation and the Deluge" (70–85); *From Shadows to Reality* bk. 2, chap. 1: "The Flood, Baptism, and Judgment in Holy Scripture" (69–84).
2. Daniélou, *From Shadows to Reality*, 82.
3. *Dialogus cum Tryphone* 138, 1–2 (*PG* 6:793).
4. *De baptismo* 8 (*SC* 35:77–78).
5. *Constitutiones Apostolicae* 2, 14, 19. The work dates from the second half of the fourth century.
6. *De Noe et arca* (*CSEL* 22:413–97; *PL* 14:361–416).
7. *De sacramentis* is a collection of notes taken by a stenographer during Ambrose's catechetical sermons to the newly baptized. *De mysteriis* was written by the saint himself.
8. See *De sacramentis* 1, 6, 23 (*SC* 25bis:72).
9. Ibid., 3, 1, 1 (*SC* 25bis:75).
10. *De mysteriis* 10–11 (*SC* 25bis:160–62).
11. *Commentaria in Evangelium secundum Matthaeum* 15, 23 (*PG* 13:1322).
12. *De peccatorum mentis et remissione* 2, 7, 10, quoted in Mouroux, *The Meaning of Man*, 294n142, alt.
13. *De vita Moysis* (*PG* 44:327).

11. Second and Third Sundays of Lent (Year B): God Has Handed over His Son for Us

1. *De sacramentis* 4, 6, 27 (*SC* 25bis:116).
2. The text as we have it is the subject of debate among scholars today. See N. Lohfink, "Les dix commandements dans le Sinaï," in his *Sciences bibliques en marche: Un exégète fait le point* (Paris, 1969), 114–27. (This is a translation by H. Savon of Lohfink's *Bibelauslegung im Wandel: Ein Exeget ortet seine Wissenschaft* [Frankfurt, 1967].)
3. *Homiliae in Exodum* 8, 1 (*PG* 12:350; *SC* 16:184–85).

12. Fourth and Fifth Sundays of Lent (Year B): The Salvation of the World

1. See C. H. Dodd, *The Interpretation of the Fourth Gospel* (Cambridge, 1953).

17. Palm Sunday, Monday, Tuesday, and Wednesday of Holy Week: Toward the Mount of Olives

1. See *Egeria: Diary of a Pilgrimage* (chap. 6, n. 19, above).

2. Ibid., chap. 31, 104–5. The procession starts at the Mount of Olives and moves through Jerusalem to the Anastasis, or rotunda church containing the Holy Sepulcher.

3. See J. Ziegler, "Die *Peregrinatio Etheriae* und die hl. Scrift," *Biblica* 12 (1931): 188–89.

4. See A. Baumstark, *Comparative Liturgy*, rev. B. Botte and trans. F. L. Cross (London, 1958), 149.

5. On Lent in Spain, see p. 197.

6. See M. Férotin, *Le Liber Ordinum en usage dans l'Eglise Wisogothique et Mozarabe d'Espagne du cinquième au onzième siècle*, Monumenta Ecclesiae Liturgica 5 (Paris, 1904), cols. 178–84.

7. *Sermo* 54, 5 (*SC* 74:35; *CCL* 138A:322).

8. The title is found in, e.g., the Gregorian Sacramentary; see J. Deshusses, ed., *Le sacramentaire grégorien*, Spicilegium Friburgense 16 (Fribourg, 1971), n. 312.

9. The Romano-Germanic Pontifical is a collection compiled at Sankt Alban in Mainz in the tenth century. Several individuals seem to have collaborated in the work. The Pontifical has been edited by C. Vogel, *Le Pontifical romano-germanique de dixième siècle*, 2 vols., Studi e testi 226–27 (Vatican City, 1963).

10. See Vogel, *op. cit.*, 2:40–54.

11. See M. Andrieu, *Le Pontifical romain au Moyen Age* 1: *Le Pontifical romain du XIIe siècle*, Studi e testi 86 (Vatican City, 1938), 210–14.

12. On all of these usages and on the history of Palm Sunday, see H. A. P. Schmidt, *Hebdomada Sancta*, 2 vols. (Rome, 1956–57), with an abundant bibliography. See also A.-G. Martimort, ed., *L'Eglise en prière: Introduction a la liturgie* (Paris, 1961), 711–13. We have frequently had recourse here to the excellent article of P. Jounel, "Le dimanche des Rameaux," *La Maison-Dieu* 68 (1961): 45–63.

18. Toward the Glorious Passion of the Lord

1. For the history of the procession, see N. Maurice-Denis Boulet, "Le dimanche des Rameaux," *La Maison-Dieu* 41 (1955): 16–33; H. J. Gräf, *Palmenweihe und Palmenprozession in der lateinischen Liturgie*, Veröffentlichungen des Priesterseminars St. Augustin Sieberg, 5 (Kaldenkirchen, 1959). The *Ordinarium* of the Hospice of St.-Jacques at Melun (thirteenth century), for example, gives a detailed description of the procession, which started outside the city gates (Bibliothèque Nationale, Paris, Latin MS. 1206). And see U. Chevalier, *Sacrament ire et martyrologie de l'Abbaye Saint-Remy de Reims* (Paris, 1900), 270–79.

2. See, for example, R. Bloch, "Quelques aspects de la figure de Moïse dans la tradition rabbinique," *Moïse, l'homme de l'Alliance* (Tournai-Paris, 1955), quoted by J. Lécuyer, *Le sacrifice de la Nouvelle Alliance* (Lyons, 1962), 98.

3. Qoheleth Rabbah 1, 28 on Qoh. 1:9, quoted in J. Jeremias, "Mōusōs," *TDNT* 4:860.

4. Lécuyer, *op. cit.*, 103–4.
5. *Sermo* 62, 5 (*SC* 74:77; *CCL* 138A:380–81).

19. Reconciliation

1. See C. Vogel, "Sin and Penance," in J. Delhaye et al., *Pastoral Treatment of Sin*, trans. C. Schaldenbrand, F. O'Sullivan, and E. Desmarchelier (New York, 1968), 178–79.
2. St. Polycarp, *Letter to the Philippians* 6, 1 (*PG* 5:1010).
3. *De paenitentia* 9 (*SC* 35:78).
4. Gel. 78–83.
5. Gel. 349–74.
6. See Vogel, *Le Pontifical romano-germanique du dixième siècle* 2:59–67.
7. M. Andrieu, *Le Pontifical romain au Moyen-Age* 3: *Le Pontifical de Guillaume Durand*, Studi e testi 88 (Vatican City, 1940), 560–69.
8. The ceremonial prescriptions are shortened and paraphrased in our account; the various texts are translated in full.
9. J. Mouroux, *The Mystery of Time: A Theological Inquiry*, trans. J. Drury (New York, 1964), 254–55, alt.
10. *Expositio Evangelii secundum Lucam* 5, 92 (*SC* 45:216; *CCL* 14:164).

20. The Ongoing Renewal of Creation

1. See A. Chavasse, *Etude sur l'onction des infinnes dans l'Eglise latine du IIIe au XIe siecle* 1: *Du IIIe siècle à la réforme carolingienne* (Lyons, 1942); Schmidt, *Hebdomada Sancta* 2:727–28.
2. See, for example, Schmidt, *op. cit.*, 2:738, 734–36.
3. See, for example, A. Chavasse, "A Rome, le jeudi saint au VIIe siècle d'après un vieil Ordo romain," *Revue d'histoire ecclésiastique* 50 (1955): 21–35; idem, *Le sacramentaire gélasien: Vaticanus Reginensis 316: Sacramentaire presbytéral en usage dans les titres romain au viiᵉ siècle* (Tournai, 1958), 126–37. The two opposed views on the origin of the prayers are related to the positions taken on the origin and use of the Gelasian Sacramentary. Chavasse regards it as a book composed at Rome for use in the presbyteral churches of the city; Schmidt considers it to be a compilation of various Roman *libelli* that made their way to Gaul in the sixth century and to which Gallican and other formularies were added.

21. Lent in the Liturgies of the Past

1. The Würzburg Epistolary (ca. 560–90), ed. G. Morin, "Le plus ancien lectionnaire de l'Eglise Romaine," *Revue bénédictine* 27 (1910): 41–74. For its history, see C. Vogel, *Introduction aux sources de l'histoire du culte chrétien au Moyen Age*, Biblioteca degli "Studi Medievali" 1 (Spoleto, n.d. [1965]), 309–10, 313–14, 321–25.
2. The Würzburg Evangeliary (ca. 645), a pure Roman document; see Vogel *op. cit.*, 313–14.
3. The Murbach Lectionary, composed at Murbach, France, toward the end of the eighth century; it was later followed at Rome, and the Missal of Pius V (15790) makes extensive use of it. Edition: A. Wilmart, "Le Comes de Murbach," *Revue bénédictine* 30 (1913): 23–69. See Vogel, *op. cit.*, 318–19.

4. The Evangeliary of Aquileia (eighth century); see Vogel, *op. cit.*, 298.

5. Liturgy of Benevento, as reflected in the Comes of Naples; see Vogel, *op. cit.*, 306.

6. A. Paredi, ed., *Sacramentarium Bergomense*, Monumenta Bergomensia 6 (Bergamo, 1962); see Vogel, *op. cit.*, 301–2.

7. M. Ceriani, ed., *Missale Ambrosianum Vetus*, Monumenta Sacra et Profana 8 (Milan, 1912); see Vogel, *loc. cit.*

8. "Per Christum Dominum nostrum. In qua ieiunantium fides alitur, spes provehitur, caritas roburatur. Ipse enim panis verus et vivus, qui est substantia aeternitatis, esca virtutis. Verbum enim tuum, per quod facta sunt omnia, non solum humanarum mentium sed ipsorum quoque panis est angelorum. Huius panis alimento Moyses famulus tuus quadraginta diebus ac noctibus legem suscipiens ieiunavit et a carnalibus cibis, ut suavitatis capacior esset abstinuit. Unde nec famem corporis sensit et terrenarum oblitus escarum est. Quia illum et gloriae tuae clarificabat as pectus et influente spiritu Dei sermo pascebat. Hunc panem etiam nobis ministrare non desinas, quem ut indeficienter esuriamus hortaris legum Christum" (*Sacramentarium Bergomense*, 100).

9. "Per Christum Dominum nostrum, qui ad insinuandum humilitatis suae mysterium fatigatus resedit ad puteum et a muliere samaritana aquae sibi petiit porrigi potum qui in ea creaverat fidei donum" (*Sacramentarium Bergomense*, 110).

10. "Qui peccantium non vis animas perire sed culpas et peccantes non semper continuo iudicas sed ad poenitentiam provocatos expectas. Averte quaesumus a nobis quam meremur iram et quam optamus super nos effunde clementiam. Ut sacro purificati ieiunio electorum tuorum adscisci mereamur collegio" (*Sacramentarium Bergomense*, 123).

11. Bobbio Epistolary. A Vatican manuscript from northern Italy (sixth to seventh century) gives a marginal list (eighth century) of readings from Paul for Advent to Holy Saturday; the list is called the "Bobbio List" or "Bobbio Epistolary." See Vogel, *op. cit.*, 292–93.

12. Bobbio Missal: eighth century, preserved at Paris. Edition: E. J. Lowe and J. W. Legg, *The Bobbio Missal* 1: *Facsimile*; 2: *Text*, Henry Bradshaw Society 53 and 58 (London, 1917, 1920). See Vogel, *op. cit.*, 293.

13. Sélestat Lectionary, in two states. I = a Merovingian lectionary (ca. 700) from northern Italy; partial edition in G. Morin, "un lectionnaire mérovingien de Sélestat avec fragments du texte occidental des Actes," *Revue bénédictine* 25 (1908): 161–66, reprinted in *Etudes, Textes, Documents* 1 (Maredsous, 1913), 404–56. The readings given run from Advent to Good Friday; see Vogel, *op. cit.*, 292. II = a fragment of a lectionary from Sélestat (also ca. 700 and from northern Italy), giving readings from Advent to the Second Sunday of Lent; see Morin, *art. cit.*, 166; Vogel, *loc. cit.*

14. Evangeliary of St. Kilian. Marginal notes (seventh and ninth centuries) in a text of the four gospels; edited by G. Morin, *Revue bénédictine* 28 (1911): 328–30. See P. Salmon, "Les système des lectures liturgiques continues dans les notes marginales du ms. M. p. th. Q. Ia de Wurzbourg," *Revue bénédictine* 61 (1951: 28–53; 62 (1952): 294–96; Vogel, *op. cit.*, 294.

15. Evangeliary of Trier. 125 marginal notes (eighth century) in an eighth-century manuscript; see Vogel, *op. cit.*, 295.

16. Toledo Missal. Really a lectionary (or more exactly a *Liber commicus*) from the ninth to tenth centuries; see Vogel, *op. cit.*, 303.

17. Toledo Lectionary. A fragmentary manuscript from the end of the ninth century; see Vogel, *op. cit.*

18. Silos Lectionary. From before 1041/1067, Abbey of Silos; see Vogel, *op. cit.*, 302.

19. San Millàn Lectionary. Written in 1073 for the Church of San Millàn; see Vogel, *op. cit.*, 304.

20. M. Férotin, ed., *Le Liber mozarabicus sacramentorum et les manuscrits arabes*, Monumenta Ecclesiae Liturgica 6 (Paris, 1912).

21. *Liber mozarabicus sacramentorum*, 166–212.

22. "Ideo igitur, etsi fatigatus ille in carne, non tamen nos sinit infirmari in sua infirmitate. Nam quod infirmum est illius fortius est hominibus: ideoque per humilitatem veniens eripere mundum a potestate tenebrarum, sedit et sitivit quando aquam petivit. Ille enim humiliatus in carne, quando sedens ad puteum loquebatur cum muliere. Sitivit aquam, et exegit fidem ab ea. In ea quipped muliere fidem quam quasivit quam que petiit, exegit: atque venientibus dicit de ea discipulis: "Ego cibum habeo manducare quem vos nescitis." Ille iam qui in ea creaverat fidei donum, ipse poscebat aquae sibi ab ea porrigi potum: quique earn dilectionis suae flamma cremabat, ipse ab ea poculum quo refrigeraretur sitien postulabat" (*Liber mozarabicus sacramentorum*, 168).

23. "Qui illuminatione suae fidei tenebras expulit mundi et fecit illos esse gratiae qui tenebantur sub legis iusta damnatione. Qui ita in iudicium in hunc mundum venit ut non videntes viderent, et videntes caeci essent; qualiter et ii qui in se tenebras confitentur errorum perciperent lumen aeternum, per quod care rent tenebris delictorum; et ii qui de meritis suis arroganter lumen in semetipsos habere se iustitiae estimabant, in se ipsos merito tenebrescent, qui elati superbia sua et de iustitia confisi propria; ad sanandum Medicum non quaerebant" (*Liber mozarabicus sacramentorum*, 180–81).

24. "Cuius nos gratia liberavit a pondere legis, et fecit filios suae adoptionis. Qui ad suscitandum veniens Lazarum, 'Tollite lapidem,' clamabat, ut pressuram au ferret ab eo damnation is, quem iam fetidum reddiderat horrenda actio supulchralis. Tollite, Iesus ait, ab eo pondus legis, quod eum deprimit in morte; ut succurrat illi gratia vocis meae. Gratia quippe Dei est cum vocem eius audivimus, ut cum Lazaro rectis Iesum gressibus adsequamur" (*Liber mozarabicus sacramentorum*, 210–11).

22. A Crucified God

1. A. Camus, *L'homme révolté* (Paris, 1951), 50–51. The passage is not in the abridged English translation published as *The Rebel* (London, 1953) and is here taken from J. Moltmann, *The Crucified God: The Cross of Christ as the Foundation and Criticism of Christian Theology*, trans. R. A. Wilson and J. Bowden (New York, 1974), 226, alt.

2. Moltmann, *op. cit.*, 226.

3. Ibid., alt.

4. On St. John, see L. Bouyer, *The Fourth Gospel*, trans. P. Byrne (Westminster, MD, 1964); C. H. Dodd, *The Interpretation of the Fourth Gospel* (Cambridge, 1953).

5. On all this, see L. Cerfaux, *Christ in the Theology of St. Paul*, trans. G. Webb and A. Walker (New York, 1959), 131–39. We have sometimes followed this book step-by-step.

6. Moltmann, *op. cit.*, 201.

7. B. Steffen, *Das Dogma vom Kreuz* (1920), quoted in Moltmann, *op. cit.*, 241.

8. Elie Wiesel, *Night* (1969), 75–76, quoted in Moltmann, *op. cit.*, pp. 273–74.

23. The Glorious Christ, Victor over Death

1. G. Martelet, *The Risen Christ and the Eucharistic World*, trans. R. Hague (New York, 1976), 91.

2. Ibid.

3. See A. Festugière, *L'idéal religieux des Grecs et l'Evangile* (Paris, 1932), 143–69; reference given in Cerfaux, *op. cit.*, 78.

4. See P. de Surgy et al., *The Resurrection and Modern Biblical Thought*, trans. C. U. Quinn (New York, 1970).

24. The Resurrection and the Eucharist

1. On all this, see E. Schillebeeckx, *Christ the Sacrament of the Encounter with God*, trans. P. Barrett, M. Schoof, and L. Bright (New York, 1963); Martelet, *op. cit.*

25. Celebrations Ancient and Modern

1. *Epist.* 23, 12–13 (*PL* 16:1030).

2. P.-M. Gy, "Semaine sainte et triduum pascal," *La Maison-Dieu* 41 (1955): 9, alt. The article gives an excellent sketch of the history of the paschal Triduum.

3. *De consensu Evangeliorum* 3, 66 (*PL* 34:1199).

4. *Epist.* 55, 24 (*PL* 33:215).

5. J. Gaillard, "Le mystère pascal dans le renouveau liturgique: Essai de bilan doctrinal," *La Maison-Dieu* 67 (1961): 85.

6. See the Capua Epistolary (ca. 545), edited by G. Morin, "Lectiones ex epistolis paulinis excerptae quae in Ecclesia Capuana saec. VI legebantur," *Anecdota Maredsolana* 1 (Maredsous, 1893): 436–44.

7. *Epist.* 25: *Ad Decentium*, cap. 7, no. 10 (*PL* 20:559).

8. *Epist.* 77 (*OL* 22:692–93), cited in P. Jounel, "Le jeudi saint: La tradition de l'Eglise," *La Maison-Dieu* 68 (1961): 15–16.

9. H. Bruns, *Canones Apostolorum et Conciliorum* 1 (Berlin, 1839), 127.

10. *Epist.* 54, 5 (*PL* 33:202).

11. *Egeria: Diary of a Pilgrimage*, chap. 35, pp. 107–8. The Martyrium is the church enclosing the place where Jesus was crucified or, more accurately, the place where the cross was found.

12. A short exposition of the various interpretations is given in H. A. P. Schmidt, *Hebdomada Sancta*, 2 vols. (Rome, 1956–57), 2:733–36.

13. *Apologia I*, chap. 65 (*PC* 6:427).

14. *La Tradition Apostolique de saint Hippolyte: Essai de reconstitution*, ed. B. Botte, Liturgiewissenschaftliche Quellen und Forschungen 39 (Münster, 1963), cc. 4 and 21, pp. 11 and 55.

15. See E. Lanne, "Textes et rites de la liturgie pascale dans l'ancienne Eglise Copte," *Orient syrien* 6 (1961): 291.

16. See *Le pontifical Romano-Germanique du dixième siècle*, ed. C. Vogel with R. Elze, Studi e testi 226–27 (Vatican City, 1962), 2:71–75 and 77–85.

26. The Pasch That Gathers

1. See Nathan Goldberg, *Passover Haggadah*, rev. ed. (New York, 1966). The prayers quoted in this outline will be found on pp. 7, 8, 25, 27, 42–43.

2. See A. Jaubert, *La date de la Cène* (Paris, 1967), a book that has occasioned further essays. Its thesis is that the Supper was celebrated on Monday evening; this would clarify certain passages in the gospels and would also make the Synoptics and John more coherent. The possibility that two different calendars, an ancient and a more modern, were in use would explain how the Lord's Supper could be located on either Monday or Thursday, but the thesis is far from having convinced all the exegetes.

3. See M. Thurian, *The Eucharistic Memorial*, trans. J. G. Davies, 2 vols., Ecumenical Studies in Worship 7–8 (Richmond, VA, 1960–61).

4. R. Aron, "La liturgie juive et le temps," *La Maison-Dieu* 65 (1961): 19.

5. St. John (18:28; 19:14) says that the Jews had not yet eaten the Passover when Jesus was put to death. The problem this statement raises is simplified if John is following a different calendar from the Synoptics (see 22. A Crucified God, n. 1, p. 493). Recent exegetes (e.g., J. Jeremias), have insisted that in any case the atmosphere of the Last Supper is clearly that of the Passover. In Luke 22:15 Jesus says he wishes to eat this Passover with his disciples before he suffers. Cf. J. Jeremias, *The Eucharistic Words of Jesus*, trans. N. Perrin (London, 1966), 41–62.

6. "Anamnesis" is a technical term meaning "remembrance" or "memorial." In the present context, it means a reminder of what Yahweh has done for his people.

7. *Didache* 10, 1–5. Text in *Prex Eucharistica: Textus e variis liturgiis antiquioribus selecti*, ed. A. Hänggi and I. Pahl, Spicilegium Friburgense 12 (Fribourg, 1968), 66–68; or in J.-P. Audet, *La Didachè: Instructions des Apôtres* (Paris, 1958), 234–36.

8. *Epist.* 55, 18–24 (*PL* 33:212–16).

9. RB 53.

10. RB 35.

11. See A. Chavasse, "A Rome, le jeudi saint au VIIe siècle d'après un vieil Ordo romain," *Revue d'histoire ecclésiastique* 50 (1955): 21–35.

12. See Lanne, *art. cit.*, 291.

13. *De sacramentis* 3, 5 (*SC* 25bis:94).

14. P.-M. Gy, "Les origines liturgiques du lavement des pieds," *La Maison-Dieu* 49 (1957): 52.

15. See G. Khouri-Sarkis, "La semaine sainte dans l'Eglise syrienne," *La Maison-Dieu* 41 (1955): 105–9; F. Mercenier and F. Paris, *La prière des Eglises du rit byzantine*, 2 vols. (Amay, 1937–39), 2:161–66.

16. See Abul'l Barakat, *La lampe des ténèbres*, cited in Lanne, *art. cit.*, 291n28. On all this development, see Schmidt, *op. cit.*, 2:763–76; Th. Schäfer, *Die Fusswaschung im monastischen Brauchtum und in der lateinischen Liturgie*, Texte und Arbeiten 47 (Beuron, 1956).

17. A wide, black cloak, which, in the case of a monk, is unadorned.

18. A white apron.

19. Mercenier and Paris, *op. cit.*, 2:164–65.

20. See B. Fischer, "Formes de la commemoration du baptême en Occident," *La Maison-Dieu* 58 (1959): 120.

21. Ibid.

22. *Didascalia Apostolorum*, trans. R. H. Connolly (Oxford, 1929), 122, 124, alt.

27. The Lord's Supper

1. CL 7.

2. *Sermo* 26, 2 (*SC* 22bis:138; *CCL* 138:126).

3. *Sermo* 53, 6 (*SC* 74:82; *CCL* 138:386).

4. CL 57.

5. *La Tradition Apostolique de saint Hippolyte*, chap. 4, p. 11.

6. Even if strict exegesis does not enable us to say that Christ celebrated the Eucharist on this occasion, surely there are eucharistic overtones to the language.

7. See M. Andrieu, *Les Ordine Romani du Haut Moyen Age* 2, Spicilegium Sacrum Lovaniense 23 (Louvain, 1948), 82.

28. The Unity of the Three Holy Days

1. *Epist.* 23, 12–13 (*PL* 16:1030).
2. *Epist.* 55, 24 (*PL* 33:215).

29. Celebrations Ancient and Modern

1. *Apologia I*, chap. 67 (*PG* 6:430).
2. CL 35.
3. See, for examples, *Ordines* 16, 17, 23, 24, and 30B (all in Andrieu, *op. cit.*, vol. 3, Spicilegium Sacrum Lovaniense 24 [Louvain, 1951]), which date from the end of the eighth century, as well as some of the sacramentaries of the same period. See also Schmidt, *op. cit.*, 2:778–84.
4. Several sacramentaries (the Gelasian, for example) showed this pattern.
5. *Egeria: Diary of a Pilgrimage*, chap. 24, p. 90.
6. The Council of Vaison (Provence, France; 529) speaks of the Italian custom of saying the *Kyrie*.
7. See B. Capelle, "Le Kyrie de la Messe et le pape Gélase," *Revue bénédictine* 34 (1924): 126–44; reprinted in his *Travaux Liturgiques* 2 (Louvain, 1962), 116–34.
8. Andrieu, *op. cit.*, 2:413, thinks that the *Ordines* began to be composed in the seventh century and even in the second half of the sixth. A. Chavasse, *Le sacramentaire gélasien* (Tournai, 1968), 171, refuses to date their appearance before the seventh century and considers the first *Ordo* to be dependent on the Gelasian Sacramentary.
9. *Egeria: Diary of a Pilgrimage*, chap. 37, pp. 110–11.
10. See H. Grisar, "Il 'Sancta Sanctorum' in Roma e il suo tesoro novamente aperto," *Civiltà Cattolica* 57 (1906): 513–44, 708–30. On the iconography, see J. Wilpert, "Le due piú antiche rappresentazioni della 'Adoratio crucis,'" *Atti della Pontificia Accademia Romana de Archeologia* (1927).
11. See M. Férotin, ed., *Le Liber Ordinum en usage dans l'Eglise Wisogothique et Mozarabe d'Espagne du cinquième au onzième siècle*, Monumenta Ecclesiae Liturgica 5 (Paris, 1904), 193ff.
12. See *Ordo* 23, nos. 9–22, in Andrieu, *op. cit.*, 3:270–72.
13. See Schmidt, *op. cit.*, 2:791.
14. *Egeria: Diary of a Pilgrimage*, chap. 37, p. 112.
15. See *Ordo* 24, no. 35, in Andrieu, *op. cit.*, 3:294–95.
16. See A. Baumstark, "Der Orient und die Gesänge des Adoratio crucis," *Jahrbuch für Liturgiewissenschaft* 2 (1922): 1–17.
17. *Liber officialis* 1, 14, ed. J. M. Hanssens, *Amalarii Episcopi opera liturgica omnia* 2 (Vatican City, 1948), 101.
18. *Ordo* 31, nos. 45–46, in Andrieu, *op. cit.*, 3:498.
19. See J. M. Hanssens, *Institutiones liturgicae de ritibus orientalibus* (Rome, 1932), 3:108–56; I.-H. Dalmais, "L'adoration de la croix," *La Maison-Dieu* 45 (1956): 76–86; H. Engberding, "Zum formgeschichtlichen Verständnis des *hagios ho theos, hagios ischuros, hagios athanatos, eleison hemas*," *Jahrbuch für Liturgiewissenschaft* 10 (1930): 168–74.
20. M. Andrieu, *Le Pontifical Romain au Moyen Age* 1: *Le Pontifical Romain du XIIe siècle*, Studi e testi 86 (Vatican City, 1938), 236. Schmidt, *op. cit.*, 2:796, cites *Ordo* 31 as prescribing the unveiling of the cross; Andrieu thinks, however, that this *Ordo* was a purely literary composition and was not used in fact for conducting a service.
21. Andrieu, *Le Pontifical Romain*, 1:237.

22. In the Antiphonary of Senlis (880); an antiphonary is a book containing the various antiphons and hymns for Mass or other services. The practice is also to be found in the Romano-Germanic Pontifical of the tenth century.

23. *Epist.* 25: *Ad Decentium*, cap. 4, no. 7 (*PL* 20:555–56). See G. Malchiodi, *La lettera di S. Innocenzio I a Decentio vescovo di Gubbio: Breve studio esegetico-storico* (Rome, 1921), 11.

24. *Ordo* 23, no. 22, in Andrieu, *Les Ordines Romani*, 3:272.

25. *Liber officialis*, in I Ianssens, *Amalarii Episcopi opera liturgica omnia*, 2:107–8.

26. C. Vogel, *Le Pontifical Romano-Germanique du dixième siècle*, 2:92–93.

27. *Ordo* 31, no. 11, in Andrieu, *Le Pontifical Romain*, 1:237.

28. Andrieu, *Le Pontifical Romain au Moyen Age* 2: *Le pontifical de la Curie Romaine au XIIIe siècle*, Studi e testi 87 (Vatican City, 1940), 469, 541–78.

30. The Blood of the Lamb

1. J. Lécuyer, *Le sacrifice de la Nouvelle Alliance* (Lyons, 1962), 17.

2. L. Moraldi, *Espiazione sacrificale e riti espiatori nel ambiente biblico e nell'Antico Testamento* (Rome, 1956), 237–38, quoted in Lécuyer, *op. cit.*, 117.

3. See Lécuyer, *op. cit.*, 17.

4. On this subject, see L. Cerfaux, *Christ in the Theology of St. Paul*, trans. G. Webb and A. Walker (New York, 1959), 122, 143. The reader will find the references to St. Paul's letters that show the link between blood and sacrifice (Rom 3:25; 5:6-11; Eph 1:7; 2:13; Col 1:20).

5. *Catecheses* 3, 13–19 (*SC* 50bis:174–77).

31. The Servant Pierced and Victorious

1. *Sermo* 61, 4–5 (*SC* 74:71; *CCL* 138A:372).

2. See page 168, "The Glorious Passion for the Sake of the Covenant."

3. *Sermo* 53, 3 (*SC* 74:29–30; *CCL* 138A:315).

4. Edited by M. Férotin (see 29. Celebrations Ancient and Modern, n. 11, p. 496).

32. Celebrations Ancient and Modern

1. See L. C. Mohlberg, ed., *Liber sacramentorum romanae aeclesiae ordinis anni circuli* (*Sacramentarium Gelasianum*), Rerum ecclesiasticarum documenta, Series maior: Fontes 4 (Rome, 1960), nos. 419–24 (henceforth cited as Gel. with number of text, e.g., Gel. 419–24); *Ordo* II, in Andrieu, *Les Ordines Romani*, 2:83–88.

2. *Rite of Christian Initiation of Adults* (Washington, DC, 1974), no. 259.

34. Celebrations Ancient and Modern

1. *Historia Ecclesiastica* 5, 24, 6.

2. *Commentaria in Evangelium Matthaei* 4, 25 (*PL* 26:192).

3. H. M. Féret, "La Messe, rassemblement de la communauté," in *La Messe et sa catéchèse*, Lex orandi 7 (Paris, 1947), 220–21.

4. Aron, *art. cit.*, 19.

5. On this subject, see Eusebius of Caesarea, *Historia Ecclesiastica* 5, 23–25; O. Casel, *La Fête de Pâques dans l'Eglise des Pères*, French translation by J. C. Didier, Lex orandi 37 (Paris, 1963), 29 (a translation of "Art und Sinn der ältesten christlichen Osterfeier," *Jahrbuch für Liturgiewissenschaft* 14 [1934]: 1–78); M. Richard, "La question pascale au IIe siècle," *Orient syrien* 6 (1961): 179–212.

6. The *Didascalia Apostolorum* is a third-century Syrian document. It was edited by F. X. Funk, *Didascalia et Constitutiones Apostolorum* (Paderborn, 1905), see nos. 18–19, p. 288. English translation by R. H. Connolly, *Didascalia Apostolorum* (Oxford, 1929).

7. *La Tradition Apostolique de saint Hippolyte*, cc. 20–21, pp. 43–55.

8. *De baptismo* 19, 1 (*SC* 35:93; *CCL* 1:293).

9. *La Tradition Apostolique de saint Hippolyte*, chap. 25, p. 65.

10. See *Ordo* 24, no. 41, in Andrieu, *Les Ordines Romani*, 3:295 and 321.

11. See *Ordo* 32, nos. 1–7, in Andrieu, *Le Pontifical Romain au Moyen Age*, 1:238–40.

12. See *Ordo* 23, no. 24, in Andrieu, *Les Ordines Romani*, 3:272.

13. See Schmidt, *op. cit.*, 2:809–12.

14. *Ordo* 50, no. 17, in Andrieu, *op. cit.*, 5, Spicilegium Sacrum Lovaniense 29 (Louvain, 1961), 267; text of hymn on pp. 396–98.

15. Andrieu, *Le Pontifical Romain au Moyen Age*, 2:565.

16. See F. C. Conybeare, ed., *Rituale Armenorum* (Oxford, 1905); H. Leclercq, "Semaine sainte," *Dictionnaire d'archéologie chrétienne et de liturgie* 15:1177–78.

17. *Ordo* 17, nos. 102–4, in Andrieu, *Les Ordines Romani*, 3:190.

18. Complete text in Schmidt, *op. cit.*, 2:629–34.

19. J. Deshusses, ed., *Le sacramentaire gélasien*, Spicilegium Friburgense 16 (Fribourg, 1971), 183.

20. Gel. 431–43.

21. *Ordo* 23, no. 26, in Andrieu, *op. cit.*, 2:27. On this whole matter, see Schmidt, *op. cit.*, 2:827–47; B. Botte, "Le choix des lectures dans la veillée pascale," *Questions liturgiques et paroissiales* 33 (1952): 65–70; A. Chavasse, "Leçons et oraisons des Vigiles de Pâques et de la Pentecôte dans le sacramentaire gélasien," *Ephemerides Liturgicae* 69 (1955): 209–26, and his *Le sacramentaire gélasien*, 113.

22. In his *Euchologion*; text in Funk, *Didascalia et Constitutiones Apostolorum*, 2:181–83.

23. *Contra Parmenianum Donatistam* 7, 6 (*CSEL* 26:153).

24. *Constitutiones Apostolorum* 7, 43; text in J. Quasten, *Monumenta eucharistica et liturgica vetustissima*, Florilegium Patristicum 7 (Bonn, 1936), 192–94.

25. L. C. Mohlberg, ed., *Sacramentarium Veronense*, Rerum ecclesiasticarum documenta, Series maior: Fontes 1 (Rome, 1956), no. 1331 (henceforth, Ver. with number of text, e.g., Ver. 1331).

26. *De sacramentis* 2, 14 (*SC* 25bis:80).

27. *Ordo* 17, no. 102, in Andrieu, *op. cit.*, 3:190.

28. *Ordo* 23, no. 28, in Andrieu, *op. cit.*, 3:273.

29. *Ordo* 16, nos. 43–44, in Andrieu, *op. cit.*, 3:153. Other *Ordines* say the same.

30. *Ordo* 31, nos. 91–95, in Andrieu, *op. cit.*, 3:503–4.

31. *Ordo* 30A, no. 21, in Andrieu, *op. cit.*, 3:457–58.

35. The Light of Christ

1. First antiphon, Vespers, Holy Saturday. [The Latin text, "O mors, ero mors tua; morsus tuus ero, inferne," represents the Hebrew text rather than the Greek and Syriac readings that are reflected in the usual English translation (for example: "Where are your plagues, O death! where is your sting, Sheol!"). —Trans.]

2. These words used to be part of the prayer of blessing but have now been omitted; see. e.g., *The Maryknoll Missal* (New York, 1964), 329, which is quoted here.

3. Blessing of the fire.

4. See B. Capelle, "L'Exultet pascal, oeuvre de saint Ambroise," in *Miscellanea Giovanni Mercati* 1 (Vatican City, 1946), 214–46.

5. The Vigil at Rome originally had six readings; later, there were twelve, and even twenty-four in the period when both Greeks and Latins attended the liturgy in the Lateran Basilica and the pericopes were read in both languages.

B. Botte, "Le choix des lectures de la veillée pascale," *Questions liturgiques et paroissiales* 33 (1952): 65–70, establishes that the traditional number of readings in the Church of Rome was six; the four readings in the Gregorian Sacramentary represent a later usage.

6. See volume 1 of this series, "The Presence of the Lord," 16–17.

7. Exod 14:15–15:1; third reading of the Vigil.

8. Exod 15:1-6, 17-18, provides the responsory for the third reading.

9. See J. Delorme, "The Resurrection and Jesus' Tomb," in P. de Surgy et al., *The Resurrection and Modern Biblical Thought*, trans. C. U. Quinn (New York, 1970), 74.

10. See the bibliography in ibid., 147–48.

11. On this and the preceding four paragraphs, see ibid., 95–100.

12. *De sacramentis* 2, 1, 1 (*SC* 25bis:74).

13. *De baptismo* 8, 4 (*SC* 35:77–78; *CCL* 1:283).

14. Complete Latin text in Schmidt, *op. cit.*, 2:854–55.

15. *Apologia I*, chap. 61 (*PG* 6:420).

16. *Sermo* 24, 3 (*SC* 22bis:114; *CCL* 138:112–13).

17. *De sacramentis* 2, 4, 12–13 (*SC* 25bis:80).

18. *De sacramentis* 2, 7, 20 (*SC* 25bis:84, 86).

19. *De sacramentis* 2, 6, 19 (*SC* 25bis:84).

20. *De sacramentis* 2, 7, 23 (*SC* 25bis:86, 88).

21. *De mysteriis* 7, 34–35 (*SC* 25bis:175).

22. *De sacramentis* 5, 3, 12–13 (*SC* 25bis:124).

23. *De mysteriis* 8, 43 (*SC* 25bis:181).

24. *Explanatio in Psalmum* 22 (*PG* 69:841).

25. *Catecheses mystagogicae* 4, 7 (*SC* 126:140).

26. *Catecheses mystagogicae* 4, 7 (*SC* 126:142).

27. See page 310 on "Three Sacramental Stages."

28. *La Tradition Apostolique de saint Hippolyte*, chap. 21, p. 55.

29. See the title of J. M.-R. Tillard's excellent book on the Eucharist: *The Eucharist, Pasch of God's People*, trans. D. L. Wienk (Staten Island, 1967).

30. G. Martelet, *op. cit.*, has provided a remarkably good discussion of the complex but essential aspects of the eucharistic celebration.

36. This Day That the Lord Has Made

1. P. Nautin, ed., *Homélies pascales* 1 (*SC* 27:158).

2. On the discourse, see J. Dupont, *Etudes sur les Actes des Apôtres*, Lectio divina 45 (Paris, 1967).

3. The gospel of the Easter Vigil (three-year cycle) may be read instead.

4. See Casel, *op. cit.*, 103.

5. See *Sur la Pâque*, ed. O. Perler, *SC* 123 (Paris, 1966). Melito was probably a bishop.

6. *On the Pasch* 1–6 (*SC* 123:60, 62).

7. *On the Pasch* 40 (*SC* 123:80).

8. *On the Pasch* 46 (*SC* 123:84).

9. See C. Mohrmann, "Pascha, Passio, Transitus," *Ephemerides Liturgicae* 66 (1952): 37–52; reprinted in her *Etudes sur le latin des chrétiens* 1 (Rome, 1961), 205–22.

10. *Catecheses mystagogicae* 3, 13–19 (*SC* 50bis:158–62).

11. *Explanatio symboli* 5 (*SC* 25bis:52).

12. *Sermo* 63, 1 and 3 (*SC* 74:78, 80; *CCL* 138A:382).

13. *Sermo* 63, 4 (*SC* 74:80–81; *CCL* 138A:384).

14. *Sermo* 63, 5 (*SC* 74:81; *CCL* 138A:385).

15. *Sermo* 63, 6 (*SC* 74:82–83; *CCL* 138A:386).

16. *Sermo* 65, 4 (*SC* 74:93; *CCL* 138A:399).

17. *Sermo* 71, 3–4 (*SC* 74:125–26; *CCL* 138A:436–37).

18. *Sermo* 72, 1 (*SC* 74:129; *CCL* 138A:441).

19. *Sermo* 72, 7 (*SC* 74:135; *CCL* 138A:447).

37. Believing without Seeing

1. *Apologia I*, chap. 67 (*PG* 6:430).

2. See M.-E. Boismard, *Quatre hymnes baptismales dans le premier épître de saint Pierre*, Lectio divina 30 (Paris, 1961).

3. See L. Bouyer, *Eucharist: Theology and Spirituality of the Eucharistic Prayer*, trans. C. U. Quinn (Notre Dame, 1968).

38. The Risen Christ Appears to His Disciples

1. See, e.g., B. Botte's preface (with its notes) to Casel, *op. cit.*, 7–10.

40. Ministries in the New Community

1. Dogmatic Constitution on the Church, no. 10. See also nos. 3, 9, 11, 31, 32.

2. *Didache* 9, 1; text in Hänggi-Pahl, *op. cit.*, 66, and Audet, *op. cit.*, 372.

41. The Spirit and the Church

1. See volume 1 of this series, pages 24–26, "Let the Mirror Be Broken!"

42. The Ascension of the Lord

1. *Sermo* 73, 4 (*SC* 74:138; *CCL* 138A:453).

2. *Sermo* 74, 1 (*SC* 74:139; *CCL* 138A:455–56).

3. *Sermo* 74, 2 (*SC* 74:140; *CCL* 138A:465–57).

4. E. Schillebeeckx, *op. cit.*, develops such a theology on the basis of the ascension.

5. Ver. 176.

43. Jesus Prays for His Disciples

1. C. H. Dodd, *The Interpretation of the Fourth Gospel* (Cambridge, 1953), 177.

2. Ibid.

44. The Mission of the Holy Spirit

1. *De resurrectione mortuorum* (PL 2:837; CCL 2:959).
2. *Commentaria in Ezechielem prophetam* (PL 25:349; CCL 75:515).
3. See J. van Goudoever, *Fêtes et calendriers bibliques*, Théologie historique 7 (Paris, 1967), 30ff.; G. F. Moore, *Judaism in the First Centuries of the Christian Era*, 3 vols. (Cambridge, 1927–30), 2:43–47.
4. On this problem, see M.-E. Boismard, "De son ventre couleront des fleuves d'eau," *Revue biblique* 65 (1958): 522–46; A. Feuillet, "Les fleuves d'eau vive de Jean 7, 38," in *Parole de Dieu et sacerdoce* (*Mélanges Weber*) (Paris, 1962), 107–20; idem, "Eau du rocher ou source de temple?," *Revue biblique* 70 (1953): 43–51.
5. See A. George, "The Accounts of the Appearances to the Eleven from Luke 24, 36–53," in P. de Surgy et al., *op. cit.*, 62–64.
6. *Sermo 75*, 1 (SC 74:144–45; CCL 138A:465–66).
7. *Sermo 76*, 3 (SC 74:151; CCL 138A:476).

46. Missal Prayers during Easter Time

1. Wednesday of second week, collect.
2. Saturday of seventh week, collect.
3. Sixth Sunday, collect.
4. Tuesday of second week, prayer over the offerings; Saturday within the octave of Easter, prayer over the offerings.
5. Thursday of seventh week, collect.
6. Monday of seventh week, collect.
7. Saturday of seventh week, prayer after Communion.
8. Second Sunday, prayer over the offerings.
9. Second Sunday, collect.
10. Easter Sunday, prayer after Communion.
11. Thursday of third week, prayer after Communion.
12. Easter Vigil, prayer after Communion.
13. Thursday of second week, collect.
14. Thursday of second week, prayer after Communion; Thursday of sixth week, prayer after Communion.
15. Wednesday of third week, prayer after Communion.
16. Thursday of third week, prayer over the offerings.
17. Friday of fifth week, collect.
18. Thursday of third week, collect.
19. Second preface of Easter.
20. First preface of the Ascension.
21. Fourth preface of Easter.
22. Third preface of Easter.
23. First preface of Easter; Good Friday, alternate collect.
24. *Exsultet.*
25. Wednesday in octave of Easter, prayer after Communion.
26. Easter Vigil, alternate prayer after third reading.
27. Easter Vigil, prayer after first reading.
28. Easter Vigil, prayer after seventh reading; Monday of second week, prayer after Communion.
29. Blessing of baptismal water; Easter Vigil, alternate prayer after third reading.

30. Good Friday, alternate prayer.

31. Fifth Sunday, collect. [This pertains to the missal Nocent was using. The same prayer is still found on the Twenty-Third Sunday in Ordinary Time. The third edition of the Missal, however, has replaced it here with a different one. —PT]

32. Third Sunday, collect.

33. Easter Vigil, prayer after fourth reading.

34. Easter Vigil, prayer after second reading.

35. Good Friday, alternate prayer.

36. Monday of second week, collect. [In the third edition of the Missal, this collect was replaced with a long-neglected one from the Gelasian Sacramentary. The prayer Nocent cites used to be offered twice—on Monday of the Second Week of Easter and also on the Nineteenth Sunday in Ordinary Time. Other Ordinary Time collects were being repeated during the year, but the third edition of the Missal has removed the repetitions. Hence, the prayer to which Nocent refers here is only found on the Nineteenth Sunday in Ordinary Time. —PT]

37. Thursday of third week, prayer over the offerings.

38. Second preface of the Ascension.

39. Thursday of fourth week, collect.

40. Monday of fourth week, collect. [In the third edition of the Missal this collect has been replaced with a long-neglected one from the Gelasian Sacramentary. At Nocent's writing, this prayer repeated the collect from the Fourteenth Sunday in Ordinary Time. It is still in place there but has a new substitute here. —PT]

41. Good Friday, prayer.

42. Saturday in octave of Easter, collect.

43. Tuesday of third week, collect.

44. Preface of Pentecost.

45. See Pentecost Sunday, collect.

46. Seventh Sunday, prayer over the offerings.

47. Fourth Sunday, collect.

48. Sunday of the sixth week; Thursday of second, fourth, and sixth weeks; Monday of third and fifth weeks, prayer after Communion.

49. Third Sunday, collect; see also the prayer after Communion.

50. Friday of second week, collect. [In the third edition of the Missal, this prayer has been replaced with a long-neglected one from the Gelasian Sacramentary. The collect to which Nocent refers duplicated the one from Wednesday of Holy Week, where it can still be found. —PT]

51. Tuesday in octave of Easter, collect. [The French translation added the aspect of passing from death to life. —PT]

52. First preface of the Ascension.

53. Third preface of Easter.

54. Ascension, collect.

55. Tuesday of second week, collect.

56. Easter Day, collect.

47. The Easter Vigil in Other Liturgies

1. Edited by G. Morin, "Le plus ancient lectionnaire de l'Eglise romaine," *Revue bénédictine* 27 (1910): 41–74. For its history, see C. Vogel, *Introduction aux sources de l'histoire du culte chrétien au Moyen Age*, Biblioteca degli "Studi Medievali" 1 (Spoleto, n.d. [1965]), 309–10, 313–14, 322–23.

2. Edited by A. Wilmart, "Le comes de Murbach," *Revue bénédictine* 30 (1913): 26–59. See Vogel, *op. cit.*, 318–19.

3. See A. Chavasse, "Le lectionnaire et l'antiphonaire romains," *Revue bénédictine* 62 (1952): 74–76.

4. Mercenier and Paris, *op. cit.*, 2:210–61.

5. O. H. E. Burmester, *Le lectionnaire de la semaine sainte* in *Patrologia Orientalis*, 25:433ff.

48. Solemnity of the Most Blessed Trinity

1. [In Christian usage, the Greek word *oikonomia* means "administration" and then "arrangement, order, plan." The "economy" of salvation is the working out of God's plan of salvation. An "economic" interpretation of the Trinity analyzes not the relation of each of the three Persons to the others within the Godhead but the relation of each to the work of salvation. —Tr.]

2. See *Vita S. Benedicti Anianensis* 26 (*PL* 103:364).

3. See P. Browe, "Zur Geschichte des Dreifaltigkeitsfestes," *Archiv für Liturgiewis senschaft* 1 (1950): 69.

4. St. Athanasius of Alexandria, *First Letter to Serapion* 28 and 30 (*SC* 15:134, 138), in *The Liturgy of the Hours*, vol. 3: *Ordinary Time Weeks 1–17* (New York: Catholic Book Publishing Co., 1975), 584–85.

5. Ibid., 30 (*SC* 15:138–39).

6. See L. C. Mohlberg, ed., *Liber sacramentorum romanae aeclesiae ordinis circuli (Sacramentarium Gelasianum)*, Rerum ecclesiasticarum documenta, Series maior: Fontes 4 (Rome, 1963), no. 286. [NB: In the older baptismal ritual and in the revised rite, the Latin text has *gloriae tuae rudimenta* (see Ordo *Initiationis Christianae Adultorum*, editio typica [Rome, 1972], p. 30, no. 87). This is translated in the official English version as "grace which has been begun" (*Rite of Christian Initiation of Adults* [Collegeville, 1988], no. 57). Mohlberg's critical edition of the Gelasian Sacramentary, from which this prayer is taken, has *magnitudinis gloriae rudimenta*, which Nocent interprets as meaning "the beginning of [the catechumen's] future great glory." —Tr.]

49. Solemnity of the Most Holy Body and Blood of Christ (Corpus Christi)

1. Thomas Aquinas, *Opusculum 57: Officium de Festa Corporis Christi*, In primo nocturno lectio 1. Text in *Opuscula theologica*, ed. R. A. Verardo and R. M. Spiazzi (Turin, 1954), 2:276, in *The Liturgy of the Hours*, vol. 3: *Ordinary Time Weeks 1–17* (New York: Catholic Book Publishing Co., 1975), 610.

50. Solemnity of the Most Sacred Heart of Jesus

1. *Opusculum 3: Lignum vitae* 47 (*Opera Omnia*, ed. Quaracchi, 8:79), in *The Liturgy of the Hours*, vol. 3: *Ordinary Time Weeks 1–17* (New York: Catholic Book Publishing Co., 1975), 636.